THIRD EDITION

INFANT DEVELOPMENT

CHARLES W. SNOW
East Carolina University

CINDY G. McGAHA
Appalachian State University

Upper Saddle River, New Jersey 07458

Library of Congress Cataloging-in-Publication Data

SNOW, CHARLES W., 1935–
Infant development / Charles W. Snow, Cindy G. McGaha.—3rd ed.
p. ; cm.
Includes bibliographical references and index.
ISBN 0-13-048144-0
1. Infants—Development. I. McGaha, Cindy G., 1969–
II. Title.
[DNLM: 1. Child Development. 2. Growth—Infant.
WS 103 S674i 2003]
RJ134 .S66 2003
305.232—dc21 2002020597

Editor in Chief: Leah Jewell
Senior Acquisitions Editor: Jennifer Gilliland
Editorial Assistant: Nicole Girrbach
Production Editor: Maureen Benicasa
Prepress and Manufacturing Buyer: Tricia Kenny
Marketing Manager: Jeff Hester
Marketing Assistant: Ron Fox
Director, Image Resource Center: Melinda Reo
Manager, Rights and Permissions: Zina Arabia
Image Permissions Coordinator: Charles Morris
Cover Image Specialist: Karen Sanatar
Cover Designer: Bruce Kenselaar
Cover Art: Getty Images Inc.

This book was set in 10/12 Times by TSI Graphics and was printed and bound by RR Donnelley & Sons. Covers were printed by Phoenix Color Corp.

For permission to use copyrighted material, grateful acknowledgment is made to the copyright holders on page 311, which is considered and extension of this copyright page.

Printed in the United States of America
10 9 8 7 6 5

ISBN 0-13-048144-0

Pearson Education LTD., London
Pearson Education Australia PTY, Limited, Sydney
Pearson Education Singapore, Pte. Ltd
Pearson Education North Asia Ltd, Hong Kong
Pearson Education Canada, Ltd., Toronto
Pearson Educación de Mexico, S.A. de C.V.
Pearson Education—Japan, Tokyo
Pearson Education Malaysia, Pte. Ltd
Pearson Education, Upper Saddle River, New Jersey

Dedicated to infants and their parents and other caregivers everywhere.

CONTENTS

THREE
THE BIRTH PROCESS AND THE NEWBORN 40

FOUR
PHYSICAL GROWTH 65

SEVEN
PERCEPTUAL DEVELOPMENT 126

EIGHT
COGNITIVE DEVELOPMENT 145

NINE
LANGUAGE DEVELOPMENT 166

THIRTEEN
INFANT CAREGIVING AND EDUCATION 241

PREFACE

This book presents a comprehensive overview of growth and development during the first three years of life. It is designed primarily as an introductory text for courses in infant development, infant care, and early intervention. The increasing popularity of courses on infant development in institutions of higher education throughout the United States is a reflection of the interest and attention currently devoted to infant development by the academic community and the general public. The development and expansion of early-intervention programs and child-care programs throughout the United States have increased the demand for a cadre of professionals who are knowledgeable about infant development. Anyone interested in learning about infants should find the third edition of *Infant Development* informative and helpful.

This edition is a completely updated and reorganized version of the previous text. In response to requests from reviewers and consumers, some of the chapters from the second edition have been combined in order to make room for additional material on other topics. Research literature on almost all aspects of infant development continues to expand. A new chapter on Perceptual Development has been added to reflect the burgeoning research and theoretical literature on infant sensory and perceptual capacities. Additional material on brain development has also been included. Each chapter has been extensively reviewed and carefully revised to include new information from theory and research.

Following the format of the previous editions, the material is organized topically, with a chapter on each developmental area. One of the unique features of this text continues to be the extended coverage of physical development, including the latest growth charts. Although coverage of nutrition, health, and safety has been reduced somewhat, these topics continue to receive important emphasis. The text is devoted primarily to typically developing infants, but the coverage on infants with special needs continues to be an important emphasis. A concerted effort has been made to achieve a balance between theory, research, and practical information. Suggestions for enhancing infant growth and development are incorporated and highlighted in the various chapters. We have tried to use terminology that reflects caring, sensitivity, and respect for infants and families everywhere regardless of gender, race, ethnicity, culture, and developmental abilities.

Through the years, numerous disciplines have contributed to our knowledge and understanding of infant development. This edition has been designed to retain the original interdisciplinary perspective. Information from child development and family relations, psychology, pediatrics, nursing, nutrition, biology, and other disciplines has been incorporated into the various chapters. The quotations from classical and contemporary literature that introduce each chapter are designed to add interest and express a major theme. We have tried to be objective in our coverage of infant development and base our conclusions on research and theory. If our coverage of any topic appears to be one-sided or uneven, it is due to an oversight rather than our own particular biases.

Several features used in the book will facilitate student understanding and learning. An introduction at the beginning of each chapter summarizes the basic topics that are covered. Important terms are highlighted and carefully defined as they occur in the text and are listed at the end of each chapter. Real-life examples are used to illustrate difficult concepts. Photographs, drawings, and tables are sprinkled throughout the book to illustrate and summarize important information. References to Internet Web sites containing supplementary information on various topics in the text have been added. A summary of the main points under each major heading is included at the end of each chapter.

In this edition, Cindy McGaha joins Charles Snow, the author of the first two editions, as coauthor. She is a rising young professional in the field of Child Development and Family Relations who has expertise in infant development and is especially interested in infants and young children with disabilities.

ACKNOWLEDGMENTS

We received help from many people in the preparation of this edition. The librarians in the Health Sciences and Joyner Libraries at East Carolina University (ECU) were extremely helpful in the process of identifying and obtaining essential materials. The support, encouragement, and cooperation of Dr. Cynthia Johnson, Chair of the Department of Child Development at ECU, and Dr. Sammie Garner, Chair of the Department of Family and Consumer Sciences at Appalachian State University, helped make it possible for us to work on this project. We want to express appreciation to Megan Richardson, a graduate student in the Department of Child Development and Family Relations at ECU, for her valuable assistance with literature searches and many other tasks in the various stages of manuscript preparation. Dora Snow, deserves special credit, not only for her suggestions on grammar and style but for her support and understanding during her husband's extensive involvement with this project.

The comments of the reviewers secured by the Prentice Hall editorial staff were also valuable in planning and completing this edition. They are Sybil Hart, Texas Tech University; Peggy O'Jessee, The University of Alabama; Kaveri Subrahmanyan, California State University.

Finally, we are especially grateful to Editor in Chief, Laura Pearson, Production Editor, Maureen Benicasa, Psychology Editor, Jennifer Gilliland, Editorial Assistant, Nicole Girrbach, and other members of the Prentice Hall editorial staff for their patience and guidance throughout the process of making this revised edition a reality.

ONE

Introduction and Theoretical Perspectives

All the world's a stage,
And all the men and women merely players.
They have their exits and entrances,
and one man in his time plays many parts,
his act being seven stages.
At first the infant, mewling and puking in the nurse's arms.
—Shakespeare

The term **infant** is derived from a Latin word meaning "without speech." If we use the literal definition, **infancy** covers the period between birth and 12 to 18 months, when the baby begins to talk. However, infancy often is used to cover a broader age range, encompassing a broader age span. In this book, infancy includes the age span from birth to 3 years of age. Older infants who have begun to walk are often referred to as toddlers. The term **toddler** (or toddlerhood) will be used in this book when the discussion is specifically limited to infants between approximately 18 and 36 months of age. Since the first act in life's drama actually begins before birth, the prenatal period is also included as an important part of our discussion.

SOME BASIC QUESTIONS

This book is designed to acquaint you with the important concepts, characteristics, stages, and underlying processes of infant development. The basic questions we consider throughout the book are:

1. How do infants grow and develop? What are the characteristic abilities and needs of infants at various stages in their development from conception to the third year of life? How do infants differ from culture to culture?
2. Why do infants grow, develop, and behave in the ways they do? What important variables or factors influence development from conception through infancy?
3. What are the characteristics of infants who are at-risk for developmental delay, or who have a disabling condition? What are their special needs and how can those needs be met?
4. What childrearing practices facilitate the development of infants into healthy, competent individuals? How do child-rearing practices differ from culture to culture?

This introductory chapter alerts you to some additional issues, recurring themes, and perspectives that are important to the study of infant development.

HISTORICAL PERSPECTIVES

Today infants are regarded as the most precious of all creatures. Whether or not this has always been true is a matter of debate by historians. In this section we take a brief look at two contrasting views about how infants have been treated in the past. It is important to look at the past before we can understand contemporary attitudes and practices in infant care.

Negative Practices. According to many historians, before the 17th century infants and young children were considered to be inferior creatures and were placed at the very bottom of the social scale (e.g., de Mause, 1974; Pollock, 1983). Parents were perceived as largely indifferent to the needs of their offspring. Until the early 1800s, infants were often subjected to very cruel treatment. For example, from ancient times until the fourth century, infanticide was practiced in many cultures. Newborn infants who were sickly, deformed, or otherwise viewed as a burden to their parents were killed, usually by exposure or starvation.

During the fourth century, the practice of infanticide was largely replaced with the practice of abandonment (de Mause, 1974). Whenever possible, problem infants were given away to be reared by substitute families or religious orders. As recently as the 1800s, many young mothers in Europe and America left their babies on the steps of a church or a mansion in the hope that they would be adopted (Langer, 1975). In addition, many wealthy parents turned their infants over to "wet nurses" for the first two years of life as a means of avoiding close contact. Love and affection generally were not considered important for infant development (Kagan, Kearsley, & Zelazo, 1978). Discipline was harsh and beating of children was common.

By the end of the 1800s, the concept of infancy as a separate and important stage in life had started to evolve. Infants were given a central role in the family, and their rights were protected by the state (Pollock, 1983). Parents gradually became more physically and emotionally involved with their infants. By the early 1900s we entered a new age of concern about the development and care of infants. Pediatrics was established as a separate field of medicine. The infant death rate declined as sanitation and medical practices improved. In the United States, public-spirited citizens worked to improve the living conditions of infants and their families. De Mause (1974) refers to current views of infancy as reflecting a "helping mode" era.

A Contrasting View of History. The harsh treatment of infants discussed previously has been widely acknowledged, but some historians (Hanawalt, 1977; Pollock, 1983) disagree with claims that the mistreatment of infants has been widespread. Pollock (1983) believes that, apart from social changes and technological advances, childrearing practices have not changed dramatically through the centuries. According to this view, infanticide, abandonment, and other forms of cruelty to infants were practiced in the past, but not by the majority of parents. Nearly all children were wanted, and most parents were not cold and indifferent to their children's welfare. Changes have occurred in specific practices, such as feeding, and changes in parental attitudes have been observed. However, for the most part, infant care has remained remarkably consistent through different historical eras (Pollock, 1983).

UNDERLYING ISSUES AND RECURRENT THEMES

The study of infancy involves struggling with several basic issues and problems. Throughout this book you will be confronted with divergent views about when, how, and why infants behave in certain ways. This means that you will need to decide which points of view or which answers make the most sense to you. You will also find that several themes reappear from time to time. These recurrent themes are as basic to human development as the underlying melody or motif is to a musical composition. This section is designed to introduce some of the themes you will encounter in the study of infant development.

The Nature-Nurture Controversy. A major question in the study of infant development is "Which is most important, heredity or environment?" There are certain physical features such as hair and eye color that are clearly controlled by heredity. When it comes to human behavior, though, philosophers and scientists for centuries have debated the relative importance of nature and nurture.

Nature. The nature side of the debate is represented by the *maturationists* and *nativists.* **Maturationists** believe that the key to growth and development is found in genetic and biological foundations. Physical growth, motor development, and other abilities proceed according to a genetic timetable. **Nativists** believe that infants come equipped with innate ideas, feelings, and personality traits. For example, they believe that infants are genetically endowed with the ability to understand the rules of grammar. Arnold Gesell (1945), one of the pioneers in the study of human development, believed that there are timetables of development when children are mature enough or "ready" to develop a particular skill. Gesell considered these periods of maturational readiness to be controlled by the unfolding of the genetic blueprint. A contemporary version of the nature point of view is presented in a controversial book by Judith Harris (1998). Although she does not rule out environmental influences, Harris asserts that genes are more important than parental influences in shaping a child's personality.

Nurture. On the other hand, the nurture point of view is advocated by the **empiricists,** who believe that the course of infant development is shaped by experience. This position is based on the proposal made by John Locke (1690/1961) in 1690 that the infant mind is a ***tabula rasa*** or "blank slate." Infants are thus viewed as passive creatures, molded by external environmental forces. An extremist version of the nurture position can be found in John B. Watson's (1924) claim that he could take 12 healthy infants and guarantee to train any one, selected at random, to be an artist, doctor, lawyer, or merchant regardless of the child's talents or characteristics of the ancestors.

Nature *and* Nurture. Although there continues to be debate about the relative importance of nature and nurture, currently biologists and social scientists tend to agree that most characteristics of individuals result from an interaction of both genetic and environmental influences. A widely accepted way of looking at heredity-environment relationships is through the **transactional perspective.** In order to understand human development we have to take into consideration the "transactions between and among individuals, their biological inner workings, and their social outer workings" (Sameroff, 1993, p. 11). A major principle of this model is that heredity and environment mutually influence each other throughout the lifespan. Developmental outcomes are viewed as the result of reciprocal influences between the child and the environment. The action of the child changes the environment and then, in turn, the changes in the environment affect the behavior of the child. The two factors interact and combine in ways that make infant development more than simply the sum of the two parts. For example, powerful environmental events, such as exposure to toxic chemicals or starvation can alter the genetic foundations of development. These transactions represent a powerful process that continues over time (Sameroff, 1993).

Some of the complexities of the transactional perspective are described in Scarr and McCartney's (1983) view of how heredity and environment interact. They believe infants' genetic endowment and environmental influences operate within the context of three types of relationships: passive, evocative, and active.

The environment that parents provide for an infant is influenced by the parent's own heredity. An example of the passive gene-environment interaction is the case in which artistic parents are likely to expose the child to play materials and experiences that emphasize art. The child who has inherited a genetic predisposition to be artistic is also the recipient of an environment that pushes the child toward the fulfillment of genetic potential. In the case of evocative gene-environment interactions, infants with certain types of genetic tendencies evoke reactions from their environment. For example, parents respond differently to a child who is generally easygoing and compliant than to a child who tends to be irritable and fussy. Within the active gene-environment, children have a tendency to seek out experiences that match their genetic predispositions. This is also referred to as **niche-picking.** For example, highly intelligent children look for experiences that are cognitively challenging; thus, in some sense, they shape their own environment. Therefore, it is practically useless to try to determine how much of a specific trait is determined by genes and how much by the environment (deWaal, 1999).

The Critical Periods Debate. Another controversial issue that is the subject of much debate is whether there are certain critical periods in human development. A **critical period** is a definite period of time when environmental events have the greatest and most lasting impact on the developing human. Environmental events include exposure to harmful substances or experiences, as well as the deprivation of essential stimuli or materials. The term *window of opportunity* that opens and closes within a certain time frame is sometimes used as an analogy for a critical period. Scientists agree that there are critical periods in some areas of physical growth. We know that various organs of the body can be irreversibly damaged by exposure to environmental hazards or by deficits of needed substances during their formative stages. Specific examples of such critical periods will be described in the discussion of prenatal development.

The critical periods debate has focused mainly on whether or not critical periods can be identified in cognitive and psychosocial domains. Questions about the existence of a critical period for the acquisition of language, the formation of infant-parent attachment bonds, and the development of brain capacity are some of the subjects of controversy. These and other related questions will be considered in chapters that deal with specific developmental areas.

A major controversy in the critical periods debate is related to the lasting effects of early experience. Some theorists believe that the presence or absence of important experiences during the first three years of life leaves an indelible, irreversible mark on a child for life (Bruer, 1999). Statements such as "The early years last forever," "As the twig is bent, so grows the tree," and "The future of our nation depends on what happens to our children during the early years of life" illustrate this position.

Sigmund Freud (1940) was one of the first psychologists to view experiences during the infancy years as having lifelong effects. He believed that all personality neuroses are acquired during the first 5 or 6 years of life (Rutter, 1987). Freud proposed that the first 2 years were the most important within that time period. For example, the child who is treated harshly during toilet training will develop personality tendencies that are likely to last a lifetime.

A famous study by René Spitz (1945) of infants who were reared in an orphanage is also used to support the critical periods hypothesis. The infants he studied had few toys and lay in their cribs most of the time with little human contact. As a result of this deprivation of normal "mothering," the infants failed to grow and became severely depressed and withdrawn. The infants had little resistance to disease, and many of them died. Spitz believed that the severe deprivation resulted in psychological damage that was practically irreversible. However, critics point out that Spitz failed to determine the condition the infants were in before they were institutionalized.

Studies are also available to support critics who are skeptical about the long-term effects of early experience. For example, Kagan and Klein (1973) observed infants who spent the first year of life in a windowless hut with little attention from caregivers. The infants were found to be silent, apathetic, and retarded. In spite of their early retardation, however, these infants grew up to be active, happy, and intellectually competent 11-year-olds. Rutter (1985) reviewed research studies on children from severely deprived backgrounds who were subsequently placed in much better environments. He concluded, "The effects of early bad experiences can be 'neutralized' to a substantial extent by good experiences in later life . . . (p. 360). The evidence runs counter to the view that early experiences irrevocably change personality development" (p. 364).

The view of infancy as a fixed and absolute critical period of psychological development that determines what happens in future stages has been, in the minds of many people, replaced with a more moderate approach (Rutter, 1985). According to this position, infants are in many ways more sensitive or vulnerable to their environment than older children. As the first stage of life, infancy provides the foundation for later development. In some cases the effects may be long lasting but not necessarily irreversible. Infants are quite adaptable and malleable and have demonstrated the capacity to overcome a lot of adversity. Not all infant experiences have an impact on later development, although some experiences can have long-term effects (Bornstein & Lamb, 1992).

The extent to which psychological disabilities or benefits from infancy persist depends upon a complex chain of events linking the first stage of life to the last (Rutter, 1987). The key condition under which early experiences are likely to continue or fade is environmental continuity. If the environment remains constant, the attributes (good or bad) developed in the early years are likely to be reinforced and remain stable. On the other hand, if the environment changes, children tend to change. For example, many infants who are born with prematurity, anoxia, or other birth complications, do not experience long-term problems if they are reared in an environment that is compensatory and supportive. However, if they are reared in environments that are stressful and deprived, the birth traumas are more likely to have long-term negative developmental effects (Kopp & Krakow, 1982).

Norms and Individual Differences. Throughout this book we consider typical patterns of growth and development, which are referred to as **norms**. The normal age ranges for major milestones, such as the first spoken word and the social smile, are discussed. However, within these average growth and developmental trends there is plenty of room for individual differences. You should always keep in mind that no two babies are exactly alike. Human infants differ in appearance and behavior within and between racial and ethnic groups. Even identical twins differ in significant ways. Although there is an average rate and sequence of development, no infant should be thought of simply as an "average" child.

Interrelations Among Developmental Areas. In this book, infant growth and development are described in seven major domains or areas: physical, motor, cognitive, language, personality, social, and emotional. These areas are closely interrelated. When an infant makes progress in one area, there is usually a chain effect whereby development occurs in other areas as well.

Numerous illustrations of how development in one area relates to that of another area can be given. For example, the development of the ability to move around and explore the environment is accompanied by marked improvement in sensory perception. When an infant advances to a higher stage of cognitive functioning, for instance, a new milestone of language development has been reached. Changes in social and emotional development, such as smiling and stranger anxiety, are apparently related to changes in the cognitive domain.

Directions of Development. Two basic laws or principles of developmental direction are evident in the growth and development of all infants. According to the **cephalocaudal principle**, development proceeds from head to foot. The head and upper extremities develop and become functional earlier than the trunk and lower extremities of the body. In accordance with the **proximodistal principle**, development proceeds from the center of the body toward the outer extremities. For example, the arms and legs develop and become useful before the fingers and toes.

The Competent Infant. Human infants are born into the world more helpless than the young of any other species. Human infancy lasts a relatively long time. However, even at birth infants possess remarkable abilities. We used to believe that infants were blind at birth. We now know that newborns not only can see, but also are capable of other sophisticated sensory functions. What you will see emerging in this study of infancy is not so much a picture of a passive infant "mewling and puking" as an active infant with an impressive amount of ability in various areas of development.

Robert White (1959) used the term **competence motivation** to describe the infant's tendency to explore and master challenges within the environment. Infants thrive on such challenges as putting a peg in a hole, finding a lost object, or saying a new word. Infants are also tough and resilient. They have a tendency to "grow toward health" (Kagan, 1979, p. 21). This means that infants are capable of overcoming a lot of adversity (see "Risk and Resiliency" later in this chapter).

Robert Emde (1996) has identified a set of five "basic motives" that infants are equipped with at birth:

1. *Activity.* The desire to explore and confront environmental challenges.
2. *Self-regulation.* The propensity for regulating physiolgical and behavioral states (e.g., wake-sleep, attention, emotions).
3. *Social-fittedness.* The desire to initiate, maintain, and discontinue interactions with other people.
4. *Affective monitoring.* The inclination to monitor situations on the basis of what is pleasurable and unpleasurable, reassuring or alarming.
5. *Cognitive assimilation.* The tendency to seek out new experiences and make them familiar.

With the help of caregivers who are emotionally available and provide growth-fostering activities, these tendencies provide the impetus for an infant to achieve social, emotional, and cognitive competence.

Reciprocal Interactions. Another theme in the study of infants is the reciprocal (mutual) nature of adult-infant interactions. The socialization of infants is not a one-way process. From the beginning, infants are interactive partners in the child-rearing process. Infants influence their caregivers in numerous ways, even as caregivers influence them. For example, parents respond differently to a male baby than to a female baby. A baby who is calm and easygoing receives different treatment than a baby who fusses a lot and is difficult to manage. Therefore, to a significant extent, infants play an active role in creating their own environment.

THEORETICAL PERSPECTIVES

Much of the literature on infant development is written in the form of theories. Developmental theories are assumptions, hypotheses, or best guesses about how and why babies develop and behave in certain ways. Theories are important because they serve as systems or frameworks for viewing infant development and conducting research. Most theories represent a particular view of such issues as human nature, the nature-versus-nurture debate, the importance of early experiences, the ways in which individuals learn, and the stages of development. Theories vary widely in scope, complexity, scientific support, and popularity.

Some of the most important and controversial theories of development are presented in this text. The major theories are briefly summarized below. More specific information about these and other theories is provided in other chapters where they relate to specific features of infant development. Most theories of child development can be divided into six general categories:

1. **Nativistic or maturational theories,** which stress the importance of innate characteristics, are represented by Arnold Gesell (1945) and Noam Chomsky (1975). These theorists give more weight to hereditary influences than environmental influences on development.

2. **Behavioral theories** emphasize the importance of the environment and experience in shaping the human infant. B. F. Skinner (1972) is the most well-known representative of behaviorism. These theorists believe that human behavior is conditioned through the processes of positive and negative reinforcement. Other theorists (e.g., Bandura, 1977) have expanded Skinner's ideas to include modeling, observation, imitation, and verbal instruction as important cognitive and social processes in the acquisition of behavior. These modifications of Skinner's ideas form the basis for **social learning theory.**

3. **Psychoanalytic** and **psychosocial theories** stress the importance of early experiences and the role of emotions in shaping human personality and behavior. Sigmund Freud (1917) and Erik Erikson (1963) are the major proponents of these points of view.

4. **Cognitive developmental theories** emphasize the interaction between genetic inheritance and environmental factors. Understanding the development of cognitive processes is the key to human behavior. Jean Piaget (1929) is a major representative of this theory. Other cognitive developmental theorists promote an information-processing approach. Rather than emphasizing stages of development, these theorists focus on the information children represent in their mind, the processes they use to transform the information, as well as their memory capacity and functions (Siegler, 1991).

5. **Social contextual theorists** believe that human beings are, to a large extent, products of their social and cultural worlds. In order to understand how children develop, we need to study their social and cultural background. Lev Vygotsky (1978) and Urie Bronfenbrenner (1979) are widely recognized as major contributors to this theory.

6. **Developmental systems theories** represent the latest attempt to describe the wholeness and complexity of human development, how new behaviors and skills are acquired, and the origin of individual differences (Fogel, 2001; Thelen & Fogel, 1989; Thelen & Smith, 1998). Human beings are made up of internal body (genetic/cellular), motor, cognitive/behavioral, and other systems that work together in complex ways. Changes in one system have an impact on the other systems. The systems within the individual are also connected to and interact with external environmental systems. Systems theorists are more interested in explaining how development occurs than identifying specific developmental

outcomes (e.g., norms and stages of development). Some theorists (Thelen & Smith, 1998) use the term *dynamic systems* to emphasize the belief that the various systems are constantly in a state of change as new abilities and behaviors continue to emerge over time.

METHODS OF STUDYING INFANTS

Although the answers to many questions about infant growth and development are tentative and incomplete, we now have more and better information than ever. During the past 20 to 30 years, our knowledge of infant development has increased dramatically. The numerous books, magazine articles, and scientific publications on infant development currently available reflect this information explosion. The rapidly growing amount of infancy research is, in part, the result of the development of some innovative methods of studying infants.

Early Techniques. The first known efforts to study and record the behavior of infants were found in several "baby diaries," the first of which was published by German philosopher Dietrich Tiedemann in 1787 (Tiedemann, 1787/1972). A **baby diary** is a day-to-day record maintained by an adult observer of an infant's behavior. Diary records published by parent-scientists Charles Darwin (1877) and William Preyer (1888) were a little more systematic than Tiedemann's records and have received wider recognition. The information reported in baby diaries is considered to have limited value because the information may not be very objective. In addition, observations of a single subject cannot be generalized to other infants.

Jean Piaget (1962) combined the naturalistic observation method used in the baby diary with informal experiments performed on his own three infants (S. Miller, 1987). For example, Piaget gave an infant an object to manipulate or a problem to solve and then systematically recorded the infant's response. Piaget's conclusions about infant development based upon such observations have been widely accepted, but only because they have been verified by other researchers using more sophisticated procedures.

Current Methods. Contemporary researchers have searched for more objective and reliable methods. However, the scientific study of infants has been extremely difficult for a variety of reasons. For one thing, young infants don't talk so we can't ask them questions. They also have limited motor abilities with which to respond to stimuli. In addition, securing the baby's attention and cooperation is a problem. The baby may be too sleepy, fussy, distractable, or active to concentrate on the experimental situation. Even when an infant is cooperative, how do researchers find out what the infant is thinking or feeling before language begins? Given the challenges imposed by these limitations, researchers have had to find creative ways to assess the infant's experience of the world.

Through the years, researchers have been persistent and ingenious in designing more and better ways to measure responses they can use to make inferences about what is going on inside the baby's body and mind (S. Miller, 1987). Sophisticated video cameras, computerized scanners, and other high-tech equipment are now available to monitor, record, and analyze the responses of infants. We will review a few of the ways researchers study infants at this point. You will find examples of additional infancy-research procedures throughout this book.

Habituation-Dishabituation and Novelty. Much of the research focuses on methods linked to visual preferences and habituation-dishabituation responses. You probably have had the experience of going into a store where background music is playing. You notice the music at first, but within a few minutes you are no longer listening to it. This progressive decline of response to a repeated stimulus is referred to as **habituation.** If a catchy tune comes on, you find yourself listening to the music again. If the music stops, you become aware of its absence. The recovery of interest in and response to a changing stimulus is called **dishabituation.**

To determine when an infant has habituated or dishabituated to a given stimulus, investigators measure changes in the infant's heart rate, breathing, visual activity, startle reflex, and other reactions. When an infant pays less attention to a picture, after seeing it a few times in succession, the infant is demonstrating the capacity to remember the picture. If the infant indicates renewed interest when a new picture is shown researchers infer that the infant can detect the difference between the two pictures (Trotter, 1987). Given a choice between a familiar stimulus and an unfamiliar stimulus (or **novelty**), infants typically respond to and focus on the novelty. Habituation-dishabituation has been used to study a variety of infant abilities, including learning, memory, visual, taste, and sound discrimination.

Visual Preference Technique. Robert Fantz (1958), a pioneer in infancy research, developed an innovative **visual preference technique** to study visual perception. In this study, an infant is placed in a special apparatus equipped with a peephole and a "looking chamber." Two pictures are hung in the looking chamber within the infant's field of vision. The pictures are separated so that the infant has to turn his or her head slightly to look from one to the other. The lighting conditions are such that an image of the stimulus is reflected in the infant's eye. The observer looks through the peephole and records what the infant is viewing and the amount of looking time the infant devotes to each picture or its parts. Using this procedure, researchers can determine what infants spend the most time watching and whether they can discriminate between various stimuli.

Other researchers (e.g., Hainline & Lemerise, 1982) have added high-tech electronic equipment to Fantz's original procedure. Projectors, video cameras, monitors, and computerized data-recording equipment are now used to record the infant's smallest eye movements and detailed visual images. With this equipment, researchers can make more accurate observations and study more complex visual behaviors, such as infant scanning patterns and form perception.

Violation-of-Expectation Method. The **violation-of-expectation method** helps researchers to determine what infants perceive, understand, and believe about the characteristics of physical objects. Researchers present infants with two test events: a possible and an impossible event (Baillargeon, 1994). Infants typically expect the possible event to occur. If an impossible event occurs instead, the infant's expectations are violated and the infant is surprised. Since the impossible event is more novel, the infant will look at it longer. For example, Baillargeon (1994) describes an experiment to test the ability of young infants to reason about support phenomenon involving a box and a platform (see Figure 1-1). In the possible event, a box is shown on top of a platform. As expected, the box does not fall off when pushed from one side to the other as long as

In both events, a gloved hand pushes a box from left to right along the top of a platform. In the possible event (top), the box is pushed until its leading edge reaches the end of the platform. In the impossible event (bottom), the box is pushed until only the left 15 percent of its bottom surface rests on the platform.

Figure 1-1. Paradigm for Studying Infants' Understanding of Support Phenomena
From R. Baillargeon. (1994). How do infants learn about the physical world? *Current Directions in Psychological Science, 3,* 34. Reprinted by permission.

most of the box remains on the platform. In the impossible event, the box is pushed almost off the edge of the platform, but the box does not fall. Younger infants (under 4 months) are not surprised, while older infants (over 6.5 months) apparently expect the box to fall. The violation-of-expectation method has also been used to study the ability of infants to reason about other phenomenon including collision of objects, object permanence, barriers to moving objects, and object number.

Physiological Responses. Researchers have used the infant's physiological responses such as brain waves, heart rate, body temperature, and body chemistry as measures of infant responses to various experimental conditions. Although the results of physiological tests are sometimes difficult to interpret, we are obtaining important new information about infants through these measures.

Brain Activity. Scientists attach a cap or bonnet containing several electrodes to a baby's head. These electrodes pick up brain wave activity by means of machines that generate electroencephalograms (EEG) or magnetoencephalograms (MEG). Changes in brain wave patterns are detected as an infant is exposed to sound, visual, or other stimuli (Gopnik, Meltzoff, & Kuhl, 1999). For example, sounds are emitted within the baby's range of hearing. If the baby's physiological hearing mechanism is functioning, the sounds produce small electrical changes in the brain that are picked up by the electrodes and shown on the EEG or MEG.

Scientists have developed more sophisticated "windows to the brain" through the use of positron emission tomography (PET) and functional magnetic resonance imaging (fMRI) (Chugani, 1993; Gopnik et al., 1999). PET technology employs scanners to detect glucose consumption. Although promising, PET technology is limited because it requires that the subject be injected with a radioactive glucose solution. Therefore, it can only be used with infants and children for clinical or diagnostic purposes. The fMRI scans are easier and more useful, especially with children, because an injection is not required. This technique measures brain activity by tracking the flow of blood and oxygen (Gopnik et al.,1999). Both PET and fMRI scans produce brightly colored images that make it possible to see what part of the brain is most active during controlled stimulation such as sounds or visual images.

Heart Rate. Changes in heart rate can also be measured with an electrocardiogram (EKG). Changes in heart rate indicate whether an infant is paying attention to and responding to a stimulus. The heart rate slows down in response to conditions that require the infant to concentrate and speeds up under conditions that cause excitement or distress. Some scientists study an aspect of heart rhythm called **vagal tone.** This particular measure of heart rate variability is controlled by the vagus nerve of the brain and is associated with breathing patterns. Vagal tone is considered to be an indicator of how well the central nervous system is functioning. Researchers have proposed that individual differences in vagal tone predict individual differences in developmental outcomes. Newborn infants with higher vagal tone may be more likely to perform better on certain tests of infant development at 8 and 12 months of age than infants with lower vagal tone (Bornstein & Lamb, 1992; Fox & Porges, 1985).

Saliva Tests. Human saliva contains a hormone called **cortisol.** Apparently, the amount of cortisol in the saliva varies with emotional changes related to stress. Since samples of saliva are easy to obtain from infants, researchers can analyze cortisol levels under varying conditions as an indicator of the stress an infant may be feeling. For example, researchers have found that infant cortisol levels increase in response to stressful events such as physical exams and medical treatments procedures (e.g., heel sticks), but decline during relaxing events such as short car rides (Stansbury & Gunnar, 1994).

Thermography. A marked change in facial-skin surface temperature is considered to be an indication of a change in an infant's emotional state. A drop in skin surface temperature may be an indication of stress. Such changes can be detected through **thermography,** using television cameras that are equipped with infrared sensors. The cameras are connected to computers for processing and evaluating the facial images. Japanese researchers (Mizukami et al., 1990) have used this procedure to study attachment of 10- to 16-week-old infants. The mother placed her infant in a crib and left the room after about 5 minutes. A stranger then entered the room and played with the infant for a few minutes. After the stranger left the mother returned. The facial temperature of the infant was recorded during each of the conditions. The infant typically experienced a decline in body temperature in response to a stranger, which was interpreted as an indication of stranger anxiety and awareness of the mother's absence. Thermography is a relatively new technique for assessing emotions and must undergo further use and evaluation to establish its validity and usefulness.

Facial Expressions. One of the most frequently used techniques for measuring infant emotions is the analysis of facial expressions. Theoretically, a specific facial expression is a reflection of a specific underlying emotional state. Researchers have developed detailed descriptions and coding systems for rating and analyzing facial expressions of infants as indicators of specific emotions. For example, Izard (1979) has developed a detailed system for measuring specific emotional expressions called the Maximally Discriminative Facial Movements Code (MAX). Videotapes of infants' facial expressions are made under conditions designed to elicit emotional changes. The tapes are then played at a very slow speed so that trained observers can code the facial movements according to the criteria defined in the MAX.

Nonnutritive Sucking. A measure that is often used to evaluate the baby's responses to visual and other stimuli is provided by the sucking reflex. Researchers place a pacifier that is connected to a pressure gauge in the baby's mouth to measure the number of times the baby sucks and the strength of sucking within a given time frame. The baby is then shown pictures or provided with sounds. In some cases the baby can control the sights or sounds by varying the sucking response. The sucking rate declines as babies lose interest in a particular sight or sound and increases as the interest level increases. By varying the stimulus conditions and measuring changes in sucking responses, researchers can get a lot of information about infant preferences and capabilities.

Parent Reports. Although the accuracy and reliability of parent reports have been criticized in the past, in recent years there has been a renewed interest in the value of using parents as sources of information. Improved strategies for obtaining information from parents have made this approach more acceptable. For one thing, parent reports are currently used mainly to record infant behavior as it occurs rather than to provide retrospective information about past events. Researchers have also developed more sophisticated techniques of training parents to be observers and record information (Parke, 1989). By asking parents to observe specific behaviors and keep systematic records, researchers are able to obtain information about infants and parents that would not otherwise be available.

Observational Strategies. In order to obtain information about certain types of infant behaviors, such as social interactions, it is necessary to make direct observations of their behaviors either in laboratory or naturalistic settings. Advances in the sophistication of observational methods and procedures have made this a more reliable and useful strategy for collecting information about infant behavior. Technological advances in portable videotape and computer equipment now make it possible to collect information in homes and other nonlaboratory settings. These recordings can be analyzed in various ways at a very detailed level

(Parke, 1989). For example, the observation of infant facial expressions in the study of emotions relies heavily on this technique (Parke, 1989). Systematic observations are an essential component of laboratory experiments and studies conducted in naturalistic settings, such as day-care centers.

RISK AND RESILIENCY

For the most part, this book deals with infants who conform to the developmental norms in all areas of growth and development and who are referred to as "typically developing" infants. However, many infants are born under circumstances and with challenges that may prevent them from following typical developmental patterns. These infants are referred to as infants at-risk. The term **at-risk** is used to refer to infants who have been exposed, or who may be exposed, to conditions that are likely to result in developmental delay or atypical development. There are many diverse and complex factors that threaten development, including genetic/biological, environmental, or a combination of factors. Two basic categories of risk have been identified: established risk and potential risk.

Established Risk. Infants placed in the **established risk** category have been diagnosed with a medical condition, physical disorder, or mental condition known to result in developmental delay or atypical development. Examples of established risk are infants with a diagnosed sensory impairment (e.g., blindness or deafness), genetic disorder, congenital malformation, or failure to thrive. These infants have a 100 percent chance of experiencing developmental problems at some point in life.

Potential Risk. In many instances, infants are exposed to adverse biological and/or environmental conditions that have the potential for causing developmental problems. Prematurity, low birthweight, bleeding in the brain, or prenatal exposure to German measles or other viruses are examples of biological concerns that represent **potential risks** of causing developmental problems. Severe malnutrition, neglect, and abuse are examples of environmental conditions that place infants at-risk. Poverty is a major condition that contributes to and interacts with other factors in placing infants in double jeopardy for adverse developmental outcomes. The degree of risk varies with the severity, timing, duration, and the interactions among these conditions.

Infants who are developmentally at-risk and their families have special needs for a variety of medical, educational, economic, and other intervention services that will help them reach their developmental potential. Additional information about conditions that place infants at-risk and infants with special needs will be discussed at other relevant places in the text.

Resilient Infants. Infants who grow up under conditions of poverty and other adverse conditions generally turn out less well than infants who grow up in more favorable circumstances. However, some infants develop into competent children and adults in spite of the odds against them. **Resilient infants** are individuals who have good developmental outcomes while living under stressful conditions such as economic hardship, child abuse, or biological risk (Werner, 2000; Werner & Smith, 1992). Researchers have been interested in identifying the protective factors and mechanisms that serve as buffers against risk and adversity while enhancing successful development (Werner, 2000).

Long-term studies (reviewed by Werner, 2000) have identified individual qualities that distinguish resilient infants and toddlers from their less-successful disadvantaged peers. These infants were described as affectionate, cuddly, good-natured and easy to manage, exhibiting good feeding and sleeping habits, not easily distressed or highly emotional, socially responsive, and at least average in intelligence. Other protective factors that were characteristic of the environment in which resilient infants were reared included small family size, supportive grandparents or other caring people, and sufficient nurturing to form secure attachment bonds and a sense of basic trust in at least one caregiver (Werner, 2000).

DEVELOPMENTAL ASSESSMENT

Developmental assessment is a process designed to obtain information about the abilities and characteristics of an infant. The information may be used for a variety of purposes, including identifying infants who may be at-risk for developmental problems (screening); verifying the presence and degree of a disability (diagnosis); planning an appropriate environment, curriculum activities, or other strategies to facilitate development (program planning); and testing theories and hypotheses about various aspects of infant development (research) (Meisels, 1996).

Assessment Instruments. There are hundreds of instruments available for screening and assessing infant development. Screening instruments are designed to identify infants who show signs of developmental delay indicating the need for further assessment. These tests usually can be administered quickly so that large numbers of infants can be screened for the early detection of a developmental disability. Other assessment instruments are designed for more in-depth testing to verify and identify the existence of a specific problem. Most assessment instruments can be classified as a norm-referenced or a criterion-referenced test.

Norm-referenced tests provide specific scores or ratings that can be used to compare one infant's performance with that of other infants of the same age. One of the most widely used norm-referenced screening tests for infants and children up to 6 years of age is the **Denver II** (Frankenburg et al., 1992). The test covers four areas of development: gross motor, language, fine motor–adaptive, and personal-social. Infants who do not pass a sufficient number of age-appropriate items are referred for further testing with another instrument such as the ***Bayley Scales of Infant Development–II*** (see Chapter 8).

Criterion-referenced instruments assess the infant's ability to achieve specific, previously determined skills without comparing one infant with a group of others. **The Hawaii Early Learning Profile (HELP)** (Furuno et al., 1988) is an example of a widely used criterion-referenced instrument. The HELP is used with infants from birth through 3 years of age to assess cognitive, language, gross motor, fine motor, social-emotional, and adaptive (self-help) skills. This instrument is accompanied by suggested teaching/remediation activities for each of the test items.

Assessment Guidelines. The National Center for Infants, Toddlers and Families has formulated some basic guidelines for the assessment of infants and young children (Greenspan & Meisels, 1996):

1. Assessment should include multiple sources of information, including parent reports and direct observation. Standardized tests provide useful information, but should not be the cornerstone of assessment.
2. Assessment is a collaborative process. Participation in the process should be open to parents and other significant caregivers, as well as a variety of professionals with special expertise.
3. The assessment process should identify the child's strengths in addition to developmental delays.
4. Infants should never be separated from their parents or familiar adults and should never be challenged by assessment by strangers without a sufficient "warm-up" time.

In addition, professionals involved in the assessment process need to be aware of and sensitive to the social, linguistic, and ethnic characteristics of the families and infants they work with (Crais & Roberts, 1996). It is beyond the scope of this text to provide a comprehensive view of the assessment process and available measurements. However, in some of the chapters that follow, we will look at a few of the most widely used instruments for assessing specific developmental areas.

SOURCES OF ERROR AND CONFUSION IN STUDYING INFANTS

As you read and think about some of the information contained in this book, you may at times become confused and frustrated. Two major sources of difficulty that you may encounter in understanding infant development are the numerous contradictory theories and inconclusive research findings.

Contradictory Theories. As described earlier, there are many theories about human development that present different views about how infants develop and why they behave in certain ways. Theories are important because they are sources of ideas for debate, study, and educational practices. However, deciding which theorist to believe or "buy into" is difficult, especially for first-time students. Keep in mind that most theories provide some "kernels" of truth and valuable insights about infant development. No one theory explains all aspects of growth and development, and each theory must be evaluated on the basis of research evidence.

Contradictory Research Findings. Unfortunately, research findings on various theoretical questions about infant development are often "contradictory and inconclusive." For example, you will find that researchers often reach different conclusions about the perceptual capacities of newborn and older infants. In many cases the differences may be attributed to the use of different research methods and interpretation of findings. One researcher may use visual preference procedures to study visual acuity, while another uses brain wave measurements to study the same question. Writers of textbooks have to sort through and interpret numerous theories and thousands of research studies. For some topics, the many available research studies reveal sufficient consistencies in their results to provide definite answers to questions about infant development. However, many other questions remain unanswered because there are not enough studies available or because several studies report contradictory findings. In addition, many studies contain methodological flaws that make their results unacceptable. Consequently, it is important to consider critically the overall weight of research evidence and avoid making firm conclusions on the basis of limited research findings.

SUMMARY

Some Basic Questions

- Some of the basic questions we consider throughout the book are: What are the abilities and needs of infants at various stages in their development? How do infants and parenting practices differ from culture to culture? Why do infants grow, develop, and behave in the ways they do? What factors influence development from conception through infancy? What childrearing practices best facilitate the development of infants?

Historical Perspectives

- Until the late 1800s, many unwanted infants were murdered or abandoned by their parents. Many others died of disease or abuse. During the 1900s, medical care, attitudes, and childrearing practices gradually improved. The current "helping" mode reflects an increased concern for the physical and psychological development of infants.

Underlying Issues and Recurrent Themes

- The relative influence of heredity and environment on infant development has been an ongoing controversy for centuries. The extent to which infancy is a critical period in human development also continues to be the subject of scientific debate.
- Additional underlying issues and recurring themes of infant development discussed in this book are norms and individual differences, interrelationships among different areas of development, laws of developmental direction, the concept of the competent infant, and ways in which infants and adults influence each other.

Theoretical Perspectives

- Theories of infant development discussed include nativistic or maturational, behavioral, psychoanalytic and psychosocial, cognitive developmental, information-processing, social contextual, and developmental systems.

Methods of Studying Infants

- Techniques for conducting research with infants have improved dramatically since the first "baby diaries" were recorded. The use of high-tech equipment and sophisticated research procedures now make it possible to assess a variety of infant responses. Methods of obtaining information about infants are often based on the infant's tendency to habituate to stimuli after a period of exposure, to be surprised by unexpected events, and to prefer new over old stimuli. Specific measures of infant responses include their visual preferences, brain waves, PET and fMRI scans, heart rate, body temperature, body chemistry, facial expressions, and sucking rates. Parent reports and behavioral observations are also used to obtain information about infant functioning.

Risk and Resiliency

- Many infants are born under circumstances and with challenges that may prevent them from following typical developmental patterns. Infants who have a genetic history, biological, or environmental background that threatens to delay or impair normal growth and development are referred to as infants at-risk. Two basic categories of risk are established risk and potential risk.
- Some infants develop into competent children and adults in spite of the odds against them. These are resilient infants who have good developmental outcomes while living under stressful conditions such as economic hardship, child abuse, or biological risk.

Developmental Assessment

- There are numerous instruments available for assessing infant development. Assessment instruments are usually classified as norm-referenced or criterion-referenced tests.
- Basic guidelines for the assessment of infants and young children include the use of multiple sources of information, collaboration between professionals and parents, identification of children's strengths in addition to developmental delays, the presence of parents or familiar adults, and sensitivity to social, linguistic, and ethnic characteristics of families and infants.

Sources of Error and Confusion in Studying Infants

- Two major sources of errors and difficulty in understanding infant development are the numerous contradictory theories and inconclusive research findings.

KEY TERMS

infant
infancy
toddler
maturationists
nativists
empiricists
tabula rasa
transactional perspective
niche-picking
critical period
norms
cephalocaudal principle
proximodistal principle
competence motivation
nativistic or maturational theories
behavioral theories
psychoanalytic and psychosocial theories
cognitive developmental theories
social contextual theorists
developmental systems theories
baby diary
habituation
dishabituation
novelty
visual preference technique
violation-of-expectation method
vagal tone
cortisol
thermography
at-risk
established risk
potential risk
resilient infants
norm-referenced tests
Denver II
criterion-referenced instruments

INFORMATION ON THE WEB*

www.srcd.org. Official Web site of the Society for Research in Child Development (SRCD). Provides information about the work of the organization, publications, membership, and ethical standards for research with children.

*Web sites are subject to change.

www.zerotothree.org. Official Web site of *Zero to Three,* a national nonprofit charitable organization to promote the healthy development of infants and toddlers. Site contains information for professionals and parents on infant development and care.

TWO

PRENATAL DEVELOPMENT

Where did you come from baby dear?
Out of the everywhere into here.
—George MacDonald

Zygote, blastocyst, embryo, and *fetus* are among the terms used to label the developing human infant at various stages of prenatal development. None of these words, however, adequately conveys the profound complexity of the drama of life before birth. For centuries, scientists have attempted to understand the process of how life begins in the hidden world of the mother's womb. Although much of the mystery remains to be solved, the intricate details of prenatal development have been meticulously catalogued through the analysis of specimens of medical and spontaneous abortions at various stages of development. This chapter provides a chronological summary of the major developments during the various stages of the prenatal period. In addition, factors that affect the health and well-being of the human infant before birth, as well as after birth, are discussed.

FERTILIZATION

Prenatal development begins the moment one of the father's sperm cells **(spermatozoa)** unites with the mother's egg cell **(ovum).** Around the 14th day after the onset of menstrual bleeding, an egg cell is released from one of the mother's ovaries into the fallopian tube (see Figure 2-1). Occasionally two or more ova are released simultaneously and, if fertilized, result in a multiple pregnancy. An ovum is about the size of the point of a needle.

Approximately 200 to 600 million sperm are deposited in the vagina close to the mouth of the uterus (cervix) during intercourse. Spermatozoa are much smaller than ova and cannot be seen without the aid of a microscope. Unlike ova, sperm have the capacity to move on their own by lashing their tails back and forth. Sperm swim

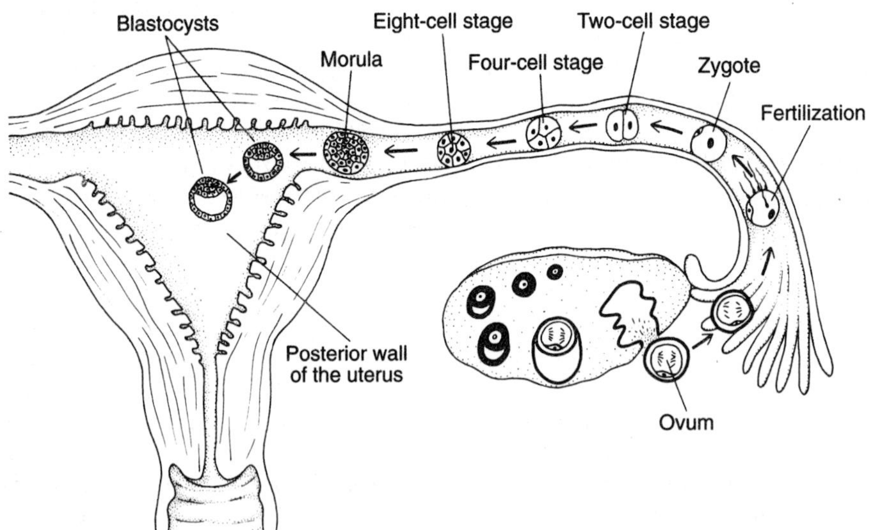

The ovum is released from the ovary and passes into the uterine (fallopian) tube, where it is met and fertilized by a sperm. The zygote divides repeatedly as it passes down the uterine tube and becomes a morula. The morula enters the uterus, develops a cavity, and becomes a blastocyst. The blastocyst usually implants itself into the lining of the posterior wall of the uterus.

Figure 2–1 Ovulation, Fertilization, and Development Through Implantation
Source: K.L. Moore (1983). *The Developing Human: Basic Embryology and Birth Defects* (2nd ed.). Philadelphia: W.B. Saunders Co., p. 32. Adapted by permission.

through the **cervix** into the uterus and up the fallopian tubes to meet the ovum. Sperm are not capable of fertilization until they undergo a seven-hour period of conditioning, called **capacitation** (Moore & Persaud, 1998). They usually remain alive for about 24 hours, but some sperm may be capable of fertilization for up to three days.

If an ovum is not fertilized in 12 to 24 hours after ovulation, it degenerates. Only about 200 sperm reach the usual fertilization site in the widest part of the fallopian tube (Moore & Persaud, 1998). Although many of the spermatozoa may contact the ovum at the same time, usually only one reaches the nucleus and accomplishes fertilization and the entry of other sperm is blocked. If more than one sperm fuses with an ovum the pregnancy will probably terminate early, or abnormal development will likely result from the presence of the extra chromosomes (Carlson, 1999; Carr, 1971). Even if one sperm fertilizes an ovum, more than one-half of all pregnancies end in a spontaneous abortion (**miscarriage**) within the first three weeks. The most common reason for such miscarriages is chromosomal abnormalities (Carlson, 1999).

Artificial Insemination and In Vitro Fertilization. When a woman has fertility problems, she may elect to utilize artificial insemination. This is a process whereby a donor's sperm is deposited by a syringe into the vagina. The sperm are then left to find their way to the ovum. A woman may also attempt to become pregnant through in vitro fertilization (IVF) and "embryo" transfer. The IVF process involves the removal of several ova from the prospective mother or from a donor. The ova are then placed in a test tube or a Petri dish within a special culture fluid. Sperm are then added to the mixture. When fertilization has occurred and the cell has divided four to eight times, the embryo is transferred through the cervical canal into the uterus. Although the incidence of spontaneous abortion is higher than it is for other pregnancies, many thousands of successful IVF pregnancies have occurred since this technique was first used in 1978 (Moore & Persaud, 1998).

PREEMBRYONIC PERIOD

Fertilization marks the beginning of the preembryonic period of human development. This is the starting point for the conceptual age or **fertilization age** on which the timetable or calendar of prenatal development is usually based. The preembroyonic period lasts until the end of the second week after fertilization when the embryo begins to form. Calculated from the date of fertilization, the prenatal period typically lasts 266 days or 38 weeks. However, another reference point used in clinical medicine for timing the prenatal period is the first day of the last normal menstrual period and is called the menstrual or **gestational age.** In that case, prenatal period is extended by 14 days to a total 280 days or 40 weeks. Unless otherwise indicated, all statements in this text about age of embryonic and fetal development are based on the fertilization age rather than the gestational age.

Once the ovum has been fertilized, a series of rapid changes takes place. The nuclei of the two parent cells merge, and the hereditary material from each is arranged into a blueprint for a new life. The gender of the baby is determined at that time. The mother contributes a sex chromosome that is always an X, whereas the father contributes, by random selection, either an X-bearing or a Y-bearing sex chromosome. If the chromosome is an X, the baby will be a girl (XX). If the chromosome is a Y, the baby will be a boy (XY). (In rare cases the sperm may carry a mixture of sex chromosomes, which results in the development of a baby that is not genetically distinguishable as either male or female.) The newly fertilized ovum is called a zygote. Within 36 hours, the zygote divides into two cells. As the zygote moves slowly through the fallopian tube on the way to the uterus, cell division continues. The series of rapid cell divisions results in a progressively larger number of increasingly smaller cells (Gasser, 1975). By about the third day after fertilization, the mass of cells is composed of 12 to 16 cells and resembles a mulberry in shape. At this point, the cell mass is called a **morula** because of its knobby appearance (Singer, 1995). The morula enters the uterus about four days after fertilization. The cells, numbering about 58, cluster around a central cavity and become known as a **blastocyst.** Inside the blastocyst a small group of microscopic cells cluster to one side and begin to form the embryo and the supporting membranes.

Implantation. For two or three days, the blastocyst floats freely in the uterus. It is about the same size as the original ovum, but its content has been dramatically altered. Around the sixth day, the blastocyst attaches itself to the lining of the uterus. By this time the blastocyst has grown an outer layer of cells called tryphoblasts, which bury into the uterine lining by secreting enzymes that break down the cells at the implantation site. After implantation is completed, around the 10th day after fertilization, enzymatic digestion stops as abruptly as it began. The implantation is usually healed over in a scarlike cyst by the 13th or 14th day. At that time the baby is connected with the mother and circulation between the two has begun. Occasionally, implantation is accompanied by bleeding that can be mistaken for menstruation.

Not all fertilized ova become attached to the uterus. Scientists estimate that about one-third to one-half of all zygotes fail to implant and are flushed out of the uterus with the onset of menstruation (Pansky, 1982; Sadler, 1990). In addition, many of the embryos that become implanted are spontaneously aborted because of severe abnormalities (Tanner, 1990). Occasionally the zygote becomes lodged in the fallopian tube or makes its way to the abdominal cavity, the ovary, or the pelvic area.

Implantation Sites. In most cases, implantation occurs in the upper half of the uterus (see Figure 2-1). If the blastocyst becomes implanted in the extreme lower part, there is a risk of bleeding after the fourth month of pregnancy. This condition is called **placental previa** and endangers both the mother and the baby (Dryden, 1978). Implantation within the opening of the uterus (cervix) is called a **cervical pregnancy.** This situation rarely occurs but usually leads to spontaneous abortion (Moore & Persaud, 1998).

Implantation outside the uterus is called an **ectopic pregnancy.** Ordinarily ectopic pregnancies lead to the death of the embryo during the second month. In some cases the health of the mother is threatened because of excessive bleeding. In instances too rare to calculate, an ectopic pregnancy may continue long enough to result in the birth of a live baby. One such exceptional case was reported in Burlington, North Carolina, where a 32-year-old woman gave birth to a normal 6-pound, 4-ounce baby boy. The baby had developed in the mother's abdomen and was removed surgically. No one knew the woman had an ectopic pregnancy until the time of delivery ("Burlington Wife," 1979).

EMBRYONIC PERIOD

By the time the process of implantation is complete at the end of the second week the inner cell, a mass clustered to one side of the blastocyst, has formed a tiny embryonic disk. The word **embryo** is based on the Greek word *embryon* meaning "a swelling." The term signifies the growth (swelling) of cells inside the fertilized ovum, as well as the beginning of all major internal and external structures of the body. The embryonic period covers the time from about two weeks after fertilization until the end of the eighth prenatal week.

The Germ Layers. During the third week, three germ layers are formed through the process called **gastrulation**—the development of body form. Each of the germ layers forms the foundation for the development of specific body structures (Moore & Persaud, 1998). One germ layer, the ectoderm, is thicker and will later form the nervous system, backbone, skin, hair, nails, and parts of the eyes and ears. The endoderm will develop into the digestive tract, respiratory system, liver, and various glands. A third layer of cells, the mesoderm, is sandwiched between the ectoderm and endoderm. This middle layer of cells forms the circulatory, excretory, and reproductive systems, skeleton, muscles, and connecting tissues. At the end of the first month of development, the embryo and its supporting membranes are about the size of a pea.

Supporting Membranes.

Chorion. Approximately three weeks after fertilization, the outer layer of cells surrounding the embryo is called the **chorion.** This membrane, which resembles a round sponge, encloses the embryo and its supporting tissues. One side of the chorion is attached to the lining of the uterus and, combined with the maternal tissues, develops into the placenta. A second cavity, called the amniotic cavity, develops inside the chorion (see "Amnion" below).

Placenta. The **placenta** provides the link between the mother and the embryo where exchanges of nutrients, waste products, oxygen, hormones, and antibodies take place. Unfortunately, viruses and other harmful substances can also cross over from the mother to the embryo. In addition to transporting substances between the mother and embryo, the placenta performs metabolic functions and produces hormones (Carlson, 1999). The placenta continues to develop throughout pregnancy. At three weeks it covers about 20 percent of the uterus. By five months, half of the uterus is covered. At full term, the placenta is about 6 to 8 inches in diameter, 1 inch thick, and weighs approximately 1 pound (Rugh & Shettles, 1971; Singer, 1995).

Umbilical Cord. The early embryo is attached to the placenta by a mushroom-shaped connecting stalk, the forerunner of the umbilical cord. The **umbilical cord** serves as the connecting link between placenta and embryo. The cord contains two arteries and a vein. The arteries carry blood containing waste products to the placenta, while the vein carries nutrients, oxygen, and other substances to the embryo. At full term, the cord is typically 1/2 to 3/4 inch thick and approximately 20 to 24 inches long (Jirasek, 1983). It is usually twisted many times, but if (in rare cases) the cord becomes tightly knotted as the result of fetal movements, the developing baby may suffer loss of oxygen leading to brain damage or death (Carlson, 1999).

Amnion. When the embryonic disc is formed, a small space, called the amniotic cavity, is formed on one side of the inner cell mass. A larger cavity, known as the **primary yolk sac,** is formed on the other side. The embryo stretches between the amniotic cavity and the primary yolk sac. As the embryo develops, the amniotic cavity enlarges within the expanding chorionic cavity. Eventually the yolk sac disappears, and the amniotic cavity totally encloses the embryo within the walls of a thin, tough transparent membrane called the **amnion.** The cavity is filled with a salty liquid called amniotic fluid. The **amniotic sac,** often called the bag of waters, serves as a shock absorber, allows freedom of movement, helps control the temperature of the fetus, serves as a barrier to infection, and prevents the amnion from sticking to the fetus (Callen & Filley, 1990). In the beginning, the amniotic fluid is mostly (99 percent) water that is changed every three hours through the placenta. As the fetus develops, urine and fecal matter (meconium) are secreted into the fluid. The fetus swallows the sterile amniotic fluid in increasing amounts throughout the prenatal period (Moore & Persaud, 1998). With the umbilical cord serving as a lifeline, the developing fetus floats freely within the amniotic cavity, somewhat like an astronaut in outer space.

Yolk Sac. As the amniotic sac expands, the primary yolk sac decreases in size and forms a much smaller **secondary yolk sac.** The human yolk sac, unlike that of bird eggs, contains no nutrients. However, it is apparently instrumental in the transfer of nutrients to the embryo before the placental connection is made with the mother. The yolk sac also serves as a source of blood cells until the liver begins to function around the sixth week (Moore & Persaud, 1998).

The Nervous System. During the third week after fertilization, the central nervous system begins to develop through a process called **neurulation.** The ectoderm (outer layer of the embryo) folds over to form the neural tube. The major divisions of the nervous system are produced along the length of this primitive structure (Nowakowski, 1987). During the process of neurulation, the tube is sealed, with the top part developing into the brain as the tail end becomes the spinal cord. Three distinct bulges that will become the forebrain, midbrain, and hindbrain soon appear at the top of the neural tube (Singer, 1995; Spreen, Risser, & Edgell, 1995). A primitive form of the spinal cord is present by the 9th or 10th week (Moore & Persaud, 1998).

Once the neural tube is formed at about four weeks, cells that store and transmit information, called **neurons,** are generated within its walls. The neurons proliferate rapidly throughout each area of the neural tube. The cells are formed in locations that are physically separate from their intended destination within the central nervous system. Therefore, the neurons must eventually migrate to their final location where they differentiate and assume their special functions (Nowakowski, 1987). The migration of neurons continues until about the 28th week (Kolb, 1989).

The formation and migration of neurons is only one of the many processes involved in human brain development. Another major critical process is the formation of communication connections between the neurons, referred to as **synapses.** The formation of synapses begins in the spinal cord as early as the fifth week and in the upper part of the brain at seven weeks (Eliot, 1999). However, this is a prolonged process that continues even in adulthood whereby intricate connections between the neurons are formed (Kolb, 1999).

The span of time between the 3rd and 16th prenatal weeks has been identified as the "most critical period for brain development" (Moore & Persaud, 1998, p. 183). This is the stage of rapid growth when the embryo is most susceptible to damage from drugs, toxins, and other environmental agents. However, different growth spurts occur at different times in different regions of the brain, so other critical periods have been identified (Kolb, 1989). Additional information about critical periods and other aspects of brain development is presented in Chapter 4.

Other Body Systems. During the second month of life, the various parts of the embryo continue developing at a fantastic rate, changing almost daily. Rapid brain growth causes the head to grow to almost one-half of the total body length. The facial region begins to develop in the fourth week, squeezed between the forebrain and the heart. Placodes, or rounded areas of specialized thickened tissue, have developed as the locations for the eyes, ears, and nose. The external face of the embroyo begins to assume human features by six weeks of age (Moss-Salentijn & Hendricks-Klyvert, 1990).

On the opposite end, the 28-day-old embryo has a pointed tail that curls up in a C-shape toward the top of the bulbous head that bends downward. The tail will disappear by the end of the eighth week. A string of budlike structures, called **somites,** have formed along the outer arch of the embryo. The somites serve as the foundation of the skeleton. The embryonic skeleton consists mostly of cartilage, a rubbery material found, among other places, in the end of an adult's nose. The limb buds are now visible as small swellings on the embryo's surface. The arm buds develop slightly ahead of the leg buds. Deciduous (temporary) teeth have begun to form beneath the gums. The primitive beginnings of some of the permanent teeth form as early as the 12th prenatal week.

The rudimentary elements of the urinary system also emerge during the first month. The embryo develops three successive sets of kidneys within the fourth and fifth weeks. The third set begins secreting urine by the eighth week and remains as the permanent kidneys.

The primitive elements of a cardiovascular system appears around the 18th day with a horseshoe-shaped tube. The heart begins its first fluttering beats around the 21st or 22nd day after fertilization. Like the head, the heart is large in proportion to the other organs at this stage. Even though it is relatively incomplete at this time, the heart is strong enough to circulate blood produced by the embryo through a primitive system of veins and arteries, the umbilical cord, and the placenta. The cardiovascular system (heart, arteries, and veins) is the first major organ system to

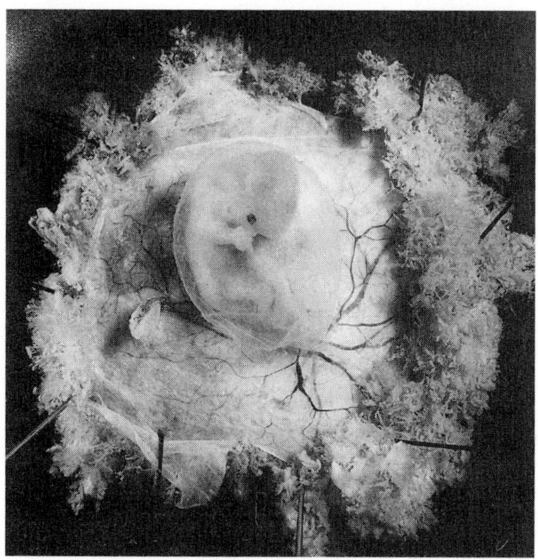

Seven-week-old embryo

begin functioning. (Carlson, 1999; Moore & Persaud, 1998).

At the end of eight weeks (56 days), the overall appearance of the embryo is unmistakably human. It measures about 1-1/2 inches long from head to buttocks and weighs about 1/3 ounce. The basic form of the skeleton is complete. The internal organs have continued to develop, and all the major systems are present. The embryo resembles a tiny doll with a large head, carefully formed arms and legs, and a protruding abdomen. The face is characterized by slitlike eyes and small ear lobes (Rugh & Shettles, 1971). From the beginning of the ninth week, the developing organism is called a **fetus**—a "young one." The name change signifies the completion of human form and the appearance of the first bone cells in the skeleton. A new act in the drama of life before birth has begun.

FETAL PERIOD

The fetal period is characterized by rapid growth in body size of the developing baby. The various body organs and systems become larger, distinct, and more complex. Most of the systems begin to take on their specific functions before birth.

Early Fetal Development: 9–20 Weeks. At the beginning of the fetal stage, the uterus has expanded to the point where the mother's pregnancy begins to "show." The head makes up at least one-half of the fetus, but the ratio gradually decreases during the remainder of the prenatal period. The development of the facial area is completed during the 12th week (Spreen et al., 1995). The eyes have undergone further development. By the third month, the various parts of the eyeball have formed, including the cornea, lens, and retina. The optic nerves, which began to develop at four weeks, now link the eyes directly to the brain. Around the ninth week the eyelids develop as two layers of skin that completely cover each eyeball and are sealed shut. They remain closed until about the 26th week.

The sex of an infant is determined at fertilization by the sperm that fertilizes the ovum. However, all human embryos go through a primitive stage of development when their genital systems are not distinguishable as male or female. Internally, sex differentiation begins toward the end of the second month. External sex organs begin to appear early in the fetal period but are similar in males and females until the end of the ninth week.

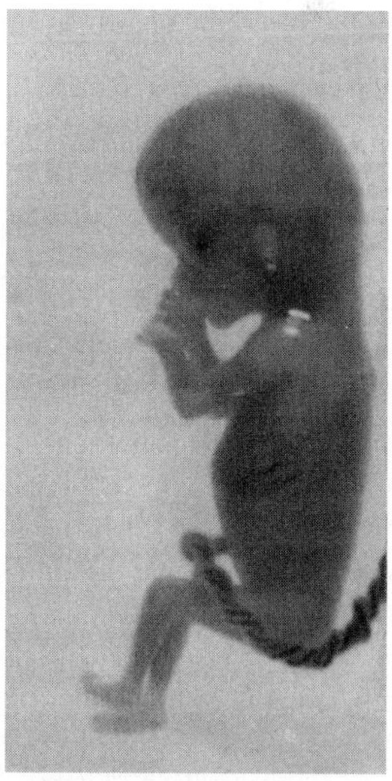

Fetus at three months

Their mature form is clearly observable and distinguishable in the 12th week (Pansky, 1982).

Between 13 and 16 weeks the fetus grows rapidly in both height and weight (Pansky, 1982). The legs grow longer as the head becomes proportionately smaller. The hands and feet are well formed. Bone cells also grow rapidly during this stage. The ears move to their normal position on the sides of the head. The fetal heart is beating at 120 to 160 beats a minute and circulating blood throughout the body (Rugh & Shettles, 1971). Heartbeats can be heard through a nonamplified stethoscope at about 16 weeks. The fetus apparently becomes sensitive to light at this time and will turn away from bright light shown on the mother's abdomen (Bernhardt, 1987).

The mother begins to feel the movements of the fetus, referred to as **quickening,** around 17 weeks of pregnancy. By that time the skin of the fetus is covered with a waxy, cheeselike substance called **vernix caseosa.** The vernix ("varnish") protects the fetus's skin from chapping and cracking during the long immersion in the amniotic fluid. By 20 weeks the fetus is also covered with tiny, downlike hairs called **lanugo.** The eyebrows and scalp hair are also visible. The lanugo usually falls out before the end of prenatal period, but some of it may still be present at birth (Moore & Persaud, 1998).

By 20 weeks, virtually all the neurons have been produced (Huttenlocher, 1994). On average, over a quarter of a million neurons are generated every minute of the prenatal period (Wortman, Loftus, & Marshall, 1992). Most of these cells are generated between 10 weeks and 20 weeks after fertilization. From then until maturity, the neurons grow in size, but not in number. They also form trillions of connections with each other. However, **neuroglia** (glial cells) that support the neurons continue to be added throughout the remainder of the prenatal period until sometime after birth (Tanner, 1990). The most important function of the glial cells is to produce a fatty lipid called myelin that forms around each neuron before the nervous system reaches maturity. This process, called **myelination,** begins around 20 weeks and increases rapidly throughout the prenatal period until the brain reaches maturity. The development of the cerebral hemispheres also proceeds at a rapid pace during this period. The increasing number of cortical cells results in the shaping of the folds and convolutions that are characteristic of the mature brain (Spreen et al., 1995).

Late Fetal Development: Weeks 21–38. A picture of the fetus at approximately 21 weeks reveals a thin layer of pinkish red transparent skin. With little fat underneath, the blood vessels are clearly visible. Although still top-heavy, the proportions of the body are now more similar to those of the newborn infant. The fetus sleeps and wakes at regular intervals (not necessarily the same as the mother's!) and has a favorite resting position. During this period, the lungs develop and become capable of functioning with the production of surfactant, a chemical that is necessary for breathing (Needleman, 1996). The fetus may suck its thumb and engage in other reflexive activities such as swallowing, grasping, stretching, and yawning. Researchers have found that fetuses blink their eyes in response to sounds between 26 and 29 weeks, indicating that the sense of hearing is functioning (Bornstein & Lamb, 1992).

The brain continues its rapid pace of growth as the outer layer of the brain (cerebral cortex) develops. The immature brain acquires its general adultlike shape by the end of the prenatal period (Spreen et al., 1995). The lungs have developed the capacity to breathe, even though they are not completely mature. During the last few weeks before birth, the fetus rapidly puts on protective fat in preparation for life in the outside world. The baby does not change much in appearance except to add weight and height. Its movements are more restricted as the living quarters becomes crowded. If the fetus is not born too early, antibodies are acquired from the mother that provide temporary protection against some communicable diseases such as measles, mumps, whooping cough, and polio. As the placenta ages and becomes less efficient, the fetus's growth rate slows down. The end of the prenatal period and the beginning of the birth process are near.

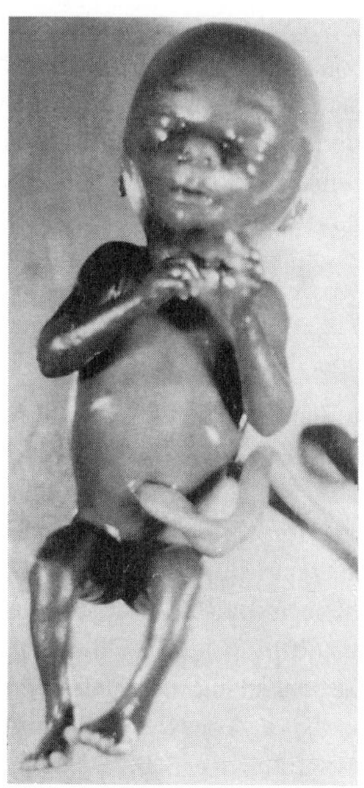

Seven-month-old fetus

MULTIPLE PREGNANCIES

When two separate ova are fertilized during the same ovulatory cycle, dizygotic (DZ) or fraternal twins are conceived. Approximately two-thirds of twins are produced from two zygotes (Moore & Persaud, 1998). Twins may also originate from a single zygote that divides into two equal parts. When that happens, monozygotic (MZ) or identical twins are the result. The incidence of DZ twins varies somewhat from country to country, but the number of MZ twins born each year is remarkably similar throughout the world (Benirschke, 1995).

Dizygotic twins have separate chorions, amnions, and placentas. If they implant close together chorions and placentas tend to grow together (fuse). Monozygotic twins usually develop within separate amnions, but are enclosed in one chorion and share a common placenta. In rare cases when the zygote divides within the first three days, the embryos will have separate placentas and chorions with two placentas that may be separate or fused (Dunnihoo, 1992). Other multiple births, such as triplets and quadruplets, are produced in various possible combinations of the above fertilizations.

In recent years the number of multiple births in the United States has increased dramatically. The rate of twin births has risen by approximately 50 percent since 1980. The increase in multiple births has been fueled by advances in the use of fertility drugs and in vitro fertilizations that increase the likelihood of such births, from twins to quintuplets (Coustan, 1995b). Twins account for about 98 percent of all multiple births. However, the number of triplet and higher-order births declined in 1999 (Ventura et al., 2001).

Multiple births, especially quadruplets and quintuplets, attract a lot of attention and delight, but they can also overwhelm their families. Unfortunately, adverse birth outcomes are more common among multiple gestations. While one twin might be healthy, the other one may experience intrauterine growth delay or fail to survive. Birth defects are twice as high in twins as in single births. Multiples are also more prone to premature birth and low birth weight (Coustan, 1995b).

INFLUENCES ON DEVELOPMENT

Each year approximately 3 to 7 percent of human newborns have a birth defect requiring medical attention (Goldman, 1984; Shepherd, 1991). It is estimated that almost half of the children being treated in hospitals are there because of prenatally acquired malformations. Birth defects are sometimes called congenital (meaning "present at birth") malformations. Congenital malformations are caused by genetic factors, environmental influences, or a combination of the two. About one-fourth of all birth defects are attributed to purely genetic factors, while environmental factors alone probably account for approximately one-tenth of such problems (Friedman & Polifka, 1994). It is difficult to separate genetic from environmental conditions, and most malformations probably come from a complex combination of both factors. Our knowledge about the cause and prevention of these problems is, in most cases, extremely limited (Shepherd, 1991).

Genetic Factors. Genetic factors play a significant role in human development throughout the life span. At the moment of fertilization, an infant receives the genetic code that is a blueprint or set of instructions for cell division and the development of individual features. The genetic code, which is unique for each individual, is carried by genes and chromosomes. Chromosomes are spiral-shaped structures within a cell's nucleus. They contain a chemical substance called deoxyribonucleic acid, or DNA. Genes are basic units of heredity that are contained within the chromosomes. Individual chromosomes contain thousands of genes. Each parent contributes one-half of the hereditary material to the infant by means of the reproductive or germ cells (sperm and ova) created in the testes of the father and the ovaries of the mother.

The human body contains two types of cells: somatic (body cells) and sex (reproductive cells). Each growth cell normally contains a total of 46 chromosomes. The chromosomes come in 23 matching pairs, except in cells containing an X and Y sex chromosome combination. Growth (somatic) cells for the development and replacement of body tissue are formed through the process of cell duplication called **mitosis.** During mitosis, cells divide and make exact copies of themselves. The process takes place during different stages when two daughter cells, containing the same genetic material, are created from one parent cell.

The process by which reproductive or germ cells are formed is called **meiosis,** or reduction division. During meiosis each chromosome pair separates to form two cells. Thus, the sperm or ova produced by meiosis normally contain only a total of 23 single chromosomes. When the sperm and ovum unite at the time of fertilization, a total of 46 chromosomes is once again attained. The process of meiosis is more complicated than mitosis. Thus, there is more room for errors that result in cells containing chromosomal numerical or structural irregularities or genetic mutations.

Genes determine the infant's individual hereditary characteristics such as eye, hair, and skin color, as well as internal organ systems. Because of the complex laws of genetics, an individual may inherit a specific characteristic, such as blue eyes, even when one parent or both parents have a different characteristic, such as brown eyes. However, all genetic disorders are not inherited. Defective genes must come from one or both parents in order for a condition to be inherited. In some cases, genetic problems result from aberrations during the transmission and recombination process at the time of fertilization (Meryash, 1995).

Some human characteristics are determined by a single pair of genes, one from the father and one from the mother, whereas other traits are controlled by multiple gene pairs. Some genes are dominant, and others are recessive. When a dominant gene is paired with a recessive gene, the hereditary trait carried by the dominant gene is always present in the individual. A hereditary trait carried by a recessive gene prevails only when it is paired with a recessive gene of the same type.

The complexity of the information contained in the human genetic program is enormous. Scientists estimate that a human zygote contains 100 billion bits of information, which is equivalent to 10 million printed pages. Considering the complexity of the genetic code, it is amazing that the large majority of infants are born without defects (Goldman, 1984). Actually most fertilized cells (ovum) with chromosomal abnormalities do not survive. In some cases though, defects in the genes or chromosomes result in the live birth of a child with a genetic disorder. Some of the genetic problems are relatively mild and do not cause major problems, whereas others result in severe developmental disabilities. Many genetic flaws are obvious at birth, but some are "time bombs" that cause problems only later in life. Genetic disorders can be classified into four types: (1) chromosomal abnormalities, (2) single gene disorders, (3) sex-linked disorders, and (4) polygenic inheritance.

Chromosomal Abnormalities. Disabilities may be caused by the presence of more or less than the normal 46 chromosomes or by a defect in the structure of one or more chromosomes (Widerstrom,

Mowder, & Sandall, 1991). The most common disorder caused by chromosomal aberrations is **Down syndrome.** In most cases (95 percent), Down syndrome is caused by the presence of an extra chromosome (No. 21), making a total of 47 instead of the usual 46 chromosomes (Stewart, Manchester, & Sujansky, 1995). Down syndrome is also caused by the presence of an extra piece of chromosome 21, which becomes attached to another chromosome (e.g., No. 14) during meiosis. In that case, an infant will have the usual 46 chromosomes, but the extra amount of chromosome 21 leads to Down syndrome. Infants with Down syndrome have distinctive features. They have a relatively small head, small ears, and slanting eyes. The infants have a large protruding tongue, thin straight hair, and small hands with stubby fingers. They are usually shorter than average in height. The condition results in moderate to severe mental disability. Down syndrome occurs in approximately 1 out of every 600 to 800 births (Meryash, 1995; Stewart et al., 1995).

Other major chromosomal abnormalities are sometimes found in the sex chromosomes (No. 23). The most frequent sex chromosome abnormality is **Klinefelter syndrome,** which occurs when a male child is born with two X chromosomes and one Y chromosome. Klinefelter syndrome may not be noticeable until after puberty. In about a third of the cases, males begin to develop feminine breasts, small testes, and very sparse beard and pubic hair. The disorder frequently results in learning disabilities and a slightly lowered level of intelligence.

A comparable sex chromosomal disorder that affects females is called **Turner syndrome.** This condition occurs when an infant is born with only one sex (X) chromosome, resulting in a total of 45 chromosomes. Turner syndrome causes delayed growth, a "webbed" neck, widely spaced nipples, and ovaries that do not function. Most females who have this disorder develop normal intelligence, but they may have visual-perceptual problems that lead to learning disabilities (Batshaw, 1997). Problems sometimes result from defects in the structure of chromosomes involving the gain, loss, or rearrangement of chromosomal sections (Widerstrom et al., 1991). ***Cri du chat* syndrome** is a disorder caused by a missing section of chromosome No. 5. The cry of the infant affected by this problem resembles the meowing of a cat. Affected infants also have an unusual facial appearance, reduced head and brain size, congenital heart disease, and severe mental disabilities (Batshaw, 1997).

Single Gene Disorders. Many genetic disorders result from a single gene, or a pair of genes, contributed by one or both parents, following the laws of genetic transmission. These abnormalities may be classified according to a dominant, recessive, or sex-linked pattern of inheritance. Hundreds of disorders resulting from dominant genes have been identified, including dwarfism (achondroplasia); some forms of glaucoma; **Huntington's chorea** (a progressive degeneration of the nervous system); and polydactyly (extra fingers or toes). If one parent has such a disorder, each offspring has a 50 percent chance of being affected by the same problem. Dominantly inherited disorders usually cause developmental problems, but their effects are relatively mild in comparison to recessive genetic disorders.

Both parents must carry the defective recessive gene before the offspring can be affected. In such pregnancies there is a 25 percent chance that the infant will have the recessive trait. **Phenylketonuria (PKU)** is one of the major recessive genetic disorders. The infant with PKU cannot produce an enzyme necessary for the digestion of an amino acid (phenylalanine) found in milk and many other foods. The unmetabolized phenylalanine accumulates in the infant's body and, over time, causes severe brain damage. Infants born in the United States are routinely tested for PKU. The ones who are affected are placed on a special diet to eliminate the offending substance. When brain development is almost complete, around 10 to 12 years of age, the child can go on a regular diet.

Other recessively linked disorders that result in severe, life-threatening problems include: **cystic fibrosis**—a disease that affects the mucous, sweat, tear, and salivary glands, causing congestion in the breathing passages; **sickle cell**

anemia—a blood disease that produces malformed red blood cells and weakens resistance to infection and other symptoms. This disease primarily affects people of African ancestry; **Tay-Sachs disease**—a fatal disease that causes the nervous system to degenerate. This condition primarily affects people of eastern European Jewish ancestry. These diseases are almost always fatal, but many affected infants live for several years.

Sex-linked Disorders. A variety of hereditary disorders are caused by defective genes carried by the sex chromosomes. Most of these are recessive genes attached to the X chromosomes. Color blindness, hemophilia (deficiency in blood clotting), gargoylism (dwarfing and body deformities), and some forms of muscular dystrophy are examples of defects caused by sex-linked genes. More male than female infants are affected by such genetic abnormalities. Since males have only one X chromosome, it automatically has freedom to express any defect inherited from the mother. Females are less likely to inherit sex-linked diseases because they have two X chromosomes.

Polygenic Inheritance. Most inherited characteristics of human beings are the result of the combined effects of many genes rather than simple combinations of single pairs of recessive or dominant genes. This is referred to as **polygenic** (or multifactoral) **inheritance.** Characteristics that result from the combined effect of genetic and environmental factors are attributed to polygenic inheritance. Among typically developing infants, most differences such as intelligence and body size are caused by several factors. A number of common congenital disorders are also attributed to polygenic inheritance (Stewart et al., 1995). Spina bifida (exposed spinal cord), anencephaly (incomplete brain and skull), hydrocephaly (enlarged head with excessive fluid), cleft lip and palate, and congenital heart disease are examples of multifactorial disorders.

Environmental Factors. Although the human embryo is well protected in the amniotic sac, a variety of toxic substances can cross the placental barrier and cause malformations or other problems. Drugs, viruses, radiation, and other agents that cause permanent defects in infants exposed during the prenatal period are called **teratogens.** Scientists have made remarkable progress in identifying products and other environmental conditions that are associated with birth defects. However, establishing definite proof that specific substances are harmful to the unborn child is difficult because of the numerous factors involved. The effects of a drug or other substance are dependent on genetic susceptibility, stage (timing) of prenatal development, amount of exposure (dosage), length of exposure, method of exposure, interactions with other substances, maternal health, nutritional status, and other conditions affecting the prenatal environment (Hogge, 1990).

Drugs and Medications. The adverse effects of a variety of drugs and medicines have been documented in numerous research studies. Maternal use of prescription, nonprescription, and illegal drugs may affect the embryo in both dramatic and subtle ways. The most clearly observable effects are physical deformities, delayed growth, central nervous system disorders, and internal organ dysfunctions. A tragic example was seen in the use of the tranquilizer Thalidomide. In the 1960s, scientists discovered that a single dose of this drug taken between 21 and 35 days after fertilization often produced babies with severely malformed or missing limbs. More subtle effects of drugs used during pregnancy include learning disabilities and behavioral problems such as irritability or hyperactivity.

Between 40 and 90 percent of pregnant women in the United States take at least one drug, and many ingest two or more compounds. While hundreds of substances have been approved as safe for use during pregnancy, the effects of many others are not known (Levy & Koren, 1992). The drugs and chemicals that may possibly produce birth defects or other problems are numerous. The list includes illegal drugs such as marijuana, heroin, and cocaine, and many prescription and nonprescription drugs and chemical compounds given to treat epilepsy, diabetes, blood disorders, acne, and infection, as well as tranquilizers, hormones, and barbiturates. A number of environmental pollutants such as lead and mercury are also listed as potential teratogens (L. Hill & Kleinberg, 1984a; Hogge, 1990; Levy & Koren, 1992).

There is growing concern about widely used over-the-counter medicines such as aspirin, antihistamines, diuretics, and antacids. Researchers have found an association between the mother's use of aspirin during pregnancy and the tendency of premature infants to bleed inside the brain. Studies have also found that heavy users of aspirin have an increased rate of infant mortality, low birth weight infants, prolonged pregnancies, and hemorrhaging before and after childbirth (Turner & Collins, 1975; Collins & Turner, 1975). Acetaminophen appears to be less risky for use during pregnancy (L. Hill & Kleinberg, 1984b). Unfortunately, there is not enough evidence for researchers to form definite conclusions about the safety of many pain-relief compounds and many other nonprescription medicines. In view of the limited but changing knowledge, women should check with their doctor before taking any medications or other substances during pregnancy.

Alcohol. During the past 20 years a large amount of research has accumulated confirming prenatal exposure to alcohol as a teratogen. Alcohol crosses the placenta and circulates in the bloodstream of the developing infant. The effects of prenatal exposure to alcohol vary on a continuum from spontaneous abortion to no observable effects (H. Olson, 1994). The consequences depend upon the amount of alcohol consumed, timing, and length of exposure. A host of other factors may also be involved, including the use of other drugs, dietary factors, health status, prenatal care, maternal age, and the infant's genetic susceptibility to alcohol effects (Eliason & Williams, 1990; Wekselman et al., 1995). Some studies indicate that consumption of alcohol combined with smoking cigarettes increases the risk of adverse developmental effects (Olsen, Pereira, & Olsen, 1991; Widerstrom et al., 1991).

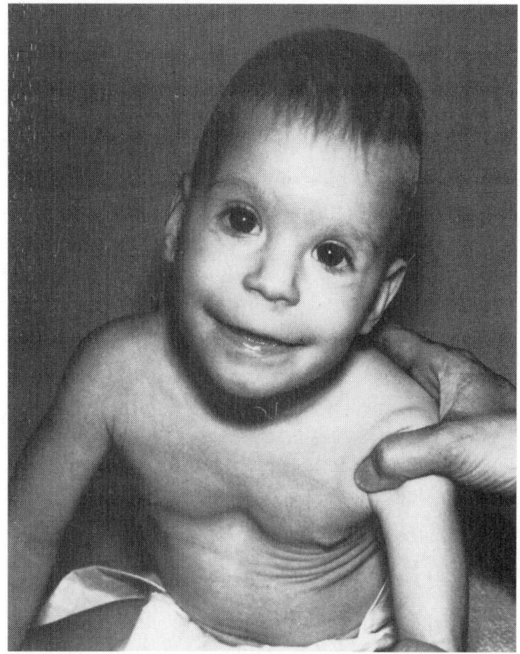

Infant with fetal alcohol syndrome. Notice the thin upper lip and wide, flat nose.

Maternal consumption of large amounts of alcohol during pregnancy can lead to full blown **fetal alcohol syndrome (FAS).** Estimates of the incidence of FAS range from 1 to 3 per 1,000 births (Olson, 1994). FAS infants suffer overall growth retardation, facial malformations, inadequate brain growth, heart defects, motor problems, skeletal defects, hyperactivity, and other difficulties. FAS has been called the leading known cause of mental disabilities in the western world (Olson, 1994). Although many of the effects may be long lasting and persistent, more information is needed about the long-term effects of prenatal alcohol exposure. Researchers have not determined why some infants of alcoholic mothers suffer from FAS, while others are apparently not affected. The risk that an alcoholic will give birth to a child with FAS during her first pregnancy has been estimated to be 6 percent, but the risk goes up to 70 percent for subsequent births (Day & Richardson, 1991).

Since there is a range of alcohol-related effects, the term possible **fetal alcohol effects (FAE)** is used in cases where the prenatal alcohol exposure has been more limited and the observable effects are not as severe as FAS. The most common results of FAE are growth retardation and central nervous system disorders. These infants tend to have decreased birth weights and suffer milder variations of some of the same problems as full-blown FAS infants, including attention deficits, impaired intellectual functioning, language deficits, sleep disorders, and impaired motor functioning (Olson, 1994; Vorhees & Mollnow, 1987; Wekselman et al., 1995; Eyler & Behnke, 1999).

Researchers have tried to determine whether there is a safe amount of alcohol that can be consumed during pregnancy. No one has yet been able to determine exactly how much alcohol is necessary to produce fetal alcohol syndrome or other developmental problems. Research evidence indicates that the consumption of one to three drinks containing 2 or more ounces of alcohol each day places the fetus at risk for growth retardation (Niebyl, 1982). Scientists are not certain about whether or not smaller amounts of alcohol produce adverse effects (Eliason & Williams, 1990). Mothers are advised to avoid consuming alcohol in any amount during pregnancy since there is no known safe amount of alcohol that can be consumed at that time.

Tobacco. When the mother smokes, the baby smokes. Exposure to tobacco smoke produces an increase in the carbon monoxide in the maternal-fetal bloodstream and reduced placental blood flow. Both of these processes reduce the supply of oxygen available to the developing baby by as much as 25 percent (Levy & Koren, 1992). Smoking also tends to cause placental abnormalities that negatively affect the flow of nutrients to the fetus. The potential problems associated with smoking during pregnancy include:

spontaneous abortion (Kullander & Kaellen, 1971)
reduced body weight, length, and head circumference (Cornelius et al., 1995; Eyler & Behnke, 1999)
increased perinatal mortality rates, including sudden infant death syndrome (SIDS) (Abel, 1983; Levy & Koren, 1992).
preterm birth (Niebyl, 1982)
cleft lip and cleft palate (Abel, 1983)
congenital heart disease (Himmelberger, Brown, & Cohen, 1978)
behavior disorders and learning difficulties (Abel, 1983)

Unborn babies are also adversely affected by "passive smoke" inhaled by the mother from other smokers (Roquer, Figueras, & Jimenez, 1995). The severity of effects of prenatal tobacco exposure, from active and/or passive maternal smoking apparently increases in proportion to the level of exposure (Cornelius et al., 1995).

Cocaine and Heroin. The use of cocaine and heroin by pregnant women appears to have become more widespread in recent years. Newborn babies whose mothers have been heavy users of cocaine or heroin (or a milder substitute, methadone) tend to be at increased risk for a number of problems including mortality, growth retardation, prematurity, physical malformations, irritability, poor behavioral organization, attention deficits, memory, and reduced ability to interact with others (Eyler & Behnke, 1999; Levy & Koren, 1992). Infants may be born in an addicted state and suffer withdrawal effects characterized by irritability, shaking, sweating, and feeding difficulties. Although we can't say for sure, the long-term effects of prenatal exposure to heroin appear, in most cases, to be less serious than the effects of cocaine.

Marijuana. Marijuana is one of the most frequently used illegal substances in the United States by women of childbearing age (Dahl et al., 1995). In contrast to the large amount of research data on alcohol and tobacco, there is less information about the effects of marijuana on unborn infants.

Studies have not found the use of marijuana to be associated with congenital malformations and physical impairments (Cornelius et al., 1995; Linn et al., 1983; Vorhees & Mollnow, 1987). However, a few well-controlled investigations have found use of marijuana during pregnancy to be associated with decreased visual responsiveness and attention, increased startles and tremors, high-pitched crying, and reduced self-quieting in newborn infants. Impaired cognitive functions at 4 years of age, as well as disturbed sleep in 3-year-olds, have also been observed (Dahl et al., 1995; Eyler & Behnke, 1999; Fried & Makin, 1987; Lester & Dreher, 1989; Vorhees & Mollnow, 1987). Some studies have found prenatal exposure to marijuana smoke to be associated with preterm births and reduced fetal growth (Barr et al., 1984; Frank et al., 1990; Zuckerman et al., 1989), whereas other studies have produced contradictory results (Cornelius et al., 1995). Overall, there appears to be sufficient evidence of adverse effects to indicate that marijuana use during pregnancy should be avoided.

Caffeine. Since most women in the United States drink coffee or other caffeinated beverages during pregnancy (Widerstrom et al., 1991), questions about the effects of caffeine on the developing baby frequently arise. There appears to be little doubt that high doses of caffeine (equivalent to 12 to 24 cups of coffee per day) produce birth defects in rats (L. Hill & Kleinberg, 1984a). A few human studies have associated high caffeine consumption with fetal death, birth defects, prematurity, decreased activity, and increased irritability in newborns and an increased risk of sudden infant death syndrome (SIDS) (Ford et al., 1998; Hronsky & Emory, 1987; Lechat et al., 1980). However, other studies have reported no such adverse effects (Alm et al., 1999; Brooten & Jordan, 1983; Linn et al., 1982). Until further evidence is available, expectant mothers should eliminate caffeine from their diets or at least limit the intake of caffeine beverages to no more than two or three cups per day.

Radiation. Accidental exposure to radiation during the early prenatal period generates a lot of concern about possible birth defects, genetic abnormalities, or other problems. A study of twins conducted at the National Cancer Institute (Harvey et al., 1985) found that children who are exposed to X-rays before birth face about two-and-one-half times the usual risk of cancer. The incidence of mental retardation in Japanese children who were prenatally exposed to the World War II atomic bomb explosions is five or more times higher than in children who were not exposed to the radiation. The most serious effects were found in the children who were exposed during the 8th to 15th prenatal weeks (Otake & Schull, 1984). During the early days of X-ray, women patients were sometimes exposed to radiation if a multiple pregnancy was suspected, but this practice has been mostly replaced by other diagnostic procedures. The use of X-rays for diagnostic purposes may be used with appropriate precautions. Radiation from the sun and other natural sources is generally not viewed as a threat to the developing baby (Eliot, 1999).

Maternal Nutrition. Good nutrition during pregnancy is essential for a successful pregnancy and a healthy baby. Severe malnutrition may cause stillbirth, preterm birth, low birthweight, mental deficiency, and infant death during the first year of life (Annis, 1978). Apparently malnutrition is most harmful during the last three months of pregnancy. This is the period when most of the weight gain and rapid growth of the brain cells occurs (Stein et al., 1974). The nutritional status of the mother at the time of fertilization is also critical. Researchers have found that adding folic acid supplements to the mother's diet before fertilization and during the early weeks of pregnancy reduces the risk of having an infant born with a neural tube defect by as much as 50 to 70 percent (Eliot; 1999; N. Rose & Mennuti, 1995). In addition, other birth defects such as cleft lip or cleft palate may be prevented by the folic acid supplements (Allen, 1996).

Maternal weight gain is considered to be one of the best overall indicators of a healthy pregnancy. Prenatal and infant mortality rates are lowest when maternal weight gains are between 24 and 27 pounds. On the average, weight gains in this range contribute to ideal infant birth weight as well as desirable maternal weight after pregnancy (Gormican, Valentine, & Satter, 1980). Women who are overweight at the start of pregnancy probably need to gain only around 16 pounds, whereas underweight women may need to gain as much as

30 pounds during pregnancy (Naeye, 1979; Satter, 2000).

When a pregnancy is planned, women frequently take prenatal vitamins in order to build up their nutritional stores before fertilization occurs. However, vitamin consumption should be carefully monitored before and during pregnancy. Studies have found that excess amounts of vitamin A (retinol) are teratogenic (Rothman et al., 1995). An excess intake of the type of vitamin A that comes from animal products, such as dairy products or liver, and from fortified foods and vitamin supplements has been associated with birth defects in both human and animal newborns. Apparently this substance interferes with the normal brain and central nervous system development during the early stages of prenatal development. It has been estimated that 1 of every 57 babies born to women who consume high levels of vitamin A is born with a birth defect (Rothman et al., 1995).

Many women report changes in food preferences and eating habits during pregnancy. In addition to craving pickles and ice cream, some expectant mothers develop a compulsion for eating nonfood substances. This phenomenon is called pica. Clay, dirt, charcoal, laundry starch, baking soda, soot, ashes, and coffee grounds are some of the items that may be consumed. Pica should be discouraged because some of the substances may be poisonous to the mother or fetus. Nonfood items replace nutritional foods in the diet and may lead to malnutrition, iron deficiency anemia, or obesity.

Some women experience changes in their sense of smell during pregnancy that in some instances result in cravings to smell a variety of substances (Cooksey, 1995). The effect of this practice is unknown. Since the sense of smell and the sense of taste interact, the mother's food preferences may be altered, resulting in changes in nutritional status.

Maternal Age. The years between 20 and 35 appear to be the "**golden age of pregnancy**" (Rugh & Shettles, 1971). Teen-age mothers (especially those under 17) experience more complications during the birth process and give birth to more low birthweight babies, preterm babies, and babies with birth defects than mothers in any other age group. The death rate for babies born to teenagers is twice as high as that of older mothers (Alan Guttmacher Institute, 1981). However, it is difficult to separate the effects of age alone from the effects of poverty, since teenagers are more likely than older mothers to be poor before and during pregnancy.

At the other end of the age continuum, fetal and infant mortality rates, genetic abnormalities, and congenital malformations increase as the mother gets older (Naeye, 1983). The risk of having a child with Down syndrome increases dramatically after a woman reaches age 35. At age 35 the risk is 1 in 365, but at age 45 the chances increase to 1 in 32 (Hook & Lindsjo, 1978).

Age of the Father. For many years the age of the father was not considered to be as much of a problem as the age of the mother for the outcome of pregnancy. However, the age of the father may be an important risk factor in prenatal development. For example, Down syndrome rates double when the father is 55 years old (Matsungaga et al., 1978; Stene et al., 1977). Rare genetic disorders such as achondroplasia (short-limbed dwarfism), Apert syndrome (facial and limb deformities), and Marfan syndrome (height, vision, and heart abnormalities) are more common among the offspring of fathers over 35 years of age (Evans & Hall, 1976). Congenital deafness, cleft palate, hydrocephaly, heart disorders, and increased prostate cancer risk may also be linked to the age of the father (Day, 1967; Savitz, Schwingl, & Skeels, 1991; Zhang et al., 1999).

The age of the sperm may also be important. Apparently sperm go through an aging process in which they become defective over the passage of time. Spermatozoa age in the male reproductive tract after long periods of sexual rest (Vander Vliet & Hafez, 1974). A prolonged interval between insemination and fertilization of the ovum may also cause a sperm to age beyond its optimum quality (Salisbury & Hart, 1970). Aging also occurs in sperm stored for artificial insemination. Spontaneous abortion (Guerrero & Rojas,

1975) and chromosomal abnormalities (Tesh & Glover, 1969) have been linked to aging sperm.

Maternal Emotions. Strong emotional stress, such as fear, anxiety, or anger, may result in chemical and endocrine changes in the mother's blood. There is a possibility that the chemicals will enter the developing infant's bloodstream or will direct blood flow away from the placenta. High levels of stress for an extended period of time during pregnancy may increase the chances of miscarriage or of giving birth to a baby with such problems as low birth weight, hyperactivity, cleft palate, and digestive disorders (Eliot, 1999; Stechler & Halton, 1982). Maternal depression during pregnancy has been linked with excessive crying and irritability in newborn infants (Zuckerman, Bauchner, & Parker, 1990). In addition, fetuses of highly anxious mothers spend more time in a quiet sleep state and exhibit less movement during active sleep than fetuses of less anxious mothers (Groome et al., 1995). Maternal stress may also contribute to other prenatal risk factors such as poor nutrition or the use of tobacco, alcohol, and drugs.

The precise relationship between maternal emotions during pregnancy and the long-term effects upon development are not known. Therefore, statements about the effects of maternal emotional states on prenatal development must be made with caution. Folklore about pregnancy and childbirth tends to perpetuate the belief that a mother may "mark" her unborn child through a traumatic experience or strong emotional desires. For example, a mother may believe that her child was born with a strawberry-like birth mark because she had a strong craving for strawberries during pregnancy. There is no scientific evidence to support such beliefs, and connections between birth defects and such maternal experiences are coincidental.

Maternal Health. Physicians monitor the health of the expectant mother very carefully. Serious illnesses and infectious diseases of the mother during pregnancy may influence the well-being of the embryo or fetus. For example, if the mother is diabetic before she becomes pregnant, her pregnancy may end abruptly with a miscarriage, the baby may gain excessive weight, or may be born with a congenital defect. A few women (3 to 5 percent) develop gestational diabetes mellitus (GDM) during pregnancy. The major risk associated with GDM is overgrowth of the fetus. Extra large babies are more likely to be injured during the birth process and have a higher death rate (Lee-Parritz & Heffner, 1995). Iron deficiency anemia and high blood pressure also are conditions that threaten the developing infant. A small percentage of expectant mothers develop toxemia (preeclampsia). This condition causes swelling and fluid retention, excessive weight gain, and high blood pressure. Severe cases can threaten the life of the mother and baby.

During the first 26 weeks of pregnancy, viral infections, such as German measles or herpes, may cause the baby to be born blind, deaf, retarded, or with other problems (Batshaw & Perret, 1997). Neural tube defects are more common among infants born to mothers who suffered from illnesses during pregnancy (Eliot, 1999). Women who are infected with the human immunodeficiency virus (HIV) can transmit the infection to their child during the prenatal period or during the birth process. Estimates of the chances that a mother with HIV will infect her infant vary from 20 to 35 percent (Avery, 1995; Oleske, 1994). However, treatment during pregnancy with a combination of drugs has been found to lower the risk of HIV transmission (see Chapter 5). Consequently, scientists recommend that all pregnant women be tested for the HIV virus. Bacterial infections such as group B strep are also potential causes of death and serious disabilities when they are passed on to the baby during the prenatal period or the birth process. Doctors are beginning to screen pregnant women for the infection and to administer antibiotics during labor if the woman is a carrier.

Rh Factor. The **Rh factor** refers to a protein found in the red blood cells of some people but not in others. A person's blood type is classified as Rh positive if the protein is found and Rh negative if the protein is absent. Since the protein is produced by a dominant gene, most people have Rh positive blood. However, in cases where the mother has Rh negative blood and the fetus has Rh positive blood, an adverse reaction can occur due to Rh incompatability.

The mother's blood and the baby's blood are separated by the placenta. However, during the prenatal period, and especially during the birth process, some of the baby's blood can leak into the mother's system. The Rh negative mother is allergic to the biochemical substances of the Rh positive blood and produces antibodies to fight off the foreign invaders. Normally, the antibodies do not build up in sufficient quantities to cause a problem during a woman's first pregnancy. However, if the woman has another pregnancy in which the baby is Rh positive, serious complications may arise. The antibodies from the previous pregnancy destroy the red blood cells of the fetus.

The effects of Rh incompatibility range from mild anemia to deafness, brain damage, cerebral palsy, and death. Fortunately, an injection of gamma globulin (antibody) can be given to the Rh negative mother soon after an Rh positive baby is born. The injection prevents the formation of antibodies so that the next Rh-incompatible pregnancy does not have serious complications. This treatment has resulted in a decline in the death and injury rates of infants due to Rh incompatibility.

Poverty. The relationship between poverty and adverse prenatal developmental outcomes is well established (Kaplan-Sanoff, Parker, & Zuckerman, 1991). Poverty affects the development of infants even before they are conceived. Economically disadvantaged mothers are more likely than wealthier mothers to have poor health and nutritional histories before becoming pregnant and are less likely to receive adequate prenatal care afterward. They tend to experience more stress and depression, and to engage in behaviors that are potentially harmful to the developing baby, such as substance abuse and inadequate eating patterns (R. Halpern, 1993). The incidence of low birth weight is two to three times higher among infants whose mothers live under poverty conditions (Kaplan-Sanoff et al., 1991).

PRENATAL TESTING

The first 38 weeks of human life spent inside the womb are potentially more dangerous than the first 38 years lived in the outside world (Bachman, 1983). Consequently, scientists are continuing to develop sophisticated techniques and equipment for monitoring the fetus and its intrauterine environment. Detection of congenital malformations or other critical problems before birth provides parents and their physicians information on which to select from the following alternatives: (1) termination of pregnancy, (2) treatment after term, (3) preterm induced delivery for early treatment, (4) delivery by Caesarean section, or (5) possible surgical or medical treatment before birth (L. Hill & Breckle, 1983). It has been estimated that prenatal testing and diagnosis are needed in 7 to 8 percent of all pregnancies (Stewart et al., 1995).

Ultrasound. Since its introduction in the early 1950s, **ultrasound** has become the most commonly used technique for prenatal assessment (L. Hill & Breckle, 1983). High-frequency sound waves are bounced off the fetus to form a live video image called a sonogram. Ultrasound can be used to assess fetal growth and gestational age, locate and examine the condition of the placenta, determine the baby's sex (week 16), check for congenital abnormalities, evaluate fetal well-being, estimate the amount of amniotic fluid, and diagnose a multiple pregnancy. Ultrasound is also used to determine fetal position and as a visual guide in performing other tests and procedures. The accuracy of the procedure in detecting developmental abnormalities varies from 14 to 85 percent in low-risk populations (Garmel & D'Alton, 1994). Ultrasound is more versatile than either X-rays or techniques that invade the uterus and is considered to be much safer. It has been estimated that 65 to 70 percent of women undergo at least one ultrasound procedure during pregnancy (Garmel & D'Alton, 1994). Concerns

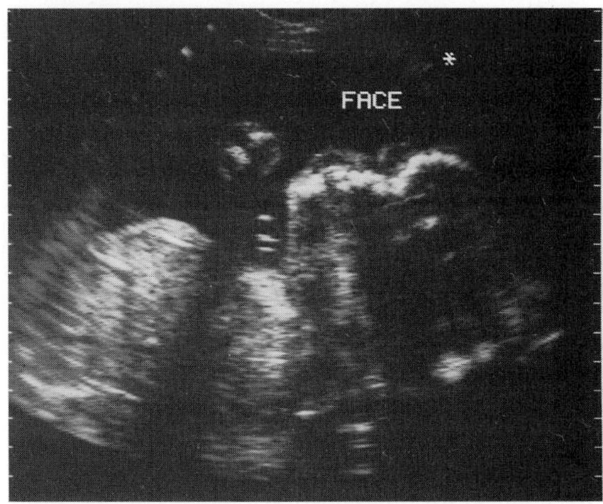

Sonogram of five-month-old fetus

about the safety of ultrasound have persisted through the years. Researchers have reported possible associations between prenatal exposure to ultrasound and dyslexia, left-handedness, and reduced birth weight. However, other studies have not confirmed those findings (Garmel & D'Alton, 1994). As yet, there are no confirmed detrimental effects on the baby from the use of diagnostic ultrasound. The benefits of limited use of ultrasound are likely to outweigh any potential risks (Garmel & D'Alton, 1994).

Amniocentesis. In cases for which ultrasound does not provide adequate information about the condition of the fetus, an **amniocentesis** test may be used. Guided by a sonogram, a skilled physician inserts a hollow needle through the woman's abdominal wall into the amniotic sac. A small amount of fluid containing cells and other substances from the fetus is withdrawn for laboratory analysis, which can detect more than 100 abnormalities, including genetic/chromosomal errors, biochemical disorders, and defects in the nervous system.

Amniocentesis is not typically used until around 16 to 18 weeks of gestation. However, medical specialists are increasingly performing early amniocentesis (EA) at 10 to 13 weeks of gestation (Stewart et al., 1995). The procedure is rather expensive and involves a waiting period to obtain the test results. Disadvantages of amniocentesis include the risk of needle-puncture injury to the fetus, spontaneous abortion, or infection. Statistics indicate that amniocentesis performed in the second quarter of pregnancy slightly (about 0.5 percent) increases the risk of spontaneous abortion (Thompson, McInnes, & Willard, 1991). The chances of fetal injury are uncertain, but estimates ranging from 0.1 to 3.0 percent of cases have been reported (D'Alton, 1994). Some studies indicate the risks apparently increase with EA, but further evidence is needed to verify those results. In either conventional or early amniotic testing, the risks are usually considered small in comparison to the benefits of the procedure.

Maternal Blood Tests. In some instances, abnormalities may be detected by testing the mother's blood for certain chemicals. The blood is analyzed to detect the presence of alpha-fetoprotein (AFP), human chorionic gonadotropin (HCG), or estriol. Steadily increasing amounts of estriol are associated with a healthy pregnancy, whereas a decrease may indicate a change in the welfare of the fetus. This test is especially useful in monitoring the pregnancy of a mother who has diabetes, hypertension, or an overdue delivery. Lower levels of estriol plus an increased amount of HCG are associated with Down syndrome. An elevated level of AFP is an indication of a possible neural tube defect in the fetus. These tests are typically done at 16 to 18 weeks of gestation. Since maternal blood tests are not extremely reliable, they must be interpreted with care. Amniocentesis or other tests are usually used to verify the accuracy if a problem is indicated (Stewart et al.,1995).

Chorionic Villus Sampling. Physicians sometimes use a procedure called **chorionic villus sampling (CVS)** to diagnose genetic diseases early in the first trimester of pregnancy before amniocentesis can be safely performed. The 9th or 10th gestational week is considered to be the most suitable time for this procedure, although it is sometimes performed a little earlier (Brambati & Oldrini, 1986). A live sonogram is used to guide a catheter through the cervix or a needle through the abdomen to the fetal chorion. A sample of the chorionic tissue, which contains the same genetic material as the fetus, is obtained. The tissue is analyzed to determine whether suspected chromosomal, metabolic, or blood disorders are present. The risks of CVS to mother and fetus have been the subject of a number of investigations. Some mothers experience minor vaginal bleeding or spotting following the procedure, but further maternal complications are rarely reported (D'Alton, 1994). Studies indicate that in comparison to amniocentesis, CVS may result in a slightly greater risk of fetal loss. CVS also appears to entail a slightly increased risk of limb deformities and blood vessel malformations (hemangiomas) that may lead to internal bleeding, port-wine stains on the skin, or benign growths (B. Burton et al., 1995; D'Alton, 1994; Wynbrandt & Ludman, 1991).

Fetoscopy. With the use of an instrument called a fetoscope and special lighting equipment, doctors can look at the fetus inside the womb. The fetoscope is attached to a hollow needle and inserted into the amniotic cavity as in the amniocentesis. The fetus can then be visually inspected for physical abnormalities such as cleft palate or defective limbs. Samples of fetal skin and cells from the fetal membranes can also be obtained. The same procedure is occasionally used to conduct corrective surgery on the fetus before birth. Fetoscopy is not used until after the 16th week of pregnancy.

Fetal Blood Sampling (Cordocentesis). Samples of the umbilical cord blood can also be obtained and analyzed to detect fetal blood disorders. This test is called **cordocentesis,** but you may also see it referred to as **percutaneous umbilical cord sampling (PUBS).** The procedure involves inserting a long needle through the mother's abdomen into a vein in the umbilical cord as it is viewed by means of an ultrasound scan. The blood is analyzed to detect genetic disorders, infections, and other disorders. One of the advantages of this procedure is that the results can be obtained in a shorter time. This procedure is also used to give fetal blood transfusions or drugs. Some studies indicate that fetal blood sampling has a greater risk of a miscarriage than amniocentesis and should be used primarily when information cannot be obtained by safer means (D'Alton, 1994).

FISH Test. Medical researchers are currently working on a promising new technique for detecting chromosomal abnormalities during the early stage of prenatal development. This method, called a **FISH test,** extracts the fetal cells that are in the mother's blood through the use of laser light to separate cells according to different characteristics. The chromosomes contained in the fetal blood cells can then be examined for abnomalities. A major advantage of the FISH test over amniocentesis and CVS procedures is that the risk of harmful fetal effects is eliminated. In addition, waiting time for the results is reduced from three weeks to less than two days (Roberts, 1991).

GENETIC COUNSELING

A genetic counselor can help prospective parents assess their chances of having a child with a genetic disorder. Prospective parents should seek genetic counseling if any of the following conditions apply: (1) either of the couple has a blood relative with a genetic disorder; (2) the woman

APPLICATIONS: PREVENTING BIRTH DEFECTS

Birth defects cannot always be prevented, but the following practices and precautions can increase a woman's chances of having a healthy pregnancy:

- Consult a health care specialist prior to pregnancy if possible. In any case, obtain prenatal care early and have regular checkups throughout the pregnancy.
- Avoid tobacco smoke, alcohol, and all drugs and medications that are not approved by a health care specialist.
- Avoid exposure to pesticides, lead, mercury, and other hazardous substances.
- Eat a healthy diet as recommended by a health care specialist. Be sure all meat is adequately cooked and raw fruits and vegetables are carefully washed. Avoid weight loss diets during pregnancy.
- Take 400 micrograms (0.4mg) (or an amount recommended by a doctor) of folic acid every day.
- Avoid hot tubs and saunas during early pregnancy.
- Get adequate rest, appropriate exercise, and take measures to reduce stress during pregnancy.

has had previous miscarriages; (3) they already have a child with a genetic disorder or with abnormal physical or behavioral development; (4) the woman is over 35 years of age; (5) they are members of an ethnic group with specific genetic disorders such as Tay-Sachs disease or sickle cell anemia; and (6) either one has a history of drug use, exposure to industrial chemicals, or other possible teratogens (Bachman, 1983).

SUMMARY

Fertilization

- Fertilization of the mother's ovum by the father's sperm cell takes place in the fallopian tube. The prenatal period, which begins with fertilization, is divided into three stages: preembryonic, embryonic, and fetal. When a woman has fertility problems, she may elect to utilize artificial insemination to become pregnant through in vitro fertilization and "embryo" transfer.

Preembryonic Period

- During the preembryonic stage, the fertilized ovum, called a zygote, changes into a morula (12 to 16 cells), and a blastocyst (58 cells). The blastocyst typically begins to implant itself in the upper part of the uterus around day 6. Occasionally an ectopic pregnancy occurs when the blastocyst is implanted outside the uterus.

Embryonic Period

- The embryonic period begins with the formation of the embryonic disc around the second week after conception and continues until the end of the eighth week of pregnancy. The growth that takes place during this period is rapid and dramatic. The size and appearance of the embryo change almost daily. During the third week, three germ layers are formed through a process called gastrulation. Each of the germ layers—ectoderm, endoderm, mesoderm—forms the foundation for the development of various body structures. The chorion, placenta, umbilical cord, and amnion develop early to function as supporting membranes for the embryo. By the end of this period the beginnings of all limbs, internal organs, and the skeleton have been established. The heart is pumping blood; the kidneys and other organs are beginning to function.

Fetal Period

- The fetal stage begins at the ninth week and continues until the baby is born. The name change from embryo to fetus signifies the completion of the human form and the appearance of the first bone cells in the cartilage of the skeleton. The body structures and organ systems develop further. The sex of the fetus is distinguishable. By mid pregnancy, the fetus begins to move and is covered with lanugo and vernix caseosa. The complete number of neuronal cells is present in the brain. The process of myelination of the nerve cells has also begun. During the last two months of pregnancy, the fetus gains weight rapidly, increases in length, and practices many of the functions that are necessary for life in the world outside the womb.

Multiple Pregnancies

- Twins may originate from a single zygote that divides into two equal parts (monozygotic or identical twins) or two separate ova that are fertilized during the same ovulatory cycle (dizygotic or fraternal twins). The number of multiple births in the United States has increased dramatically in recent years.

Influences on Development

- Both genetic and environmental factors influence growth and development during the prenatal period. Genetic disorders are classified as chromosomal abnormalities, single gene disorders, sex-linked disorders, and polygenic inheritance. The most common disorder caused by chromosomal aberrations is Down syndrome. Huntington's chorea is a disorder resulting from a faulty dominant gene. Phenylketonuria is one of the major recessive genetic disorders. Color blindness and hemophilia are examples of defects caused by sex-linked genes. Spina bifida represents a polygenic disorder.
- Numerous drugs, viruses, and other environmental factors have been associated with birth defects and developmental problems. The list of substances pregnant women should avoid includes a variety of drugs and medications, alcohol, tobacco, cocaine, heroin, marijuana, large quantities of caffeine, and exposure to radiation. Inadequate nutrition during pregnancy may also cause problems such as low birth weight and mental deficiency. Maternal age, paternal age, maternal stress and health problems, maternal-fetal blood incompatibility, and poverty are additional risk factors.

Prenatal Testing

- Techniques that are used to monitor the condition of the baby and to detect developmental problems include ultrasound, amniocentesis, maternal blood tests, chorionic villus sampling, fetoscopy, and fetal blood sampling.

Genetic Counseling

- Information obtained from tests performed before pregnancy and during the early stages of prenatal development can be used to provide genetic counseling to the parents.

KEY TERMS

spermatozoa
ovum
cervix
capacitation
miscarriage
fertilization age
gestational age
morula
blastocyst
placental previa
cervical pregnancy
ectopic pregnancy
embryo
gastrulation
chorion
placenta
umbilical cord
primary yolk sac
amnion, amniotic cavity
secondary yolk sac
neurulation
neurons
synapses
somites
fetus
quickening
vernix caseosa
lanugo
neuroglia
myelination
mitosis

meiosis
Down syndrome
Klinefelter syndrome
Turner syndrome
cri du chat syndrome
Huntington's chorea
phenylketonuria (PKU)
cystic fibrosis
sickle cell anemia
Tay-Sachs disease
polygenic inheritance
teratogens
fetal alcohol syndrome (FAS)
fetal alcohol effects (FAE)
golden age of pregnancy
Rh factor
ultrasound
amniocentesis
chorionic villus sampling (CVS)
cordocentesis, percutaneous umbilical cord sampling (PUBS)
FISH test

INFORMATION ON THE WEB*

www.babycenter.com. This site provides an illustrated month-by-month summary of prenatal development. Pull-down menus provide more detailed information. Additional information is provided on preconception concerns plus a variety of other topics of interest to expectant mothers and fathers.

www.modimes.org. Official web site of the March of Dimes. Site provides information about reducing infant mortality and birth defects and offers a health library, information about research, and prevention programs. Also available in Spanish.

*Web sites are subject to change.

THREE

The Birth Process and the Newborn

My mother groan'd, my father wept,
Into the dangerous world I leapt;
Helpless, naked, pipin' loud,
Like a fiend hid in a cloud.
—Blake

Be careful with that new baby—it leaks.
—American Greeting Cards

Childbirth is a relatively brief period of transition between prenatal development and life in the outside world. Montagu (1964) refers to birth as a bridge between two stages of life. The birth process is marked by a series of dramatic events affecting all the participants. For the fetus, the tranquility of the mother's womb is abruptly interrupted, for better or worse, by powerful forces projecting the fetus through the birth canal. For the parents, particularly the mother, the months of waiting are coming to an end, but only after a few more exciting and stressful hours. For the physicians, nurses, or other birth attendants, decisions must be made about when and how to assist mother and baby in the process.

LABOR AND DELIVERY

The process of childbirth is commonly referred to as **labor** because the mother works to give birth. Normally she exerts a considerable amount of energy in pushing the baby out of the uterus. However, the process is more complex than the term labor implies. Labor is affected by the interplay of various physiological conditions, including hormonal substances, contractions of the uterus, dilation of the cervix, and the position of the fetus. In addition, psychological factors such as the mother's anxiety level and pain threshold play important roles.

Onset of Labor. Calculated from the first day of the last menstrual period, the average pregnancy lasts 280 days. Approximately 95 percent of all babies are born within two weeks of this time period (or between the 266th and 294th day) (Nilsson & Hamberger, 1990). The date of birth can be estimated but not accurately predicted. Actually, scientists do not clearly understand what causes labor to begin. The answer to this mystery is obviously very important for predicting and controlling labor as well as for preventing premature births.

Researchers have tried for years to identify the factors that lead to the onset of labor. In addition to finding the mechanism controlling labor, scientists are also faced with the task of identifying whether the mother, the fetus, or both are responsible for its initiation. The process is very complicated due to the separate physiological events involved, including cervical dilation, rupture of the amniotic sac, contractions of the uterus, and placental separation.

Recent investigations have focused on the identification of hormones and other biochemical substances that may, either singly or in combination, trigger the birth process. Some researchers believe that prostaglandins, fatty acids found in most body tissues and fluids, play a key role in the ripening of the cervix and the onset of labor (Gibb, 1998; Lu & Goldenberg, 2000). Apparently, labor begins when prostaglandins, in combination with estrogen and other substances, reach a critical level. However, other factors, such as intrauterine infections or the size, health, and nutritional state of the fetus, may influence the onset of the birth process (Lu & Goldenberg, 2000; R. Smith, 1999). A complete and precise explanation for the timing of birth remains somewhat of a mystery because of the complex interplay among various contributing factors.

Contractions. The onset of labor is signaled by regular contractions of the uterus. A **labor contraction** is the tightening and shortening of the muscles in the uterus. The mother has no control over the contractions. When labor begins, the contractions are usually 10 to 30 minutes apart and last for 30 to 45 seconds. At the end of labor, the contractions are closer together and last from 60 to 90 seconds (Benson & Pernoll, 1994). Contractions usually begin at the top of the uterus and move downward, reaching a peak and then becoming weaker. Typically, contractions become stronger, last longer, and get closer together as labor progresses. During the process, the baby's head is pushed into the lower part of the uterus. As labor progresses, the upper part of the uterus becomes thicker and smaller, while the lower portion stretches thinner and larger. The uterus is slowly pulled upward, as if a turtleneck sweater is being pulled over the baby's head (Oxorn, 1980).

Braxton Hicks Contractions (False Labor). The muscles of the uterus contract every 5 to 20 minutes, increasing in frequency throughout the prenatal period. These contractions are usually not strong enough to be felt by the mother until approximately the last month of pregnancy. When they are perceived by the mother, usually in late pregnancy, they are called false labor, or **Braxton Hicks contractions.** At that time the mother may believe that labor has begun. Unlike true labor contractions, these contractions are irregular, short, mild in intensity, and do not cause cervical change (Troyer & Parisi, 1993).

Dilation and Effacement. The cervix is the lower part, or mouth, of the uterus that protrudes into the vagina (see Figure 3-1). During most of the pregnancy the cervix is about 1 inch (2.5 centimeters) long, with an opening about the width of the end of an unsharpened pencil (Oxorn, 1980). During pregnancy the opening is closed with a mucous plug to protect the fetus.

Throughout the prenatal period, physical and chemical changes in the uterus soften or "ripen" the cervix in preparation for the birth process. During labor, the cervix becomes shorter and thinner through the process of **effacement.** Before the baby can leave the uterus, the cervix must open to its widest capacity, which is about 4 inches (10 centimeters), or about the size of five fingers on an average hand. This process is called **dilation.** Usually effacement and dilation occur simultaneously.

Position of the Fetus. The process of labor is dramatically affected by the position of the fetus and the body part that first enters the birth canal. Approximately 96 percent of all babies are born in the head-first (vertex or cephalic) position as shown in Figure 3-1 (Hamilton, 1984). Ideally, the smallest part of the baby's head is directed down the birth

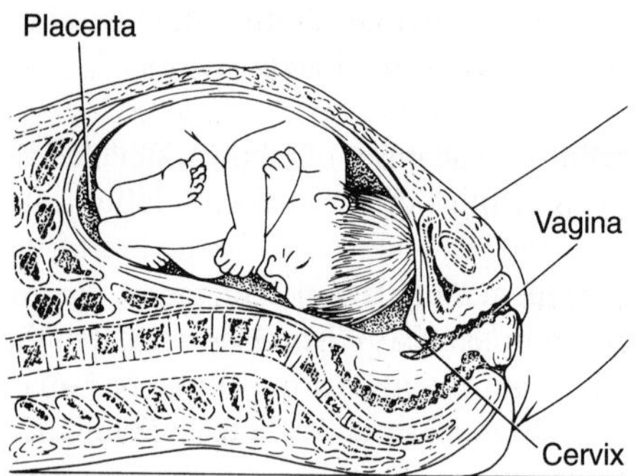

A. Prelabor. The cervix is thick and closed.

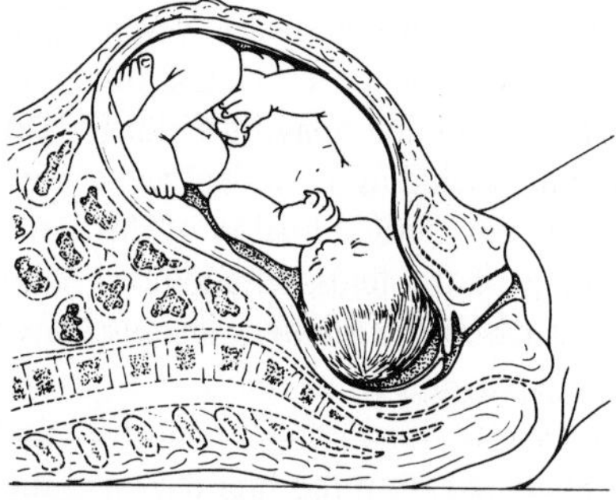
B. Early labor. Contractions, dilation, effacement, and head engagement.

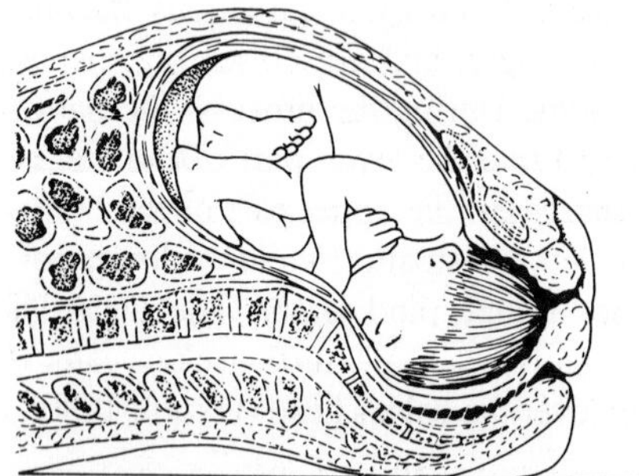
C. Late labor. Cervix is completely dilated; head is in the birth canal.

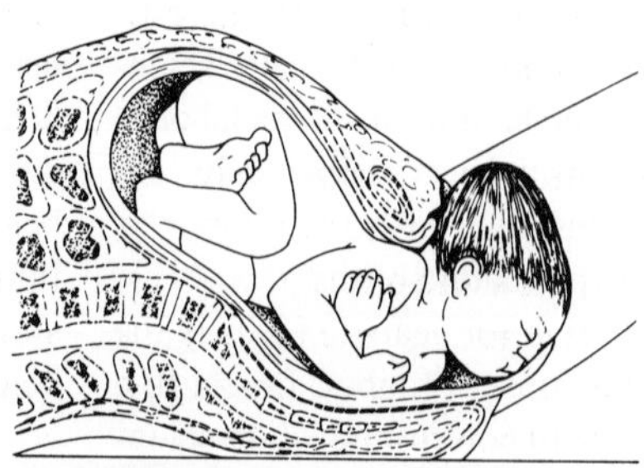
D. Delivery. Baby's head begins to emerge.

Figure 3-1 Labor and Delivery.

canal first, with the face turned toward the spinal column. However, the presenting part may be the face or the brow, with the head turned, in relation to the spinal column, at one of a variety of angles.

In approximately 3 to 4 percent of pregnancies, the fetus is in a **breech position** when labor begins (Hamilton, 1984). In a breech delivery, the baby is born with the buttocks, feet, or knees first. A variety of breech presentations are possible. The **frank breech** is the most common, in which both feet are extended straight up beside the ears, and the buttocks enter the birth canal first. Breech births are more difficult and may take longer than normal births. In a few deliveries (less than 1 percent) (Hamilton, 1984), the fetus is turned crosswise in the uterus in a transverse presentation. The shoulder blade is typically positioned in the birth canal. In a transverse presentation, the baby must either be turned or be surgically removed through a Caesarean section.

Stages of Labor.

Preliminary Signs. Toward the end of pregnancy there are a number of signs that labor is approaching. Approximately two to four weeks before labor begins, the head of the fetus usually moves or "drops" downward into the pelvic cavity. This is called "lightening," since there is less pressure on the mother's diaphragm, allowing her to breathe more freely. Other warning signs include a pink vaginal discharge or a bloody "show" caused by the loss of the mucous plug from the cervical opening. Diarrhea, stomach upset, increased Braxton Hicks contractions, low back pain, and a 2- to 5-pound weight loss are other prelabor symptoms.

Stage 1: Dilation of the Cervix. The first stage of labor, called dilation, begins with the first true contractions of the uterus and ends when the cervix is completely effaced and fully dilated (10 cm). This stage of the birth process is the longest. The dilation stage typically lasts from 6 to 18 hours for women delivering their first baby, and 2 to 6 hours for the second and subsequent deliveries. The time, however, varies widely with individuals and may be shorter or longer depending upon a variety of individual factors.

Contractions are usually mild in intensity to begin with, but normally become increasingly strong as labor progresses. During the early part of labor, they occur from 5 to 8 minutes apart and last about 30 seconds. As labor continues, the time between contractions decreases while the contractions last longer and increase in intensity. When the cervix is almost completely dilated (8 cm), the mother enters a **transition phase.** This is the most difficult time during labor. The contractions are stronger, last longer (about 80 seconds), and are closer together. These contractions have been compared to the ocean waves on a beach during a storm, with one coming in on top of another. Feelings of irritability, discouragement, loss of control, and panic are common. Other difficulties include hot and cold flashes, disorientation, nausea, and vomiting. The mother usually feels a strong desire to push, comparable to having a bowel movement. Fortunately the transition phase is relatively short, lasting 30 to 60 minutes for first births, and about 20 to 30 minutes for subsequent births (Hassid, 1984).

Stage 2: Expulsion. The second stage of labor begins as soon as the cervix is completely open and lasts until the baby is born. The expulsion stage is usually a welcome relief after the difficult transition phase. The mother may have a chance to recover her equilibrium and possibly doze between contractions. The contractions are long but less frequent. The mother can now use her abdominal muscles and diaphragm to help push the baby out of the birth canal. The baby is usually born within 30 minutes to 2 hours after this stage begins. For mothers who have given birth before, however, expulsion may last only about 20 minutes to 1-1/2 hours (Novak & Broom, 1999).

If the baby is in the head-first position, the head advances through the birth canal with each contraction and recedes slightly as the uterus relaxes, as if taking two steps forward and one step back. The baby's head must rotate to move through the mother's pelvic structure. The top of the head eventually becomes visible at the vaginal opening. The term **crowning** is used when the largest part of the scalp appears and does not recede between contractions.

About the time an inch (3 cm) of the baby's head is visible, the physician usually makes a surgical incision (**episiotomy**) in the perineum—the tissue between the vagina and rectum. The routine performance of episiotomies is controversial and has been questioned as unnecessary surgery. Some physicians argue, however, that it shortens the delivery time and spares the baby's head from excessive pressure, and is easier to repair and heals better than a ragged, uncontrolled natural tear (Pritchard, MacDonald, & Gant, 1985; Wheeler, 1995).

Once the baby's head is out of the birth canal, the head rotates to become aligned with the baby's shoulders. The shoulders must also rotate to pass through the pelvic structure. First one shoulder emerges and then the other, followed by the buttocks and lower limbs. This part is relatively easy, since the larger head has paved the way.

Obstetrical forceps (metal clamps shaped like salad tongs) are used in some deliveries to rotate the baby's head when the mother cannot push the baby out, or to speed delivery in case of an emergency such as fetal distress. In some instances a **vacuum extractor** is applied to facilitate the movement of the head. This device consists of a metal or plastic suction cup that is placed on top of the baby's head and attached to a suction pump. In recent years, however, the use of forceps and the vacuum extractor has declined markedly because of the risk of injury to the baby's head or brain (Dunnihoo, 1992; Ventura et al., 2001).

When the baby emerges from the uterus, the umbilical cord is still attached. When the cord stops pulsating (or sooner if the baby is premature or in distress), clamps are applied to the umbilical cord in two places. The cord is then cut between the two clamps. Usually the physician keeps the head lowered below the vaginal opening and waits about 30 seconds before clamping the cord to allow placental blood to drain from the placenta to the newborn (Benson & Pernoll, 1994; Pritchard et al., 1985).

Stage 3: Placental Expulsion. The third stage of labor begins as soon as the baby is completely out of the birth canal and ends with the expulsion of the placenta and fetal membranes (the afterbirth). The stage of placental expulsion usually lasts about 5 to 20 minutes. If it extends beyond 30 minutes, the danger of excessive bleeding becomes a problem.

As soon as the baby is born, the contractions usually stop for a few minutes and then start again to expel the placenta. Oxytocin may be administered to the mother to stimulate contractions. The uterus shrinks dramatically so that the implantation site of the placenta is reduced. Since the placenta stays the same size, it typically separates or "peels off" from the lining of the uterus and is expelled during the final contractions.

Stage 4: Recovery. The recovery stage usually lasts for about an hour after the delivery of the placenta is complete. However, the length of this stage varies with hospital and cultural practices. During this period, the mother and baby are carefully observed for complications of the birth process. The stage of expulsion and the first hour after birth are considered to be the most dangerous periods in the birth process for the mother because of the risk of excessive bleeding (Zlatnik, 1995).

Caesarean Delivery. A variety of conditions can prevent or interfere with a vaginal childbirth. When complications occur, the baby may be removed through a surgical incision in the abdomen and uterus, called a **Caesarean section (C-section).** The transverse or breech position of the fetus, failure of the cervix to dilate, obstructions in the uterus or pelvis, excess bleeding, and signs of fetal distress are some of the conditions that might necessitate a Caesarean delivery (Hawkins & Higgins, 1981).

The number of Caesarean births in the United States more than quadrupled from 1970 to the mid-1980s, rising from 5.5 per 100 deliveries in 1970 to a peak of 24.7 per 100 live deliveries in 1988. By 1996 the rate of C-sections had declined to 20.7 per 100 births. However, between 1998 and 1999 the C-section delivery rate rose again to a total of 22 per 100 births (Ventura et al., 2001).

Even under ideal conditions, the surgical procedures used in C-sections carry greater health risks for the mother and baby than normal vaginal delivery (Clarke & Taffel, 1995). Consequently, the high number of Caesarean births has generated a lot of concern among physicians and public health officials and has resulted in continuing attempts to reduce the number of such births.

Multiple Births. Labor and delivery of more than one fetus presents special problems. The extra crowding of the uterus frequently results in early rupture of the membranes, leading to premature labor. Although labor and delivery proceed satisfactorily in most cases, the overstretching of the uterus sometimes causes weak and inefficient contractions, delaying the progress of labor. There is also an increased risk of maternal bleeding after the birth process has been completed (Oxorn, 1980).

The birth of twins and other multiple conceptions may be complicated by the position of the fetuses. Usually both twins are in the ideal head-first position when labor begins, but other combinations of positions are possible. One twin or both may be in a breech position or in a transverse lie. Another rare combination is for the first twin to be in a breech position while the second twin is in a head-first lie. In that case, the possibility exists for *interlocking* twins whereby the body of the first twin is born, but the head of the second twin descends in the pelvic structure underneath the head of the first twin. In this position the head of the first twin is trapped and cannot be born (Coustan, 1995b). The second twin faces a greater risk because it occupies the less favorable position, and the uterine capacity to supply oxygen to the placenta may be reduced after the first twin is born (Oxorn, 1980).

Position of the Mother. Women in different cultures labor and give birth in a variety of positions, including kneeling, squatting, standing, sitting, or on hands and knees. For example, Mexican Tarahumara women often deliver outdoors. As delivery begins, the mother finds an overhead tree limb to hang on to and gives birth in a standing position. The baby falls into a soft bed of grass underneath the mother (Broude, 1995). In some places, "birth chairs" are used to support the mother as she delivers the baby in an upright sitting position.

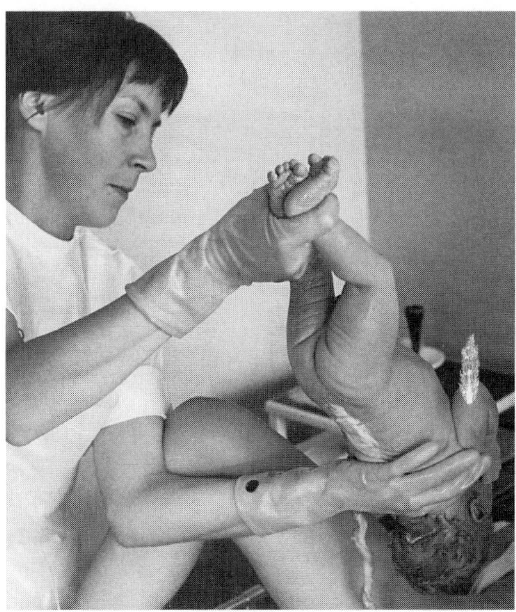

This baby was born while the mother was in a semi-reclining position on her back.

In contrast, the mother in the United States usually labors and delivers while lying on her back (recumbent) in what is sometimes called the "stranded turtle" position. Traditionally, during delivery, the head of the delivery table is raised as the mother's knees are bent toward the abdomen with the feet flat on the surface or in stirrups (Hamilton, 1984). European women frequently lie on their sides during the delivery of the baby. Numerous studies on posture and movement by women in labor indicate that variations of upright posture, such as standing, sitting, squatting, or walking, tend to facilitate labor progress and reduce the need for pain medication. No adverse effects of these practices on the baby were reported (Troyer & Parisi, 1993).

PAIN AND LABOR

The reality of childbirth pain is universal and well documented. Melzack (1984) reviewed studies indicating that labor is one of the most intense types of pain reported by women in all cultures. There are many causes of pain during labor and delivery, including both physiological and psychological. The contractions of the uterus restrict the blood supply to the muscles, creating a painful shortage of oxygen. Pain signals are sent to the brain by the stretching of the cervix and other organs, as well as the pressure and friction on sensitive nerve endings by the baby's descent through the birth canal.

People vary widely in their anatomy as well as in their sensitivity to pain. The mother's pelvic structure, the size of the baby, previous birth experience, childbirth preparation, and support affect the extent to which labor is painful. In addition, the amount of pain actually experienced may be increased or diminished by the mother's emotional state. Fear, anxiety, and stress create muscle tension and may initiate chemical changes that intensify the pain of labor and delivery.

Methods of Pain Relief. Before the discovery of ether and chloroform in the mid-1800s, people resorted to chants, rituals, body contortions, and folk medicine in attempts to find relief from the pain of childbirth. Currently, modern medicine offers women numerous choices of obstetric medications that partially or completely eliminate the pain of childbirth with or without the loss of consciousness. Obstetric medications are broadly classified as analgesics (relieve pain) and anesthetics (block sensations). A very popular method of pain relief in labor is an **epidural block** (Zwelling, 1996). In this procedure, a local anesthetic is delivered through a thin tube inserted in the epidural space between two lower spinal vertebrae, which reduces all sensations from the waist to the feet. The main advantage of epidural and other types of regional anesthesia is that the mother can be awake, comfortable, and participate in the birth process. Disadvantages of epidural and similar types of medication include increased risks of reduced blood pressure, severe headaches, convulsions, and urinary retention. If given too early, or in large doses, these substances may interfere with contractions, delay labor, and increase the need for the use of forceps.

Effects of Obstetric Medication. Ideally, the goal in the use of pain medications is to provide a safe, more comfortable, and satisfactory delivery for the mother without adversely affecting the baby. Since most obstetric medications rapidly cross the placental barrier, scientists have been concerned about the possibility of adverse affects on the fetus and the newborn infant (Brackbill, McManus, & Woodard, 1985). The length and severity of the effects are related to the potency of the drug, the dosage, and time the drug is administered (Golub, 1996). In most cases, the effects of a small to moderate amount of obstetrical medication are considered to be short-term and rather benign. However, additional research is needed before the effects of obstetrical medication are clearly determined.

PREPARED CHILDBIRTH

Many women attempt to avoid or minimize the need for medication during childbirth by attending childbirth education classes. Prepared childbirth training has gained popularity since the 1960s as the result of concerns about the undesirable effects of medication and the desire of both mothers and fathers to participate more actively in the birth process. Childbirth education is now widely accepted and sponsored by health care providers (Zwelling, 1996).

There are several specific methods of prepared childbirth. The Dick-Read (1972), Lamaze (1970), and Bradley (1974) methods have provided the basic theoretical and methodological foundations of prepared childbirth training in the United States. The various theoretical approaches are similar in that they were developed to empower expectant parents to become active participants in the birth process and to minimize the medical management of childbirth (Zwelling, 1996). Class sessions typically include information about the physiology of labor and delivery, breathing exercises, massage, relaxation techniques, positions for labor, and various body-conditioning exercises. The father is also encouraged to attend classes, be present for the delivery, and assume a supportive role in the birth process. The **Lamaze method** has been the most widely used approach to childbirth education in the United States (Leifer, 1999). Currently, most childbirth educators are utilizing a more integrated and diverse approach to childbirth preparation rather than a strict adherence to a specific theoretical perspective (Novak & Broom, 1999).

The Leboyer Method. The methods of prepared childbirth discussed up to this point are procedures designed to control pain during labor and delivery. The **Leboyer method** is different from the others in that it involves procedures for controlling the environment in the delivery room and for handling the infant during the first few minutes after birth. This method is based on Leboyer's (1975) belief that the process of birth is traumatic for the infant and potentially leads to emotional difficulties later in life. Leboyer's method of gentle birth, sometimes called "birth without violence," is designed to help minimize the shock of the birth experience and make the transition easier from the uterus to the outside world. The delivery room is warm and quiet. The lights are dim as the baby emerges from the uterus. The newborn baby is handled gently and placed on the mother's stomach where it is lightly massaged until the umbilical cord stops pulsating. The baby is then moved to a tub of warm bath water designed to resemble the uterine environment. The complete Leboyer method is not widely practiced in the United States because research studies (Maziade et al., 1986; N. Nelson et al., 1980; Rappoport, 1976) have not yet sufficiently proved its effectiveness.

Effects of Childbirth Preparation. Some studies support claims that women who participate in childbirth preparation classes tend to (1) experience reduced pain during labor and delivery, (2) have less need for medication, (3) have lowered rates of forceps delivery, and (4) demonstrate a more positive attitude toward childbirth than women who do not receive such training (Cogan, 1980). A major factor contributing to the mother's overall favorable evaluation of childbirth is a feeling of being able to maintain control over pain perception, emotions, and behavior. Many women who participate in childbirth training believe that it boosts their confidence and sense of control (Mackey, 1995). However, some studies report no differences between women who attend childbirth training and those who don't participate (L. Bradley, 1995; Monto, 1996). The results of prepared childbirth classes vary widely with instructors and individual patients.

Fathers' Participation. An important outcome of the prepared childbirth movement in the United States has been increased participation by fathers in the birth process. Several years ago hospitals were very reluctant to allow fathers in the delivery room because of concerns about increasing the risk of infection and about legal issues that might arise. Hospital personnel also feared that the husband would faint or otherwise interfere with the birth process. However, hospitals now routinely allow the father to enter the labor and delivery room. Many fathers choose to be present for the birth of their child. The use of local anesthesia makes it possible for the father to attend even a Caesarean birth.

The presence, effective coaching, and encouragement of the father during childbirth have been associated with the mother's positive evaluation of the birth experience. Mothers sometimes perceive the father's absence or inadequate coaching as contributing to a less satisfactory childbirth experience (Mackey, 1995). From the father's perspective, being present during childbirth tends to be a positive experience. In one study, 95 percent of the fathers who were in the delivery room were enthusiastic about the experience (Entwisle & Doering, 1981). The presence of the father during childbirth may facilitate attachment (Bowen & Miller, 1980) and later involvement in caregiving (Parke, 1995).

The role of the father in childbirth varies from culture to culture. The term **couvade** is sometimes used to refer to the behavior that is typical of expectant or new fathers. Such practices are usually related to magical or religious beliefs that are meant to protect the mother and baby. For example, Cubeo fathers of the Northwest Amazon are expected to stay at home during the birth process and avoid strenuous activities that might magically be harmful to the mother and baby. A widely reported, but rarely practiced, form of the couvade is associated with cases where the expectant father goes to bed and complains of abdominal pain, exhaustion, and other symptoms identified with the birth experience (Broude, 1995). Although various couvade practices are not common in industrialized societies, they illustrate the power of culture over childbirth practices.

Alternative Childbirth Practices. As a result of the childbirth education movement in the United States and other countries, hospitals have responded to parental demands for family-centered childbirth and maternity care. Hospitals now allow patients to choose a **rooming-in** arrangement in which the baby stays in a private room with the mother immediately after birth or as soon as she desires. In this arrangement, the father is allowed to visit and participate in the care of the baby. Also, siblings are allowed to visit the mother and baby.

The increased interest in family-centered labor and delivery has also led some hospitals to develop **birthing rooms** and **maternity centers**. These facilities more closely resemble the home environment and are usually less expensive than the standard hospital labor and delivery rooms. The mother labors and delivers in the same room, with the father and possibly other family members present.

Some birthing centers are located in conventional hospital settings, whereas other units are structures built separately from the main hospital. In each case, the facilities attempt to combine the best of both the home and the hospital (Baruffi et al., 1984).

Although 99 percent of all births in the United States are carried out in hospital settings (Ventura et al., 2001), some women choose **home birth** as an alternative. Comparisons of home births with hospital births have found no significant difference in the death rates or other risk factors, such as prolonged labor or fetal oxygen deprivation (e.g., Durand, 1992; Mehl & Peterson, 1981). Women who have pregnancies complicated by diabetes, hypertension, Rh incompatibility, multiple pregnancy, breech or transverse presentation, or other high-risk factors are advised not to consider home birth (Vedam & Kolodji, 1995).

THE NEWBORN: LIFE IN THE OUTSIDE WORLD

The **newborn period** begins with the cutting of the umbilical cord and ends when the part that remains attached to the baby falls off to form the navel. Normally this takes about two weeks. However, not everyone agrees on when the newborn period ends, so infants as old as 4 to 6 weeks of age are often classified as newborns. In this text, the newborn period is defined as the first two weeks of life after birth. You should keep in mind, however, that when the results of research studies on neonates are discussed, the subjects may include babies who are older than 2 weeks of age. The newborn period is also referred to as the **neonatal period** and the two terms are used interchangeably.

Adjustments to Birth. The transition from the uterus to the outside environment is one of the most traumatic periods in life. At birth the baby is cut loose from the placental life-support system and virtually every system of the body must adjust to a new and hostile world. The newborn infant emerges from a world of darkness and relative quiet into a world of light and noise. Within the first 12 to 24 hours after birth the newborn must make several major adjustments, including respiration, body temperature regulation, elimination of body waste, and nutritional intake. However, the stress and strain of labor and delivery trigger a surge of hormones (catecholamines) that help the baby make the transition to life outside the uterus (Lagercrantz & Slotkin, 1986). The extra dose of "stress" hormones apparently helps protect the infant from asphyxia during the birth process, enhances the newborn's ability to breathe, and increases the flow of blood to the vital organs.

Respiration. Most infants begin to breathe within 20 to 30 seconds after birth (Cockburn,

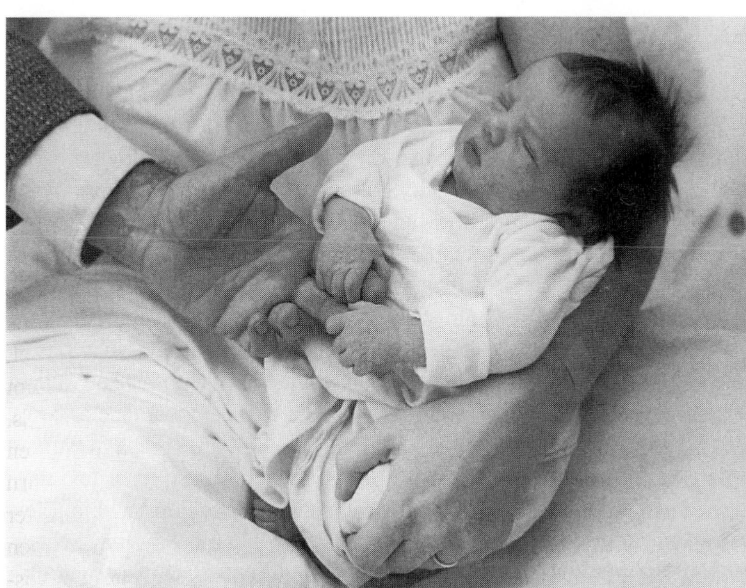

This baby is only a few hours old. Notice the grasp reflex. She is in a state of regular sleep with the eyelids tightly closed (See sleep states).

1984). The first breath is largely reflexive. It is probably initiated by stimulation in the brain stem triggered by skin contact with the cold air, along with decreased oxygen and higher levels of carbon dioxide (Vulliamy, 1982). The newborn may have difficulty breathing because of fluid in the lungs from the amniotic sac. Normally, much of the amniotic fluid is squeezed out of the lungs as the baby passes through the birth canal. In addition, the physician removes fluid and waste products from the mouth and throat by gentle suction immediately after birth.

Temperature Regulation. The temperature of the fetus is approximately 1°F higher than that of the mother. At the time of birth, the infant's temperature drops immediately. The decrease in temperature may be one of several mechanisms that cause the newborn to begin breathing (Ensher & Clark, 1994). Normally, the body temperature goes back up within two to four hours if the temperature-regulating mechanism located in the hypothalamus of the brain is functioning properly (Lowrey, 1978). However, even at best, temperature control in the newborn is not well established. Adults shiver or sweat to get warmer or cooler, but these mechanisms are not very efficient in the newborn. In addition, there is also less fat beneath the skin for insulation. A newborn baby thus loses heat about four times as fast as an adult (Bruck, 1961).

Eating and Digestion. Within a few hours after birth, the baby needs to begin eating or to receive nourishment through other means. Many infants show signs of hunger and are ready to utilize their sucking, rooting, and swallowing reflexes as soon as they are born. However, eating and digestion are not very efficient, so babies tend to lose a few ounces of weight during the first two weeks of life.

Elimination. The kidneys are functional even before the baby is born. Infants typically urinate within the first 24 hours after birth (Novak & Broom, 1999). The frequency of urination gradually increases during the first few days after birth to about once an hour. The volume of urine also increases but varies with fluid intake. The newborn's kidneys do not function at full efficiency, which means that the ability to withstand dehydration or process a large amount of salty substances is very limited (Vulliamy, 1982).

The first bowel movement usually takes place within 24 to 48 hours after birth. The material eliminated is called **meconium.** This is a greenish black, semisolid substance consisting of amniotic fluid, mucus, bile, and other body secretions. If the baby is in distress during prolonged labor, elimination may occur in the amniotic fluid before birth. When that happens, there is a danger that some of the particles of meconium can be inhaled into the baby's lungs, possibly leading to pneumonia (Vulliamy, 1982).

Physical Appearance. As seen through the eyes of the typical parent, the newborn infant is simply beautiful. Many other people, however, have images of the newborn that are not quite as flattering. Shakespeare pictured the infant as "mewling and puking in the nurse's arms." G. Stanley Hall's (1891) classic description of the newborn as "an ugly creature with its red, shriveled, parboiled skin . . . squinting, cross-eyed, pot-bellied, and bowlegged" has been widely quoted. The beauty of the neonate is thus likely to lie in the eyes of the beholder.

At birth, the baby may be covered with a cheeselike vernix that is especially noticeable in the folds and crevices of the skin. The baby may also be splattered with spots of blood, along with bruises, scratches, and skin discolorations from the birth process. The ears may be folded or creased, but they soon reach their normal shape. The head may be elongated, lopsided, or otherwise misshapen from the passage through the birth canal. Fortunately, the skull is soft and pliable, with separate pieces of cartilage designed to overlap during the birth process. Thus, the only problem from the normal molding of the head at birth is one of temporary appearance. The genitalia of both male and female newborns are typically swollen.

The color of the Caucasian newborn's skin ranges from pale to bright pink. It may have a bluish tint if there has been a decrease in oxygen. Some babies have large red patches of skin, called strawberry nevi, which become especially noticeable during crying episodes. These and other skin discolorations tend to disappear within a few days after birth. Infants of color tend to have lighter shades of skin at birth than they do at maturity. The skin reaches its natural hereditary coloring within a few days after it is exposed to light. Infants of African, Indian, Asian, or Mediterranean descent tend to have blue-black colorations on their buttocks or lower backs called Mongolian or Asian spots. These spots usually fade in early childhood and are not associated with central nervous system disorders or other developmental problems (Novak & Broom, 1999).

The individuality of the infant is obvious at birth. Some babies are born with a head full of hair, whereas others have the appearance of being bald. In addition, some of the prenatal lanugo may remain on parts of the body for a few days after birth. Permanent hair develops within a few weeks after birth. The newborn's hair may eventually change color. The newborn's eyes may also change to a darker shade or a different color. True eye color is not usually established until 3 to 6 months of age (Novak & Broom, 1999).

Newborn infants have little voluntary control over their body posture and movements due to the immaturity of the nervous system and lack of muscular strength. They are equipped with a variety of reflexes that exert control over their patterns of movement and other activities in response to stimuli in the environment. Newborn reflexes will be identified and discussed in Chapter 6 on motor development.

Sensory and Perceptual Abilities. In typically developing infants, the five basic senses—sight, hearing, touch, taste, and smell—are functioning at birth. By the second trimester of prenatal development, the eyes, ears, nose, tongue, and skin are approaching functional capacity (Bornstein & Lamb, 1992). The idea that infants are passive creatures with a mind that is comparable to a blank slate (or a computer disc) is no longer widely accepted. Infants are currently viewed as partially equipped at birth to participate actively in their experiences of the world. The notion that the neonate's sensory experiences amount to only "buzzing confusion" has also been replaced with the view of the infant as capable of organizing and processing discrete impressions. However, the quantity and quality of information newborns obtain through the senses and how it is organized and interpreted continue to be the subject of scientific debate and investigation. We will examine the amazing variety of sensory capacities of newborn infants more completely in Chapter 7 on perceptual development.

States of Arousal. Even before they are born infants display patterns of sleep and waking. The degree to which an infant is awake, alert, active, or sleeping is defined as a **state of arousal.** Researchers have distinguished as many as 11 different states of arousal (Zeskind & Marshall, 1991). However, the following six states identified by Wolff (1966) are most frequently used to describe distinct periods of rest and activity that newborns exhibit within a 24-hour period:

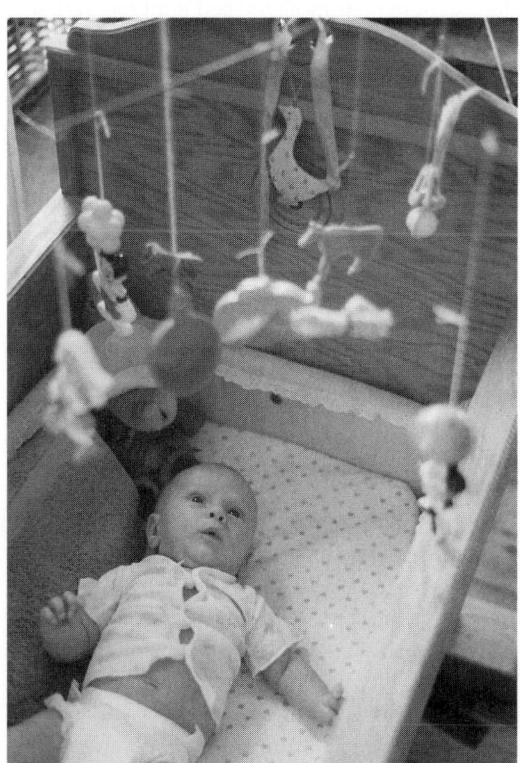

This infant is in a state of waking activity, gazing intently at the crib mobile.

1. *Regular sleep (quiet sleep).* The baby lies very still with the eyelids firmly closed. Breathing is smooth and even. Facial muscles are relaxed and the skin is pink. Regular sleep is often referred to as **non-rapid-eye-movement (NREM) sleep** because the baby's eyes do not display patterns of movement beneath the eyelids.
2. *Irregular sleep (active sleep).* The baby may jerk and startle and occasionally whimper. Facial expressions change frequently and include smiling, frowning, and pouting. Breathing is irregular and the skin may become flushed during activity. The eyelids are usually closed but may occasionally open and close, or remain half-open for a brief period. Irregular sleep is also called **rapid-eye-movement (REM) sleep** because the eyes move rapidly from side to side beneath the eyelids due to increased brain wave activity.
3. *Drowsiness (indeterminate sleep).* This is a transition period from waking to sleeping and from sleeping to waking. The eyelids open and close intermittently and are unfocused. Breathing is regular but rapid. Periods of drowsiness decline with age.
4. *Alert inactivity (quiet alert).* The baby is awake, with bright, shiny eyes. The face is relaxed; breathing is regular but faster than it is during sleep. The baby is happy, alert, and curious without fussing or crying. This is the ideal state for interacting with baby and for administering newborn assessments.
5. *Waking activity.* There are frequent bursts of vigorous movements. The skin becomes flushed and breathing is very irregular. The baby may moan, grunt, or whimper.
6. *Crying.* The baby cries consistently and engages in vigorous movements. The face is twisted into a cry grimace and becomes flushed.

Newborns typically spend most of their time (67 percent) in one of the states of sleep or drowsiness (8 percent). They are alert and quiet about 10 percent of the time, and awake and fussy approximately 10 percent of each day (Berg, Adkinson, & Strock, 1973). Although it probably seems longer to parents, babies spend about 5 percent of their time crying. It is important, however, to keep in mind that babies vary widely in the amount of time spent in each state. Infant states are altered by caregiving activities and environmental conditions such as movement and noise.

Approximately 50 percent of the full-term newborn's sleep time is spent in active, REM sleep. (See preterm infant states later.) In comparison, adults spend about 20 percent of their sleep time in REM sleep. The newborn infant's active and quiet sleep state cycles are also more irregular than the cycles displayed by adults (DeHart, Sroufe, & Cooper, 2000). Fluctuation between active and quiet sleep states is mainly attributed to brain wave activity. Brain wave patterns are different for each state of awareness and change rapidly with maturity of the brain (Myers et al., 1997). By 3 months of age, infants display more adultlike quiet and active sleep patterns (DeHart et al., 2000).

Caregivers need to determine the infant's state of arousal because it reflects the infant's needs and availability for contact with the outside world. For example, infants who are in the alert inactive state tend to turn away from louder voices to more gentle voices (Parmelee & Sigman, 1983). From a scientific perspective, the emergence of regular sleep-wake cycles may provide valuable information about the maturity and integrity of the nervous system. Assessment of sleep-wake development may be useful in the identification of infants at risk for later developmental problems (Myers et al., 1997).

Infant Sleeping Arrangements. In the United States, most infants from middle-class families sleep in their own bed, either in their own or a sibling's bedroom. Although many parents place their newborn infant in a bassinet or crib in the parents' bedroom, this is a usually a temporary arrangement. In contrast to the United States, in most societies throughout the world, infants tend to sleep in the same bed with the mother for the first few years of life. In some instances the infant sleeps with the father, or with both mother and father (Broude, 1995). This practice is referred to as **cosleeping** or **bed sharing.** Cultures that practice cosleeping include rural and urban as well as technological and less technologically advanced communities (Morelli et al., 1992). Even in the United States, cosleeping is widely practiced in some cultural groups. For example, infants from the eastern Kentucky Appalachian Mountains sleep with their parents until age 2 (Abbott, 1992). African American infants are more likely than Caucasian American infants to sleep with their parents (Lozoff, Wolff, & Davis, 1984).

Through the years, American pediatricians and other child-rearing experts have advised parents to make separate sleeping arrangements for infants (e.g., Spock & Rothenberg, 1992). Some of the concerns about cosleeping are that it may interfere with the child's independence, become a habit that will be difficult to break, interfere with the parents' privacy, be overstimulating as infants get older, and cause sleep problems (Lozoff et al., 1984).

Morelli and colleagues (1992) interviewed mothers from urban middle-class families in the United States who did not sleep with their infants. They also interviewed a group of mothers from a rural Guatemalan Mayan community whose children slept in their mothers' bed until toddlerhood. The reasons given by the American mothers for placing infants in a separate bed were based primarily on the belief that babies need to be trained to be independent, and sleeping apart facilitates that process. Other concerns of these mothers related to safety issues (smothering), establishing a difficult-to-break habit, loss of privacy and sexual intimacy, and just being uncomfortable with the idea.

Mayan mothers regarded their sleeping arrangement as "the only reasonable way for a baby and parents to sleep" (Morelli et al., 1992, p. 608). In contrast to U.S. mothers, Mayan mothers emphasized the need to establish interdependence between parent and child. They believed that cosleeping fosters security and closeness, as well as facilitating feeding and other caregiving activities. The available space for sleeping appears to play only a minor role in sleeping arrangements.

There is little scientific evidence on the effects of cosleeping versus independent sleeping arrangements. Currently researchers are debating whether cosleeping prevents or contributes to sudden infant death syndrome (see Chapter 5). Theoretically, infant sleeping arrangements have implications for the psychological development of infants. However, isolating the effects of where the infant sleeps from the effects of other cultural practices is a difficult task.

Infant Mortality. In recent years there has been a steady decline in the rate of infants who die during the first year of life. The United States' infant mortality rate of 7.0 percent for 1999 (7 deaths per 100 live births in 1999) was down 21 percent from the rate of 8.9 in 1990 (Matthews, MacDorman, & Menacker, 2002). In spite of recent improvements, however, the United States ranks 23rd among other industrialized nations in the prevention of infant mortality. (Children's Defense Fund, 2001). Approximately two-thirds of the infant mortality rate is accounted for by infants who die during the first 27 days of life. In the United States, African American infants are twice as likely to die during the first year of life as Caucasian American infants. Research indicates that this gap may be due primarily to the higher rates of low birth weight and SIDS among infants born to black mothers. The infant mortality rate is approximately 22 percent higher for male infants than it is for female infants (Matthews et al., 2002).

A number of factors have been associated with infant mortality. The 3 leading causes of first-year infant death in 1999 were congenital abnormalities, prematurity/low birth weight, and sudden infant death syndrome (SIDS). Together these factors accounted for almost one-half of all infant deaths. In addition, complications of pregnancy, injuries, and infectious disease, poverty, poor nutrition, insufficient prenatal care, maternal health, and behavioral risk factors such as substance abuse, smoking, multiple births, maternal age, and sexually transmitted disease contribute, directly or indirectly, to the death of infants during the first year of life (Matthews et al., 2002).

BIRTH WEIGHT AND GESTATIONAL AGE

Infants are usually classified according to gestational age, birth weight, and size for age. The classifications used to designate the newborn infant's developmental status are listed in Table 3-1. These factors dramatically affect the newborn's ability to survive and thrive in the outside world.

Birth weight is easily and routinely measured, but gestational age is more difficult to ascertain. An estimate of gestational age can be made from the first day of the last menstrual period. However, this information is frequently unreliable because of reporting inaccuracies and irregular menstrual cycles. An ultrasound scan prior to 18 weeks of pregnancy can provide a fairly good estimate of gestational age. Chemical analysis of substances found in the amniotic fluid can also be used for

Table 3-1 Classification of Newborn Infants by Gestational Age, Birth Weight, and Size for Gestational Age

Gestational Age (GA)	
Preterm (premature)	born before 37 weeks of gestation
Extremely premature	born before 28 weeks of gestation
Full-term	born between 37 & 42 weeks of gestation
Postterm (postmature)	born after 42 weeks of gestation
Birth Weight	
Low birth weight (LBW)	less than 5 1/2 lbs (2,500 grams)
Very low birth weight (VLBW)	less than 3 1/2 lbs (1,500 grams)
Extremely low birth weight (ELBW)	less than 2 lbs (1,000 grams)
Size for Gestational Age	
Appropriate for gestational age (AGA)	birth weight between the 10th & 90th percentiles*
Small for gestational age (SGA)	birth weight below the 10th percentile*
Large for gestational age (LGA)	birth weight above the 90th percentile*

*as measured on a standard growth chart

estimating gestational age. The Dubowitz Scale (L. Dubowitz, Dubowitz, & Goldberg, 1970), or a newer abbreviated version (Ballard et al., 1991), is frequently used to assess gestational age after the baby is born. In this test, the baby's physical flexibility, muscle tone, and physical appearance are observed to obtain a maturity rating. Scientists (e.g., Lubchenco et al., 1963) have developed special growth charts to classify newborns on the basis of size for age of gestation.

Preterm and Low Birth Weight Infants. Doctors delivered Quentin four months premature to save his mother's life. He surprised them by exhibiting a healthy heartbeat, a pinkish color, open eyes, and a strong cry. He weighed only 14 ounces and was small enough to fit into the palm of your hand (Knight-Ridder News Service, 1991). Medical science keeps pushing back the **boundary of viability,** or how early infants can be born and still survive. Neonatal intensive care units with sophisticated equipment and health care personnel who specialize in neonatology are now available in most regional medical centers. With aggressive perinatal intervention infants born as early as 23 weeks of gestation and weighing as little as 1 pound (454 grams) are now surviving (Wyly, 1995). However, only 15 percent of infants born at such an early age survive, and 98 percent of the survivors have significant brain damage (Allen, Donohue, & Dusman, 1993).

Preterm or **premature** infants (those born before 37 weeks of gestation) make up approximately 11 percent of all infants born in the United States (Ventura et al., 2001). Premature deliveries are higher among African American and Hispanic mothers, but the rate has been declining in recent years (Hogue & Hargraves, 1995; Ventura et al., 2001). Approximately 90 percent of all infants who die soon after birth were born preterm. More than three-fourths of preterm infants who die were born before 32 weeks of gestation (Ventura et al., 2001). In this section we consider preterm and **low birth weight (LBW)** infants together because they share many of the same characteristics, risk factors, and problems. Low birth weight infants who are products of full-term pregnancies are discussed in a separate section on small for gestational age (SGA) infants.

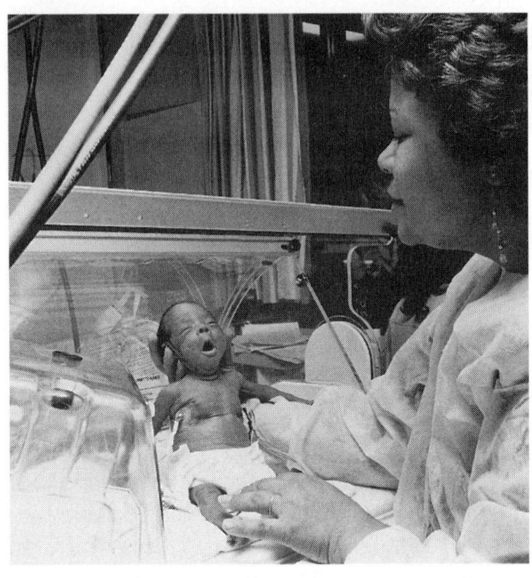

A preterm infant in a neonatal intensive care unit.

Risk Factors. In most cases it is not possible to determine exactly why a mother has given birth to a preterm baby. Many diverse factors may increase a pregnant woman's chances of a preterm delivery. The largest single factor appears to be immaturity of the uterus. Mothers younger than 20 years of age account for 20 percent of all preterm births (Bernbaum & Batshaw, 1997). Other factors associated with premature births include poor maternal nutritional status, inadequate prenatal care, poor socioeconomic status, alcohol or drug abuse, smoking, multiple pregnancy, high blood pressure during pregnancy, premature opening of the cervix, hormonal deficiency, fetal malformations, premature rupture of the amniotic sac, and unusual physical or psychological stress (Committee to Study the Prevention of Low Birth Weight, 1985; Johnston, 1998). A common vaginal infection (bacterial vaginosis) may be responsible for about 6 percent of all preterm births (Hillier et al., 1995). Scientists are also studying the possibility that maternal gum disease is a major contributing factor (Associated Press, 1997).

Many of these risk conditions for having a preterm or low birth weight infant are interrelated. For example, poor socioeconomic status is associated with poor nutrition, stress, lack of prenatal care, and other adverse conditions. Not all of the factors carry the same weight. Even if one or more factors are present, the mother is still likely to give birth to a **full-term, appropriate for gestational age (AGA)** infant (Redshaw, Rivers, & Rosenblatt, 1985).

Physical Characteristics. Preterm babies are not just smaller versions of a full-term baby, but continue to be a fetus developmentally in some respects. The youngest of these infants are covered with the downy hair (lanugo) that normally is lost before birth. The skin is paper thin and transparent. Since little fat has accumulated beneath the skin, the baby looks scrawny and has the wrinkled appearance of a wizened, elderly person. The ears are wrinkled and lie flat against the head, since the cartilage is not well formed. The nipples on the breast may be barely visible. The genitals are not fully developed and may be swollen in appearance. The relatively large head and abdomen are particularly striking. In contrast to those of full-term infants, the movements of preterm infants are wild and bizarre. When lying on the stomach, the knees are stretched out to the side of the body rather than drawn underneath the abdomen. These infants do not attempt to change position very often. Unlike a full-term infant their limbs are very limp and floppy and are not likely to resist forced movement. The youngest preterm infants display few reflexes since some of the reflexes do not develop until 30 to 32 weeks of gestation (Bernbaum & Batshaw, 1997).

Preterm Infant States. The organization of states in preterm infants depends upon the infant's level of maturity. In very young premature infants (23–27 weeks), states are diffused and not well organized. These infants display jerky movements and irregularity of breathing and heartbeats. They sleep most of the time, but their sleep is restless (active) with twitching muscles and rapid eye movements (REMs). The cries of these very young preterm infants are comparatively weak, short, and infrequent. They have difficulty swallowing and sucking. Between 30 and 37 weeks of gestational age, preterm infants begin to display quiet, REM sleep with regular respiration and less movement. However, other states are not clearly distinguishable until approximately 37 weeks (Wyly, 1995).

Problems and Complications of Prematurity. A number of problems make survival difficult for infants who are born too early and too small. Some of the most serious and commonly observed problems include respiratory disorders, temperature regulation, heart problems, bleeding in the brain, eye problems, blood disorders, nutritional difficulties, and infections.

Respiratory Distress Syndrome. The most frequent cause of death among preterm infants is **respiratory distress syndrome (RDS),** sometimes referred to as hyaline membrane disease (HMD). The risk of death from RDS increases as birth weight and gestational age decrease (Henig & Fletcher, 1983). RDS occurs more frequently in males than in females, and in Caucasians than in infants of color (C. Gleason & Durand, 1993). The problem is caused mainly by incomplete lung development and the lack of a chemical called surfactant. The underdeveloped lungs are leaky and fragile, making them susceptible to damage from ventilators. Without surfactant, the air sacs in the lungs tend to collapse between breaths. This makes breathing more difficult and inhibits the efficient exchange of oxygen and carbon dioxide. Infants do not usually have adequate levels of surfactant until about the 34th or 35th week of gestation (Ensher & Clark, 1994).

Improved treatment methods have reduced the number of deaths from RDS dramatically. Several years ago, almost three out of every four infants with RDS died. Today the large majority of infants recover from RDS within 10 days to two weeks. Treatment of RDS includes carefully controlled delivery of pressurized oxygen through a tube to keep the lungs from collapsing. Another treatment method is the administration of surfactant replacement into the lungs of the baby (Bernbaum & Batshaw, 1997). In some cases, steroids are injected into a mother who is about to have a preterm delivery to stimulate the baby's lungs to make surfactant (C. Gleason & Durand, 1993).

Bronchopulmonary Dysplasia. In some cases, when preterm infants who have been affected by RDS are taken off the respirator, they develop a chronic lung disease called **bronchopulmonary dysplasia (BPD).** The walls of the lungs thicken and the mucous lining of the lungs is reduced along with the airway diameter. Therefore, the infant has to work harder to breathe. BPD can also be caused by infections, inhaling meconium into the lungs, or asphyxia. Months of oxygen therapy and treatment with various medications to keep the lungs open may be required (Bernbaum & Batshaw, 1997).

Temperature Regulation. Another problem faced by preterm infants is maintaining a stable, normal body temperature. The layer of fat needed for insulation has not yet developed, and the skin surface area from which heat can be lost is relatively large. Premature infants cannot sweat to keep cool because their sweat glands are not completely developed. In addition, the temperature-control mechanism in the brain is not sufficiently mature to regulate the body's responses to environmental temperature changes. At birth, these babies are placed in an incubator, where the temperature can be carefully maintained. For very sick newborns who require access to therapeutic devices, a radiant heater is sometimes used (C. Gleason & Durand, 1993).

Heart Problems. Before birth the infant's heart circulates the blood through the placenta, where it receives a supply of oxygen. Most of the blood bypasses the baby's own lungs. In full-term infants, a blood vessel (ductus arteriosus) closes automatically soon after birth so that the full blood supply is channeled into the lungs. In approximately one-third of preterm infants, the duct does not close (Bernbaum & Batshaw, 1997). If this happens, the infant will have an insufficient oxygen supply. The condition can be life threatening, and emergency surgery may be necessary. However, in many cases medication can be given that is effective in stimulating the duct to close on its own (Sammons & Lewis, 1985).

Bleeding in the Brain. In premature infants, the small blood vessels in the brain are more immature and have fewer supporting cells in the surrounding tissue. Therefore, sudden changes in blood pressure or blood oxygen levels may cause blood vessels to rupture and bleed inside the skull (Sammons & Lewis, 1985). Less serious bleeding may also result from trauma to the head during the birth process. Sometimes there are no symptoms when bleeding occurs, but with severe bleeding the blood count may drop, the head may swell, and seizures may develop. Bleeding in or around the brain is most likely to occur in the youngest and smallest infants. Intracranial bleeding takes place in approximately 30 percent of infants who weigh less than 3-1/2 pounds (Ensher & Clark, 1994). In some cases, the bleeding is so slight that it has little or no impact on the functions of the brain. More massive or more frequent bleeding may result in long-term motor and mental difficulties, or even death.

Retinopathy of Prematurity. A common problem found among very small and immature newborns is **retinopathy of prematurity (ROP).** The problem occurs when the normal progression of newly formed vessels in the retina is interrupted. If this condition continues, it causes scarring or detachment of the retina, which may lead to visual impairment or blindness (Graeber & Schwartz, 1993). ROP has been attributed to exposure to excessive oxygen in the hospital nursery. Through the years, careful control of supplemental levels of oxygen has resulted in a dramatic decline in the incidence of ROP. However, in recent years, as more and more extremely low birth weight (ELBW) and premature infants have survived, the incidence of ROP has increased (D. Gibson et al., 1990). Even with careful control of oxygen exposure, many of the smallest and youngest infants develop ROP (Teplin, 1995). Few infants who are born later than 28 weeks of gestational age, or weighing 3-1/2 pounds or more, develop this condition. Infants of multiple births are more likely to develop ROP than singletons. Fortunately, new techniques in laser and other surgeries offer promise for treatment of ROP (Ensher & Clark, 1994).

Excess Bilirubin. Preterm and LBW infants frequently have a yellow-orange skin color similar to a fading tan. This condition, referred to as jaundice, is caused by an excess accumulation of **bilirubin** in the bloodstream and body tissues. Bilirubin is a pigment formed when red blood cells are destroyed. Premature infants are especially susceptible to jaundice because the liver is likely to be too immature to remove the bilirubin from the blood. Normally, this problem can be corrected with phototherapy by placing the baby under a special light. In some cases a blood-exchange transfusion may be required. This can be done before birth if needed. Treatment of this problem is a high medical priority because extremely high bilirubin levels can eventually lead to brain damage.

Nutrition. Nutritional needs of preterm infants are generally higher than those of full-term infants. The precise quantities of nutrients needed by infants born prematurely are still being defined (Trahams & Pipes, 1997). Meeting the nutritional needs of preterm and LBW infants is also a problem because of the immaturity of sucking and swallowing abilities and the digestive system. The stomach is small and the passage of its contents is very slow. The infant's capacity to metabolize fat and protein is inefficient. In addition, premature infants are born with low nutritional stores plus the need to grow faster in order to achieve optimal "catch-up" growth (Anderson, 1993).

Infants who are born after 32 to 34 weeks of gestation are usually able to coordinate sucking and swallowing and may feed themselves through a nipple. Infants who are born earlier or who are critically ill are usually fed through a tube inserted through the nose or mouth into the stomach and/or may be given intravenous solutions containing glucose, fat, amino acids, and other nutrients (Committee on Nutrition, 1993). The intake of fluids and other substances has to be carefully controlled because the kidneys of the premature infant have a limited capacity to eliminate waste products. In spite of these difficulties, however, considerable progress has been made in providing nutritional care of preterm and LBW infants. One current technique is the use of breast milk fortified with supplementary nutrients as the main diet for tube-fed premature infants (Schanler & Hurst, 1994).

Infections and Other Problems. Preterm infants are very susceptible to infections from bacteria and viruses. Immunity to diseases, which the infant receives from the mother, is not present until 28 weeks of gestational age, and the level of immunity is rather limited at first (Vulliamy, 1982). Some of the problems, such as blood poisoning, probably result from the invasive procedures used in inserting tubes, taking blood samples, and other routines used in intensive-care nurseries. **Necrotizing enterocolitis,** a life-threatening disease that affects the bowel wall, is a special hazard of prematurity. This disorder is caused by an inadequate blood flow to the intestines or from infectious bacteria (Novak & Broom, 1999). Other problems experienced by preterm infants include apnea (a prolonged pause in breathing) and inefficient kidney function.

Prevention. Research studies have consistently shown that prenatal care can be effective, especially among women in high-risk categories, in preventing low birth weight and prematurity (Committee to Study the Prevention of Low Birth Weight, 1985). Pregnant women are less likely to smoke or to use alcohol, drugs, and other harmful substances when they are aware of the adverse effects on the baby. They also are more likely to maintain better nutrition and health when they receive appropriate prenatal care. Detection of bacterial vaginosis infections and treatment with antibiotics reduces the risk of premature delivery (Hauth et al., 1995).

The early detection of premature labor symptoms is the most important step in preventing preterm birth. Low back pain, cramps, mild contractions, increased vaginal discharge, pelvic heaviness, and diarrhea are some signs of preterm labor (Rust & Morrison, 1993). The mother can be hospitalized and treated with labor-stopping drugs if the beginning of premature labor is detected early enough. A variety of medications are effective in postponing a preterm delivery, but there is some risk of undesirable effects on the infant. Consequently, the use of such drugs is a dilemma for patients and their physicians who must weigh the benefits versus the risks involved. Extended bed rest for mothers who are considered to be at risk for preterm delivery is one commonly used treatment approach. However, unless the mother is actually experiencing premature labor, bed rest has not proved to be very beneficial (Rust & Morrison, 1993). While some progress is being made in preventing preterm births, the prevention of preterm delivery continues to be one of the major challenges in modern medical care.

Small for Gestational Age Infants. An infant whose weight is below the 10th percentile (i.e., who weighs less than 90 percent of infants of the same gestational age) is, by definition, **small for gestational age** (SGA). The majority of these infants are born at term, although some are classified as preterm SGA or postterm SGA (Cockburn, 1984). Full-term SGA births are usually caused by intrauterine growth retardation. Known causes of this problem include genetic conditions, congenital infections, maternal malnutrition, placental abnormalities, and maternal ingestion of adverse substances. Rates of mortality and health problems are highest among infants at the lowest weight levels (3rd percentile or below) even if they are born full-term (McIntire et al., 1999).

The majority of full-term SGA infants appear to have starved in the uterus. SGA infants tend to have even less fat and muscle tissue than premature infants. The head appears to be larger and even more out of proportion to the rest of the body. The skin is loose and dry with very little lanugo or vernix. Typically SGA babies have more hair than preterm infants (Sammons & Lewis, 1985). These infants are often very active and cry vigorously (Cockburn, 1984).

SGA infants have some of the same problems as premature infants, such as temperature regulation, but they develop some special complications of their own. They are more likely to have problems such as asphyxia (low oxygen and high carbon-dioxide blood level) before they are born. SGA infants also frequently have trouble with hypoglycemia (low blood sugar). Since they are stressed, these infants tend to inhale meconium, which they excrete into the amniotic fluid before birth. Inhaled meconium causes breathing difficulties after birth and often leads to pneumonia. The stress placed on the heart by these breathing difficulties may result in death (Vulliamy, 1982). However, SGA babies rarely are affected by RDS (Bernbaum & Batshaw, 1997).

Large for Gestational Age Infants. **Large for gestational age (LGA)** infants weigh above the 90th percentile (or more than 90 percent of infants of the same gestational age). Although there is much less written about LGA babies than SGA babies, they have problems that are equally serious. LGA is most frequently caused by maternal diabetes. At birth LGA babies are likely to have too much insulin in their blood. This condition results in overgrowth of fatty tissue, the heart, liver, and the adrenal gland. Fortunately, brain growth is not usually affected. LGA infants are likely to have respiratory distress because excess insulin prevents the lungs from maturing. Congenital defects and injuries during birth are also more prevalent among LGA babies. Other problems include an extra large tongue and other body organs. The neonatal mortality rate is higher among LGA infants than AGA infants (Ensher & Clark, 1994).

Postterm Infants. Babies born after 42 weeks of gestational age are considered to be **postterm** or **postmature.** The main risk these infants face is the aging of the placenta. After about 40 to 42 weeks of gestation, the placenta loses efficiency in supplying nutrition and carrying off waste products. The amount of amniotic fluid also tends to diminish in a postterm pregnancy. As a result, postmature babies are long and skinny and have dry skin that may be cracked and peeling. Asphyxia, inhalation of meconium, pneumonia, and hypoglycemia are typical problems they experience at birth (Johnston, 1998). With more accurate methods of assessing gestational age, physicians are now better equipped to prevent pregnancies from continuing too long.

Effects of Prematurity and Low Birth Weight. The vast majority of preterm and low birth weight infants grow up to be normal, healthy infants with little or no traces of their former condition. Advances in medical knowledge and technology since the 1960s have resulted in a decreased incidence of major disabilities and sensory impairments (Allen, 1993). Unfortunately, though, many of these infants suffer one or more developmental problems. These infants will have moderate to serious degrees of such problems as visual impairment, hearing loss, learning disabilities, epilepsy, cerebral palsy, mental retardation, and anxiety and behavioral problems (Courage & Adams, 1997; Modi, 1999). The chances of having one or more developmental problems increase as gestational age and birth weight decrease. Some reports indicate that the severe disability rate is about 18 percent for very low birth weight (VLBW) infants, and about 20 to 25 percent for extremely low birth weight (ELBW) infants (Courage & Adams, 1997; Hall, 1985; Wood et al., 2000). Follow-up studies of ELBW, including extremely prematurely born infants without major impairments, suggest that 40 to 65 percent require special education or additional services in school (Collin, Halsey, & Anderson, 1991; Courage & Adams, 1997). Boys are more likely than girls to have problems (Wood et al., 2000).

Healthy AGA premature or low birth weight infants who have adequate nutrition usually catch up to full-term infants of the same birth date by 40 to 42 weeks of age. After that time, AGA preterm infants grow at the same rate as full-term infants (Desmond et al., 1980). However, even healthy preterm infants have been found to differ from full-term infants in the structural development of the brain. They have less gray/white matter differentiation and myelination, which may explain their poorer neurobehavioral performance (Modi, 1999). As a group, premature infants demonstrate a normal range of intelligence as they grow up. However, their average IQ score is slightly below the norm for the general population (Allen, 1993).

SGA infants tend to have a higher incidence of developmental disabilities than babies whose weight is appropriate for gestational age (Bernbaum & Batshaw, 1997). Infants who are born with VLBW and SGA have been found to be at increased risk for developmental problems in cognitive and motor functioning (Smedler et al., 1992). SGA infants are also more likely to grow up to be smaller than their full-term peers (D. Hall, 1985). For example, Willie Shoemaker, the famous jockey, was an SGA baby (2½ pounds at 36 weeks of gestation). His parents kept him in a shoe box in the oven with the door open during the neonatal period (Shoemaker & Tower, 1970). Shoemaker's adult height reached only 4 feet 11½ inches.

In summary, during the first two or three years of life, preterm infants typically display deficiencies in behavioral organization, visual attention, information processing, motor skills, and language acquisition. Most of these problems tend to disappear with age, but the effects may be permanent for some children. In some instances, prematurity and low birth weight have a "sleeper effect" whereby developmental problems do not show up until these children enter school. It is almost impossible at birth to predict how being born too soon and too small will affect any particular baby. In most cases, parents and others must "wait and see" (Ensher & Clark, 1994).

Caring for Preterm and Low Birth Weight Infants. During the past 30 years hospital workers and researchers have attempted to design neonatal intensive care units (NICUs) to meet the unique psychological and physical needs of infants who have been born too early and too small. Investigators have experimented with a variety of sensory stimulation or stress-relieving activity interventions in order to facilitate the development of these fragile infants. Studies have been conducted on the effectiveness of the use of water beds and air mattresses (with or without built-in rocking mechanisms), use of pacifiers, sound recordings of the mother's heartbeat and other intrauterine noises, parental voices, classical music, and high-contrast pictures, mobiles, or other materials placed in the infant's field, as well as a variety of infant massage therapy techniques. These interventions are referred to as a "deficit model" based on the assumption that preterm infants are deprived of stimulation they would normally receive in the womb or postnatal experiences that are usually provided for full-term infants. The goal is to compensate for lost intrauterine sensory experiences.

Other researchers (e.g., Thoman,1993) prefer interventions that are based on a "minimal stimulation" approach whereby nursery lights are dimmed, sounds are reduced, isolettes are covered with blankets to provide shade from the light, and infants are snugly surrounded with blanket rolls. Handling and routine medical checks are minimized. This approach is designed to simulate the protective features of the intrauterine environment and minimize stressful stimulation until the infant is better equipped to cope.

An example of the minimal stimulation approach is Thoman's (1993) "**gentlest intervention**" procedures. This approach is based on the theory that infants benefit most when they are allowed to respond to or ignore the stimulation provided. Examples of interventions that allow infants to self-regulate the stimulation include opportunities for nonnutritive sucking that premature infants could respond to or ignore and provision of a small beanbag so that infants can mold to it and make their own "nest." Another intervention developed by Thoman is a "breathing teddy bear" that is placed in the isolette with the infant. A special air pump located outside the isolette makes the bear "breathe" in adjustable rhythms to match the baby's own breathing patterns, or at a slower rate.

The findings of studies evaluating the effectiveness of the various NICU intervention techniques and models vary somewhat and must be carefully interpreted. For the most part, the combined results of numerous studies support the view that VLBW and LBW infants benefit from various NICU interventions (Field, 2000; Linn, Horowitz, & Fox, 1985; C. Mueller, 1996). For example, some researchers have concluded that low birth weight and preterm babies gain weight faster and go home from the hospital sooner if they are exposed to sensory interventions such as massage therapy (Field, 1995). On a cautionary note, however, some scholars note that many of the studies reporting positive results have serious flaws and the results have not been reproduced in other studies (Bennett, 1987; Modi, 1999; Palmer, Capute, & Shapiro, 1988).

In any case, there is general agreement that caregivers who work with premature infants should be aware of the infant's state and avoid intrusive or overstimulating activities. Stimulation should be provided in small increments and withdrawn if the baby appears stressed. Signs that a baby is overstressed include color changes, yawning, sneezing, vomiting, eye aversion, or crying. Recent investigations by Modi (1999) support the belief that infant massage and other interventions are effective only when performed at times suitable to the infant.

Parent-Infant Interactions in the NICU. Preterm, low birth weight, and other infants who need to be cared for in a NICU are at increased risk for problems in early parent-child interaction patterns. These infants are more likely to be perceived by parents as less physically attractive and less responsive than babies who are born on schedule with appropriate weight. The early birth of a tiny baby is likely to be accompanied by parental feelings of guilt, anxiety, and uncertainty. Mothers of preterm infants are more likely to become depressed and develop mental health problems than mothers of full-term infants (Modi, 1999).

NICU babies tend to avoid eye contact, smile infrequently, have difficulty sending clear signals, and are difficult to cuddle and console. Consequently, parents of these children may respond differently than parents of healthy infants. Many parents smile less, spend less time in face-to-face contact, and make less body contact. In some cases though, parents use overstimulating touching and talking interactions in attempts to obtain responses from their baby. Infants respond to such "intrusive" behaviors by gaze aversion and turning away. Thus, parents and infants have difficulty in establishing satisfying patterns of interactions (Modi, 1999; Wyly, 1995).

Recognizing the importance of early parent-infant contacts, many NICUs have established liberal visitation policies and encourage parent involvement in the nonmedical care and feeding of their infants. They also have parent education programs, support groups, and other interventions that promote parent involvement. A special type of intervention that is being used in some NICUs is **kangaroo care.** This approach originated in Bogotá, Colombia, as a means of using mothers as "human incubators" because of the lack of hospital equipment. The practice was introduced in the United States and other countries as a means of promoting tactile stimulation for the baby and facilitating parent-infant bonding through skin-to-skin contact. The mother holds the diaper-clad baby between or near her breasts so that the baby has self-regulatory access to breastfeeding. The time at which kangaroo care is begun and the length of caregiving episodes vary with the condition of the baby. Fathers may also hold the baby kangaroo-style. Research studies have found that this type of care provides at least some short-term benefits for both premature infants and their families. The long-term effects have not yet been evaluated (Charpak et al., 1997; Wyly, 1995).

NEWBORN SCREENING TESTS

Apgar Scale. Many physicians routinely use the **Apgar Scale** to evaluate the vital signs of newborn infants in the delivery room. The scale is administered within the first 60 seconds after birth to check the baby's heart rate, breathing, muscle tone, reflex irritability, and color (Table 3-2). A second assessment is usually made about 5 minutes later. Infants who are in the best condition score in the 8–10 range. A score of 5–7 warns the doctor that the baby may need help and should be carefully observed. If the score is 4 or below, the infant is in critical condition and requires emergency care. The large majority of infants score in the 7–10 range.

Brazelton Scale. The **Brazelton Neonatal Behavior Assessment Scale (BNBAS)** was designed to assess the newborn infant's responses to the environment (Brazelton, 1973). One section of the test contains 20 items that measure the intactness of the nervous system through elicited reflexes such as rooting and sucking (see Chapter 6). The examination also contains items that score an infant on 26 kinds of behavior, including sensory responses (e.g., vision, hearing), motor maturity,

Table 3-2 Apgar Scale

SIGN	*0*	*1*	*2*
A—appearance (color)	blue, pale	body pink (extremities blue)	completely pink
P—pulse (heart rate)	absent	below 100	over 100
G—grimace (reflex irritability, response to stimulation of sole of foot by a glancing slap)	no response	grimace	cry
A—activity (muscle tone)	limp	some flexion of extremities	active motion
R—respiratory effort	absent	slow, irregular	good strong cry

Source: J. Butterfield and M. Covey (1962). Practical epigram of the Apgar Score. *Journal of the American Medical Association, 181,* 353. Copyright © 1962, American Medical Association. Reprinted by permission.

APPLICATIONS: FACILITATING DEVELOPMENT OF THE NEWBORN

The most important thing parents and caregivers of newborns can do to facilitate the development of newborn infants is to meet their basic needs, including adequate nutrition, good health care, and affection. Giving an infant a "feeling of being loved and cared for" is the best thing parents can do to get their child off to a good start (White, 1985, p. 26). The following child-rearing practices are recommended during the first four to six weeks of life:

- Handle the newborn frequently and respond promptly to its cries. A crying infant who is not hungry or in need of a diaper change can usually be calmed by swaddling (wrapping tightly in a blanket), gentle rocking, burping, holding and cuddling, humming, trying different types of stroking or massage, shielding the baby from bright light, or adjusting clothing or room temperature (Ramey & Ramey, 1999; White, 1985).
- Provide a crib mobile with contrasting colors. This is about the only enrichment material a newborn needs. The mobile should be designed so that it can be enjoyed from the perspective of an infant looking up rather than an adult looking down (White, 1985).
- Change the position and location of the baby several times during waking hours. A baby should be placed on its stomach frequently during the day. This position induces head lifting and increases the visual field (White, 1985). However, the baby should be placed on its back to sleep (see sudden infant death syndrome, Chapter 5).
- Develop the habit of talking to the baby when it is alert. Diaper changing and other caregiving activities are usually good times to get the baby's attention and engage in play (White, 1985).
- Pay attention to the infant's state of awareness for the timing of activities.

alertness, self-quieting activity, and social interaction (cuddliness). The BNBAS scale is about 80 percent effective in detecting abnormalities of development in newborns; the device has been used widely in research and is also used in teaching parents about the behavior of their baby (Heidelise et al., 1979).

Assessment of Preterm Infant Behavior Scale. One of the most widely used instruments for evaluating the developmental status of preterm infants is the **Assessment of Preterm Infant Behavior (APIB) Scale** (Als, 1982). The APIB is based on the BNBAS and includes some of the same items. It is designed to assess signs of stability and instability in each of the following areas: physiological functioning (e.g., heart rate, color changes), motor functioning, state organization, attention or interaction, and self-regulation. The examiner observes how well the infant responds to a series of increasingly demanding stimuli.

SUMMARY

Labor and Delivery

- Scientists believe that the birth process begins when a combination of prostaglandins and other substances reach a critical level. The process of childbirth begins with involuntary contractions of the uterus. As labor progresses, the contractions occur closer and closer together with increasing regularity, intensity, and duration. Before labor actually begins, the mother may experience false labor, sometimes referred to as Braxton Hicks contractions.
- Labor is affected by the position of the fetus and the body part that first enters the birth canal. Almost all babies are born in the head-first position. A few babies are born in a breech position with the buttocks, feet, or knees first. Normal labor and delivery consist of four stages: dilation of the cervix; expulsion of the baby; delivery of the placenta; and a recovery period.
- When complications occur, the baby may be removed through a surgical incision in the abdomen

and uterus, called a Caesarean section (C-section). The high number of Caesarean births in the United States has generated a lot of concern among health care officials.

- Around the world, women give birth in a variety of positions, including kneeling, squatting, standing, sitting, or on hands and knees. Mothers in the United States most often labor and deliver while lying on their back, but this practice is changing.

Pain and Labor

- A variety of medications are available for the treatment of labor pains. The epidural block appears to be the most popular method. The use of small to moderate amounts of pain medications is considered safe, but the extended use of strong pain medication can have an adverse effect on the baby.

Prepared Childbirth

- Approaches to prepared childbirth include the Dick-Read, Lamaze, and Bradley methods. These methods differ somewhat in theory and specific procedures, but they are similar in their goal of achieving a relatively pain-free childbirth without the use of medication, while involving the father as an integral part of the birth process. Prepared childbirth can be effective, but the results may vary with the instructors and individual participants. The role of the father in childbirth varies from culture to culture. In the United States, the presence, effective coaching, and encouragement of the father during childbirth have been associated with the mother's and father's positive evaluation of the birth experience.
- Current alternatives to traditional hospital procedures used in childbirth and postpartum care include rooming-in, the use of homelike birthing centers, and home delivery.

The Newborn: Life in the Outside World

- The newborn period is defined as the first two weeks after birth. Adjustments newborn infants have to accomplish include breathing, temperature changes, taking in nourishment, eliminating body waste, sleeping, and waking. Infants vary widely in physical appearance at birth, but the effects of the birth process are usually obvious. Skin discolorations, bruises, and a misshapen skull are some of the features displayed by many infants.
- The five basic sensory systems—vision, hearing, touch, taste, and smell—are functioning at birth, at least to a limited extent. Six states of arousal are typically exhibited by newborns: regular/quiet sleep, irregular/active sleep, drowsiness/indeterminate sleep, alert inactivity, waking activity, and crying. Infant sleeping arrangements vary among different cultures. Most newborn infants in the United States sleep in a separate bed in a separate room. In most other cultures throughout the world infants sleep with their mother.

Birth Weight and Gestational Age

- The infant's birth weight and gestational age are critical factors that have a major impact on growth and development. Preterm and low birth weight infants have numerous problems including respiratory distress syndrome, chronic lung disease, temperature-regulation difficulties, heart problems, intracranial bleeding, eye problems, excess bilirubin, nutritional difficulties, and infections. Small for gestational age (SGA), large for gestational age (LGA), and postterm infants also have many problems when they are born.
- Preterm and low birth weight infants may have developmental disabilities and sensory impairments. The risk of disabilities increases as gestational age and birth weight decrease. Most of these problems tend to disappear with age, but the effects may be permanent for some children.
- Researchers have experimented with a variety of NICU stimulation and intervention activities for preterm and low birth weight infants with contradictory results. There is general agreement that NICU interventions should be carefully controlled and based on the individual needs of the infant.

Newborn Screening Tests

- The Apgar Scale, the Brazelton Neonatal Behavior Assessment Scale, and the Assessment of Preterm Infant Behavior Scale are assessment instruments that are widely used to determine the developmental status of newborn infants.

KEY TERMS

labor
labor contraction
Braxton Hicks contractions
effacement
dilation
breech position
transition phase
crowning
episiotomy
vacuum extractor
Caesarean section (C-section)
epidural block
Lamaze method
Leboyer method
couvade
rooming-in
birthing rooms
maternity centers
home birth
newborn period
neonatal period
meconium
state of arousal
non-rapid-eye-movement (NREM) sleep
rapid-eye-movement (REM) sleep
cosleeping, bed sharing
boundary of viability
preterm (premature)
low birth weight
full-term
appropriate for gestational age
respiratory distress syndrome (RDS)
bronchopulmonary dysplasia (BPD)
retinopathy of prematurity (ROP)
bilirubin
necrotizing enterocolitis
small for gestational age
large for gestational age
postterm (postmature)
gentlest intervention
kangaroo care
Apgar Scale
Brazelton Neonatal Behavior Assessment Scale (BNBAS)
Assessment of Preterm Infant Behavior (APIB) Scale

INFORMATION ON THE WEB*

www.childbirth.org. The site provides many links to information and resources related to pregnancy, giving birth, and newborns.

www.parentsplace.com/expert/pediatrician. Provides links to newborn care, including Apgar scores and other helpful information for parents.

www.aapi-online.com. Valuable information provided by the American Association for Premature Infants. AAPI is an organization dedicated to improving the quality of health, developmental, and educational services for premature infants, children, and their families.

*Web sites are subject to change.

FOUR

PHYSICAL GROWTH

There's only one beautiful baby in the world and every mother has it.
—An English Proverb

As surely as life continues outside the uterus, the baby grows. At no other time period following birth is growth so rapid, dramatic, and clearly observable as it is during infancy. Adults are constantly amazed at how quickly an infant changes in physical appearance. Physical growth results from two processes—cell division and the increase in the size of existing cells. Before birth, the increase in cell number resulting from cell division is the main type of growth activity. After birth, the process shifts to the enlargement of existing cells. This does not mean that no new cells are formed, but the main growth function is to build on existing structures and to replace cells that are lost through aging, wear and tear, and physical injury.

In this chapter we consider physical changes that occur during infancy. Clearly observable changes in height, weight, head circumference, teeth, and skin are discussed. We also give attention to less obvious growth processes occurring in the internal organs such as the brain, muscles, skeleton, and cardiovascular system. Finally, procedures for evaluating and enhancing physical growth are considered.

FACTORS INFLUENCING PHYSICAL GROWTH

Human growth is an extremely complicated process that is affected by numerous forces including interactions among genes, hormones, health, nutrition, socioeconomic status, sex, race, and emotional stress. Some of these factors are considered in other chapters in connection with specific aspects of growth, whereas others are discussed at this point. Keep in mind, however, that the precise influence of each factor is almost impossible to determine because of the complex ways in which heredity and various environmental conditions intermix.

Socioeconomic Status. Social and economic factors (socioeconomic status, SES) are very important influences on human growth and development. Children from higher social class groups are taller, heavier, and grow faster than children from lower socioeconomic groups in the same part of the country. In England, children of fathers employed in professional jobs average about ¾ to ½ inch taller at age 3 than those of fathers working in unskilled occupations (Tanner, 1990). Everywhere, infant mortality and health problems are most common among children of lower socioeconomic status. Social class differences simply reflect the nutrition, health care, and other environmental conditions to which infants are exposed.

Illness. The effects of garden-variety childhood diseases (measles, colds, viruses, etc.) on the growth rate of well-nourished children are hardly noticeable. In some cases, growth may be slowed down slightly, but once the disease is cured, the growth rate resumes and the infant makes up for "lost time" (Tanner, 1990). Undernourished children do not catch up as easily. Children from economically deprived environments, who have a long history of frequent colds, ear disease, sore throats, and skin infections, tend to be smaller than other children (Tanner, 1990). In all children, major diseases delay growth, but the effects on body size are seldom lasting. However, some of the illnesses to which infants are exposed have the potential to cause severe sensory or nervous system impairments leading to physical disabilities.

Culture and Race. Many aspects of physical growth during infancy, such as height and weight, vary widely around the world, depending upon gene pools, nutrition, and other environmental factors. At 1 year of age, infants living in different regions of the world differ as much as 5⅕ inches in average height and 9 pounds in average weight. The shortest and lightest infants come from South-central and Southeast Asia (India, Vietnam, Pakistan). The tallest and heaviest infants come from the United States and Europe (Werner, 1979). Nail and hair growth are more advanced in African infants in comparison to American babies (Broude, 1995).

In the United States, black infants tend to be slightly smaller at birth than white infants, but their skeletal development is slightly more advanced. Black infants soon surpass white infants in size and are a little taller and heavier throughout childhood as long as socioeconomic factors are equivalent (Eichorn, 1979). Birth weights of Mexican Americans are similar to those of white Americans. Japanese and Chinese infants are shorter and weigh less, on average, than infants of European ancestry (Malina & Bouchard, 1991). Japanese infants reared in America are more advanced in height, weight, and skeletal growth than Japanese infants living in Japan (Broude, 1995). The difference is assumed to be at least partially related to dietary influences. The largest physical differences among races are those of body proportion, especially of the lower extremities (Tanner, 1990; Malina & Bouchard, 1991). However, differences in shape are more observable in later years than in infancy.

Hormonal Influences. Hormones secreted directly into the bloodstream by the endocrine glands play a major role in physical growth, particularly height. Although numerous hormones affect all growth throughout the life cycle, the hormones that are particularly influential during infancy are thyroxine and human growth hormone (HGH).

Thyroxine. The thyroid gland releases **thyroxine** in response to chemical messages from the pituitary gland. Adequate quantities of this hormone are necessary for cell multiplication and subsequent growth in size. Thyroxine also is important for the stimulation of brain growth during the fetal and early infancy periods (Lowrey, 1978). To meet this need, it is secreted in greater quantities during the first two years of life, after which the amount is reduced until adolescence. Insufficient thyroxine (hypothyroidism) leads to brain growth failure and mental diasbility. If hypothyroidism is discovered and treated within the first three months of life, an infant has an 85 percent chance of developing an IQ of at least 85. The outlook is more dismal if treatment is delayed (Tanner, 1990).

Human Growth Hormone. Normal physical growth from infancy to maturity depends upon an adequate supply of **human growth hormone (HGH),** which also comes from the thyroid gland. Human growth hormone is apparently not necessary for normal prenatal growth. However, if there is a deficiency of HGH, growth after birth is less than normal and is increasingly evident by 2 years of age (Tanner, 1990). Human growth hormone affects cell multiplication and expansion in all organs of the body except the central nervous system and some of the endocrine glands (Lowrey, 1978). Deficiency of HGH is found in approximately one out of 4,000 children (Gotlin et al., 1995). Growth hormone deficiency (GHD) of infants is considered to be the result of anatomical malformations of the brain or genetic defects (Vance & Mauras, 1999).

The extent of growth retardation is related to the amount of HGH available. Partial GHD results in slightly short stature. Children who have severe GHD grow to be about one-half the size of other children (Gotlin et al., 1995). However, their skeletons are normally proportioned (Tanner, 1990). Fortunately, growth hormone replacement therapy can be given to stimulate body growth. Early diagnosis of GHD is important in order to obtain maximum benefit from the treatment. Children who begin HGH replacement therapy at the earliest ages and who have the most severe GHD tend to respond best to the treatment. Gains in height are most pronounced during the first two years of treatment. HGH supplements are not recommended for use with children of short stature who have a normal amount of growth hormone (Vance & Mauras, 1999).

Emotional Disturbances. Disturbances in the parent-child relationship or other causes of continuing severe emotional stress result in growth failure. This condition is sometimes referred to as psychosocial or deprivation dwarfism. Apparently, young children respond to stress by reducing or completely inhibiting the secretion of growth hormone. When the stress is alleviated, the child resumes growth and usually catches up with age mates (Tanner, 1990). Short-term emotional stress connected with normal daily family living has no marked impact on growth patterns.

BODY SIZE AND FEATURES

The major indicators of normal body growth during infancy and childhood are weight, height, body mass index (based on weight and height), and head circumference. Measurements of these body features should be made periodically as a part of a child's routine health care. Standard growth charts developed by the National Center for Health Statistics (2000) are widely used to evaluate and monitor the growth of infants. These are new charts based on information that more accurately represents the cultural and racial diversity in the United States than previous charts published 25 years ago (National Center for Health Statistics, 1976). Examples of the new charts are available in Appendixes 1–4. The complete set of charts is available through the Internet at www.cdc.gov/growthcharts.

Weight. When the birth of a baby is announced, one of the first questions people ask is "how much did the baby weigh?" This is an important question because birth weight is a good indicator of the baby's health and well-being. Body weight is probably the best single indicator of growth in infancy because it represents a summary of all changes in size.

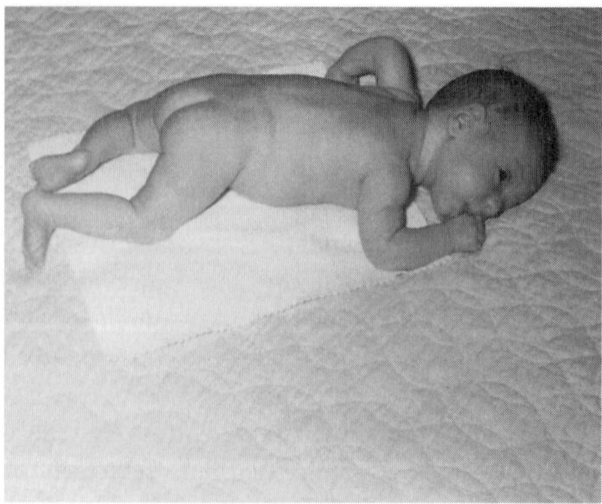

This infant weighed 7 lbs. 7 ozs. and was 19 inches long at birth. At two months of age, when this picture was taken, she weighed 11 lbs. 7 ozs. and was 23 inches long.

The average birth weight (50th percentile) for a newborn infant is approximately 7¾ pounds for males and 7½ pounds for females (National Center for Health Statistics, 2000; see Appendixes 1 & 2). Typically, a newborn baby is expected to gain about 1 ounce each day, averaging about 2.2 pounds each month for the first six months of life (Silver, 1984). During the last half of the first year, the weight gain slows down to about ½ ounce per day. Healthy infants usually double their birth weight by 4 or 5 months. Birth weight is tripled by 1 year, and quadrupled by 2 years of age. Thus the infant who weighs 7 pounds at birth will probably weigh about 14 pounds at 4 months, 21 pounds at 1 year, and 28 pounds at 2 years of age. During the remainder of infancy and early childhood, the average annual weight gain is about 5 pounds. However, individual variation from these weight gain patterns is to be expected.

The growth of the skeleton, muscles, and body organs contribute to weight gains in infancy, but much of the body weight is due to the addition and enlargement of fatty tissue. The layer of fat beneath the skin of the fetus begins to develop during approximately the 30th week of the prenatal period. Body fat continues to increase until reaching a peak in growth rate from six to nine months after birth. The rate of fat cell growth then gradually declines throughout infancy. Although male infants, on average, weigh a little more than female infants at the same ages, females have a little more total body fat than males at birth, and the difference tends to increase throughout infancy (Tanner, 1990). Males tend to be less mature at birth in several aspects of physical growth including skeletal and respiratory development (Pressman et al., 1998).

Height. The average birth length (50th percentile) is approximately 19½ inches for females and 19¾ inches for males (National Center for Health Statistics, 2000; see Appendixes 1 and 2). The first year of postnatal life brings rapid change in height. By the first birthday, an infant has usually increased the birth length by approximately 50 percent. Thus, the infant who measures 20 inches at birth would be about 30 inches tall at the end of the first year. During the second year, the increase is less dramatic, with a gain of about 4.5 to 5 inches, or about 24 percent of the full length. On the average, infants grow about 3 to 4 inches in the third year and measure about 3 feet tall (Silver, 1984). Typically, males remain about ¼ to ½ inch taller than females throughout the infancy period. Growth in height can be restricted by chronic infections, malnutrition, malabsorption of nutrients, severe chronic diseases, cystic fibrosis, and other developmental disorders (Illingworth, 1991). Genetic control over height is considered to be greater than genetic control over body weight (Malina & Bouchard, 1991).

Prediction of Adult Height. Tanner's (1990) **relative maturity percentages** are sometimes used as a rough estimate of adult height. At 2 years of age, a boy growing up in the United States will be 49.2 percent as tall as he will grow to be as an adult. A girl of the same age has reached 52.5 percent of her mature height. An average 3-year-old American female has reached 57.8 percent of her mature height, while the typical male has obtained 53.9 percent of his adult height. In general, taller-than-average 2-year-olds tend to become taller-than-average adults. However, it is not possible to accurately predict the final adult body size of an infant because there are too many unknown variables that can affect growth. Generally, tall parents tend to have tall children, but there are many exceptions to this trend (Malina & Bouchard, 1991).

Body Mass Index. Body Mass Index (BMI) is a new and important guideline that is used after infants reach 2 years of age to determine whether a child is underweight or overweight in relation to the child's height. When height and weight measurements have been obtained, the BMI can be calculated with the following formula: *BMI = pounds ÷ by inches ÷ by inches × 703*. For example, a 3-year-old girl who measures 37.2 inches and weighs 31.0 pounds would have a BMI of 15.7. The BMI value can be plotted on a growth curve percentile (Appendix 4) to determine the child's relative standing in relation to other children of the same age and gender (Centers for Disease Control and Prevention, 2002). Thus, the 3-year-old girl with a BMI of 15.7 would be at the 50th percentile, indicating an average and healthy weight for her height. The BMI will be further discussed later in this chapter in the section on evaluating physical growth.

Head Growth. The circumference of an infant's head is a major index of normal growth during infancy because it is closely related to brain weight. At birth, head circumference normally ranges from approximately 12 to 15 inches, with an average of 13¾ inches for females and 14⅛ inches for males (see Appendix 3). Males usually have a slightly larger head (¼ to ¾ inch) than females during the infancy period. On average, the head circumference increases about 3 inches during the first six months of life. Growth in head circumference continues at a slower pace as infants get older. There is an average gain of about 1 inch from 6 to 12 months of age and an average gain of about another inch during the next year (National Center for Health Statistics, 2000).

The shape of the young infant's head is noticeably different from that of an adult (see Figure 4-1). The cranium, or top of the head, is proportionately larger and more prominent in the infant. The face constitutes a much smaller part of the head. At birth, the head of an infant is approximately one-fourth of the total body length, whereas for an adult the head is only about one-eighth of total height. During infancy, the head grows slower than the rest of the body, so there is a noticeable change in its proportion to body length.

The shape of an individual's skull is influenced by sex, race, and other factors, but the facial size is closely related to the overall growth of the head. If the brain grows as it should, the head circumference will equal the expected measurements. Head growth is considered to be a good index of brain growth. An extremely small or large head may be an indicator of atypical brain growth. However, the total body size should be considered, because a large baby will typically have a large head and a small baby will usually have a small head (Illingworth, 1991).

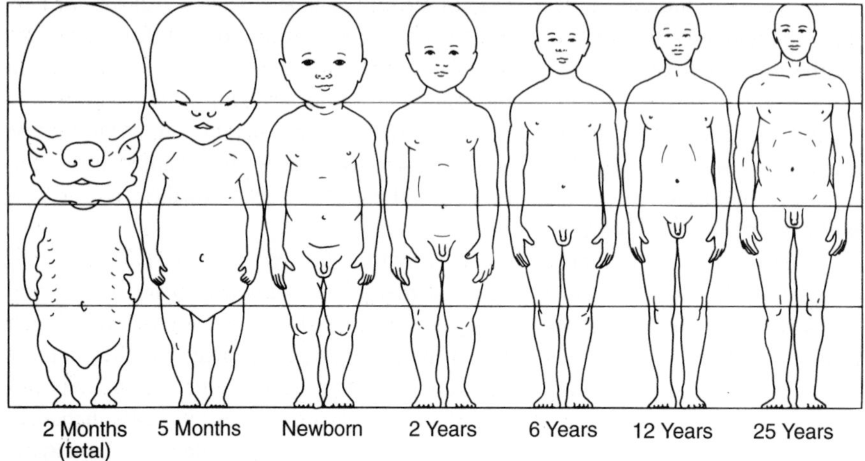

Figure 4-1 Proportionate Changes in Growth of the Head, Trunk, and Limbs.
Source: B. Anson, (Ed.) (1966). *Morris' human anatomy* (12th ed.). New York: McGraw-Hill. Used by permission.

Fontanels. The skull of an infant consists of eight pieces of bone held together by softer cartilage and connecting tissue. At birth the bones are soft and movable and may overlap so the head can more easily move through the birth canal. The narrow seams of cartilage are called sutures, while the wide sections of cartilage are called **fontanels,** or "soft spots." Four sutures and six fontanels are usually present at birth.

The two larger fontanels can easily be felt with the fingertips as soft spots in the skull. The sutures are more difficult to find and typically cannot be felt after the first few weeks. However, the sutures are not completely closed until adolescence. The largest fontanel is located in the front of the cranium. It is usually diamond shaped and measures about 0.4 to 2.5 inches at birth (Nelms & Mullins, 1982). The front fontanel is usually closed by 18 to 20 months of age (Valadian & Porter, 1977). The fontanel on the back of the skull is typically shaped like a triangle and measures about 0.2 inches in diameter at birth. As the skull hardens, this fontanel gradually gets smaller and is completely closed by 3 or 4 months in most infants. In some infants it may already be closed at birth (Behrman & Vaughan, 1983).

The Face. The most noticeable and complex growth of the head can be observed in the facial features. The front view of the newborn infant reveals a broad, flat appearance in comparison to the face of an adult. The flat facial appearance is a result of the baby's small, almost bridgeless nose, and cheekbones that are barely distinguishable. The profile (side view) is dominated by the cranium and forehead since the lower jaw is underdeveloped and receded (Ranly, 1980). Lorenz (1965) has noted that these facial features, in combination with the infant's small size, form the "cuteness" that attracts adults to infants. This infant shape triggers nurturing behaviors, including human affection for the young of other species.

With age, the lower part of the face undergoes "catch-up growth" that changes the infant's overall appearance. The length of the face is about 40 percent complete at birth. Facial growth proceeds very rapidly during the first three years of life, after which growth is slower and steadier until maturity (Ranly, 1980). The middle of the face emerges from beneath the cranium and grows forward and downward. The bony bridge and soft tissue of the nose grow while the front sinus cavities expand so that the flat appearance of the face diminishes. In spite of the rapid growth, however, the face of an infant remains considerably less mature in appearance than an adult face.

The Eyes. One of the most striking features of an infant's face is the eyes. The eyes dominate the face of the infant until the nose becomes large enough to provide a definite separation between them. Apparently, the infant is equipped with a small nose to prevent the mother's breast from pressing against it and cutting off the air supply. In the normal full-term newborn, the eyes are approximately three-fourths of normal adult size. They grow rapidly during the first year and at a rapid but decelerating rate until the third year. Although growth of the eyes continues after infancy, it proceeds at a much slower rate (Nelson, 1996).

Various parts of the eye have different growth rates. The front part of the eye is relatively large at birth and grows less than the structures in the back of the eye. The cornea is large at birth and reaches mature size at about 2 years of age. It tends to flatten with age. The small pit near the center of the retina, known as the fovea, changes rapidly during the first year of life (Banks & Shannon, 1993). The fovea is the area of the eye that provides the sharpest vision. Overall, the shape of the eye becomes more clearly spherical with growth.

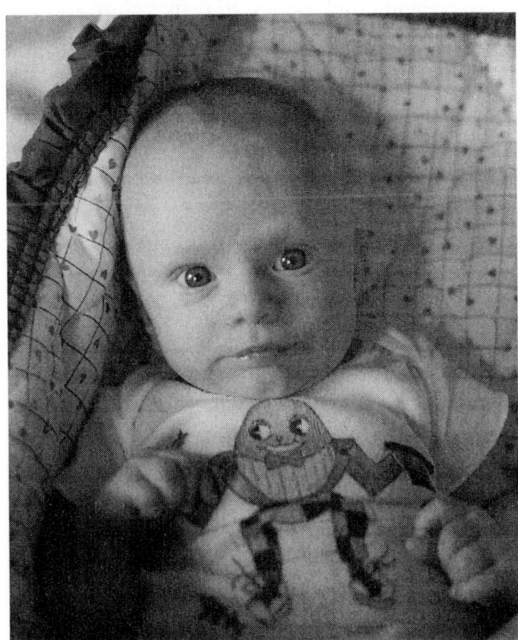

The eyes are the dominant feature of the young infant's face. Notice, also, the relatively large skull and small jaw.

The color of the eyes tends to get darker with age in many children. In Caucasians, the eyes are typically light blue at birth but get darker and may change color as pigment is added. Infants of color typically have dark eyes at birth, so the addition of pigment is not as noticeable. Tears are often not produced when the baby cries until approximately 1 to 3 months. Periodic eye examinations are recommended beginning at birth and throughout infancy and childhood to detect and treat such problems as strabismus (cross-eyes), amblyopia ("lazy eye"), refractive disorders, or other problems. Visual acuity is usually measured at 2½ to 3 years of age (Nelson, 1996).

The Ears. The external, middle, and internal parts of the human ear form the auditory system. The development of the ear begins with the inner ear during the fourth prenatal week (Moore & Persaud, 1998). Most of the components of the auditory system are functionally complete at birth. However, the ear canal of the newborn is shallow and straight. The supporting structure is mostly cartilage. The tympanic membrane (eardrum) is not completely closed and lies at a horizontal angle. During the first three years of life, the tympanic membrane closes and assumes a more mature verticle position. The ear canal gradually changes to the adult S-shape. The bends in the canal protect the eardrum from foreign bodies and sounds that are too loud. Bony formation takes the place of the cartilaginous tissue. The structure of the outer ear (pinna) has typically reached its adult form by the time of birth. Both the pinna and the ear canal continue to grow until age 7 to 9 when adult size is attained (Ballachanda, 1995).

Throughout the infancy period, routine physical exams of the ear should be conducted, along with hearing screening tests, to detect any structural defects, infections, or problems that might lead to hearing loss. There are two main types of hearing loss. **Conductive hearing loss** results from abnormalities in the ear structure, or fluid in the middle ear. **Sensorial hearing loss** results from abnormality of the inner ear, or failure of the nerves to carry sound signals from the inner ear to the brain (Shelov, 1998).

Catch-up Growth. An individual's potential body size is controlled by several genes, each of which has a small effect. Some genes do not begin to function until after birth. During the prenatal period the baby's growth is affected by the size of the mother's uterus. The uterus of a small mother thus may have a restraining effect on a baby who has the genetic potential to grow larger than average. On the other hand, an infant born to a larger mother may be larger than average even though genetically programmed to reach a relatively small adult height.

After birth, small infants who have a genetic heritage to be tall adults will usually grow faster than average for the first few months of life. Such rapid growth after the period of intrauterine growth restriction is called **catch-up growth** (Tanner, 1990). By the same genetic principle, larger-than-average infants who are destined to be small adults will grow slower than average. Thus, the baby's length at birth is not a good indicator of height at maturity. Generally, an infant will reach the genetically determined growth channel by 12 to 14 months of age. The smaller infants "catch up" earlier than larger infants who "lag down" a little later in infancy (Bax, Hart, & Jenkins, 1990). Consequently, an individual infant's height and weight percentile rankings often change considerably on a growth chart during the first two or three years of life (Malina & Bouchard, 1991).

SKELETAL GROWTH

Ossification. At birth an infant's skeleton is made up mostly of semihard, gristlelike tissue called cartilage. The skeleton is softer and more flexible in the joints. This makes it possible for babies to suck on their toes as well as their fingers! As the baby grows, the skeleton becomes harder and less flexible. The process by which minerals and other substances are added to the cartilage so that it hardens into bones is called **ossification.** Bone growth and ossification are largely dependent upon an adequate supply of nutritional and hormonal substances. Different parts of the skeleton grow and ossify at different rates. On average, girls are more typically advanced in skeletal ossification than boys at birth. The sex difference tends to increase with age because female infants mature at a faster rate during infancy. In addition, the rate of ossification is less variable for girls than for boys (Sinclair, 1978). In general, the growth curves for skeletal weight tend to be similar to the curves for overall body weight and height (Malina & Bouchard, 1991).

Limbs. The bone-hardening process begins in an ossification center in each piece of cartilage. At birth, primary ossification centers have begun in all of the long limb bones. Shortly before and immediately after birth, secondary ossification centers, or epiphyses, form near each end of each separate piece of cartilage. Ossification then proceeds from the end of each bone to the middle.

New ossification centers appear continuously throughout the skeleton until maturity is reached. At the same time ossification is proceeding, new layers of bony tissue are deposited on the outside of the basic structure so that the bones grow in width. The bones also grow in length and change in shape as cells are added to the epiphyses. At birth, the bones of the lower limbs and pelvic area are proportionately shorter and less advanced than the upper limbs and shoulders. However, the lower limbs grow at a faster rate and catch up with the upper part of the skeleton (Sinclair, 1978). The genetic contribution to the length and thickness of the long bones in the body has been estimated to be approximately 60 percent (Malina & Bouchard, 1991).

Feet. The feet of the normal newborn infant are proportionately longer and thinner than those of older children. The toddler's feet are somewhat chubbier and wider than the feet of older children. The bottom typically appears flat because of external fullness of the foot pad. Since the ankle joints are very flexible, the toes may appear to be turned too far in or out. Intoeing, a condition in which the front part of the entire foot turns in, is a common problem in young infants. This condition can result from confinement in the uterus, sleeping on the stomach, or genetic predisposition. When the baby begins to stand and walk, the problem tends to correct itself. In some cases, however, an orthopedic exam and corrective treatment may be necessary (Behrman & Vaughan, 1983).

Muscles. The muscle tissue makes up about 20 to 25 percent of an infant's weight at birth. The newborn's muscle fibers are small, watery, and underdeveloped. As the baby grows, the proportion of water in the muscles decreases as protein and other substances are added. These changes result in an increase in strength and stamina. Growth of the muscle fibers is influenced by nutrition, hormones, metabolism, exercise, and health (Valadian & Porter, 1977).

Scientists generally believe that the total number of muscle fibers the human body needs are present at birth or develop shortly afterward (Tanner, 1990). Muscle fibers become longer and thicker throughout infancy and childhood. Muscles grow at about twice the rate of bones. Following the cephalocaudal principle, the muscles in the top part of the body develop a little faster than those in the lower part of the body.

Skin. A newborn infant usually comes equipped with five complete layers of skin. However, the outer layers are thinner and more delicate. The baby's outer layers of skin are also more loosely connected to the inner layers than are those of an adult. Although all of the sweat glands are present at birth, they function poorly. The glands that produce the oily secretions that form the vernix caseosa covering the baby at birth decrease production and remain relatively inactive until puberty (Lowrey, 1978). The infant's skin is thus normally dry and may flake or peel easily. Diaper rash, heat rash, allergic reactions, and skin infections are common in infants because of their delicate skin (Valadian & Porter, 1977).

In comparison to older children and adults, infants' skin contains less pigment (color). Infants of dark-skinned parents thus tend to have lighter skin coloring than they will have at maturity. Pigment in the skin of infants of all races increases throughout the infancy period, but the process proceeds more slowly in children with light skin (Nelms & Mullins, 1982).

Infants have a larger skin surface in proportion to their body weight than adults. Thus, an infant loses more water through the skin and has more potential for heat loss and dehydration than an adult. In proportion to adults, a baby needs more calories for maintaining basal metabolism (Eichorn, 1979).

Teeth. Ordinarily humans grow two sets of teeth in the course of a lifetime. The first set includes 20 teeth that are referred to as the primary or **deciduous teeth.** The word *deciduous* literally means to "fall off." Primary teeth are also called milk teeth, baby teeth, or temporary teeth. Unfortunately such names may lead parents to mistakenly think that these teeth are not important (Woelfel, 1984). The primary teeth begin to develop beneath the gums as early as the sixth week of prenatal life. The process of calcification begins in the second trimester (W. Mueller, 2001). The buds of some of the permanent teeth also begin to form during the fourth or fifth month of the prenatal period (Beedle, 1984).

The timing of tooth formation and eruption is largely controlled by genetic programming, but the environment can accelerate or delay the rate of development to some extent. Severe nutritional deficits, hormonal imbalances, various genetic disorders (e.g., Down syndrome, sickle cell anemia), and prolonged or serious illnesses may disturb the formation or hardening of the teeth. Ethnic differences have been observed in dental maturation. Caucasian Europeans are typically behind Caucasian Americans in dental development, while Africans in some nations as well as African Americans display earlier dental development

(E. Harris, 1998). Sex differences have also been found in dental development, with females usually slightly ahead of males in tooth formation and eruption (Goldman, 1998).

The development of a tooth begins with a bud that forms the crown and grows downward to form the root. The enamel (outer portion) is formed slightly ahead of the dentin (inner portion). The enamel develops in microscopic layers, comparable to the rings of a tree. Usually none of the infant's teeth are visible at birth. The first tooth normally begins to appear around 8 months (Harris, 1998). The central incisors (front and center teeth) are typically the first teeth to cut through the gums, followed by the lateral incisors. The sequence and approximate ages at which the primary teeth erupt are presented in Figure 4-2. The lower front teeth and second molars tend to cut through the lower jaw before their counterparts are visible in the upper jaw. The lateral incisors, canines, and first molars tend to emerge in the upper jaw earlier than in the lower jaw (Lunt & Law, 1974).

Infants vary considerably in the order, as well as the timetable, of tooth development. Variations of as much as six months from the average dates, either earlier or later, are not unusual (McDonald & Avery, 1983). The 12-month-old typically has

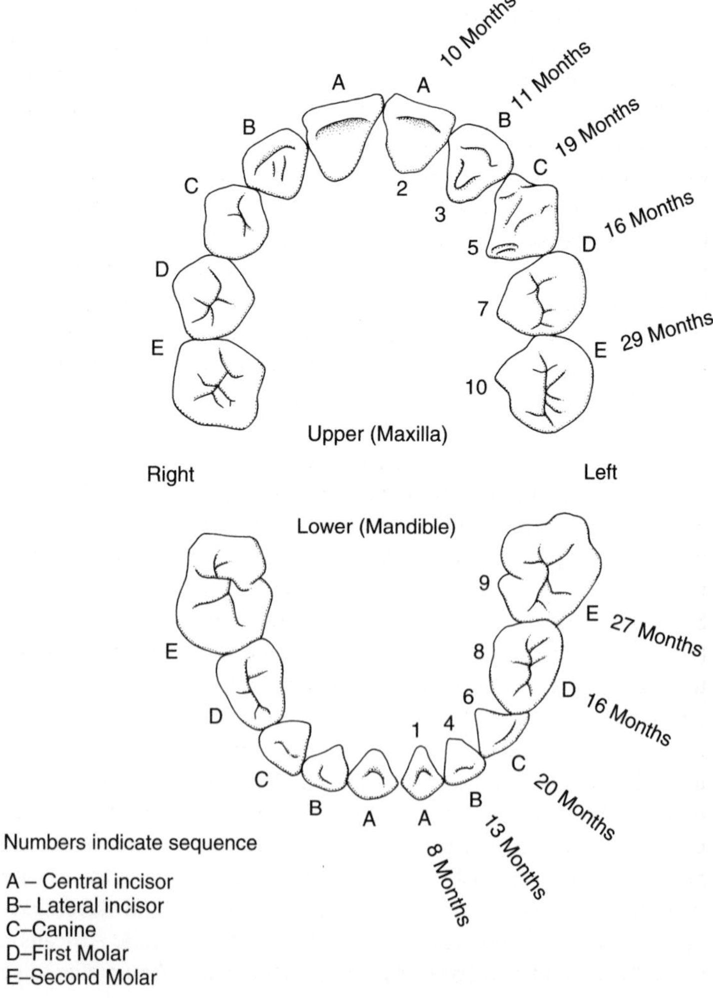

Figure 5-2 Eruption of the Primary Teeth—Age and Sequence.
Data from R. Lunt and D. Law, (1974). A review of the chronology of eruption of deciduous teeth. *Journal of the American Dental Association, 89,* 872–879. Used by permission.

six to eight teeth. The 18-month-old has from 12 to 14 teeth, and the 2-year-old usually has approximately 14 to 16 teeth. The complete set of 20 deciduous teeth is present by 30 to 36 months in most infants.

Infants also vary in their responses to teething. Some babies are very cranky and fussy when they are cutting a tooth, whereas other babies appear to be affected very little by the process. Teething usually causes the gums to be sore, but contrary to popular opinion, teething does not cause fever or diarrhea (Beedle, 1984). Babies try to bite on objects placed in their mouths during this stage. When teeth begin to erupt, the biting behavior may present problems for the nursing mother, who may decide to wean the baby at that point.

Good dental care is important even for the temporary teeth. These are the only teeth a child will have until around the sixth birthday. Young children need primary teeth for chewing of food, normal appearance, and clear speech. They may reject food needed for a proper diet, such as raw fruits and vegetables, because of missing or decayed teeth. Also, decay and abscess in a primary tooth may cause the permanent tooth developing beneath it to have a dark spot (Woelfel, 1984). More important, premature loss of primary teeth may result in problems with the timing of the eruption, spacing, and occlusion (bite) of the permanent teeth.

An infant should begin regular visits to the dentist by the time all of the primary incisors have erupted, or at least by the age of 2, to check for cavities (caries or decay) or other problems. Although the rate of dental caries in the United States has decreased considerably in recent years (Brunelle & Carlos, 1990), dental health continues to be a major concern during the infancy period. Nutrition plays a critical role in the development of healthy teeth from the sixth week of the prenatal period through the adolescent period. The state of dental health is, to a large extent, a reflection of dietary adequacy. The major nutrients required for normal tooth development are protein, calcium, phosphorus, vitamin A, vitamin D, and ascorbic acid. The value of fluoride, in combination with an adequate diet, in the prevention of dental caries has been well documented (Committee on Nutrition, 1979; Trahams & Pipes, 1997).

A characteristic pattern of dental decay that is frequently observed in infants and young children is **bottle-mouth syndrome** (also called nursing-bottle syndrome, and baby-bottle tooth decay). The problem is characterized by extreme damage to the upper and sometimes the lower front teeth. The teeth decay and may break off at the gum line. The pattern of decay results from the pooling of milk or sugary substances around the teeth. Children who are habitually given a bottle while going to sleep are particularly susceptible to bottle-mouth syndrome.

BRAIN GROWTH

During the past 20 years, our knowledge of how the brain grows and functions has increased by leaps and bounds with the development of increasingly sophisticated procedures for assessing brain activity, such as positron emission tomography (PET) and functional magnetic resonance imaging (fMRI) technology (see Chapter 1). Although we have only begun to understand the complexity of brain development, we now know that important and dramatic changes in the structure and function of the brain occur during the infancy period. Researchers have verified the importance of early experiences in shaping brain development.

The brain of a newborn infant is relatively large and well developed. All major lobes (sections of the brain) are clearly distinguishable. At birth, the brain typically weighs about 1 pound (DeKaban, 1970), which is roughly 15 percent of the newborn's total body weight. The brain is nearer to its adult weight than any other organ of the infant's body, except the eye. At birth, the brain has grown to approximately 25 percent of its mature weight, and by 6 months of age, nearly one-half of its adult weight has been obtained. Growth of the brain is slower during the second year, during which it reaches about three-fourths of its mature size (Tanner, 1990).

The tissue of the human brain is made up of basic nerve cells, called **neurons,** supporting cells called **neuroglia, myelin,** and various chemical substances. Neurons store information and carry impulses from one part of the body to another. They are the "hardwiring" of the nervous system (Kolb, 1999). The cell body of each neuron grows treelike branches called **dendrites,** and a longer extension called an **axon.** Dendrites are receptors of nerve impulses, and axons are the transmitters (Figure 4–3). Dendrites and axons of separate neurons lie close together but do not touch. These connecting gaps, called synapses, are where nerve impulses are passed from one neuron to another by releasing small amounts of chemicals. Several brain chemicals, called **neurotransmitters,** which mediate transmission of impulses between neurons and synapses have been identified (Spreen et al., 1995). Three of the more familiar ones are dopamine, epinephrine, and catecholamines. Concentrations of these chemicals rise and fall with brain growth activity and environmental experiences. The brain also uses glucose to perform its functions.

The human brain has approximately 80 billion neurons (Kolb, 1999). Recall that around the 20th week of the prenatal period the total number of neurons the infant will ever have is practically complete. At this time, unlike other body cells, they can no longer divide and multiply, or repair themselves if damaged (Dobbing, 1993). Fortunately, the human body produces an excess number of neurons. Neuroglia (glial) cells begin forming about the 15th prenatal week. Unlike the neurons, glial cells continue to increase in number until maturity of the central nervous system (Spreen et al., 1995). The glial cells, named after the Greek word for glue, make up about one-half of the brain's size and serve as support structures for the neurons. They are smaller and more numerous than neurons and do not carry messages. Approximately 100 billion glial cells are eventually formed (Kolb, 1999). Once they are formed, nerve cells grow to about 200,000 times their original size. Thus, most postnatal brain growth occurs because of an increase in the size of the neurons, the addition of glial cells, and the proliferation of synaptic connections.

The brain follows an **asynchronous growth** pattern, which means that different parts of the brain develop at different rates. The lower part of the brain develops and becomes functional before the higher structures. The brain stem and spinal cord that control the basic body functions and early reflexive activities are most fully developed at birth. The upper, or cortical, parts of the brain that control voluntary movements, speech, and other cognitive processes, are comparatively undeveloped at birth but grow at a rapid pace throughout infancy.

Myelination. The process of **myelination** is another very important part of brain development. Myelin, a fatty substance produced by the glial cells, forms a sheath around the nerve fibers (see Figure 4–3). The myelin sheath functions like the insulation on an electric wire to prevent short circuits. Myelination affects the rate at which impulses travel through the nervous system. Consequently, the infant's brain performs less efficiently than an adult's. From infancy through adolescence the formation of myelin makes the neurons more functionally capable and efficient (Spreen et al., 1995). The increase in the myelin content of the brain cells is also accompanied by the addition of connections between neurons.

Apparently, myelin begins to form on the nerve cells in the spinal cord and some areas of the brain before birth. The process continues rapidly during infancy, slowing down after the fourth or fifth year of life. Myelination is not complete in some parts of the nervous system until adulthood. Some scientists believe that myelination is related to the development of specific abilities of an infant. The appearance of specific motor abilities and muscle control thus corresponds with the formation of the myelin sheath in the area of the brain that controls those functions. However, motor abilities and sensory functions may occur without myelination, although they function less efficiently (Spreen et al., 1995).

Lateralization. The brain is divided into various parts, including the hindbrain, midbrain, and

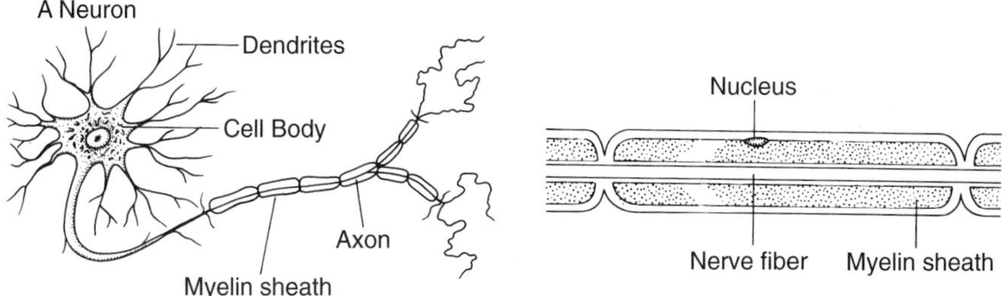

Figure 4–3 Myelination of a Neuron.
Source: I. Valadian and D. Porter, (1977). *Physical growth and development.* Boston: Little, Brown & Co. p. 134. Copyright by Little, Brown, & Co. 1977. Adapted by permission.

forebrain. Each area of the brain is capable of performing specialized functions in controlling body functions and mental processes. The largest part of the brain is the cerebral cortex. It surrounds the inner parts of the brain like a cap or helmet. The cortex controls thinking, memory, and language. Since the cortical areas of the brain are the most undeveloped parts of the brain at birth and the last to stop growing, they are most susceptible to postnatal environmental influences (Suomi, 1982).

The cortex is divided into two hemispheres—left and right—that basically match each other in size and appearance. The cerebral hemispheres are physically connected and interact with each other, but perform different functions. For example, scientists believe the left half of the brain controls such functions as speech and language, verbal memory, mathematical reasoning, and positive emotions. The right hemisphere controls visual memory, musical functions, sense of direction, and negative emotions (Kolb & Whishaw, 1990). The process by which the different hemispheres of the brain take on special functions is called **lateralization.** Even though certain areas of the brain appear to be highly specialized in their functions, the brain is remarkably adaptable and capable of recovery from injury. For example, very young children who suffer strokes or other brain injuries can still develop into fully functioning adults (Nash, 1997).

Synaptogenesis. Synaptogenesis, the formation of synapses or connections between the neurons (via their dendrites and axons), is a critical feature of brain growth and functioning. Synaptic development is often referred to as "brain wiring." The formation of synapses depends on complex interactions between genetics, experience, and biochemistry (Kolb, 1999). Once a neuron has migrated to its relatively permanent location during the prenatal period, its axon develops an enlarged tip equipped with tentacles that branch out in all directions. The axons, guided by chemical cues and tiny electrical signals, form a synaptic connection with the dendrites of compatible neurons. In early brain development, neurons rapidly expand their dendritic surfaces to make places for the formation of new synapses. As a result of rapid dendritic growth, the cerebral cortex (large outer layer of the brain) triples in thickness during the first year of life (Eliot, 1999).

PET scans show patterns of brain glucose utilization that are consistent with dramatic expansion of synaptic activity during the early months of life (Chugani, 1993). The timing and sequence of synaptic development coincides with the appearance of various skills. During the first six months or so after birth, there is a 10-fold increase in the number of synapses formed in the visual control center of the brain, and the connections needed for sight are essentially complete (Huttenlocher, 1994). Beginning around 2 months of age, synaptogenesis progresses rapidly in the motor cortex areas. Synaptic formation is also rapid during the first 24 months in areas of the brain that control memory functions and emotional development.

From birth to age 3, brain circuits that are critical for language development are established. Infancy is also an important period for the generation of synaptic connections that establish the foundations for the development of math and logic functions during the childhood years (Begley, 1996, 1997).

Synaptic Pruning. The development of neuronal connections in the brain involves both additive and subtractive processes. During the early stages of brain development, an excess number of neurons is produced and eventually eliminated. Similarly, there is evidence of overproduction of synaptic connections among the neurons. By 2 years of age, the infant's brain contains twice as many synapses as the brain of a typical adult (Nash, 1997). After maximum synaptic density is reached in an area of the brain, fine-tuning of the brain occurs through the process of synaptic elimination. This "pruning" process begins to take place as early as 6 to 12 months of age (Huttenlocher, 1994). Some scientists estimate that at the peak of synaptic loss as many as 100,000 unnecessary or unused connections may be lost per second. Yet even at that rate, we only lose about one 10-millionth of our total final synapses (Kolb,1999).

Scientists are not exactly sure why or how neuronal death and synaptic loss occur. Neurons may die because they do not succeed in forming connections with other neurons (Spreen et al., 1995). Synapse elimination appears to be related to experience. To some extent, the specific experiences of the infant may determine which of the connections survive and which are "pruned." Because humans share a common genetic history of predictable experiences, the newborn's brain apparently sets up special synaptic connections that are "**experience-expectant**" (Greenough, Black, & Wallace, 1987). That is, the human species has come to anticipate and expect certain experiences in the process of development, such as the sound of the human voice. Therefore, the brain pathways are ready and waiting for something to happen (e.g., visual or motor activity) within a given time period.

Neurons that are stimulated by sensory and perceptual activities continue to thrive and expand, while those that are not activated do not survive. The "use it or lose it" principle is at work here. For example, at birth infants have a large pool of synapses that make it possible to discriminate between sounds common to all human speech (see Chapter 7). However, this ability declines during the first year of life. A possible explanation is that necessary neuronal connections are lost over time because the infant's exposure to sounds is usually limited to those of a specific language (Kolb, 1989).

Other types of experiences are needed for the brain to establish new synaptic connections and expand the wiring of the brain. This process by which the brain is wired through experiences when a child is exposed to unique stimulation has been referred to as **experience-dependent** programming (Greenough et al., 1987). In this case the brain is not prewired to expect certain experiences in order to maintain connections already established. However, the formation and maintenance of new brain connections needed for the brain to function at its maximum capacity is dependent upon the stimulation to which an individual is exposed throughout the formative years.

Critical Periods. Scientists who study the brain (neuroscientists) have tried to identify critical periods of very rapid brain growth, sometimes referred to as brain growth spurts during which the brain is highly susceptible to environmental influences. Recall from Chapter 2 that the 3rd through the 16th prenatal weeks are considered to be a critical period for brain development. During this period the brain is particularly vulnerable to teratogenic influences because the brain cells, particularly the neurons, are in a delicate stage of formation. Some neuroscientists have identified a second critical period beginning during late fetal life and continuing through early infancy, when the brain cells increase in size and complexity (Dobbing, 1976). However, not all scientists agree about the peak or critical periods, especially for postnatal brain growth. Epstein (1978) has proposed that postnatal brain growth occurs mainly during two periods—3 to 10 months of age and 2 to 4 years of age.

Scientists generally agree that there are periods of time when the brain is most susceptible to the effects of toxins, viruses, or other adverse conditions that may cause significant damage, even though they sometimes disagree on the exact beginning and end points of such time periods. There is much less agreement about the existence of critical periods during which the brain is particularly efficient at specific types of learning and needs to be exposed to appropriate amounts and types of stimulation in order to achieve optimum development.

It is likely that each area of the brain has its own critical period when stimulation is needed. Researchers have recently identified critical periods of growth when the brain is especially devoted to the development of control of a particular sense or ability (Ramey & Ramey, 1999). For example, animal studies are often cited as evidence for a critical period in brain centers that control vision. A frequently cited study found that kittens deprived of light during the period of brain development beginning around one month after birth experience permanent damage to the visual system of the brain if they are kept in the dark for two months (Hubel & Wiesel, 1970). Although similar experiments cannot be performed with human infants, scientists believe that the development of the human visual system would be seriously damaged if deprived of appropriate experience during the first two years of life (Spreen et al., 1995).

Importance of Early Experience. Each individual's brain is wired through a complex interplay between hereditary foundations and environmental experiences. The genetic code mainly directs the growth of neurons and their migration to proper locations within the brain where they begin linking together. After genetic programming sets the process of brain development in motion, environmental experiences begin to play a major role in the final outcomes in determining how the brain is "wired."

The importance of environmental stimulation is seen in a series of studies of rats exposed to different levels of stimulation (Rosenzweig, Bennett, & Diamond, 1972). In one group, rats were reared in a complex environment with various play objects, while another group of rats were reared in cages with nothing but food and water. The rats exposed to the enriched environment were superior to the other rats on problem-solving tasks. The environmentally enriched rats also had several regions of the cerebral cortex that were heavier and thicker, with larger neurons and more neuroglial cells. Subsequent research has also found that rats raised in an enriched environment develop a greater number of synaptic connections (Greenough et al., 1987). However, it is important to note that the enriched laboratory environment was actually more like the normal environment of a rat living in the wild. The survival of wild rats is dependent upon eluding their enemies, fighting and mating with other rats, and finding the best places for food. Thus, it is probably more accurate to conclude from these studies that a more normal environment leads to a better brain than a deprived environment (Gopnik, Meltzoff, & Kuhl, 1999).

Evidence is thus rapidly accumulating to show that appropriate environmental stimulation is essential for the growth and maintenance of synapses that affect the complexity of the nervous system. However, the amount, type, and quality of the stimulation are important factors. "If the normal pattern of experience occurs, a normal pattern of neural organization results. If an abnormal pattern of experience occurs, an abnormal neural organization pattern results" (Greenough et al., 1987, p. 544). Consistent and repetitive activities rather than infrequent experiences build the brain's circuitry. Certain types of experiences are more beneficial than others. For example, the stimulation infants receive from listening to TV is apparently less effective in producing language development than parent talk (Begley, 1997). Too much sensory stimulation may be just as detrimental to brain development as too little stimulation. Typically developing infants receive adequate experience for normal brain development through "average" experience and do not need "super" enrichment. However, infants with sensory impairments and environmental deficits need special compensatory stimulation activities.

CARDIOVASCULAR SYSTEM

Heart. Growth of the heart during the first four to six weeks after birth is very slow. Following this period, the heart grows steadily and rapidly throughout infancy. At the end of the first year, the weight of the heart has doubled; by the second year it has tripled (M. Moore, 1978). The shape of the heart also matures rapidly. At birth, both sides of the heart are about the same size. After birth, the left side of the heart typically grows more rapidly than the right side (Malina & Bouchard, 1991). By the second or third year of life, the outline of the infant's heart is very similar to that of an adult (Lowrey, 1978).

The heart rate of the newborn infant is rapid and subject to wide fluctuations. The 120 to 140 beats per minute is about twice the normal rate of an adult. The heart rate decreases to about 110 beats per minute between 1 and 2 years, and to 105 beats per minute between 2 years and 4 years of age (Stangler, Huber, & Routh, 1980). Heart rates are more variable in infants than in adults, and heart murmurs are common. In most cases, such murmurs do not indicate a serious problem and usually disappear by age 1 (Lowrey, 1978). There are no sex differences in heart rate averages during infancy, although slight differences appear at around 10 years of age (Malina & Bouchard, 1991).

Blood Pressure. Normally blood pressure increases throughout infancy. The blood pressure of the full-term newborn is 75/50 as compared with the typical 100/60 of an infant 2 to 4 years of age (Stangler et al., 1980). Premature infants typically have lower blood pressure readings than full-term infants. Blood pressure is more variable in infants than in adults. However, some of the variability reported in blood pressure is probably a result of the difficulty of obtaining accurate and consistent measurements. Some of the fluctuations may be attributed to rapid shifts in infant states, such as sleeping or crying, which tend to cause the blood pressure to change.

EVALUATING PHYSICAL GROWTH

Records of an infant's height, weight, and head circumference should be maintained and compared periodically with normative growth standards. Various tables and growth charts are available for this purpose, but the National Center for Health Statistics (2000) charts are the best ones currently available. There are separate charts for boys and girls. The growth status of any infant can be compared with that of other children of the same sex and age. There are other specialized charts available for assessing the growth status of infants and children affected by Down, Turner, and Klinefelter syndromes and achondroplasia, a form of short-limbed dwarfism (Needham, 1996).

The child's status is interpreted according to percentile rankings. Various measurements can be plotted on a growth-curve chart (see Appendixes 1–4), which gives a graphic illustration of the child's relative standing in comparison to that of other infants of the same age. To use one of the charts, find and point with one index finger to the child's measurement in the vertical column. With the other index finger, point to the child's age in the horizontal row. Move the two fingers along the two lines until they meet. The intersection represents the child's percentile ranking. Measurements should be plotted at three- to six-month intervals throughout infancy to obtain the growth curve.

The middle line, or 50th percentile, in each chart represents the median or standard value and is a commonly used point of reference. Infants with measurements between the 25th and 75th percentiles are considered to be growing normally. Rankings between the 10th and 25th percentiles or between the 75th and 90th percentiles may or may not represent typical growth. Infants who fall above the 95th percentile or below the 5th percentile, or whose growth drops down more than 2 percentiles, should be evaluated for nutritional, health, or other problems that might be affecting their growth trajectory (Needham, 1996; Stangler et al., 1980). If head circumference measures below the 3rd percentile or above the 97th percentile, the infant should be carefully evaluated for such problems as **microcephaly** (underdeveloped brain) or **hydrocephaly** (excess fluid on the brain) (Valadian & Porter, 1977).

The new body mass index (BMI) (see Appendix 4), based on both height and weight, provides a more accurate method of tracking weight gain than

APPLICATIONS: FACILITATING PHYSICAL GROWTH

The infant's basic physical needs include food, elimination, warmth, sleep, rest, exercise, cleanliness, health, and safety. As long as caregivers consistently meet these basic needs, infants usually grow to fulfill their full genetic body-size potential. Facilitating physical development thus means routinely providing adequate nutrition, bathing, diapering, dressing, as well as sleep and rest periods for an infant (Gonzalez-Mena & Eyer, 1980). In addition, regular health-maintenance checkups (including appropriate dental care) and prompt medical treatment for illnesses are extremely important. The infant's social, emotional, and other psychological needs are closely linked to the physical needs. Therefore, the manner and attitude with which caregivers meet the infant's physical needs are important. Caregivers should not be aloof or indifferent as they provide routine physical care. Rather, parents and other caregivers should touch, cuddle, and talk to the infant in tender, loving ways as they meet basic physical needs.

weight charts used alone. This information can identify children early who have a high ratio of body fat. Combined with a family history of obesity, these children have the potential to become overweight later in life. If the BMI-for-age is below the 5th percentile, the child is considered underweight. The child is considered to be at risk for becoming overweight if BMI index is above the 80th percentile. BMI-for-age rankings above the 95th percentile indicate that a child is overweight. An early warning gives parents and other caregivers an opportunity to shape eating habits before a problem develops (Center for Disease Control and Prevention, n.d.).

SUMMARY

Factors Influencing Physical Growth

- Physical growth is influenced by a variety of environmental factors. The factors discussed in this chapter are socioeconomic status, illness, culture, race, hormonal influences, and emotional disturbances.

Body Size and Features

- The major indicators of body growth are height, weight, body mass, and head circumference as assessed by standardized growth charts. Male infants usually weigh a little more and are slightly taller than female infants at birth and throughout the infancy period. Infants normally double their birth weight during the first four or five months, triple it by the end of the first year, and quadruple it during the second year of life. They usually increase their birth length by 50 percent during the first year and an additional 24 percent during the second year of life.
- Two soft spots, called fontanels, may be felt on the newborn infant's head. The fontanel on the back of the head is usually closed by 3 or 4 months of age. The larger fontanel in front is closed by approximately 20 months of age.
- The infant's facial features are broader and flatter in appearance than an adult's. The lower jaw is underdeveloped and receded.
- The ear canal of the newborn is shallow and straight. The tympanic membrane (eardrum) is not completely closed and lies at a horizontal angle. During the first three years of life, the tympanic membrane closes and assumes a more mature S-shaped position.

Skeletal Growth

- As the baby grows, the bones that make up the skeletal system become harder and less flexible through a process called ossification.
- An infant's feet are proportionately thinner and longer than those of older children, but the feet of toddlers are somewhat chubbier and wider.
- Muscle tissue makes up about one-fourth of the newborn baby's weight. As the baby grows, the muscle fibers become longer and thicker.

- A newborn infant comes equipped with five complete layers of skin, but the outer layers are thin and delicate. The infant's skin is dry and may flake or peel easily. In comparison to older children and adults, the skin of an infant contains less pigment (color).
- The infant's deciduous teeth begin to develop as early as the 12th prenatal week. The first tooth, however, is not visible until approximately eight months after birth. The complete set of 20 temporary teeth is usually present by 30 to 36 months.

Brain Growth

- The brain of the newborn infant is relatively large and well developed, but continues to grow rapidly during infancy, reaching 75 percent of its mature size by the end of two years. The infant brain may be especially vulnerable to environmental disturbances. Brain growth after birth consists primarily of increases in the size of the neurons, the growth and formation of neuroglial cells, the formation of synaptic connections, and the myelination of the nerve cells.
- The formation of synapses, or connections, between the neurons is critical to brain functioning. Infancy is an important period for the establishment of synaptic connections. The development of the neuronal connections in the brain involves both additive and subtractive processes. As the baby grows, the different parts of the brain become more specialized through the process of lateralization.
- Scientists generally agree that environmental conditions, including sensorimotor experiences, play a major role in the formation of synaptic connections in the brain.

Cardiovascular System

- The heart of the infant grows rapidly during infancy and triples in size by the second year. The heart rate gradually decreases, while the blood pressure increases during infancy.

Evaluating Physical Growth

- New standardized growth charts for height, weight, and head circumference should be used to monitor the infant's growth status. After age 2, a body mass index-for-age can be plotted on a chart to assess weight gain problems.

KEY TERMS

thyroxine
human growth hormone (HGH)
relative maturity percentages
Body Mass Index (BMI)
fontanels
conductive hearing loss
sensorial hearing loss
catch-up growth
ossification
deciduous teeth
bottle-mouth syndrome
neurons
neuroglia
myelin
dendrites
axon
neurotransmitters
asynchronous growth
myelination
lateralization
synaptogenesis
experience-expectant
experience-dependent
microcephaly
hydrocephaly

INFORMATION ON THE WEB*

www.cdc.gov/growthcharts. The complete set of growth charts in a variety of forms can be viewed and downloaded. This site also contains news releases and updates on the development and use of the charts. Links to the National Center for Health Statistics home page.

www.zerotothree.org/brainwonders. This site provides information about how the brain develops within the context of relationships from conception through 3 years of age. Contains sections for parents, child-care providers, and health care professionals.

*Web sites are subject to change.

FIVE

Health, Safety, and Nutrition

Eat no green apples or you'll droop
Be careful not to get the croup
Avoid the chickenpox and such
And don't fall out the window much.
—Edward Anthony

A baby is fed with milk and praise.
—Mary Lamb

From the beginning of life, infants are confronted with countless hazards that threaten their health and well being. Numerous viruses, bacteria, and other microorganisms can invade an infant's body, resulting in reactions ranging from the common cold to life-threatening infections such as acquired immune deficiency syndrome. Infants are also confronted with a plethora of safety hazards, such as poisons and unsafe toys, as they explore their world. Unfortunately, we have to add abusive treatment and neglect to the list of obstacles that potentially threaten the survival of many infants. Nutritional problems represent another set of obstacles to infants' healthy growth and development.

In the first part of this chapter we consider the immunizations and other precautionary measures that can be taken to protect infants and prevent the spread of deadly communicable diseases. We will look at the major symptoms of illness in infants along with some of the garden-variety and the life-threatening illnesses for which no permanent immunizations are available. We also consider the horrors of child abuse and neglect, including treatment and preventive measures. The second part of this chapter is devoted to a discussion of the leading causes of death due to unintentional injuries among infants and how such injuries can be controlled. In the third part of this chapter we consider the nutritional needs of infants and how these needs can best be met.

IMMUNITY DURING INFANCY

Newborn infants have some resistance to a number of infectious diseases because of the antibodies they receive from the mother during the prenatal period. The mother may be immune to communicable diseases such as diphtheria, German measles, mumps, and polio because she has had either the disease or a vaccine (Reinisch & Minear, 1978). Even so, newborns are especially vulnerable to infection. If the mother does not have immunity against the disease, no protection can be passed on to the baby. In addition, the newborn's immune system is relatively immature and does not provide the same level of protection against most diseases as adults.

Infants are especially vulnerable to infections between 6 months and 2 years of age. Most immunities received from the mother are gone by 6 to 12 months of age. Infants may then become more vulnerable because their immune systems are still not sufficiently mature to fight off many organisms. Also, they have not had sufficient exposure to accumulate a repertoire of antibodies in combating many common infections. Fortunately, infants do not have to fight the battle alone. There are hundreds of antibiotic and therapeutic drugs to help fight off most infectious microorganisms and other diseases, in addition to vaccines available to protect infants against some of the serious contagious illnesses. By 3 years of age the immune system is much more mature (Andersen et al., 1994).

IMMUNIZATION AGAINST COMMUNICABLE DISEASES

Through the years, a number of vaccines have been developed to provide immunity against many of the life-threatening communicable diseases infants and young children face in growing up. Routine immunization of infants and young children has dramatically decreased the rates of serious illness and death from infectious diseases. If 95 percent or more of infants and children worldwide can be immunized, it may be possible to virtually eliminate many other communicable diseases as well (Gold, 1996). Immunization is begun early in life so that the baby will have time to build up the level of protection necessary to avoid getting the diseases.

Immunization against specific communicable diseases is required in all 50 states before a child can enter school or a child day care program. Unfortunately, many infants do not get their vaccinations early enough to prevent the outbreak and spread of the diseases. However, special government programs launched in the early 1990's have increased immunization rates in the United States, particularly among low-income

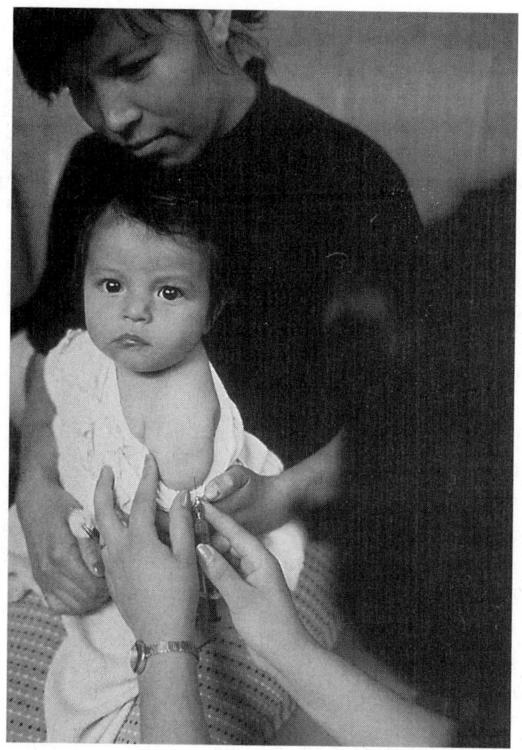

This infant is receiving an immunization.

families. As of 1999, 80 percent of the 2-year-olds in the United States had received the recommended vaccines. Immunization rates were lower among Black, Hispanic and American Indian infants than White infants (Children's Defense Fund, 2001).

Immunization Schedule. The schedule currently recommended for the routine immunization of healthy infants is given in Table 5-1. Currently, vaccines are recommended to protect infants against 12 infectious diseases. The legally required immunizations are controlled by state laws rather than federal regulations.

Adverse Reactions. Although modern vaccines are extremely safe and effective, there is a slight risk of side effects with all of these substances. Minor reactions, such as a fever, swelling around the site of the injection, and general discomfort for a few hours are common. However, the possibility of more severe complications has been associated with some of the vaccines. The greatest concern has centered around the potential risk of the **polio** and the **pertussis (whooping cough)**

Table 5-1 Recommended Immunization Schedule (Birth–6 years)—2001

VACCINE	*AGE FOR ADMINISTRATION*
Hepatitis B (HiB)	Birth–3 mos. (1st); 1–4 mos. (2nd); 6–18 mos. (3rd)
Diptheria Tetanus Pertussus (DtaP)	2 mos. (1st); 4 mos. (2nd); 6 mos. (3rd); 15–18 mos. (4th); 4–6 yrs (5th)
Haemophilus influenzae	2 mos. (1st); 4 mos. (2nd)
Type b (Hib)	6 mos. (3rd); 12–15 mos. (4th)
Inactivated Polio (IPV)	2 mos. (1st); 4 mos. (2nd); 6–18 mos. (3rd); 4–6 yrs (4th)
Pneumococcal Conjugate (PCV)	2 mos. (1st); 4 mos. (2nd); 6 mos. (3rd); 12–15 mos. (4th)
Measles, Mumps, Rubella (MMR)	12–15 mos. (1st); 4–6 yrs (2nd)
Varicella	12–18 mos.
Hepatitis A	24 mos. (In selected areas)

Note: This schedule was approved by the Advisory Committee on Immunization Practices, the American Academy of Pediatrics, and the American Academy of Family Physicians. It was effective for 2001 but is subject to change. Check with a physician or a local Department of Health for updates. Recommended age or age range for administering the vaccine may be affected by the child's health, date of visit to health care provider, state mandates, physician preferences, or other factors. DtaP and MMR vaccines are usually combined and given in a single injection.

Source: Centers for Disease Control and Prevention (2001). Recommended childhood immunization schedule - United States, 2001. *Morbidity and Mortality Weekly Report, 50(1). 10.*

vaccines. There are two types of vaccine available for immunization against polio: oral polio vaccine (OPV) and inactivated polio vaccine (IPV). Use of the OPV is controversial because there is a slight possibility that the vaccine can cause paralytic polio. Since IPV is made from a killed virus and carries no risk of polio, health officials currently recommend use of the safer IPV vaccine (Center for Disease Control and Prevention, 2001). In response to concerns about the safety of the pertussis vaccinations, a newer type of vaccine has been developed. This currently recommended vaccine (referred to as aP for "acellular pertussis") is safer because it is made with only part of the pertussis germ instead of the entire bug. An additional controversy has focused on a claim made in a leading medical journal that the MMR vaccine may cause autistic disorder and bowel problems (Wakefield, 1998). However, follow-up studies have led scientists to conclude that there is no link between the MMR vaccine and either of the two conditions (Bower, 1999).

Newer Vaccines.

Varicella (Chickenpox). Varicella, commonly called **chickenpox,** is a relatively mild, highly contagious disease caused by the varicella zoster virus. Nearly everyone in the United States who is not immunized will develop chickenpox. Most cases of chickenpox occur among children between 2 and 10 years of age (Gershon & LaRussa, 1992). Chickenpox causes itchy blisters that may spread over most of the body and in some of the mucous membranes, depending on the severity of the infection. Complications from chickenpox in otherwise healthy infants are uncommon but can be serious. The greatest risk is for infants under 1 year of age and older adults. The most common complications include bacterial skin infections, pneumonia, encephalitis, meningitis dehydration, and hepatitis. After many years of scientific research, a safe and effective vaccine is now available to prevent infants and children from being infected with the chickenpox virus (Holmes et al.,1996). Research shows that 85 percent of children who are vaccinated do not get chickenpox. Even if an inoculated child gets chickenpox, chances are the effects will be mild (Arvin, 2001).

***Haemophilus Influenzae* Type B.** Although it is not as well known, ***Haemophilus influenzae* type b (Hib)** is more dangerous than most other childhood diseases. Hib has been compared with paralytic polio in the seriousness of its effects. Hib occurs most frequently, and is most serious, among infants between 6 months and 1 year of age. Before the availability of an effective vaccine, Hib was the most common cause of meningitis in infants and children, and a major cause of pneumonia and severe infections of the skin, throat, ears, joints, and bloodstream. Approximately 3 percent of infants and children who are infected with Hib in the United States die, while many others suffer permanent brain damage, hearing loss, mental disability, or learning problems. The use of the Hib vaccine in recent years has resulted in a dramatic decline in the incidence of this devastating disease among infants and young children (Clements, 1998).

Hepatitis. The term **hepatitis** refers to an inflammation of the liver caused by viruses, toxic substances, or drugs. The most common forms of hepatitis that infect infants are type A and type B (Andersen et al., 1994). These illnesses, especially hepatitis A, often go undetected because many infected infants do not display any symptoms (Townsend, 1993). Hepatitis B is less contagious and therefore less common among infants and young children. However, hepatitis B is more serious because the virus can continue in the body and eventually cause chronic infections, cancer, or cirrhosis of the liver. Symptoms of both hepatitis A and B infections are similar and include fever, diarrhea, a general sick feeing, dark urine, light-colored stools, and jaundice (Andersen et al., 1994; Townsend, 1993).

Hepatitis B is mainly transmitted through infected blood products and saliva. Hepatitis A is extremely contagious, especially in large daycare centers with infants under 2 years of age. This infection spreads primarily from contact with feces during the diaper-changing process.

Lack of sanitation, particularly hand washing, is one of the major factors contributing to its spread. A new vaccine for hepatitis A is available and is recommended for use with children age 2 and older in certain areas of the United States.

Pneumococcus. The newest vaccine on the list of recommended childhood immunizations, the pneumococcal conjugate vaccine, is given for protection against ***Streptococcus pneumoniae*** **(pneumococcus)** bacteria. This strain of bacteria is the leading cause of pneumonia, bacterial meningitis, sinusitis, and bloodstream and middle ear infections. This vaccine is currently recommended for all infants who are 2 months and older. The peak age range for these infections is 6 to 11 months (Centers for Disease Control and Prevention, 2000). A study of Finnish children who were given the vaccine found that it is safe and effective in reducing the episodes of middle ear infections (otitis media) caused by various types of pneumococcal bacteria (Eskola et al., 2001). This vaccine will reduce the need for the use of antibiotics, which in turn will slow the development of antibiotic-resistant bacteria.

SYMPTOMS OF ILLNESS IN INFANTS

Numerous symptoms accompany illness in infants. Some of the more common symptoms parents and other caregivers should attend to include general discomfort (malaise), loss of appetite, vomiting, congestion, runny nose, fever, cough, diarrhea, skin rash, listlessness, incessant crying, and irritability. An infant may exhibit one or more of the symptoms, and the symptoms could be caused by one problem or a combination of problems. Generally, parents tend to be most concerned about fever, vomiting, and diarrhea. Health specialists recommend that a health care provider be contacted when one of these conditions occur, or if the parent has other concerns.

Fever. A temperature higher than 100°F by mouth or 101°F by rectum is usually considered to be a fever (Schmitt & Roxann, 1994). Parents should call a doctor if an infant is (1) younger than 3 months and has a rectal temperature of 100.2°F or higher; (2) between 3 and 6 months of age and has a rectal temperature of 101°F or higher; (3) older than 6 months and has a fever of 103°F or higher (Shelov, 1998). However, parents are advised to avoid "fever phobia"—the tendency of overanxious parents to treat low-grade fevers with unnecessary medications (Schmitt & Roxann, 1994).

Vomiting. Vomiting may result from one or more of a long list of causes, ranging from food reactions to motion to viral infections. Generally parents are advised to contact a doctor if any of the following apply (Shelov, 1998):

1. The baby vomits strenuously and repeatedly.
2. Vomiting is accompanied by diarrhea, a fever, or convulsions.
3. The baby has ingested something unusual that may be poisonous.
4. Vomiting follows a fall or blow to the head.
5. There are indications of a swollen stomach, stomach pain, or other discomfort.
6. Vomiting episodes extend beyond 24 hours.
7. Blood or bile (greenish material) appears in the vomit.

One of the main dangers associated with vomiting is dehydration. To prevent this from happening, the child should be given water and other fluids especially prepared to treat diarrhea as recommended by the doctor.

Diarrhea. Diarrhea is defined as an increase in the frequency, fluidity, and volume of bowel movements. One or two watery bowel movements a day is not unusual for an infant, but three to five is considered mild diarrhea. Diarrhea is one of the most frequent problems encountered by infants and young children. Diarrhea is often preceded or accompanied by other symptoms, such as respiratory congestion or a cough (Gellis & Kagan, 1986). An infant is in danger of dehydration if severe diarrhea continues. The risk of dehydration is increased if diarrhea is accompanied by vomiting.

COMMON ILLNESSES AND HEALTH CONCERNS

While many of the life-threatening infectious diseases of infants can be controlled through immunizations, there are numerous other illnesses and health problems for which there are no vaccines. It is not possible in this chapter to consider all the diseases to which infants are susceptible, but some of the disorders that occur most frequently are briefly discussed. In addition, we will consider two relatively infrequent but life-threatening health concerns. Parents should obtain a medical guide such as the American Academy of Pediatrics' *Caring for Your Baby and Young Child* (Shelov, 1998). The American Academy of Pediatrics recommends that parents take an infant to a doctor at least eight times before age 2 for checkups, immunizations, and screening for disabilities. Annual checkups are recommended after 2 years of age (Shelov, 1998).

Colds and Respiratory Infections. Infections of the respiratory tract include a wide variety of problems ranging from the common cold to severe pneumonia. This class of diseases represents by far the most frequent illnesses of childhood in the United States. Most infants have 8 to 10 colds in the first two years of life (Shelov, 1998). Infants who attend a group child-care facility have more colds and other infectious illnesses than infants who are not in group care (see Chapter 13). More than 150 different viruses have been identified as possible causes of colds and coldlike illnesses. Infants are more likely than adults to have a fever with a cold (Marks, 1985). They have special difficulty with the nasal congestion caused by a cold because of the inability to blow their nose and clear the nasal passage. Furthermore, very young infants are often instinctive nose breathers and have a great deal of difficulty breathing through the mouth when the nasal passage is obstructed. The main concern about colds is not so much the cold itself, but the potential side effects, such as ear and throat infections, bronchitis, and pneumonia. Although there is no prevention or cure for the common cold, secondary infections can be treated with antibiotics.

Ear Infections. Inflammation of the middle ear, **otitis media,** is the most common infectious illness of childhood in the United States. Approximately 85 percent of all U.S. infants have at least one middle ear infection before they are 3 years old (Arnold, 1996). The highest incidence is in children 6 to 24 months of age (Shelov, 1998). Otitis media is found more frequently among male infants, lower socioeconomic groups, Native Americans, infants with cleft palate or other craniofacial anomalies, and those with allergic rhinitis (Arnold, 1996).

Otitis media is a secondary infection caused by bacteria that are usually not associated with the primary illness. (*Streptococcus pneumoniae* and *Haemophilus influenzae* are the most common infecting bacteria.) The infection produces a sticky fluid that may gradually accumulate because the tubal passage tends to be swollen and blocked. The symptoms include earache, fever, drainage, and hearing impairment in those who have recurrent infections. However, infants cannot be relied on to give direct signs that they have otitis media. They tend to give only general signs of distress, such as irritability, crying, and loss of appetite. Some infants and toddlers may rub their ears or stop babbling or talking as much. The condition may persist for weeks without any signs of ear pain or other symptoms. Otitis media is usually treated with antibiotics. However, questions have been raised about the effectiveness of antibiotics in fighting ear infections (Watson & Stone, 1997).

In some cases fluid buildup in the middle ear may persist after earaches and other signs or symptoms are gone. This condition is referred to as **otitis media with effusion.** In persistent cases, tubes, resembling small buttons, may be inserted into the ear to promote drainage of fluid (Klein, 1992). However, there are are potential complications from this type of surgery (Watson & Stone, 1997). Chronic ear infections may cause hearing loss, which can interfere with language acquisition and/or cognitive and social development.

Colic. Infantile colic is one of the most common complaints for which parents seek medical assistance. Approximately 10 to 30 percent of all babies in the United States develop colic (Overby, 1996). **Colic** may be defined as inconsolable crying for long periods of time, day in and day out, in an otherwise healthy baby. The cry has been described as a loud, high-pitched, intense, piercing, angry scream that may be accompanied by breath holding (Lester et al., 1992). Crying is often accompanied by arching of the back, extending or pulling up the legs, or other agitated motor movements. Other symptoms of colic include an enlarged stomach, increased bowel sounds, spitting up, and difficulty sleeping. Episodes of colic occur most frequently between 6:00 P.M. and midnight. The condition usually begins around 2 weeks of age and may persist for four months or longer (Treem, 1994). Health care professionals have found colic difficult to define, explain, and treat.

In general, there is no one condition that causes colic in all babies. In some cases, colic may be caused by an allergic reaction to protein in formula milk or allergens in breast milk. In other cases, the problem may stem from various gastrointestinal problems such as irritable bowel syndrome, esophageal reflux (flowing back of digestive juices into the esophagus), or the production of excessive stomach gas due to the inability to absorb carbohydrates (Treem, 1994). Colic is sometimes attributed to unusual sensitivity of an infant to stimulation (Shelov, 1998). Although there is no conclusive evidence that colic originates from parental stress or anxiety, parents may compound the problem in frustrated efforts to stop the crying.

Recommendations for treating colic vary as widely as explanations of why colic occurs. Apparently breast-feeding does not protect infants from colic since a similar number of breast-fed and formula-fed infants have this problem. Changing the bottle-fed baby's formula or eliminating cow's milk and other potentially irritating foods from the nursing mother's diet is often recommended. Other treatments that are recommended include swaddling, rocking, walking with the baby in a body carrier, running an appliance (e.g., a vacuum cleaner) that has a rhythmic sound, playing soothing music, giving the baby a pacifier, and placing the baby stomach down across one's arm or legs (Shelov, 1998). Some pediatricians have found that counseling parents on how to respond to excessive crying can be helpful (Taubman, 1984).

Acquired Immune Deficiency Syndrome. Anyone who has watched television or read a newspaper since the early 1980s is familiar with the term **acquired immune deficiency syndrome,** commonly referred to as **AIDS.** This relatively new and terrifying disease results from infection with the human immunodeficiency virus (HIV). Infants acquire HIV from their infected mothers during the prenatal period, the birth process, or during breast-feeding. Infants can also become infected with the HIV virus through blood transfusions. However, this route of transmission has been virtually eliminated in the United States since careful testing and treatment of donated blood began in 1985. Without medical intervention, the chance of an infant of an infected mother being born with HIV is approximately 20 to 25 percent (Boland & Oleske, 1995). Scientists have found that the risk of perinatal transmission of HIV can be reduced by approximately 30 to 50 percent if the mother is treated with special medication during pregnancy (Fiscus et al., 1996; Parks, 1996; Wortley, Lindegren, & Fleming, 2001). However, concerns have been expressed about the possibility that infants who are exposed to such medication during the prenatal period may face an increased risk of developing cancer in childhood (Health Watch, 1997).

The HIV virus attacks the immune system and eventually results in acquired immune deficiency syndrome (AIDS). Infants with AIDS are at extremely high risk for infection with many different viruses, bacterial infections, and other disorders. By contrast, such infectious agents pose little or no risk to infants with normal immune systems (Bale, 1990). The onset of AIDS is usually marked by a variety of medical problems. The symptoms include intermittent fevers, recurrent diarrhea, weight loss, and failure to thrive. The liver, spleen, and lymph nodes are often enlarged. As time passes, almost all infants are affected by opportunistic and recurrent infections such as middle ear infections, eye infections, cold sores and thrush in the mouth, pneumonia, herpes, bronchitis, bacterial infections, salmonella, bone and joint infections, and internal organ abscesses (Rutstein, Conlon, & Batshaw, 1997).

Infants with AIDS do not produce antibodies in response to vaccines for common childhood diseases. Consequently, they are at increased risk for life-threatening complications from episodes of diseases such as measles and mumps. HIV-infected infants may also experience a variety of neurologic complications, including central nervous system infections, lymphomas of the brain, strokes, and abnormalities of the peripheral nerves. The neurologic features of AIDS lead to a progressive decline in motor, cognitive, social, and language functions, as well as the development of weakness, spasticity, loss of balance, paralysis, or seizures (Bale, 1990).

In most cases, HIV is dormant for a period of time before AIDS symptoms appear. Approximately 20 percent of infants who are infected with HIV at birth quickly develop full-blown AIDS. In the majority of cases, though, the disease progresses more slowly. There is some evidence that the AIDS symptoms appear earlier in infants whose mothers are seriously affected by the disease at the time of delivery (Blanche et al., 1994). Until recently, most HIV-infected infants displayed AIDS symptoms by 2 years of age and died by age 6. Currently, the median age at which AIDS is likely to be diagnosed has been estimated to occur at 4.1 years, somewhat later than previous occurrences (Mawhinny & Pagano, 1994). With recent advances in medical treatments, many HIV positive infants survive into their teens (Oleske, 1994).

Sudden Infant Death Syndrome. On a warm, sunny afternoon Sharyn and Joe sat on their deck while their infant daughter, Lynn, slept in a baby carriage between them. When Joe picked up Lynn a few minutes later, inexplicably she was dead (Hermes, 1981). Similar incidents are repeated all too often throughout the United States. In most cases of this type, the cause of death is attributed to sudden infant death syndrome since no medical reason can be found.

Sudden infant death syndrome, usually referred to as **SIDS,** is defined as the sudden death of any infant under 1 year of age that cannot be explained by medical history, a complete autoposy, and examination of the death scene (Willinger, James, & Catz, 1991). The terms *cot death* and *crib death* are also used to describe this phenomenon. The number of SIDS deaths reaches a peak between 2 and 4 months of age with the incidence decreasing as infants get older (Dwyer & Ponsonby, 1995). SIDS rarely occurs before 1 month of age. SIDS is a threat to the well-being of young infants everywhere.

Risk Factors Associated With SIDS. During the past 25 years a massive amount of information has been accumulated in the search for an answer to the SIDS mystery. Scientists have identified a number of factors that are statistically associated with an increased risk of SIDS. The following trends have been reported:

1. Exposure of a baby to tobacco smoke before or after birth increases the risk of SIDS (Blair et al., 1996; Dwyer & Ponsonby, 1995).
2. SIDS occurs more frequently among economically disadvantaged families (Guntheroth, 1995).
3. The risk of SIDS is highest for firstborn infants (Guntheroth, 1995).
4. Preterm, low birth weight infants, and infants of multiple births are at increased risk for SIDS (Dwyer & Ponsonby, 1995).
5. The incidence of SIDS is higher among infants whose mothers are characterized by one or more of the following conditions: are less than 20 years of age, do not receive adequate prenatal care, engage in substance abuse, have a short interval between pregnancies, suffer from anemia or an infectious disease during pregnancy (Dwyer & Ponsonby, 1995; Willinger, 1995).
6. SIDS occurs at increased rates during the winter months (Dwyer & Ponsonby, 1995).
7. The incidence of SIDS is higher among male infants than it is among female infants (Centers for Disease Control, 1996).

Possible Causes. The factors just described provide information that can be used in reducing the chance of an infant being affected by SIDS. However, the exact medical explanation for SIDS remains elusive. Through the years researchers have pursued several theories in attempting to solve the SIDS mystery, including the search for a faulty gene, virus, and irregular heart rythmns (T. James, 1985; Kelly & Shannon, 1982). Currently, investigators are trying to find the physiological mechanisms associated with the prone (stomach) sleeping position, because SIDS rates are higher for infants who sleep in that position (Dwyer & Ponsonby, 1995). A leading hypothesis is that there is a developmental delay or abnormality in the part of the brain that controls breathing and waking during sleep. It appears likely, however, that SIDS may result from a variety of causes rather than one single explanation (American Academy of Pediatrics, 2000; Freed et al., 1994).

SIDS Prevention. Until the cause (or causes) of sudden infant death is determined, no completely effective means of prevention can be developed. However, since 1992, the American Academy of Pediatrics has recommended that infants be placed on their backs to sleep. Due to the public awareness **Back to Sleep campaign,** the number of SIDS deaths has declined by more than 40 percent (American Academy of Pediatrics, 2000).

In addition to placing an infant on its back for sleeping, the Back to Sleep campaign recommends keeping the infant in a smoke-free environment before and after birth. British researchers have concluded that the number of SIDS deaths can be reduced by almost two-thirds if parents follow both recommendations (Blair et al., 1996). Parents are also advised to keep the sleeping room temperature at a comfortable (moderate) level, participate in prenatal and postnatal health care, obtain immunizations for the infant on schedule, and when possible, breast-feed the baby. Caregivers should not place soft bedding such as pillows, comforters, cushions, or stuffed toys under the baby, and should ensure that the baby's face does not become covered (Willinger, 1995).

Physicians sometimes recommend the use of breathing and heart rate monitoring devices for infants who have been exposed to one or more risk factors for SIDS. The use of such devices has been controversial because the monitor are not totally reliable. Although some studies have found home monitoring programs to be associated with a decrease in the incidence of SIDS (Freed et al., 1994), the weight of evidence shows that use of monitors does not lower the risk of SIDS (American Academy of Pediatrics, 1985, 2000).

Currently researchers are trying to decide whether infant-parent cosleeping (see Chapter 3) may be a means of preventing SIDS, or actually a risk factor for SIDS occurrence. McKenna and colleagues (1994) have found that cosleeping alters sleep patterns so that infants are aroused more frequently during the night. The researchers believe that these partner-induced sleep interruptions and transitions may provide the infant with practice in self-arousal or the use of other physiological mechanisms that may prevent SIDS. Other scientists believe cosleeping may actually be a risk factor for SIDS due to possible suffocation (Byard, 1994). In New Zealand and Australia, bed sharing has been associated with a higher incidence of SIDS (Kilkenny & Lumley, 1994; McKenna & Mosko, 1993). Additional research is needed before this question will be resolved. In the meantime, the American Academy of Pediatrics (2000) recommends that parents consider placing the infant's crib near their bed as an alternative. Parents who choose to bed share should place the infant in the supine (face up) sleep position and exercise the other precautions that are recommended for infants who sleep alone.

CHILD MALTREATMENT

Each year thousands of children in the United States are victims of various forms of child maltreatment. The highest rates of victimization occur between birth and 3 years of age. Approximately 13 percent of the victims of child maltreatment are under 1 year of age, while about 25 percent are from 2 to 5 years of age (U.S. Census Bureau, 2000). Maltreatment is the most frequent single cause of death in infants between 6 and 12 months of age. Approximately 40 percent of children who die because of maltreatment are under 1 year of age (U.S. Department of Health and Human Services [USDHHS], 2001). Child maltreatment takes many forms, including neglect, physical abuse, sexual abuse, and emotional abuse. The two most frequent forms of child maltreatment are neglect and physical abuse (USDHHS, 2001).

Neglect. **Child neglect** refers to the willful failure of parents or other designated caregivers to meet the child's basic needs for food, clothing, shelter, medical treatment, and affection. Child neglect does not typically receive as much public attention as physical abuse, but it is the most frequent form of child maltreatment. Children under the age of 2 are especially vulnerable to **nonorganic failure to thrive (NOFTT).** Most cases of NOFTT can be attributed to inadequate feeding. These infants do not gain weight and grow on schedule. In most instances emotional neglect is also involved. Approximately 5 to 15 percent of these infants also suffer physical abuse. A few of these infants actually die of starvation (C. Johnson, 1996). NOFTT occurs less often after age 2 because older infants are better able to obtain food for themselves (Mrazek, 1993).

Physical Abuse. **Physical abuse** can be defined as nonaccidental physical injury to a child that is the result of acts or omissions on the part of parents or other caregivers (Kempe & Helfer, 1972). Abused children are beaten severely, burned, poisoned, and punished in many other ways. A variety of "weapons" may be used to inflict injury on a child, such as a belt, a pan, a fist, or a lighted cigarette. The extent of injuries varies from minor bruises and abrasions to broken bones, permanent nervous-system damage, and death.

The form of abuse most frequently reported for victims younger than 1 year of age has been called the **shaken infant syndrome** (J. Leventhal, 1996). Adults often grab an infant by the arms or shoulders and shake vigorously. This action may cause stretching and tearing of the tender blood vessels in the brain. The brain can also be damaged from bumping against the inside of the skull. Violent shaking can lead to bleeding in the brain and eyes as well as whiplash injury to the neck bones and muscles. The following is an excerpt from a case report:

> An 11-month old female was taken to the emergency room after she was found lying on the floor unconscious. The stepfather reported that the child fell from the couch but later admitted that he had "shaken" the child to wake her from her nap in an attempt to adjust her sleep schedule and "slapped" her to gain her attention (Eagan, Whelan-Williams, & Brooks, 1985, p. 505).

Recent studies indicate that shaking alone may not be responsible for the more severe brain injuries observed. Many of the shaken babies also display signs of injuries that are likely to have been caused by the impact of the head striking the crib, bed, floor, or other hard surface as the baby was being shaken. Because physicians often have trouble determining whether bleeding in the brain results from the shaking and/or an impact, the term shaken infant syndrome has been replaced with **shaken impact syndrome** in some of the medical literature (J. Leventhal, 1996).

Characteristics of Child Abusers. Why does child abuse occur? How could any sane parent or adult abuse a helpless child? Attempts to find answers to such questions have focused largely on the characteristics of abusive parents. Many abusive parents have little knowledge of normal child growth and development, and their ignorance results in unrealistic expectations of a child. They also tend to be afraid of spoiling their children, or they strongly believe in the value of physical punishment as a means of discipline (Mayhall & Norgard, 1983). Being maltreated as a child puts a person at risk for becoming abusive. However, the majority of mistreated children do not grow up to be abusive parents. Approximately one out of three people who were abused or neglected as children will mistreat their own children (Kaufman & Zigler, 1987).

Child maltreatment occurs among families of all economic and educational levels. However, child maltreatment tends to be reported more frequently among parents and adults who are poor and less educated, or isolated without friends and support from relatives (J. Leventhal, 1996).

Effects of Child Maltreatment. The effects of child maltreatment are devastating and long-lasting in most cases. Children less than 3 years of age are biologically more vulnerable than older children. Consequently, the effects of abusive treatment are more devastating. Most fatalities due to maltreatment occur within this age group (Mrazek, 1993). If they survive, abused infants suffer long-lasting physical and mental disabilities. Damage to the brain leaves them with mental retardation, seizures, learning disabilities, and hearing or other sensory impairments. Even when severe physical impairments are not obvious, mistreated children may have lower-than-average intellectual, language, and motor abilities, leading to lower academic achievement and developmental delays (Mayhall & Norgard, 1983). Abused children also suffer emotional scars, which may make them extremely shy, withdrawn, depressed, or angry (Mrazek, 1993).

Treatment and Prevention. The complexities of child abuse require a wide range of treatment and prevention strategies. Efforts to treat abusive parents and their victims include individual therapy, family counseling, placing children in foster care or crisis nurseries, and short-term residential treatment for the entire family (Starr, 1979). Parents Anonymous is a volunteer organization that has been very effective in working with abusive families. The large majority of abusive parents can be helped with appropriate treatment and support. Approaches to the prevention of child abuse include parent-education programs, and hospital maternity-ward practices to facilitate parent-child bonding. The most effective method of preventing physical abuse and neglect has been extended home visitation (MacMillan, MacMillan, & Oxford, 1993). Home visitor programs usually focus on providing training in parenting along with emotional support for parents who may be at risk for becoming child abusers.

INFANT SAFETY

Nearly all children are involved in one or more accidents while growing up. An **accident** is that occurrence in a sequence of events that produces unintended injury, death, or property damage. The term *accident* refers to the event, not the result of the event (see *unintentional injury*). Actually, medical and safety experts are attempting to get people to use **unintentional injury** and **injury control** instead of *accidents* and *accident prevention*. The term *accident* implies a chance event, or even an "act of God" that cannot be controlled. This often leads to a fatalistic attitude that becomes a barrier to decreasing the number and the severity of injuries among infants and children. Use of the terms *unintentional injury* and *injury control* are more personal and focus on the possibility of injury reduction (Rivara & Brownstein, 1996).

Risk factors that are related to the frequency of injuries include age, sex, and socioeconomic status. The first year of life is the most dangerous. Injuries take the lives of more babies during this period than any other age under 16 years. Unintentional injuries are the fourth leading cause of death for infants under 1 year of age (National Safety Council, 2000). Male injury rates exceed those of females. Whether by nature or nurture, or both, males tend to be more active and aggressive in exploring the environment. Infants and children growing up in poverty conditions tend to have higher injury rates because they are exposed to more environmental hazards than their peers from more economically advantaged backgrounds (Kroenfeld & Glick, 1995). Toddlers are especially susceptible to burns, drowning, falls, and poisoning. They are increasingly mobile and curious but lack judgment to know what safety hazards to avoid.

Causes of Unintentional Injury Deaths. By far the leading cause of deaths attributed to unintentional injuries during infancy is motor vehicles,

Table 5-2 Leading Causes of Unintentional Injury Deaths Among Infants and Children (Birth–5 Years)*

RANK	*CAUSE*	*NUMBER*
1	Motor vehicle	933
2	Drowning	516
3	Fires and burns	399
4	Ingested food/object	147
5	Falls	62
6	Poisoning (solids and liquids)	39
7	Firearms	20

*Based on latest available data = 1997

Source: National Safety Council (2000). *Injury Facts.* Chicago: Author. Used by Permission.

as indicated in Table 5-2. The death rate attributed to motor vehicles is highest for infants under 12 months of age (National Safety Council, 2000). Very young infants are more likely to be riding in the front seat held in someone's arms. They are especially vulnerable to head injury because of the soft spots in the skull and a top-heavy body.

Water is another safety hazard for infants. Drowning is the second leading cause of fatal injuries for infants and young children. Drownings are most likely to happen when infants are left in bathtubs or near swimming pools. Fires and burns represent the third leading cause of injury deaths during the first four years of life. Most fire victims die of asphyxiation and inhalation of poisonous substances rather than from burns, but infants are more sensitive to heat from flames than older children or adults because of their thin, tender skin. In addition, infants suffer burns from hot water, grease, steam, heating and cooking appliances, and electrical shocks. Infant deaths also result from choking on food, balloons, buttons, or small parts of toys (Rimell et al., 1995). Deaths due to falls have been declining in recent years, but continue to be ranked as the fifth leading cause of unintentional injury deaths (National Safety Council, 2000). Falls occur mainly when caregivers leave children unattended in hazardous places.

Nonfatal Injuries. Fortunately most unintentional injuries are not fatal. Each year, countless numbers of infants are treated in physicians' offices and hospitals for a variety of injuries. The leading causes of nonfatal unintentional injuries to infants and children are falls, motor vehicles, drowning, fire and burns, and poisoning (Rivara & Brownstein, 1996). Unfortunately many of these injuries are severe and result in long-term or permanent physical disabilities, neurological impairments, or other problems.

Injury Control. Scientists estimate that 90 percent of childhood injuries can be avoided. Efforts to control injuries include public safety awareness and educational campaigns, the development of new safety devices (e.g., car safety seats), stricter government-mandated product-safety standards, and environmental control (Rivara & Brownstein, 1996). Most motor vehicle deaths and serious

This toddler is in a very dangerous situation which could have been avoided if these toxic substances had been properly stored in a "childproof" location.

injuries could be prevented through the proper use of infant safety seats. A 10-year research study conducted in the state of Washington found safety seats to be 80 to 90 percent effective in preventing deaths and major injuries to infants and children under 5 years of age (Scherz, 1981). For maximum protection the seat should be certified as meeting government safety standards. The seat must be buckled tightly and securely, preferably in the center position of the rear seat. An infant safety seat should not be installed in the front passenger seat within range of an air bag that can strike a severe blow to the baby's head.

One of the most important steps an infant caregiver can take in injury control is to **babyproof the environment** by making regular safety checks of the home and other places where infants live and play. For example, medicines, cleaning supplies, and other substances with toxic-warning labels should be kept in a locked cabinet or a place that is not accessible to an active toddler. Food, cleaning products, and medicines should never be stored in the same area. Plants should be kept out of reach. Razor blades, knives, and other sharp objects should be removed from drawers within the reach of infants and toddlers. Electrical outlets not in use should be covered with safety plugs. Cords on appliances should not be accessible to infants. Floors should be checked regularly for small objects such as coins, tacks, pins, paper clips, and marbles. Smoke detectors should be installed on each floor of the house and in all bedrooms.

Equipment or furnishings may need to be moved, added, removed, or modified. For example, stair railings, baby cribs, or playpens that might trap a baby's head should be modified. Stairs should be blocked at the top and bottom. Play yards should be fenced in. Severe burns from tap water can be avoided by lowering the thermostat setting to below 120 degrees. Infants should not be placed in mobile walkers. The American Academy of Pediatrics has recommended a ban on the manufacture and sale of infant walkers because of the risk of injury associated with their use (Committee on Injury and Poison Prevention, 1995). Numerous other things can be done to provide a hazard-free, babyproof environment. However, there is no substitute for constant vigilance on the part of caregivers.

Caregivers should be prepared in case an injury occurs. Emergency telephone numbers, including the number of a poison-control center, should be posted on or near the telephone. A first-aid kit and an emergency-action chart should be readily available. In case poisoning occurs: (1) remove any remaining substance from the skin or mouth, (2) call the doctor or a poison control center immediately, and (3) follow their instructions. A bottle of ipecac syrup should be kept on hand to induce vomiting. However, it should be used only if recommended by a medical specialist.

Toy Safety. All toys and play materials for infants should be selected with safety precautions in mind. Toys that have small parts that can come off and become lodged in the windpipe, ears, or nostrils are among the most hazardous. Materials such as balloons, buttons, marbles, and chalk should not be available to young infants. Toys for infants and toddlers should not have sharp edges or points, should not be made of glass or brittle plastic, should not have cords or strings more than 12 inches long, and should not be put together with easily exposed straight pins, wires, or nails. Balls or other spherical objects less than 1 3/4 inches in diameter have been banned in toys designed for infants (Rimell et al., 1995). Even after carefully selecting toys, adults should supervise their use and examine them from time to time to be sure that wear and tear have not made the toys unsafe.

MEETING NUTRITIONAL NEEDS

Nutrition is fundamental to growth and development. The maintenance of nutritive balance during the early months of life is especially important because it lays the foundation for physical health and mental functioning throughout life. Prenatal and infant nutrition affects the quality and quantity of body cells and fluids, skeletal and dental development, and the body's susceptibility to disease. It is difficult to think of any aspect of infant growth and development that is not directly or indirectly influenced by nutrition.

Nutrition is the process by which the body uses food and other substances in the digestive system (McLaren & Burman, 1982). Infants need nutrients for the maintenance and growth of the skeletal system and body tissues, as well as energy to support activity and life-sustaining processes. Nutritionists have had difficulty determining the exact quantities of nutrients needed by infants or humans in general, so opinions vary as to ideal diets for individuals at all ages. Factors that affect an individual's nutrient needs include body size, rate of growth, activity level, basal metabolism, and nutritional reserves stored in the body. Nutrient needs in proportion to body size are greatest during infancy and decline with age (Trahms & Pipes, 1997).

Basic categories into which nutrients are divided include energy, carbohydrates, fat, protein and amino acid, vitamins, minerals, and water. An infant's diet must provide sufficient energy to maintain physical activity, growth, and physiological processes such as breathing, digestion, and blood circulation. Energy needs are met by foods containing fats, carbohydrates, and protein (Pipes & Trahms, 1997). Infants also require protein for the development of new body tissue as well as the synthesis of enzymes, hormones, and other compounds (Worthington-Roberts & Williams, 1996). A healthy supply of vitamins is needed for the metabolism of energy and protein, to supply nutrients for the growth of bones and mucous membranes, and for the synthesis of vital compounds (Trahms & Pipes,1997)

Feeding Newborns and Young Infants. As soon as an infant is born there are several decisions parents have to make about how to meet their baby's nutritional needs. One of the first and most important decisions that parents face is whether the newborn baby will be fed with maternal milk or a processed formula. Parents must also decide when the baby should be fed, how to wean the baby from breast or bottle, and when to begin adding other foods, such as strained vegetables, to the baby's milk diet.

Choice of First Food: Breast or Formula Milk. At the turn of the century, almost all infants in the United States were breast-fed (E. Martin & Beal, 1978). Over the years, cow's milk and other types of commercial formula gradually replaced breast milk as the most frequently used alternative for meeting nutritional needs during the early months of life (Committee on Nutrition, 1976). A resurgence of interest in breast-feeding in the United States occurred during the 1970s as more mothers from all socioeconomic classes breast-fed their babies (Martinez & Dodd, 1983). Breast-feeding rates have fluctuated during the past 30 years, but are currently on an upward trend. Approximately 67 percent of new mothers in the United States begin breast-feeding their newborns. However, only 31 percent of these mothers continue breast-feeding for the recommended minimum of six months (Ryan, 2000).

The choice of feeding the baby from breast or bottle is usually made by the sixth month of pregnancy. A variety of social, cultural, educational, and psychological factors are involved in the decision. The mother's decision about breast-feeding may be based more on the advice of family members, friends, and cultural norms than on scientific arguments (Alexy & Martin, 1994). Maternal employment can adversely affect the length of breast-feeding but does not appear to be a major factor involved in the initial decision. Strong approval of breast-feeding by the father has been associated with a high incidence of breast-feeding among middle-class families (Littman, Medendorp, & Goldfarb, 1994).

Benefits of Breast-Feeding. Nutritional experts and health care specialists recommend breast milk as the best food for newborn infants. Breast-feeding is especially important in underdeveloped countries where poor sanitation, poor nutrition, and a high incidence of infectious diseases exist. Apparently some breast-feeding is better than no breast-feeding, but mothers are encouraged to continue the process for at least six months, especially in underdeveloped countries.

The reasons cited for breast-feeding include both physiological and psychological advantages

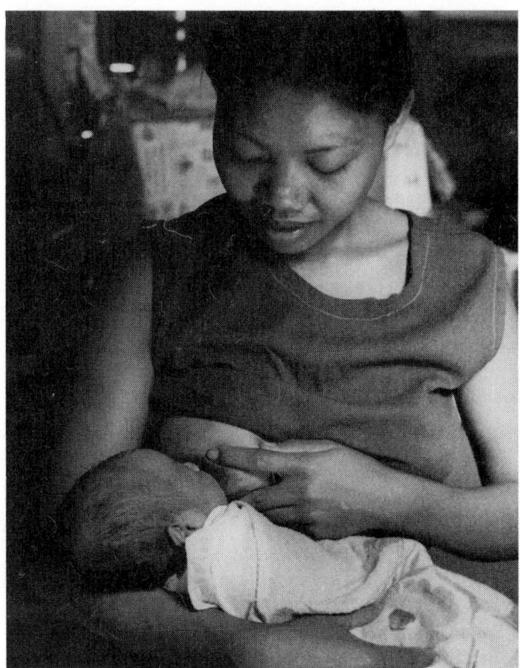

The importance of breastfeeding is emphasized by nutritionists and health care specialists.

for the infant and the mother. The major reasons that are given for breast-feeding are:

1. Breast milk is best because it contains nutrients that most adequately meet the infant's nutritional needs for the first six months of life. The components of breast milk, such as proteins and fat, are easier for the infant's body to digest and absorb. The waste products are more easily processed by the immature kidneys of the infant (Foman, 1993).
2. Breast milk is sterile and is less likely to be contaminated (World Health Organization/UNICEF, 1981).
3. Human milk contains substances that provide infants with protection against viral and bacterial infections (Dewey, Heinig, & Nommsen-Rivers, 1995). Death rates and incidences of illnesses, such as otitis media and repiratory infections, are lower in breast-fed than bottle-fed babies throughout the world (Pipes, 1997).
5. Breast-feeding facilitates the return of the mother's uterus to its normal size and reduces the danger of postpartum bleeding (Martin & Beal, 1978).
6. Breast milk is inexpensive and convenient (Marotz, Cross, & Rush, 2001).

Other benefits need to be confirmed by additional research evidence. However, breast-feeding may: facilitate mother-to-infant bonding (Klaus & Kennell, 1982); promote mother's earlier return to prepregnancy weight; enhance infant motor coordination; boost cognitive development, especially for preterm infants (Lucas, Morley, & Cole, 1992; Rogan & Gladen, 1993); reduce the risk of osteoporosis for the mother (Byers et al., 1985; Kalkwarf & Specker, 1995; Rosenblatt & Thomas, 1993); and offer the infant protection against SIDS (Willinger, 1995), allergies (Pipes, 1997), and asthma (Komaroff, 1999).

Barriers to Breast-Feeding. The evidence favoring breast milk as the best food for young babies is conclusive and compelling. Consequently, the superiority of breast-feeding over formula-feeding is rarely questioned. It is considered by most experts to be the only food that the baby needs during the first six months of life (including vitamins or other supplements). In some cases, though, there are conditions that prevent mothers from breast-feeding. Some mothers do not produce an adequate milk supply, and other mothers cannot breast-feed because of illness, alcoholism, or use of certain medications. There is a possibility that the AIDS virus can be transmitted through breast milk, so infected mothers are generally advised not to breast-feed (Nicoll et al., 1994)

Some mothers prefer not to breast-feed because of feelings of revulsion, embarrassment, fear, or uncertainty. In addition, there are restrictions placed upon many working mothers that make it difficult for them to breast-feed satisfactorily. As an alternative, some mothers pump the milk out of their breasts and store it for bottle-feeding when they are not available for nursing. In some cases resistance to breast-feeding is associated with the father's limited opportunity to participate in feeding the baby.

Formula-Feeding. The mother who bottle-feeds her baby has several options in the selection of formula. Formulas made from cow's milk are available under different brands, in concentrated liquid or ready-to-feed containers, with or without iron fortification. Formula milk fortified with iron is generally recommended (Satter, 2000). Milk substitute formulas, usually made from soy milk or protein hydrolysate, are available for infants who are allergic to cow's milk protein. However, some infants who are allergic to cow's milk are also allergic to soy-based formula. Condensed milk, skim milk, low-fat milk, goat's milk, and nondairy creamers are not nutritionally acceptable for infants during the first two years. Regular whole cow's milk should not be given to infants under 12 months of age because it may cause a small amount of intestinal bleeding resulting in iron deficiency anemia (Committee on Nutrition, 1998).

Schedule versus Demand Feeding. Another decision that must be made in feeding infants is whether to schedule feedings every three or four hours, or to follow a baby-led, self-demand approach. In many cultures, such as Chimalteco infants of Guatemala, a baby is nursed throughout the day and night any time it cries. However, in other cultures babies are fed on a more limited schedule. For example, many Jamaican mothers tend to nurse their babies an average of four times a day (Broude, 1995). Over the years, recommendations in the child-rearing literature have variously emphasized feeding babies on a schedule or feeding them any time they get hungry. In recent years the emphasis has continued to favor demand feeding and self-regulation by the infant (Foman, 1993; Satter, 2000). On a cautionary note, parents must be careful to distinguish hunger cues from other distress signals in order to avoid overfeeding or underfeeding.

Weaning. The World Health Organization (WHO/UNICEF, 1981) defines **weaning** as the process by which milk-fed infants gradually become accustomed to the range of foods characteristic of the society into which they are born. Parents are likely to interpret weaning as the process of taking away the breast or bottle. The process of weaning may include a partial transition from breast to bottle, from a bottle to cup, from liquids to solids, and from caretaker-administered feeding to self-feeding (Gesell & Ilg, 1937). In most cases, the method and timing of weaning tends to be based on cultural traditions and personal preferences rather than scientific recommendations. In the United States, infants are typically weaned by 1 year of age, if not sooner. However, in 83 percent of 159 societies across the world, mothers wait until infants are at least 2 years of age before weaning. In some cultures children may still be nursing at 3 years or older.

Whether weaning is easy or difficult depends upon the readiness of the infant and the pressure exerted by the parent. In some cultures, such as Mixtecans of Mexico, infants are weaned abruptly. Once the mother decides to wean her baby, she never offers the breast again. If the baby protests, a woman may attempt to make nursing distasteful by rubbing bitter herbs or dirt on her nipple. In some cases the baby may be sent to stay with relatives for a day or two (Broude, 1995). Experts tend to favor gradual weaning rather than an abrupt cold turkey approach (B. Wood & Walker-Smith, 1981).

Age to Begin Semisolid Food. The process of weaning actually begins with the introduction of semisolid food into the diet. **Semisolid food** commonly refers to the thin, strained food that is typically introduced as the baby's first nonmilk food. The age to begin giving an infant semisolid food has been the subject of debate and controversy through the years. Currently, there is wide agreement among health care professionals and nutritionists that the best time to introduce semisolid food is from 4 to 6 months of age. Various medical groups (Canadian Paediatric Society Nutrition Committee, 1979; Committee on Nutrition, 1998) have expressed concern about possible harmful effects of introducing significant amounts of semisolid food at 1 or 2 months of age. The practice of feeding infants any food other than breast or formula milk before 4 to 6 months of age is strongly discouraged because the nutritional values of solid foods are inferior to milk or formula in meeting specific needs of young infants. In addition, semisolid foods impose a higher eliminative load upon immature kidneys.

Nutritional experts generally recommend starting out with baby cereal, mixed with formula or breast milk (Satter, 2000). The order of introduction of other semisolid foods, including fruits, vegetables, and meats is not important. However, caregivers are advised to introduce one new single food ingredient at no less than weekly intervals so that specific food allergies can be identified as they occur. Juices should be given to the baby when the ability to drink from a cup has developed Fruit juice should be limited to less than 8 to 10 ounces per day, and should not be given in a bottle (Committee on Nutrition, 1998).

Feeding Older Infants and Toddlers. Minimum daily nutritional requirements for older infants and toddlers can be met with menus prepared from the basic food groups identified on the **Food Guide Pyramid for Young Children** 2 to 6 Years Old published by the United States Department of Agriculture (www.usda.gov/cnpp/KidsPyra/). Five major food groups are placed from the base to the top of the pyramid according to the number of servings (most to least) recommended. The pyramid recommendations begin at age 2, but the requirements for nutritional adequacy are the same for 1-year-olds as well. However, the portion sizes are smaller in keeping with the younger infant's needs and appetite (see Satter, 2000). The number of servings for each food group is:

Grain (bread, cereal, rice, and pasta) group: 6 servings
Fruit group: 2 servings
Vegetable group: 3 servings
Meat (poultry, fish, dry beans, eggs) group: 2 servings
Milk (and dairy products) group: 2 servings

Recommended portion sizes for children ages 1 to 3 years are 1 to 2 tablespoons for most foods (Satter, 2000).

An adequate supply of iron (as recommended by a health care specialist) should be included in the diet. Meats and iron-enriched cereal products are recommended sources of iron (Committee on Nutrition, 1998). Unless adequate fluoride is available in the water supply, an infant should be given fluoride supplements beginning at 6 months of age (Satter, 2000). However, the fluoride intake should be carefully monitored to avoid tooth pitting and discoloration. Fluoride supplements should be given at evening bedtime for maximum benefit (Committee on Nutrition, 1998). Additional mineral or vitamin supplements for infants should only be given when recommended by a health care provider.

Consequences of Malnutrition. Worldwide, malnutrition is one of the leading causes of illness and death in infancy (Barness & Curran, 1996). **Malnutrition** is a condition in which there is either a deficit or an excess of one or more essential nutrients needed by the body tissues (Santos, Arrendo, & Vitale, 1983). This condition can result from either insufficient or excessive nutrient intake, or inadequate absorption of food into the infant's system. There are various degrees of malnutrition, ranging from mild to severe.

Malnutrition is considered to be the most widespread and serious problem affecting infants and young children in the world (Santos et al., 1983). Nearly a third of the children under age 5 in underdeveloped nations are severely malnourished (United Nations Children's Fund, 1996). The effects are numerous and varied. Specific symptoms or conditions resulting from varying nutritional problems include growth delay or failure, rickets, anemia, dental caries, obesity, and lowered resistance to disease. Malnutrition also has serious behavioral consequences such as listlessness, withdrawal, and mental retardation. The ultimate outcome of malnutrition depends upon its timing, severity, and duration.

Iron-Deficiency Anemia. Iron deficiency is the most common specific nutritional deficiency usually encountered in infants and young children in the United States (Committee on Nutrition, 1998). An inadequate supply of iron in the diet can lead to iron-deficiency anemia. This condition involves an insufficiency in the number or size of blood cells which limits the ability of the blood to carry oxygen (Shelov, 1998). Premature infants, infants with growth delay, and infants of diabetic mothers are very susceptible to iron deficiency. Iron deficiency is most prevalent between 6 months and 3 years of age (Committee on

Nutrition, 1998). Iron deficiency anemia results in poor growth and lowered resistance to infection. Long term iron deficiency anemia may have detrimental effects on psychomotor and intellectual development (Filer, 1990; 1995; Holst, 1998). Symptoms of iron deficiency anemia include poor appetite, irritability, poor skin color, and listlessness.

Protein Energy Malnutrition. On a worldwide scale, **protein energy malnutrition (PEM)** is a major health problem (Avery & First, 1994). This condition results in growth retardation or failure and possibly mental disabilities (McLaren & Burman, 1982). Cases of PEM become evident between 4 months and 2 years of age, when infants from poverty backgrounds have been weaned from breast milk. The main features of mild to moderate PEM are growth retardation, lowered resistance to infectious diseases, and a diminished activity level. Growth retardation may be compounded by the higher incidence of infectious diseases that occurs in an infant subjected to PEM.

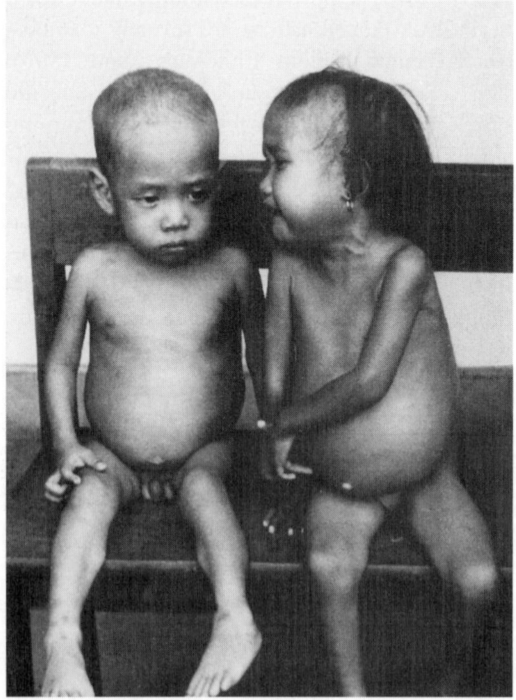

These children are suffering from kwashiorkor. Notice the swollen stomach, skinny arms, and loss of hair.

The most severe forms of malnutrition include the conditions known as kwashiorkor and marasmus. **Kwashiorkor** is caused primarily by insufficient protein in the diet and usually occurs in the second, third, or fourth year of life (Wood & Walker-Smith, 1981). The child who suffers from kwashiorkor has a swollen appearance (edema) but has little muscular tissue under the skin. Skin ulcers, loss of hair, irritability or lethargy, weakness, and growth failure are other characteristics of the condition. **Marasmus** is caused by insufficient food intake (starvation) in general, but a deficiency of calories in particular. It typically appears in the early months of life. The marasmic child has lost most of the subcutaneous fat and appears to be mostly skin and bones. The condition may include chronic diarrhea, vomiting, irritability, or apathy (McLaren & Burman, 1982). Marasmus is more frequent in children under 1 year of age and kwashiorkor is found more frequently among children 1 to 6 years of age (Monckeberg, 1991). Either condition leads to death if left untreated. These diseases are rarely found in the United States.

Malnutrition and Brain Growth. The effects of malnutrition on brain growth and mental functioning have been the subject of speculation and intensive investigation. Evidence is accumulating to show that severe early malnutrition is likely to alter the structure and function of the brain. Both animal and human studies have found that early malnutrition of the marasmus type reduces the number of brain cells, brain size, and head circumference. In addition, myelination, structural organization, and biochemical composition of the brain may be adversely affected (Winick, 1979). However, the timing of the nutritional deficit is critical and the starvation must be severe. The periods of growth when the brain is most vulnerable to damage coincide with times "when the brain is increasing its weight particularly rapidly" (Dobbing & Smart, 1974, p. 164).

APPLICATIONS: SUGGESTIONS FOR FEEDING INFANTS

Unfortunately, feeding infants is not an exact science and the advice given to parents is often contradictory and controversial. Parents should make decisions about feeding practices only after obtaining current information from their pediatrician and other professional sources. The following are some examples of generally recommended feeding practices for each feeding stage (Hinton & Kerwin, 1981; Satter, 1990, 2000):

Nursing Infants.

- Breast-feed the baby for the first 6 months of life if possible.
- Engage in eye contact and cuddle the infant during feeding sessions. Talk and smile but not constantly. Look for and respond to infant cues.
- Hold the baby securely but allow freedom to move. Avoid using bottle props to replace a caretaker's lap.
- Allow infants to decide how much to eat as well as the feeding tempo. Allow the baby to pause and return to eating as desired. Discontinue feeding when the infant loses interest in feeding. Avoid giving infants breast or bottle to stop their crying that results from needs other than hunger.
- To avoid bottle-mouth syndrome (see Chapter 4), do not allow an infant to go to sleep with a bottle containing anything but water after teeth begin to appear. Sweetened liquids should not be given in a bottle.
- Avoid giving an infant honey in any form because of the risk of botulism.

Older Infants.

- Let the child take the lead. Allow the child to touch the food and finger-feed.
- Do not give cereal or other foods mixed with milk in a bottle.
- Make the first solid food thin and smooth. Use a small spoon to place the food on the middle of the tongue, but do not exert pressure. Give very small amounts of any new food at the beginning.
- Introduce new foods one at a time at one- or two-week intervals and watch for allergic reactions. Do not mix foods until each has been introduced separately.
- Allow all infants to have food preferences. Offer infants a variety of foods over time.
- Do not add salt or sugar to an infant's food. Foods containing refined sugar should be limited.

Toddlers.

- Serve food at lukewarm temperature in bite-size pieces and small portions. Provide child-size utensils and comfortable seating. Provide soft finger foods, with no choking hazards, for self-feeding.
- Encourage self-feeding as soon as the infant can hold a spoon, manage a cup, or use other culturally appropriate utensils. Be tolerant of spills and messiness.
- Establish mealtimes and feeding routines.
- Provide meals in a pleasant, relaxed atmosphere. Keep mealtime conversation happy and pleasant. Allow for a rest period before meals when possible.
- Avoid rigid rules about the amount of food to be eaten. Do not force toddlers to eat by coaxing or by offering treats or bribes.
- Give toddlers between-meal snacks; toddlers need more frequent feedings than adults. Snacks should consist of small amounts of nutritious, low-sugar foods and should be carefully spaced, usually midway between meals.
- Children over 2 years of age may begin following adult guidelines, which limit dietary fat to no more than 30 percent of total calories.

SUMMARY

Immunity During Infancy

- Newborn infants usually have some temporary resistance but become especially vulnerable to infections between 6 months and 2 years of age.

Immunization Against Communicable Diseases

- Infants should receive a complete series of immunizations at the recommended ages for hepatitis B, diphtheria, tetanus, pertussis, polio, *Haemophilus influenzae* type b, measles, mumps, rubella, hepatitis A, chickenpox, and *Streptococcus pneumoniae*.
- The polio and pertussis vaccines have been controversial because of concerns about the risk of severe adverse reactions. However, the benefits of all immunizations far outweigh any risks involved.

Symptoms of Illness in Infants

- Of the common symptoms of illness in infants, parents are usually most concerned about fever, vomiting, and diarrhea.

Common Illnesses and Health Concerns

- Common illnesses and health problems of infancy include colds and respiratory infections, ear infections, and colic.
- AIDS is a relatively new and deadly disease that results from the human immunodeficiency virus (HIV).
- The leading cause of death among infants between 1 month and 1 year of age is a mysterious condition called sudden infant death syndrome (SIDS). Recommendations for preventing SIDS include placing infants on their back for sleeping and avoiding exposure to tobacco smoke.

Child Maltreatment

- Each year thousands of infants are victims of neglect, physical or emotional abuse, and sexual abuse.
- Child neglect is the most frequent form of child maltreatment. Children under the age of 2 are especially vulnerable to nonorganic failure to thrive (NOFTT).
- The most common form of physical abuse suffered by infants under 1 year is shaken impact syndrome.

Infant Safety

- Each year many infants are seriously injured or killed by a variety of unintentional injuries. The first year of life is the most dangerous.
- The leading causes of unintentional injury deaths during infancy are motor vehicle collisions, drowning, fires and burns, choking on ingested food or objects, falls, poisoning, and firearms.
- Parents and infant caregivers should take careful steps to prevent injuries by babyproofing the environment and selecting toys that are free of safety hazards.

Meeting Nutritional Needs

- For healthy growth and development, infants need a diet that provides a daily balance of fats, carbohydrates, protein, vitamins, minerals, and water.
- Nutritional experts and health care specialists recommend that mothers breast-feed their newborn infants for six months if possible.
- Generally, professionals recommend feeding infants on demand rather than on a predetermined schedule.
- Recommendations on the age for weaning infants vary widely. In the United States, most infants are likely to be weaned by the end of the first year of life. However, weaning practices vary widely from culture to culture.
- The recommended age for the introduction of semisolid food into the diet of an infant is from 4 to 6 months.
- After 1 year of age an infant's basic nutritional needs can be met with menus planned from the basic food groups identified on the Food Guide Pyramid for Young Children.
- The most common nutritional problem of infants in the United States is iron deficiency anemia.
- Protein energy malnutrition (PEM) is a common nutritional problem among infants throughout the world. The physical effects of PEM include retardation of physical growth, lowered resistance to infectious diseases, and diminished activity level. Kwashiorkor and marasmus are severe forms of malnutrition rarely found in the United States.
- Severe early malnutrition is likely to alter the structure and function of the brain.

KEY TERMS

polio
pertussis (whooping cough)
varicella (chickenpox)
Hemophilus influenza type b (Hib)
hepatitis
Streptococcus pneumoniae (pneumococcus)
diarrhea
otitis media
otitis media with effusion
colic
acquired immune deficiency syndrome (AIDS)
sudden infant death syndrome (SIDS)
Back to Sleep campaign
child neglect
nonorganic failure to thrive (NOFTT)
physical abuse
shaken infant syndrome
shaken impact syndrome
accident
unintentional injury
injury control
babyproof the environment
nutrition
weaning
semisolid food
Food Guide Pyramid for Young Children
malnutrition
iron deficiency anemia
protein energy malnutrition (PEM)
kwashiorkor
marasmus

*INFORMATION ON THE WEB

kidshealth.org/parent/general/sleep/sids.html This site is operated by the Nemours Foundation and provides information on general health, medical problems, first aid and safety, nutrition, and other topics of interest to parents.

www.nlm.nih.gov/medlineplus/suddeninfantdeathsyndrome.html Information from the National Institutes of Health on a variety of topics related to SIDS, including the Back to Sleep campaign, can be obtained from this site. There are also links to SIDS support organizations and the Medline Plus National Library providing access to a medical encyclopedia and dictionary.

www.cincinnatichildrens.org/Health_Topics This site, sponsored by the Cincinnati Children's Hospital, provides infant safety tips plus information on a variety of other topics relating to children's health.

www.usda.gov/cnpp/KidsPyra/ The Food Guide Pyramid for Young Children can be downloaded from this site along with a publication on *Tips for Using the FGP for Young Children.*

*Web sites are subject to change.

SIX

MOTOR DEVELOPMENT

The loving mother teaches her child to walk alone. She is far enough from him so that she cannot actually support him, but she holds out her arms to him. She imitates his movements, and if he totters, she swiftly bends as if to seize, so that the child might believe that he is not walking alone. . . . And yet, she does more. Her face beckons like a reward, an encouragement. Thus, the child walks alone with his eyes fixed on his mother's face, not on the difficulties in his way. He supports himself by the arms that do not hold him and constantly strives towards the refuge in his mother's embrace, little suspecting that in the very same moment that he is emphasizing his need of her, he is proving that he can do without her, because he is walking alone.

—Søren Kierkegaard

Cradling a newborn in your arms is like "holding a three-pound bag of loose corn; the baby has about as much motor control as the sack of kernels" (Wingert & Underwood, 1997, p. 14). But, as soon as an infant is born, or perhaps even before, the struggle to establish control over the body begins. The changes that occur in the infant's ability to control the movement of the muscles of the body are referred to as motor development. During the first three years of life, the child progresses from a relatively helpless infant state of uncontrolled motor activity to a state of independence and mobility. The development of basic motor skills during infancy forms the foundation for the more elaborate and refined motor acts of later childhood.

The numerous motor behaviors that emerge during the infancy period will be considered in the following major categories: (1) reflex activities, (2) fine motor skills, (3) gross motor movements, and (4) self-care activities. Reflexes are motor responses that an infant is equipped with at birth. The development of fine motor skills involves use of the small muscles of the body that control the use of eyes, fingers, and hands. Gross motor activities involve the large muscle groups such as the ones used in body movements. Self-care activities include both fine and gross motor movements that are needed to meet one's personal needs such as eating, dressing, and toileting. This chapter focuses on the characteristic patterns and processes of motor development in each of these categories. However, the classification of motor skills into distinct categories such as fine motor and gross motor actions is somewhat arbitrary and simplistic. You should keep in mind that most motor actions are dependent upon the functioning of mutually interdependent muscles groups and other body systems. For example, the ability to pick up an object depends upon the joint coordination of the muscles in the shoulder, arm, and elbow with the small muscles in the hand and fingers.

Before we discuss the specific motor skills that emerge during infancy, we need to consider how motor development is interrelated with other areas of infant development, the factors that influence the acquisition of motor skills, and some general trends in motor development.

INTERRELATIONSHIPS OF DEVELOPMENTAL AREAS

The development of motor skills is a complicated process involving coordination between the nervous system, the skeleton, muscles, and sensory mechanisms. Consequently, motor development influences and is influenced by other components of the growing infant. During infancy an important indicator of mental functioning is the ability to carry out motor acts. At the same time, the acquisition of motor skills allows the infant to move and explore the environment in order to satisfy curiosity and obtain knowledge. In Piaget's (1952) view, the sensorimotor activities of infancy provide the foundations of intelligence (see Chapter 8).

Held and Hein's (1963) classic study of kittens showed that self-produced movement (e.g., creeping, walking, reaching) is important for perceptual development. More recent evidence from a variety of studies with human infants shows that dramatic changes in perceptual-cognitive, social, and emotional changes occur when infants begin to move around on their own (Bertenthal, Campos, & Bennett, 1984). Self-produced locomotion promotes the development of perceptual abilities, spatial orientation, fear of heights, and the ability to remember where hidden objects are located (see Chapter 8). It also facilitates concept formation and the differentiation of emotions (Bertenthal & Campos, 1987, 1990).

The development of an infant's body awareness and self-image are also derived to some extent from information obtained through sensorimotor activities. As infants use their bodies and experience success or failure in motor acts, they form self-opinions that are closely interrelated with overall personality development. The establishment of physical independence through motor control leads to feelings of self-confidence, psychological security, and independence. On the other hand, feelings of dependency and inadequacy tend to inhibit the acquisition of motor control.

FACTORS INFLUENCING MOTOR CONTOL

Maturation Versus Learning. As in other areas of development, scientists debate the relative contributions of maturation and learning to motor development. Several classic research studies have been used to support the view that motor development is largely controlled by the process of maturation. For example, Gesell and Thompson (1934) gave one identical twin six weeks of practice in a variety of motor tasks, while they gave the other twin no opportunity for practice. Within a three-week period after the training ended, the twin who had not been given special instruction made more progress than the twin who had been trained. These researchers concluded that practice does not make any difference until a child is biologically ready to acquire a particular motor skill.

Myrtle McGraw (1935) conducted another classic study on the long-term effects of early practice on the acquisition of motor skills by a set of twins called "Johnny and Jimmy." At appropriate ages, Johnny was given intensive training in sitting, crawling, climbing, and other activities. After Johnny mastered each skill, Jimmy was also given the same training exercises. Jimmy quickly caught up with Johnny. McGraw concluded that the training had not been effective. The results have been interpreted to support the maturational theory.

Further support for the importance of maturational influences on motor development is cited by Casaer (1992). Infants who remained in a cast between 5 and 12 months of age began to walk soon after the cast was removed. After a few days there was no difference in their walking ability as compared to children who started earlier. Another classic study, by Dennis (1941), reached a similar conclusion. Hopi Indian infants who were tied to a cradleboard on their mother's backs for much of the first nine months of life were compared to a group of infants from Western culture who were allowed relatively unrestricted movement. Since both groups of infants began to walk at about the same age, Dennis concluded that walking must be maturationally determined.

On the other side of the question, Bower (1977b), a Scottish psychologist, believes that opportunities for learning "have a great deal to do with the rate and direction of motor development" (p. 91). In one of Bower's experiments, babies were given practice in reaching for a dangling object. These babies obtained a more mature pattern of reaching and grasping several weeks earlier than a control group of infants who had no comparable experience. Learning experiences were thus considered to have been influential in the acquisition of these particular skills.

Results of cross-cultural research (discussed later) are also cited to support the view that childrearing practices can influence the acquisition of motor skills. Currently, scientific opinion tends to support the view that both maturation and experience are important. Thelen (1995) believes that

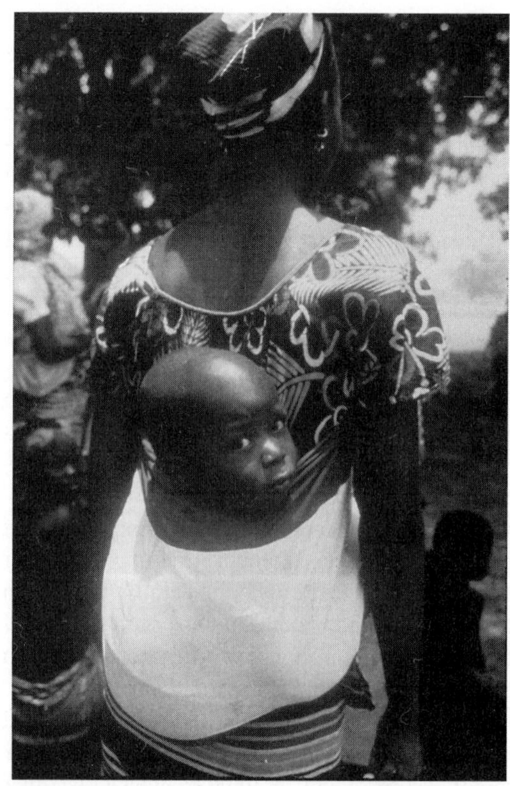

In some cultures, infants are carried on the mother's back for several months.

more recent theory and research on motor development have silenced the nature-nurture debates.

Dynamic Systems Approach. Esther Thelen and her associates explain the development of motor skills in terms of a **dynamic systems approach** (Thelen & Fogel, 1989; Thelen & Smith, 1998). This perspective represents a compromise between extreme maturation and learning points of view. Multiple factors and processes contribute to the acquisition of motor skills. The human body is composed of biological systems. The sensory, skeletal, muscular, and motor systems are examples of some major components. In order for the infant to accomplish the tasks involved in walking and other motor skills, the body systems must work together. These body systems develop within a cultural context and are influenced by social systems such as mother-infant dyads. Emphasis is placed upon ways in which these biological and social systems cooperate and interact in the process of acquiring motor skills. Motor development thus develops as a "continual dialogue between the nervous system, body, and environment" (Thelen & Spencer, 1998, p. 507). The term *dynamic* reflects the concept that changes involving growth and skill acquisition in one area or system will have an impact on performance in another.

An increasing number of researchers are using dynamic systems as a theoretical framework for conducting studies on motor development. Researchers are less concerned about the milestones of motor development and more concerned with the underlying explanations of how motor skills are acquired (Thelen, 1995). For example, researchers have used a "moving room" situation to study how the development of postural control of infants is affected by information obtained from the visual and vestibular (balance) sensory systems (Bertenthal & Campos, 1990). Infants sit or stand on a platform inside a room constructed with hanging walls that swing back and forth while the floor remains stationary. When the walls move forward, observers determine if the infants are tricked into the false perception that they have swayed backward and react by swaying forward to maintain balance rather than falling down.

The results of moving-room studies show that 3-day-old infants integrate visual information with postural responses by moving their heads in the opposite direction of the moving wall (Woollacott, 1992). By 7 to 9 months of age infants make appropriate adjustments in posture to compensate for the perceptions of the wall movements. According to Bertenthal and Campos (1990), this is a significant development because it means that infants are capable of monitoring their motor movements through both visual and vestibular information at about the time they start creeping.

Researchers have found that there are plateaus and regressions throughout infancy in the ability to use visual and vestibular information in maintaining balance. For example, after the onset of creeping there is a decline in the infant's ability to effectively use visual information from the moving wall to maintain balance. However, this ability returns again about the time the infant learns to stand (Woollacott, 1992). The changes in sensitivity to visual information in maintaining posture control and balance are not easy to explain. They may be the result of changes in the nervous system that occur during transition periods after infants accomplish one task and get ready for another (Haywood, 1993; Woollacott, 1992).

Body Size. The sizes of the various parts of the body affect its resistance to movement (Newell, 1984). Body size and proportions are apparently related to the age at which some of the motor milestones are achieved. The relationships are not simple, however, and are most clearly observed in infants who represent extreme differences in body measurements (Malina, 1973). For example, slender infants with relatively long legs walk earlier than shorter infants with shorter legs (Bayley, 1935; Shirley, 1931). Garn (1966) found that leaner infants attained better scores on a variety of early motor tasks than heavier infants.

Muscle Strength and Tone. The development of the ability to control body movements and postures is affected by muscle strength and muscle tone. **Muscle strength** involves the amount of force that the muscles in a particular body part can exert while pushing or pulling against resistance. Muscle strength is affected by a number of factors including exercise, body chemistry, nervous system activity, skeletal size, and the amount and properties of muscle tissue (Fetters, 1996). In general, muscle strength improves as fibers increase in size and overall mass throughout the infancy period (Malina & Bouchard, 1991). Muscle strength also improves as infants increase activity and mobility.

Muscle tone refers to the amount of tension in the muscles when the body is in a state of rest (P. Smith, 1989). Muscle tone provides the foundation for the control of body posture, balance, stability, and voluntary movements. Muscle tone is controlled by the central nervous system. Underlying muscle tone is usually viewed in terms of a continuum ranging from **hypotonia** (decreased tone) at one end to **hypertonia** (increased tone) at the other end (Fetters, 1996). Normal muscle tone is dynamic and fluctuates according to movement requirements. Muscle tone that is too limp (hypotonic) or too rigid (hypertonic) interferes with the control of motor activity. Muscle tone quality generally improves with the maturation of the nervous system during the infancy period. Infants with neurological impairments may have motor problems due to atypical muscle tone or strength.

Cultural and Ethnic Influences. Cross-cultural studies consistently show that traditionally reared infants from underdeveloped countries are more accelerated in motor performance than infants from Western culture (Werner, 1979). Their advanced motor development has been attributed to such child-rearing practices as frequent sensorimotor stimulation, participation in adult activities, exposure to multiple caregivers from extended families, and freedom from restrictive clothing and playpens. For example, West Indian mothers use a series of stretching exercises and massage routines from about the second or third months to stimulate active movements (Hopkins & Westra, 1988). At the end of bathing, usually when the baby is wet, the baby is suspended by both arms and gently shaken up and down. Next the mother holds the baby up by one arm and then the other, and then holds the baby upside down by the ankles. The mother also grasps the baby's head on both sides while pulling upwards to stretch the baby's neck. Infants are also propped with cushions that are gradually removed for independent sitting. Later in the year, the baby is held and stimulated to walk up the mother's body, and eventually encouraged to take steps on the floor while being held by the arms in a standing position. Researchers found these infants to be superior in head control, sitting alone, and standing up when held, in comparison to infants who do not receive this type of stimulation (Hopkins & Westra, 1988). On the other hand, infants reared in cultures where they are restricted by heavy clothing and where interactions with caretakers are quiet and passive tend to lag behind in motor activities. Differences in motor development that result primarily from cultural influences, however, tend to disappear by the end of the infancy period.

Research studies comparing infants from different racial and ethnic groups in the United States on motor performance are rather limited. There is some evidence that African American infants demonstrate precocity in motor development (King & Seegmiller, 1973). Studies tend to show that, on average, African American infants reach the motor milestones identified in the Bayley Motor Scales at a younger age than Caucasian American infants (Bayley, 1965; Capute et al., 1985; Haywood, 1993). However, socioeconomic differences and other environmental conditions may account for the differences since those factors have not been well controlled in existing studies. Comparisons of motor development among preschool-age African American and Caucasian American children have found no conclusive differences (Haywood, 1993).

Nutrition. Nutrition may affect motor development in two ways. First, inadequate nutritional intake may cause damage to the nervous system, resulting in impairment of intersensory functioning. The child may thus have problems in processing and efficiently utilizing sensations, perceptions, memory, and attention in acquiring motor skills. Second, nutrition affects strength and energy level.

Undernourished infants are apathetic and lack sufficient physical vigor and endurance to pursue motor activities (Smoll, 1982).

The relationship of nutrition to motor development is dramatically illustrated by cross-cultural studies of infants from poverty-stricken environments where breast-feeding is heavily utilized. During the first six months of life, infants from these cultures compare very favorably with infants from more economically advantaged environments. However, during the second half of the first year, when breast milk alone becomes insufficient to meet nutritional needs, there is a steady decline in the psychomotor performance of these infants. Motor development begins to decline even earlier if the period of breast-feeding is shorter (Werner, 1979).

Sleep Position. The position in which an infant sleeps apparently affects the age at which some of the motor milestones are achieved. Traditional norms of motor development were developed in the United States when most infants slept on their stomach (prone). The Back to Sleep campaign designed to lower the risk of sudden infant death syndrome has resulted in a dramatic increase in the percentage of infants who sleep on their back (supine) in the United States. Researchers have recently found that infants who sleep in the supine position roll over, sit up, creep and crawl, or pull to a standing position later than infants who sleep prone (B. Davis et al., 1998; C. Dewey et al., 1998). However, parents need not be concerned about differences between back-sleepers and stomach-sleepers in the achievement of motor milestones. Infants who sleep on their back still attain the motor milestones within the accepted normal range. The American Academy of Pediatrics (1996) recommends that infants be placed in the prone position when they are awake and observed, but that parents continue to position infants on their back when they are sleeping.

DEVELOPMENTAL TRENDS

Motor Biases. Infants demonstrate **motor biases** or preferences in motor activities. They generally prefer to work on developing the newest body movements they have learned. Levin (1983) points out that babies tend to give themselves homework assignments such as "work on crawling," or "practice standing now." For example, once infants discover that the hand can be used to touch an object, they practice over and over until they have achieved and refined their ability to reach, touch, and pick up an object. Fourteen-month-old Kristin tried to make a lid fit on a small plastic bottle. She had formed the idea that caps go on bottles if you twist them. However, she could not quite get the threads on the cap to fit the threads on the bottle. She would twist and turn until she became frustrated. Then she would throw the pieces away in anger. She returned to the same task over and over until she had mastered the skill.

Infants can be observed engaging in repetitive movements such as rocking on hands and knees, head banging, kicking, and scratching. Such a pattern of movements is sometimes referred to as a **rhythmical stereotypy** (Thelen, 1981). Infants tend to use stereotypies as a means of preparing for later, more coordinated movements. Thelen (1981) believes that infants are programmed at birth to engage in rhythmic movements. These activities are viewed as normal responses that facilitate future motor development.

General to Specific. The **general to specific** trend refers to the fact that control over general movements of the body develop before specific body movements are mastered. In the newborn, the legs and arms usually move at the same time. As the baby grows, the capacity to make specific movements with individual body parts increases. An infant can eventually move the arms without moving the legs, then one arm without the other, and finally one finger at a time. For example, if a newborn's foot is touched with an ice cube, the whole body moves in a generalized response. An older infant responds to the ice cube by withdrawing the specific foot that has been touched.

Hierarchical Integration. The simplest and most elementary skills develop first and become more complex as they are combined to form more elaborate movements in a process called **hierarchical integration.** An infant who grasps a raisin between the thumb and index finger and places it in a bottle is integrating four basic skills—reaching, grasping, placing, and releasing—to complete a more difficult pattern of activity.

Developmental Direction. Motor development generally follows the laws of developmental direction. According to the **cephalocaudal principle,** the infant obtains control of the arms before the legs. Reaching develops before walking. Following the **proximodistal principle,** control of the arms is established before control over the wrist and fingers is obtained. In the hand, control over the index finger develops first, followed by control over the third, fourth, and fifth fingers in that order (Tanner, 1990). While the laws of developmental direction are generally true, there are exceptions, according to Cratty (1979), particularly in the proximodistal principle. In his estimation, the laws of developmental direction need further refinement.

REFLEXES

The first movements newborn infants exhibit consist mostly of reflex activities. A **reflex** is an automatic or involuntary response to a specific stimulus. The reflexes are controlled by the lower brain stem and spinal cord. As the upper part of the brain matures, the reflexes are mostly replaced with voluntary movements. The newborn infant is equipped with a variety of primitive reflexes (Illingworth, 1991). Some of the reflexes, such as sucking, have obvious survival value. However, the importance of many of the reflexes is not clear. In general, the reflexes are considered to be indicators of the maturity and intactness of the nervous system. Several reflexes can be easily observed in young infants. If a reflex fails to appear or disappear at the appropriate age, some type of neurological problem may exist. A few of the key reflexes are described here.

Rooting and Sucking. Newborn infants are equipped with rooting and sucking responses that allow them to obtain nourishment. Touching a newborn infant in the corner of the mouth will trigger a **rooting reflex** in which the head is turned in the direction of the stimulus in search of something to suck, preferably a breast or a bottle containing milk. In concert with the rooting reflex, the **sucking reflex** occurs as soon as a finger or a nipple touches the newborn's mouth. The rooting reflex begins to disappear by 3 months of age. The sucking reflex is gradually replaced by voluntary sucking.

Grasp. The **palmar grasp reflex** is easily elicited by placing a finger or small object in the palm of the baby's hand. The grasp may be so tight and strong that the baby's weight can be supported for an instant. The palmar grasp becomes weaker after the first month and is replaced by voluntary grasping by 3 or 4 months of age.

Moro. The **Moro reflex** is a response to a loud noise or sudden loss of support. It may be elicited by holding an infant with one hand supporting the head and the other behind the back. The hand supporting the head is lowered abruptly, allowing the infant's head to fall an inch or two. The baby responds by quickly stretching the arms outward and bringing them together in a hugging motion. The back is arched and the hands curl slightly, while the knees are drawn toward the stomach. The Moro, sometimes called the embracing reflex, is typically present at birth and begins to disappear around 3 months of age. It cannot be observed in most infants after 4 or 5 months of age. The Moro is one of the most widely used reflexes in the neurological examination of infants (Bench et al., 1972).

Babinski. If a finger or a pencil is rubbed along the inner side of the young infant's foot from heel to toe, the big toe will move upward while the other toes fan inward toward the bottom of the foot. This is the **Babinski reflex,** which develops just before birth in full-term infants and typically disappears between 12 and 16 months of age.

Tonic Neck. The **tonic neck reflex,** in which one side of the body is dominant, can be elicited by

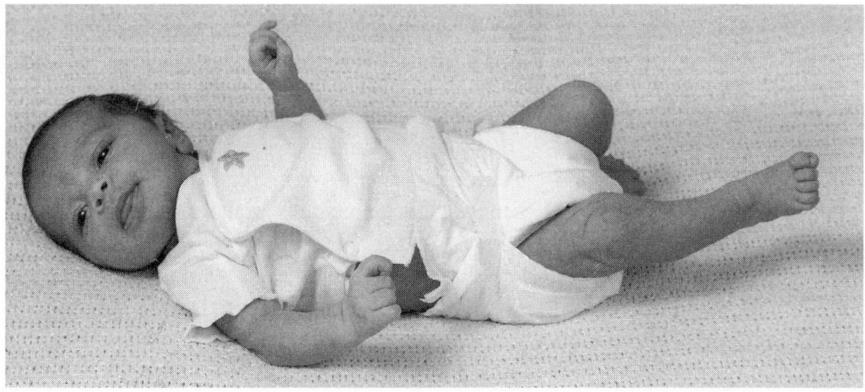

The tonic neck reflex position.

placing an infant on its back and turning the baby's head to one side. One arm and leg are extended in the direction in which the head is facing. The other arm is bent at the elbow with the hand placed near the head. This is similar to a fencing position. The tonic neck is most commonly observed during the first two or three months of life. It usually fades out by the fourth to sixth month.

Stepping. Infants typically exhibit a walking or **stepping reflex** at birth or soon afterward. When held upright with bare feet touching a flat surface, an infant will take rhythmic steps forward. The stepping reflex usually disappears by 5 months of age. However, Thelen and her colleagues (Thelen, 1995; Thelen, Fisher, & Ridley-Johnson, 1984) believe that the stepping reflex cannot be elicited after 5 months because the infant's legs have grown too heavy to lift. She found that infants who gained weight most rapidly between 2 and 6 weeks of age made the fewest reflex stepping movements during that time period (Thelen, Ulrich, & Jensen, 1989). Additional experiments were conducted in which 4-week-old infants were partially submerged in water to reduce the effects of leg weight (Thelen, Ulrich, & Jensen, 1989). The results revealed that stepping movements increased in rate and speed.

Influence of Reflexes on Voluntary Movement. The extent to which reflexes facilitate or interfere with voluntary movement is a major question in infant motor development. From one point of view, reflexes form the basis for later voluntary motor activities (Newell, 1984). Reflexes are considered to be responses that an infant may incorporate efficiently into the process of establishing voluntary motor skills. In support of this position, researchers have found that exercise of the stepping reflex during the first nine weeks of life can lead to an earlier beginning of voluntary walking (Zelazo, Zelazo, & Kolb, 1972). Similar effects of reflex exercise have been found for crawling (Lagerspetz, Nygard, & Strandwick, 1971) and grasping (Bower, 1977a).

On the other hand, reflexes are sometimes viewed as behaviors that inhibit the onset of voluntary movements (Newell, 1984). According to this position, a reflex response must disappear before a related voluntary motor movement can be established. For example, the plantar reflex must disappear in the feet before an infant can stand and walk. Otherwise the bottoms of the feet tend to curl up and fail to provide a firm foundation for walking. In children with cerebral palsy some primitive reflexes tend to continue longer and often last into adult life (Pellegrino, 1997).

The relationship between the establishment of voluntary motor skills and reflex activities is obviously a complex issue. Both points of view have some validity. Apparently some of the reflexes evolve into voluntary motor responses, and with practice, facilitate their early onset. At the same time, other reflexes stand in the way of emergence and development of some motor skills. From a dynamic systems perspective, reflexive activities are viewed as interacting with other body systems in the emergence of motor skills.

FINE MOTOR DEVELOPMENT

Eye-Hand Coordination. The development of the ability to locate, grasp, and manipulate objects is a major task in motor development. This very complex task requires the voluntary coordination of eye, arm, hand, and finger movements. There are two major stages in the development of eye-hand coordination, which include a variety of changes during the infancy period.

Stage 1: Prereaching. Some scientists (Cratty, 1979; Trevarthen, 1978; Williams, 1983) believe that infants are equipped at birth with an underlying "motor prewiring" through which vision and kinesthetic sensations (from movement of muscles and joints) work together to produce reaching and grasping movements. Newborn infants apparently reach for or swat at objects in their visual field (Bower, Broughton, & Moore, 1970; Von Hofsten, 1982). Moving objects are more likely to elicit arm movements than stationary objects. Such movements, however, are referred to as **prereaching,** in contrast to later reaching (Bushnell, 1985; Von Hofsten, 1984).

Researchers have identified several characteristic features of prereaching activities. During this stage, infants are rarely successful in touching, not to mention grasping, the target object. They do not shape the hand to correspond with the object properties. They move their arms very rapidly, withdrawing the hand immediately without making corrective adjustments in the trajectory or path of the hand (Bower, 1982; Bushnell, 1985). Prereaching infants do not appear to look at both the reaching hand and the target object in their reaching attempts. Rather, the eye-hand coordination of newborn and very young infants seems to be based on a primitive combination of kinesthetic and visual responses.

Prereaching movements are visually elicited rather than visually guided (Bushnell, 1985). That is, an infant sees an object and reaches out for it automatically as part of the same response pattern. The reaching response is apparently triggered by the sense of vision rather than the thought of obtaining and manipulating the object. The main function of prereaching behavior is thus considered to be attentional rather than intentional (Von Hofsten, 1982).

The quantity and quality of prereaching activities change with age. Major changes become evident by 7 weeks of age (Von Hofsten, 1984). The amount of reaching activity declines while the intensity of staring increases. A baby seems to grasp an object with the eyes, mentally dropping it and picking it up again (Williams, 1983). Around this age, infants have a tendency to spend a lot of time looking at their hands. Apparently the increased visual attention inhibits and alters reaching behavior. Burton White (1975) believes that the visual discovery of the hands around 6 or 7 weeks is a major milestone in infant development.

When the 7-week-old infant occasionally reaches for an object, the form is different from neonatal reaching. The hand is held with the fist closed during reaching rather than remaining open as it was earlier. As the infant gets older, the amount of reaching activity goes up again, and the hand opens as it reaches an object. The changes that occur in reaching activities have been attributed to reorganization of the systems of the brain as the baby matures and moves from reflexive to voluntary responses (Von Hofsten, 1984).

Stage 2: Visually Directed Reaching. The infant begins to acquire the ability to engage in **visually directed reaching** sometime between 3 and 5 months (Bushnell, 1985). During this stage the regulation of grasping/manipulative responses is intensified through visual activity (Williams, 1983). Vision is involved in determining both the position of the target and the position of the hand (Von Hofsten, 1992). The infant first locates an object with the eyes and attempts to pick it up. Frequently, the baby loses sight of the object and fails as in earlier eye-hand coordination efforts.

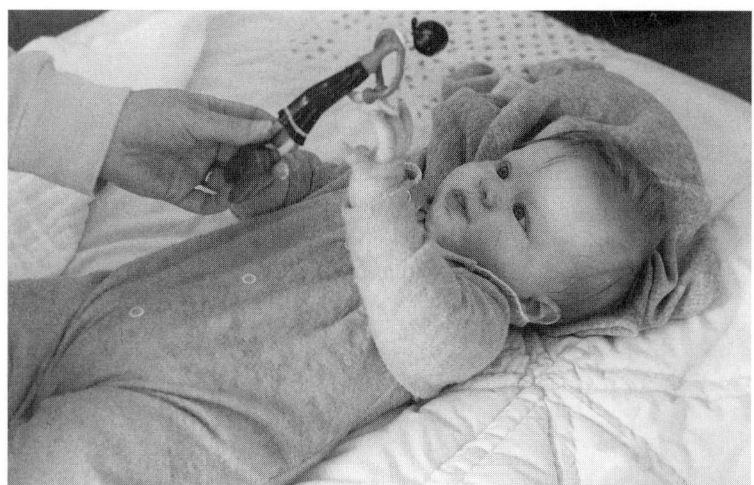

This baby is engaged in visually directed reaching.

However, when this happens, the baby intensifies visual fixation and adjusts the reaching movements, keeping the hand and object in view until the goal is obtained.

There are indications from research studies that the infant must establish control over the head and torso of the body before efficient reaching is established. Thelen and Spencer (1998) have concluded on the basis of their research and studies of others that infants cannot hold their arms steady or keep a steady view of a target object if the head is wobbly. In addition, postural control must be established for the infant to have a stable base from which to reach.

As the infant learns to hold the head and torso steady, visually directed reaching becomes smoother and more successful over time. Toward the end of the first year, infants are very accurate in reaching so that targeted objects are obtained with few, if any, corrections in hand trajectories. In order to pick up and manipulate large objects, infants need to use both hands in coordinated movements. At around 7 months of age infants reach for an object with one hand or both hands simultaneously, depending on the size, weight, and shape of the object (Fagard, 1990). They begin to coordinate the movements of both arms independently and use both hands cooperatively in reaching for and grasping objects around 8 months of age (Haywood, 1993).

Prehension. After the grasp reflex disappears at approximately 4 months of age, the infant begins to work on **prehension**—grasping an object between fingers and thumb. Halverson (1931) identified 10 stages that occur between 26 and 52 weeks of age in the acquisition of adultlike grasping skills (see Table 6-1 and Figure 6-1). In the early stages, the infant uses only the fingers and the palm in picking up an object, such as a small cube. Initially an infant rakes at a tiny object, such as a pellet, without picking it up. As soon as the ability to use the thumb (finger-thumb opposition) is acquired at approximately 9 months, grasping skills develop faster. By approximately 1 year of age, an infant can pick up cubes and pellets in an adultlike fashion, with a thumb and forefinger pincer grasp.

Object Manipulation. Once infants develop the ability to grasp and pick up objects, they spend a large amount of time engaging in manipulative activities. The way in which an infant interacts with an object varies according to age. Uzgiris (1967) observed how infants between the ages of 2 and 24 months manipulate a variety of objects

Table 6-1 Milestones of Fine Motor Development

MOTOR ACTIVITY	AVERAGE AGE (MONTHS)	MOTOR ACTIVITY	AVERAGE AGE (MONTHS)
Prehension of cubes		Prehension of pellets	
Reaches—no contact	4	Rakes with whole hand	5.5
Reaches—makes contact	5	Inferior scissor grasp	7.4
Primitive squeeze	5	Scissors grasp	8.2
Squeeze grasp	6	Inferior pincer grasp	9.2
Hand grasp	7	Neat pincer grasp	11
Palm grasp	7	Inserts pellet in bottle	12
Superior palm grasp	8	Other	
Inferior forefinger grasp	9	Turns pages, two or three	
Forefinger grasp	12	at one time	18
Superior forefinger grasp	12	Inserts shoelace through	
Voluntary release of cube	11	safety pin	24
Builds tower of four cubes	18	Turns single page	30
Builds tower of seven cubes	24	Tries to cut with scissors	36
Aligns train of four cubes	24		
Builds tower of ten cubes	36		

Sources: H. Halverson (1931). "An Experimental Study of the Prehension in Infants by Means of Systematic Cinema Records," *Genetic Psychology Monographs, 10,* 107–286. Reprinted with permission of the Helen Dwight Reid Foundation. Published by Heldref Publications, 4000 Albermarle St., NW, Washington, DC 20016. Copyright © 1931; H. Knobloch, F. Stevens, & A. Malone (1980). *Manual of Developmental Diagnosis.* New York: Harper & Row. Used by permission.

including a rattle, a small doll, and a piece of aluminum foil. The earliest infant interactions with objects were characterized by holding, mouthing, and visual inspection. As they grew older (4 to 10 months), infants acquired the ability to manipulate objects by banging, shaking, examining (turning, poking, probing, etc.), dropping, and throwing. Between 1 and 2 years of age, their object manipulations became more socially oriented through showing, extending, or naming activities.

Bushnell and Boudreau (1993) condensed patterns of object manipulation by infants into the following stages:

1. *Clutching (birth through 3 months).* During this stage, object manipulation is largely controlled by the palmar grasp reflex. Typically, objects are clutched in one hand and brought to the mouth. The fingers may move in a "kneading" pattern.
2. *Rhythmical Stereotypies (4–10 months).* At the beginning of this stage infants establish elementary eye-hand control and exhibit more differentiated finger movements. They engage in repetitive finger and hand movements (rhythmical stereotypies) that peak in frequency at 6 or 7 months. These stereotypies include scratching, rubbing, banging, squeezing, poking, waving, and passing objects from one hand to the other.
3. *Complementary Bimanual Activities (10 months plus).* At this point the infant uses both hands in object manipulation. One hand may be used to hold an object in place, while the other hand is used to manipulate or explore its parts. The hand and finger movements are more focused on exploring object properties rather than repetitive movements. At approximately 1 year of age infants are able to make the complex hand movements essential for advanced haptic (tactile) perception, or the recognition of object properties through handling (see Chapter 7).

Hand Preference. Many organisms display a preference for one side of the body in performing certain movements. Rats tend to exhibit a paw preference, and even grasshoppers have a favorite scratching leg (Hecaen & Ajuriagurra, 1964).

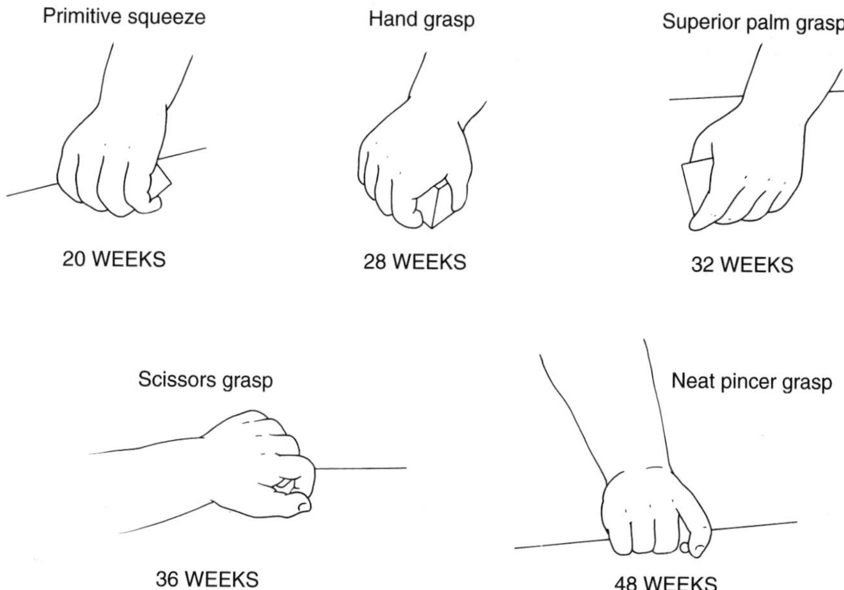

Figure 6-1 Types of Grasping Behavior

Sources: H. Halverson. (1931). "An Experimental Study of the Prehension in Infants by Means of Systematic Cinema Records," *Genetic Psychology Monographs, 10,* 107–286. Reprinted with permission of the Helen Dwight Reid Foundation. Published by Heldref Publications, 4000 Albermarle St., NW, Washington, DC 20016. Copyright 1931.; H. Knobloch, F. Stevens, & A. Malone, (1980). *Manual of Developmental Diagnosis.* New York: Harper & Row. Used by permission.

Human beings may begin to demonstrate a preference for one hand or the other in reaching and grasping as early as the infancy period.

Infants begin to demonstrate a hand preference when they reach for objects as early as 5 months of age (C. McCormick & Maurer, 1988; Butterworth & Hopkins, 1993). At that age, most infants reach predominantly with their right hand, although the incidence of left-handedness is higher than it is in the adult population. However, many infants display an irregular pattern of handedness, shifting from one side to the other or using both hands about same amount of time (Butterworth & Hopkins, 1993). By 18 months to 2 years of age, most infants have established a hand preference that does not change as they get older. In some cases, though, permanent hand preference is not established until 3 or 4 years of age.

Scientists have long debated whether hand preference is controlled by heredity or environmental influences. Some scientists believe that, although genetic factors may be involved, handedness is largely controlled by environmental factors related to imitation and instruction (Illingworth, 1991). Support for this position is found in a study that showed that young infants imitated the hand preference of their mothers during episodes of manual object play (Harkins & Uzgiris, 1991).

Overall, scientific evidence tends to support the position that hand preference is mainly determined by biological (including genetic) factors (Butterworth & Hopkins, 1993). Boklage (1980) believes that hand preference is linked to the organization of the brain, which is established early in the prenatal period. Evidence from his study of 800 twins reveals that if either one or both parents were left-handed, they were 50 percent more likely to have a left-handed child. Left-handedness occurs almost twice as often in twins as in singletons. These findings are consistent with the theory that hand dominance is a reflection of brain lateralization. That is, a left-handed person has a dominant right hemisphere and vice versa.

Other researchers have found that the incidence of left-handedness is higher among infants who are born prematurely, and/or who experienced respiratory distress or other trauma during a difficult birth process (N. Fox, 1985). The reason for this may be that the prenatal or birth-related damage to the left hemisphere switches hand control to the right hemisphere (Eliot, 1999). Still other scientists suggest that left-handedness is a result of increased testosterone levels during fetal development (Bryden & Steenhuis, 1991). We need more research to better understand the biological mechanisms related to handedness and how environmental factors are involved.

Throwing and Catching. Infants do not develop much proficiency in throwing. However, the ability to throw objects begins to emerge as early as 6 months, when babies accidentally release and hurl objects they are waving about or shaking (Espenschade & Eckert, 1967). As voluntary release is established, infants soon learn that dropping objects has an interesting effect. They delight in dropping or throwing spoons and other objects from the high chair to hear the noise as well as to watch someone pick them up. The first attempts at throwing are usually a stiff underhand motion (Cratty, 1979). Seventy-five percent of infants develop the ability to throw a small ball overhanded by 24 months of age (Frankenburg et al., 1992).

The ability to catch an object requires much more eye-hand coordination and perceptual ability than does throwing an object. Consequently, infants make little progress in this area. The baby's first efforts at catching are typically trying to stop a rolling ball (Hottinger, 1977). The first successful attempts to catch an object thrown into the air usually occur around 3 years of age (Williams, 1983).

GROSS MOTOR DEVELOPMENT

The development of gross motor skills involve using the large muscles of the body to control body posture and movements. **Posture** represents the adjustments of the body in relation to the forces of gravity. Postural abilities an infant must develop include achieving head control, sitting, and standing. Posture provides the base of support for body movements. **Locomotion** is the ability to move from place to place, which involves coordinating posture and controlling various body movements.

Prerequisites for Locomotor Skills. The development of locomotion involves the strength and coordination of the muscles and joints in organized response patterns. The ability to maintain a sense of balance and postural control under changing conditions, such as the location of objects and surface slopes, are related processes. These abilities gradually emerge after 6 months of age. By the time an infant is ready to crawl, the senses of vision and balance are sufficiently integrated for the infant to coordinate arm and leg movements with environmental cues. The ability to creep and crawl sets off a chain of experiences that lead to new and increasing levels of perceptual abilities and motor achievements (Bertenthal & Campos, 1990; Bushnell & Boudreau, 1993).

Emerging Locomotor Skills. The achievement of mobility increases the infant's opportunities for exploration and is necessary for learning and the development of independence. Although learning to walk is the most dramatic and important locomotor task of infancy, it is preceded and followed by an orderly progression of several other significant milestones (see Table 6-2).

Head Control. Establishing control of the head is the first step toward achieving an upright position and independent locomotion (Gesell, 1954). Head control is defined as the ability to keep the head steady in an upright position and move the head at will. The neck muscles of the newborn are not strong enough to support the weight of the disproportionately large head for more than a few seconds. In addition, the relative immaturity of the nervous system makes voluntary control of head movements difficult for the newborn.

Table 6-2 Milestones of Gross Motor Development

MOTOR ACTIVITY	*AVERAGE AGE (MONTHS)*
Sits with support—head steady	2.3
Rolls over—back to stomach and stomach to back	3.2
Sits alone—steadily	6.6
Crawls	7.0
Stands—holding on	7.2
Creeps	9.0
Walks—holding on	9.2
Walks alone—steadily	12.3
Walks up steps alone (can hold to rail)	16.6
Throws ball overhand	20.3
Jumps up—both feet off floor	23.8

Sources: W. Frankenburg, J. Dodds, P. Archer, B. Bresnick, P. Mashka, N. Edelman, & H. Shapiro (1992). *Denver II Training Manual* (2nd ed.). Denver, CO: Denver Developmental Materials, Inc.; H. Knobloch, F. Stevens, & A. Malone (1980). *Manual of Developmental Diagnosis.* New York: Harper & Row. Used by permission.

The beginning of head control may be observed when the baby raises the head far enough to clear the chin from the surface for a few seconds. Most infants accomplish this task during the first two months of life. When lying on the stomach, an infant can routinely hold the head so that the face makes a 45-degree angle with the surface at approximately 2 months of age (Frankenburg et al., 1992). On average, infants acquire the ability to hold their head steady when held in an upright position at around three months (B. White, 1975).

Rolling. The infant's first attempt at locomotion is rolling from one side to the other. An infant rolls by turning the head, twisting the trunk, and using a leg to push the body over. Cratty (1979) believes that the body-righting and visual-tracking reflexes are responsible for the infant's first attempts to roll over. The baby catches sight of a moving object and turns the head to follow it. The turned head triggers the righting reflex, which causes the body to flip over. Another possible explanation for some of the early rolling activity is that an infant accidentally turns from the stomach to a side position due to poor control of a shift in weight. From the side position the infant can turn to the stomach or back. As an infant gains more muscle strength and control, rolling movements become smoother, more coordinated, and deliberate.

Ordinarily an infant accomplishes the ability to roll from stomach to back before working on the more difficult task of rolling from back to stomach. Infants typically develop the ability to roll over completely from stomach to back and from back to stomach between 2 and 6 months of age (Frankenburg et al., 1992).

Sitting. As the infant gradually gains control over the muscles in the trunk of the body, sitting alone becomes possible. Most babies are able to sit alone momentarily without support between 6 and 7 months of age (Frankenburg et al., 1992). During their first attempts at sitting alone, infants lean forward to gain added balance and support (Gallahue, 1982). On average, an infant can maneuver into a sitting position from lying down, standing, or other postures by 8 to 9 months of age (Frankenburg et al., 1992).

Crawling and Creeping. About the time an infant can sit alone and roll onto the stomach, crawling movements are likely to follow. In **crawling,** the head and chest are raised while the stomach maintains contact with the surface. The weight of the head and shoulders rests on the elbows and hands, which are used to slide the body forward or backward. The legs usually drag, although they may sometimes be used to push forward or pull backward. Most infants begin crawling around 7 months (range = 4.5 to 9.5 months) (Burnett & Johnson, 1971).

As the baby becomes a proficient crawler, and muscle strength increases in the legs, efforts are made to advance to the creeping stage. Infants begin to creep around 9 months (range = 5.0 to 14.5 months) (Burnett & Johnson, 1971). **Creeping** is defined as locomotion on the hands and knees or hands and feet. The technical definitions

This baby is beginning to make **crawling** movements on his hands and stomach.

of crawling and creeping may be confusing because the meanings are usually reversed in common usage. Keep in mind also that different sources may use these terms interchangeably or in different ways. Thinking of the terms alphabetically—crawling before creeping as it occurs developmentally—may help you remember their sequence and therefore the technical definitions.

When infants first attempt to creep, they slowly and deliberately move one limb an inch or two at a time. With practice, the movements become smoother, more efficient, and faster. Most babies exhibit a pattern in which the arm movement is followed by movement of the opposite leg. However, about 20 percent of all infants follow the arm movement by moving the knee on the same side of the body (Cratty, 1979). Infants are individuals, though, and tend to use a variety of positions and movements in creeping and other forms of locomotion.

The importance of self-produced locomotion for perceptual, emotional, and social development in infancy was emphasized in the beginning of this chapter. Bertenthal and colleagues (1984) have linked the acquisition of the ability to move around on four limbs to the emergence of many of the developmental changes (e.g., wariness of strangers and heights) taking place between 7 and 9 months of age. Once infants begin to creep, their view and experience of the environment changes in important ways. Creeping contributes to the emergence of other abilities by enhancing the infant's ability to extract information from the environment and make more precise calculations of distances through the coordination of visual-motor cues (Bertenthal et al., 1984).

Hitching. A few infants learn to move around by an unusual method referred to as hitching or scooting. **Hitching** is defined as locomotion in a sitting position. The baby uses the legs, heels, and sometimes the hands to slide the buttocks along the floor. Some infants can scoot along quite rapidly and may use hitching as a substitute for creeping or walking. For example, at 20 months of age, Sue was attending a nursery-toddler class in which she was the only child who had not learned to walk. However, she could participate in the activities and keep up with the others by skillful hitching movements. Although her parents and teachers were concerned, physical and neurological examinations revealed no problems. She was walking by 2 years of age.

Standing. Infants typically begin to stand by pulling themselves up and holding on to furniture. One of the infant's motivations for standing is to extend the range of grasping and reaching for attractive objects above eye level. Most infants begin to pull themselves to a standing position by using chairs or other furniture between 8 and 10 months of age (Frankenburg et al., 1992).

Standing up to furniture is followed by **cruising.** This activity consists of moving around, usually sideways, holding on to furniture or other objects. As infants gradually gain stability in pulling up and cruising, they develop enough confidence to let go of their support for a few seconds. Infants typically accomplish the task of standing alone with stability between 10 and 13 months (Frankenburg et al., 1992). Once they achieve this milestone, they soon proceed to the more interesting task of walking alone.

Walking. From the parents' point of view, the baby's first independent steps may represent the most significant accomplishment of infancy. From the baby's perspective, walking opens up a new world. The average age for walking alone is approximately 12 months. However, 25 to 90 percent of infants walk alone steadily between 11 to 15 months (Frankenburg et al., 1992). Infants are often referred to as toddlers from the time they begin to walk until they achieve a stable pattern of walking around 24 to 36 months of age. In comparison to other species, human infants walk relatively late. Thelen and her colleagues (1984) believe this happens because infants are top-heavy, with large heads and short legs, and, therefore, have trouble balancing their bodies in an upright position.

In the initial stage of walking, the legs are spread apart for a wide base of support (Cratty, 1979). The toes are pointed outward with the knees slightly bent. The arms are held out for balance as the legs move in rigid, high-stepping, halting movements. The baby has difficulty maintaining balance and falls easily (Gallahue, 1982). Some infants may walk sideways as a carry-over from early cruising movements.

One of the tasks in learning to walk is to move over surfaces with different slopes without falling. Apparently infants acquire experience with slanted surfaces during the creeping stage that prepares them for this activity. Researchers have found that creeping infants differentiate between shallow and steep slopes but do not use that information to avoid hazardous inclines. By 14 months of age, toddlers make adjustments in their movement patterns to compensate for different surface levels (Eppler, Adolph, & Weiner, 1996).

Toddlers progress to a more advanced stage of walking rather quickly, although for several weeks they may resemble a "duck out for a jog" (Fogel, 2001, p. 289). With practice, the walking pattern becomes more balanced and smoother, the toes point straight ahead, and heel-to-toe contact replaces flatfooted slipping (Gallahue, 1982). The length of the steps tends to increase with age. Walking improves throughout the infancy period, but a mature, adultlike pattern does not emerge until around 4 to 7 years (Scrutton, 1969).

Running. Young children begin to run soon after they begin to walk. Toddlers may take a few rapid steps to maintain balance even before they master walking. Toddlers who are just beginning to walk sometimes move their feet as rapidly as possible in order to reach the next base of support (Williams, 1983). Running is defined as "a series of smoothly coordinated jumps during which the body weight is borne on one foot, becomes airborne, is then carried on the opposite foot and again becomes airborne" (Slocum & James, 1968, p. 205). The feature that distinguishes running from fast walking is the phase in which the body briefly leaves the supporting surface (Wickstrom, 1983).

Running begins its developmental course around 18 months of age. In the initial stage of running, the leg swing is short and limited. The stride is stiff and uneven. There is no observable time when the feet are not in contact with the surface. By 2 years of age, most infants can run well enough to meet the minimum standards of true running (Gesell, 1940). They can move a little faster and the length of the stride has increased. There is a limited but clearly observable flight phase. The arm and leg movements are more balanced and coordinated (Gallahue, 1982). Although a mature running pattern is not established during the first three years of life, infants make a remarkable amount of progress.

Climbing. An infant may attempt to go up stair steps on all fours before developing the ability to stand alone or walk. These initial climbing efforts are an extension of creeping and generally coincide with early attempts to stand. After they begin to walk, infants will attempt to climb stairs in an upright position with the assistance of an adult. These early efforts consist of a "mark time" pattern in which the child leads with the same foot on each step. Wellman (1937) found that children, using this same pattern, can climb a long flight of stairs or a ladder by 24 months of age. Climbing with an alternating foot pattern begins to occur around 3 years of age (Cratty, 1979).

Jumping. The first attempts to jump (off low steps) may be observed in infants at about 18 months of age (McClenaghan & Gallahue, 1978). Infants like to jump off the last step as they are descending stairs with assistance. This seems to be a preliminary phase in development before they obtain the ability to jump up and down from a standing position (Williams, 1983). The average age for jumping off the floor with both feet is approximately 24 months (Frankenburg et al., 1992).

SELF-CARE ACTIVITIES

Self-care skills such as dressing, toileting, and self-feeding vary widely among infants and toddlers. The development of these abilities is largely dependent upon biological maturation but is also related to internal motivation and parental influences. Some infants insist on doing things for themselves very early, whereas others are more passive and dependent. Self-care activities are sometimes called **adaptive behaviors** and are closely associated with social development as well as motor development. The infant cannot develop into an independent and autonomous individual until self-care activities are mastered.

Dressing. Gesell (1940) observed that infants learn many things in reverse order. This observation is especially applicable to dressing skills. Infants begin to remove articles of clothing long before they can put them on. During the first 12 to 18 months of infancy they are more concerned about taking clothes off than putting them on. They take special delight in pulling off their shoes, tied or untied, as well as their socks. By 20 months, most infants (75 percent) can purposefully remove at least one article of clothing (Frankenburg et al., 1992).

Infants begin to push their arms through sleeves and hold out their feet for shoes shortly before they are 1 year old. However, most of their dressing skills develop between 18 months and 3 years. During this period, most infants begin to put on their shoes, shirts, sweaters, and most other articles of clothing. Most children accomplish the task of self-dressing without help by 3 years of age except for tying shoes and buttoning or zipping difficult garments.

Self-Feeding Skills. By 4 or 5 months of age, the feeding reflexes have been replaced by voluntary muscle control. Sucking and rooting are voluntary, and the extrusion reflex of the tongue that pushes food out of the mouth has diminished or disappeared. The mouth is larger in proportion to the tongue and more easily accommodates a spoon. The normal infant is able to maintain a sitting position and hold the head erect without support.

Beginning around 1 year of age, many of the skills that are essential for self-feeding are being developed and refined. The average baby has changed the pattern of eating from sucking to rotary chewing movements. Some of the teeth have developed to the point of being useful in biting and chewing solid food. Control of the lips and tongue, which is essential in drinking from a cup, has developed. Infants usually manage to hold a cup and drink with only minor spilling early in the second year. Voluntary hand-to-mouth movements, a finger-thumb grasp, and the ability to hold and let go of eating utensils have developed around 7 or 8 months of age. Wrist control, essential in using a spoon efficiently, develops between 12 and 18 months. According to Gesell and Ilg (1937), the 2-year-old is relatively efficient at spoon-feeding. The willingness of the parent to allow the baby to practice self-feeding is a very important factor in determining when the skill is accomplished.

The age at which children are expected to feed themselves varies widely among cultures. For example, in Tarong families of the Phillipines, infants are encouraged to eat by themselves by 1 or 2 years of age. In Indonesia, Javanese mothers may feed their children until they are 5 or 6 years old (Broude, 1995). In many cultures, the task of self-feeding involves the ability to use a spoon, chopsticks, and other eating utensils. However, in others the process of self-feeding is simplified because few, if any, eating utensils are available.

Elimination Control. A major developmental task that begins during infancy is the establishment of control over the sphincter muscles, which control bowel and bladder movements. At birth, elimination is a reflexive act that is subject to conditioning. Infants can be conditioned to empty the bladder or bowels as early as 1 or 2 months. However, infants are not usually ready to begin to establish voluntary control over these functions until they are 15 to 18 months old (Illingworth, 1991).

Many child development experts advise parents to wait until an infant is at least 2 years old before beginning toilet training. B. White (1975) believes that toilet training should not be attempted between 14 and 24 months of age, because the infant is entering a period of negativism. Two-year-olds are more cooperative and usually train themselves in a short period of time. Infants who begin the process of toilet training before 18 months of age tend to take longer to be completely trained than infants who start around 24 months (Shelov, 1998).

Across cultures, toilet training practices vary widely. For example among the Gussi people of Africa, toilet training begins after the child is weaned and can walk well. The mother takes the child to a spot outdoors and tells the child what to do, or tells the child to do what the other children do. Factors that influence cultural traditions and practices include the availability of indoor plumbing, climate, modesty standards, the amount of clothing children wear, and sanitation standards. In most societies, serious toilet training begins between 1 and 3 years of age (Broude, 1995).

Elimination control is usually established in the following sequence: bowel control, daytime bladder control, nighttime bladder control. Children are usually ready to begin toilet training when they can use a word (such as "pee-pee") to label the process, remain dry for 2-hour intervals or naps, express discomfort with wet diapers, and display signs that a bowel movement or urination is about to occur (American Academy of Pediatrics, 1993). Some children are cooperative and accomplish training easily with minimum guidance and assistance. In some instances, parents have to initiate the process with more structure and guidance. The process works best when parents are relaxed, use lots of praise, provide clear, consistent instructions, and avoid conflicts of will.

IMPEDIMENTS TO MOTOR DEVELOPMENT

Some atypical variations in motor development are common among infants and disappear with age. However, persistent delays and variations in motor performance may be signs of a neuromotor disorder. Conditions that interfere with the motor development of infants are numerous and varied. Vision problems, mental disabilities, and cerebral palsy represent developmental challenges to an infant's motor functioning.

Visual Impairment. Vision is obviously a very significant factor in motor development. Surprisingly, though, blind infants tend to achieve some of the tasks of motor development at about the same time and in the same sequence as infants who can see. Blind infants look at their hands with their unseeing eyes (Illingworth, 1991), begin to sit alone, roll from back to stomach, take stepping movements when their hands are held, rise to their hands and knees, and stand alone within the normal age range (Adelson & Fraiberg, 1974). However, blind infants experience considerable delay in achieving self-initiated mobility and in reaching for objects.

Fraiberg and her colleagues (Fraiberg, 1971; Fraiberg, Smith, & Adelson, 1969) developed a guidance program to help blind infants with the achievement of reaching and mobility. Their program focused on the coordination of the ear and hand in reaching for objects, parent-child games, and the use of sound lures as incentives to mobility.

Bower (1977a) equipped a 16-week-old blind infant with a device that produced echoes from objects. The baby was able to reach accurately and grasp silent objects, even distinguishing two different objects. Scott, Jan, and Freeman (1977) have produced a guidebook for parents of visually impaired infants and toddlers, which contains suggestions for helping these children with motor-skill development.

Mental Disabilities. Research findings generally indicate that infants with lower-than-average intelligence experience delay in achieving the normal milestones of motor development (Wickstrom, 1983). The extent of the delay depends on the level of mental disability and physical or nervous-system disorder. Studies of infants affected by Down syndrome (see Chapter 2) have found timing problems in the activation of muscle responses needed for posture control (Woollacott, 1992). Infants with Down syndrome tested at 22 months of age displayed muscle response behaviors comparable to patterns found at 8 to 10 months of age in typically developing infants. **Hypotonia,** muscle weakness, and joint instability are other problems that contribute to delays in motor development (Fetters, 1996). As a group, infants with Down syndrome experience delays in achieving most motor milestones such as sitting, stepping, creeping, and standing. However, the delays are not uniform and a wide range of individual differences have been documented (Cobo-Lewis et al., 1995).

In some areas of motor functioning, children with mental disabilities may be more similar to than different from other children. For example, Kaminer and Jedrysek (1983) recorded the age of walking in 200 infants representing all levels of mental disability. The majority of children walked by the normal age of 17 months. Only when the babies were extremely disabled was walking delayed beyond 17 months. Also, early walkers were found even among this group.

Cerebral Palsy. One of the most common and serious disorders associated with motor impairment in infants and toddlers is **cerebral palsy.** Infants with cerebral palsy have difficulty with movement, posture, and muscle tone. This condition is caused by brain damage that occurs during the prenatal period, the birth process, or after birth. The incidence of cerebral palsy is higher among preterm and low birth weight infants than in full-term infants (Pellegrino, 1997). There are different types of cerebral palsy depending on the severity of the problem. The type of cerebral palsy is usually classified in terms of the quality of muscle tone and the areas of the body affected (Fetters, 1996). The effects of cerebral palsy vary from mild motor problems involving one side of the body to severe impairment involving the trunk and all four extremities. Some of the signs of cerebral palsy in infants include the persistence of primitive reflexes, weak and prolonged head lag, muscle tone that is unusually floppy or stiff, and lopsided or unusual creeping movements (Pellegrino, 1997; Shelov, 1998).

ASSESSING MOTOR PERFORMANCE

Numerous multidomain scales include components for the assessment of gross and fine motor development during infancy. For example, the motor scale from the **Bayley Scales of Infant Development - II** (described in Chapter 8) is one of the most reliable and widely used norm-referenced instruments for assessing motor development of infants. The other two instruments described here were exclusively designed to evaluate the motor performance of infants.

The **Alberta Infant Motor Scale (AIMS)** (Piper & Darrah, 1993) is one of the newest tools designed to evaluate motor performance of infants from birth to 18 months of age. Infants are observed in a variety of postures by a trained professional. One strength of the AIMS is that it includes evaluation of the quality of motor movements and is not based merely on major milestones or reflexes. The AIMS can be administered in 20 to 30 minutes.

The **Movement Assessment of Infants (MAI)** (Chandler, Andrews, & Swanson, 1980) is one of the most widely used tools designed to identify infants with cerebral palsy and other motor problems (McLean, Bailey, & Wolery, 1996). This test covers muscle tone, primitive automatic reactions, and voluntary movement in infants from birth to 12

APPLICATIONS: FACILITATING MOTOR CONTROL

A variety of infant-stimulation programs have been developed to assist parents and other caregivers in helping infants enhance their motor skill development. Some of these programs have been designed specifically for infants with motor delays (e.g., Connor, Williamson, & Siepp, 1978), and others are intended for use with typically developing infants (e.g., Gerber, 1981; Levy, 1973; Prudden, 1964). Ridenour (1978) advises parents to avoid motor-stimulation programs that claim to greatly enhance an infant's future motor or intellectual performance.

The following principles are recommended for use by parents and caregivers in promoting infant motor development:

- Activities and materials should be developmentally appropriate within the various stages of motor development (Weiser, 1982).
- Caregivers should not try to hurry development. Babies get ready for the next stage by mastering what they are doing in the present stage (Gonzalez-Mena & Eyer, 1980).
- Stimulation activities, such as games and exercises, should be provided in each area and stage of motor development (Weiser, 1982). The Uzgiris-Hunt Scales of Psychological Development suggest many age-appropriate motor activities (Uzgiris & Hunt, 1975).
- Movement activities should be staged so that infants can solve problems without relying on adult help or encountering adult interference (Weiser, 1982).
- A variety of toys and materials designed to facilitate motor development should be made available to an infant. However, such objects should usually be placed within the infant's reach rather than directly in the hands (Pikler, 1968).
- Infants should be placed in situations where they are most free and least helpless during the waking hours (Gonzalez-Mena & Eyer, 1980). Playpens, infant seats, highchairs, swings, and jump chairs should not be used for extended periods of time (Gerber, 1981; Prudden & Sussman, 1972). Parents should carefully supervise infants who are using such equipment because of the risk of injury (Ridenour, 1978). Infant walkers should not be used for safety reasons (Committee on Injury and Poison Prevention, 1995).
- Infants should be placed on their stomachs during waking hours (American Academy of Pediatrics, 1996).
- Infants should frequently wear as little clothing as temperature and social settings allow in order to facilitate maximum freedom of movement (Pikler, 1968; Prudden, 1964).
- Caregivers should model and demonstrate some activities for infants to imitate, such as banging two blocks together, stacking blocks, and putting objects in containers (Machado & Meyer-Botnarescue, 1997).

months of age. An overall score of normal, abnormal, or questionable is calculated. Norms are not available for comparison at the present time. The MAI is administered by a physical or an occupational therapist trained in its use.

SUMMARY

Interrelationships of Developmental Areas

- Motor development plays an important role in the development of intelligence, perceptual skills, emotional development, self-awareness, and other aspects of infant development.

Factors Influencing Motor Development

- Factors influencing motor development include maturation and learning, body size, muscle strength, muscle tone, cultural practices, nutrition, and sleep position.
- According to the dynamic systems approach, the human body is composed of various biological systems (e.g., sensory, muscular) that must work

together for the acquisition of motor skills. Through the use of a "moving room," researchers have found that development of postural control of young infants is affected by the use of information from the visual and vestibular (balance) sensory systems.

Developmental Trends

- Infants display a tendency to practice a new motor activity until it becomes a skill. Motor development proceeds from general to specific responses and from simple to complex skills. Motor development follows the cephalocaudal law of developmental direction and, with some exceptions, the proximodistal law as well.

Reflexes

- Newborn infants are equipped with numerous reflexes. Key reflexes observed during infancy are rooting, sucking, grasping, Moro, Babinski, tonic neck, and stepping. These reflexes are considered to be indicators of the maturity and integrity of the nervous system. Some of the reflexes apparently facilitate the development of motor skills with practice, whereas others may inhibit the emergence of voluntary control.

Fine Motor Development

- Eye-hand coordination is established in two stages between birth and 3 to 5 months of age. Prehension, the ability to grasp an object between fingers and thumb, develops in several stages between 6 months and 12 months of age. The infant who has developed prehensory skills spends a lot of time mouthing, visually inspecting, examining, and manipulating objects in numerous ways.
- Permanent hand preference is established in most infants by 2 years of age. Although evidence is not conclusive, research tends to support the position that hand preference is mainly determined by biological factors.

Gross Motor Development

- To achieve an upright position, the infant establishes head control (3 months), sitting alone (5–6 months), and standing alone (6–10 months). The development of locomotion begins with rolling (2–6 months) and progresses through the stages of crawling, creeping, and sometimes hitching. Infants usually begin to walk alone by around 12 months of age. Climbing, running, and jumping develop toward the end of the infancy period.

Self-Care Activities

- Infants typically accomplish most of the skills needed for dressing and feeding themselves between 8 months and 3 years of age. Parents are advised to wait until the infant is 2 years old before beginning toilet training.

Impediments to Motor Development

- Some of the conditions that delay and impede motor development include visual impairment, mental disabilities, and cerebral palsy.

Assessing Motor Performance

- Numerous scales are available for the assessment of motor development during infancy, including the motor scale from the Bayley Scales of Infant Development – II, the Alberta Infant Motor Scale, and the Movement Assessment of Infants.

KEY TERMS

dynamic systems approach
muscle strength
muscle tone
hypotonia
hypertonia
motor biases
rhythmical stereotypy
general to specific
hierarchical integration
cephalocaudal principle
proximodistal principle
reflex
rooting reflex
sucking reflex
palmar grasp reflex
Moro reflex

Babinski reflex
tonic neck reflex
stepping reflex
prereaching
visually directed reaching
prehension
posture
locomotion
crawling
creeping
hitching
cruising
adaptive behaviors
cerebral palsy
Bayley Scales of Infant Development–II
Alberta Infant Motor Scale (AIMS)
Movement Assessment of Infants (MAI)

INFORMATION ON THE WEB*

www.nichcy.org. This is the official Web site of the National Information Center for Children and Youth with Disabilities. The national information and referral center provides information on disabilities and disability-related issues for families, educators, and other professionals.

www.geocities.com/SouthBeach/Pier/2682/. Web site of Dr. Esther Thelen's Infant Motor Development Laboratory. Contains information about Dr. Thelen's research studies on various aspects of motor development based on dynamic systems theory.

*Web sites are subject to change.

SEVEN

PERCEPTUAL DEVELOPMENT

Baby infant, Baby dear,
What do you see and what do you hear?
What do you taste and what do you smell?
Oh, how I wish that you could tell!
—C. Snow

How do infants begin to learn about their world? What sights, sounds, tastes, and odors do infants perceive and discriminate? How do infants begin to make sense out of the world to which they are exposed? The basis for human learning is sensation and perception. Even in utero, the developing fetus begins to learn about the world through perception. In fact, a very important job for the newborn is to begin to take in information (**sensations**) and organize and interpret it in a way that is meaningful (**perception**). This organization facilitates all other areas of development, including motor, cognitive, language, and social development. In this chapter, we explore the development of the different sensory systems and perceptual abilities, both before and after birth.

PHILOSOPHICAL AND THEORETICAL FOUNDATIONS

Of all the areas of development, perception and how it develops is the most closely tied with the nature-nurture debate (Bornstein, 1988). Theorists who support the nature side are referred to as **nativists.** According to their view, infants come into the world with perceptual systems and mental structures in place that help them organize new experiences. Individuals are born with perceptual categories for size, form, position and motion, as well as for time and space (Bornstein, 1988). Theorists who favor the nurture side of the debate are called **empiricists.** They believe that infants come into the world with no knowledge or "prewiring" with which to view the world or organize their perceptions. They gain perceptual knowledge through sensory experiences (Bornstein & Arterberry, 1999).

This debate continues even today, but current writings about infant perceptual development reflect a modification and, in some instances, a blend of the earlier, more extreme theories. Today theorists tend to hold the view that infants are not born with sophisticated perceptual systems, but there is something special and innate about infants that enables them to *more easily* perceive certain types of sensory stimulation. This view is reflected in the work of James and Eleanor Gibson.

James Gibson (1979) and his wife Eleanor have developed a theory of perceptual development known as **direct perception.** Infants are viewed as "preattuned" to pick up the features that are consistent and unchanging and are able to filter out irrelevant information (P. Miller, 1993). According to Eleanor Gibson (1969, 1992; E. Gibson & Pick, 2000), perception is a process that develops over time as the baby becomes capable of increasingly finer, more complex, discriminating, and accurate perceptions. In the process, infants search for information from the environment in the form of invariant features of objects and events. For example, they detect overall patterns in the shape of objects, such as squares and forms. Infants also tend to look for distinctive features that distinguish one object from another. This tendency enables the infant to distinguish between faces on the basis of differences in noses, ears, hairline, and other individual features.

An important component of Gibson's theory is the concept of **affordances.** What the individual perceives is related to what the environment provides to the individual or what the environment affords (E. Gibson, 1995). Affordances are affected by developmental level and previous experiences. For example, a rattle may afford sucking to a 3-month-old, but to a 2-year-old it may afford a tool for banging a sibling's head. Many of Gibson's ideas have been supported by existing research and her theory is finding increasing acceptance. The theory, however, has been criticized for not identifying what structures in the mind support direct perception (Bremner, 1998).

DEVELOPMENT OF THE SENSORY SYSTEMS

Operating from various theoretical perspectives, researchers are accumulating an increasingly large body of literature on the perceptual and cognitive abilities of infants. We now consider how perceptions change from conception through the infancy period. Current views of perception emphasize that we are biologically equipped at birth to perceive the world in certain ways, that newborns have amazing (although limited) perceptual abilities, and that many aspects of perception reach adultlike capacity during the second six months of life (Siegler, 1998). In this section, we will explore the development of the taste, olfaction, touch, hearing, and vestibular input in the prenatal period and infancy. Vision, which has been researched more extensively, will be covered in a separate section.

Taste. Research indicates that infants can taste even before birth. Taste buds begin developing on the tongue of the human fetus at 7 to 8 weeks of gestational age with mature cells appearing at approximately 14 weeks (Bradley, 1972; Eliot, 1999). Mistretta and Bradley (1975) found that the swallowing patterns of fetuses changed when a flavored chemical was injected into the uterus. Studies with premature infants, who have had no taste experiences, also support the early development of taste (Maone et al., 1990; Tatzer et al., 1985). Amniotic fluid is rich with different tastes and the taste experiences of the fetus may bias later taste preferences (Eliot, 1999). The findings of animal studies are consistent with this conclusion. A study of rats prenatally exposed to apple juice found that they preferred apple juice to other liquids after birth (Smotherman, 1982).

Physiologically, infants enter the world prepared to experience various taste sensations. A newborn infant will smile with satisfaction when a drop of sugar is placed on its tongue and will frown with distaste in response to a drop of lemon juice or a bitter substance (Steiner, 1977). Thus, newborns discriminate between three basic tastes—sweet, sour, and bitter. Studies about newborn infants' responses to salty substances are less conclusive.

The newborn's taste for sweet is by far the dominant taste. Researchers have consistently reported that newborn infants all over the world prefer sweet substances to plain water or other substances, including milk. Infants demonstrate their preference for sweet solutions through facial expressions (Rosenstein & Oster, 1990; Steiner, 1977), faster heartbeats (Lipsitt, 1977), and faster, longer, and stronger sucking episodes (Crook, 1977). Apparently the sweeter the solution is, the better they like it (Desor, Maller, & Greene, 1977). There are indications that babies respond positively to sweet-tasting substances even before birth (Mennella & Beauchamp, 1993b). The preference for sweet substances appears so early and so strong that many scientists believe the "sweet tooth" infants have at birth is an innate characteristic.

Researchers have confirmed (what every mother knows) that the taste of sucrose, given in combination with a pacifier (oral-tactile) or separately, has a calming effect on crying newborns (Blass & Ciaramitaro, 1994). It is believed that the taste sensation of sucrose or milk activates the production of opioids (substances that protect against pain).

Newborns find sour flavors distasteful. They frown and grimace when given citric acid. They even reduce their intake of a sweetened liquid when a sour substance is added (Desor, Maller, & Andrews, 1975). Newborn infants display highly negative facial reactions when given a strong bitter concentration of quinine or urea. However, they do not reject moderate concentrations of urea. Infants do, however, show a rejection of these bitter tastes between 14 days and 6 months of age (Kajuira, Cowart, & Beauchamp, 1992).

In general, newborns react indifferently to salty substances. Studies measuring the facial expressions and intake amounts indicate that newborns may not detect salt (Beauchamp et al., 1994; Mennella & Beauchamp, 1993f). Salt was accidentally substituted for sugar in the formula of newborns in a hospital nursery. All of the infants drank the formula until they became quite ill (Finberg, Kiley, & Luttrell, 1963). In view of contradictory research findings, additional studies are needed to clarify the newborn's response to the taste of salt as well as bitter substances. Around 4 months, however, babies undergo a change in salt preference (Beauchamp et al., 1994; Harris & Booth, 1987). They prefer a salty solution to plain water. By age 2, children begin to reject salt solutions and seem to be developing a sense of what should and should not be salted (Eliot, 1999).

For infants, the experience of taste is provided through gestation of milk. Several studies have been conducted to determine the effect of the mother's diet on the breast-feeding infant. These studies indicate that the mother's food intake affects the feeding behavior of the infant. For example, researchers gave a group of nursing mothers garlic or placebo pills prior to breast-feeding (Mennella & Beauchamp, 1991a). Infants nursed longer and ingested more milk when their mothers were given the garlic capsules. The same result was achieved when the mothers were given vanilla. Interestingly, the opposite infant behavior was found when the mother ingested a small amount of alcohol (Mennella, 2001; Mennella & Beauchamp, 1991b, 1993a).

Smell. The **olfactory system** that controls the sense of smell is well developed before the baby is born (Bossey, 1980). The amniotic fluid contains odor that can be affected by maternal disease (Mace et al., 1976) and diet (Mennella, Johnson, & Beauchamp, 1995). Although research with animals supports the view that prenatal odor experiences affect later odor preferences, it is not known whether the sense of smell is functional before birth in humans. One study with human subjects, however, is consistent with the findings of the animal studies. Varendi, Porter, and Winberg (1997) presented newborns with an unwashed breast and a breast treated with amniotic fluid. The infants preferred the treated breast, although this preference declined over time.

There is relatively little research on the development of the sense of smell during infancy, because odor preferences are difficult to assess. Some researchers (e.g., Guillory, Self, & Paden, 1980) argue that ability to discriminate odors does not develop until 1 month of age. However, the bulk of evidence indicates that infants have the ability to smell, at least some odors, as soon as they are born.

Within hours after birth, infants respond to a variety of odors. For example, newborns smile pleasurably when a piece of cotton with a banana odor is waved under their nose, but frown in protest at the smell of rotten eggs. Like adults, newborns prefer the smell of vanilla to the odor of fish (Steiner, 1977). Newborns are especially sensitive to odors associated with their mothers and are apparently able to recognize their mothers within hours after birth through the sense of smell alone. Breast-fed newborns are able to detect the difference between the breast pad of their mothers and those of a lactating stranger. In addition, newborns can discriminate between the underarm and neck odors of their mothers and those of a stranger (Mennella & Beauchamp, 1993b). The sense of smell may play a role in the formation of attachments in humans, just as it does in animals (Lamb & Campos, 1982).

The sense of smell improves rapidly during the first few days of life. Infants are able to detect weaker odors as they get older. Lipsitt, Engen, and Kaye (1963) discovered the amount of asafetida odor needed to elicit a response in newborns decreases with age. Breast-fed babies soon learn to detect the differences between the odor of milk from the mother's breast and milk from the breast of a stranger. MacFarlane (1975) found that such distinctions could be made by 6-day-old infants but not by 2-day-old infants. However, Russell (1976) concluded that this ability did not occur until 6 weeks of age.

Research with older infants suggests that infants are aware of and remember information related to smell. Mennella and Beauchamp (1998) conducted a study in which they presented infants with three toys: a vanilla-scented toy, an ethanol-scented toy, and an unscented toy. Infants spent most of the time looking at the vanilla-scented toy and less time manipulating the ethanol-scented toy versus the unscented toy. In addition, infants' responses were affected by consumption of alcohol or vanilla scent by the mother.

Touch. Touch has been referred to as the "mother of the senses" (Montagu, 1971). Between 7½ and 14 weeks of gestational age, almost the entire surface of the embryo becomes sensitive to tactile stimulation (Hooker, 1952). It is the first sensory system to develop (Gottfried, 1984) and is considered to be one of the baby's most advanced abilities (Eliot, 1999). Touch is the most complex of the senses and the most difficult to study as a separate modality. The word *touch* and its synonyms, *contact* and *feel,* usually refer to sensations that occur when receptors in the skin are stimulated.

The sense of touch also encompasses perceptions of pain, temperature, pressure, weight, texture, firmness, and many other feelings. Touch is closely linked with sensations of the muscles and joints and with sensations of movement (S. Rose, 1984).

Touch plays a very important role in infant development. One of the most effective ways to soothe crying babies is to pick them up and hold them close to the body or to swaddle them tightly in a blanket. There are indications that touch or related sensations influence parent-infant attachment, cognitive development, sociability, ability to withstand stress, and immunological development in infants (Gottfried, 1984). Tiffany Field (1995) believes that touch or massage therapies can be used to enhance several behavioral processes and physiological functions. Massage therapy with infants involves movement of the hands over the body, stroking with pleasure, and pressure without movement. She reports that infant massage has been effective in enhancing growth and development, reduction of pain, and increased attentiveness.

However, touching an infant can have a positive or negative effect. The type of touching and when it occurs are important factors. Stroking, as opposed to tickling and poking, has been linked to infants spending a greater proportion of time making eye contact, smiling, and vocalizing and less time spent crying (Pelaez-Nogueras et al., 1997). A sick infant responds differently to vigorous stroking than does a well infant. The precise effects of touch are not entirely clear because of the difficulty encountered in separating touch from other sensations (Gottfried, 1984).

Perception of Pain. For many years, doctors have performed surgery on newborn infants with little or no anesthesia. This practice was based on the rationale that anesthesia is risky, and the immaturity of the infant's brain blocks out significant perceptions of pain. We now know that even premature infants experience pain. The neurological structures and pathways for the transmission and perception of painful stimuli are developed by 29 weeks of gestation (Walco, Cassidy, & Schechter, 1994; Walco & Harkins, 1999).

Newborn infants respond to pain in ways that are similar to those of adults. Harrigan-Hamamoto (1983) observed crying, changes in facial expressions, fist clenching, and changes in color, blood pressure, and other vital signs in newborns during a procedure used to draw a sample of blood. Lipsitt and Levy (1959) found that newborn infants are sensitive to the pain of a mild electric shock at birth. Their responsiveness gradually increased over the first four days of life. Premature infants who have surgical procedures performed with little anesthesia display more stress responses and have higher rates of complications and mortality than infants given deeper anesthesia (Walco et al., 1994). Infants as young as 25 weeks of gestational age are sensitive to heel-stick procedures to obtain blood samples (Craig et al., 1993). Studies indicate that perception of pain changes with age, and infants learn to more effectively cope with pain as they get older (Craig et al., 1994; Lilly, Craig, & Grunau, 1997).

Painful experiences during infancy can affect later behavior. Taddio and colleagues (1997) conducted a study comparing boys who were uncircumcised, boys who were circumcised using a topical anesthesia cream, and boys who were given a placebo topical cream. They videotaped the children at 4 and 6 months when they came in for routine vaccinations. They found differences in pain responses between the children who were circumcised without anesthesia and those who were uncircumcised or who had been circumcised with anesthesia. Infants who were circumcised without anesthesia demonstrated more intense pain responses, suggesting that early pain experiences can sensitize children to later painful experiences.

Haptic Perception. In recent years, researchers have been increasingly interested in the ability of infants to acquire information about the properties of objects through touch and handling sensations (Bushnell & Boudreau, 1993). This process is referred to as **haptic perception.** Infants rub their hands and fingers back and forth across the surface of objects, enclose their hands around an object, squeeze objects, push, pull, and move objects up and down. Researchers are finding that infants learn about the size, shape, temperature, texture, and weight of objects through these haptic exploratory procedures.

An example of how researchers have studied haptic perception is found in the experiments of Streri and Spelke (1988, 1989). They conducted experiments to determine whether infants can perceive the unity and boundaries of objects they touch and manipulate but cannot see. Four-month-old infants were given two separate rings, one in each hand, under a cloth that blocked their view. In a separate condition, the rings were also connected to each other with a rod so that they moved only together. Under a third condition the rings were connected with elastic so they could be moved independently. The infants were found to perceive the two rings as separate objects when they could be moved independently and as a single object when they were held rigidly together.

Bushnell and Boudreau (1991, 1993) used findings from existing research studies to project a general timetable for the development of haptic perception. Infants can probably distinguish size and distinct object shapes (e.g., a solid disc from a ring) with their hands beginning at approximately 3 months of age. Haptic perception of temperature, hardness, and texture begin to emerge at approximately 6 months of age. Weight perception becomes evident at about 9 months of age. Haptic perception of shapes that are similar in features but differ in spatial arrangement (configurational shape) emerges last at 12 to 15 months.

Hearing. Contrary to early theories that infants are born deaf, we now know that babies hear and respond to sounds even before birth. The development of the hearing apparatus is basically complete and functional around the fifth or sixth month of fetal life (Bredberg, 1985; Lecaunet, 1998). Researchers have noted movements (Fleischer, 1955) and heart rate changes (Kisilevsky, Muir, & Low, 2000; Murphy & Smyth, 1962) following auditory stimulation as early as 26 weeks of gestation. Infants prefer the sound of an "intrauterine" recording of their mother's voice over a regular version of their mother's voice (Fifer & Moon, 1989; Moon & Fifer, 1990).

Newborns do not hear as well as adults. They can detect sounds within the range of 40 to 50 decibels. In comparison to the typically hearing adult who detects sounds around 10 decibels, the newborn has a moderate hearing impairment (Werner & VandenBos, 1993). However, a wide range of individual differences in hearing abilities among newborns has been identified (Siegler, 1998).

Changes in sensitivity to sounds are to be expected throughout the infancy period for several reasons. Structurally, the size and shape of the external ear, the ear canal, the middle ear cavity, and the sound conductive mechanism continue to change until middle childhood. In addition, the part of the brain in which sound is interpreted is quite immature at birth and improves with age (Muir, 1985). Finally, as the nervous system matures, the ability of the infant to concentrate, select, and attend to sounds improves. Until about 3 months of age, infants hear lower-pitched sounds better than higher-pitched sounds. As they get older, this pattern reverses so that by 6 months of age, infants are more sensitive to sounds at higher frequencies (pitch). By 24 months of age, an infant's ability to detect sounds of the highest frequencies is much like that of an adult (Werner & VandenBos, 1993).

Sound Localization. In spite of their limitations, newborn infants are amazingly sensitive to sounds. Several studies have shown that neonates are capable of **sound localization,** that is, identifying the direction from which a sound originates (Aslin, Pisoni, & Jusczyk, 1983). Infants as young as 2 to 4 days turn their head toward the correct location of a sound (Muir & Field, 1979).

For reasons not altogether understood, however, the ability to orient toward sound apparently declines during the second and third months. It reappears by 4 months of age (Aslin et al., 1983). This is called a *U-shaped curve* of development, since the ability is present at first, then declines, then reappears. By 6 to 7 months of age, infants use sounds to locate objects in space when no visual cues are available. For example, infants can reach accurately for a noise-making object coming from a variety of locations in total darkness (Clifton, Perris, & Bullinger, 1991; Perris & Clifton, 1988). One of the sound features they apparently use at 6 months of age for auditory depth perception is changes in sound pressure level (intensity of decibels) (Litovsky & Clifton, 1992). The ability to identify the location of sounds continues to improve throughout the infancy period.

Sound Discrimination. Newborn infants are able to distinguish between sounds of different pitch, loudness, and duration (Leventhal & Lipsitt, 1964). They are capable of distinguishing the difference between tones that are about one note apart on a musical scale as early as 36 to 39 weeks in utero (Lecaunet et al., 2000). They also appear to be capable of distinguishing between words. In one study, newborns (1 to 2 days old) were able to recognize a word after a 24-hour delay (Swain, Zelazo, & Clifton, 1993). Neonates prefer music to noise, and vocal music to instrumental music (E. Butterfield & Sipperstein, 1974). Moderately low-pitched sounds and continuous or rhythmic sounds have a soothing effect on newborns. Very low-frequency and high-pitched sounds produce an opposite effect (Appleton, Clifton, & Goldberg, 1975). In addition, newborns apparently are more attentive to sounds that are of moderate duration (5 to 15 seconds) than shorter or intermittent sounds (Eisenberg, 1976).

Sound Preferences. Neonates demonstrate a preference for sounds within the range of the human voice (Eisenberg, 1976). They have been observed moving their arms and legs in rhythm to voices (Bernhardt, 1987; Condon & Sander, 1974) and tend to prefer music that is accompanied by vocal sounds (E. Butterfield & Sipperstein, 1974). Given a choice, newborns prefer their mother's voice to other female voices (DeCasper & Fifer, 1980). They also would rather listen to the voice of a female than the voice of a male. However, they do not prefer their father's voice to those of other males, even though they can detect the differences in voices (DeCasper & Prescott, 1984; Ward & Cooper, 1999).

The preference for female voices in general and the mother's voice in particular may originate with their prenatal auditory experiences. DeCasper and Spence (1986) found that newborn infants whose mother had read *The Cat in the Hat* to them during the prenatal period preferred that story to *The King, the Mice and the Cheese,* after they were born. Not only do newborns prefer the mother's voice, they also prefer her language. Moon, Panneton-Cooper, & Fifer (1993) presented 2-day-old infants with a recording of their mother's language (but not in the mother's voice) and an unfamiliar language. The infants in the study preferred their mother's language to an unfamiliar language. Prenatal auditory experiences seem to play a strong role in infants' auditory preference after birth.

Not only are infants aware of differences in voice inflection (Morse, 1972) and pitch (Moffitt, 1971), but they can also discriminate between very similar speech sounds (Eilers & Minifie, 1975; Moffitt, 1971). One group of researchers (Eimas et al., 1971) taught two groups of 4-week-old babies how to turn a tape on by sucking on a pacifier connected to a control device. While one group of babies was allowed to listen to "pa pa pa" sounds, the other group heard "ba ba ba" sounds. The babies in both groups soon habituated to the sounds and stopped sucking, which turned off the speakers. When the taped sounds were reversed between the two groups, renewed sucking was generated to keep the new sound going. The researchers concluded that the infants could discriminate between the very similar sounds of *p* and *b*. They also hear the difference between a variety of vowel sounds, such as *a* and *e* (Kuhl, 1981). At 4 months of age infants can match vowel sounds to the face of the person making the sound (Kuhl & Meltzoff, 1982).

Research has also shown that infants can detect differences in sounds of languages that are not their own (Lasky et al., 1975; Lisker & Abramson, 1970; Streeter, 1976), whereas adults have difficulty discriminating sounds that are in their nonnative language (Lisker & Abramson, 1970). In fact, this decline in discriminating sounds of nonnative language occurs between 6 and 12 months of age (Werker, 2000; Werker & Lalonde, 1988; Werker & Tees, 1984).

As infants get older, it becomes important for them to begin to distinguish between words. Infants have also been shown to attend more to patterns of speech evident in their native language (Echols, Crowhurst, & Childers, 1997). For example, in English, words with two syllables tend to have a strong-weak stress pattern (e.g., baby, former). Infants prefer to listen to words that follow this pattern. Recent brain research suggests that infants may be able to make these distinctions as early as 3 months (Shafer, Shucard, & Jaeger, 1999). Brain activity patterns indicate that infants at this age are sensitive to the patterns of their native language. As early as 4.5 months, infants show a preference for their own names (Mandel, Jusczyk, & Pisoni, 1995). By 9 months of age, infants make distinctions between a variety of sound clusters in speech (Jusczyk, Houston, & Goodman, 1998; Juszcyk, Luce, & Charles Luce, 1994).

Vestibular Sensation. Bouncing is a popular activity with infants. It seems that almost all infants like to be gently bounced on the knee of an adult. This type of action produces a type of sensory input called vestibular stimulation. **Vestibular stimulation** tells us information about our body's movement and our degree of balance (Eliot, 1999). We gain vestibular information through the inner ear. Changes in the fluid in the inner ear tell us whether we are bending forward, backward, or sideways. The vestibular system is also responsible for coordinating the vestibulo-ocular reflex. This is a reflexive action that keeps the eyes pointed in a particular direction, even when the head is moving (Bear, Connors, & Paradiso, 2001).

The vestibular system consists of the otolith organs and the semicircular canals. The otolith organs are responsible for detecting gravity and head tilt, while the semicircular canals detect head rotation (Bear et al., 2001). The vestibular system begins to develop at the same time as the auditory system, but develops more quickly. "By just five months of gestation, the vestibular apparatus has reached its full size and shape, vestibular pathways to the eyes and spinal cord have begun to myelinate . . . however, myelination of some other vestibular pathways progresses at a very slow pace, all the way to puberty" (Eliot, 1999, p. 149).

Vestibular input is important because it provides the foundation for movement and posture (Woollacott, 1992). Vestibular information has been found to increase the development of motor skills. D. Clark, Kreutzberg, and Chee (1977) conducted a study in which they exposed babies (3 to 14 weeks) to spinning in a chair on an adult's lap. They compared these subjects with babies who were not given vestibular stimulation. The babies who received the spinning stimulation developed better reflexes and motor skills.

THE DEVELOPMENT OF VISION

Vision is considered to be the most important of the senses because it serves to integrate information from the other senses. In other words, vision helps the infant to pull together what is tasted, smelled, felt, and heard. Ironically, vision is the least developed sensory system at birth (Banks & Shannon, 1993). In fact, it wasn't long ago that people believed that infants were blind at birth and only learned to see a little later (Bremner, 1998). The development of the sense of vision during infancy involves improving visual acuity, tracking and scanning, the ability to discriminate between colors, and other perceptual skills described later.

Visual Acuity. The physical structure of the visual system is immature at birth. The newborn's eyes are shorter and flatter than those of an adult. The pupils are significantly smaller, the ciliary muscles that control the lens (focus) do not function well, and the retinas are relatively immature (Banks & Bennett, 1991). The visual centers in the brain are not fully developed at birth. These immaturities affect the ability of infants to see objects clearly (**visual acuity**) and to bring objects into focus at various distances (**visual accommodation**). These limitations do not hamper development and may promote development by removing distractors (Hainline, 1998; Slater, 2000).

Estimates of the visual acuity of newborns vary widely, but generally indicate that newborns see about 1⁄30 as well as adults with perfect vision (Bremner, 1998; Courage & Adams, 1990). This means that their visual images, even from close up, are somewhat blurred. However, the limited vision of newborns is not the result of deficiencies in the range or depth of focus. Evidently, newborn babies can keep objects in focus as well as or better than adults. This ability doesn't help much though because they "see equally unclearly across a wide range of distances" (Banks, 1980, p. 663). In the first six months after birth the infant's visual acuity improves dramatically. By 1 year of age, visual acuity is estimated to be approximately 20/50. Normal adult 20/20 vision is typically achieved by about 4 years of age (Teplin, 1995). Visual acuity is affected by the amount of contrast between an object and its background, and by spatial frequency of an object's patterns, such as squares on a checkerboard. Young infants see best at low spatial frequencies (e.g., a checkerboard with a few, larger squares) for maximum contrast. As they get older, infants prefer to look at progressively higher spatial frequencies and do not need as much contrast (e.g., a checkerboard with a larger number of smaller squares). This indicates they are able to see more details (Siegler, 1998).

Tracking and Scanning. Even though their visual clarity is limited, newborns can locate and follow a single moving object with their eyes (tracking) for about 90 degrees. Another important accomplishment for infants is to learn to stabilize gaze on a new target once they change focus (Von Hofsten & Rosander, 1998). Infant eye pursuit, however, is slow and jerky for a small target (Bloch & Carchon, 1992; Dayton & Jones, 1964). Tracking movements become smoother and more coordinated as early as 6 weeks of age. By 12 weeks, the eyes are often focused on the moving target (Aslin, 1981). The ability to track moving objects improves dramatically from 2 to 5 months of age (Von Hofsten & Rosander, 1996).

A skill that contributes to the ability to track is the ability to turn the head. As infants gain head control, the ability to track increases. Initially, infants track with eyes as far as possible before turning the head (Bloch & Carchon, 1992). By 1 month old, infants are using the head in tracking objects (Roucoux, Culee, & Roucoux, 1983). In later studies, Von Hofsten and Rosander (1996, 1997) found that some 5-month-old infants used head movements almost entirely.

Newborn infants also engage in visual scanning of stationary objects. They apparently scan the environment, even in the dark, to find something to look at. Haith (1979) believes that neonates operate according to the following "rules" in their attempts to locate and look at interesting things:

> When awake and the light is not too bright, open eyes.
> If it is dark, look intensely for shadows or dimly illuminated objects.
> If it is light, search widely for something with edges.
> If an edge is found, scan up and down or back and forth across it.

Newborns tend to prefer angles to straight lines. When given a choice between horizontal and vertical contours, they prefer the vertical (Banks & Salapatek, 1983). Their visual exploration of faces and other objects is apparently limited to the borders and a single feature at a time, but by 2 months of age they begin to scan internal features (Haith, Bergman, & Moore, 1977). Newborn infants appear to have the innate capacity to perceive that objects remain the same size even when they are viewed from different distances (Siegler, 1998).

Color Vision. We know that newborn infants are capable of responding to variations in brightness of lights. Infants as young as 2 to 4 days old prefer to look at lights of medium brightness rather than at brighter or dimmer lights (Hershenson, 1964). Do newborn infants also have the ability to see color, or is their vision limited to a black-and-white view of the world? Some researchers have concluded that infants as young as 3 days old distinguish between the basic color categories of red, yellow, green, and blue (Adams & Maurer, 1983,

1984; Adams, Maurer, & Davis, 1986). Other researchers (Adams, Courage, & Mercer, 1994) found that most newborns in their study only distinguished between red and gray. In any event, newborn babies do not do well in distinguishing between similar shades within specific color ranges (Banks & Bennett, 1991).

Some researchers think that infants may simply be responding to different degrees of brightness along the color spectrum rather than color per se. Banks and Shannon (1993) have concluded that newborn infants do not consistently demonstrate the ability to discriminate between stimuli that differ in color shade only. There is general agreement that newborns do not see colors well, if at all, either because of immaturity of color receptors in the eyes (cones), immaturity of the brain, or overall visual inefficiency. In the future, researchers using better techniques to control for brightness may eventually discover more definitive answers to questions about color visual capacities of newborns (Teller & Lindsey, 1993).

Scientists generally agree that by 2 months of age infants can perceive the difference between two of the primary colors. The ability to discriminate among different degrees of brightness increases rapidly. This is consistent with findings that by 2 months of age, infants make discriminations among degrees of brightness almost as well as adults (Peeples & Teller, 1975). Many of the fundamental aspects of color vision are reasonably adultlike by 3 months of age (Banks & Salapatek, 1983).

Scientists have speculated about whether or not color perception is culturally related. That is, do infants from different cultures classify the same wavelengths as different colors? Generally, research studies indicate that people all over the world share similar color perceptions (Bornstein, 1981). These findings support the theory that biology plays a dominant role in color perception.

Depth Perception. Much of the research on visual capabilities of infants has been directed toward finding out when depth perception develops. **Depth perception** involves such things as seeing objects in three dimensions, judging the size and distance of objects, and perceiving heights of drop-offs. Infants need to be capable of depth perception in order to avoid falling down stairs or bumping into furniture, and to become capable of grasping objects.

Monocular and Binocular Cues. Through the years, researchers have explored questions about the ability of infants to use monocular and binocular cues in depth perception. **Monocular cues** are cues that can be perceived through one eye working alone. By placing a blindfold over one eye of an infant, researchers are able to observe the infant's reactions to pictorial cues, such as shading and textures used by artists to create depth. Infants are capable of accurate depth perception through the use of pictorial and other types of nonmoving monocular cues by approximately 7 months of age (Granrud & Yonas, 1984; Granrud, Yonas, & Opland, 1985). However, infants perceive depth on the basis of monoucular cues as early as 1 month of age if the stimuli are moving (Siegler, 1998).

Bincoluar cues are cues that are only available when both eyes focus on an object. Since the two eyes are separated, each eye picks up information from a slightly different angle. Try closing one eye and then the other to view a scene. You can easily perceive that it is not necessary to use both eyes to perceive depth. However, depth perception is more accurate and efficient with the use of binocular cues. For example, infants are more accurate in judging the distance of objects when using binocular vision than monocular vision (Granrud et al., 1984).

How soon do infants view the world from a binocular perspective? While infants can focus both eyes on the same target (convergence) as early as 1 month of age, they evidently do not have the capacity to use binocular cues efficiently until about 3½ months of age (Held, 1993). Binocular perception, as well as other aspects of perceptual development, are heavily dependent upon maturation of the nervous system, but visual experience plays a significant role.

There may be a critical period for the development of binocular perception. Researchers (Banks, Aslin, & Letson, 1975) have studied binocular functioning in children who were born with strabismus. Children who have this condition cannot focus both eyes on the same target and do not perceive binocular cues. Fortunately, this problem can be corrected by surgery. If normal focus is restored before 3 years of age, complete binocular depth perception is achieved. However, if the condition is corrected later than 3 years of age, binocular vision appears to be permanently impaired.

The Visual Cliff. The most well known studies of depth perception are based on the **visual cliff** technique performed by E. Gibson and Walk (1960; Walk & Gibson, 1961). These innovative researchers created the illusion of a visual cliff by using a special table with a checkerboard-patterned surface covered by a sheet of clear plexiglas. One side of the table has a drop-off of several feet. Infants who can crawl typically avoid the side with the drop-off even though it is covered by plexiglas (E. Gibson & Walk, 1960). However, infants as young as 1½ to 3 months of age respond differently to the deep drop-off than they do to the shallow side of the visual cliff (Bertenthal & Campos, 1990). These responses can be interpreted to mean that babies perceive depth before they become mobile. An alternative explanation is that the infants are simply responding to two different visual patterns without any appreciation for the differences in depth.

In any case, though, infants do not display fear or wariness of the visual cliff, regardless of age, until they gain experience in moving around by themselves (Campos, Bertenthal, & Kermoian, 1992). Thus, motor activities play an important role in the type of depth perception that causes an infant to avoid heights. Experience obtained through independent locomotion apparently allows the infant to judge height more accurately and develop the impression that heights are dangerous and should be avoided.

Motion Cues. One of the most important factors in an infant's ability to perceive depth and discriminate properties of moving objects is motion. Infants are attracted to moving objects from the beginning of life. As described earlier, their eye movements are jerky at first and do not reach adult efficiency until about 6 months of age (Aslin, 1993). However, their sensitivity to rapidly moving objects is high during the first month of life.

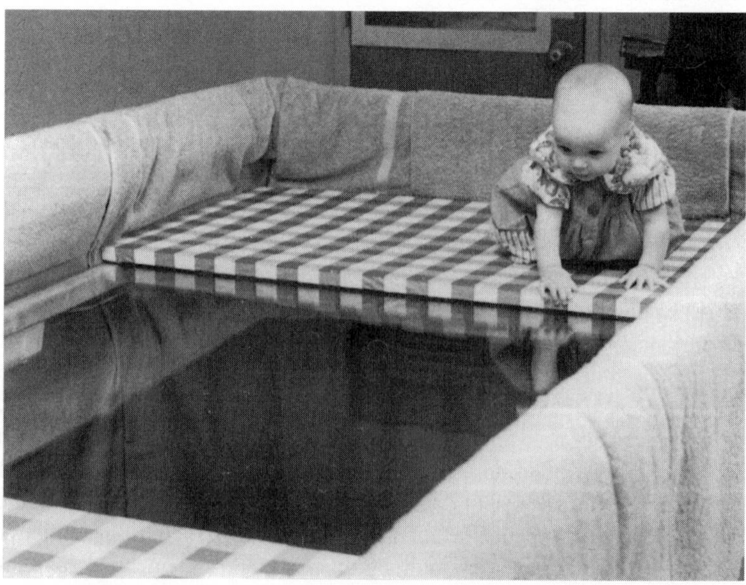

This infant is facing the challenge of the "visual cliff"

The ability to perceive depth through monocular and binocular cues involving motion develops well ahead of depth perception limited to cues from motionless stimuli (Arterberry, Craton, & Yonas, 1993). For example, infants blinked more at an object that was moving toward them than at an object that appeared to be moving away (Nanez, 1988). Apparently the ability to perceive rapidly moving objects develops ahead of the ability to respond to very slowly moving objects (Kaufmann-Hayoz, 1991). By 3 months of age, infants have an uncanny ability to use motion-carried information in their perceptions. For example, infants are able to extract information from visual motion patterns to distinguish objects from their background surfaces (figure-ground relationships), as well as to perceive object shapes, spatial relations, and other properties (Arterberry et al., 1993; Kaufmann-Hayoz, 1991). Motion studies also show that young infants perceive that (1) objects move cohesively and maintain their external boundaries; (2) objects move continuously, tracing a path as they move; and (3) objects move independently and influence each other's motion only on contact (Spelke & Hermer, 1996).

Perception of Faces. Much attention has been given to how infants respond to other humans. Infants seem to be remarkably responsive to the human face. One study found that infants' smiling declined and their visual attention decreased whenever adults looked away (Hains & Muir, 1996). The response of infants to human faces is not only important for social development, but it tells us something about their ability to see.

Facial Recognition. Over the years researchers have tried to determine whether newborns can distinguish one face from another and discriminate faces from other similar stimuli. We now have reasonably good evidence that newborns are capable of detecting and discriminating human faces from other stimuli under certain conditions. When they view moving facial images, with the features highlighted, newborns demonstrate a preference for faces over other patterns (Morton & Johnson, 1991). Shortly after birth, infants also appear to discriminate their mother's face from that of a stranger (Bushnell & Sai, 1987; Field et al., 1984). However, newborns have difficulty discriminating faces if a surrounding border (e.g., a shower cap) is placed around the face (Atkinson, 1995), and most research has found that infants do not reliably discriminate faces of strangers until around 3 months (Bushnell, 1998). Although the evidence isn't conclusive, these studies provide support for the theory that newborns are endowed with an innate preference for the human face and the ability to recognize faces.

In spite of this impressive beginning, studies indicate that this preferential tracking of faces disappears between 4 and 6 weeks of age (M. Johnson et al., 1991). The disappearance is probably due to inhibition of a reflexlike behavior by the development of higher forms of brain activity. By 2 to 3 months of age, infants again clearly demonstrate a preference for the natural arrangement of human facial features over various scrambled facial images (Maurer & Barrera, 1981). At this stage, infants do not need motion to detect facial features. By 6 months of age, infants have developed the ability to discriminate young from old faces and male from female faces. They also remember and discriminate between the faces of strangers (Carey, 1996). Six- to eight-month-old infants display a relatively sophisticated ability to discriminate facial features. Like adults (Rhodes, Sumich, & Byatt, 1999), they tend to demonstrate a preference for attractive faces (Langlois et al., 1987). Infants show this preference as early as 3 days after birth (Slater et al., 1998).

Facial Imitation. If you stick your tongue out at an alert newborn infant, you are likely to find that the infant will stick his or her tongue out at you in return. Researchers have verified the ability of newborns to imitate tongue protrusion modeled by other people (Meltzoff & Moore, 1989, 1994). Researchers have also concluded that newborn infants can imitate a variety of other facial gestures including mouth opening, lip protrusion, and head movement (Meltzoff & Moore, 1977, 1983, 1992, 1994). Cross-cultural studies conducted among newborn infants in rural Nepal,

An example of neonatal imitation

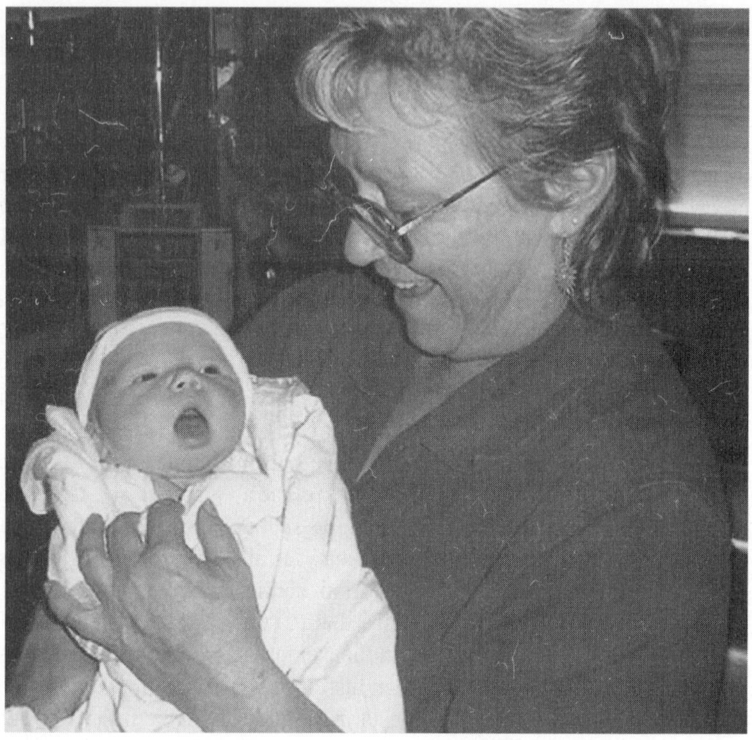

Israel, Switzerland, and France (Meltzoff, Kuhl, & Moore, 1991; Reissland, 1988) have reported this behavior to be universal. Newborns apparently are biased in favor of human facial gestures since they do not imitate tongue protrusion or mouth opening modeled by inanimate objects (Abravanel & DeYong, 1991; Legerstee, 1991). Imitation of tongue protrusion begins to decline after 2 to 3 months of age (Abravanel & Sigafoos, 1984; Fontaine, 1984; Vinter, 1985). However, at the same time facial imitation begins to decline, imitation of sounds and vocalizations begins to increase (Maratos, 1998).

Not all scientists agree, however, that newborns can imitate a wide variety of facial gestures. After critically reviewing the studies on neonatal imitation, Anisfield (1996) concluded that infants only imitate the tongue protrusion gesture. Therefore, additional evidence is needed to resolve this controversy. The resolution of this question is important because if newborns only have the ability to imitate tongue protrusions, it means this early form of imitation can be explained as a type of reflex response elicited by the behavior of a model. On the other hand, if infants can imitate a variety of facial gestures, their abilities may be more advanced and complex. This would support the view that newborn infants have the ability to engage in cross-modal transfer of information from one sensory modality to another (Anisfield, 1996). That is, newborns actively link facial expressions they see others exhibit with internal motor sensations they feel when they engage in the same behavior.

Perception of Objects. Infants spend much of their time looking at objects. Recall that newborn infants scan the edges of faces and still objects. It has been proposed that there are two stages of visual information processing of objects (Bhatt, 1997; Neisser, 1967). The first stage, the preattentive stage, is characterized by focus on features such as line segments, line crossings, and color. This focus, however, is not intentional. The second stage, the attentive stage, is characterized by intentional focus and involves item-by-item processing. This type of processing also involves the use of memory. Infants begin to compare objects with memories of other objects.

Research on infant attention to objects indicates that by 2 months of age, infants tend to focus on the internal features of objects (Haith et al., 1977). Objects are perceived as distinct, single units that are separate from other objects and surfaces (Spelke & Hermer, 1996). At this age infants prefer to look at stimuli with more complex patterns (Brennan, Ames, & Moore, 1966) and stimuli that have highly contrasting contours and curves (McCall & Melson, 1970). By 3 to 4 months of age, object perception skills have blossomed. For example, infants are sensitive to three-dimensional cues in static images (Bhatt & Waters, 1998). In another study, 4-month-old infants were exposed to a rod that was moving back and forth behind a block so they could see only the rod's top and bottom. The infants' responses indicated that they perceived the rod as a unified object rather than two separate pieces (Kellman & Spelke, 1983). Other studies have observed that infants perceive the rod as a whole as early as 3 months (S. Johnson, 1997).

By 12 months, infants can perceive several properties of objects such as object number, shape, and length (Arterberry, 1997). Research on object number has shown that infants can discriminate between small numbers of items. Groups of 8-, 10-, and 12-month-old infants were habituated to two objects (rabbits) as they disappeared and reappeared in a gap between two curtains—an expected event (Arterberry, 1995). The situation was changed whereby only one rabbit appeared in the opening—an unexpected event. Even 8-month-old infants looked more at the unexpected event, suggesting they have a rudimentary form of counting. However, when the ability to perceive number over time was considered, only the 12-month-olds looked longer at the unexpected than at the expected event. These finding suggest that by 12 months of age, infants are capable of perceiving and remembering number over time.

Other studies, however, indicate that by 4 or 5 months of age, infants can discriminate one or two objects from three. For example, Wynn (1992) presented 5-month-old infants with a series of displays in which two objects were manipulated in various numerical combinations. She concluded that these infants could clearly perceive the arithmetical operation being performed and calculate the results. There is no suggestion, though, that infants actually count the objects. Rather, infants identify numbers through **subitization**, a quick and effortless perceptual process that people can apply in looking at three or four objects and knowing how many there are without going through the process of enumeration. Some researchers (e.g., Wynn, 1992) believe that this means human infants are innately endowed with the ability to perform simple mathematical operations. However, others (e.g., Haith & Benson, 1998) argue that infants can detect differences in the number of objects in small sets of perceptual images without necessarily understanding numeric relations or engaging in arithmetic as simple as subitization.

Infants also develop shape and size constancy early, and these abilities may be present at birth (Slater, 2000). Shape constancy is the recognition of a shape even though its orientation has changed. Size constancy is the realization that size is the same regardless of the distance of the object from the viewer. Studies indicate that newborn infants differentiate size and that newborns were able to detect the difference between objects of different size and shape at various locations within their field of vision (Slater, Mattock, & Brown, 1990; Slater & Morison, 1985).

The Importance of Vision: Insights From the Blind. While vision is the least well developed sensory system at birth, it may very well be the most important sensory system. Vision serves as an integrating sense that helps us to put together information from all the other sensory systems. Observation and research of individuals with visual loss have demonstrated how critical vision is to development.

Much of the research on the importance of vision to development has been done with animals.

Research with animals has shown that the absence of vision affects the development of the brain. In classic studies by Hubel and Weisel (1959, 1963, 1965) the eyelids of newborn and 3-month-old kittens were sewn shut (a procedure that might be considered unethical today). While this procedure was devastating to the newborn kittens, the kittens who received the treatment at 3 months showed little effect from it. Just as there is a critical period in visual development for kittens, there also appears to be a critical period for human visual development. Human vision is highly malleable until around 2 years of age (Eliot, 1999).

Research with animals also indicates that vision is of critical importance for the development of other skills. For example, Hein and Held (1967) conducted a study in which they raised kittens without allowing them to see their own limbs. They found that the experience of not seeing their own paws prevented the kittens from being able to guide their paws accurately. Held and Bauer (1974) found similar results with monkeys. Those monkeys who were allowed to see their own hands reached accurately, but monkeys who were not allowed to see their own hands had difficulties not only in reaching, but in tactile control of the object as well.

Children with visual impairments show delays across all developmental areas. Research indicates that infants who are blind are responsive to stimuli from birth, but because they do not have vision, many characteristics of development appear later. For example, remember that infants can distinguish between the faces of mother and stranger shortly after birth. Infants with visual impairments have to make these distinctions through voices. The ability of infants with visual impairment to make this distinction does not occur until two to three months after birth (Fraiberg & Freedman, 1964). Infants who are blind do not distinguish objects until 6 months of age (Burlingham, 1964).

INTERSENSORY PERCEPTION

Most of our experiences involve simultaneous impressions from more than one sensory modality. Sights occur in combination with sounds; tastes and odors are often experienced as a blend of sensations. Newborn infants are faced with the task of integrating information they receive from different sensory systems into a unified, meaningful experience. The ability to combine information from different senses is referred to as **intersensory perception** (or **intermodal perception**). For example, when infants recognize that an object that is seen can also be touched, they are engaging in intermodal or intersensory perception. As part of their perceptual experiences, infants also need to use information from one sensory system to "inform" other sensory systems. Infants identify an object with one of the senses (e.g., vision) through the use of information obtained only by a different sensory mechanism (e.g., touch). This process is referred to as **cross-modal transfer**.

Research evidence tends to support the belief that infants are capable of intersensory integration at birth, at least to a limited extent. When newborns hear a sound, they attempt to find the source of the sound, apparently for visual inspection, thereby integrating sounds and sights into a single experience (Mendelson & Haith, 1976). They are also more interested in visually tracking moving objects that make a sound than objects that are silent (Rose & Ruff, 1987). In addition, newborns appear to be capable of coordinating the senses of vision and touch. Experiments show that they reach out to touch objects that move back and forth in their field of vision (Von Hofsten, 1982).

Some researchers believe that very young infants focus on redundancy in intersensory coordination (Bahrick, 2000). In other words, they look for information that occurs in synchrony across two of the senses. For example, when infants were shown a video of a hammer tapping out two different rhythms, they were able to distinguish the rhythms when accompanied by the visual image but not when presented with the rhythm alone (Bahrick & Lickliter, 2000). Later, infants begin to make connections between more arbitrary stimuli, such as associating hair style with the sound of a voice.

In a rather ingenious experiment, Meltzoff and Borton (1979) provided 1-month-old infants with a smooth object attached to a pacifier and a rough nubby one attached to another pacifier. The infants were allowed to suck, but not view, each of the two objects. They were then given the pacifiers to look at, along with new objects larger than those used for sucking. The infants showed a definite preference for looking at the objects with which they had become familiar through sucking. This experiment indicates that very young children have the ability to engage in cross-modal transfer from the oral-tactile to the visual-perceptual systems.

The ability to coordinate and integrate information from different sensory modalities continues to improve with age (Bahrick & Pickens, 1994; S. Rose & Ruff, 1987). At the age of 3 or 4 months, infants can match pictures with recorded sounds. This ability can be assessed by showing infants two different films at the same time. As the moving pictures are projected side-by-side, a soundtrack that matches only one of the films is played. When infants look longer and more often at the pictures that are synchronized with the sounds, it is assumed that they have made a correct match (Spelke, 1979). Infants from 2 to 5 months old can match a face with a voice based on the synchrony between the movements of the mouth and the timing of speech (Lewkowicz, 1996). Not only can infants match voices and faces, they can recognize themselves by using contingency cues. Infants can watch live video of themselves and other infants and recognize themselves (Bahrick, 1995).

By 5 months of age infants are able to coordinate visual-distance perceptions with auditory-distance cues. At this age, infants correctly match increases or decreases in sounds with the images of approaching or retreating toy trains and automobiles (Pickens, 1994; Schiff, Benasich, & Bornstein, 1989). Additional studies, reviewed by Bahrick and Pickens (1994) indicate that by 5 or 6 months infants are capable of a wide variety of rather complex intersensory functions. For example, 4- and 7-month-old infants were shown films of the faces of an unfamiliar child and an adult of the same gender positioned side-by-side. The child and the adult recited a nursery rhyme in synchrony with one another. The synchronized voice of only one of them was also played. While the 7-month-old infants were able to match the appropriate faces and voices, the 4-month-olds could not (Soutullo, Hernandez, & Bahrick, 1992). Seven-month-olds also coordinate facial motion and/or vocal sounds with facial expressions to discriminate happy and angry expressions (Soken & Pick, 1992). In addition, they can match the corresponding pitch of an impact sound with the color and shape of the object that strikes the surface (Walker-Andrews, 1994).

However, there is some evidence that infants who are at-risk because of prematurity and/or social factors (e.g., poverty) have problems in cross-modal transfer (S. Rose, 1994). It is very common for children who are visually impaired, who have cerebral palsy or attention deficit disorder, or who exhibit self-injurious behavior to have problems with sensory integration. These types of problems are known as **sensory integration dysfunction**. Children who have this disorder have been shown to exhibit attentional, emotional, organizational, and motor delays as well as tactile defensiveness, distractibility, and poor language and visual-spatial skills (DeGangi & Greenspan, 1989; McLean, Bailey, & Wolery, 1996; Sears, 1994).

EVALUATING PERCEPTUAL DEVELOPMENT

Evaluating perceptual development in infants and toddlers can be difficult. Many of the tests we use with older children and adults rely on their ability to tell us what they are able to perceive. With infants, much of our assessment relies on observation of infant behavior.

Evaluating Touch and Vestibular Stimulation. The **Test of Sensory Function in Infants** (DeGangi & Greenspan, 1989) can be used to assess sensory processing and reactivity abilities of infants who are 4 to 18 months old. There are other instruments that measure several areas of development but specifically include items related to tactile and vestibular abilities. These tests include the **Carolina Curriculum for Infants and Toddlers With Special Needs** (Johnson-Martin et al., 1991)

APPLICATIONS: FACILITATING PERCEPTUAL DEVELOPMENT

Perceptual skills are facilitated through a sensory-rich environment. Fortunately, most home environments provide an ever-changing variety of stimuli through the natural progression of the day (Gestwicki, 1999). However, careful planning can also enhance the sensory richness of an environment. First and foremost, safety is critical. Infants need an environment where they can freely and safely explore. Attention to different types of sensory input is also important. Infants like to explore through taste and touch. It is important to have materials that are soft and cuddly, but that also have different textures, such as warm, fuzzy, rough, smooth (Cryer, Harms, & Bourland, 1987; Gonzalez-Mena & Eyer, 1997). It is also essential to provide materials that infants can explore orally. In addition to materials, opportunities for messy play where infants can freely manipulate materials can enhance the use of touch and taste (O'Brien, 1997), as well as vision, hearing, and smell. The development of haptic perceptual abilities can be enhanced by making it possible for infants to engage in numerous motor activities (Bushnell & Boudreau, 1993).

Hearing can be enhanced in many different ways. Provision of toys that make sounds is one way. However, calling attention to the many natural sounds in the environment (e.g., bird and animal noises) can also be used in the development of hearing. Interactions and the use of language with the infant can be another way to encourage the use of hearing. Infants and toddlers love to hear stories read from books (O'Brien, 1997).

Providing visually interesting toys and mobiles in places where infants have access to them can be beneficial for visual development. Toys should vary in shape and color (Cryer et al., 1987). In addition, pictures and mirrors placed low on the walls as well as on the floors will be stimulating to infants (Gestwicki, 1999). Because the human face is so visually interesting, many opportunities for social interaction can also facilitate visual development. Including infants in the natural routine of the day, by moving them around as caregivers move around, can also provide different visual stimuli from different perspectives and angles.

It is important, nevertheless, to be aware of sensory overload. Too much stimulation in an environment can result in stress and can cause the infant to disengage from the environment. Gestwicki (1999) recommends that providers change materials as infants lose interest and remove items that infants are not interested in or that do not have meaning to the infant. In addition, she recommends that stimulation not be provided in the crib. The crib is a place for sleeping, and providing extra stimulation can send confusing signals. Attention to signals from the infant can help gauge what is the appropriate level of stimulation for each infant.

and the **Bayley Scales of Infant Development–II** (Bayley, 1993).

Evaluating Hearing. All newborn infants should be tested for hearing loss. One method for testing infants prior to 6 months of age is the use of **behavioral observation audiometry (BOA)**. BOA relies on behavior to indicate the child's level of hearing (McLean et al., 1996). Infants are presented with acoustic toys (squeak toys, rattles, bells, etc.) in a soundproof environment, and their reactions to those sounds are observed. This type of assessment is problematic, however. A child may not attend to the noise for reasons other than hearing loss or may not respond because of the presence of other disabling conditions (Hyvarinen, 1988).

The **otoacoustic emissions test** may be the best method of detecting loss in newborn infants. It is frequently used to screen infants for hearing problems before they leave the hospital. In this test, which takes about 15 minutes, a probe through which sounds are emitted is placed into each ear canal. If the hearing mechanism is functioning properly, an "echo" from the baby's inner ear is transmitted through the probe and registered on a computer screen.

Visual reinforcement audiometry (VRA) is a technique that is used to detect hearing problems of older infants. VRA is appropriate for infants who are 6 months of age and older (McLean et al., 1996). In this type of assessment infants are exposed to auditory stimuli paired with visual stimuli in a variety of ways. They are rewarded for correctly associating the sound with the visual object. Their responses or lack of responses are used as indicators of the ability to hear.

Evaluating Vision. A thorough eye examination is recommended at birth, 6 months, 3½ years, and 5 years (American Academy of Pediatrics, 1986). This eye exam should consist of an examination of "the structural integrity of the external eye, the pupillary reflexes, range of the extraocular movements, ocular alignment and binocularity, acuity, visual fields, depth perception, and color perception, if possible" (McLean et al., 1996, p. 143). Infant vision can be tested through several techniques including **visual evoked responses**. In this procedure, electrodes are placed on an infant's head to measure brain waves in response to visual stimulation.

SUMMARY

Philosophical and Theoretical Foundations

- The philosophical and theoretical views on which the study of infant perception is based include nativism, empiricism, and direct perception.

Development of the Sensory Systems

- The five basic sensory systems—vision, hearing, touch, taste, and smell—are functioning at birth, at least to a limited extent.
- As soon as they are born, infants apparently have the capacity to distinguish among the four basic tastes. The taste for sweet substances is predominant over other taste preferences and is probably innate.
- Infants can detect strong odors at birth but do not respond to weaker odors until they are a few days older. Like adults, infants prefer pleasant to unpleasant odors. The sense of smell improves rapidly as infants grow, enabling them to become increasingly aware of and remember information related to smell.
- The sense of touch is one of the earliest and most important senses to develop. It is the most complex of the senses to study and understand but plays a very important role in development.
- Contrary to previous opinion, newborns respond to pain in ways that are similar to how adults respond to pain.
- Between 3 and 12 months of age, infants develop the capacity to discriminate between the size, temperature, hardness, texture, weight, and shape of objects through the use of haptic perception.
- Newborn babies cannot hear as well as adults, but they are sensitive to sounds even before birth. They are capable of identifying the direction from which a sound originates, distinguishing between sounds of different pitch, loudness, and intensity. They prefer to listen to sounds within the range of the human voice, and the sound of their mother's voice over other voices.
- Infants hear better as their auditory system matures. By 6 to 7 months of age, infants can use sounds to locate objects in the dark. By 9 months, infants are making distinctions of a variety of sound clusters in speech.
- The vestibular system provides the foundation for body movements and posture. This system is intact at birth but improves in function throughout infancy.

The Development of Vision

- The vision of newborns is blurred but improves rapidly with age. Their eye movements are jerky but become well coordinated by 12 weeks of age as head-turning ability improves.
- Newborns scan the edges of objects and do not look much at the overall shape of objects until around 2 months. As they get older, infants prefer to look at more complex and detailed patterns.
- Newborn infants appear to be capable of limited color vision. The perception of colors improves rapidly and become almost adultlike by 3 months of age.
- Infants use both monocular (one eye) and binocular cues (two eyes) in depth perception. Depth

perception is more accurate with the use of binocular vision. Infants indicate a sophisticated ability to perceive when they avoid the "visual cliff." This form of depth perception is affected by the infant's experiences obtained through self-produced locomotion.

- The ability of infants to perceive depth and discriminate object properties is heavily influenced by motion cues. The ability to perceive the properties of moving objects develops ahead of the ability to detect the features of immobile objects.
- Under certain conditions, newborns recognize and prefer to look at human faces more than other images. They can discriminate between a variety of human faces and facial features as they get older. Newborns imitate tongue protrusion, but their ability to mimic other facial gestures has not been determined.
- The ability to perceive objects blossoms by 3 to 4 months of age. The ability to discriminate various features of objects—number (subitization), shape, and length—reaches adultlike levels by 1 year of age.
- Infants with visual impairments tend to be delayed in many aspects of development.

Intersensory Perception

- Research evidence tends to support the view that infants are capable of limited intersensory perception at birth. The ability to coordinate and integrate information from different sensory modalities improves with age.

Evaluating Perceptual Development

- Evaluating perceptual development in infants and toddlers can be difficult but should be done at regular intervals. A variety of screening and assessment tests are available to detect vestibular function, hearing, and vision.

KEY TERMS

sensations
perception
nativists
empiricists
direct perception
affordances
olfactory system
haptic perceptions
sound localization
vestibular stimulation
visual acuity
visual accommodation
depth perception
monocular cues
binocular cues
visual cliff
subitization
intersensory perception/intermodal perception
cross-modal transfer
sensory integration dysfunction
Test of Sensory Function in Infants
behavioral observation audiometry (BOA)
otoacoustic emissions test
visual reinforcement audiometry (VRA)
visual evoked responses

INFORMATION ON THE WEB*

psych.wisc.edu/gradstudies/infant.html. University of Wisconsin Web site with links to Dannemiller's Perceptual Development Laboratory, Goldsmith's Twin and Temperament Laboratory, and Saffran's Infant Learning Lab.

www.shriver.org. Web site of the Eunice Kennedy Shriver Center. Contents include information about Infant Vision Lab, including a summary of milestones in visual development, plus many other topics related to infant perception and cognition.

*Web sites are subject to change.

EIGHT

Cognitive Development

What is the little one thinking about?
Very wonderful things no doubt! . . .
Who can tell what a baby thinks.
J. G. Holland

When do infants begin to think? How do they think? How soon do learning and memory begin? What does an infant know? These and other questions about the development of intelligence in infants have been the target of numerous inquiring minds. One of the characteristics of human intelligence is to try to find out how that intellectual capacity evolved. During a child's infancy, we have opportunities to observe the development of intelligence almost from the very beginning. Although we have only scratched the surface, our knowledge of cognitive development has increased dramatically during the past 30 years.

Cognition and perception are interdependent processes to the extent that it is difficult to determine where one leaves off and the other begins. Therefore, this chapter is, to some extent, a continuation of the previous chapter on perceptual development. Here we focus on some of the factors that influence intelligence, some important theories of cognitive development, the development of infant memory, and some of the ways infants learn. We also look at some of the instruments that are used to assess infant intelligence. Finally, suggestions for facilitating cognitive development during the infancy period are considered.

DEFINITIONS

Definitions of intelligence are numerous and varied. Wechsler (1944) defined **intelligence** as "the capacity of the individual to act purposefully, think rationally and deal effectively with the environment" (p. 3). Piaget (1954) defined intelligence in terms of an individual's capacity to adapt to the environment. There is widespread agreement among experts from various fields that intelligence consists of at least three elements—the ability to think abstractly or reason, the capacity to accumulate knowledge (memory), and the ability to solve problems (K. McCormick, 1996).

Cognition is a term that is closely associated with intelligence. The two terms are frequently used to mean the same thing. Technically, though, cognition refers to all the mental processes, such as thinking, remembering, use of language, problem solving, and concept formation. The cognitive processes thus make up the functional component of intelligence. In this chapter, the terms *cognition* and *intellectual development* are used interchangeably.

INFLUENCES ON INTELLIGENCE

The extent to which intelligence is controlled by heredity or by environment has been intensely debated for centuries. Today the most widely accepted point of view is that heredity and environment interact in complex ways to shape intelligence. However, researchers have attempted to determine the relative contribution of each factor.

Heredity. The position that heredity is the dominant force in intellectual development has been represented most vigorously by Arthur Jensen (1969). Jensen claims that approximately 80 percent of the differences in IQ scores is the result of genetic factors. Thus if one child obtains an IQ score of 120 and another obtains a score of 100, 16 points of the 20-point difference (.80 × 20) are the result of heredity. Jensen's claims have been controversial and not widely accepted. Still, there is no doubt that intelligence is influenced by heredity. Plomin and colleagues (Plomin & Defries, 1980; Plomin, DeFries, & McClearn, 1990) have concluded that the difference in IQ scores that can be attributed to genetic factors is no more than 50 percent. Most researchers have been reluctant to accept a specific percentage as valid because of the difficulties involved in separating genetic from environmental factors. Scientists such as Scarr and Weinberg (1978) believe that it is impossible to assign a specific percentage to the proportion of intelligence that is controlled by heredity.

Environment. In combination with heredity, numerous environmental influences potentially affect intellectual development. Most of these factors, including health, nutrition, and prenatal and perinatal influences, are covered in other chapters. At this point we need to consider three additional potential sources of influence during infancy: the family environment, socioeconomic status, and cultural factors.

Family Environment. Research studies have tended to confirm the assertion that family influences play a very important role in the development of intelligence. In the Harvard Preschool Project, B. White and Watts (1973) conducted extensive observations of the home environment of 31 infants through the first three years of life. They concluded that the infants who were assessed to be the most intellectually competent experienced parent-child interactions superior to those of the infants who were less competent. A four-year longitudinal study of 193 mothers and their infants (Bee et al., 1982) found that measures of home-environmental quality and parent-infant interaction taken in the first year of life are good predictors of later IQ and language development.

Socioeconomic Status. Children from low-socioeconomic backgrounds consistently score lower on measures of intelligence than do their middle-class peers. However, these differences do not begin to appear until after the first 18 months of life (Golden & Birns, 1976). By 3 years of age, the child's IQ score has been affected by such socioeconomic indicators as parental education, occupation, and income (Bayley & Schaefer, 1964). For infants living in poverty, a variety of factors can lead to cognitive delays. Adverse conditions commonly faced are inadequate nutrition, insufficient health care, exposure to toxic substances, and inappropriate stimulation (Kaplan-Sanoff, Parker, & Zuckerman, 1991). Fortunately, infant intervention programs can prevent the decline of IQ scores attributed to the effects of poverty.

Cultural Factors. Cross-cultural studies have generally found more similarities than differences in cognitive development of infants throughout the world. The sequence and timing of sensorimotor milestones, smiling, separation anxiety, the order of stages of language development (Rogoff & Morelli, 1989), and the ability to interpret the meaning of facial expressions and perceive whole-part relationships (Berk & Winsler, 1995) are similar for infants from all cultures. After reviewing numerous investigations, Super (1981) concluded that infants from one particular culture or race generally do not show more rapid cognitive development than infants from other cultures or races, except under conditions of minimal stimulation or malnutrition. Kagan and Klein (1973) found that infants living in an isolated village of Guatemala were delayed two to three months in achieving a variety of cognitive milestones such as object permanence and symbolic aspects of play. The delays were attributed to the inadequate stimulation they experienced during their first year.

Even though infants from all cultural backgrounds are alike in many ways, cultural influences are a primary factor in infant development. There is increasing evidence that social and cultural factors are a powerful source of influence in shaping and transforming children's thinking (Berk & Winsler, 1995). According to Vygotsky (1978), learning is inseparable from social and cultural activities. In order to understand children, therefore, we must understand the social and cultural contexts in which they develop (Berk & Winsler, 1995). Vygotsky's ideas will be considered in more detail after we look at Piaget's cognitive developmental theory.

PIAGET'S THEORY

The theory of Jean Piaget has most widely influenced contemporary understanding of the development of infant intelligence. Piaget did not agree with the nativist view that infants are born with basic concepts and knowledge structures. He also disagreed with the empiricist position that the newborn infant's mind is a *tabula rasa* (blank slate) and all knowledge is acquired through experience. Instead, Piaget's theory is based on the belief that intelligence develops through an interaction between internal (genetic) and external (environmental) influences.

Key Concepts. For Piaget (1952), making progress in cognitive development is based on scheme building. A **scheme** is a basic pattern of action, thought,

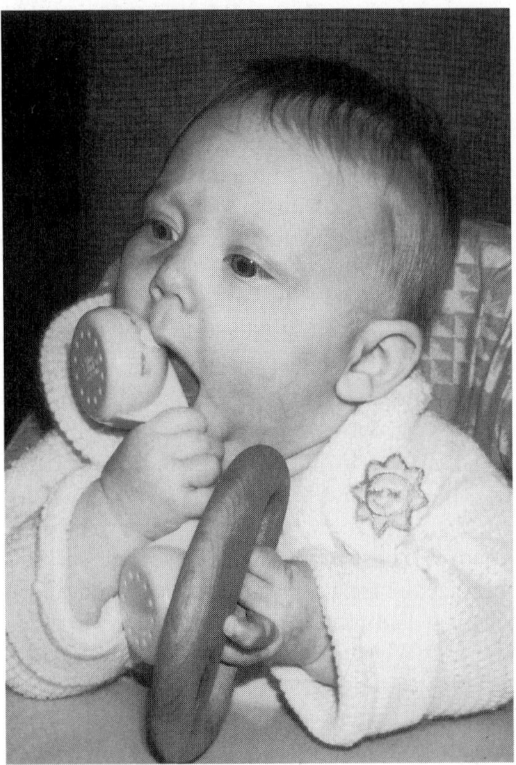

This infant is practicing assimilation by exploring the object with the mouthing scheme.

or knowledge that is used to interact with the environment. Schemes can be classified as either motor or mental. Motor schemes are organized patterns of action such as sucking a bottle, picking up a toy, or walking. Mental schemes are concepts, ideas, or images that make up the thought processes. Mental and motor schemes are used together and are difficult to separate, as when an infant produces a sound (motor) to form a word (mental). Schemes are the building blocks of intelligence. They make up the structure of the mind and serve as basic units of behavior. At any given age, a person's intelligence is based upon the number, complexity, and flexibility of the available schemes.

Schemes are built and modified through the process of **adaptation.** Piaget believed that adaptation is the key to intellectual functioning. In order to survive and get along in the world, an individual must make changes and adjustments in thought and action to fit new situations. Adaptation takes place through two related processes—assimilation and accommodation. **Assimilation** is making the environment fit you. In assimilation, the individual makes use of substances or information through existing schemes. A young infant who spots a new object will probably pick it up and try to eat it or bang it on something. If the toy is small enough, the baby can exploit it without making any modifications in existing behaviors. In some cases an infant assimilates information (perceptions) from the environment by forcing it to conform or fit in with existing ideas or understandings (schemes). For example, an infant may learn the word *cat* and associate it with a four-legged, furry animal. The infant may then use that particular scheme (cat) to apply to a dog or other animals. Thus, in assimilation, the infant uses and tries to preserve existing structures.

Accommodation is making yourself fit the environment. It is the process whereby an individual's schemes are altered to fit new information or experiences. When a breast-fed baby is given a bottle for the first time, the sucking scheme has to be modified to fit the shape, size, and milk flow of the new nipple before it is effective. The infant who calls all four-legged animals "cat" will eventually learn that the "cat" scheme only applies to certain animals. In some cases a new scheme has to be created because there is no existing scheme available into which new information can be accommodated. Accommodation is the mechanism through which variability, growth, and change occurs.

Assimilation and accommodation are complementary processes that usually operate in concert. The two processes may be observed when an infant adjusts the mouth (sucking) to accommodate the shape of a new nipple while at the same time taking in or assimilating nourishment and pleasurable sensations. In this instance, assimilation and accommodation have reached a state of equilibrium or balance. The infant has reached a state of adaptation to the environment. However, the equilibrium or state of balance between assimilation and accommodation does not last, and one process or the other dominates temporarily. When assimilation and accommodation are out of balance, the result is usually cognitive conflict. The infant is then motivated to restore equilibrium by searching for a solution. Cognitive development advances as the baby produces more sophisticated schemes in order to adapt and change.

Piaget's Stages. According to Piaget, cognitive development proceeds through a series of orderly stages. Although the approximate age at which each stage occurs has been identified, not everyone goes through the stages at the same rate or chronological age. In some instances, a person may "straddle" or be in two stages at the same time. However, the order in which individuals progress through the stages does not vary. The basic stages Piaget identified are the *sensorimotor period* (birth to 2 years), the period of *preoperational thought* (2 to 7 years), the *period of concrete operations* (7 to 11 years), and the *period of formal operations* (11 to 15 years). The sensorimotor period, which corresponds with infancy, is considered further.

Sensorimotor Period. The first two years of life are called the **sensorimotor period** because the baby relates to the world by coordinating information from the senses with motor activities of the body. Piaget (1952) introduced the idea that thought arises from action. In the beginning of life, knowledge is not separated from activities. The young infant looks at an object and reflexively reaches for it without thinking about the process. As the baby gets older, the repetition of motor activities provides the basis for development of mental schemes, or ideas of the mind. During most of the sensorimotor period infants do not have concepts or ideas and thus are not capable of true thinking (Mandler, 1990).

The period of sensorimotor intelligence is divided into six stages. The infant is working on several tasks during the various substages. These tasks include imitating the behavior of others, developing intentional behavior, and understanding object permanence, cause-effect relationships, and time and space concepts. A summary of the cognitive changes that occur during each of the stages of the sensorimotor period follows.

Stage 1: Exercising Reflex Schemes (Birth–1 Month). A newborn infant is equipped with some basic reflex schemes such as sucking, looking, and crying. The baby's actions during this stage consist primarily of exercising these innate reflexes. The main accomplishment during this substage is the increased efficiency and complexity of reflexive behaviors. For example, the baby uses the sucking scheme on different objects and assimilates taste and other pleasurable sensations in the process. With experience and practice, the sucking reflex becomes more efficient and adapted to satisfying both nutritive and non-nutritive sucking needs. The other reflexes are also modified and become more efficient and discriminating if the infant has opportunities for practice.

Stage 2: Primary Circular Reactions (1–4 Months). The reflex schemes have become more complex through repeated use and now serve as the basis for new patterns of behavior. Piaget labeled these new schemes primary circular reactions. Responses in this stage are called primary because they are centered in the baby's own body, and because they are the first of a series of circular reactions. A **circular reaction** is a response that stimulates its own repetition.

At the beginning of this stage, the baby may be observed repeating over and over interesting and pleasurable behavior patterns that have been accidentally discovered. One of the first primary circular responses an infant demonstrates is thumb-sucking. A major accomplishment in this stage is the infant's growing ability to coordinate and combine various schemes. Piaget (1952) observed his daughter Jacqueline turning her head to locate the sound of his voice at age 2 months and 12 days. Her action represents the intercoordination of the looking and hearing schemes. At this stage, the infant also begins to anticipate the occurrence of events on the basis of past experience. An infant may begin sucking movements the minute it is picked up and placed in the position to nurse. In so doing, the infant demonstrates an elementary understanding that there is a sequence to certain events. This forms the basis for the infant's understanding of time.

Stage 3: Secondary Circular Reactions (4–8 Months). The circular reactions are now labeled as secondary for two reasons. For one thing, this stage represents the second in the series of circular reactions. The main reason, though, is that the infant's repetitive behaviors now focus on events or objects outside the body. The stage 3 infant is concerned with a result produced in the external environment. Unlike primary circular reactions, these are not reflexive behaviors, but schemes that have been acquired through learning.

Secondary circular reactions are the result of accidental or random behaviors, which produce something that attracts the infant's attention. The following is an example:

> One day when Dimitri was 4 months old, he was lying on his back in his crib looking at his multicolored animal mobile . . . when he suddenly kicked one of his feet and banged the side of the crib. The movement of his leg against the crib bars caused the mobile to sway . . . Dimitri watched the mobile's movement until it stopped. As soon as the mobile was still, he looked away and then looked back at it again. No movement. Now he again looked away, but this time catching sight of his foot. Then he kicked his foot again but not hard enough to make the crib, and hence the mobile, move. He became slightly agitated and kicked both feet, this time with success. Dimitri lay perfectly still, his eyes fixed on the dancing animals. When they stopped moving, he kicked both feet and waved his arms until he moved the crib enough to activate the mobile. (Sherrod, Vietze, & Friedman, 1978, p. 104)

When Dimitri made the connection between the moving mobile and his own movements, he repeated the action and established a secondary circular response.

The stage 3 infant begins to develop an awareness of the object concept. Infants have to learn that objects are external or separate from themselves and continue to exist even though they are not visible (**object permanence**). At this point the infant will search for an object if it is partially visible. If an infant drops an object and loses sight of it, the infant will attempt to visually anticipate its new location. This usually happens only if the baby has caused an object to disappear. The concept of object permanence thus is only partially developed in stage 3.

Stage 4: Coordination of Secondary Circular Reactions (8–12 Months). For the first time, the infant exhibits behaviors that Piaget called truly intelligent. Schemes are now mobile and flexible enough to be generalized to new situations. Babies can use existing schemes to overcome obstacles or solve simple problems. The infant can also combine and coordinate several different schemes to reach a goal. This stage is thus called coordination of secondary circular reactions (schemes).

Stage 4 infants demonstrate intentional, goal-directed activity, which is one of the first signs of intelligent behavior. Piaget described how he placed his hand in front of a matchbox his son Laurent was trying to obtain. Laurent hit his father's hand to move it aside in order to get the box. When Piaget replaced the hand with a cushion as an obstacle, Laurent also hit the pillow so that he could grasp the box. In this example, we see how an existing scheme is adapted to apply to a new situation. The "hitting" scheme from stage 3 was applied to obtain the desired object.

We can also see in Laurent's means-to-an-end behavior a major step in the understanding of *cause-effect relationships.* Up to this point, an infant acts and waits for something to happen, but with no real understanding of how effects occur. It was as if things happened by "magic" or that objects obeyed the baby's wishes. At this stage, however, infants begin to be aware that their own actions create results: If you hit a mobile, it moves.

The development of the object concept takes another step forward in this stage. The infant's increased understanding of the permanence of objects is evident when the infant searches for an object that has disappeared. If a ball rolls under a chair, the infant will try to find it there. An infant will also remove a cover from an object that is completely hidden. At this stage, infants love to play peekaboo and hide-and-seek games based on the disappearance and reappearance of people and objects. The concept of object permanence is not completely established, though. The infant cannot think of an object as having an independent existence apart from the actions performed on it. If an object is placed under one cover (A) and then under another (B), the infant will look only under the first cover (A). The infant will find a ball that is hidden under a handkerchief but will continue to look under the handkerchief if the ball is hidden the second time under a pillow even while the infant watches. At this stage, the object is still connected with the infant's previous success in locating it at point A, so the search ends at that location. Piaget believed that the infant thinks there is more than one object involved in the game. In other words, there is an object at A and another just like it at B.

According to Piaget, the beginning of true imitation occurs in this stage. Imitation involves the capacity to copy the actions, sounds, or other characteristics exhibited by a model. Before stage 4, infants engage in what Piaget called reflexive or **pseudoimitation.** This is an early form of imitation that is based on a response the child has already demonstrated or finds easy to mimic. For example, an infant will readily imitate cooing and other sounds the infant has already made. Infants can be taught to imitate adults waving "bye-bye" and performing other actions, but Piaget did not call these behaviors true imitation because they require constant practice and encouragement.

Now, at stage 4, infants can imitate actions that involve movements they cannot see themselves perform, such as wrinkling the nose. They also begin to imitate new sounds. For example, one mother was surprised after she angrily hung up the phone to hear her 1-year-old mimic her perfectly with the word "*Damn*!" (Pulaski, 1978).

Stage 5: Tertiary Circular Reactions (12–18 Months). Tertiary means third-order, or third in a series. Piaget used this term to describe how the baby's intellectual activities reach a more complex and advanced level of proficiency. The infant still engages in repetitive activity, but deliberately makes variations to see what happens. The stage 4 infant was satisfied with producing the same result over and over. The stage 5 infant wants to use a familiar combination of schemes to produce something new and different. This marks the beginning of curiosity and creative activity.

Piaget (1952) described how Laurent dropped pieces of bread and other objects from various body positions and locations. In the previous stage he would have been interested simply in the act of letting go, to observe the same result over and over. At stage 5 he was more interested in observing where the object landed, particularly in relation to the position from which he let it fall. Piaget referred to this type of activity as directed groping.

Through the use of tertiary circular reactions, the infant solves simple problems by trial and error. Like a budding scientist, the infant experiments to find new ways to accomplish a goal or solve a problem. New combinations and variations of schemes are attempted until the infant finds one that works. For example, babies discover they can obtain an object that is out of reach by pulling on the tablecloth on which the object is resting. Such behavior indicates that the stage 5 baby displays a certain amount of practical intelligence.

The infant continues to make progress in understanding the various features and functions of objects. The stage 5 infant is able to walk, which brings increased opportunities for contact with more objects and opportunities to see their relationship to one another in space. The baby learns more about physical properties such as size, weight, and texture. During the previous stage, the infant was interested in taking objects apart, putting them into containers, and dumping them out. Now the infant is interested in putting the pieces of an object together and exploring the relationship between different objects and their containers.

The understanding of cause-effect relations reaches a new level during this stage. Infants now begin to recognize that actions result from the behavior of other people as well as their own. They are thus becoming slightly less egocentric. When an object moves, they may look for the source of the movement outside of their own activities. For example, Piaget (1954) slowly moved Laurent's stroller with his foot. Laurent leaned over to the edge of the carriage to find what was making it move. As soon as he saw his father's foot on the wheel, he gave a smile of understanding.

The concept of object permanence also improves. The infant can now follow and locate an object that has been hidden in three successive locations. However, the infant must see the movements. If not allowed to watch where the object disappears at any point, the baby becomes confused and will look for it only at the first location. Apparently it is not yet possible for the infant to imagine what might be happening to an object while it is out of sight.

Like the object concept, the development of imitation parallels cognitive development. Stage 5 infants are capable of more accurate and extensive imitations. They can imitate behaviors that are not in their repertory, but they require some "groping," or trial and error. In keeping with the tendency to experiment, they vary the actions or sounds of the model to observe the result.

Stage 6: Invention of New Means Through Mental Combinations (18–24 Months). At last the infant begins to think before acting. The ability to represent objects and events by mental images (symbols) develops during this stage. The infant no longer has to "discover" solutions to problems through trial and error, but is capable of inventing solutions by combining mental schemes.

Piaget (1952) gave his daughter, Lucienne, a matchbox containing his watch chain. He left a small opening so that she could see the chain inside. Her first efforts to get it out with her index finger were unsuccessful. Next, she looked at the opening and began to open and close her mouth, wider and wider. She then put her finger into the opening of the box and slid the cover back far enough to reach the chain. Lucienne gave an indication of what she was thinking when she opened and closed her mouth. Piaget concluded: "This new type of behavior pattern characterizes systematic intelligence" (Piaget, 1952, p. 331).

The ability to represent actions through mental pictures makes it possible for an infant to imitate a model faster and more accurately. The infant can, for the first time, imitate a model that is no longer present. Jacqueline observed a little boy stamping his feet while engaging in a temper tantrum. The next day she screamed and stamped her feet in a similar fashion (Piaget, 1962). This is called **deferred imitation.**

The concept of object permanence is fully developed at this stage. The baby now has a mental image of the object that is independent of an immediate sensory impression of the object itself. The object has an independent, enduring existence even though it cannot always be seen. Infants are not as easily fooled when an object disappears, even though part of the process may be invisible. They search in various places where they have found objects hidden before.

Evaluation of Piaget's Theory. Presently, there is sufficient evidence to support some of the basic sequences of development outlined in Piaget's sensorimotor stages. On the other hand, researchers have found evidence to challenge many of Piaget's assumptions. There is an increasing amount of research indicating that infants accomplish some of the cognitive tasks earlier than Piaget's timetable suggests. The studies of Mandler (1990) and Baillargeon (1993) indicate that infants are far more sophisticated in their cognitive abilities than Piaget believed. The results of several studies on object permanence are viewed as incompatible with Piaget's ideas. Piaget based his belief about the timetable for the development of the object concept on the willingness or ability of an infant to manually or physically search for a hidden object. It is possible, however, that infants do not manually search for an object because of motor limitations, memory limitations, motivational factors, or the understanding of how to search. Bower (1982), Baillargeon (1993), and others conducted studies that relied on looking rather than the manual tasks used by Piaget and others. The results of these investigations indicate that infants develop a concept of object permanence earlier than Piaget assumed, although there is no general agreement about when it is developed (Lutz & Sternberg, 1999).

In spite of findings that apparently contradict Piaget's theory, many scholars have rushed to defend Piagetian theory (e.g., Glassman, 1994; Lourenco & Machado, 1996). G. Decarie and Ricard (1996) contend that upon closer examination, research findings on object permanence and imitation do not necessarily constitute evidence of cognitive skills that violate Piaget's basic theory. These and other supporters of Piaget are convinced that his theory continues to provide a valuable framework for understanding infant development. Even if Piaget underestimated the timetable for the emergence of some of the infant's cognitive abilities, his portrayal of the sequence in which cognitive functions emerge remains less controversial. As Piaget's theory undergoes reappraisal, other theories are gaining popularity. Two such theories that we will consider are Vygotsky's sociocultural theory and information-processing theories.

VYGOTSKY'S THEORY

Piaget emphasized the importance of the biological and maturational determinants of cognitive development. Vygotsky believed that environmental and social interactions are the critical factors in intellectual development (Lutz & Sternberg, 1999). For Piaget, sensorimotor activities are the most important activities during infancy. For Vygotsky (1978), the interchanges between the infant and other people represent the key to cognitive change. He agreed with Piaget that infants learn through the manipulation of objects. However, Vygotsky believed that the significance of object play cannot be separated from the cultural context. "The path from object to child and from the child to object passes through another person" (Vygotsky, 1978, p. 30). All higher mental activities, such as attention, memory, and problem solving are rooted in social behavior that becomes internalized by the child. The next section is a brief overview of some of Vygotsky's main ideas.

Key Concepts. Vygotsky believed that language plays a central role in shaping mental functioning. Language is considered to be a "tool of the mind" that enables the infant to transfer socially generated knowledge to internal, self-regulated thought (Berk & Winsler, 1995). The language environment in which the child is reared is crucial to intellectual growth. Vygotsky's ideas about language development will be considered further in the next chapter.

Vygotsky described the key to learning in terms of the **zone of proximal development (ZPD).** At any given time in a child's life the continuum of learning includes tasks that a child can do without assistance, tasks that a child can do with help or guidance, and tasks that are completely beyond the child's capacity. The ZPD represents the middle region, which consists of the motor activities or concepts a child is capable of mastering with the help of an adult or a more advanced peer. For example, 2-year-old Pia could only put together a four-piece puzzle, but with some coaching from her mother she quickly learned to "work" a more difficult puzzle of six pieces.

Barbara Rogoff (1990) introduced the term **guided participation** to describe the process by which children develop through involvement in the practices of their community. Children learn as they actively participate in culturally structured activities with the guidance, support, and challenge of companions who impart a wide variety of skills and knowledge. Children are not just passive recipients of cultural experiences, but are viewed as "apprentices" who collaborate and participate in real-life activities and problem solving with more skilled and knowledgeable, but supportive, others.

Rogoff and her collaborators (1993) examined how toddlers (12 to 24 months old) and their caregivers in four cultural communities shared activities through guided participation. They observed families in two middle-class communities from Turkey and the United States. These families were compared with Guatemalan Mayan and Indian tribal families from two non-middle-class communities. In the two middle-class communities, the goals and methods of guided participation involved an emphasis on verbal instruction, adult play with young children, and provision of "lessons" within single events and dyadic participation. Within the non-middle-class communities, the toddlers were more likely to be exposed to guided participation that involved nonverbal instruction. They were also expected to learn through observation and participation in multiple events in a larger group context. Similiarites in guided participation as well as differences were found. The results were not viewed as establishing the superiority of one cultural practice over another, but rather as support for Vygotsky's views on the importance of cultural influences on cognitive development.

Evaluation of Vygotsky's Theory. Vygotsky's theory has been given high marks for how well it reflects the real world of children (R. Thomas, 1996) and for its sensitivity to the diversity of children (P. Miller, 1993). Vygotsky's concept of the zone of proximal development is viewed as one of his major contributions. As a result, observers of infants and children have been encouraged to look beyond a child's behavior that is being displayed at a given time to the child's potential accomplishment (Lutz & Sternberg, 1999). Educators have been interested in finding ways (e.g., see "Learning Through Scaffolding" later) to extend and faciliate development of children's cognitive abilities within the ZPD.

On the other hand, Vygotsky's theory has been criticized for the vagueness of some of the concepts related to the zone of proximal development and for insufficient attention to how children develop within the zone (P. Miller, 1993). In comparison to Piagetian theory, there is much less research on Vygotsky's theory, especially on infant development, due to the complexities of studying children in a cultural context. Vygotsky's ideas have been mostly applied to older age groups because of his emphasis on the importance of language (Berk, 1996). In recent years, however, Rogoff (1990) and others (Berk & Winsler, 1995) have extended some of his ideas downward to the infancy period.

INFORMATION-PROCESSING

Although information-processing theories are quite different from Piagetian theory, Piaget's ideas have had a formative influence on their development. Some theorists (e.g., Rutkowska, 1993; Siegler, 1998) have used an information-processing approach to revise, refine, and rethink Piaget's theory. However, unlike Piagetian theory, the **information-processing approach** is not based on developmental stages, but focuses on the operations of the mind (Lutz & Sternberg, 1999). Actually information-processing theories are numerous and varied. Consequently, they are often referred to as a framework rather than a single theory. For our purposes we will look at a few basic ideas that characterize this approach.

Key Concepts. According to the information-processing framework, the functions of the brain are compared to the internal operations of a computer (R. Thomas, 1996). Information is entered into the computer (input), processed within the machine (throughput), resulting in a response (output). The input and output features of information processing can be observed, but what happens during the internal processing phase remains unseen and is, therefore, the key to understanding human cognition. Information-processing theorists vary among themselves but generally agree that thinking is information processing (Siegler, 1998). Therefore, information-processing theorists attempt to explain the infant's internal mechanisms for manipulating information and the way the components interact to produce behavior (R. Thomas, 1996).

A key element in our understanding of cognitive functioning is the process by which information is entered (encoded) into the brain through the sense organs and how it is perceived (processed) by the infant. Other key components of the information-processing approach are the structure and function of attention, perception, and memory. The quality of a child's thinking at any age depends on the capacity to receive and store information, how much information a child can access and keep in mind at one time, and the ability to operate on the information to solve problems and achieve goals (Siegler, 1998).

A basic goal of information-processing theorists is to identify the inner mechanisms that are responsible for developmental changes and how they work to produce cognitive growth (Siegler, 1998). The acquisition of cognitive skills that improve the way information is processed is one mechanism of development. As children get older, their knowledge about various aspects of the physical world (e.g., objects) and social world (e.g., people), knowledge about memory, and strategies for remembering information improve. Another proposed mechanism of development is the changes that take place in the rate of acquiring and processing information. Theoretically, these abilities improve with age and experience.

Evaluation of the Information-Processing Approach. The information-processing approach has been a useful model for analyzing the complexities of the thought processes. This approach has been rated highly for the emphasis that is placed on the use of research findings in analyzing and forming conclusions about cognitive processes. Much of the research on infant perception and memory is currently conducted from an information-processing perspective (P. Miller, 1993). This approach has contributed greatly to new research findings and to our understanding of the cognitive, "computational" competencies of infants described in the next section on memory.

On the other hand, information processing has been criticized for failing to come up with a comprehensive, integrated theory of human development. This approach focuses primarily on how infants think and does not adequately consider how they develop physically, emotionally, and socially within a cultural context (R. Thomas, 1996). In addition, some people object to depicting infants and children as "little computers." However, proponents of information-processing views are quick to point out that the computer model is just an analogy that helps us understand cognitive development. Infants are not reduced to "robots" or "machines." Understanding how babies process information will also help scientists develop more sophisticated computers, although that is not a primary reason this approach was developed (Gopnik et al., 1999).

MEMORY

Do infants remember what they perceive and learn? How soon does memory begin? How long do infants remember? Questions such as these are significant because memory is one of the most important components of intelligence. Information-processing theorists focus on the infant's capacity to encode (take in) information, store it, and selectively bring it to mind as needed. Various terms are used in discussing memory development, including the *sensory register,* and *working, short-term, long-term, recognition,* and *recall memory.* These terms can be confusing at times because the way they are used may vary somewhat among different texts.

The **sensory register** consists of the immediate sensory impressions that persist for a brief interval after a stimulus is gone. This information is replaced by other sensory stimulation unless it receives further attention. We know that the sensory register is functional at birth since newborn infants attend to sights and sounds and tend to prefer some stimuli to others. The ability of the sensory organs to register information accurately improves rapidly during early infancy (refer to the previous chapter).

Working memory consists of information that the brain is actively working on at the moment. The brain processes information from the sensory register, rehearsing and organizing it for transfer into storage. The current sensory information may be combined with information that has been previously stored. For example, an infant may see an animal and remember that it is called a cow. The amount of time information is stored in working memory is generally considered to be about a minute or less (Helms & Turner, 1976; Siegler, 1998). Infants apparently develop the brain capacity for this type of memory from 6 to 12 months of age (Papalia, Olds, & Feldman, 2002). For example, studies on object permanence suggest that 8-month-old infants can remember the location of a hidden object for approximately 70 seconds (Arterberry et al., 1993). The capacity to retain more information in the working memory improves as infants grow older and are able to retain and process larger chunks of information (Siegler, 1998). The term **short-term memory** is often used to mean the same thing as working memory (e.g., Papalia et al., 2002). However, some scholars (e.g., Fogel, 2001) extend short-term memory to include the ability to remember events for several hours or days.

Long-term memory involves the ability to recall information after days, weeks, and even years have passed. Some information and experiences are stored permanently. Memory length will be discussed further, in connection with two basic types of memory—recognition and recall.

Recognition Memory. The ability to recall whether a stimulus has been previously experienced is referred to as **recognition memory.** An infant who, upon request, selects a picture of a cat from an animal book is demonstrating this type of memory. There is little doubt that newborn infants display recognition memory. The ability to recognize a stimulus that triggered a response is not possible without some information in storage for use in working memory. The conditioned responses that have been demonstrated in numerous experiments with newborns constitute evidence of their capacity to remember (G. Olson & Strauss, 1984). The ability to store information in working memory increases dramatically in infants from all racial and ethnic groups around the world between 8 and 12 months of age (Kagan, 1981b).

There is also evidence that newborns have the capacity for long-term recognition memory. Babies less than 55 hours old remembered a specific reinforcement schedule for as long as 10 hours after a single learning session (Panneton & DeCasper, 1982). Newborn infants (over 24 hours old) also appear to remember specific sounds for at least a 24-hour period (Swain, Zelazo, & Clifton, 1993). However, due to the immaturity of the nervous system, the newborn's capacity to remember is probably limited to a primitive form of recognition memory.

Within the first month or two, infants show signs of an increasing capacity for long-term retention of information. Researchers have found that 1-month-old infants can remember a conditioned response for about two days in some experiments (Ungerer, Brody, & Zelazo, 1978) and for as long as 10 days in others (Little, Lipsitt, & Rovee-Collier, 1984). By 2 months of age, infants have demonstrated that they remember for almost three weeks how to move a crib mobile (J. Davis & Rovee-Collier, 1983). However, the infants remember the response only if they receive some prompting (called reactivation). As you would expect, 2-month-olds forget more rapidly than 3-month-olds, who remember the procedure for a month or more with prompting (Greco et al., 1986).

The period between 3 and 7 months of age is a time in which memory shows a dramatic improvement (G. Olson & Strauss, 1984). The information-processing skills have improved remarkably as the result of physiological maturation, increased attention span, improved motor skills, and the acquisition of a substantial amount of knowledge. The infant can learn more complex information faster and remember it for longer periods of time (Rovee-Collier & Shyi, 1992). Fagan (1971) found that 6-month-old infants recognize a variety of stimuli for as long as 14 days without prompting. Long-term recognition memory is routinely displayed by infants between 3 and 6 months of age (Daehler & Greco, 1985).

Researchers have found that the physical setting or context in which learning takes place is an important factor in memory retrieval for young infants. Six-month-old infants who learned to move a mobile by kicking or who pressed a lever to view a moving toy train had difficulty remembering how to do the same task when they were placed in a different environment after a short delay (Borovsky & Rovee-Collier, 1990; Hartshorn & Rovee-Collier, 1997). The relatively weak memory of young infants depends on contextual cues that serve to prime and facilitate recall. After about 1 year of age, infants can remember what they learned in one place when tested in another without the benefit of contextual cues, except after a relatively long time delay (Rovee-Collier, 1999).

The speed of memory retrieval increases between 3 and 6 months, indicating that information is processed more rapidly with age (Rovee-Collier & Shyi, 1992). As infants get older, they also demonstrate more accurate recall of specific events over increasingly longer periods of time. Children as young as 11 months have accurate recall for specific events after a short delay. Infants as young as 13 months can recall events for as long as eight months. Over short delays of a week or less, infants do not need to be reminded. If the delay is one month or longer, memory is enhanced with repeated experience, or reminding, or both (Bauer, 1996).

Recall Memory. The ability to remember something that is currently not available to direct sensory perception is called **recall memory** (Mandler, 1984). A baby who can tell you the name of the family dog is demonstrating recall memory. The ability to think begins with recall memory. Piaget linked recall memory with deferred imitation and symbolic thinking (mental images) and the use of language. Piaget thus argued that this type of memory does not emerge until 18 to 24 months of age. However, there is an increasing amount of evidence that infants are capable of elementary recall memory much earlier.

Results of studies on infant attachment and separation anxiety are sometimes used to argue that infants possess at least a rudimentary form of recall memory by around 6 months of age (Schaffer, 1979). Since attachment and separation anxiety (typically established at around 6 months of age) involve the ability to remember that the parent exists even when out of sight, this capacity implies that recall memory has been established. Studies (see Schneider & Bjorklund, 1998) have reported demonstrations of deferred imitation in 9-month-olds after a 24-hour delay. Deferred imitation has been reported after delays as long as two days for 11- to 20-month-old infants. The neurological systems needed to support long-term recall memory are apparently present around the beginning of the second year of life (Schneider & Bjorklund, 1998).

One method researchers have used to study recall memory has been to ask parents to keep diaries of their child's memory behavior over a period of time. Using this approach, Ashmead and Perlmutter (1980) found examples of recall memory in infants between 7 and 9 months of age. In one case, a 9-month-old girl kept some ribbons that she played with in the bottom drawer of a chest. One day she opened the drawer but could find no ribbons. She opened all the drawers until she found her ribbons in the top drawer. The next day she looked for her ribbons in the top drawer. Anecdotal records such as this seem to provide evidence of long-term recall memory. However, other researchers believe that this type of research lacks scientific objectivity (Daehler & Greco, 1985).

Researchers have also used **elicited imitation** to test nonverbal infants' recall memory (Bauer & Wewerka, 1995). In elicited imitation, props such as nesting cups are used to model an action or a sequence of actions. The props are then given to an infant who is encouraged to imitate the actions observed. After a period of hours or days, controlled by the researchers, the props are made available again to the infant to determine if the original actions will be repeated without the benefit of a model to observe. By 9 to 11 months of age, infants reproduce actions involving a single object after a 24-hour delay (Meltzoff, 1988a). At 13 to 14 months of age, infants can reproduce limited actions after a one-week delay (Bauer & Hertsgaard, 1993; Meltzoff, 1988b). Toward the end of the second year of life, infants remember multistep sequences for two to six weeks, and for as long as eight months if they are given verbal reminders (Bauer & Wewerka, 1995).

Infants remember for increasingly longer periods of time as they get older. Deferred imitation experiments indicate that duration of memory is also affected by the amount of exposure to stimuli. For example, 18-month-olds were asked to imitate the actions of an adult model manipulating an object. These infants were able to exhibit deferred imitation over a four week time period after one session, but extend the memory time to 10 weeks after two sessions (Rovee-Collier, 1999).

Infant Thinking. A question that is often the subject of debate among theorists and researchers is "When do babies begin to think?" The answer to the question depends upon how *thinking* is defined.

Some dictionary words that are used as synonyms for thinking include pondering, reflecting, knowing, reasoning, remembering, intending, and deliberating. Thinking is also viewed as a computational or mediating process that occurs between perceptions (input) and actions (output) (Gopnik et al., 1999).

If we define **thinking** in terms of what happens between input and output, and as a process that includes elementary knowledge and memory, it is apparent that babies begin thinking at birth or during the early days after birth. As described in the previous section, they have the ability to remember events for at least a short period of time. They translate information from the world into coherent images, interpret their experiences in particular ways, and generate responses to stimulation within their limited abilities. While many of their responses are automatic reflexes (e.g., sucking), others involve a higher level of information processing. Gopnik and colleagues (1999) believe that

> Even the youngest infants seem to have representations of the world. They have symbols inside their minds that represent the world outside, in much the same way the symbols of computer programs do. They take input from the world, the light waves and sound waves, and they make rules that transform that high input into very different kinds of representations. Those representations are responsible for the output: the babies' expressions, gestures, and actions. (pp. 144–145)

For example very young babies distinguish between sounds, imitate some facial expressions, and when they see a toy train disappear behind a screen, anticipate that it will appear at the other side (Gopnik et al., 1999).

As neurological structures mature and experiences accumulate, thinking processes improve. Rochat (2001) has identified 2 months and 9 months as key ages at which infant thinking takes a leap forward. At 2 months of age (Piaget said 8 to 12 months.) infants begin to shows signs of planning intentional actions. They change from being "direct perceivers and actors to active thinkers, evaluators and planners" (Rochat, 2001, p. 183). Another revolution in thinking occurs at 9 months of age with the emergence of triadic competencies. The term *triadic* refers to the three-way transactions that take place between the infant, another person, and objects in the environment. An example of a triadic transaction is joint attention (see Chapter 9) when a baby and an adult attend to the same object simultaneously (Rochat, 2001).

The emerging sense of self (see Chapter 10) is another key event that facilitates thinking. The capacity to monitor one's thoughts or to "think about thinking" is contingent on the development of the awareness that you are a distinct individual, separate from other people. Thinking also takes a leap forward with the development of the use of words as symbols or "tools" that can be used in the thought processes. Obviously, the capacity of infants to think and reason is a "work in progress" that becomes more efficient and complex with age.

HOW INFANTS LEARN

Learning is the acquisition of knowledge or skills through experience. Infants begin to learn even before they are born. However, for a number of reasons, learning is generally more limited during infancy than at other stages. For one thing, the brain and nervous system are very immature. The interconnections between the various cells have not yet been completely established. The sensory organs that affect the infant's perceptual capacity have not reached their peak functional capacity. The infant's limited attention span, motor skills, and language ability are additional factors affecting the capacity to learn. All of these limitations affect the infant's ability to collect, process, store, and retrieve information. In spite of these immaturities, however, much learning takes place rapidly during infancy. The ways in which infants learn are numerous and varied.

Conditioned Responses. Behavioral psychologists believe that all learning is the result of conditioned responses. This theory is based on the principle that infants learn through actions that are reinforced, punished, or ignored. There are two types of conditioned responses—classical and operant.

Classical Conditioning. Infants frequently exhibit the same response to a particular stimulus each time it is encountered, such as turning the head when the cheek is stroked (rooting reflex). In **classical conditioning,** an infant learns to transfer the response to a different stimulus than the one that initially elicits the response. This type of conditioning is based on the principle that when two different stimuli appear close together, the response to one of them will be transferred to the other (Baldwin, 1967). For example, a buzzer can be set off each time the cheek is stroked to elicit the rooting reflex. A baby will eventually turn its head in response to the buzzer alone. An infant thus learns to associate a new stimulus (buzzer) with an old response (rooting reflex). This is referred to as a new stimulus-response connection. Researchers have observed classical conditioning in unborn infants during the last three months of the prenatal period. Spelt (1948) found that a loud sound would cause a fetus to move each time the noise was made. The loud sound was paired with a vibration of the mother's abdomen. After a number of simultaneous repetitions, the vibratory stimulus alone was effective in causing the infant to move. A later study using ultrasound images confirmed Spelt's conclusion (Birnholz & Benacerraf, 1983).

Researchers have also demonstrated classical conditioning in infants soon after birth. Connolly and Stratton (1969) paired the Babkin reflex, in which the mouth opens when pressure is applied to the palms, in 2- to 4-day-old infants, with a neutral buzzing noise. When the noise was presented by itself, the infants exhibited mouth-opening movements characteristic of the Babkin reflex. Researchers (Blass, Ganchrow, & Steiner, 1984) also gently stroked the foreheads of newborns (2 to 48 hours of age) while feeding them a sucrose solution. The infants were thus conditioned to exhibit the facial expressions related to sucking through stroking alone. The use of classical conditioning is limited to the responses that infants already exhibit.

Younger infants are harder to condition than older infants. The emotional responses of older infants are particularly susceptible to classical conditioning. Numerous environmental encounters become sources of infant fears. Carla, a toddler, was stung by a bee while she was playing on her swing set. After that experience she was afraid of all flying insects. Babies frequently begin crying as soon as they see a doctor or anyone else dressed in a white coat. They have learned to associate the coat, initially a neutral stimulus, with painful examining or treatment procedures such as injections.

Operant Conditioning. If a response to a stimulus is followed by reinforcement, the chances are increased that the response will be repeated when the stimulus is repeated. By the same token, responses that are punished or receive no reinforcement are less likely to be repeated. In **operant conditioning,** the reinforcement follows the response that, in the beginning, occurs spontaneously. In classical conditioning, the infant has no control over the events through which stimuli occur. However, in operant conditioning the infant's response, or lack of response, determines whether a reinforcer will follow (Sameroff & Cavanagh, 1979).

Researchers have not found a method by which operant conditioning can be studied in the unborn infant. However, there is ample evidence that newborn infants can be conditioned. In fact, operant conditioning is easier to obtain in newborns than classical conditioning (Columbo, 1993). Examples of this type of learning are found in experiments that have successfully conditioned newborns to alter their head-turning (Siqueland, 1968) and sucking (Sameroff, 1968) responses to receive a reinforcer.

Operant conditioning, like classical conditioning, depends upon the ability of an infant to emit a specific response. Consequently, the variety of behaviors that can be conditioned in infancy is limited. As with classical procedures, the operant-conditioned responses are obtained easier and faster as the infant gets older, especially after 6 months of age (Lamb & Bornstein, 1987). Sameroff and Cavanagh (1979) believe that there is a shift in the behavioral organization of an infant between 7 and 9 months of age. During this time, changes occur in the emotional, cognitive, and physiological domains, which greatly facilitate conditioned responses as well as other types of learning. The acquisition of the ability to move around on all four limbs (creep) is a major factor in the developmental advances taking place between 7 and 9 months (Bertenthal, Campos, & Barrett, 1984).

In older infants, operant-conditioning procedures are often used to shape behavior. This involves reinforcing gradual changes, or successive approximations, in the infant's behavior until the desired behavior is obtained. Parents often use this procedure with their infants. An example is found in the infant's use of the word "Da-da." When the baby first says "Da-da," it is reinforced by praise, hugs, and other positive responses no matter when the sound is made. Later, parents respond positively only if "Da-da" is repeated in the presence of the father. Finally, the term is reinforced only when the infant uses it to designate the father.

Imitation. One of the most easily observed ways that infants learn is through **imitation.** At around 6 weeks of age, imitation begins to play an increasingly important role in learning (Rosenblith & Sims-Knight, 1985). Older infants imitate actions from a variety of models, including adults, children, and television characters. Parents are primary models, as the following example indicates: At 15 months, Candy is very imitative—"Often when she picks something up from the floor, she wipes it on her dress. That's what her mother does with anything Candy will put in her mouth again" (Peterson, 1974, p. 37).

Imitation is frequently combined with operant conditioning in the learning process. An initial response is produced by an infant because it has been copied from a model. If the behavior is considered desirable, the infant receives responses that are rewarding so the behavior will continue. At 2 years of age, Kristin was encouraged to observe her mother use the bathroom as a way to begin toilet training. As soon as Kristin began to imitate her mother's behavior she was reinforced with verbal praise, "Good, Kristin! That's good!" The verbal reinforcement that was used in facilitating toilet training was so effective that Kristin began to imitate her mother in the use of praise. One day, while observing her mother use the bathroom, Kristin said, "Good, Mommy! That's good!"

Learning Through Play. Play is one of the basic ways infants learn. To an infant, "play is learning and learning is play" (Sroufe, 1977, p. 93). No one needs to teach infants to play. Their play is voluntary, intrinsically motivated, and freely chosen (J. Johnson & Ershler, 1982). Piaget (1962) viewed play as opportunities for infants to test reality through acts of assimilation. Sounds, objects, and other stimuli are freely manipulated to serve the infant's own particular needs. Piaget divided cognitive play during infancy into two basic stages: sensorimotor play and symbolic play. Within each stage, the complexity of play changes with the baby's cognitive maturity and competence.

Sensorimotor Play. During the first three or four months of life, infant play is focused on body movements that provide sensory pleasure. Repetitious kicking movements and sucking the fist are typical activities. Infants also begin to play with cooing and other sounds as soon as they are capable. At approximately 6 months of age, an infant typically plays with one object at a time (Fenson et al., 1976). This earliest object play involves mouthing, shaking, banging, inspecting visually, and shifting from one hand to the other.

After about 9 months of age, the simple, undifferentiated type of play declines and is gradually replaced by function-relational play with two or more objects (Belsky and Most, 1981). The infant begins to figure out how some objects "work" (e.g., a toy telephone dial). At first, two objects may be used together indiscriminately, without regard to their appropriate relationships (e.g., placing a hairbrush in a cup). Later the infant learns to combine objects in ways that exploit their appropriate relationships, such as placing a

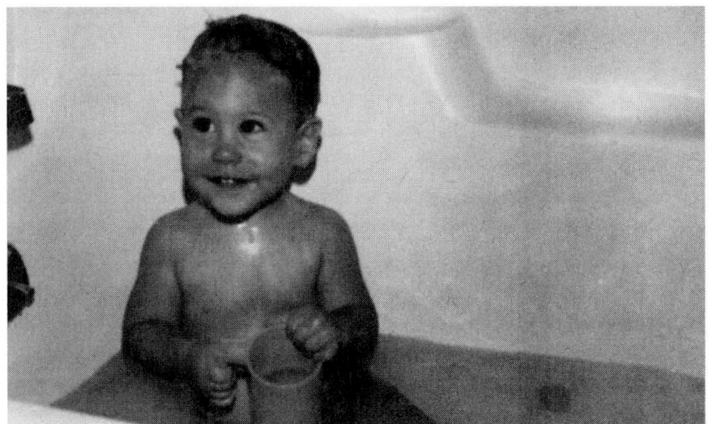

Infants are sensory creatures who use simple, everyday experiences, such as bathing, for play and stimulation.

lid on a pot. During this stage, infants usually prefer new toys to old ones (Ross, 1974), and complex toys to simple ones (McCall, 1974).

Pretend (Symbolic) Play. The earliest form of symbolic play begins around 12 months of age when the infant begins to perform simple "pretend" activities. In the beginning, pretend play involves activities directed toward the self, such as making drinking sounds using an empty cup, or using a doll brush on the infant's own hair (Belsky & Most, 1981). As infants get older, their pretend play is directed toward others (dolls are fed "pretend" bottles of milk), and they begin to substitute "pretend" objects for the real thing (a stick becomes a bottle of milk). The most sophisticated level of pretend play is called double substitution (Belsky & Most, 1981). This happens when a toddler uses two "pretend" materials in a single play sequence. Thus, a stick becomes a "doll" and a bottle cap is used as a "cup" to feed the doll.

Learning Through Scaffolding. Theorists and educators who share Vygotsky's views (Berk & Winsler, 1995) use the concept of **scaffolding** to describe how infants benefit from their experiences. The term scaffolding (as in building construction and repair) is used to describe how adults use special structures of social encouragement to promote children's learning. Basically, scaffolding takes the form of tutoring that offers assistance when necessary for mastery, but prompts children to assume responsibility for their own learning as much as possible (Berk & Winsler, 1995). The following is an example of how a mother helps her 2½-year-old child put a puzzle together:

Child: *Oh, now where's this one go?* (Picks up a blue piece and looks at the form board.)

Mother: *Which piece might go here?* (Points to the bottom of the puzzle.)

Child: *His hat?* (Picks up another piece, but tries the wrong one).

Mother: *See if you can find a piece that looks like this shape.* (Points to the bottom of the puzzle again).

Child: *The red one!* (Tries it, but can't quite get it to fit.)

Mother: *Try turning it just a little more this way.* (Gestures to show her.)

Child: *There it fits!* (Picks up another piece and says:) *Now this green one should fit here. Oh, I need to turn it just a little! Look, Mom, this one fits too!* (Adapted from Berk & Winsler, 1995, p. 27.)

Adults should be careful, though, not to interfere unnecessarily with the child's attempts to solve a problem. The key to scaffolding is to wait until the child is about to give up and provide just enough assistance to keep the child working on the task (Gonzalez-Mena & Eyer, 1997).

ASSESSING INFANT INTELLIGENCE

"Intelligence is what the tests test" (Boring, 1923, p. 35). Although this widely quoted statement is not an adequate definition of intelligence, it is an indication of the importance that has been attributed to testing intelligence. The assessment of intelligence in infancy is viewed as especially important in the early detection of mental disabilities, as well as in determining the extent to which intelligence changes from infancy to adulthood.

The accurate measurement of infant intelligence has proved to be very difficult, from the standpoint of both test construction and test administration. Eliciting an infant's attention and cooperation can be a major obstacle to testing, especially when the infant is being tested by a strange person in a strange place. Intelligence tests for children and adults typically have a large verbal-skills component, whereas intelligence tests for infants are composed primarily of sensorimotor functions. Scarr-Salapatek (1983) believes that the type of intelligence displayed by infants during the first two years is not comparable to the cognitive skills that evolve later in life. Thus, infant test scores are not reliable predictors of intellectual functioning in later years.

In spite of these problems, though, infant intelligence scales (sometimes referred to as developmental schedules) are useful for specific purposes when interpreted appropriately. They are widely used in screening programs to identify infants with potential mental disabilities. Researchers have also used these measures for a variety of purposes, such as assessing the influence of intervention programs on the development of intelligence during the infant years. The following examples represent some of the older and newer instruments that are available for assessing infant intelligence:

Gesell Developmental Schedules. Arnold Gesell (1925) was one of the pioneers in the assessment of infant development. Gesell and his coworkers at Yale University made extensive observations on the normal developmental patterns of infants and young children. The **Gesell Developmental Schedules** were designed primarily for the purpose of determining the integrity and functional maturity of the nervous system between 1 month and 6 years of age. The schedules are divided into five major areas: adaptive (e.g., problem solving), fine motor, gross motor, language, and personal-social. A separate score is obtained for each of the five areas, plus an overall score that is labeled the Developmental Quotient (DQ). Gesell intended for this instrument to be used as an indicator of total development rather than of intelligence per se. A short version of the test is available for use as a developmental screening inventory. Cattell (1940) used Gesell's schedules as a basis for the development of a test (**Cattell Infant Intelligence Scale**) specifically designed to measure intelligence over the age span of 2 months to 30 months.

Bayley Scales of Infant Development–II. The **Bayley Scales of Infant Development–II** (Bayley, 1993) is the most widely used norm-referenced instrument for assessment of the cognitive performance of infants and toddlers (Meisels, 1996). It is used in early intervention programs and research settings. The Bayley–II is administered to infants from 1 month to 42 months of age. This test is divided into three separate scales that can be used independently or in combination for assessment purposes. The Mental Scale is designed to assess such functions as sensory/perceptual abilities, memory, learning, language development, and problem-solving ability. This scale results in a standard score that is labeled the Mental Development Index (MDI). The Motor Scale measures skills such as body control, gross and fine motor skills, and manipulatory ability. The results of this scale are expressed as the Psychomotor Development Index (PDI) score. The third scale, the Behavior Rating Scale, allows the examiner to rate the infant's attention, orientation, motor quality, and emotional regulation. It provides four subscale scores in addition to an overall score.

Uzgiris-Hunt Scales. The **Uzgiris-Hunt Ordinal Scales of Psychological Development** (Uzgiris & Hunt, 1975) are based on Piaget's description of cognitive development during infancy. The term *ordinal* indicates that the test items are arranged, or ordered, according to the

APPLICATIONS: FACILITATING COGNITIVE DEVELOPMENT

There are numerous reliable publications that offer widely accepted suggestions for facilitating cognitive development during infancy (e.g., Fowler, 1980; Gonzalez-Mena & Eyer, 1997; P. Leach, 1976; Lehane, 1976; Machado & Meyer-Botnarescue, 1997; Marzollo, 1977; Painter, 1971; Ramey & Ramey, 1999; Sparling & Lewis, 1979). Greenfield and Tronick (1980) have developed a list of techniques for use in teaching babies how to use play materials, solve problems, and learn by scaffolding. Some of these techniques, listed in order from the simplest to most complex, are as follows:

- Simplify the activity. For example, in introducing nesting cups, give the infant only the smallest and largest ones in the set. This is a useful teaching technique for infants under 6 months of age.
- Point to and touch the important parts of a new activity, such as the space on a puzzle board that matches the piece of puzzle the baby is holding.
- Show the infant how to do an activity or solve a problem (after about 6 months). For example, let the infant watch you place one block on top of another.
- Tell the baby what to do next in an activity. This technique, obviously, is only appropriate when words that an infant can understand are used. Use short, simple phrases, such as "Turn it over" and "Put it here." The other techniques may be used in combination with telling.
- Allow infants to use self-teaching as much as possible. Avoid interfering in activities when help is not needed or wanted.

On a cautionary note, parents and other caregivers are advised to avoid the "pressure-cooker" approach to early learning in an attempt to create a "super-intelligent" baby. Numerous Internet sites offer books, music tapes and CDs, toys, and other products created to accelerate learning. Parents should be aware that scientific evidence is not available to support claims made for the value of some of these products. For example, some researchers claim that there is a "Mozart Effect" whereby early exposure to classical music enhances brain development (Rauscher & Shaw, 1998). Tapes and CDs of selections from Mozart are sold or distributed free to help parents improve their infant's brain. However, attempts to verify the existence of a Mozart Effect for infants or older children have not been successful (Steele, Bass, & Crook, 1999).

When infants are expected to achieve too much, too soon, a level of stress is created that may result in behavior problems at the time or at a later stage of development. Too much emphasis on early intellectual achievement can result in the hurried-infant syndrome (Elkind, 1981). White (1985) believes that superiority in the intellectual domain is frequently obtained at the expense of progress in other areas of equal or greater importance. Infants learn more efficiently with better results when they are developmentally ready to master a task.

level of difficulty. The first items on the scale should be passed at an earlier age than subsequent items. These scales provide the most in-depth assessment of infant cognitive development of any instrument available (Horowitz, 1982). However, this instrument has not been used as widely as other infant assessment scales because of its complexity and the amount of time required for administration. Dunst (1980) has developed a simplified version of the scales that requires less time to administer.

SUMMARY

Definitions

- Cognition refers to all the mental processes, such as thinking and remembering, that make up the functional component of intelligence. Intelligence consists of the ability to think, to solve problems, to learn, to remember, and to adapt to the environment. The terms *intelligence* and *cognition* are used interchangeably.

Influences on Intelligence

- Intelligence is influenced by heredity and environmental influences. The family environment, socioeconomic background, and cultural experiences are important environmental factors.

Piaget's Theory

- The theory of Jean Piaget has been widely influential in the contemporary understanding of intellectual development during the infancy period. Piaget's theory is based on the development of schemes through the process of adaptation and two related processes: assimilation and accommodation.
- Piaget identified four basic stages in the development of intelligence. The stage that corresponds with the first two years of life is the sensorimotor period. This period is divided into six substages: (1) exercising reflex schemes; (2) primary circular reactions; (3) secondary circular reactions; (4) coordination of secondary circular reactions; (5) tertiary circular reactions; and (6) invention of new means through mental combinations.
- By the end of the sensorimotor period, infants have typically developed the ability to understand cause-effect relationships, object permanence, simple problem solving through insight, and deferred imitation. However, evidence is accumulating to indicate that infants accomplish some of these tasks earlier than Piaget's estimated ages.

Vygotsky's Theory

- According to Vygotsky's theory, cultural influences play a central role in shaping cognitive development. Language development provides the foundation for intellectual advancement. Learning takes place within the zone of proximal development and is facilitated through guided participation.

Information-Processing Approach

- The key elements of cognitive development, according to the information-processing approach, include the individual's capacity to perceive, store, recall, and utilize information.

Memory

- Newborn infants are capable of both short- and long-term recognition memory at a very elementary level. Memory capacity improves with age, especially between 3 and 7 months. Recall memory develops later than recognition memory. Infants are capable of the recall memory based on situational cues at approximately 7 to 9 months of age. During the second year of life, infants display an increasing ability to recall more complex events for longer periods of time.

Infant Thinking

- In the broadest meaning of the word, infants begin to *think* around the time they are born. Their thought processes improve and become more sophisticated with age.

How Infants Learn

- Infants are capable of learning through both classical and operant conditioning processes from birth. Imitation is another mechanism through which infants learn, beginning at approximately 6 weeks of age. Infants also learn through play, which progresses through two basic stages: sensorimotor and pretend, or symbolic, play. Adults can use a special form of tutoring called "scaffolding" to promote learning.

Assessing Infant Intelligence

- Infant intelligence test scores are not reliable predictors of intellectual functioning in other stages of life. However, infant intelligence scales, or developmental schedules, are used for screening programs and research purposes. The Bayley Scales of Infant Development–II is the most widely used instrument for assessment of the cognitive performance of infants and toddlers.

KEY TERMS

intelligence
cognition
scheme
adaptation
assimilation
accommodation
sensorimotor period
circular reaction
object permanence
pseudoimitation
tertiary circular reactions
deferred imitation
zone of proximal development (ZPD)
guided participation
information-processing
sensory register
working memory
short-term memory
long-term memory
recognition memory
recall memory
elicited imitation
thinking
learning
classical conditioning
operant conditioning
imitation
sensorimotor play
pretend (symbolic) play
scaffolding
Gesell Developmental Schedules
Cattell Infant Intelligence Scale
Bayley Scales of Infant Development–II
Uzgiris-Hunt Ordinal Scales of Psychological Development

INFORMATION ON THE WEB*

www.members.aol.com/Jmed64/journals.htm. This site includes brief summaries of articles from a variety of recent professional journals concerning research and theory on infant/toddler cognitive development.

www.sesameworkshop.org/babyworkshop. Web site sponsored by the *Sesame Street Magazine for Parents.* Contains information about cognitive development of infants along with information about language and other areas of development.

*Web sites are subject to change.

NINE

LANGUAGE DEVELOPMENT

Out of the mouths of babes and sucklings
Thou hast brought perfect praise.
—Psalm 8:2; Matthew 21:16

One of the most fascinating and exciting things to observe about babies is the process of language development. Parents and scientists alike are captivated by how children learn languages. For parents, language represents a communicative link with their child and the key that opens the door to the child's inner world. Communication is at the center of the relationship between the parent and child. **Language** is a complex system of mutually agreed-upon symbols used to express and understand ideas and feelings. In its broadest meaning, language refers to an act or acts that produce some kind of interchange or communication between two or more people (Bangs, 1982). The symbols used in language include vocal utterances, written expressions, and body movements such as hand gestures and facial expressions. **Speech** is the vocal or oral component of language and refers to the production of spoken words or other meaningful sounds. The terms speech and language are frequently used interchangeably, but technically they are not synonymous.

Scientists have been astonished at the predictability of language development and at how easily babies learn to talk. Normally, all children pass a series of milestones at approximately the same age, regardless of the language they acquire (McNeil, 1970). For a long time, observers of language development were content to plot these major milestones and record children's utterances. More recently, however, they have been concerned with why and how language is acquired. This chapter summarizes the processes involved in language acquisition, the progress infants make in developing language competence, and some of the biological, psychological, and social influences.

THEORIES OF LANGUAGE DEVELOPMENT

There are several theories about how human language is acquired. Theorists differ on the relative influence of innate biological mechanisms and environmental experiences in language acquisition. Theorists also differ in their views about the relationship between thought and language. Some of the major theories representing extreme and moderate views are described here.

Behavioristic Theory. Skinner (1957) proposed that language, like any other behavior, can be explained as conditioned responses. When infants make sounds that resemble adult speech, such as "ma-ma," adults reinforce them with smiles, hugs, or other positive responses. Other behaviorists (e.g., Bandura, 1977) add imitation as a factor that plays a key role in language acquisition. These behaviorists stress the importance of the language environment, especially the availability of speech models to copy. Behaviorism has been criticized, among other things, for failing to adequately explain the creative use of language, the production and comprehension of novel utterances (Bryen, 1982), and the rapid rate of language development during infancy.

Nativistic Theory. There is little doubt that human infants are uniquely equipped to acquire language. However, the extent to which language development is controlled by biology has been the subject of extensive debate. Nativists argue that progress in language development is closely linked to the maturation of the brain. Language acquisition is remarkably predictable and similar among humans. Children normally pass a sequence of milestones at about the same age, regardless of the language or cultural conditions. In addition, progress in language development during the early years appears to be synchronized with progress in motor development. The two functions thus appear to be commonly controlled by the maturation of the central nervous system.

Nativistic theory is based on neurological studies that have shown that verbal function in humans is controlled by specific speech centers in the brain. For most people, perhaps as many as 95 percent, language is located in the left cerebral hemisphere. Lenneberg (1967) maintains that speech functions have not been localized in a particular region of the brain as early as infancy. His theory is based on studies showing that if injury occurs to the left side of the brain in infancy or childhood, the right side of the brain apparently takes over the language functions so that normal speech is possible. As the child grows older, the speech functions become increasingly lateralized, with less flexibility to compensate for damage. Other theorists (Kinsbourne, 1978; Krashen, 1973) assert that lateralization of the brain occurs much earlier than Lenneberg proposed.

Chomsky (1968), another leading proponent of nativism, has proposed that human infants are equipped at birth with a language acquisition device (LAD). This device is analogous to a computer that is prewired or programmed to acquire language. Babies are programmed to sort out the underlying rules and principles of their native language. Thus, children's language develops rapidly and with few errors, with little help from language partners (Barnet & Barnet, 1998). The many similarities in the timetable of language acquisition for children all over the world tend to support Chomsky's theory. However, infants do not acquire language as quickly or as easily as his theory proposes. Chomsky's theory does not provide a complete explanation for the hows and whys of language development.

Cognitive Developmental Theory. According to Piaget (1952, 1954), language development is rooted in the cognitive development that occurs during the sensorimotor period (see Chapter 8). The infant has to develop the concept of self as a distinct person separate from other objects and understand the concept of object permanence before speech can begin. In Piaget's view, development of language also depends upon the acquisition of knowledge through touching, tasting, manipulation, and other experiences with objects and people. As the child's cognitive capacities and thoughts become more elaborate and complex through the years, language acquisition becomes more sophisticated and complete.

Not all cognitive developmental theorists agree with Piaget's view that thought shapes language development. Whorf (1956) took the opposite view when he hypothesized that the language we learn determines the way we think. For example, we view an orange as a round piece of fruit because we have attached those verbal labels to it. If oranges had originally been labeled as square, purple smalzes, we would perceive oranges in those terms. Thinking is thus dependent upon language.

Vygotsky's Theory. Vygotsky's (1962) theory represents a middle ground on questions about the relationship between thought and language. He proposed that language and thought develop at the same time and eventually become interdependent. In early infancy, language and thought develop separately along parallel lines because they are both related to the same underlying cognitive ability. However, at about 2 years of age, language and the thought processes merge as the infant acquires the capacity to understand the symbolic meanings of words. Language then begins to facilitate thought, and the two processes become interdependent. Siegler (1998) has concluded that, overall, the research evidence tends to support Vygotsky's position.

Vygotsky also viewed language as socially generated rather than biologically given. The social origins of language are found in the cultural group as infants, children, and adults interact and communicate. Language starts out as a means for social communication and interpersonal influence. Eventually, language that starts out as a social tool for mediating relationships between people becomes internalized. When that happens (during the second year of life), language becomes "a tool of the mind" to direct thinking, organize perceptions, and to communicate with one's self (P. Miller, 1993). Advances in thinking are made possible as the child's language tools become increasingly more sophisticated. However, language development always occurs within the sociocultural context. Children are not just passive recipients of cultural influences, but are active participants in the process.They use their own mental processes to make sense of the information and experiences they encounter (Berk & Winsler, 1995).

Vygotsky believed that language is initially transferred from the social world to the child's cognitive world through **private speech.** This type of speech appears around 30 months of age and is defined as inner speech or "self-talk." Private speech is not addressed to other people but is used for self-communication in solving problems and regulating one's own behavior. Through the use of private speech, older infants begin to transfer the regulation of behavior from others to the self (Berk & Winsler, 1995). For example, Tyrone's mother told him not to touch the buttons on the television. One day Tyrone's mother observed him looking at the TV, shaking his head, and saying "No! No!" to himself.

Interactionist Theory. The **interactionist** perspective emphasizes the interplay between biological abilities and environmental influences in language acquisition (Bohannon, 1993). This approach to language development combines elements of other theories including nativist, behavioral, and sociocultural theories. The innate capacities of the infant provide the structural foundations, determine the sequence, and set the timetable for language acquisition. The specific elements and characteristics of the language the child acquires are determined by environmental influences. Thus, both biology and environment are indispensable and work together in language development. However, the two are not simply added together, but interact in complex ways to produce language. Bruner (1982) explains the role of environmental experiences in language acquisition as ". . . a subtle process by which adults artificially arrange the world so that the child can succeed culturally by doing what comes naturally, and with others similarly inclined" (p. 15). An example of the infant's early sensitivity and responsiveness to the language environment can be found in studies by Condon and Sander (1974). They found that newborn infants sometimes move their limbs in synchronous rhythms that match the tempo and sounds of adult speech. Interactionist theorists also emphasize the important contribution of the infant as an influence upon the people who provide the language environment.

According to Bloom (1998), language acquisition must be considered as one part of the whole child in the larger context of the child's overall development. Language depends upon the mutual influence of all other areas of development including physical, cognitive, social, emotional, and motor abilities (Bloom, 1998). Language acquisition proceeds as "a process of transaction between the child's internal processes (e.g., state of mind) and the external social and physical world" (Bloom, 1998, p. 310).

STRUCTURAL COMPONENTS OF LANGUAGE

To understand the process of language acquisition, we must first know something about the nature and structure of language. All spoken languages consist of five basic components:

1. **Phonology:** the distinctive sound features of speech and the rules for their combinations.
2. **Morphology:** the way sounds are combined to form words and other units of meaning.
3. **Semantics:** the definitions of words and the meanings of words as they are used in relation to other words.
4. **Syntax:** the way words are combined to form sentences.
5. **Pragmatics:** the practical functions of language and the ways it is used to communicate.

These components overlap and are interrelated in usage. Each language has a set of rules governing the components and their relationships. Developing language proficiency involves mastering these rules. Considering the complexities involved, human infants typically make remarkable progress toward mastering their native language. Infants are mostly occupied with developing phonological proficiency. However, they also work on the other features of language, sometimes separately and sometimes simultaneously, until the five components are combined in an elementary fashion by the end of the first three years of life. A summary of the major milestones in language development, shown in Table 9-1, illustrates the progress made in the various components during the first two years of life.

Table 9-1 Milestones of Language Development

AGE	*PHONOLOGY*	*MORPHOLOGY AND SEMANTICS*	*SYNTAX*	*PRAGMATICS*
Birth	Crying			
1 Month	Attends and responds to speaking voice			
2 Months	Cooing, distinguishes phoneme features			
3 Months	Vocalizes to social stimulus			
4 Months	Chuckles			Pointing and gestures
6 Months	Babbling			
9 Months	Echolalia	Understands a few words		Understands gestures; responds to "bye-bye"
12 Months	Repeated syllables, jabbers expressively	First word		Waves "bye-bye"
18 Months		Comprehends simple questions, points to nose, eyes, and hair; vocabulary of 22 words	Two-word utterances, telegraphic speech	Uses words to make wants known
24 Months		Vocabulary of 272 words	Uses pronouns and prepositions; uses simple sentences and phrases	Conversational turn taking

Sources: Taken from the Bayley Scales of Infant Development, Copyright © 1969 by the Psychological Corporation. Reproduced by permission. All rights reserved. E. Lenneberg, *Biological Foundations of Language.* Copyright © 1967. John Wiley and Sons, Inc. Reprinted by permission of John Wiley and Sons, Inc. D. McCarthy, "Language development in children." In L. Carmichael (Ed.), *Manual of Child Psychology.* Copyright © 1954 by John Wiley and Sons, Inc. Reprinted by permission of John Wiley and Sons, Inc.

Phonological Development. Each spoken language is made up of a set of basic, distinctive sounds, sometimes referred to as **phonemes,** which are used to form words. There are two major classes of phonemes—segmented and suprasegmented. The segmented phonemes consist of the vowels and consonants. The suprasegmented phonemes include the sounds of pitch, intonation, juncture, and stress, which constitute the "melody" of a language (Bryen, 1982). To master the sound system of a language, infants must learn to discriminate and combine the phonemes into meaningful words. Apparently infants master the phonemes of their language by discovering the contrasting or distinctive features. Each phoneme is learned in context with another sound rather than one at a time. The first distinction infants make is between vowels and consonants.

Early Sound Perception. You will recall that most babies are born with the sensory capacity to hear distinction between sounds. Within a few days after birth, infants are responsive to speech and other sounds resembling the human voice.

Very young infants are capable of discriminating practically every phonetic contrast on which they have been tested (Aslin et al., 1983). Not only do infants hear subtle differences between sounds, but also they can organize many of them into distinct categories (e.g., *p*'s and *b*'s). Young infants are able to distinguish between sounds even when the rate at which they are spoken varies (J. Miller & Eimas, 1983).

Studies also show that very young infants perceive sound contrasts even in languages other than their own (Juscyck, 1995). Thus infants are equipped with the capacity to make sound discriminations necessary for learning any of the world's languages to which they are exposed. During the second half of the first year the general capacities for sound perception begin to evolve so that infants are more specifically equipped to deal effectively with native sound patterns (Juscyck, 1995). Weir (1966) found that the babbling sounds produced by Polish infants can be distinguished from the babbling sounds of English infants at 5 months of age. Other cross-linguistic studies confirm that by the end of the first year infants select and prefer sounds and arrangements of sounds from their own linguistic background (Boyson-Bardies, 1994). The sounds that babies hear during the early months of life apparently plot the sound map for hearing and producing words that make up a specific language (Kuhl, 1999).

Development of the Speech Mechanism. The production of meaningful utterances involves the complex coordination of the respiratory system and vocal tract by the nervous system. To produce a desired sound, we transmit a set of instructions, usually unconsciously, from the brain to our respiratory system and vocal tract. When we are ready to speak, an airstream is released from the lungs into the vocal tract, which includes the throat, mouth, tongue, nasal cavity, and other organs. The type of sound produced depends upon the tautness of the vocal cords; the position of the tongue; the shape of the lips; whether the air passes through the mouth, nasal cavity, or both; and the speed and continuity of the airstream (Lindfors, 1980). Obviously, defects in the speech mechanism, such as a cleft palate or brain dysfunction, will affect sound production.

The speech mechanism of an infant is in an almost constant state of anatomical change. According to Kent (1980):

> The infant's vocal tract differs from that of an adult in four major respects: The infant's tract is shorter; the pharynx is shorter and wider in relation to its length . . . ; the mouth is flatter than in the adult because of the absence of teeth, and the tongue more evenly fills the mouth. (p. 39)

The vocal tract lengthens and changes its relative anatomical relationship as the baby grows. These changes affect the patterns of sound produced, which means that the motor control of speech has to be continuously modified during the course of development.

Crying and Reflexive Vocalizations. The first sound a baby makes is likely to be a cry. In the beginning, crying and "vegetative noises" such as burps, hiccups, coughs, grunts, and sneezing are involuntary behaviors that are biologically rooted (Menn & Stoel-Gammon, 1993). The crying of the newborn thus serves no intentional communicative purpose. However, as the baby grows older, crying becomes associated with specific stimuli, such as hunger pains, and is a signal to the caretaker that the baby has a need to be met.

Wolff (1969) studied the cries of infants during the first six months of life to identify the emotional quality conveyed by sounds. Of the four main types of cries that were identified, the "basic," hunger cry was the type that occurred most frequently. Other types of cries were a "mad" or angry cry, a cry caused by pain, and a "fake" cry. Fake crying is a more purposeful type of crying behavior that begins around the third week and is described as "of a low pitch and intensity; it consists of long drawn out moans which occasionally rise to more explicit cries, and then revert to poorly articulated moans" (Wolff, 1969, p. 98).

Crying usually means that the baby is trying to get the attention of the caregiver.

Both adults and children can distinguish between various types of cry sounds. In one study, adults were able to distinguish between tape-recorded cries of pain and cries indicating hunger (Zeskind et al., 1984). Even children as young as 7 years of age are capable of distinguishing different types of cries (Berry, 1975). There is some indication that mothers are more skillful than nonmothers in identifying infant cries (Sagi, 1981), but not all studies support this conclusion (Rosenblith & Sims-Knight, 1985). However, parents are more accurate in identifying the different types of cries of their own babies than those of a strange baby (Wiesenfeld, Malatesta, & Deloache, 1981). Some scholars believe that caregivers interpret the cries of infants not simply on the basis of precise sound quality, but within the context of situational cues (e.g., nap time, feeding time) as well (Adamson, 1995; Siegler, 1998).

Researchers have also studied the cries of babies with developmental abnormalities. In one such study (Wasz-Hocket et al., 1968), the cries of infants with brain injuries were compared with the cries of babies without such injuries. The researchers concluded that the sounds produced by the babies with brain damage were quite different from the cries of infants with no signs of brain injury. Variations in cry characteristics have been documented in infants born with developmental problems such as *cri du chat* syndrome and Down syndrome (Lester & Boukydis, 1992). Such differences are apparently obvious to parents. Zeskind (1983) found that the cries of high-risk infants could be distinguished from low-risk infants' cries by Anglo-American, Cuban American, and African American mothers, regardless of their previous experience with infants.

Cooing. Sometime between 1 and 3 months of age, the types of prespeech sounds commonly referred to as **cooing** begin to emerge. In contrast to crying sounds, which are signals of distress, cooing sounds are usually sounds of contentment and happiness. Babies everywhere cry and coo alike. The appearance of cooing is related to physical and sensory changes that take place around 6 or 8 weeks of age, including increased visual attention and greater control of the tongue (Mussen, Conger, & Kagan, 1974).

Cooing sounds are open, vowellike, gurgling noises, such as "aaah" and "oooh." Unlike crying, cooing involves the use of the tongue and lips in sound production. The earliest cooing sounds consist of vowels that come from the front of the mouth and use the tongue, such as /e/ as in bee and /u/ as in blue (Irwin, 1948). The term cooing most likely arises from the predominance of the /u/ sound (Dale, 1976). A few consonants formed in the back of the mouth appear in cooing, such as /k/ as in kite and /g/ as in goat (Cruttenden, 1970). Vowel sounds are frequently preceded by a consonant to form sounds like "coo" and "moo."

Babbling. Between 6 and 10 months of age, the infant's vocalizations take on an increasingly speechlike quality. At this point, the baby enters the babbling period. **Babbling** is the repetition of consonants and vowels in alternating sequences ("ba ba ba," "ga ga ga," "da da da"). The emergence of repetitive syllables in the infant's vocal repertoire is one of the most important milestones of speech development. The sounds are sometimes referred to as reduplicated babbling (Stark, 1979). Babbling is distinguished from cooing by a closer resemblance of sounds to the syllables of words. The transition from cooing to babbling is due to increasing control over the vocal mechanisms (Menyuk, 1982). However, babies continue to coo and tend to shift back and forth between cooing and babbling in their vocalizations for several weeks.

During the babbling period, the repetition of syllables (e.g., "na na na") is accompanied by distinctive intonational patterns as babies begin to explore the suprasegmental aspects of phonology. The sounds take on a definite rhythmic and melodic quality. The sound play of this period has been compared to practicing scales on a piano (Hopper & Naremore, 1978). Apparently, the sounds an infant practices more frequently in babbling are instrumental in determining the first words the infant acquires (Bloom, 1998).

Between 6 and 12 months, the infant's sound repertoire expands. While vowel sounds predominate during the cooing stage, with the onset of babbling there is a shift toward the dominant use of consonants (Menn & Stoel-Gammon, 1993). Sounds and sound combinations never heard from parents have been identified in the babblings of infants. As strange as it may seem, sounds that babies find difficult to produce later in words are produced frequently in babbling (Ervin-Tripp, 1966). Toward the end of the babbling period, the sounds that are not included in the native language begin to drop out of the infant's repertory. Many infants go through a period, immediately before the onset of speech, when they babble less frequently.

The babbling sounds of infants from all language backgrounds are remarkably similar. The babbling of an American infant cannot be distinguished from that of Chinese or Mexican infants (Oller & Eilers, 1982; Olney & Scholnick, 1976). Although we cannot say for sure that no differences in babbling occur, studies suggest that differences are hard to find in the light of overwhelming similarities and rare occurrence of nonuniversal sounds. Even deaf infants babble (Lenneberg, Rebelsky, & Nichols, 1965). Babbling begins at about the same age in deaf children as in hearing children and is similar, though perhaps a little more monotonous. Deaf babies tend to stop babbling earlier than hearing children because of the lack of auditory feedback (Whetnall & Fry, 1964). They replace babbling with gestures (see "Nonverbal Communication" later in this chapter).

Significance of Prespeech Sounds. The relationship of crying, cooing, and babbling to each other and to later stages in the acquisition of speech has been the subject of debate and controversy. Some theorists believe that crying sounds have no relationship to cooing and babbling, and that none of the **prespeech sounds** are important in the development of speech. According to this discontinuity view, cooing and babbling sounds are simply vocal play and have little, if any, effect on later speech.

Research evidence now favors a continuity view of the relationship between early sounds and speech development. According to this perspective, these early sounds that infants make are the elements from which speech develops (Bloom, 1998; Hopper & Naremore, 1978). Stark (1978) found indications that early crying and later cooing vocal behaviors are integrally related. Sound features present in crying and reflexive vocal tract activity are apparently incorporated in vocal expressions of pleasurable cooing. The voice and breath control developed during crying and fussing are important factors in the emergence of cooing.

Other researchers (Oller et al., 1976) also offer support for the significance of babbling in the development of speech. For example, the phonetic content of babbling indicates that infants exhibit preferences for certain consonant-vowel clusters that are later found in meaningful words. Longitudinal studies indicate that children's phonological patterns in early meaningful speech consist of many of the sound patterns they used in babbling (Menn & Stoel-Gammon, 1993). Although the role of babbling and other prespeech utterances in language development is still not clear, this experience appears to be an important preliminary step in gaining articulatory control of the vocal apparatus. Infants use this sound play to explore the potentials of their vocal tract as neuromotor and other biological foundations of speech mature (Papousek & Papousek, 1991). In addition, these sounds provide practice in the production of certain sound sequences, intonations, and pragmatic aspects of speech.

Morphological Development. When an infant has learned to pronounce phonemes, the next task is to combine them into units of meaning, referred to as **morphemes.** At this stage the child begins to work on the morphological component of language—the formation of words with the proper endings to express grammatical elements such as tense, gender, number, person, and case. Morphemes are the smallest meaningful units of language (J. Gleason, 1993). Some words consist of a single morpheme, while others are composed of multiple morphemes. For example, the word *boy* is a single morpheme, *trustworthy* consists of two morphemes, *trust* and *worthy,* and the word *opened* consists of the morphemes *open* and *ed.* A sentence is a collection of morphemes, but there may be more morphemes than words.

First Words. The baby's first word is generally considered one of the most significant milestones in speech development. Researchers have difficulty in determining precisely when an infant utters a first word because of the difficulty in separating babbling sounds from meaningful utterances (Adamson, 1995). Near the end of the first year of life, babbling consists largely of reduplicated monosyllables, (e.g., "na na" or "ma ma"). Infants practice babbling sounds until they typically arrive at a stage referred to as **canonical babbling** around 10 months of age. Canonical babbling consists of well-formed vowel and consonant sound combinations, such as "da da," that resemble words (Oller et al., 1999). These sophisticated babbling sounds are rich in intonation and are frequently made with gestures and eye contact. Although these vocalizations may be a complex form of sound play, in many instances they appear to reflect an infant's effort to engage in conversation. Parents tend to respond to such sounds positively and shape them into real words through reinforcement. Thus, the first word is thus likely to be a babbled utterance such as "ma-ma" or "da-da," which becomes associated with a specific person as parents reinforce increasing accuracy in their usage. The mother doesn't appreciate the baby referring to a strange man as "da-da," so she says, "No! That man is not your daddy!" Infants' first words are similar in all languages because they tend to begin with consonants and end with vowels that are repetitive. It is therefore no accident that all over the world the names for parents, *mama, papa,* and *dada,* are often the first words babies begin to use (Siegler, 1998).

Various researchers have reported different ages for the appearance of the first word. This is partly due to the difficulties involved in interpreting the meaning of specific sound combinations as well as individual differences in speech development. Generally, the average age cited in these reports is about 11 to 12 months. The range of 8 to 18 months includes most observations recorded for typically developing children (Darley & Winitz, 1961; McCarthy, 1954). If the first word does not appear by 18 months, there may be reason to suspect problems in the physiological, cognitive, or environmental foundations of language (Whitehurst, 1982).

Characteristics of First Words. The first words produced by infants are mostly nouns and references to people or objects such as things that move, things that can be acted upon, or objects of particular interest or familiarity (e.g., ball, car, cat) (Haslett & Samter, 1997). Verbs, adjectives, adverbs, and prepositions are acquired later, usually in that order. While vowels dominate the cooings and babblings of the infant, consonants occur more frequently than vowels during this phase (Bryen, 1982). The first words tend to:

1. be single syllable words such as "go" or "no";
2. be reduplicated (repeated) monosyllables such as "ma-ma" or "bye-bye," or
3. end with ie or y (birdie, doggie, sissy);
4. begin with consonants such as /s/, /b/, /d/, /t/, /m/, or /n/ followed by a variety of vowel sounds that are made at the front of the mouth (Beck, 1979);
5. appear one at a time;
6. refer to objects or events familiar to the child.

The repetitive quality of the babbling period carries over into many of the child's early words. Babbling continues during this period but diminishes in frequency as the repertory of meaningful words expands.

Many of the infant's early words are learned through the process of association between objects, people, and actions (Bloom, 1993). The infant hears a word and enters it into memory along with information about the context in which it is used. For example the word "shoe" takes on meaning as the parent uses the word in dressing the child. After sufficient encounters with the word, the infant vocalizes the word "shoe" during the dressing sequence. Later the parent may show the child a shoe, or a picture of a shoe, and ask "What is this?" The word is thus reinforced in a more general context. The first 50 distinct words infants produce include words for people (mommy, baby), household objects (clock), utensils (cup), animals (dog), activities and states (up, on), and routines (night-night) (Clark, 1995).

Development of Meaning (Semantics). Mastery of the semantic features of a language includes vocabulary development and understanding word meanings and relations of words within sentences. Infants concentrate mainly on the first task of developing a mental dictionary of individual word definitions. As the baby grows, new words are added and definitions of old words are revised and expanded. Toward the end of the second year of life, infants demonstrate a developing cognitive sophistication that provides the basis for the development of meaning (Bangs, 1982).

Vocabulary Development. Building up a repertoire of words is a critical task in language acquisition. From the time the infant utters the first word, vocabulary development proceeds at an increasingly rapid rate. The vocabulary grows rather quickly during the last half of the second year with the infant's increasing mobility and expanding knowledge and experience with people, objects, and events. The rate of spoken vocabulary

Reading to a toddler and naming pictures is an excellent way to enhance language development.

Table 9-2 How the Infant's Vocabulary Grows

AGE (MONTHS)	*NUMBER OF WORDS*	*GAIN*
8	0	
10	1	1
12	3	2
15	19	16
18	22	3
21	118	96
24	272	154
30	446	174
36	896	450

Source: Adapted from M. E. Smith (1926). An investigation of the development of the sentence and the extent of vocabulary in young children. *University of Iowa Studies in Child Welfare, 3,* (5), p. 54. Used by permission.

acquisition is depicted in Table 9-2. By the time a child is 30 months of age the vocabulary should be too large for a parent to easily count. If it is less than 150 to 200 words, it is probably too small (Coplan, 1995). Although some research suggests that in the English language infants learn nouns before verbs, the proportions probably depend upon the words they hear (Clark, 1995).

Vocabulary development involves expansion and elaboration of the various meanings of words already acquired. Many words used by infants are **overextended** or overgeneralized to apply to situations, objects, or persons not included in the conventional adult meaning. For example, Eva first said the word "moon" while actually looking at the moon. She then used the word "moon" while looking at half of a grapefruit, a lemon slice, a crescent shaped piece of yellow paper, and other similarly shaped objects (Bowerman, 1978).

Infants also **underextend** words by using them too narrowly and specifically. A child may think that the word car applies only to the family car rather than to cars on the street or to cars in picture books. A word such as "bye" may be used only when someone is leaving the child's own house. According to E. Clark's (1973) semantic features hypothesis, underextensions represent the first stage in the process of learning new words. The child begins by identifying one or two meanings of a new word and adding more features until the word, over a period of time, corresponds to the adult definition. Thus, in the process of adding new meanings to words, children often use words too broadly. Overextensions and underextensions are often reported in children's speech throughout the single-word period (Bloom, 1993).

One of the most interesting aspects of vocabulary development is the way infants create their own versions of adult words. A child's version of "Santa Claus" may be "Slaus Slaus," or a bottle may be a "baber." Obviously, such words are the product of mispronunciations or simplifications of adult usage. However, other words are the result of the child's own creation for which there is no adult version. The infant who called a pacifier a "bye" and money "bee" was not approximating adult word sounds. English-speaking infants make up their own version of nouns, verbs, and adverbs beginning around 2 years of age (E. Clark, 1995).

Why babies simplify adult words is not clearly understood, but it probably results from their limited articulatory skills (H. Clark & Clark, 1977). Children have been observed simplifying words by omitting final consonants ("out" = "ou"), reducing consonant clusters ("step" = "dep"), or reduplicating syllables ("water" = "wa wa") (Bryen, 1982; N. Smith, 1973). In other instances, infants create their own words from sounds or features associated with an object. A bell is called a "ding-ding," or a cow a "moo-moo." E. Clark (1995) suggests that infants construct new words from elements they already know (word roots and endings), and rely on simplicity to make the least adjustment possible. She gives the example of a child describing a wet newspaper as "soaky" (instead of soak+ed).

Word learning proceeds rather slowly until about 18 months (Siegler, 1998). Many infants experience a rapid increase in the number of words they add to their vocabulary between 18 and 24 months. This is sometimes referred to as a **vocabulary spurt.** At this point, infants appear to "soak up" new words as a sponge soaks up water.

This explosion in vocabulary growth is probably due to a number of factors. For one thing, major improvements in the thought processes take place toward the end of the second year of life. Advances in the understanding of object concepts and in the ability to sort objects into categories leads to increased ability and motivation to learn words. At this time infants also discover that everything has a name. Bloom (1993) also suggests that the vocabulary spurt is related to the infant's increased understanding of the relation between words and the ability to use one word to recall another. Finally, increases in social interactions and verbal exchanges with caregivers, connected with the infant's growing awareness of the value of words, may be a major impetus in learning words at this time.

Receptive versus Expressive Speech. The meaning the infant attaches to what other people say is called **receptive speech.** The meaningful sounds and words that infants use in communicating with others is referred to as **expressive speech.** Babies usually understand more words than they can say at all stages of language development. The first signs of word comprehension appear at approximately 9 to 10 months of age when infants respond to verbal commands such as "No!" or "Clap your hands!" (Adamson, 1995). Infants typically understand a few words such as mommy, daddy, and bye-bye, well before they say their first word (Ervin-Tripp, 1966). They may understand words for three or four months before they try to say them. By 13 months of age, an infant typically has a receptive vocabulary of about 50 words (Adamson, 1995). Toward the end of the second year, 2-year-olds usually can understand and carry out two or three related requests combined in a single utterance (Bzoch & League, 1991).

Mastery of Syntax. Children learn the syntax of a language when they (1) can join words into sentences and (2) understand multiple-word sentences said by others (B. Wood, 1976). Infants begin to put two words together around 18 months. This stage represents an important milestone in language acquisition. The infant's utterances become more representative of formal grammar as many of the rules of syntax are applied without explicit guidance.

One-Word Phrases. Between 12 and 18 months of age infants usually begin to use single words to convey larger meanings (Siegler, 1998). These single-word utterances are referred to as **holophrases** because they are roughly equivalent to whole phrases or complete sentences (McNeil, 1970). For example, when baby Maria says "ball," she may mean "There is a ball" or "Bring me the ball." Children normally use variations in voice inflections or gestures to help the listener distinguish between ambiguous meanings. In some instances, however, such words are hard to interpret without gestures or situational cues. Adult responses to these short utterances provide a context for the baby's language development to emerge. Holophrases are considered to be the product of the child's increasing cognitive awareness and limited verbal skill for self-expression (de Villiers & de Villiers, 1978).

Two-Word Utterances. Some infants remain in the one-word stage for several weeks or months, but others begin to combine words soon after they produce their first single-word utterance (E. Clark, 1995). The typically developing infant begins in a halting and uncertain manner to put two words together at approximately 18 months of age. The transition from one-word to two-word utterances has begun. Infants in the one-word stage use verbal interactions with language partners to move on and create two-word and longer sentences (Barnet & Barnet, 1998).

Many infants go through a brief phase in which strings of single words are produced in succession with pauses and separate intonations for each word. When the child reaches that point, the appearance of two-word utterances is imminent, and "Baby. Chair." becomes "Baby chair." (Bloom, 1973). During the early stage of language acquisition some two-word utterances can be interpreted as either a combination of two one-word sentences or a single two-word sentence. Emphasis or pauses between words usually indicate their meanings (Haslett & Sampter, 1997). The appearance of two-word combinations typically coincides with the time when the child has acquired a vocabulary of about 50 words (Lenneberg, 1967).

Two-word utterances are more definite indicators than holophrases that the child is learning the rules for putting words together in proper order. Such utterances are almost always constructed according to basic grammatical rules, with the subject first and the verb second. Even at this early stage, infants combine words with meanings that fit together in a sensible statement. For example, you may hear a toddler say "Daddy eat!" but not "Eat Daddy!" Some children build up word combinations through the use of a small number of words they combine with a variety of other words in fixed patterns, such as *more* milk and *more* juice (E. Clark, 1973).

Roger Brown (1973) identified five stages of language acquisition based on the average length of the child's utterances. An infant enters the first stage when the average sentence length is more than one word. The infant enters a new stage each time the average increases by about 50 percent. Infants work carefully on the correct grammatical structure of their sentences as they increase the average length of their utterances. Brown (1973) studied the speech of infants from such diverse languages as Spanish, Finnish, and Russian. He found that children from each of the different language environments used words with similar meanings and combined them in the same way.

Brown (1973) referred to the two-word expressions of infants as **telegraphic speech** because they are similar to a telegram, which omits all but the key words. The concept of telegraphic speech focuses on the efficiency and simplicity of the child's speech, as in "See truck?" instead of "Do you see the truck?" Such sentences consist mainly of nouns and verbs occurring in the order that corresponds to adult usage (Brown & Fraser, 1963).

Elaborated Sentences and Clauses. At approximately 2 years of age, infants begin producing three-word sentences. Between 2 and 2 1/2 years of age infants produce many two- and three-word sentences, and a few utterances with as many as six words (Crais & Roberts, 1996). With increasing age and a more extensive vocabulary, infants form longer, more complex sentences. They add other parts of speech to noun and verb combinations. As grammatical development advances, they begin to use conjunctions such as *and, then, after,* and *if* to link sequences of words (E. Clark, 1995). At first they learn to add *ed* to form the past-tense of verbs, but do not learn exceptions to the rule until later (Siegler, 1998). They also work on using negativies (e.g., "not"), imperatives (e.g., "must"), and the grammatical forms for asking questions (e.g., "Where mommy go?"). They begin to add the letter "s" to words to show possession (e.g., "baby's juice") and to form plurals (e.g., "dogs") (Haslett & Sampter, 1997). By 3 years of age typically developing children often speak in grammatically correct sentences (Coplan, 1995). The average length of their utterances is three to four words (Brown, 1973), but some children use as many as eight words in a sentence by 30 months of age (Fenson et al., 1994).

Pragmatic Aspects of Language. At the same time that infants are working on phonology, semantics, and other components of language, they are becoming increasingly proficient in the pragmatic aspects of language. Pragmatics refer to affective language behavior or social competency in language (Bangs, 1982). The essence of pragmatics is that language is used functionally—to do things (Hopper & Naremore, 1978). Pragmatics include the following features: (1) rules governing conversations, (2) selection of appropriate verbal as well as nonverbal language to convey intended meaning, and (3) proxemics—the proximity of physical distance people maintain in their interpersonal interactions (B. Wood, 1976).

Early Language Functions. Very young infants learn to use crying, cooing, and other prespeech sounds as well as body language to communicate their needs and influence the behavior of others. Halliday (1975) identified seven basic functions of language that may be practiced by infants:

1. Instrumental—getting needs met *(I want).*
2. Regulatory—controlling the behavior of others *(Do as I tell you).*
3. Interactional—relating to others *(Me and you).*
4. Personal—expressing self-awareness *(Here I come).*
5. Heuristic—exploring the environment *(Tell me why).*
6. Imaginative—creating an environment *(Let's pretend).*
7. Informative—communicating information *(I've got something to tell you).*

Halliday concluded that infants are capable of using the first four functions by 10 1/2 months, and that functions five and six are added by 18 months of age. The seventh function appears around 22 months. Children learn how to use different forms of language when addressing different people to achieve different goals. From a young age they realize that not everyone should receive the same type speech (E. Clark, 1995). For example, 2-year-olds have been observed using a small, high-pitched voice and very short sentences in talking to dolls, talking for dolls, and in talking to babies (Sachs & Devlin, 1976).

Nonverbal Communication. Nonverbal communication includes various body movements, postures, facial expressions, and gestures such as pointing, reaching, approach-avoidance behavior, smiling, and eye contact. The acquisition of nonverbal communication apparently parallels verbal expression. As verbal abilities become more complex, the child acquires greater varieties and fluency in the use of gestures and facial expression (Hopper & Naremore, 1978).

Out of 63 gestures identified in a study of 1,803 infants, the one most frequently reported at 8 months of age was "extends arms upward" in the unmistakable universal signal that says "Hold me" or "Pick me up" (Fenson et al., 1994). The pointing gesture (extended arm and index finger) that emerges between 9 and 14 months of age is another major communication device used by babies everywhere to attract the attention of another person (E. Bates, O'Connell, & Shore, 1987; Butterworth, 1998; Desrochers, Morissette, & Ricard, 1995). It is also a means of saying "Look at that!" or "I want that!" (Bower, 1977a). The comprehension of pointing gestures made by others may emerge before infants produce pointing gestures of their own (Butterworth, 1998). At approximately 1 year of age, babies begin to look at objects other people point to (Lempers, Flavell, & Flavell, 1977). Infants begin to point to themselves at approximately 18 months of age (Bates et al., 1987). The amount of pointing at 12 months may be an indicator of language production rates when an infant is 2 years of age (Butterworth, 1998). However, language development does not appear to be related to the amount of hand gestures used by a child after 2 years (Haslett & Sampter, 1997).

Parents often use both verbal labels and gestures in the same episode to communicate with infants. Consequently, infants acquire both words and gestures as object names or references early in development (Acredolo & Goodwyn, 2000). This experience apparently influences infants to continue using gestures after they begin to talk. The toddler who can say "milk" may still point to the refrigerator instead of speaking or may point at the same time a request is made.

Eye contact plays a major role in the communication rituals between caregiver and child very early in an infant's life. Smiling also is a very important early facial expression that facilitates adult-infant interactions. Eye contact and smiling are complementary behaviors that serve to instigate and maintain interaction sequences with infants. The absence of eye language and smiling presents extraordinary problems for a parent in communicating and establishing emotional intimacy. Mothers of blind infants sometimes find their babies perplexing and unresponsive and have difficulty knowing what their babies want (Fraiberg, 1974). However, even infants who are born blind communicate with gestures to a limited extent (Iverson, Tencer, & Goldwin-Meadow, 2000).

There are indications that deaf infants babble with their hands. Research evidence also suggests that timing of the milestones for the acquisition of sign language among nonhearing babies coincides with spoken language milestones (Peperkamp & Mehler, 1999). For example, babies who do not hear babble with their hands at about the same age hearing infants engage in voice babbling (Petitto & Marentette, 1991). Infants who are deaf can begin to form sentences with sign language at about the same age that hearing infants begin to use spoken sentences (Meier, 1991).

Some language experts recommend that parents of hearing babies teach them signs as a means of communication during the preverbal stage. Infants may learn gestures more easily than words (Goodwyn & Acredolo, 1993). Infants reduce frustrations that lead to whining and temper tantrums by expressing their needs with signs. For example, 13-month-old PJ used her hands to say "thank you," "please," "milk," and "more" (Baca, 2001). Apparently teaching signs to an infant does not interfere with spoken language development and may even enhance language acquisition and cognitive functioning (Fawcett, 2001; Goodwyn & Acredolo, 1998). The use of standard sign language is recommended, but caregivers can make up their own signs for words and objects. Some babies are interested in signing by 8 months, while others may not be interested until 12 months of age (Fawcett, 2001). Books by Acredolo and Goodwyn (1996) and Garcia (1999) provide instruction on how parents can teach an infant to sign.

Conversational Turn Taking. Infants apparently learn some of the basic rules of polite conversation such as taking turns, recognizing one's turn to speak, and not dominating the conversation even before they say their first words. Parents apparently encourage **conversational turn taking** in interactions with infants as early as 1 month of age by phrasing questions and responses in such a way that burps, yawns, and blinks may be considered as a conversational turn (Snow, 1977). Infants reciprocate by making sounds such as a coo and waiting for responses. Apparently, the baby is almost instinctively following the rules of polite conversation. These playful "dialogues" prepare the infant for more sophisticated conversations during the linguistic stage. As caregiver and child take turns vocalizing to each other, the process evolves into what has been referred to as the "fine-tuning" of the baby's language by the parent. Parental vocalizations are thus adjusted to match the child's changing linguistic abilities according to cues from the child (Bruner, 1978).

Proxemics. The use of space in communication is referred to as **proxemics.** Hall (1969) identified four zones of space people maintain in communicating under various circumstances: (1) the intimate zone (0–18 inches); (2) the personal zone (1½–2½ feet); (3) the social zone (4–7 feet); and (4) the public zone (12–25 feet). Children learn to use space in their communications in developmental stages. Infants typically prefer to communicate in the intimate zone. They engage in touching, hugging, and vocal interchanges in the intimate and personal zones. After 3 years of age, children gradually establish preferences for the less intimate zones, which involve less body contact and greater physical distance (B. Wood, 1976).

Crib Talk. Not all infant speech involves interactions with other people. Between 2 and 3 years of age, some toddlers talk to themselves just before going to sleep. These monologues are referred to as **crib talk.** This is a form of private speech as described in the discussion of Vygotsky's theory earlier in this chapter. Katherine Nelson (1989) analyzed tape recordings of the speech of an infant named Emily made over a 15-month period between 21 and 36 months of age. Some examples of Emily's earlier and later crib talk are (K. Nelson, 1989):

(22 months) . . . when Daddy comes in . . . then Daddy get Emmy . . . (p. 221)

(28 months) . . . we are going at the ocean . . . ocean is a little far away . . . (p. 163)

(33 months) . . . actually it's Stephen's koala bear . . . when Stephen wakes up, I'll have to throw his koala bear in his room . . . (p. 160).

These crib monologues are used by infants (1) as a pleasurable form of advanced vocal play; (2) to practice and expand their emerging language skills; and (3) to represent, sort out experiences, and make sense of their world (K. Nelson, 1989).

FACTORS INFLUENCING LANGUAGE DEVELOPMENT

Critical Periods and Language Development. Lenneberg (1967) asserts that there is a critical period for the acquisition of one's first or native language beginning around the age of 2 and ending at puberty. The case of Genie is sometimes cited as support for this claim (Bruer, 1999). Genie was an abused child who was discovered confined to a small room isolated from social and linguistic stimulation at around 12 years of age (Curtiss, 1977). In spite of concentrated intervention efforts, Genie never achieved proficiency in the use of language. Newport (1990) found that deaf children who were exposed to sign language before 4 to 6 years of age were more proficient in signing than children who were not introduced to sign language until 12 years or later. Studies of immigrants indicate that they never completely master all the components of their new country's language if learning begins after approximately 15 years of age (Bruer, 1999). Overall, the research evidence tends to support the existence of a critical period for language development. However, the critical period should be viewed as a "window of opportunity" that stays open well beyond the infancy period rather than a window that abruptly slams shut at an early age.

Parent-Child Interactions. Researchers and language specialists emphasize the importance of the interactions between infants and their caregivers, particularly the mother, in the acquisition of language (L. Leavitt, 1980). During the early months of life, parent-infant interactions provide the natural environmental context and foundations for language acquisition. Bruner (1983) believes parents create a language acquisition support device (LASD) that equals Chomsky's LAD in importance. Opportunities for learning experiences that foster language occur daily in conjunction with routine caregiving activities. During diaper changing, feeding, and other daily dyadic interactions, parents tend to encourage eye contact, vocal production, vocal imitation, turn taking, and the use of gestures. Many of the interactions involve contingent responses in which the baby's behavior depends upon a response from the parent and vice versa (Papousek & Papousek, 1991).

The mere presence of a newborn infant elicits vocal overtures from adults. By 2 months of age infants begin to reciprocate with sounds that sometimes match the pitch of the parent's voice. Vocal play interactions between infants and adults increase in number with the infant's age. In one study of vocal interactions between 2-, 3-, and 4-month-old German infants and their parents, 82 percent of the episodes were initiated by the infant (Papousek, Papousek, & Harris, 1987). Parents answered the infant's sounds with matching turns almost two-thirds of the time. In contrast, the infant answered only 17 percent of parent-initiated sounds. Other researchers have found that when an adult vocalizes just after the baby, infants tend to make sounds in response that take on a more speechlike quality (Bloom, 1998). Interactional vocal play between infants and their caregivers is considered a powerful influence on language acquisition.

Variations in vocabulary size have been attributed to the amount of language exposure provided infants by their parents. Talkative parents tend to have children with larger vocabularies. Parents who use complex sentence structures in parent-child discourse tend to influence their toddlers to produce complex sentences (Huttenlocher,1999). Hart and Risley (1995) conducted a two-year study on 42 infants, ages 1 to 2 years, and their families in which they observed the amount of speech parents used with their infants and other parenting characteristics. By 3 years of age, 86 to 98 percent of the words recorded in each child's vocabulary consisted of words also recorded in their parents' vocabularies. The characteristics of parental language and interactions that fostered speech competency included large amounts of diverse speech, responsiveness to child utterance, encouragement of autonomy, and talk about relations between things and events. Parents use these as well as other specific practices and parent-child interactions to support language acquisition. Some of these—"parentese," fine-tuning, and joint attention episodes—will be described here.

Parent-Infant Speech. The special language mothers use in talking to their infants is sometimes referred to as **motherese** (Newport, Gleitman, & Gleitman, 1977) or baby talk (Brown, 1977). The term **parentese** is currently being used to include the baby talk of fathers as well as that of mothers. Mothers from all linguistic communities tend to talk to their babies in much the same way. The mere presence of an awake infant elicits baby talk (Trehub, Trainor, & Unyk, 1993). Kaye (1980) has summarized the following characteristics of motherese:

1. A higher pitch, greater range of sound features, more varied tones.
2. Simplified words and special forms, such as *potty* and *mama.*
3. Shorter and simplified utterances, slower pace, and occasional whispering.
4. Immediate repetition and more repetition of the same words or phrases over a period of time.
5. Restriction of topics to the child's world.

The rise in pitch that generates a falsetto quality is perhaps the most notable aspect of baby talk. Mothers, fathers, other adults, and even children in cultures all over the world adjust their speech when addressing infant listeners (Trehub et al., 1993). However, some studies indicate that fathers, in contrast to mothers, tend to omit the falsetto rise in pitch (Trehub et al., 1993). Fathers also tend to use fewer repetitions and expansions in child utterances (Giattino & Hogan, 1975).

Fernald and her associates (1989) compared sound modification in mothers' and fathers' speech to preverbal infants in French, Italian, German, Japanese, British English, and American English. In all languages, mothers and fathers spoke with higher-pitched sounds, shorter utterances, and longer pauses in infant-directed speech than in speech directed to adults. Fernald (1989) found that objective adult listeners could identify the communicative intent (e.g., comfort, attention-bid) of the speaker in infant-directed speech more accurately than in adult-directed speech.

Cultural variations in baby talk have also been reported. For example, Japanese mothers tend to use repetitive nonsense syllables and imitations of their infants' sounds more than American mothers. Japanese mothers also seem to spend more time soothing their infants with vocalizations as compared with American mothers (Trehub et al., 1993). Higher pitch and exaggerated baby-talk sounds do not appear to be as prevalent among southern rural African American parents, Kaluhi families in New Guinea, and Quiche-Mayan parents in Guatemala (Sachs, 1993).

There are indications that a type of parentese extends into the songs mothers sing to their infants. The practice of singing to infants is observed throughout the world. Apparently, mothers and other caregivers almost everywhere sing lullabies to soothe their babies and put them to sleep. This practice has been observed in cultures as diverse as the Cuna Indians of Panama, the Hazara tribe of Afghanistan, and traditional Vietnamese families. Trehub and her colleagues (1993) identified the following characteristics of lullabies similar to infant-directed speech: word reduplication, sequence repetition, a low and narrow pitch range, elongated vowels, and common words incorporated into rhythmic patterns. However, fathers are less likely than mothers to sing lullabies to infants. Instead, they tend to sing popular songs or folk tunes, improvising words or melodies and often embedding the infants' names into the words (Trehub et al., 1993).

The importance of parentese is more than the provision of sounds or words for the baby to imitate. What caregivers are mainly attempting to accomplish when they use baby talk is to communicate, to understand, to be understood, to engage and maintain infant attention, to communicate affect to the infant, and to facilitate speech and language comprehension (Brown, 1973; Fernald, 1984). Evidently the mother's efforts are not wasted. Studies of vocal interactions between young infants and their mothers have found that infants as young as 3 months of age vocalize in response to their mother's speech (Bates et al., 1977; M. Lewis & Freedle, 1973). Infants match the pitch of the parent's voice, sometimes engaging in vocal "duets." They prefer infant-directed speech over adult-directed speech, and approving over disapproving infant-directed tones (Trehub et al., 1993).

Parentese and other forms of vocal play between caregivers and infants eventually include a variety of playful interactions and ritualized games. German mothers have been observed engaging in playful "headbutting" games with their infants as they make playful flow of rhythmic sounds (Papousek et al., 1987). Blowing on the baby's stomach, tickling, playing "I'm gonna getcha" are other examples of the types of games parents everywhere play with their infants. Some theorists believe that other forms of children's play originate in these early dyadic interactions combining vocal and social games (Papousek et al., 1987). Many of these play interactions involve turntaking such as peek-a-boo and build-and-bash (the parent builds and the child bashes) games (de Villiers & de Villiers, 1979).

Fine-Tuning. The process of fine-tuning the baby's speech may involve the techniques of prompting, echoing, and expansion (Dale, 1976). For the preverbal child, a parent may talk and make sounds while feeding or bathing the child, such as "You are a sweet baby—Yes—Ooh—Ooh—," which prompts the child to reciprocate with sounds. For the older infant, the parent may prompt by asking, "What do you want?" as the child points to the refrigerator. In echoing, the parent imitates or repeats the child's utterances, which stimulate the child to continue to vocalize. Expansion is similar to echoing, but with something added to the child's utterance by the adult, as in: "Mommy's dress." "Yes, this is Mommy's blue dress." In the following interchange all three processes are used:

Mother: (Pointing to a ball) *What's that?* (Prompting)
Child: *Ball.*
Mother: *Ball.* (Echoing)
Child: *Blue ball.*
Mother: *Yes! It's a round, blue ball.* (Expansion)

These techniques represent a form of scaffolding (discussed in Chapter 8) and are consistent with Vygotsky's theory of facilitating language acquisition within the zone of proximal development.

Joint Attention. Parents and infants often communicate through the process known as **joint attention.** This happens when infant and caregiver focus on the same object, sounds, or events. Most of what we know about joint attention involves episodes of joint visual attention (shared looking). For example, an adult might notice a bright red ball that has captured the baby's attention. The adult looks back and forth from the infant to the ball to indicate mutual interest and attention. The adult then comments, "Ball! Red ball!" Adults also initiate shared looking episodes by moving objects into the baby's field of vision, by pointing at objects, and by making eye contact with the baby and then shifting their gaze to something they want the baby to see. Infants call attention to objects they want to share with adults by shifting gaze, pointing, making sounds, and by physical contact (e.g., tugging). Such interactions usually elicit adult naming or other comments that help infants label objects and other features of the environment. Babies typically engage in sustained shared looking with adults at approximately 12 months of age (Corkum & Moore, 1995).

There is a growing amount of evidence to support the significance of joint attention as a powerful means of communication and language acquisition. For example, infants are more likely to acquire a correct word for a novel object (*dodo*) if they are looking at the object while it is being named than if their attention is focused on something else (Dunham, Dunham, & Curwin, 1993). Toddlers make faster progress in vocabulary acquisition when adults label features of the environment during joint attention episodes (Dunham & Dunham, 1992). On the basis of existing studies it is not possible to determine whether the adult contributes more to the language acquisition in joint attentional episodes, or whether the child controls the process. An alternative explanation favored by Dunham and Dunham (1992) is that the process is a mutual one in which both adult and child make important contributions to language acquisition during joint attention episodes.

Gender Differences. Through the years researchers and scholars have had difficulty deciding whether or not gender is an important factor in language acquisition. In 1982, Shepherd-Look concluded that research has not found gender differences in the age of beginning to talk, age of first sentences, mean length of utterances, picture vocabulary ability, word comprehension, or word production.

More recently, studies of infants and toddlers have found a female advantage in certain aspects of verbal ability, such as vocabulary and length of utterances (Morisset, Barnard, & Booth, 1995). For example, a study of gender differences among toddlers from economically disadvantaged families found differences favoring girls on spontaneous utterances at 20 to 30 months of age. However, no gender differences were found at 24 and 36 months on standardized tests of language development (Morisset et al., 1995). A large-scale study to develop norms for a parent-report inventory of infant communicative development found female scores on several aspects of language ability to be slightly higher than male scores (Fenson et al., 1994). A study comparing the receptive and expressive speech of twins 14, 20, 24, and 36 months of age, found that the scores of girls on a variety of measures were higher than those of boys at each age tested (Young et al., 2001).

Overall, the evidence from existing studies tends to show that female infants and toddlers, on average, display superior performance on some measures of language development. However, gender differences are much smaller than previously believed and probably account for no more than 1 to 2 percent of individual differences in language ability during the early years (Fenson et al., 1994).

Twins. Researchers have found that twins and other children of multiple births have more problems in language development than children from single births. In comparison to singletons, twins tend to lag behind in language ability (Drillien, 1964; McCarthy, 1954). These speech problems have been attributed largely to the fact that twins are frequently premature or low birth weight babies, and their parents may have less time to attend to them individually and to help them develop verbal skills. Some of the problems may also be due to twins' tendency to develop a "twin language," referred to as **idioglossia.** This is a private communication system of their own that includes gestures and jargon (Bowen, 2001). However, there are indications that this type of language may not be used exclusively by twins, but may be communication patterns used by other children to communicate with their peers (Bakker, 1987). In any case, research on language development in twins is complicated by factors such as prematurity, low birth weight, and other developmental problems that are more prevalent among twins than singletons. A study on language development among twins conducted in Sweden did not find any significant delays in language development among twins at 4 years of age when birth weight was controlled (Akerman & Thomassen, 1991). Thus, factors other than "twinness" per se may account for much of the language delay found among many twins.

Multilingualism. Under certain circumstances, being born into a family in which more than one language is spoken may be an obstacle in the early stages of language acquisition. Infants from bilingual families have trouble separating phonological components of the languages until about 3 years of age, unless there is a marked separation of a situation or speakers (Ervin-Tripp, 1966). However, many children who are exposed to two languages during infancy tend to show few differences in language development when compared to monolingual children (Padilla & Lindholm, 1976). Even when early difficulties are present, children eventually speak each language without one interfering with the other (Obler, 1985). The optimal way for infants and young children to learn two languages at the same time is keeping the contexts in which they are used separate. For example, one parent can use one language consistently, while the other parent uses the second language. Another approach is for one language to be used in the home, while the second language is used in the child-care facility or preschool environment (Taber-Flusberg, 1994).

Socioeconomic Status. Infants from upper and middle social-class environments are generally considered to have a linguistic advantage over infants from lower social classes. Socioeconomic status (SES) is generally found to be associated with the quality of the language environment, including the amount of talk and complexity of expression. Hart and Risley (1995) found that middle-SES parents of 11- to 18-month-old infants average 535 utterances per hour of which 321 were addressed to the baby. By comparison, lower-SES parents average 521 utterances per hour, of which 283 were addressed to the baby. The crowded conditions in the homes of families living in poverty make it difficult for parents to be individually verbally responsive to their babies (Evans, Maxwell, & Hart, 1999). However, the effects of social class on language acquisition do not, in most cases, become evident until the second and third years of life (Golden & Birns, 1976). Morisset and her colleagues (1995) studied language development among toddlers 13 months through 36 months of age who were from poverty backgrounds. Language delays did not become observable until after 24 months of age. This finding is consistent with other studies demonstrating the emergence of social-class differences in language during the third year of life (Fenson et al., 1994).

Individual Differences. The study of language development involves, to a large extent, the identification of typical patterns displayed by infants all over the world. Researchers, however, are also interested in individual differences in language acquisition. Some infants are producing two- or three-word sentences while others of the same age are still struggling with the first words. One study (Snyder, Bates, & Bretherton, 1981) found variations in the one-word vocabularies expressed by 13-month-old infants ranging from 0 to 45 words. An interesting (but not verified) anecdote about the famous Scottish philosopher, Thomas Carlyle, is sometimes used to illustrate precocious language development. At 10 months of age, Carlyle had not said any words, but when he heard a baby crying was reported to have said, *"What ails thee, Jock?"* From then on he spoke in complete sentences (Illingworth, 1991).

K. Nelson (1973) identified individual stylistic differences in how children acquire and use early words. Some toddlers use a **referential style** whereby they acquire a large number of words that refer mainly to objects. Their speech is used mainly for sharing information about objects ("ball"), one word at a time. Other toddlers use an **expressive style.** Their speech is more socially oriented and consists mainly of pronouns and action words. Expressive toddlers tend to have smaller vocabularies, but compress them into phrases ("getit") to communicate feelings and wants.

Individual difference in language styles and other aspects of language acquisition have been attributed to variations in caregiver styles and interaction patterns. Researchers have found that parents use verbal styles of interaction that tend to match and support the style (referential or expressive) used by the child (Goldfield, 1987). Other possible sources of individual variations include maturational status at birth, disabilities, intelligence, underlying brain mechanisms, and personality factors.

PROBLEMS IN LANGUAGE ACQUISITION

Most infants appear to master language with little difficulty if they have a reasonably stimulating language environment. However, some infants suffer language delay and communication disorders due to nervous system disorders or other impairments. Communication disorders are often not detected during the early months of life unless an infant has an obvious developmental disability such as cerebral palsy, Down syndrome, or a cleft lip. Communication disorders are usually much harder to identify in infants who are typically developing in other areas. Approximately 3 to 6 percent of children who are following other

APPLICATIONS: FACILITATING LANGUAGE DEVELOPMENT

Although theorists differ about the extent to which language development can be facilitated through environmental stimulation, the importance of exposure to a supportive and enriched environment is being increasingly recognized. The following are examples of activities that can be used by parents and other caregivers to enhance communication and language development during the various stages of infancy. Keep in mind, however, that these activities should be natural, spontaneous, informal, and free from pressure on the infant to "perform."

Birth to 6 Months.

- Imitate the baby's facial expressions, gestures, and sounds. Maintain frequent eye contact and talk to the baby during diapering, feeding, and other routines (Ramey & Ramey, 1999; Senter, 1983).
- Engage in turn taking with the infant. Initiate the cycle when the baby is quiet and alert by making a series of sounds ("ooh-ooh," "ah-ah") (Senter, 1983).
- Play records with soothing sounds for the baby. Sing lullabies while rocking the baby.
- When talking to an infant at this age, frequently keep your face about 6 to 18 inches from the baby's, so that the baby can watch your face and lips (Meier & Malone, 1979).
- Gently bounce the baby on your knee and sing songs like "trot-a-little-horsey" (Sparling & Lewis, 1979). Speak with "parentese" types of sounds.
- Say the baby's name frequently (Cataldo, 1983).

6 to 12 Months.

- Continue activities suggested for birth to 6 months (except face-to-face distance).
- Play peekaboo. Vary the game by attaching a cloth to the top of a mirror. Ask "Where is [baby's name]?" and raise the cloth to let the baby see the reflected image (Sparling & Lewis, 1979).
- Say "Hi" when you come close to the baby. Wave and say "bye-bye" when you are leaving the room (Sparling & Lewis, 1979).
- Play pat-a-cake.
- Toward the end of this age period, read simple short stories when baby is quiet and

developmental norms have problems in speech acquisition (Bruer, 1999). Parents should have an infant screened for potential problems if the infant has not spoken any words by 2 years of age or is not responsive to words and sounds of others.

The number one cause of speech and language delays during infancy is hearing loss (Billeaud, 1993). Consequently, hearing loss should be identified as early as possible. Hearing screening tests should be administered periodically, especially to infants who are at-risk for developmental delay, who have persistent incidents of otitis media, or who display any indications of hearing loss. Some possible signs of hearing loss that parents, caregivers, and teachers should look for are:

1. lack of responsiveness to loud noises;
2. cessation of babbling after a few months;
3. failure to produce words soon after the first year of age;
4. failure to form two-word phrases by 2 years of age;
5. failure to produce simple sentences by 3 years of age;
6. cessation of vocabulary growth after it begins (Tweedie, 1987).

LANGUAGE ASSESSMENT INSTRUMENTS

Most general infant-assessment scales, such as the Bayley–II (Bayley, 1993), have sections for measuring language performance. In addition, there are several instruments specifically designed for screening and assessing infant-toddler alert. Avoid forcing the child to be quiet or sit still (B. White, 1975).

- Carry the child around the house or other places on "word walks," pointing to and naming objects of interest (Meier & Malone, 1979).
- Use a tape recorder to record the infant's sounds and play them back (Meier & Malone, 1979).

12 to 18 Months.

- Continue activities suggested for 6 to 12 months.
- Talk to the baby during bath time about soap, water, washcloth, and toys. Discuss how they feel and what they do (Sparling & Lewis, 1979).
- Use learning exercises such as the following: Find a book with stiff pages with only one brightly colored object on each page. Place the book where the baby can see it, point to the picture of an object, and say, "See the ———." (Point to the ———.) "Where is the ——— ?" If the baby makes any sounds, repeat the sounds or words vocalized (Meier & Malone, 1979).

18 to 24 Months.

- Continue reading and naming objects from books at least once a day.
- Listen carefully to what the child is trying to say, and respond positively. If the words are not clear, venture a guess (e.g., "You want some water?")
- Repeat and expand the child's one- or two-word utterances into complete sentences. For example, if the baby says, "Go bye-bye," respond by saying, "You want to go outside?"
- Continue to structure games and activities to stimulate language (e.g., This Little Piggy).
- Be very specific when giving instructions and directions to your child. Instead of saying, "Bring me your things," say, "Bring me your shoes and socks." Then expand further by saying, "I see you brought your blue socks." (Sparling & Lewis, 1979).
- Raise or lower your voice from time to time to make sounds more interesting. Sing your words at times.

communication skills. Two examples of the instruments available are the Receptive-Emergent Language Test-2 and the MacArthur Communicative Development Inventories.

The **Receptive-Emergent Language Test-2** (Bzoch & League, 1991) or **REEL-2** is a checklist that is used to screen infants from 1 to 36 months of age for potential delays in receptive and expressive speech skills. The examiner obtains information about the child by means of a parent interview. The scale provides receptive and expressive communication quotients, an age-equivalent score, and an overall language score.

The **MacArthur Communicative Development Inventories:** Infant and Toddler Versions (Fenson et al., 1993) are designed to assess vocabulary comprehension and production, word endings and forms, and syntactic development between 10 months and 3 years of age. The MacArthur is classified as a parent-completed checklist in which the respondents indicate whether their child currently has a particular communication skill (McLean et al., 1996).

SUMMARY

Theories of Language Development

- Language is a complex system of mutually agreed-upon symbols used to express and understand ideas and feelings. Speech is the vocal component of language, which includes expressive and receptive functions.

- Behaviorists maintain that language is acquired through systematic reinforcement, whereas nativists claim that infants are innately equipped to master language. Cognitive developmental theorists stress the importance of cognitive processes. Vygotsky emphasized the cultural origins and functions of language. Interactionist theorists stress the interplay between biological and environmental influences in language acquisition.

Structural Components of Language

- Language consists of five components: phonology (sounds), morphology (words), semantics (meaning), syntax (structure), and pragmatics (social usage). Developing proficiency in a language involves mastering the rules governing the various components.
- The ability to produce speech sounds is affected by the development of the vocal mechanism, which changes rapidly during infancy.
- The prespeech sounds include crying, cooing, and babbling. Research studies indicate that each type of prespeech sound is an important link in the chain of language acquisition.
- The first word represents a major milestone in morphological development and usually appears around the child's first birthday. The first words produced by infants are mostly nouns and references to things that move and capture their interest.
- Semantic development is based upon the infant's growing cognitive capacity to acquire new words, add new meaning to old words, and understand relationships among words.
- Vocabulary development is an important task in language acquisition that proceeds rapidly after 18 months of age.
- Word comprehension (receptive speech) progresses ahead of word production (expressive speech) during all stages of language development.
- Infants begin to acquire the grammar (syntax) of their language when they can understand and produce multiple-word utterances. The first two-word combinations, sometimes called telegraphic speech, are usually produced around 18 months. However, some linguists believe that sentencelike words, called holophrases, may be the first indicators of syntactic awareness.
- Infants demonstrate their growing competency in the pragmatic aspects of language early in life by using crying, cooing, and other prespeech sounds to interact with adults and get their needs met. They use "crib talk" as a form of vocal play, to practice language usage, and make sense of their experiences.

Factors Influencing Language Development

- Evidence exists to support the idea that there is a critical period for mastering the components of language, but the period ends gradually and extends well beyond infancy.
- Parent-child interactions are an important influence on language acquisition during infancy. Mothers and fathers use their own special language, called "parentese," in talking to their babies. Language acquisition is facilitated by parent-infant interactions that are characterized by episodes of fine-tuning and joint attention.
- Gender differences probably account for only 1 to 2 percent of individual differences in language acquisition during infancy.
- Twins may be at a disadvantage in language acquisition, but other correlated factors may be responsible for their language delay.
- Infants from bilingual families are faced with challenges in language acquisition, but usually demonstrate few problems in language ability. The best way for infants and young children to learn two languages at the same time is for adults to keep the contexts in which they are used separate.
- Infants from economically impoverished environments are generally considered to have a disadvantage in language development. However, the effects of social class on language acquisition do not usually become evident until the second and third years of life.
- Individual differences in language development have been attributed to stylistic differences in how children acquire and use early words, variations in caregiver styles and interaction patterns, maturational status at birth, disabilities, intelligence, underlying brain mechanisms, and personality factors.

Problems in Language Acquisition

- The number one cause of speech and language delays during infancy is hearing loss. Parents should have infants screened periodically for potential problems.

Language Assessment Instruments

- Examples of instruments that are used to assess the language competency of infants are the REEL-2 and the MacArthur.

KEY TERMS

language
speech
private speech
interactionist
phonology
morphology
semantics
syntax
pragmatics
phonemes
cooing
babbling
prespeech sounds
morphemes
canonical babbling
overextended words
underextended words
vocabulary spurt
receptive speech
expressive speech
holophrases
telegraphic speech
conversational turn taking
proxemics
crib talk
motherese
parentese
fine-tuning
joint attention
idioglossia
referential style
expressive style
Receptive-Emergent Language Test-2 (Reel-2)
MacArthur Communicative Development Inventories

RESOURCES ON THE WEB*

www.kidsource.com/ASHA/index.html Link to American Speech-Language-Hearing Association site containing articles providing questions and answers on language development issues and problems, such as otitis media, hearing, and bilingualism.

members.tripod.com/Caroline_Bowen/devel1.html Presents information on the key stages in the development of language in young children, including a listing of developmental milestones in the first five years of a child's life.

www.enfagrow.com/index.html Provides information on a variety of language development topics including lists of activities for promoting language development from birth to 4 years of age. Links to discussion of topics related to other areas of development.

*Web sites are subject to change.

TEN

PERSONALITY

I am the only ME I AM
who qualifies as me;
no ME I AM has been before
and none will ever be.
—Jack Prelutsky

An infant is a person, even from the beginning of life. Although parents are frequently preoccupied with routine caregiving activities, they quickly recognize the uniqueness and individuality of their newborn infant. Even identical twins display their own unique behavior patterns. Jan is quiet and placid, while her sister Jean is active and exuberant. One of the most important features distinguishing one baby from another is personality.

The term *personality* has many general meanings as well as specific definitions. The following definition has been widely used: "**Personality** refers to more or less stable internal factors that make one person's behavior consistent from one time to another, and different from the behavior other people would manifest in comparable situations" (Child, 1968, p. 83). Personality is thus viewed as the sum total of the internal qualities and enduring patterns of behavior that establish a person's individuality. In this chapter we examine a number of concepts and theories associated with the development of infant personality. Two important components of personality that emerge during the infancy period—temperament and the concept of self—are discussed. Finally, the practical implications of the theoretical and research literature for facilitating personality development during infancy are considered.

THEORIES OF PERSONALITY DEVELOPMENT

There are numerous theories about what makes up human personality and how it develops. For our purposes, however, we consider the three most influential and prominent theories: the classical psychoanalytic theory of Sigmund Freud; Erik Erikson's contemporary psychosocial theory; and the behavioristic theory of B. F. Skinner.

Freud's Psychoanalytic Theory. Freud was probably the first theorist to emphasize the importance of infancy and the first few years of life in personality development. He believed that the "child is father of the man," and that the basic personality structure is formed by the fifth year of life (Hall & Lindzey, 1978). Consequently, the experiences a person has during infancy have a profound influence on the adult personality.

Freud identified three major components of personality: the id, the ego, and the superego. The **id** is the biological part of personality that is present at birth. It includes the basic instincts and physiological urges such as hunger and libido (sexual energy). The id provides the energy that motivates the personality. According to Freud, the newborn infant has a very simple personality consisting solely of the primitive urges of the id. The infant seeks immediate gratification and has little ability to tolerate tension created in the id when needs are not met.

The irrational, pleasure-seeking, uninhibited id remains part of the personality throughout life. However, people cannot realistically always have what they want as soon as they want it. Consequently, a second part of the personality, the **ego,** develops during infancy to exercise control over the id's instinctual urges. The ego is the rational, planning, and organizing part of the personality. Its primary function is to help the id find ways to achieve gratification that are, in the long run, most satisfactory.

The gradual emergence of the ego during the infancy period lays the foundation for the formation of the **superego** during preschool years (ages 3 to 5). The superego consists of the conscience and the ego-ideal (the person you would like to be). It functions primarily to inhibit the impulses of the id that are socially unacceptable and works to perfect moral behavior (C. Hall & Lindzey, 1978). The superego is often in conflict with the id, while the ego works to reconcile the differences. If the ego is not successful in resolving the conflict, personality problems may develop.

According to Freud, personality develops through a series of stages: oral, anal, phallic, latency, and genital. The personality is shaped by the quality of the experiences related to the area of the body that is dominant in each stage. Only the two stages, oral and anal, that occur during the infancy period will be discussed in more detail.

The Oral Stage (Birth to 18 Months). During the first part of infancy, the oral region—the mouth, tongue, and lips—is dominant. Feeding experiences, nonnutritive sucking, and other sensations incorporated through the mouth provide the infant's first experiences of pleasure and frustration. If the baby receives too much or too little gratification through the mouth, oral fixation is likely to occur. Oral fixation through deprivation results in such personality traits as pessimism, self-depreciation, and passivity. Opposite personality characteristics develop from overindulgence in the oral stage.

The Anal Stage (18 Months to 3 Years). Toward the end of the infancy period, the anal region of the body gradually becomes the focal point of the baby's experiences. During this stage, bowel movements become a source of pleasure and potential conflict. The toilet training that typically begins during this period is likely to have long-term consequences. If the infant is treated too harshly, a personality dominated by excessive orderliness, stinginess, stubbornness, and compulsivity is likely to develop. On the other hand, overpermissiveness in toilet training can result in the opposite personality traits.

Erikson's Psychosocial Theory. Erik Erikson was a follower of Freud, but he disagreed with some of Freud's ideas. Erikson (1963) reinterpreted Freudian theory, with more optimism about human nature and an emphasis on cultural influences. He translated Freudian theory into completely different, more contemporary terms.

Erikson's psychosocial theory is usually discussed in relation to eight psychosocial stages of development, from birth through old age. The personality forms as the individual passes through this series of interrelated stages. Each stage involves a conflict, or crisis of emotional opposites. The quality of the individual's experience in each stage determines how the conflict is resolved. The emotional crisis that occurs in each stage must be resolved before personality development can proceed smoothly in succeeding stages. The first two stages—trust versus mistrust, and autonomy versus shame and doubt—occur during the infancy period.

Trust Versus Mistrust (Birth to 18 Months). Erikson's first stage, trust versus mistrust, roughly parallels Freud's oral stage. The trust versus mistrust stage is considered to be the most critical because it provides the foundation for resolving crises and developing a healthy sense of identity in other stages of life. The basic psychosocial attitude the infant must develop in this stage is that the world and the people in it can be trusted. According to Erikson (1963), consistency and continuity of experience provide the foundation for the sense of trust to develop.

Infants are inclined to be uncertain and mistrusting because their knowledge about the world is very limited. Some feelings of mistrust are normal and healthy. However, if the baby is treated harshly and the basic needs are not consistently met, feelings of mistrust are reinforced and become dominant. Distrustful infants have difficulty separating from their mothers and may exhibit other emotional problems later in life.

Autonomy versus Shame and Doubt (18 Months to 3 Years). The second period coincides with Freud's anal stage. Developing a sense of autonomy begins with the feeling of being in control of one's body during infancy. With increasing mobility, infants begin to explore their environment. They want to see new places and things, undertake new activities, and generally do things for themselves. During this period they also become capable of establishing bowel and bladder control. They frequently have difficulty staying within designated boundaries and complying with adult wishes. The negativism that is characteristic of toddlerhood results from the need for autonomy.

The crisis of this period occurs when the infant's natural inclination to be self-assertive collides with adult demands and restrictions. A major area of potential conflict is toilet training. The successful resolution of the crisis involves the parents' willingness to allow reasonable freedom without being overly permissive. Problems occur when parents are too restrictive or overprotective and impose unrealistic expectations. The child may develop a dominant sense of shame and doubt. Such a child suffers from feelings of incompetence, insecurity, and unworthiness.

Skinner's Behaviorism. According to B. F. Skinner (1961), personality is nothing more than a collection of behavior patterns. The personality is acquired over time, response by response. In contrast to Freud, Skinner rejects the idea that there are internal personality mechanisms, such as an ego, or unconscious motivational forces. He identified no personality components or developmental stages. To Skinner, we are products of our environment (C. Hall & Lindzey, 1978).

The main concern of Skinner and other behaviorists is how behaviors are acquired and extinguished. Skinner's system consists mainly of laws or principles that control the formation of stimulus-response relationships. To understand personality, you need only to understand an individual's conditioning history. An infant becomes passive and compliant if the responses of parents and other caregivers reinforce that particular type of behavior. The infant's personality is not as complex and fully developed as an adult's because the infant has had fewer experiences. Each infant develops a unique personality because of a history of unique experiences (Hjelle & Ziegler, 1976).

As he explores the environment, this toddler is developing a sense of autonomy.

Evaluating Personality Theories. Personality has proved to be as difficult to study as it has been to define. Consequently, there is no overwhelming research evidence in favor of any single theory. Each theory has been praised as well as criticized. As a student of infant development, you will have to decide which theory you prefer. Many people prefer an eclectic approach, combining the best and most promising ideas from several different theories. In the remainder of this chapter, some of the attributes of infant personality that have become the focal points of current research are considered.

TEMPERAMENT

Much of the theoretical debate, as well as research, on infant personality has focused on the development of temperament. There are numerous theories of temperament. Definitions of temperament vary somewhat among theorists. One of the earliest definitions was developed by Chess, Thomas, and Birch (1965): **Temperament** is "the basic style which characterizes a person's behavior" (p. 32). Temperament has also been defined as individual differences in the behavioral expressions of emotionality and arousal (Campos et al., 1983). The following definition of temperament combines most of the common features of various theories: Temperament "refers to the stable behavioral and emotional reactions that appear early and are influenced in part by genetic constitution" (Kagan, 1994, p. 40).

Some theorists believe that temperament is the developmental forerunner of personality, or the basic early raw material from which adult personality is formed (Buss, 1989). The terms *temperament* and *personality* are thus often used as synonyms. Other theorists, however, view temperament as one of the components of personality (Strelau, 1994). Personality is thus perceived as containing other characteristics, such as the self-concept, values, and motivation, that are broader than those encompassed by temperament. Currently researchers are trying to determine the extent to which infant temperament characteristics can be accounted for by five major adult personality factors (Angleitner & Ostendorf, 1994; Hagekull, 1994). However, the debate about the relationship between temperament and personality is likely to continue for some time.

Measurement of Temperament. The most frequently used method of assessing infant temperament is parent and caregiver reports (J. Bates, Wachs, & Emde, 1994). The **Infant Temperament Questionnaire** (Carey & McDevitt, 1978) is an example of a commonly used scale. However, temperament researchers question the accuracy and validity of parental and other caregiver questionnaires. Parent ratings of the same child may vary from time to time and from parent to parent. Parental perceptions of an infant's temperament are influenced by the parents' sex, race, socioeconomic status, mental health status, marital status, and marital satisfaction. Parents who report higher levels of anxiety and make more negative statements about themselves rate their infant's temperament more negatively (Wolk et al., 1992). Thus, temperament may be in the minds of parents as much as in the behavior of the infant.

Consequently, laboratory observational ratings of temperament (e.g., *Laboratory Temperament Assessment Battery;* in Goldsmith & Rothbart, 1991) and naturalistic observation rating scales (e.g., J. Bates & Bayles, 1984) have been developed as alternatives to parental ratings. In addition, psychophysiological measures such as heart rate, cortisol secretion, and electrical activity in the brain are currently used as measures of emotional changes that are considered to be indicators of temperament. A combination of measures is considered to be the best approach to the assessment of temperament for research purposes (R. Thompson, 1999a). Parent and teacher questionnaires can be useful in clinical and educational settings as long as the potential inaccuracies are kept in mind (J. Bates et al., 1994).

Dimensions of Temperament. A variety of dimensions or components of temperament have been identified (e.g., Buss & Plomin, 1975; Rothbart, 1981; A. Thomas & Chess, 1977). The nine components developed by A. Thomas and Chess (1977) in a long-term research study have been widely used:

1. *Activity level.* Inactive versus active motor behavior (reaching, crawling, sleep-wake cycle).
2. *Rhythmicity.* Regularity of schedule; predictability versus unpredictability of behavior (eating, sleeping, etc.).
3. *Approach or withdrawal.* Typical initial response to a new stimulus (people, food, toys, etc.).
4. *Adaptability.* Response to change in routine (bedtime, feeding, travel, etc.).
5. *Sensory threshold.* Level of stimulation needed to evoke a response (noise, pain, light, etc.).
6. *Intensity of response.* Energy level of response (crying, body movements, etc.).
7. *Quality of mood.* The degree of pleasant, happy, and friendly behavior versus unpleasant, unhappy, and unfriendly behavior.
8. *Distractibility.* The extent to which extraneous stimuli (noise, objects, etc.) interfere with or change ongoing behavior.
9. *Persistence and attention span.* Length of time an activity is pursued and the continuation of an activity in the face of interruptions or obstacles.

A. Thomas and Chess (1985) found that three basic temperamental patterns of behavior could be identified soon after birth. About 65 percent of the infants in their study were classified in one of the following groups:

1. *The **Easy Child.*** Babies in this group display regularity, respond positively to new situations, adapt quickly to change, and exhibit a relatively mild and generally positive mood. These babies quickly develop regular schedules of sleeping and eating. They smile a lot, accept most frustrations with little protest, and are easily comforted. They are a joy and a delight to their caregivers. About 40 percent of the babies in the Thomas and Chess study displayed this temperament pattern.

2. *The **Difficult Child.*** At the opposite end of temperamental extremes, these babies are irregular in body functions and are slow to develop good eating and sleeping routines. They cry longer and louder than other babies. The difficult child does not adjust easily to new foods, strangers, or changes in routine. This group composed about 10 percent of the sample. Such an infant requires a lot of patience, stamina, and resourcefulness on the part of parents and other caregivers.
3. *The **Slow-to-Warm-Up Child.*** These babies are characterized by mild intensity of reactions (positive or negative). Although they are very active, infants in this group do not respond well initially to new situations. A mildly negative response can be observed in such a baby's first bath or encounter with a new person. However, over time and without pressure, the slow-to-warm-up infant will make appropriate adjustments and display quiet interest and enjoyment. About 15 percent of the infants studied were in this category.

Not all infants can be placed into one of these three groups on the basis of temperamental characteristics. Also, the percentage of infants identified by Thomas and Chess in each group does not necessarily represent the general population. Most children display a wide range of behavioral styles between the extremes and do not fit neatly into a particular category. Easy children are not always easy, and difficult children are not difficult in all situations (A. Thomas & Chess, 1985).

The concept of the difficult child has been especially controversial. Doubts about the usefulness of this classification have been expressed (Rothbart, 1982). If an infant is labeled "difficult," parents and other caregivers may focus on the negative characteristics of the child. By expecting the child to be difficult, problem behaviors may develop as a kind of self-fulfilling prophecy in which the child behaves as expected. On the other hand, the difficult child classification has been defended as a useful way of explaining to parents how infants vary in behavioral style and for planning child-rearing strategies.

Other temperament researchers believe the nine dimensions or components of temperament identified by Thomas and Chess should be reduced to a smaller list. For example, J. Bates and colleagues (1994; J. Bates, 1994) have proposed the following three general dimensions, or dispositions, that characterize temperament: (a) *negative emotionality,* including anxiety, inhibition, irritability, and fearfulness; (b) *positive emotionality,* which includes enthusiasm, excitement, happiness, and sociability; and (c) *constraint,* consisting of responsiveness to social control and self-restraint versus impulsivity. Kagan (1994) has summarized temperament characteristics into two basic contrasting types: *inhibited* and *uninhibited.* Inhibited infants display a shy, timid, and fearful profile of behaviors. Uninhibited infants present a behavioral profile that is bold, sociable, and outgoing. Currently, researchers are trying to reach an agreement on the basic dimensions of temperament.

Origins of Temperament. There appears to be widespread agreement that temperament is based on inborn biological foundations that interact with environmental influences to produce individual behavior characteristics (J. Bates, 1994). Researchers and clinicians are continuing their efforts to sort out the relative contributions of genetic, biological, and environmental influences. Twins and adopted children have been used as subjects in attempts to isolate genetic influences. If temperament is inherited, identical twins should be more alike temperamentally than fraternal twins. Adopted children would be expected to display temperamental characteristics that more closely resemble those of their biological parents than of their adoptive parents. Evidence from these studies indicates that genetic factors are at least in part responsible for an individual's temperament (Plomin, Chipuer, & Loehlin, 1990).

The results of extensive studies comparing siblings, twins, and adopted children have produced estimates of the contribution of heredity to temperament ranging from 10 percent (Plomin & DeFries, 1985) to 57 percent (Braungart et al., 1992; Plomin & Saudino, 1994). Traits that appear to be inherited include shyness (Daniels & Plomin, 1985), behavioral inhibition (Manke, Saudino, & Grant, 2001), emotionality, activity level, and attention span (Braungart et al., 1992; Campos et al., 1983; Goldsmith, 1983; Saudino & Eaton, 1991). There are indications that genetic influences on temperament become more evident as the infant grows older (Plomin & DeFries, 1985).

Researchers have used laboratory analysis to identify specific genes, or a combination of genes, that affect temperament in humans as well as animals (J. Bates, 1994). For example, Plomin and Saudino (1994) compared nine children who were rated by their mothers as being low in activity with nine children who were rated as highly active. They found that highly active children more frequently had a genetic marker that might be associated with their elevated activity. However, this is only a preliminary finding that must be confirmed in future studies, and scientists are a long way from establishing a definite link between temperament and specific genes.

Other scientists have attempted to locate biological roots of temperament within the brain (Steinmetz, 1994) and body chemicals (Gunnar, 1994), although studies have yet to produce conclusive findings. For example, the level of progesterone has been linked with the temperamental traits of intensity and approach-withdrawal. Infants who are classified as "easy babies" tend to have higher amounts of progesterone (Weissbluth & Green, 1984). Synthetic progestins administered to mothers to prevent threatened abortions may increase aggressive behavior in their infants after birth (Reimish, 1981). Our knowledge about hormones and infant temperament is limited, but the list of body chemicals that are potential sources of influence is growing.

Cultural and ethnic factors play an important role in the development of temperament. Freedman (1981) compared the temperament of newborn Chinese American, Japanese American, and Caucasian American infants. Chinese and Japanese infants were calmer, more passive, less excitable, and more adaptable than Caucasian infants. Chisholm (1981) found that Australian aboriginal infants were less irritable and more easily soothed than Caucasian American infants. Thus, we cannot fully understand individual differences in temperament without considering the cultural context. Characteristics that are considered desirable in one culture may not be accepted in another culture. For example, the behaviors associated with a difficult child in one culture may not be viewed in the same way in another culture (Wachs, 1999).

The extent to which individual differences in temperament are attributable to variations in genetic backgrounds, child-rearing practices, or other cultural influences has not been determined. However, it is still important to view temperament as developing within a complex system of multiple developmental influences even though we don't know the exact contributions of each factor (Wachs, 1999).

Continuity of Temperament. There is an increasing amount of agreement among researchers that at least some characteristics of temperament are relatively enduring. The identification of temperamental characteristics that are consistent and stable throughout the life span continues to be the subject of numerous investigations. For example, does a baby who is highly active continue to display similar temperamental characteristics as an older child and an adult? Some characteristics, such as fear, frustration-anger, and approach tendencies have been found to be stable, while others, such as activity level, have not (Rothbart, Derryberry, & Hershey, 2000). Hagekull (1994) found that intense and active infants tended to be active 4-year-olds. Behavioral inhibition in infancy has also been linked with behavioral inhibition at age 4 (N. Fox et al., 2001). Negativity, shyness, and impulsivity are also temperamental characteristics that persisted from infancy into childhood. Kagan (1994) found that the response styles of inhibited and uninhibited 2- to 3-year-olds continued to be evident when they reached adolescence. Extreme temperamental characteristics appear to be somewhat more persistent over the years than more moderate temperamental characteristics.

Temperament does not, however, always follow a consistent, predictable course over time. A. Thomas and Chess (1985) traced the development of temperamental traits from infancy through adolescence. Some of their subjects displayed clear-cut consistency in one or several characteristics. On the other hand, some subjects were consistent in certain aspects of temperament during one period and in other aspects during other times. They found that some of the subjects changed completely on a number of temperament traits. The age at which temperament is measured appears to be an important factor. Measures of temperament obtained during the newborn period or at 1 year of age are not reliable in predicting temperamental characteristics that persist over a long period of time. However, measurements taken after the second year of life are much more reliable in determining which temperament characteristics remain stable over time (R. Thompson, 1999a).

Temperament and Parent-Infant Interactions. An infant's temperamental characteristics obviously have an impact upon interactions with caregivers and other people. Fussy babies who cry a lot are likely to evoke more negative social responses than infants who are calmer and more easygoing. The baby who is friendly and approachable is likely to obtain more positive responses than the infant who is shy and withdrawn. Of course, the temperament and expectations of parents and other primary caregivers have to be taken into consideration.

The way the temperament of an infant matches the caregiving style of the parents greatly influences the socialization process. This is referred to as the **goodness-of-fit** between infant and caregiver (A. Thomas & Chess, 1977). Different styles of parenting are needed for the shy, inhibited infant than for the infant who is bold and uninhibited. Researchers have found that infant temperament and parenting reactions play an important role in development. Halpern and colleagues (2000) found that temperament and maternal responsiveness contribute to the mental development of infants. Irritable infants who had angry, punitive parents, displayed more angry, noncompliant, and less confident behavior as 2-year-olds than less irritable infants who experienced similar parental responses (Crockenberg, 1987). Other researchers have found that the combination of difficult temperament and poor parent-infant relationships increases the risk of hostile behavior problems at 7 to 8 years of age (Sanson et al., 1991).

THE DEVELOPMENT OF SELF

Two-year-old Ginny grabs her doll from Michael and says, "Mine." Another toddler, Tanya, notices her picture on the nursery school bulletin board and tells her teacher, "That's me." As these incidents clearly indicate, 2-year-old children have developed an awareness of themselves as individuals distinct and separate from others. In all probability, a primitive form of self-awareness exists much earlier than this (Brownell & Kopp, 1991; M. Lewis & Brooks, 1978).

Many psychologists believe that the self-concept is the core of the personality and a primary determinant of behavior. In many ways the cognitive, social, and emotional competencies of infants and toddlers are tied to the development of a sense of self. The self serves as a frame of reference for organizing and integrating the experiences of infants in relation to where they are, what they do, and what they want or intend (Kopp & Brownell, 1991). Generally, **self-concept** refers to the images, attitudes, and feelings one uses to describe or think about oneself as an individual. Self-image is another term that is used to mean the same thing as self-concept.

Levels of Self-Understanding. Psychologists do not agree on exactly when or how the infant's self-concept develops and functions. Several theorists (M. Lewis, 1991; Stern, 1985) believe that the self consists of multiple components or levels. They use different labels, such as the ecological self, the interpersonal self (Neisser, 1991), the physical self, the social self, the active self, the interpersonal self (Damon & Hart, 1982), the core self, or the verbal self (Stern, 1985) to identify various *selves*. The extent to which multiple selves function as separate entities or represent parts of a single, unified self is a matter of debate.

Much like other concepts, the self-concept is subject to change throughout the life cycle. Infants gradually progress through various stages, or levels of self-understanding. Early in life, primitive, subjective forms of self-awareness emerge out of perceptions associated with body functions and sensorimotor experiences. These initial subjective glimmerings of self-awareness gradually evolve into more sophisticated, objective self-awareness that involves the ability to think about oneself "thinking about oneself" and "knowing that one knows" (M. Lewis, 1991).

Subjective Self-Awareness. Subjective self-awareness includes experiences connected with one's own motor movements, body functions, and internal states such as hunger, pain, and temperature (M. Lewis, 1991). The subjective self also includes the awareness of oneself as distinguished from other people and objects in the world. Rochat and Hespos (1997) reported that newborn infants distinguish between a touch on their cheek by themselves and others. Through their actions and perceptions, infants discover the characteristics of their bodies, what they can do with various body parts. The early inclination of infants to explore their own bodies provides the information needed for the emergence of self-knowledge. For example, researchers found that 3-month-old infants could discriminate between a correct view of their own legs projected on a TV screen and a view showing their legs in a distorted, incorrect position (Rochat, 2001). The level of subjective self-awareness obtained through perceptions of body experiences is sometimes referred to as the **ecological self** (Neisser, 1991; Rochat, 2001).

Infants gain subjective self-awareness through social interactions as well as perceptions of physical (body) activities. Neisser (1991) refers to the subjective self-awareness that arises from social interactions as the **interpersonal self.** Social interactions can occur at several levels of intimacy and have such characteristic features as mutual gaze, contingent gestures, and reciprocal vocalization (Neisser, 1991). From earliest infancy, infants are responding in contingent ways. According to Trevarthen (1988), an infant is pretuned to pick up many sensations, including maternal odors and visual, auditory, tactual, and gustatory stimulation. Imitation, joint attention, and the formation of attachments are other types of social interactions that contribute to the emergence of self-awareness. By the end of the first year, infants demonstrate self-awareness through sounds or gestures to indicate a need or intention. Such actions indicate that infants recognize that their behavior can alter the emotions or activities of others (R. Thompson, 1999a).

Objective Self-Awareness. Objective self-awareness involves the capacity of infants to know that they know and to remember that they remember (M. Lewis, 1991). The objective self includes the ability to observe and talk about the experiences of the subjective self. According to M. Lewis (1991), objective self-awareness is necessary to experience certain emotions, such as shame, guilt, and embarrassment. One of the first indicators of objective self-awareness is the ability of infants to identify their own images.

Self-Recognition. The ability of infants to correctly identify images as their own is called **self-recognition.** The development of visual self-recognition has been explored in experiments designed to determine when infants can understand the significance of their own image. M. Lewis and Brooks-Gunn (1979) conducted a clever series of studies using mirrors, photographs, and videotapes of infants. The studies included the presentation of two types of cues: contingency cues and feature cues. Feature cues refer to the child's recognition of particular body and facial features that are familiar to the child. Contingency cues refer to the recognition that movements in the mirror or on videotape are exactly the same as the child's own movements.

M. Lewis and Brooks (1978) observed infants from 6 to 24 months of age with a mark of rouge on their faces. If an infant touched the spot of rouge on the nose rather than the reflection in the mirror it was assumed that the infant was engaging in self-recognition. None of the 9- to 12-month-old babies responded to the mark when they looked in the mirror. One-quarter of the babies in the 15- to 18-month age range and three-quarters of the 21- to 24-month-olds touched the

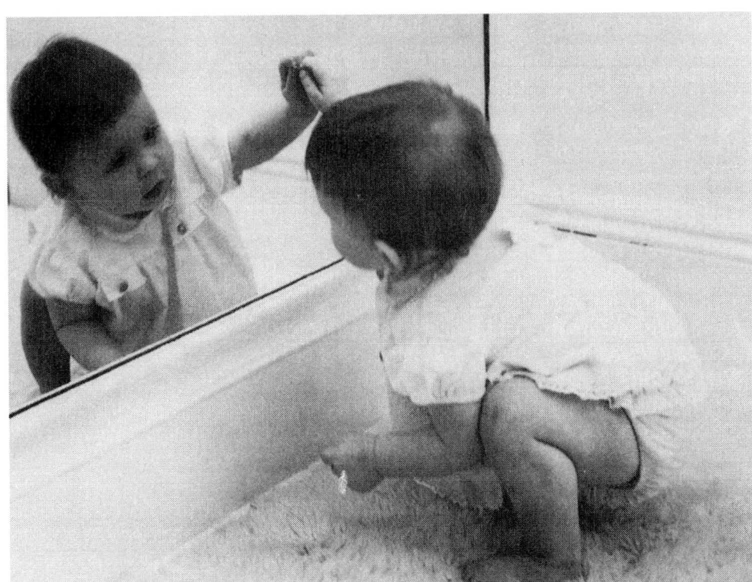

This toddler is beginning to recognize the reflection in the mirror as her own image.

mark on their own face as if to say, "That's me!" M. Lewis and Brooks (1974) also found that infants recognize their own pictures at about the same age as they identify their reflections in a mirror. By 2 years of age most infants can recognize a picture as their own and distinguish between it and a picture of another baby. Infants also recognize videotaped body movements as their own through contingency cues at 2 years of age (Brooks & Lewis, 1976). Some researchers believe that experience can lead to earlier successful performance on self-recognition tasks. Bahrick, Moss, and Fadil (1996) concluded that infants with daily mirror experiences distinguished between self and other as early as 3 months.

Bertenthal and Fischer (1978) believe that the development of self-recognition is related to the acquisition of the object concept (Chapter 8). These researchers presented a series of tasks designed to assess the development of the concept of object permanency in a group of infants between 6 and 24 months of age. The same infants were also given a test to determine their ability to recognize their own mirror image. The ages at which the infants achieved each of the stages of self-concept development closely coincided with the ages at which they progressed through a series of steps leading to the acquisition of the object concept. The concept of self apparently develops in much the same way as other concepts (Maccoby, 1980).

In summary, research studies indicate that some infants begin to recognize their own visual images by the end of the first year, but this ability is not very well developed at that age. By approximately 18 months of age, a more sophisticated level of visual self-recognition can be clearly observed in some infants. Almost all infants demonstrate the ability by the time they are 2 years old (M. Lewis & Brooks, 1978). Toddlers from nomadic tribes in the Middle East who have never seen a mirror demonstrate self-recognition when they see themselves in the mirror for the first time (Pipp-Siegel & Pressman, 1996). The emergence of self-awareness thus closely parallels the development of intelligence.

Self-Definition. With advances in cognition and expressive language ability, infants progress beyond self-recognition to **self-definition.** When infants have a concept of themselves as physical beings, they begin noticing differences and making comparisons between themselves and others on various dimensions such as age, size, and gender

(Stipek, Gralinski, & Kopp, 1990). Self-definition occurs when the self-concept is further defined and elaborated through the use of verbal labels. Stern (1985) referred to this level of self-concept formation as the **verbal self.** At this stage, they can define themselves categorically in terms of personal pronouns (*I, me, you*), gender identity, personal attributes (*little, curly hair*), and possessions (*mine, yours*).

The appropriate use of the pronouns *I, me,* and *you* represents the acquisition of verbal labels for the self. It is also an indication that an infant has developed a self-concept that includes the perspective of others. Some infants begin to use their own name as early as 15 months (Brooks-Gunn & Lewis, 1982). Personal pronoun usage follows a few months later. Most toddlers use *I* (along with *me, my,* or *mine*) as their first personal pronoun around 20 to 22 months of age (Charney, 1980; Maccoby, 1980). This pronoun is frequently used interchangeably with the child's own name or the word *baby* (Maccoby, 1980). The second pronoun most toddlers use is *you,* which appears at about 2 years of age (Charney, 1980).

Young children have difficulty using pronouns correctly because they can be used to refer to different people. For example, *I* and *my* sometimes refer to the child's mother, the father, or other people, depending on who is speaking. The pronoun *you* is even more confusing because it is frequently used to refer to the baby as well as other people. Consequently, an infant may say such things as "you go" for "I go." Surprisingly, though, most infants have little difficulty using pronouns correctly (Maccoby, 1980). The proper use of pronouns is an indication that the infant's self-concept is becoming more objective, more socialized, and slightly less egocentric.

Self-descriptive statements such as "I play" or "I can do this" increase in frequency around 2 years of age (Kagan, 1981a; Stipek et al., 1990). In addition to knowledge about the self's physical features (e.g., "I have red hair"), the 2-year-old is aware of the self's capabilities and actions ("I play"). Awareness of capabilities ("I can't!") is cognitively more advanced than the awareness of physical features (Damon & Hart, 1982). An infant who demonstrates such awareness has taken a further step in the development of self-knowledge.

Sperry and Sperry (1995) studied the self-references of rural African American toddlers recorded from their conversations about past and fantasy events with parents and other adults. Their statements reflected objective understanding of self in relation to physical, social, active, and psychological dimensions. Some of their comments were: "I have a stomach" (physical); "I gonna bite you" (active); "nobody let me" (social); "I'm not crying" (psychological) (Sperry & Sperry, 1995, p. 53). Boys tended to describe themselves in the context of fantasy events, whereas girls talked more about past events.

Age (or size) and gender are also features that infants use very early in the development of a self-concept. Infants between 6 and 12 months of age are able to distinguish adults from babies (M. Lewis & Brooks-Gunn, 1979). By the time they are 1 year old, infants exhibit more social responses to strange babies than to strange adults (Brooks-Gunn & Lewis, 1979). Presumably, infants perceive other infants as more similar to themselves than adults. Infants discriminate between male and female adults on the basis of voice and facial differences by the end of the first year of life (Fagot & Leinbach, 1993). The ability to tell the difference between boys and girls emerges in the second year of life. Gesell (1940) found that one-third of the 2-year-olds and three-quarters of the 3-year-olds he questioned knew whether they were boys or girls. Most children can correctly label photographs of themselves and others as a "boy" or "girl" by 2½ to 3 years of age (Etaugh, Grinnel, & Etaugh, 1989). However, they do not yet understand that gender is constant, as the following quotation indicates:

Teacher: *"Lisa, are you a girl or a boy?"*
Lisa (age 3): *"I'm a girl, but when I'm 4, I'll be a boy"* (Edwards, 1995, p. 54).

Self-Esteem. An infant's self-concept and self-esteem develop together. **Self-esteem** is one's self-evaluation based on the self-concept. The self-concept is the descriptive part of the self, whereas self-esteem is the evaluative and emotional component of the self. Other terms that are sometimes used as synonyms for self-esteem are self-love, self-respect, self-acceptance, and self-worth. A child who has a positive self-concept will have a high level of self-esteem, whereas a negative self-concept will result in a sense of low self-esteem.

The amount of respect, acceptance, and concerned treatment infants receive from their caregivers is especially important in developing a healthy sense of self-esteem (Coopersmith, 1967). Infants learn very powerful lessons from the countless small interchanges that occur with the caregiver each day. Encounters with caregivers have an impact on the infant's sense of worthiness. The development of feelings of love-worthiness is viewed as a forerunner of self-esteem (Mruk,1999). According to Stern (1985), the response of the parent must match or be harmonious with the baby's response. For example, the infant squeals with delight and the mother, in turn, gives the baby a gentle bounce. This is a response that matches and acknowledges the baby's level of excitement. If the parent consistently overresponds or underresponds, the baby's sense of self will be negatively affected. The development of a sense of worthiness or unworthiness is affected by the extent to which infants perceive themselves as good or bad, pleasing or displeasing to their caregivers.

The development of self-esteem is also influenced by the child's ability to control the behavior of others and cause things to happen (Coopersmith, 1967). This ability is referred to as the infant's **perceived personal effectance** (Lamb, 1981a). Infants learn very early in life the extent to which they can or cannot control their world. At approximately 12 months, they are typically capable of determining when their behavior has had an effect and when it has not (Piaget, 1952).

Infants experience a sense of power or helplessness depending upon whether or not they can accomplish what they set out to do. Gunnar (1978, 1980) found that 12-month-olds were considerably less afraid of a scary toy when they could control it than when they could not. Before

An infant's self esteem is influenced by the ability to solve problems and "make things work."

that age, infants could not determine that they were completely in control of the circumstances activating the toy. Realistically, infants experience feelings of power at certain times and a sense of weakness at other times. For healthy self-esteem to develop, an infant needs to learn how to manage both types of feelings. When one feeling or the other—power or weakness—predominates, self-esteem suffers. "Healthy personality growth is always between the extremes" (Weiner & Elkind, 1972, p. 32).

The importance of caregiver-child interactions and other relationships are critical in the establishment of a healthy self-image. However, it is also important to recognize multiple influences and sources of information in the development of self-knowledge and self-esteem, including biological changes and experiences affecting central nervous system functions, cognitive and perceptual development, temperament, and emotional differentiation.

Self-Development of Infants With Developmental Disorders. Infants with developmental disorders, such as Down syndrome, are vulnerable to problems in the development of the sense of self. Many of these infants are confronted with a variety of neurologically and other biologically based limitations that inhibit their perceptual processes and delay progress in self-understanding. Self-recognition of visual images by infants with Down syndrome does not occur until around 3 years of age (Mans, Cicchetti, & Sroufe, 1978). Infants with Down syndrome are also delayed in using personal pronouns and other language to describe their actions and internal states. However, even though they lag behind, these infants go through the same stages in the development of self-understanding as typically developing infants. Their responses to visual images indicate that their feelings about themselves are basically positive (Cicchetti, 1991).

THEORY OF MIND

The infant's self-concept is developed in relation to other people. At some point in time the child recognizes that other people are separate individuals who have internal mental states including thoughts, feelings, intentions, and beliefs that are different from the child's own states of awareness. The ability to consider the psychological states of other people is referred to as **theory of mind.** In order to have a fully developed theory of mind a person must (1) understand that others have thoughts and beliefs that may differ from one's own, and (2) understand that others sometimes have beliefs that may be false (Tomasello, 1995). For example, when children have developed an operational theory of mind they can hide from other people and reason as follows: "Mommy is looking for me in the closet, because she thinks I am hiding there; she doesn't know I am under the bed!" (Baron-Cohen, 1994). Theory of mind is viewed as a central mechanism that underlies communication, social development, and self-reflection. Children use their theory of mind to make sense of the behaviors of other people and events in the world.

The age at which children typically develop a theory of mind is a matter of debate. According to Piaget, children are ignorant about the theory of mind until 6 or 7 years because of egocentric thinking. Researchers and scholars generally believe that by 4 years of age, and possibly by 3 years of age, children have a rather sophisticated level of reasoning about their own mental states and those of other people (Wellman, 1994). For example, 3-year-olds use mental terms such as *think* and *know,* and have begun to understand that people have, at times, beliefs that are false. They also understand that adults can be deceived, and they will tell lies to adults under certain conditions (M. Lewis, Stanger, & Sullivan, 1989).

Some scholars (e.g., Thomasello, 1995) believe infants exhibit the first glimmerings of a theory of mind between 1 and 2 years of age. For one thing, infants begin to demonstrate a sensitivity to the desires of other people when they point to and hand objects to adults in joint attention episodes (see Chapter 9). Joint attention episodes imply that infants understand that their own visual field is shared with others. In addition, young infants look at the facial expressions of adults as social reference cues to guide their own behavior. Thomasello (1995) views such episodes as evidence that infants understand other people as having intentions or feelings that may be different from the infant's own experiences. At least these behaviors appear to be forerunners to a fully formed theory of mind (Charman et al., 2001).

Infantile Autism and Theory of Mind. Infantile autism or **autistic disorder** is a disorder of the brain that typically affects a person's ability to communicate, form relationships with others, and respond appropriately to the environment. An estimated 10 to 20 of every 10,000 infants born in the United States will be affected by this disorder with varying degrees of severity. Autism has no single cause but researchers have identified a number of genes that may play a role in the disorder. Environmental factors, such as brain injury, viruses and chemicals, may be involved in some cases. Autism affects males about four times as often as females and tends to run in families (National Institute of Neurological Disorders and Stroke, 1999). Approximately eighty percent of autistic children develop signs of the disorder in the first year of life. Most cases of the disorder are diagnosed by 3 years of age (Ciaranello, 2002).

APPLICATIONS: ENHANCING PERSONALITY DEVELOPMENT

Parents and other caregivers can make a positive contribution to the personality development of infants in numerous ways. The following are examples of some recommended activities and practices:

Promoting a Positive Sense of Self.

- Select a baby's name with great care. Names should not be sexually ambiguous, difficult to spell or pronounce, or the basis for undesirable nicknames, initials, or rhymes; nor should they be otherwise exceptionally odd within the context of the child's cultural heritage.
- Hold the young baby in front of a mirror and play games such as touching and naming body parts or making faces; say "See ——— in the mirror?" (Sparling & Lewis, 1979). Give the baby an unbreakable mirror to play with at about 2 months of age.
- Take the baby's picture at various ages and look at them together with the baby, pointing out such characteristics as hair and eyes (McDonald, 1980).
- Give infants dolls and toys that match their color and ethnic heritage, along with other dolls, toys, and materials. Parents should talk positively about characteristics of the body in ways that include skin color. In naming colors, point to the child's arm and name its color (Comer & Poussaint, 1976).
- Play games using various body parts (e.g, This Little Piggy). Sing songs about feet, hand, noses. Make up your own songs (Machado & Meyer-Botnarescue, 1997).

Establishing Basic Trust.

- Respond to the infant's cries and other signals promptly and consistently. Smile, talk, and relate to the infant cheerfully during caregiving routines.
- Don't try to sneak away unnoticed when leaving the baby with a substitute caregiver. Never leave without saying goodbye.
- Peek-a-boo and hide-and-seek are excellent games for teaching the baby that people disappear and return (Sparling & Lewis, 1979).

Promoting Autonomy.

- Encourage infants to do things for themselves as much as possible (e.g., pull a sock part of the way off or on and let the infant finish the task). Suggest solutions to problems without taking over.
- Give the infant choices when possible and reasonable (e.g., what to eat or wear, things to do, materials to use, and ways to spend time).
- Handle the infant's negativism with positive responses, firmness, and understanding. Avoid using shame as a response to undesirable behavior.
- Allow the child to explore the environment, particularly new places, as freely as possible within the limits of safety, available supervision, and situational restraints.
- Play games with infants that facilitate motor control (see Chapter 6).

Matching the Baby's Temperament.

- Accept and enjoy each baby's individuality.
- Try to find caregiving strategies that match the baby's behavioral style. For example, infants who are more active and difficult to manage need more structure, more environmental control, and less stimulation. Very young infants who are sensitive to being touched sometimes respond favorably to being held on a pillow. Avoid trying to force noncuddlers to be held closely (see Brazelton, 1992; Chess, Thomas, & Birch, 1965).

A major characteristic of infants with autistic disorder is their lack of responsiveness to other people. These infants usually do not make eye-to-eye contact or hold out their arms to be picked up and held. They are typically "noncuddlers," although at times they may cling to a caregiver. Autistic infants apparently do not give or receive pleasure in their relationships with others. Caregivers find them unaffectionate and difficult to engage in games such as peekaboo. They tend to be easily upset by changes in their environment and caregiving routines.

Infants with autism tend to be delayed in or rarely display many of the early behaviors that indicate an emergence of the theory of mind (Acredelo & Goodwyn, 1997). For example, they do not visually attend to social cues (Phillips, Baron-Cohen, & Rutter, 1992; Tantam, 1992). They also rarely use imitation (Meltzoff & Gopnik, 1994). In addition, joint attention does not look the same for children with autism as for typically developing children. Charman and colleagues (2000) found that children with autism do not use social gaze to communicate, show poor response to the other individual in the joint attention task, and do not produce spontaneous play.

SUMMARY

Theories of Personality

- Personality is the total of the internal qualities and enduring, observable patterns of behavior that make up a person's individuality.
- Freud emphasized the importance of child-rearing experiences during infancy in shaping personality development. He identified three components of personality: id, ego, and superego. Personality development progresses through the oral and anal stages during infancy. If infants and children are treated too harshly or too permissively in each stage, personality problems are likely to arise.
- The two stages of personality growth identified by Erikson that occur during infancy are trust versus mistrust, and autonomy versus shame and doubt.
- According to Skinner, personality is simply a collection of behavior patterns that are acquired over time through the process of conditioning.

Temperament

- Temperament refers to the relatively stable behavioral and emotional reactions that appear early and are influenced, at least in part, by heredity. Many infants can be classified as temperamentally easy, difficult, or slow-to-warm-up. Currently, researchers are trying to reach an agreement on the basic dimensions of temperament.
- At least some characteristics of temperament, such as negativity, shyness, and impulsivity, appear to be relatively enduring from infancy through childhood. Temperament does not, however, always follow a consistent, predictable course over time. Researchers and clinicians are continuing their efforts to sort out the relative contributions of genetic, biological, and environmental influences.
- Parents and other caregivers are advised to use child-rearing strategies that promote a positive sense of self, establish basic trust and autonomy, and fit the baby's temperament.

The Development of Self

- One major component of personality that emerges during the infancy period is the self-concept, or the sense of self. Infants gradually progress through various stages or levels of self-understanding, including subjective and objective self-awareness.
- Infants gain subjective self-awareness through social interactions as well as perceptions of physical (body) activities during the first year of life.
- Objective self-awareness includes self-recognition, the ability of infants to correctly identify mirror or other images as their own. Self-recognition is demonstrated by most infants around 2 years of age.
- The next level of objective self-awareness is self-definition. Infants engage in self-definition when they begin to use pronouns, notice differences, and make comparisons between themselves and others on various dimensions such as age, size, and gender.
- Self-esteem is one's self-evaluation based on the self-concept. Infants need respect, acceptance, and positive treatment from caregivers for the development of a healthy sense of self-esteem.
- Infants with Down syndrome experience delays in self-concept development but go through the same stages in the development of self-understanding as typically developing infants.

Theory of Mind

- Theory of mind, or the ability to consider the psychological states of other people, is viewed as a central mechanism that underlies self-reflection. Infants may be exhibiting the appearance of a primitive theory of mind between 1 and 2 years of age when they point to and hand objects to adults in joint attention episodes and use social reference cues to guide their own behavior.

- Infants with autistic disorder are characterized by their lack of responsiveness to other people. Infants who suffer from autism apparently have not developed a well-functioning theory of mind.

KEY TERMS

personality
id
ego
superego
oral stage
anal stage
trust versus mistrust
autonomy versus shame and doubt
temperament
Infant Temperament Questionnaire
easy child
difficult child
slow-to-warm-up child
goodness-of-fit
self-concept
subjective self-awareness
ecological self
interpersonal self
objective self-awareness
self-recognition
self-definition
verbal self
self-esteem
perceived personal effectance
theory of mind
infantile autism, autistic disorder

INFORMATION ON THE WEB*

www.personalityresearch.org/papers.html This site is an online source of publications on personality theories and research findings.

www.b-di.com Information is available from this site on a variety of issues related to temperament, including frequently asked questions, how temperament affects parenting, instruments for assessing temperament, and temperament research studies.

*Web sites are subject to change.

ELEVEN

SOCIAL DEVELOPMENT

When the first baby laughed for the first time, the laugh broke into a thousand pieces, and they all went skipping about, and that was the beginning of fairies.

—J. M. Barrie

Babies are social beings from birth. The newborn's slightest expressions elicit responses from parents, siblings, and strangers. As they get just a little older, infants become partners in the give-and-take of human relationships. Their interactions with other people, including adults and peers provide the cornerstone for developing awareness and social competency. In this chapter we explore social development during infancy. As you read this material, keep in mind that social development is largely inseparable from emotional and personality domains.

SOCIALIZATION PROCESSES

Socialization is the "process by which the newborn child is molded into the culture . . . and hence becomes an acceptable person in that society" (Smelser & Smelser, 1963, pp.102–103). Socialization involves establishing satisfactory relationships with other people and conforming to the cultural standards. Infants become socialized through interactions with parents and other people. The process of socialization involves learning that other people are necessary and becoming dependent on them. Almost as soon as this awareness develops, however, infants must begin to move in the direction of establishing independence. The crying, clinging behavior of the baby must be eventually replaced by more mature forms of social behavior, such as verbal requests and independent locomotion.

THE SOCIALLY COMPETENT INFANT

Social competence refers to an infant's ability "to make use of environmental and personal resources to achieve a good developmental outcome" (Waters & Sroufe, 1983, p. 81). Socially competent infants possess the skills necessary to get their needs met and to accomplish their desired social goals. Burton White (1985) has identified some of the abilities an infant must eventually develop to become socially competent:

1. Getting and holding the attention of adults in socially acceptable ways.
2. Expressing affection and annoyance when appropriate.
3. Using adults as resources if a task is too difficult to accomplish alone.
4. Showing pride in personal accomplishments.
5. Engaging in role-play and make-believe activities.
6. Leading and following peers.
7. Competing with peers.

These social abilities gradually emerge and develop during the first two years of life. The socially competent infant makes behavior changes as needed to conform with age-appropriate expectations. For example, very young infants get the attention of adults by crying, but older infants are expected to use other means to get their needs met.

Parents of socially competent infants are accessible (but not overwhelming) and spend time interacting with their babies (White & Watts, 1973). They organize a stimulating, safe, and nonrestrictive environment in which the infants can develop a sense of autonomy. The type of discipline that is positive, affectionate, and encouraging of autonomy is also a very important ingredient in the development of social competence. Infants who are exposed to discipline that is negative, rigid, and overprotective demonstrate less social competence (Clarke-Stewart & Fein, 1983).

EARLY SOCIAL BEHAVIORS

The social behaviors of the infant are numerous and varied. A timetable for the development of some of the major milestones of social development is given in Table 11–1. Keep in mind that social and emotional development are closely interrelated and most of the topics discussed under the heading of social development are applicable to the discussion of emotional development in the next chapter. Social relationships have a strong emotional component. The infant's social behaviors are based on emotional states of the infant as well as the emotional responses of others. Some of the early emotional indicators of the infant's growing social awareness and responsiveness include smiling, laughing, and crying.

Table 11–1 Milestones of Social Development

BEHAVIOR	*USUAL AGE (MONTHS)*
Knows mother by sight	1–2
Social smile	2–3
Social laughter	3–4
Notices and begins to interact with peers	3–6
Holds out arms to be held	5–6
Plays peekaboo	5–8
Shy with strangers	8–10
Plays pat-a-cake	9–10
Waves bye-bye	9–10
Gives a toy when asked	11–12
Negativism begins	11–12
Plays interactive games (e.g., tag)	24–30
Dresses self with supervision	30–36

Sources: Taken from N. Bayley (1969). *Bayley Scales of Infant Development,* Copyright © 1969 by the Psychological Corporation. Reproduced by permission. All rights reserved. W. Frankenburg, J. Dodds, & A. Fandel (1973). *Denver Developmental Screening Test.* Denver, CO: Denver Developmental Materials, Inc. Used by permission. H. Knobloch, F. Stevens, & A. Malone (1980). *Manual of developmental diagnosis.* New York: Harper & Row. Used by permission.

Smiling. One of the earliest social behaviors is the social smile. Smiling usually reflects positive affect (joy, pleasure, delight) and is the "most significant aspect of social development to occur in the first half-year of life" (Bower, 1977b, p. 49). The onset of a true social smile is a major milestone in social development. However, distinguishing social smiling from other types of smiling behavior is not an easy task. Infants' smiles have been classified in two categories—endogenous and exogenous (Spitz, Emde, & Metcalf, 1970).

Newborn infants can sometimes be observed smiling while they are asleep. These smiles are called **endogenous,** or spontaneous, smiles because they are passive and internally controlled. They appear to be triggered by changes in the level of arousal affecting central nervous system activity (Wolff, 1963). Contrary to what parents are sometimes led to believe, the newborn is not smiling because of "gas" or hunger sensations. Endogenous smiles cannot be thought of as indicating any conscious awareness of happiness or other emotions (Sroufe, 1977).

Within a week or two after birth, another type of smile can sometimes be elicited by gentle stimulation such as high-pitched baby talk or blowing on the baby's stomach. Such stimulation apparently increases the level of nervous-system excitation or arousal. A tiny smile follows within 6 to 8 seconds as the baby relaxes (Sroufe, 1977). These smiles are labeled as **exogenous** because they are triggered by stimuli that are outside the infant (Wolff, 1963). The first elicited smiles, like the spontaneous smiles, are only partial smiles limited to the corners of the mouth.

During the second week of life, infants begin to smile when their eyes are open. Such smiles usually occur only when an infant is sated with food, drowsy, and glassy-eyed (Wolff, 1963). The smiles may occur spontaneously or can be elicited by the caregiver's voice. By the third week of life, babies begin to smile when they are fully awake and attentive. These smiles are fuller and more expressive. A nodding head accompanied by a high-pitched voice is a more potent stimulus for eliciting smiling at this age than a voice alone (Sroufe & Waters, 1976).

As they get older (4 to 5 weeks), infants smile in response to interesting sights such as silent moving faces, sudden appearance of objects, and pat-a-cake games. At this point, sights are more effective than sounds in evoking smiles. As Bower (1977b) points out, "the first complete smile appears to be elicited by the human voice; later the controlling stimulus shifts to the human face" (p. 38).

The age at which a **true social smile** appears is a matter of debate. Wolff (1963) considers the infant's first smile in response to a human voice, which occurs around 3 or 4 weeks of age, to be the beginning of true social smiling. The prevailing opinion, though, is that the social smile appears at approximately 6 to 8 weeks. At this point, the stimulus is clearly social, because the infant smiles in response to human faces (Emde, Gaensbauer, & Harmon, 1976).

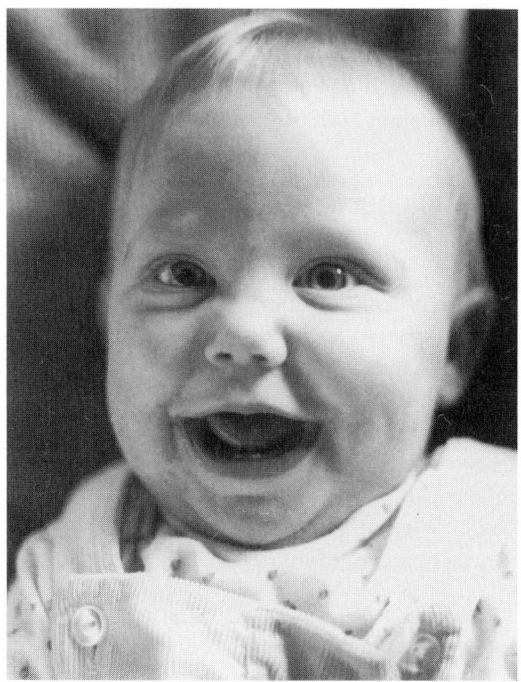

The social smile displayed by this infant is a major milestone of development.

Between 3 and 6 months of age, infants become more discriminating in their smiling behavior. Adults have to work harder to elicit smiles from them. They are less likely to smile at familiar stimuli unless a new feature is introduced. At the same time, however, infants smile at a wider range of stimuli and smile more often over the first two years of life. The frequency of smiling increases during the third and fourth months at about the same rate in infants from many cultures around the world (Super & Harkness, 1982). Mothers from all cultures and races appear to be equally capable of eliciting smiles from their infants, although their techniques vary from culture to culture (Super, 1981).

By 8 to 12 months, infants begin to smile in anticipation of social events and this anticipation has been connected with the child's increasing cognitive abilities (Jones & Hong, 2001). Apparently the development of smiling is related to the infant's growing cognitive awareness and sophistication (M. Lewis & Michalson, 1983).

Laughing. There is a considerable amount of individual variation in the age at which infants begin to laugh. Infants typically begin to laugh between 2 and 4 months of age (Walden & Garber, 1994). At first, infants laugh only in response to physical stimulation such as tickling or to intense sounds such as "boom boom boom." Beginning at 6 months of age, infants laugh more at visual and social stimuli. Interactions such as peekaboo games or the mother shaking her hair or crawling on the floor elicit laughter (Sroufe & Wunsch, 1972).

During the second year of life, infants begin to laugh at things they can participate in, such as reaching for a protruding tongue (Sroufe & Waters, 1976). Babies thus progress developmentally from laughter produced from physical stimulation to laughter based on cognitive interpretations (Sroufe, 1977). The developmental progression of laughter may be seen when the same stimuli that make younger babies cry (e.g., mother wearing a mask) make older babies laugh.

Crying. Crying has been defined as the highest "state of arousal produced by nervous system excitation triggered by some form of a biological threat . . . such as hunger, pain, sickness or insult, or individual differences in threshold for stimulation" (Lester, 1985, p. 12). Crying begins as a reflex response that has survival value. It is designed to elicit nurturing and protective responses from the baby's caregivers. Crying gradually becomes intentional to communicate emotional states such as fear and anger (Kostelnik et al., 2002).

The amount of crying typically increases until about 6 weeks of age, followed by a gradual decline as the infant gets older (Milgrom, Westley, & McCloud, 1995). On average, infants cry about two hours per day during the first three months of life. During the first year, the peak time for crying is in the evening (Fabes & Martin, 2000). Although the evidence is not conclusive, it appears that babies cry less often when their caregivers respond promptly and consistently (Bell & Ainsworth,

1972). Decreased crying and fussiness at night have been associated with increased holding and carrying throughout the day (Hunziker & Barr, 1986). Cross-cultural studies have found less prolonged crying in societies in which infants remain close to the caregiver and in which extended carrying and rocking are practiced (Hunziker & Barr, 1986). However, infant caregivers should not get the impression that they need to extinguish all crying. A certain amount of crying is necessary for the infant's behavioral organization and normal physiological functioning. Crying allows the infant to reduce tension and serves an as important regulatory mechanism for adjusting internal states.

The social functions of crying change with age. For the first six months of life, infants cry to attract attention so that their physical and psychological needs will be met. Crying is also one way an infant tells a caregiver that it wants to be left alone. In other cases, crying may be used as a means of releasing energy or tension. There are periods when infants cry for no apparent reason. Some of the young infant's unexplained crying may be due to maturational changes in the brain that occur between 3 and 12 weeks of age (Emde et al., 1976).

Crying, like smiling, progresses from internal to external sources of stimulation and control (Hodapp & Mueller, 1982). During the newborn period, infants cry primarily because they are hungry, too hot or cold, or otherwise physically uncomfortable. Crying is also used by infants as a self-calming mechanism and a means of emotional regulation. As they get older, infant cries can be traced to external stimuli such as loud noises, looming objects, frustration with play objects, fear of strangers, and the disappearance of the mother. After three months, crying changes its function to take on more intentional social, cognitive, and emotional communicative expressions (Lester, 1985; Milgrom et al., 1995). Infant cries reflect an increasingly negative emotional tone from 12 to 18 months of age. Excessive crying and temper tantrums tend to reach a peak from 15 to 18 months of age. Around 24 months of age, there are fewer crying episodes and a shift toward more positive emotional expression (Kopp, 1992). During the toddler years, crying behaviors are frequently connected with caregiving episodes (e.g., diaper changing), getting hurt from falls or other injuries, and separation from parents (Kopp, 1992).

INFANT-ADULT PLAY

Although the importance of play has been emphasized in previous chapters, play also is an important process in social development. Play is the vehicle by which infants and toddlers practice the social skills needed for successful interactions with others. During the first year, infants' play partners are usually adults. The characteristics of infant-adult social play change as the infant matures. Whaley (1990) proposes the following stages, or levels, of infant-adult social play:

1. *Complementary/Reciprocal Social Play* (birth to 4 months). During this phase, play consists mainly of face-to-face interactions such as smiles, sounds, and gazes, with the adult as the "object."
2. *Complementary/Reciprocal Play With Mutual Awareness* (4 to 8 months). The focus of play shifts to objects provided by the adult, who observes and provides support as needed.
3. *Simple Social/Simple Object Play* (7 to 13 months). The role of the adult shifts to that of a "consultant" and base of support as infants locate their own objects and playthings. They begin parallel play with peers.
4. *Object Play With Mutual Regard* (13 to 18 months). The infant attends to objects and adults at the same time through games and conversations.
5. *Simple Parallel Play* (18 to 24 months). The toddler now plays independently, but with adults or peers nearby.

Beginning with the first phase, play progresses from mutual engagement to independent play by the child during the last phase.

Uzgiris and Raeff (1995) have identified three types of parent-child play that evolve during the infancy period: interpersonal play, object play, and symbolic play. **Interpersonal play** involves face-to-face interactions, social games, or routines. These playful interactions provide opportunities for infants to enjoy and practice socially appropriate ways of interaction and communication. In many cultures, parents play interactive games such as "peekaboo," "I'm gonna getcha," and "this little pig went to market" as soon as babies are responsive. Infants as young as 4 months begin to distinguish characteristics of such play. For example, Rochat, Querido, and Striano (1999) found that 4-month-olds smiled and gazed more in a disorganized game of peekaboo than an organized game, while younger infants made no distinction. Rock, Trainor, and Addison (1999) found that infants become quiet when hearing lullaby songs, but become more focused on the external world when they listen to playtime-style songs. Imitation is another type of interpersonal game. For example, the infant coughs reflexively and the mother playfully imitates the cough. The infant coughs again intentionally, the mother coughs, and the game has begun (Whaley, 1990). Physical play, particularly among fathers and infants, is another form of interpersonal play that occurs as infants get older.

Object play involves toys and play materials and is characterized by less mutual engagement than interpersonal play (Uzgiris & Raeff, 1995). During object play, parents serve as the infants' audience and function as a facilitator through comments and other responses. Parents structure and guide play through the provision of objects. Object play reflects the infants' culture and parental values in the socialization of infants and toddlers. For example, some American parents and child-care providers attempt to promote multicultural awareness through the provision of dolls or other figures representing people of different races. Among !Kung families of Africa, objects are valued as things to be shared, rather than personal possessions. Natural objects, such as grass, stones, and nutshells are used as objects of play. Grandmothers train infants to share objects by guiding them in handing objects to other people (Draper & Cashdan, 1988).

Symbolic play is the use of pretend games and/or objects to represent something else (e.g., a block becomes a hammer). Between 1 and 2 years of age, infants and parents engage in joint episodes of symbolic play (Dunn, 1986). Both parents and infants initiate symbolic play at various times. As infants get older, symbolic play involves less parent participation and more independent play by the children (Uzgiris & Raeff, 1995). Symbolic play provides important socialization experiences by enabling toddlers to act out social roles (e.g., "mothers" and "fathers") that are not available to them in real life. Since symbolic play frequently involves the use of objects, it is difficult to distinguish from object play (Uzgiris & Raeff, 1995).

SOCIAL BEHAVIOR WITH PEERS

The socialization process involves interactions with the child's age mates, or peers. Infants in most societies begin to interact with each other very early in life. Whaley (1990) believes that early adult-infant play provides the foundation and social skills needed for infant-peer interactions. However, Hanna and Meltzoff (1993) point out that competence with peers and adults may develop simultaneously. That is, at the same time they are developing competence in their interactions with adults, infants are developing competence in relating to their peers. In any event, research evidence is accumulating to show that meaningful social encounters occur among infant peers in everyday encounters.

Early Peer Interactions. Information about peer interactions during the first year of life is limited because the significance of these early interactions for socialization has been questioned (Whaley & Rubenstein, 1994). However, the existence of social exchanges between infants during the first year of life is well documented (Eckerman & Whatley, 1977). Early infant behavior directed toward a peer is relatively infrequent, brief, and simple. One study (Finkelstein et al., 1978), conducted in a day-care center, found that infants made contact with adults about seven times as often as they did with other babies.

The earliest infant interactions take the form of exploratory behaviors. At about 2 months of age, infants begin to look at other infants. Around 3 or 4 months of age, an infant will reach out and touch another infant. Most interactions of infants consist of a single overture and a response. At this stage babies treat each other as interesting toys or objects to explore. In many instances (38 to 50 percent), social overtures of one infant to another do not elicit a response (Hartup, 1983). Even at this age, though, infants direct more sociable reactions (smiling, vocalizations, reaching) toward an actual infant than a mirror image (Field, 1990).

Smiles and vocalizations may be observed between infants by 6 months of age. When infants master a particular skill, such as babbling, they begin to use it to relate to a peer (E. Mueller & Vandell, 1979). Infants exhibit turn-taking behaviors in peer play at the end of the first year of life (Ross & Lollis, 1987). As soon as they become mobile, infants follow and attempt to make physical contact with one another, exploring each other's eyes, mouths, and ears (Vandell & Mueller, 1980). Their interactions become increasingly social and more complex as their skills in other areas (e.g., language) become more fully developed (Campos et al., 1983).

Toddler-Peer Interactions. The frequency and complexity of peer interactions increase rapidly with age. The ability to walk and talk facilitates social interactions. By 2 years of age, toddler-peer interactions are characterized by more repetitive, reciprocal, and cooperative patterns (Asher, Erdley, & Gabriel, 1994). They play run-and-chase and a variety of active games. Observations of peer interactions in group day care and informal play groups have shown that toddlers use imitation as a principal mechanism for relating to each other as well as extending their knowledge and skills (Meltzoff & Moore, 1994). Negative and aggressive behaviors, such as biting and hair pulling, increase during the second year (Mueller & Vandell, 1979) along with positive social behaviors. However, as infants get older, the proportion of negative interchanges relative to positive ones decreases.

Observations of toddlers, ages 18 to 25 months, in a French child-care center revealed various patterns of peer interactions (Sinclair, 1994). One pattern of play involved collaboration between two, and occasionally three, partners. In these episodes, the toddlers exchange objects. One child gives a small toy to the other child, who hands it back to the first one. This pattern may be repeated over and over. The children are more interested in the interactions of giving and taking than in the objects that

An infant will reach out and touch another child at an early age.

are passed back and forth. Another pattern of peer interaction involved shared activities and division of labor. One child performs part of a task, while other children carry out other parts. For example, one child puts a cylindrical container on a table, a second child adds another beside it, followed by several other children who put all the similar containers they can find on the table. These observations are consistent with those of Verba (1994), who found that peers as young as 13 to 17 months put together their ideas and actions to solve problems and achieve shared goals.

More than half of children ages 3 to 4 have at least one mutual friend. Toddlers begin to demonstrate playmate preferences as early as 18 months of age. At this point they are capable of forming genuine friendships with each other. An infant-peer friendship has been defined as a relationship characterized by "proximity seeking, sharing, positive affect, and play, . . . with the two friends specifically preferring each other as interaction partners" (Vandell & Mueller, 1980, p. 190). Howes (1987) found that 51 percent of children between 16 and 33 months of age engaged in reciprocal friendships that were maintained for at least a year. Toddler friendships are characterized by loyalty, helping, sharing, togetherness, and mutual interests and preferences (Whaley & Rubenstein, 1994). Almost from the beginning, friendships tend to be based on gender preferences. Beginning around 2 years of age, most toddlers prefer same-sex peers for their playmates and friends (Bee, 2000).

Press and Greenspan (1985a) followed the development of a friendship between two children in a toddler play group over a year's time. During that year their friendship progressed through several stages, from attraction and exploration to including other children in their friendship circle. They shared such activities as looking at books, working puzzles, and loading and unloading trucks and containers together. The following incident illustrates how their friendship included the discovery and sharing of humor:

> Dan and Ned's first shared joke happened like this: One day at snack time, when the children were 21 and 23 months old, respectively, Dan slapped his hand on a small blob of applesauce that had fallen from his spoon onto the table. He then looked across the table at Ned and wriggled with pleasure. Ned stared, caught his breath in surprise, and then laughed the most infectious belly laugh ever heard in that room. Dan was delighted and responded by repeating his act, after which Ned again dissolved in laughter. (Press & Greenspan, 1985a, p. 28)

Like older children and adults, toddlers are distressed when their friendships are terminated. Whaley and Rubenstein (1994) reported a case in which Orly left a child-care group, leaving her friend Carly behind. Carly "regressed to using a bottle more frequently and went back to wearing diapers" (p. 396).

Toddler-Peer Cultures. Corsaro and Eder (1990) believe that children form a "peer culture" that includes a set of shared routines, productive activities, values, and concerns that are separate from the world of adults. In some ways peers are as important as adults in children's acquisition of social skills and knowledge. Experiments with 14- to 18-month-old infants show that they observe and readily imitate behavior modeled by their peers in laboratory, home, and day-care settings even after a 48-hour delay (Hanna & Meltzoff, 1993). The extent to which infants form their own peer culture has not been determined. However, an increasing number of infants participate daily in some type of group child care. Once they enter child-care settings, toddlers begin to develop a strong group identity.

Researchers are studying the nature and characteristics of infant-peer interactions in groups and other contexts along with questions about the influence of peers on individual development. A major feature of peer culture from the earliest years consists of challenges to adult authority and attempts by children to gain autonomy and control over their own activities (Corsaro & Eder, 1990). Between 14 and 24 months of age, toddlers begin to find amusement in forbidden behaviors and share in the laughter of their older siblings as a challenge to adult authority (Dunn, 1988). Nursery school children find ways to circumvent rules imposed by teachers. For example, they "smuggle" forbidden toys or other objects from home to covertly share with their peers (Corsaro & Eder, 1990).

Influences on Peer Interactions. Peer interactions are affected by a variety of factors. Prior experience with peers, siblings, and older children tends to contribute to the ability of an infant to engage in peer interactions (Campos et al., 1983; Howes, 1997a; Lee & Jessee, 1997; Shirley, 1931). These interactions are more frequent and complex among infants who are acquainted with each other and who play in dyads (twos) rather than in larger groups (Campos et al., 1983). Infants from disadvantaged backgrounds tend to be less willing to interact with peers than infants from middle-class families (Press & Greenspan, 1985b).

Infants interact more with peers when they are in a familiar setting than in an unfamiliar place. Infants typically reach out to peers more frequently in their own home than in someone else's home (Field, 1990). The availability of toys, the types of toys, and the play space available also affect peer interactions. Infants interact more with peers in floor play with several toys than in playpens with a more limited number of toys (Field, 1990). Large, nonportable toys facilitate more frequent and positive interactions, whereas small toys generate more exploration, conflict, and negative interactions (Brownell & Brown, 1992). Infants tend to interact more with each other under "toy absent" conditions than they do under "toy present" conditions (Vandell, Wilson, & Buchanan, 1980). Several studies indicate that infants and toddlers are more sociable and display more complex interactions with each other in the absence of toys (Brownell & Brown, 1992).

Familiarity with playmates also affects peer interactions. Studies of infants in group settings indicate that infants engage in more body contact, touching, imitative behaviors, and smiling with acquaintances than with strangers. Peer interactions were observed in a nursery school at the beginning and the end of a semester in a group of infants younger than 15 months of age and in another group of older toddlers (Roopnarine & Field, 1983). The number of interactions increased in both age groups during the semester.

The influence of parents appears to be critical in determining the quantity and quality of peer interactions. Toddlers who are not securely attached to their mothers have been observed initiating the greatest number of social overtures to unfamiliar peers. However, toddlers who are securely attached to their mothers are more effective in peer interactions (Jacobson et al., 1986). Socially competent infants typically have socially competent parents. Researchers (Vandell & Wilson, 1987) found that 6- and 9-month-old infants who had extensive turn-taking experiences with their mothers engaged in extensive turn-taking interactions with peers.

MORAL DEVELOPMENT

The process of **moral development** involves learning and internalizing the rules and principles that govern human behavior. Moral values include such universal standards as honesty, truth, justice, respect for life, and concern about the welfare of others. Morality also includes social conventions concerned with manners and other rules that vary from culture to culture. Moral development includes cognitive functions involved in making moral judgments and the development of a set of emotions (e.g., feelings of guilt) related to the development of a conscience and other internal mechanisms for regulating actions. Infants function at a premoral level and are not expected to understand moral principles. Neither are they considered to be morally accountable for their actions. However, moral development has its roots in infancy. The socialization of moral behaviors begins as soon as infants understand their first words and become mobile. Very early infants hear words such as "No!" and "Don't touch!" that are designed to set limits on their activities. In addition, the emergence of feelings of empathy and guilt are viewed as motivating factors in early moral behavior (see Chapter 12).

Emde and his colleagues (1991) have identified some of the processes through which morality is shaped during infancy. They believe that early moral development is based on information and feelings acquired as procedural knowledge. This type of knowledge is obtained through experiences outside of awareness and memory. For example, infants demonstrate procedural or functional knowledge of one of the rules governing reciprocity of human behavior when they engage in turn-taking interactions with caregivers. The infant's turn-taking capacity may be the earliest expression of the golden rule (do unto others as you would have them do unto you). Although infants demonstrate the capacity to behave in accordance with a variety of moral rules, they do not need to remember or conceptualize these rules before they are acquired.

Infants internalize "do's" and "don'ts" through social referencing and negotiation with caregivers (Emde et al., 1991). During the second year of life, toddlers increasingly turn to caregivers for behavioral cues about how to deal with uncertain situations. Such repeated interactions with caregivers lead to the internalization of some rules for the self-regulation behavior. Emde, Johnson, and Easterbrooks (1987) found that 2-year-olds behave in accordance with social rules and expectations as long as a caregiver is present for social referencing. They also found that toddlers often tested the limits of mild parental prohibitions. For example, if an infant was moving toward a tape recorder and the parent expressed a slight "No, No" head shake, the infant might continue toward the tape recorder until the parent responded with a sterner prohibition. At this stage, toddlers often negotiate with caregivers about the rules by persistence, charm, or acts of cutenes. Through such interactions with their caregivers, infants internalize strategies of negotiation. These negotiation strategies are useful in helping one resist temptation or gain approval for behaviors that might otherwise be questioned.

The toddler years lay the foundation for moral development, including respect for authority, and compliance with reasonable rules and requests. By 3 years of age, children typically have internalized rules that govern the "do's" and "don'ts" of behavior in a variety of situations. They have also formed a set of moral emotional signals that guide their behaviors (Emde et al., 1991). Their language ability and cognitive capacity now make it possible to discuss moral rules and principles. The results of studies using "moral dilemmas" indicate that, at this age, children show evidence of having internalized rules and feelings of empathy involved in acts of compassion. For example, Buchsbaum and Emde (1990) presented a play situation to 3-year-olds that involved the need to get a bandage for a hurt child. The children were told that there was a rule prohibiting them from going to the bathroom shelf where the bandages were located. The children understood and struggled with the dilemma and many found a way to achieve a positive outcome.

Most children tend to value kindness over cruelty and good over bad behavior (Kagan, 1994). However, during the second and third years of life children also display evidence of immoral behavior. In spite of their capacity for empathetic feelings, they take pleasure in breaking rules and exhibit behaviors that are intended to upset or hurt others (Dunn, 1987). Thus, the process of socialization for moral development not only involves encouraging prosocial acts, but helping children control antisocial behavior as well.

Prosocial Behaviors. In general, parents and other caregivers encourage infants to display prosocial responses in their interactions with others. **Prosocial behaviors** include a variety of positive, socially desirable activities, including sharing resources, nurturance, helping, and cooperation. Such prosocial behaviors are considered to be important for the development of character—an individual's "general approach to the dilemmas and responsibilities of social life" (Hay et al., 1995, p. 24). Character is an important component of moral development.

Sharing. One of the earliest prosocial behaviors exhibited by humans is sharing. Shortly before their first birthday, infants begin to share resources with other people, including their own age mates (Hay et al., 1995). At around this time, infants begin to offer their food, toys, and other possessions, including their pets, to their companions.

They point to objects they wish others to see. They share new toys as often as old ones, scarce resources as well as ones that are plentiful (Hay et al., 1991). For example, Joshua, a toddler who came to his neighbor's door for Halloween "trick or treat," attempted to dump his bag of candy into the bowl of candy that was held out for him to select a treat. At first a toddler may extend an object, but show ambivalence about giving it up. However, by 18 months of age, virtually all toddlers everywhere show, offer, and give objects to others (Hay et al., 1995).

Because sharing is so strong and common among toddlers, this behavior is considered to be innate. At this age, sharing behaviors do not appear to be affected by social reinforcement or modeling. Simply requesting an object from a toddler and engaging in games of give-and-take have been found to be the most effective ways of increasing rates of sharing (Hay, 1994). Children who do not share at all between the ages of 18 and 36 months are more likely to display behavior problems (Hay et al., 1995). Since young autistic children do not show or offer objects to their companions, the absence of sharing behavior may be an early sign of autism (Hay, Castle, & Jewett, 1994).

As infants grow older, the tendency to share with others evidently becomes weaker and more individualized (Hay et al., 1999). Twenty-four-month-olds are less likely to share in response to a peer's interest in an object than are 12-month-olds (Hay, 1994). In both a laboratory and home setting, 3-year-olds are less likely to share objects with their mothers than are 2-year-olds (Hay et al., 1995; Hay et al., 1999). Researchers have found that sharing occurs at relatively low rates in preschool classrooms (Hay, 1994). As children grow older, they become aware that it is not always in their own best interest to share indiscriminately. This may be the reason why preschool children are more likely to share with their friends than with casual acquaintances (Hay et al., 1994).

Compliance. The child's willingness to modify behavior in accordance with the expectations of caregivers is generally considered to be a prominent indicator of prosocial tendencies. Even though toddlers are notorious for their negativism, they tend to comply with requests more often than they refuse (Hay et al., 1994). Children generally tend to become increasingly obedient during the second and third years of life (Howes & Olenick, 1986). However, compliant behavior is likely to vary according to the situation (what is being demanded) and a child's relationship with the person making the request (Schneider-Rosen & Wenz-Goss, 1990). It is easier for toddlers to suppress pleasant activity than it is for them to comply with unpleasant, tedious behavior (Kochanska, Coy, & Murray, 2001). Their compliance also tends to be greater for property, safety, and interpersonal behaviors than for other issues (Smetana, Kochanska, & Chuang, 2000). When commands are unambiguous and are made with sensitivity, toddlers tend to take delight in pleasing their caregivers (Edwards, 1995).

Negativism and Aggression. About the time they start becoming mobile, infants begin to hear commands from caregivers intended to protect them from dangers and disapproval, such as "Get that button out of your mouth!" or "Don't pull on the cat's tail!" In many instances, older infants and toddlers refuse to comply with caregiver requests. In other instances, children do not comply because they do not understand the request or have forgotten a previously stated limit. Kopp (1992) has identified a variety of behaviors that are characteristic of resistance including negativism (No!), physical resistance (kicking, throwing), crying, ignoring, arguing (Why?), and negotiation (excuses, bargaining). Toddlers may refuse to eat, take a bath, or go to bed. Ignoring, or other passive behaviors, and direct defiance are strategies used by younger toddlers. Bargaining and direct refusal are more typical of older toddlers (Kopp, 1992).

Noncompliance. Noncompliant and negativistic behavior reaches a peak at about 2 years of age and gradually declines during the preschool years (Edwards, 1995). This is why the stereotype of "the terrible twos" has been applied to this age period. However, this pattern of behavior does not apply to all 2-year-olds and may be more prevalent among Caucasian American toddlers reared in highly stimulating and demanding middle-class families than in other cultures (Kopp, 1992).

Adults can encourage compliance by telling the child in advance when a change of activity is necessary. "As soon as the cartoon is over, we will be going home." Adults should not insist on instant obedience. Parents and other adults should also avoid nagging and repeating demands over and over. The adult should be sure that the child hears and understands the instructions (Laishley, 1983). The toddler's "no" should not be interpreted literally (Weiser, 1982), because it may be an experimental response to see what will happen. Children usually comply willingly if the adult is firm and positive, as in the following example:

> Two-year-old Karen was busily engaged in caring for her baby doll right before lunch time. The teacher approached, saying "Let's go to the sink, Karen, and I'll help you wash your face and hands." "No!" replied Karen. The teacher smiled, took Karen by the hand, and said "Come on, Karen, it will only take a minute, and then it's time to eat. Let's go." Karen smiled and teasingly pretended a reluctant walk over to the sink. (Weiser, 1982, p. 197)

If adults are reasonable, firm, and kind in their demands, children tend to respond favorably.

Temper Tantrums. Negativism and noncompliance often take the form of kicking, screaming, throwing objects, and other violent behavior. Temper tantrums are the toddler's way of responding to behavioral restrictions, denial of wishes, and other frustrations that conflict with the desire for control and independence. Tantrums are common around the world, although parental responses vary among and within cultures (Broude, 1995). If adults respond appropriately, most toddlers grow out of this behavior. Brazelton (1992) believes that temper tantrums at this stage result from the toddler's inner turmoil and a struggle between dependence and independence. He advises parents to stand back and allow the child to gain inner control. In some cases it may be necessary to prevent the child from attacking someone or destroying property. In a group situation the child needs to be removed until the tantrum subsides. However, the child should not receive special attention in the process. Above all, this behavior should not be reinforced. A child should not be allowed to use a tantrum to obtain a desired goal. Adults need to remain as calm as possible and avoid angry, violent responses.

Hitting. Toddlers hit each other to protect or regain possessions or out of a sense of frustration and loss of control. Hitting is also a means of playful aggression without hostile intent. Most toddlers use physical aggression, but by kindergarten they have learned alternative means for dealing with conflict (Tremblay, 2001). When one child hits or pushes another, the caregiver quickly assesses the situation to see what happened. For older toddlers it may not be necessary to intervene because they often work things out on their own. For younger toddlers and in cases of a child being a bully, the caregiver needs to respond. The caregiver should make eye contact with the aggressor and state firmly: "Hitting is not allowed because it hurts!" At the same time, an alternative response is suggested: "I know that Seth made you angry when he took your hat, but you need to ask him to give it back or come to me for help" (Leavitt & Eheart, 1985). Keep in mind that toddlers who are more sensitive to peers' possible intentions are more likely to hit their peers (Hay, Castle, & Davies, 2000). The child who continues to be aggressive can be removed from the situation briefly but should be given praise and reinforcement for solving conflicts at other times in nonaggressive ways.

Biting. Day-care providers who work with toddlers typically report biting to be one of the most common and difficult behavior problems. Caregivers need to understand that infants bite other people for different reasons. Some bite out of a sense of curiosity, playfulness, or the need to satisfy oral urges. For other infants, biting may result from attempts to protect their space, their possessions, or to obtain scarce resources. Biting can be handled in much the same way as other aggressive acts, with firmness and suggestions for alternative ways (e.g., "Use your words!") to respond to frustration. Most of the attention should be focused on the child who has been bitten. It is not advisable to bite the child in return or to tell the victim to bite back. This response is generally not effective and may only reinforce biting behavior. In group situations, biting behavior can be prevented or minimized by providing plenty of toys, interesting activities, and close supervision, while avoiding too many adult restrictions.

GENDER-ROLE SOCIALIZATION

Gender-role acquisition is a critical component of the socialization process. To some extent, gender differences in behavior can be attributed to genetic factors and hormonal influences. The degree to which actual behavioral differences between males and females are determined by biological endowment or child-rearing practices has not been determined. Similarities as well as differences in male and female behaviors have been found in different cultures. Scientists generally believe that from the beginning of life, a wide variety of social and cultural influences combine with biological influences in shaping gender-related behaviors. Cross-cultural studies show that parents in different societies throughout the world socialize their sons and daughters in different ways (Garcia Coll & Meyer, 1993). The infancy period is often considered unimportant in sex-role development. However, upon close examination we find that powerful environmental influences are in operation during this period and an impressive set of gender-related concepts and behaviors have been acquired by 3 years of age (O'Brien, 1992).

In the United States, babies typically receive the "pink" and "blue" treatment with color-coded blankets, presents, and clothes as soon as their gender is known (Fagot, 1995). Adult perceptions, expectations, and treatment of an infant depend to some degree upon the infant's gender. Researchers have found that adult descriptions of infants vary depending upon sex-stereotyped dress. An infant dressed as a girl is more likely to be described as "frail" and "sweet," whereas a baby dressed as a boy is more likely to be described in terms such as "tough" and "sturdy." Babies' facial expressions are also interpreted differently depending upon their perceived gender identity (Condry & Condry, 1976). Research has also suggested that mothers interpret motor behavior differently based on gender (Mondschein, Adolph, & Tamis-LeMonda, 2000).

The extent to which parents provide different socialization experiences for male and female infants varies among families. In most American families, boys and girls have different sets of toys. Generally, girls are given more latitude than boys to display cross-gender behaviors, especially by fathers. For example, when a 2-year-old boy pushed his sister's doll carriage down the sidewalk, the father commented, "Look at the little sissy!" However, studies indicate that differences in parental sex-role socialization practices for male and female infants may not be as consistent and widespread as commonly believed (Fagot, 1995; Fagot & Hagan, 1991). Parents often use the child's behaviors as cues to guide their responses. There are some indications that parents begin to display more traditional gender-stereotyped responses to infants about the same time infants display gender-related knowledge and behaviors (Fagot, 1995). This indicates that infants are not passive creatures but active participants in the sex-role socialization process. Even though parents may try to avoid gender stereotyping in their child-rearing practices, the effects of other caregivers, peers, television, and other cultural influences often counteract parental efforts.

Researchers have looked at the emergence of gender-based behaviors during the infancy period. Some gender differences such as aggression and assertiveness in play emerge very early (Jacklin & Maccoby, 1983). Males tend to be more physically active in utero (Almli, Ball, & Wheeler, 2001) and after birth (Campbell & Eaton, 1999). Brain research suggests that from birth to 6 years, female brains are more active in language processing, fine motor skills, and social cognition, while male brains are more active in spatial-visual discrimination, visual targeting, and planning related to gross motor development (Hanlon, Thatcher, & Cline, 1999). In line with these findings, Weinberg and colleagues (1999) found that males have more difficulty maintaining synchronous interactions with caregivers.

As early as 9 months, male infants show a preference for male toys (Campbell et al., 2000). The appearance of other infant sex-typed behaviors evidently coincides with the ability of infants to label their own gender between 2 and 3 years of age (Fagot, 1995). Male toddlers who understand labels for boys and girls tend to play more with same-sex playmates, avoid female-typed toys, and play longer with male-typed toys than the toddlers who cannot label their gender (Fagot & Leinbach, 1989; Weinraub et al., 1984).

Gender awareness affects children in other ways. In one study, when asked to approach another child, children as young as age 3 stopped farther away when the other child was of the opposite gender (Wasserman & Stern, 1978). Previously unacquainted 33-month-old children were observed to engage in higher levels of social behavior when playing with a same-sex peer than an opposite-sex peer (Maccoby, 1990) As they approach 3 years of age, children begin to increasingly demonstrate a preference for same-sex peers as play partners. Although many of their gender-based perceptions and behaviors are somewhat fragile and unstable, by 3 years of age children have adopted much of their culture's sex-typed division of activities and attributes (O'Brien, 1992).

ASSESSING SOCIAL DEVELOPMENT

There are relatively few standardized instruments specifically designed to assess social skills of infants. The **Vineland Adaptive Behavior Scales** (Sparrow, Balla, & Cicchetti, 1984) are available in three forms to assess the ability of individuals to take care of themselves and get along with others from birth to adulthood. Since these scales cover a wide age range, their usefulness in screening young infants for social competence is somewhat limited. Several standardized instruments, such as the **Battelle Developmental Inventory** (Newborg et al., 1988), contain subscales for assessing social skills. Assessments of infant social skills are best observed in natural contexts such as play (Odom & Munson, 1996). The observation of infants as they play in structured and unstructured settings is a relatively new procedure for assessing social development as well as other abilities. Although various scales are available for use in play-based observations, **Transdisciplinary Play-Based Assessment (TPBA)** is one of the most widely used approaches (Linder, 1993). TPBA is conducted by a team of professionals and a parent who observe the child in a play session. The session consists of various phases of structured and unstructured activities in which the child interacts with a facilitator, plays alone, with a parent, and with a peer. Team members record their observations on forms provided and determine the child's level of functioning. The information is used to make recommendations for facilitating development.

SUMMARY

Socialization Processes

- Socialization is the process by which infants learn to behave in accordance with cultural expectations through interactions with parents and other people.

The Socially Competent Infant

- Socially competent infants possess the ability to relate to other people effectively and to get their needs met. Parents of socially competent babies are accessible, create a safe, stimulating environment, and provide appropriate discipline.

Early Social Behaviors

- Social smiling, laughing, and crying are the first indicators of the infant's social awareness. The age at which the first true social smiles typically appear is debatable and depends on the criteria that are used to define smiling. The earliest age at which social smiling is considered to appear is 3 or 4 weeks. Babies begin to laugh between 2 and 4

APPLICATIONS: FACILITATING SOCIAL DEVELOPMENT

There are numerous practices and activities that parents as well as other caregivers can use to promote healthy social development. In general, the most important thing is to give the infant a feeling of being cared for and loved. The following are some recommended principles and practices:

- Allow babies to have moments of peace. It is important to respect an infant's desire not to interact with people or other outside stimuli from time to time (Provence, 1967). However, the infant's cries for help should never be ignored.
- Read toddlers stories that have very simple moral lessons (Lickona, 1983).
- Make up rhymes for rules to help toddlers remember (Lickona, 1983).
- Encourage independency and self-sufficiency. In general, avoid doing things for infants that they can do for themselves.
- Plan time for the baby to be part of the adult world. An infant should have opportunities to interact with adults of both sexes of various ages, racial, and ethnic backgrounds.
- Provide a variety of culturally and developmentally appropriate toys and materials for infants (see Chapter 13), but do not allow toys to substitute for personal interactions.
- Play interactive games with infants such as peekaboo and pat-a-cake as soon as they can reciprocate such interactions. Increase the complexity of games (e.g., pretend "tea parties") as infants get older.
- Provide opportunities for toddlers to play with other toddlers in carefully supervised situations.

Additional suggestions may be found in other sources (e.g., Bromwich, 1980; Cryer, Harms, & Bourland, 1987; Grasselli and Hegner, 1980; Karnes, 1982; Silberg, 1993; Sparling and Lewis, 1979; Weiser, 1982; White, 1985).

months of age. Crying is a reflexive activity that is present at birth but becomes more socially responsive with age.

Infant-Adult Play

- Play is an important vehicle by which infants and toddlers practice the social skills needed for successful interactions with others. Infant-adult social play goes through five phases, progressing from mutual engagement to independent play. Three types of parent-child play evolve during the infancy period: interpersonal play, object play, and symbolic play.

Social Behavior With Peers

- The earliest infant-peer social interactions begin at approximately 2 months of age, when infants look at each other. Their interactions become more complex and frequent with age, as they begin to combine smiling and laughter with playing games.
- By 2 years of age, toddler-peer interactions are characterized by more repetitive, reciprocal, and cooperative patterns. Toddlers form genuine friendships that include loyalty, helping, sharing, togetherness, and mutual interests and preferences.
- Peer relationships are important in children's acquisition of social skills and knowledge. Toddlers form a "peer culture" that includes a set of shared routines, productive activities, values, and concerns that are separate from the world of adults. Peer culture encourages challenges to adult authority and attempts by children to gain autonomy and control over their own activities.
- Peer interactions during infancy are influenced by social class, the social setting, availability of toys, and parent-infant attachment.

Moral Development

- The process of moral development involves learning and internalizing the rules and principles that govern human behavior. Moral development has its roots in infancy as infants learn "do's" and "don'ts" through social referencing and negotiation with caregivers. By 3 years of age, children typically have internalized rules and formed morally based emotional signals that govern behavior in a variety of situations.

- Prosocial behaviors exhibited by infants include sharing and compliance with adult requests.
- Antisocial behaviors include noncompliant and negativistic behaviors that reach a peak at 2 years of age. Negativism and noncompliance often take the form of temper tantrums. Infants and toddlers express their aggressive tendencies through hitting and biting their peers.

Gender-Role Socialization

- Gender-role acquisition is a critical component of the socialization process that begins during infancy. Although many of their gender-based perceptions and behaviors are somewhat fragile and unstable, by 3 years of age children have adopted much of their culture's sex-typed division of activities and attributes.

Assessing Social Development

- Instruments and procedures that are used to assess infant social development include the Vineland Adaptive Behavior Scales, Battelle Developmental Inventory, and Transdisciplinary Play-Based Assessment.

KEY TERMS

socialization
social competence
endogenous smile
exogenous smile
true social smile
interpersonal play
object play
symbolic play
moral development
prosocial behaviors
Vineland Adaptive Behavior Scales
Battelle Developmental Inventory
Transdisciplinary Play-Based Assessment (TPBA)

INFORMATION ON THE WEB*

www.parentsplace.com/toddlers This site has links to information on the social development of toddlers as well as other topics of interest to parents.

childdevelopmentweb.com/Milestones/milestones.htm This site identifies milestones of infant development, including socialization. Toys to assist development are identified.

*Web sites are subject to change.

TWELVE

EMOTIONAL DEVELOPMENT

Moving between the legs of tables and chairs,
Rising or falling, grasping at kisses and toys,
Advancing boldly, sudden to take alarm,
retreating to the corner of arm and knee,
Eager to be reassured, taking pleasure
In the fragrant brilliance of the Christmas tree. . .
—T. S. Eliot

The opening quotation illustrates the richness of the emotional life of infants as they explore their world. Virtually all the infant's interactions with people and things in the environment are punctuated with various nuances of emotional moods and expressions. Emotional development encompasses the origin and differentiation of specific emotions. It also includes developmental changes in emotional expression and the infant's understanding of emotions in themselves and others. In this chapter we will take a look at the general course of emotional development during the first three years of life. We will consider some of the theoretical issues involved in scientific discussions of emotional development along with potential influences on emotional expression. The formation of attachment between infants and their caregivers and the importance of infant-caregiver interactions will be discussed. The infant's self-regulation of emotions and the understanding of emotions expressed by others will also be considered. Finally we will look at infant mental health along with some ways to facilitate emotional development.

DEFINITIONS

The first question we must consider is "What is an emotion?" The term **emotion** comes from a Latin word meaning to "excite," "stir up," or "agitate." In common usage, emotions are often described simply as feelings. Scientifically, however, emotions are defined more broadly than mere feelings. Greenspan and Greenspan (1985) define emotions as "complex, subjective experiences that have many components, including physical, expressive, cognitive, and organizing, as well as highly personalized, subjective meanings" (p. 7). **Affect** is a term that is often used interchangeably with emotion. Technically, affect is used to refer to the subjective feeling component and the expressive component of emotion (Sroufe, 1996). The experience and expression of emotion involve complex changes in facial expressions, body movements, respiration, heart rate, blood pressure, hormones, and other bodily functions. Current views of emotional development emphasize the complexity of emotions, the role emotions play in motivating an individual to action and in affecting interactions between an individual and others.

THEORIES OF EMOTIONAL DEVELOPMENT

The varying definitions of emotions are the result of many divergent theories about their nature, function, and development. Theories of emotional development can be summarized in terms of biological theories, socialization (learning) theories, interactionist positions, and dynamic systems perspectives. The biological model emphasizes that an infant is innately equipped, or prewired, with emotions. The young infant's emotions are viewed as comparable to sneezes and knee jerks. They are "unlearned, biologically controlled and subject to relatively little socialization influence" (M. Lewis & Saarni, 1985, p. 2).

According to socialization, or learning, theories, emotional development is shaped chiefly by social influences. This approach does not deny the existence of biological foundations but places more emphasis on environmental experiences. In recent years, theorists have tended to adopt an interactionist perspective whereby emotions are seen as a synthesis of biological and socialization processes. The innate potential for emotional expression is realized in different ways, depending on the infant's experiences with caregivers and other socialization circumstances (Murphy, 1983).

A widely accepted variation of the interactionist perspective is dynamic systems theory (see also Chapter 6). According to this theory, emotional development involves the complex interplay between multiple response systems within the infant and external sociocultural influences. Response systems within the infant include cognitive, motor, and neurophysiological processes. Examples of influential social systems are parent-child dyads and other caregiver-infant combinations.

INFLUENCES ON EMOTIONAL DEVELOPMENT

Physiological Factors. Most definitions of emotion acknowledge the involvement of numerous body processes. Researchers are still trying to determine the extent to which physiological processes influence emotion, on the one hand, and are influenced by emotions, on the other hand. According to Sroufe (1996), developmental changes in the brain parallel emotional development during the infancy period. We know that certain regions or networks of the brain and nervous system are connected with emotional activity. For example, the area of the brain referred to as the amygdala appears to be a key structure in mediating fear and anger responses (LeDoux, 1993). In addition, numerous neurochemicals (e.g., catecholamines) and hormones (e.g., cortisol) have been identified as possible influences on emotionality (Panskepp, 1993, 2000; Ryan, Kuhl, & Deci, 1997; Schore, 2000; Walden & Gerber, 1994).

Emotional experiences are affected by a complex interplay between various structures of the brain and body chemistry that mutually influence each other in ongoing processes. For example, researchers have found that stress elevates the level of cortisol in the brain. Over time, high cortisol levels contribute to the death of brain cells, reduce the synaptic connections, and alter the emotional circuitry of the brain (Gunnar et al., 1996). Affected infants have more difficulty in developing feelings of empathy, forming attachments, and establishing emotional control. In contrast, infants who develop positive attachments to their caregivers not only maintain lower levels of cortisol, but also recover from stressful situations more quickly (Newberger, 1997).

Temperament. Recall from Chapter 10 that various theories of temperament include emotional reactions and sensitivity as major components. The infant's temperamental characteristics probably exercise a major influence on emotional expression. Researchers have found temperamental characteristics such as activity level, soothability, reactivity, and affect to be related to the expression of both positive and negative emotions (Derryberry & Rothbart, 1984; Fish, 1998; Young, Fox, & Zahn-Waxler, 1999). Temperament may also affect the type and intensity of environmental stimuli that elicit emotional responses in infants (N. Fox, 1998; Yarrow, 1979).

Socialization of Emotions. Emotions develop within the context of social and cultural environments. The term **socialization of emotions** means that the infants' emotions are influenced, over time, by the responses of parents and other caregivers. Processes that contribute to the socialization of emotions include classical and operant conditioning, punishment, direct instruction, imitation, and identification (Walden & Garber, 1994). Parents influence their babies' emotions through selective reinforcement with facial expressions and other behaviors. A study by Malatesta and Haviland (1982) illustrates how parents condition the emotional expressions through the use of facial responses. The researchers videotaped mothers interacting with their infants during a period of a few months. The mothers tended to respond with more facial expressions that reinforced the display of positive behaviors in their infants. Over time, the infants' number of positive behaviors increased while the negative behaviors declined. Parents also adapt their responses to the child's developmental level. Grolnick and colleagues (1998) found that parents increased verbal strategies at 12 to 18 months to help infants regulate distress, but decreased this activity as their infants grew older.

The sex of an infant is likely to influence the socialization of emotional behavior. In face-to-face play, mothers tend to respond differently to the same emotional expressions of male and female infants. Mothers tend to smile more at boys than at girls (Malatesta & Haviland, 1985). When female infants display anger, mothers tend to display angry facial expressions in return. However, mothers are more likely to display facial expressions of sympathy when male infants display anger (Malatesta & Haviland, 1982). Mothers also give a greater variety of emotional responses to a female's emotional expressions than to a male infant's. Malatesta and Haviland (1985) believe that male infants are more excitable, so mothers soon learn to limit their range of emotional response to avoid overstimulation. The exposure to more diverse emotional stimuli may partially explain why girls are better than boys at understanding emotional expression. However, few sex differences in the expression of emotions emerge during the infancy period (Zahn-Waxler, Cummings, & Cooperman, 1984). Researchers have not found any evidence of gender differences in security of attachment formed between infants and parents (Carlson et al., 1989).

Since parent-infant interactions are partially controlled by the infant, it is necessary to look at differences in the behaviors of male and female infants that are likely to have an impact on parent-infant relationships. According to Benenson (1996), males prefer physically assertive behavior while females prefer a more gentle style of interaction. Male infants tend to engage in more gross motor activity than females. In the first year of life, males tend to be more irritable than females. Newborn females, more than males, engage in eye contact, are more sensitive to the sound of another infant's crying, and are more responsive to caregivers' efforts to relieve the infant's emotional distress.

Culture. Cultural influences play an important role in establishing the emotional climate and the extent to which infants are exposed to various emotions. Each culture has patterns of emotional expression that are somewhat distinctive. For example, Utku eskimo people do not traditionally express anger overtly, nor use anger in child rearing (Briggs, 1970). They disapprove of anger and seek to suppress it in their children. In a cross-cultural study (Caudill & Schooler, 1973), American infants made more happy vocalizations than Japanese infants. At 30 months of age, American infants were more emotionally expressive and independent. Japanese parents are indulgent with their infants and tend to shield them from exposure to strong emotional reactions such as anger and sadness. Thus, when anger is expressed, Japanese children tend to be more upset than children who have been more often exposed to such outbursts (Miyake et al., 1986). In contrast, Banoi infants in Thailand are encouraged to vent their anger very early in life (Broude, 1995). Expression of hostility is accepted throughout the childhood years.

Social-class differences in maternal interpretations of infant emotions have also been found. Lower-class mothers who were separated from their infants labeled their infants' reactions as anger more frequently than middle-class mothers (Lewis & Michalson, 1983). Thus, adults from various cultural and subcultural backgrounds are likely to socialize the emotional displays of their infants in different ways (Zahn-Waxler et al., 1984).

Cognitive Factors. Emotional development and cognitive development in infancy are generally viewed as interdependent processes. Most emotional responses are based on the interpretation of stimuli and events as pleasant or unpleasant, threatening or nonthreatening, or neutral. The emergence of advanced emotions is dependent upon the infant's cognitive ability to interpret specific eliciting conditions. For example, stranger fear does not emerge until an infant can make cognitive comparisons between faces and perceive a strange face as unfamiliar and threatening (M. Lewis, 1993). Guilt, shame, and embarrassment are emotions that depend on cognitive functions associated with the emergence of self-awareness (Walden & Garber, 1994). Sroufe (1996) contends that emotional development during infancy parallels cognitive changes outlined by Piaget during the sensorimotor period (see Chapter 8).

THE EMERGENCE OF EMOTIONS

Scientists who study emotional development have been interested in determining when various emotions first appear. There is general agreement that most of the emotions emerge and develop during the first three years of life. However, due to differences in theories, terminology, and research methods, researchers disagree on the exact timetable for the development of specific emotions. Scientists also debate whether or not emotions can be classified within two or three overall categories (e.g., anger/frustration, wariness/fear, pleasure/joy) or as seven or more separate and distinct emotions (fear, anger, sadness, etc.). Research tends to support the existence of a number of discrete emotions (Izard, 1993). In this text, an effort has been made to combine information from a variety of viewpoints and research findings. Table 12-1 encompasses the approximate ages, ranging from youngest to oldest in months, identified by various researchers for the appearance of various emotions.

Newborn infants display general emotional states of distress, discomfort, or pain. They also display signs of excitement and interest in the environment, and they seem to be relaxed and content at times (M. Lewis, 1993). However, the emotional life of the newborn is rather limited. Yet, within the first three years of life emotions develop rapidly in concert with developing self-awareness and cognitive understanding. Between the first few days of life and 3 months of age, infants begin to display signs of sadness and disgust. By the time an infant is 6 to 9 months old, surprise, joy, fear, and anger have emerged. The more complex emotions, including affection/love, sympathy/empathy, guilt, embarrassment, pride, and shame are not expressed until sometime between 18 and 36 months (see Table 12–1). We will consider the development of pleasure/joy, anger, anxiety/fear, and sympathy/empathy in more detail as they emerge during the infancy period. Information on the development of other emotions during the infancy period is more limited.

Table 12-1 Infant Emotions: Age Range of Development

EMOTION	*AGE (MONTHS)*
Distress/Discomfort/Pain	Birth
Interest/Excitement	Birth
Disgust	Birth–3
Sadness	Birth–3
Pleasure/Delight/Joy	2–7
Surprise	3–6
Anger	4–7
Wariness/Fear	4–9
Rage	7–18
Affection/Love	18–36
Empathy/Sympathy	18–36
Embarrassment	24–36
Guilt	24–36
Pride	24–36
Shame	24–36

Sources: Izard & Malatesta, 1987; Lewis, 1993; Sroufe, 1996

Pleasure/Joy. The development of pleasure and joy in young infants is revealed mainly through their smiles and laughter (see Chapter 11). The exact age at which the infant's smiles and laughter actually reflect an underlying state of pleasure and happiness is not known. The argument has been made (Emde et al., 1976) that the neonatal smile represents a positive or pleasurable emotional tone, since smiling has not been observed when infants are distressed. However, the signs of pleasure and joy are more definite by 3 months of age when infants smile at familiar events and faces they recognize (M. Lewis, 1993). Sroufe (1996) believes smiling and laughter responses mostly result from the buildup and release of tension as infants encounter various exciting and uncertain events.

Anger/Rage. Mothers and scientists alike have reported expressions of anger in the cries and facial expressions of infants as early as the neonatal period. Sroufe (1979) believes that these early "mad" expressions are more correctly identified as primitive responses to extreme distress. Anger is more differentiated and readily identified in infants between 4 and 7 months of age. Stenberg and Campos (1990) found that 4-month-old infants displayed angry facial expressions directed toward the source of their frustration (e.g., restraint). Expressions of anger become more frequent during the latter half of the first year (Emde et al., 1976; Sroufe, 1977) and gradually increase with age throughout infancy (M. Lewis & Michalson, 1983). Parents report an increase in the frequency and intensity in their infant's expression of anger after infants begin to creep (Campos, Kermoian, & Zumbahlen, 1992). Obstacles that prevent the infant from obtaining a goal, such as an attractive object, can elicit an angry response.

Young infants usually express anger through crying, angry flushed facial expressions, and increased motor activity. By 1 year of age an infant's angry reactions are likely to include foot stomping, kicking, throwing, or knocking away objects (Sroufe, 1979). Two-year-olds also use defiant verbal expressions ("No!") and aggressive acts such as pushing, biting, and hitting. Their responses are more directly targeted toward the source of anger. The intensity of anger in reaction to frustration or other stimuli at this age is referred to as rage (Sroufe, 1996).

Babies react with anger to a variety of situations. The earliest sources of anger are physical restraints that inhibit an infant's movements. Barriers that prevent a baby from reaching a goal, such as a toy, also cause anger. The developing sense of self-awareness and the need for independence result in new sources of anger as the infant's goals come into conflict with parental demands and expectations. For example, infants often react angrily when caregivers put them to bed (Stenberg & Campos, 1990). "The terrible twos" are characterized by increased resistance to adult demands as temper tantrums reach a peak.

Anxiety/Fear. Infants typically begin to show signs of anxiety and fear between 7 and 9 months of age (Izard, 1977). Sroufe (1996) thinks of fear as emerging throughout the infancy period from a more general state of wariness or apprehension rather than an emotion that appears at a specific age. Infants react negatively or warily to strangers, heights (visual cliffs), approaching (looming) objects, separation from their attachment figures, and stimuli associated with pain (e.g., doctors' offices). Fear responses in infants include crying, clinging to the caregiver, and a fearful facial expression. The stimuli that elicit fear in infants generally increase in number over the first 18 months of life (M. Lewis & Michalson, 1983) and are connected with the changes in the object concept and other aspects of cognitive development (Sroufe, 1996). During the third year of life, the sources of fear change and begin to include imaginary stimuli such as wild animals. The development of two types of fear—stranger anxiety and separation anxiety—parallel the development of attachment.

Stranger Anxiety. A 9-month-old infant is sitting on the living room floor playing with a ball. A new neighbor who is visiting walks over, kneels down close to the infant, and says, "She is a beautiful baby!" The baby takes one look at the stranger and begins to cry. **Stranger anxiety** or fear of strangers emerges during the last half of the first year of life and reaches a peak frequency around 12 months. Girls tend to display negative reactions to strangers a little earlier than boys (M. Lewis & Michalson, 1983). The incidence declines slightly at the beginning of the second year and rises once again between 18 and 24 months (M. Lewis & Michalson, 1983; Scarr & Salapatek, 1970). After that time, stranger anxiety gradually declines.

An infant is less likely to show a fear of strangers if the infant is being held by a primary caregiver (Mussen, Conger, & Kagan, 1974) and if the strangers are children, especially of the same sex (Brooks & Lewis, 1976a). Infants react more negatively to strangers who intrude in familiar, predictable settings (Brookhart & Hock, 1976). Babies who are free to move away are less likely to cry in response to a strange person than babies who are restrained (Bronson, 1972). They also are more likely to be afraid of male than female strangers (Lewis & Brooks, 1974). The extent to which a stranger's behavior is predictable or contingent upon the infant's own responses (e.g., a smile for a smile) is likely to affect the amount of anxiety exhibited (Bronson, 1972).

The infant's responsiveness to strangers is affected by the security of attachment to the mother and experiences within the family. Infants who are securely attached to the mother are much more sociable with strangers than less securely attached infants (Thompson & Lamb, 1984). The quality of the baby's attachment to other family members is also an important influence in stranger sociability. No consistent relationship has been found between the infant's previous experiences with other people outside the family and stranger anxiety (Thompson & Lamb, 1984). However, cross-cultural studies suggest that stranger anxiety is more intense and lasts longer in societies in which infants have more limited contact with strangers than they typically do in America (Super & Harkness, 1982).

Separation Anxiety. An 11-month-old boy is playing in the living room of a neighbor. He looks up and sees his mother disappear into the kitchen with the neighbor. He begins to follow as quickly as possible, crying loudly. This is an example of **separation anxiety** that is typically seen in infants around 8 or 9 months of age. It reaches a peak around 12 months and begins to disappear toward the end of the second year (M. Lewis & Michalson, 1983). However, displays of separation anxiety continue longer in some cultures than in others. Separation distress remains longer in infants who are cared for exclusively by the mother than in infants who are also cared for by siblings and other persons (Super & Harkness, 1982).

Both separation and stranger anxiety are emotions that typically are not learned through unpleasant experiences, although that is possible. Some theorists believe that these are among a group of innate emotions that have survival value by keeping the infant close to the parent. The emergence of stranger fear and separation anxiety has also been attributed to cognitive growth, including changes in recall memory and the object concept (Bronson, 1972). With growing cognitive maturity, infants learn more about the environment and develop a set of expectations. Unfamiliar persons are perceived by infants as discrepant or contradictory stimuli that do not match familiar mental images. The infant thus responds with expressions of anxiety.

Empathy/Sympathy. The experience of participating in the emotional state of another person is referred to as **empathy** (Bischof-Kohler, 1991). Empathy means "feeling as," or sharing the same emotion that another person is experiencing at a given time. **Sympathy** is an emotional response that involves feelings of sorrow and compassion for another person who is in pain and distress. Empathy usually results in expressions of sympathy, such as hugs or other comforting behaviors. On a behavioral level it is difficult to determine when a person is experiencing empathy or sympathy or both. Both empathy and sympathy require the cognitive ability to identify the emotions of others. The term **empathic concern** is sometimes

A case of separation anxiety and protest. This infant is reluctant to leave the mother.

used to describe feelings and behaviors that are a combination of sympathy and empathy (Zahn-Waxler & Radke-Yarrow, 1990).

The capacity to respond to the emotions of others appears so early in life that it is considered to be innate (Bischof-Kohler, 1991). When newborns hear the cries of other babies, they tend to join in with cries of their own. Very young infants also imitate, or match, the facial expressions of adults (e.g., a frown or a smile) that convey emotional states. However, these emotional "mimicry" responses may be attributed to the process of emotional contagion. As such, an infant can share an emotion with others without awareness that the emotion also belongs to someone else. Episodes of emotional contagion are viewed as forerunners or empathy, or the raw material from which empathy develops (Bischof-Kohler, 1991). Infants move from displaying "self-distress" to more varied and complex expressions of caring. Emotional concern thus gradually becomes more outer and other directed (Zahn-Waxler et al., 2001). By 2 years of age, children have the cognitive, emotional, and behavioral capacities to display empathic concern for others in distress (Zahn-Waxler & Radke-Yarrow, 1990).

The emergence of empathy may correspond with the achievement of self-recognition. Bischof-Kohler (1991) found that infants, between 16 and 24 months of age, who could recognize themselves in a mirror, expressed empathy in an experimental play situation. Infants who did not pass the self-recognition test did not react with empathy-related behaviors. Zahn-Waxler and Radke-Yarrow (1990) observed expressions of empathic concern in 21-month-old infants. They responded to their mother's simulated sadness by looking into her face and making verbal inquires about what is wrong. These expressions were accompanied by looks of concern, hugs, consoling sounds, and statements of sympathy. During the second and third years, children acquire an emotional language through which they can interpret and articulate the distress of others (Hay et al., 1994).

The family environment provides the context for the development of empathic concern. Infants whose parents display affectionate and sensitive interactions are likely to express empathic concern for others. Infants and young children whose parents display extended depression may develop too much empathy that results in exaggerated feelings of responsibility. Later in life, these experiences can lead to preoccupation and over-involvement with the problems of others, or avoidance of others in distress as a defense mechanism (Zahn-Waxler & Radke-Yarrow, 1990).

INFANTS' UNDERSTANDING OF EMOTIONS

The development of empathy and sympathy or other emotions is related to the infant's understanding of their own emotions and those of others. There is no general agreement about when infants recognize their own emotions (Yarrow, 1979). Due to the neurological immaturity of the newborn and very young infant, it seems likely that external indicators (e.g., crying, facial expressions) of emotional expressions are not reliable indicators of the underlying emotional experience (Campos et al., 1983). For example, when a baby first smiles, it is not necessarily an expression of joy, as it is in an adult. After the first few weeks of life, the baby's emotional expressions more closely match the underlying emotional experiences.

When do infants begin to recognize the feelings of caregivers and other people? This question is important because it involves the infant's capacity to receive emotional signals. There are indications that infants show awareness of different facial expressions of emotions at approximately 2 months of age. Between 4 and 8 months of age, the baby begins to understand and interpret the emotional significance of various facial expressions. (Bornstein & Lamb, 1992; Michalson & Lewis, 1985). At this point, they begin to respond positively or negatively on the basis of emotions exhibited by other people (Campos et al., 1983). Infants, however, need visual cues to determine emotion. D'Entremont and Muir (1999) found that infants smiled more to a happy face and less to a sad face, but when the face was taken away, infants made no distinction between a happy and sad voice. They also discriminate joy from anger and neutral expressions, as well as surprise from happiness and sadness (Bertenthal & Campos, 1990).

The ability to interpret the emotions of others improves with age. Around 9 months of age, infants begin to look for emotional indicators in the faces, voices, and gestures of their caregivers to decide what to do in uncertain situations. The term **social referencing** is used to describe this tendency (Campos & Stenberg, 1981). For example, infants are more willing to explore a strange toy when the mother smiles than when her facial expressions show fear (Zarbatany & Lamb, 1985).

At about 18 months to 2 years of age, babies begin to comprehend verbal labels that adults use to describe emotional expressions. Michalson and Lewis (1985) found that most 2-year-olds they studied (80 percent) could point to pictures of happy and sad faces. Some of the infants (40 percent) correctly selected surprised and angry faces. The ability to produce these verbal labels ("What kind of face is this?") began to develop at 3 years. The first words infants use to correctly label corresponding facial expressions are "happy," "sad," and "angry" (Michalson & Lewis, 1985). The following incident illustrates the infant's growing recognition of emotions:

> Today, my husband Jack came home . . . in a really good mood. He came in, dancing around, and he kept picking me up and hugging me. Our daughter Jennie (18 months) came running out of the bedroom to see her daddy. When she saw us, she stopped dead in her tracks and started giggling and laughing and started saying, "Kiss, kiss." Then Jack put me down and she came up to us and said, "Me, me, kiss, kiss, love, love," and we gave her a hug. (Zahn-Waxler et al., 1984, p. 45)

Two- and three-year-old children also begin to associate emotional expressions with the situations that produced them (Michalson & Lewis, 1985). Bretherton and her colleagues (1980) found that the 28-month-old infants they studied made such cause-effect statements as "I cry [so] lady pick me up and hold me," and "Grandma angry [because] I write on wall." At this stage, infants have begun to understand that others have the same feelings as they do (Zahn-Waxler et al., 1984).

EMOTION REGULATION

The ability of an infant to regulate emotions is increasingly being viewed as a critical process in healthy emotional development. **Emotion regulation** involves the capacity of individuals to monitor and modify their emotional states and emotional reactions in order to accomplish their goals (R. Thompson, 1994). Self-regulation of emotions is a key to maintaining self-control, self-reliance, and self-esteem. One group of researchers found that young infants who demonstrated low levels of regulatory behavior were more likely to display noncompliant behavior as toddlers (Stifter, Spinrad, & Braungart-Ricker, 1999).

Infants move from heavily relying on adults to help them regulate emotions to more of a partnership with adults in emotional regulation during the preschool years. Eventually children must rely on their own resources to control their emotions (Denham, 1998). Currently researchers are studying how physiological processes, such as maturation of forebrain inhibitory centers, changes in the production of cortisol and other body chemicals, and vagal (heart rate control) processes affect the expression and control of emotions during the infancy period. Emotional regulation, however, develops within the context of the infant's interactions with other people. Thus, major emphasis is placed on how emotional communication between infants and their caregivers plays a critical role in the infant's self-regulatory abilities (Fox, 1998; Tronick, 1989).

During the first year of life, infants have limited abilities to control emotional states, so they are largely dependent upon adults to regulate their environment and emotional stimulation (Cole, Michel, & Teti, 1994; Denham, 1998). Gaze aversion, head turning, pushing away, and crying are some of the ways infants attempt to control overstimulating and unpleasant sensations. Around 6 months of age infants put their hands in their mouths or stare at what their hands are doing (e.g., exploring their clothing) as self-calming mechanisms (Toda & Fogel, 1993). Rocking, kicking, and other stereotypical body movements are additional self-calming mechanisms used by infants as they gain control over their body movements. Smiling behavior, vocalizations, and leaning toward the caregiver are some mechanisms infants use for eliciting stimulation and maintaining positive emotional states.

Young infants depend upon caregivers to respond to their signals for help in reducing negative emotional states or maintaining desirable emotions. The infant's crying or other emotional signals elicit emotions from the caregiver and influence (regulate) caregiver responses, which in turn influence the baby's emotions. This process is sometimes referred to as **mutual regulation** (Robinson & Glaves, 1996). For example, crying usually signals the need for help in regulating distress, while cooing sounds signal a pleasant emotional state the infant wishes to maintain. If the caregiver is emotionally available and responsive, the crying baby receives soothing touch and rocking; or providing time away from stimulation helps the infant reduce stress and restore emotional stability. The cooing baby receives reciprocal "coos" or other caregiver sounds needed to continue the desired feeling (Cole et al., 1994). Researchers found that infants whose mothers were responsive, stimulating, and visually attentive displayed more emotional control in a variety of situations than infants of mothers who were less sensitive and responsive (Crockenberg & Leerkes, 2000).

These early synchronous interactions are critical in helping the infant establish feelings of adequacy and control. As they become mobile, infants obtain information for regulatory assistance through social referencing. In uncertain situations infants look for cues from parents before they react. Verbal commands, facial expressions, touch, and gestures are parental signals that affect infant responses (Crockenberg & Leerkes, 2000). As infants mature, they become increasingly less dependent on caregivers for assistance in regulation of their emotions (Campos, Campos, & Barrett, 1989). However, infants with Down syndrome, maltreated infants, and infants of mothers with mood disorders are at risk for developing emotion regulation difficulties (Cicchetti, Ganiban, & Barnett, 1991).

ATTACHMENT

Attachment is not typically listed as a basic, discrete emotion because it is viewed as a special emotional relationship between the infant and caregiver (Sroufe, 1996). **Attachment** is defined as "a relatively enduring emotional tie to a specific other person" (Maccoby, 1980, p. 53). Infants display attachment by behaviors such as maintaining close physical contact with the other person, crying when that person leaves, and expressing joy when the person returns (Ainsworth, 1967). The quality of parent-infant attachment has a lasting influence on socioemotional development. The formation of attachment is a two-way process in which the parent becomes attached to the child (bonding) and the child becomes attached to the parent.

Early theories and research on attachment were largely devoted to mother-infant attachment. In recent years however, the importance of concurrent attachments between infants and other caregivers, including fathers, grandparents, or other family members, as well as child-care providers has been recognized. Bowlby (1969) believed that, at first, infants do not have the capacity to form more than one attachment bond. We now know that infants have the capacity to form multiple attachments (Levitt, 1991). Information is lacking about the relative strength and influence of various attachment relationships. It appears reasonable to expect that infants typically form a hierarchy of attachments, with some relationships being more important, at certain times, than others. In most families, the mother appears to be the most important attachment figure

Infant-to-Mother Attachment. The most widely used method of assessing infant-mother attachment is the Ainsworth Strange Situation (Ainsworth et al., 1978). This procedure is used in the study of infants 12 to 18+ months of age. An infant is observed during a series of eight episodes in an unfamiliar room with the mother and a stranger. The mother is present part of the time and absent part of the time. The episodes provide an opportunity for researchers to observe the infant's reunion with the mother after being under the stress that results from being alone with a strange person in a strange situation.

Using this procedure, Ainsworth and her associates (1978) initially identified three basic patterns of attachment in 12-month-old infants. The largest number of infants (66 percent) was classified as **securely attached.** These babies were able to use the mother as a secure base to explore the environment. They were interested in the objects in the room, did not cling to the mother, and interacted positively with the stranger. Although they were distressed when the mother left the room, they were easily comforted when the mother returned and soon resumed their play.

A second group of infants was rated as insecurely attached. Two patterns of this type of attachment were observed. A few of the infants (12 percent) were labeled as **avoidant.** They did not protest when separated from their mothers. When the mothers returned, the infants avoided or completely ignored them. Another group (22 percent of the infants) displayed an **ambivalent** or resistant pattern of attachment. These infants were very upset when their mothers left the room. Although they ran to their mothers when they were reunited, they demonstrated insecurity by a mixture of clinging and resistant (kicking and pushing away) behavior.

The attachment behaviors of some infants, however, do not fit well within any of the categories already identified. More recently, an additional type of insecure attachment has been identified. Some infants display behaviors that are labeled as **disorganized-disoriented** attachment. Behaviors observed in these infants during the Strange Situation include freezing all movement, approaching the parent with head averted, stereotypies such as rocking on hands and knees, screaming for the parent upon separation but moving silently away when the parent returns, or turning to greet the parent, and then falling on the floor (Main & Hesse, 1990). These infants' behaviors are viewed as indicating extreme internal conflict. Their mothers often have a history of early psychological trauma and loss in their own lives (Main, Kaplan, & Cassidy, 1985).

Much of the research on infant-mother attachment has been based on the theory of John Bowlby (1969), who identified four stages in the formation of attachment:

1. *Preattachment: Undiscriminating social responsiveness* (birth to 8–12 weeks). During this phase, infants do not typically differentiate one person from another and can be comforted by anyone.
2. *Beginnings of attachment: Discriminating social responsiveness* (3 to 6–8 months). The infant begins to recognize the primary caregiver and a few other familiar people. These preferred adults are usually able to soothe the baby and elicit social responses more quickly than strangers.
3. *Clear-cut attachment:* Maintaining proximity (6–8 months to about 3 years). Around the middle of the first year, infants are typically attached to one specific person. This person is usually the mother, although some infants prefer the father or other caregivers.
4. *Formation of a goal-corrected partnership* (3–4 years and on). This phase begins when children recognize that other people have needs and desires of their own and that the mother has to give priority to other activities at times.

Mother-to-Infant Attachment. The process by which a parent becomes attached to an infant is sometimes called **bonding** (Klaus & Kennell, 1982). In some cases, however, bonding is used more specifically to refer to the establishment of an enduring affectionate attachment of a mother to her infant as the result of skin-to-skin contact during the first few hours after birth (Campos et al., 1983).

The belief that the first few hours after birth represent a "sensitive period" for maternal-infant attachment originated in the study of animals. In some species, such as sheep and goats, the mother will reject her offspring if they are separated from her for a short period of time as soon as they are born. In recent years, researchers have attempted to determine whether or not the sensitive period hypothesis applies to human infants.

Some studies have reported increased frequencies of affectionate behaviors by mothers who were given extended early contact with their infants (Klaus & Kennell, 1976; Svejda, Pannabecker, & Emde, 1982). These studies, however, have been criticized for serious methodological problems as well as their failure to find any long-term effects (Lamb, 1982a). More carefully controlled studies (e.g., Svejda, Campos, & Emde, 1980) have failed to find evidence that early contact experiences are necessary for bonding to occur. Furthermore, in 80 percent of the world's cultures, mother and infant do not have immediate skin-to-skin contact, and nursing is not started until three days after birth (Super, 1981). Consequently, the belief that mothers will not love their infants adequately if extended skin-to-skin contact does not occur soon after birth seems to be unfounded.

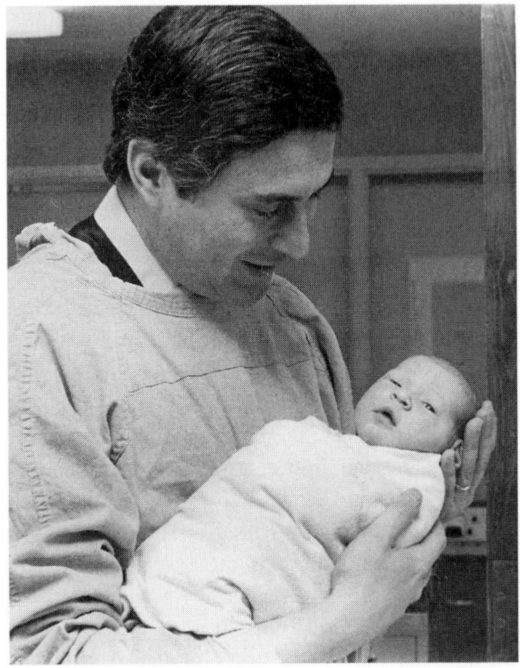

A father becomes as attached to an infant as the mother does.

Father-Infant Attachment. Research studies have shown that most babies become attached to both mother and father at about the same time—7 months (Lamb & Bornstein, 1987). Infants tend to have similar types of attachment to both parents (Pruett, 1998). Although infants spend less time interacting with their fathers than their mothers, they seek physical contact and comfort from both parents in about equal proportions (Baildum et al., 2000; Lamb, 1982c). Infants react to separations from their fathers in much the same way as they do their mothers in laboratory experiments and naturally occurring separations (Parke, 1996). However, infants apparently go through a period, between 12 and 18 months, when they turn to their mothers more than their fathers in stressful situations. The preference for the mother when under stress disappears around 24 months of age (Lamb, 1982c). It appears that attachment to father supports different skills than attachment to mothers. Kazura (2000) found that secure attachment with fathers facilitated play skills while secure attachments with mothers was associated with social interaction skills. Thus, both relationships are important for supporting development.

Fathers become just as attached to infants as mothers. Studies (Parke & O'Leary, 1976; Parke & Sawin, 1977) have found fathers to be as interested as mothers in their infants during the newborn period. Fathers tend to be as nurturing and stimulating with their infants as mothers. Like mothers, fathers touch, talk to, look at, and kiss their newborns. Fathers have been found to be equally anxious as mothers about leaving their infants in the care of someone else (Pruett, 1998). They are competent caregivers and are responsive to infant distress such as spitting up (Belsky & Volling, 1987).

Importance of Infant-Caregiver Attachment. The formation of attachments is considered to be one of the most important processes of infant development. Bowlby (1969) used a metaphor called an **internal working model** to describe the influence of attachment on human behavior. The concept of an internal working model refers to understandings and expectations about oneself and other people in the world that serve as a script or a guide for interpersonal relationships. The infant's internal working model develops out of patterns of interactions and attachment relationships with primary caregivers (Bretherton, 1996). Over time, an individual forms and revises the internal working model in response to cognitive changes and new experiences in caregiving. These models determine how infants interpret and anticipate the interpersonal responses from others, what cues they select, and how they respond. Theoretically, infants who have formed secure attachments perceive and respond to people and events very differently from infants whose attachments are insecure.

The importance of attachments is also described in terms of the availability of a **secure base** (Ainsworth et al., 1978). With the mother, or other attachment figure, available as a base of support, an infant moves away to explore the environment. When frightening or disturbing stimuli are encountered, the infant returns to the mother as a safe haven. Securely attached infants are more likely to use this strategy to learn from the environment. On the other hand, insecurely attached infants are more reluctant to venture from their base of support into strange places. Therefore, these infants have fewer opportunities for learning and establishing feelings of mastery and control over the environment. Even securely attached infants return to their attachment figures from time to time for emotional "refueling."

The security of early attachment establishes the foundation for future behavior (Laible & Thompson, 2000; Thompson, 1999b). Researchers have found that infants who were securely attached to their mothers as toddlers were likely to become kindergarteners who demonstrated emotional stability and expression in situationally appropriate ways; insecurely attached toddlers were more likely to overcontrol impulses and emotions as kindergarteners (Easterbrooks & Goldberg, 1990; Kochanska , 2001). Infants who were securely attached to their mothers and fathers tended to exhibit higher levels of social competency and more positive peer relations as they grew up than insecurely attached infants (Ladd & Le Sieur, 1995; Schneider, Atkinson, & Tardif, 2001). Longitudinal studies indicate that the type of attachment security established in infancy tends to persist into adulthood. However, no one claims that attachment security established during infancy cannot be changed as the result of later experiences (Waters, Hamilton, & Weinfield, 2000).

Influences on Attachment.

Caregiver-Infant Interactions. The characteristics of the infant's interactions with the primary caregiver (usually the mother) are probably the most important factor in the attachment process. Caregiver behaviors associated with secure attachment include acceptance, warmth and affection, accessibility, responsiveness, and cooperation with the infant (Maccoby, 1980). Mothers of securely attached infants have been found to be more accepting, sensitive, emotionally expressive, and responsive to needs than mothers of insecurely attached infants (Rosen & Rothbaum, 1993: Ziv et al., 2000). On the other hand, mothers of insecurely attached infants have demonstrated behaviors such as inconsistent care, parental intrusiveness, overstimulation, insensitivity, and negligence. Isabella and Belsky (1991) found that securely attached infant-mother relationships were characterized by a predominance of synchronous interactions. As expected, insecure infant-mother relationships were associated with a disproportionate number of behaviors that were uncoordinated or asynchronous. Interactional synchrony will be further discussed later in this chapter.

Parental Depression. Infants of depressed parents are likely to experience interactions that lead to insecure attachments. A higher proportion of insecure attachments are found in children of parents who suffer major depression than among other groups of children (Cummings & Cicchetti, 1990). Psychological unavailability of parents has been linked with insecure attachments in infants. Depression contributes to attachment problems by interfering with parental responsiveness and availability, and disrupting interactional synchrony. Tronick (1989) found that depressed mothers tend to look away from their infants more, display more anger, are more intrusive, and display less warmth and affection than other mothers. Infants of depressed mothers express more negative affect and more avoidant behavior in mother-infant interactions than infants of mothers who are not depressed (Crockenberg & Leerkes, 2000).

Contact Comfort. Harlow's studies of infant monkeys reared in isolation from their mothers may offer some clues about the formation of attachment bonds (Harlow & Zimmerman, 1959). The monkeys were reared in a cage with two artificial mothers. One of the mothers was made of wire mesh, and the other consisted of wire mesh covered with terry cloth. The monkeys invariably became attached only to the terry cloth mother, even when the plain mother held the nursing bottle. Harlow concluded that contact comfort is an important variable in the formation of attachment. Recent research with low birth weight babies indicates that the type, rather than the amount, of touch is the most important factor. Apparently a gentle, nurturing type of touch is the kind that best facilitates attachment (Weiss et al., 2000).

Temperament. The temperament of the infant may be an important influence on the way attachment develops. Theoretically, the infant's temperament affects the quality of the parent-infant interaction, which subsequently determines the quality of attachment. For example, infants who are ambivalently attached tend to have characteristics of temperament (e.g., irritability, crying) that fit the difficult child classification (see Chapter 10) (Miyake, Chen, & Campos, 1985). The interaction between the caregiver's sensitivity and the infant's temperament play important roles in the attachment process (Goldsmith & Alansky, 1987). However, researchers have not been able to confirm a strong relationship among all aspects of temperament and attachment behavior (Bretherton & Waters, 1985). It is important to note that temperament alone does not determine attachment relationships. The relationship between temperament and attachment is extremely complex.

Multiple Caregiving. In many societies, infants are exposed to a variety of caregivers. Does an infant suffer emotional harm as the result of having to develop emotional ties with several different people? Evidence from infants reared in the Israeli kibbutzim is relevant to this question. A kibbutz is an agricultural settlement where infants are, to a large extent, reared outside the home. Their time is spent largely in "infant houses" under the care of professional caregivers called metaplot (singular: metapelet). The parents, however, are accessible and frequently spend time with their infants, usually sleeping with them at night. Researchers have found that kibbutzim-reared infants demonstrate normal patterns of attachment and emotional development (Super, 1981). In comparison to American infants cared for at home, kibbutz infants demonstrate no significant differences in attachment to their mothers (Maccoby & Feldman, 1972). However, among kibbutzim-reared infants, those who slept away from their mothers were more likely to develop insecure attachments (Crockenberg & Leerkes, 2000).

The Efe (pygmies) people of the Northeastern Zaire represent another society in which infants are exposed to multiple caregiving (Morelli & Tronick, 1991). The Efe are a seminomadic people who hunt and forage for food and physical necessities. Although the basic social unit is the nuclear family, caregiving by individuals other than the mother is a cultural practice. Immediately after birth the infant is passed around among the other women present so that a mother's first contact does not occur until several hours after birth. Infants are sometimes nursed by another lactating woman. The mother may leave the baby in the camp with other individuals when she leaves to gather food. Infants are also often taken care of by other people even when the mother is in camp. Morelli and Tronick (1991) observed that the number of different people caring for an infant during the first 18 weeks of life average approximately 14. Observations of infant behaviors around 1 year of age indicate they have no problem developing primary attachments to their mothers in the context of multiple caregiving practices. American parents worry about the disruption of attachment when placing an infant in a child day-care center. The effects of nonparental care on attachment will be discussed further in Chapter 13.

Culture. Cultural variations have also been noted in research examining patterns of attachment. Secure attachments seem to be the most common pattern in most cultures within the United States, but other types of attachment are more prevalent in cultures around the world (Harwood, Miller, & Irizarry, 1995). For example, avoidant attachment has been observed more frequently in western European samples, and ambivalent attachment has been observed more frequently in Israel and Japan. There have also been regional and socioeconomic differences noted within a country (Bretherton & Waters, 1985; van IJzendoorn & Kroonenberg, 1988). Does this mean that American parents are better at supporting the development of a secure attachment relationship? Not necessarily. The differences observed may be the result of the Strange Situation as a test of attachment and the types of behaviors that various cultures encourage among infants (DeVries, 1984; Harwood, Miller, & Irizarry, 1995; Hinde, 1982). For example, German parents are more likely to encourage independent behavior, which may account for the higher incidence of avoidant attachment. Zach and Keller (1999) found that while physical touch is related to play in U.S. samples, it was not for German infants. For German infants, the best predictor of exploration was a decrease in visual contact. As Hinde (1982) noted "there is no best mothering style, for different styles are better in different circumstances. . . . Optimal mothering behavior will differ according to the mother's social status, caregiving contributions from other family members, the state of physical resources, and so on. . . . a mother-child relationship which produces successful adults in one situation may not do so in another" (pp. 71–72).

INTERACTIONAL SYNCHRONY

In order for caregiver-infant relationships to function in ways that promote optimum attachment and emotional development of infants, the interactions must represent a goodness-of-fit between the behavior of the infant and the behavior of the caregiver. Both baby and caregiver contribute to the interactions and are responsive to each other (Van-Egeren, Barratt, & Roach, 2001). Successful relationships are characterized by a predominance of **interactional synchrony.** This term is used to refer to behavioral exchanges between caregiver and infant that are reciprocal, harmonious, and mutually rewarding (Isabella & Belsky, 1991; Rochat, 2001).

Synchronous relationships are characterized by contingency and entrainment (Brazelton & Cramer, 1990). **Contingency** means the behavior of one partner in the relationship is dependent upon the behavior of the other partner. For example, if the baby smiles in response to a caregiver's "peekaboo," the game will continue. If the baby's expression does not change, the caregiver will turn away or try something else. Research suggests that infants detect and respond differently to caregivers based on whether their interactions are contingent or not (Nadel et al., 1999). The term **entrainment** is used to describe the momentum of the interactional sequences. Once a synchronous turn-taking interaction is established, it moves and flows with each partner adding to the momentum until a peak of intensity is reached. The process is sometimes described as a "dance" between the caregiver and the infant.

The first step in establishing a synchronous relationship requires caregivers to adapt their behavior to fit the rhythms of the baby. Initially babies are also dependent upon adults to assume a leadership role in initiating interactions. As they get older, infants assume more initiative and become more active participants in the interactions. An example of a synchronous interaction is seen in the following sequence: The mother smiles and the baby smiles back. After two or three interchanges of smiles that increase in expressiveness, the mother or the baby may add cooing sounds to the interchange. The partner responds with a matching vocalization. After a few such interchanges, the baby looks away to end the sequence (Brazelton & Cramer, 1990).

Infant-caregiver behaviors can quickly become **asynchronous.** This term refers to interactions, or co-occurrences of behaviors, that are not reciprocal and mutual (Isabella & Belsky, 1991). Asynchronous interactions occur when behavior becomes one-sided, unresponsive, or overly intrusive. For example, the infant becomes sleepy and closes its eyes. The caregiver jiggles and talks to the baby to keep it awake. The infant becomes agitated and starts fussing or crying. The caregiver then tries to feed the baby who rejects the nipple. The caregiver then puts the baby, who is now wide awake, to bed.

MENTAL HEALTH AND EMOTIONAL DISORDERS

We don't usually think of babies as having mental health problems. Until recent years relatively few emotional disorders of infants were specified in the professional literature. During the past 20 years, however, knowledge about infant mental health has mushroomed. The Zero to Three/National Center for Clinical Infant Programs (1994) has published *Diagnostic Classification: 0-3,* a manual for use by clinicians and other professionals in identifying mental health and developmental disorders in the early years of life. The manual identifies approximately 29 general diagnostic categories under which a variety of specific disorders are described.

Understanding the quality of the parent-infant relationship is an important part of diagnosing and treating emotional, behavioral, and other disorders of infants and children. When infants have mental-health problems, relationships with primary caregivers may be part of the problem. Significant relationship difficulties are characterized by negative attitudes, perceptions, emotions, and behaviors of either the parent, the child, or both that lead to disturbed parent-child interactions (Zero to Three, 1994). A **Parent-Infant Relationship Global Assessment Scale (PIR-GAS)** (Zero to Three, 1994) is available for use by clinicians and researchers in assessing the strengths of relationships, as well as the severity of a relationship disorder. Parent-infant (or other caregiver) relationship problems range from less than optimal interaction patterns (perturbed) that last for a short period of time, to grossly impaired interactions that are so dangerously disorganized and so disturbed that the infant is in danger of physical harm.

The behavioral quality of the interaction, the affective tone, and the level of psychological involvement are used in deciding whether or not there is a relationship disorder. Along with the PIR-GAS, a classification manual is available for use in diagnosing and classifying a variety of relationship disorders. For example, relationships characterized by physical and/or psychological intrusiveness, interference with infant goals, overcontrol, and developmentally inappropriate demands by the parent are classified as **overinvolved parenting.** At the other extreme, relationships in which parents are unresponsive and insensitive to infant cues and provide low quality of care are classified as **underinvolved parenting.** Other relationship disorders include those classified as anxious/tense, angry/hostile, and abusive.

A potential result of parent-infant relationship problems is the development of an attachment disorder. Children who are exposed to abusive environments or unstable living conditions, such as foster care, have been shown to display disturbances in attachments (Albus & Dozier, 1999; Ward, Lee, & Lipper, 2000). Research on Romanian children who were institutionalized but later adopted in the United Kingdom found a relationship between early deprivation and attachment disorder behaviors (O'Conner, Bredenkamp, & Rutter, 1999).

Psychologists and psychiatrists are increasingly attributing a variety of problems displayed by older children and adults to **disorders of attachment.** These problems include aggressive, disruptive behaviors, or the inability to form and maintain close relationships later in life (Chinitz, 1995; L. Smith, 1996). Reactive attachment disorder is characterized by a pervasive disturbance of relationships that occurs before age 5. There are two types: inhibited and disinhibited (Greenberg, 1999). In the inhibited subtype, children are hypervigilant and withdrawn. The disinhibited subtype is characterized by indiscriminate friendliness and absence of selective attachment. It has

APPLICATIONS: FACILITATING EMOTIONAL DEVELOPMENT

Parents cannot control all the factors that influence an infant's emotional development. However, there are numerous practices and activities that parents as well as other caregivers can use to promote healthy emotional development. In general, the most important thing to give the infant is a feeling of being cared for and loved. The same caregivers should be consistently available to play and interact with the baby. The following are some recommended principles and practices:

- "Woo" the baby. Fall in love with the baby and allow it to fall in love with you. Set aside time for loving and pleasant interchanges, including rocking, hugging, cuddling, smiling, touching, eye contact, talking, and singing.
- Carefully observe and interpret the baby's cues and signals for attention and distress. Provide prompt, tuned-in responsiveness to the baby's need for play, comfort, or "time-out" (Greenspan & Greenspan, 1985; Honig, 1993).
- Reassure distressed infants with caresses, calming voice tones, and facial expressions. Massage or gently rock tense, crabby babies to induce body relaxation and reduce tension (Honig, 1993).
- Accept an infant's feelings as real and valid even if the behavior is not acceptable. For example, say, "I can't allow you to hit me, but I understand that you are angry with me right now" (Gonzalez-Mena & Eyer, 1980).
- Express your own emotions honestly but appropriately. Infants benefit from being exposed to a wide range of emotions (Greenspan & Greenspan, 1985).
- Help infants identify and label their feelings through reflective listening. ("You feel sad because Mommy has gone to work." "Look at your brother smile. He looks happy!")
- Help toddlers find appropriate and alternative ways to express emotional intentions, such as "Show me what you want without crying" (Greenspan & Greenspan, 1985).
- Permit the toddler to use a stuffed animal, blanket, or other "security" object to ease the transition from parental dependency to personal independence. This is not a problem as long as it does not represent a deficit in parental attention.
- Insofar as possible and appropriate, control the stimuli that evoke negative feelings such as anger and fear (e.g., a night light can be provided for the infant who is afraid of the dark). However, infants should not be overprotected.
- Never use fear and guilt to control an infant's behavior. Avoid statements such as "There is a ghost in that closet that will come out and get you if you don't stop crying!"
- Provide everyday experiences that are predictable and reassuring (e.g., bathing and naptime) so that the baby gets a secure sense of what to expect and in what sequence (Honig, 1993).
- Child-care facilities should arrange for each caregiver to have responsibility for the same infants each day and move with them when they change age groups or rooms.
- Additional suggestions may be found in other sources (e.g., Bromwich, 1980; Butterfield, 1996; Emde, 1996; Fenichel, 1996; Gonzalez-Mena & Eyer, 1997; Grasselli and Hegner, 1980; Greenspan & Greenspan, 1985; Honig, 1993; Karnes, 1982; Ramey & Ramey, 1999, Sparling and Lewis, 1979; Weiser, 1982; B. White, 1985.).

been proposed that a more useful way to think of attachment would be to classify disorders of attachment as nonattachment, disorders of attachment, and disruption of attachments (Lieberman & Zeanah, 1995). Researchers have yet to validate such classifications or to verify any connection between attachment problems and extreme behavioral problems later in life.

SUMMARY

Definitions

- Emotions are generally viewed as complex, subjective experiences that are influenced by a combination of biological and social forces. Affect refers to the subjective feeling component and expressive component of emotion.

Theories of Emotional Development

- The various theories of emotional development include biological, socialization, interactionist, and dynamic systems perspectives.

Influences on Emotional Development

- The infant's physiology, temperament, socialization, culture, and cognitive sophistication are included among the factors that affect emotional responses.

The Emergence of Emotions

- Even though the emotional life of the newborn infant is limited, infants begin to exhibit many of the basic emotions within the first six to nine months of life (e.g., disgust, sadness, surprise, joy, anger, fear). Most emotions have emerged by 3 years of age.

Infants' Understanding of Emotions

- Infants begin to use social referencing around 9 months of age as they look for emotional expressions of other people to guide their own behavior. The ability to interpret, label, and comprehend emotions improves with age.

Emotion Regulation

- The ability of infants to monitor and modify their emotional states and emotional reactions in order to accomplish their goals is a critical process in healthy emotional development.
- During the first year of life, infants have limited abilities to control emotional states so they are largely dependent upon adults to regulate their environment and emotional stimulation. As infants mature, they become increasingly capable of regulating their emotions without assistance.

Attachment

- Basic patterns of infant-mother attachment include securely attached, avoidant, ambivalent, and disorganized-disoriented. Infants become equally attached to both fathers and mothers when given appropriate opportunities.
- The formation of attachment is one of the most important processes of infant development because it affects the formation of one's internal working model or view of the world and relationships with people. The importance of attachments is also described in terms of the availability of a secure base for exploring the environment.
- Influences on attachment relationships include caregiver-infant interactions, parental depression, contact comfort (touch), temperament, multiple caregiving, and culture.

Interactional Synchrony

- Both baby and caregiver contribute to interactions and are responsive to each other. Successful relationships are characterized by a predominance of interactional synchrony, that is, behavioral exchanges between caregiver and infant that are harmonious and mutually rewarding. Synchronous relationships are also characterized by contingency and entrainment. Infant-caregiver behaviors can quickly become asynchronous and not mutually rewarding

Mental Health and Emotional Disorders

- A manual for use by clinicians and other professionals in identifying mental-health problems covers approximately 29 general diagnostic categories under which a variety of specific disorders of infants are described.
- A Parent-Infant Relationship Global Assessment Scale (PIR-GAS) is available for use by clinicians and researchers in assessing the strengths of relationships, as well as the severity of a relationship disorder.
- Psychologists and psychiatrists are increasingly attributing a variety of problems displayed by older children and adults, including aggressive and disruptive behaviors, to disorders of attachment. However, there is disagreement among mental-health specialists about the use of attachment disorder as a diagnostic category.

KEY TERMS

emotion
affect
socialization of emotions
stranger anxiety
separation anxiety
empathy
sympathy
empathic concern
social referencing
emotion regulation
mutual regulation
attachment
securely attached
avoidant attachment
ambivalent attachment
disorganized-disoriented attachment
bonding
internal working model
secure base
interactional synchrony
contingency
entrainment
asynchronous interactions
Parent-Infant Relationship Global Assessment Scale (PIR-GAS)
overinvolved parenting
underinvolved parenting
disorders of attachment

INFORMATION ON THE WEB*

www.babyparenting.tqn.com/library/AmerBaby/blamericanbaby1.htm This Web site, sponsored by *American Baby* magazine, provides information on a variety of issues related to emotional development, including attachment and bonding.

www.dir2.nichd.nih.gov/nichd/ssed/infant.html The National Institutes of Health operates this Web site, "Section on Social and Emotional Development." It provides information about ongoing research studies and a list of articles on social and emotional development of infants and children.

*Web sites are subject to change.

THIRTEEN

INFANT CAREGIVING AND EDUCATION

Your children are not your children
They are the sons and daughters of Life's longing for itself.
They come through you but not from you,
And though they are with you yet they belong not to you . . .
You are the bows from which your children as living arrows are sent forth . . .
Let your bending in the archer's hand be for gladness.

—Kahlil Gibran

Most infants experience the world and the people in it within the setting of a family. Society assigns primary responsibility for the care of the young to the family. The infant must receive a certain amount of personal care and nurturing for healthy growth and development to occur. The crucial nature of those family experiences for every aspect of infant development cannot be overstated. But the influence is mutual. Infants interact with their caregivers from the beginning. In those interactions, infants influence parents and others just as they are influenced. Infants give as they receive.

In this chapter we consider some of the changes occurring in the American family that have implications for infant development, such as single parenting and maternal employment. A major portion of the chapter is devoted to the experiences infants have in nonparental care outside the home. We also look at various types of early-intervention programs designed to enhance the development of infants from impoverished families. In addition, we consider the characteristics of a favorable home environment, including the processes of parent-infant interaction, discipline, and the provision of appropriate toys and play materials.

FAMILY SYSTEMS PERSPECTIVES

We have long recognized that "the parent-child relationship is unique among human ties" (Maccoby & Martin, 1983, p. 1). More recently, we have begun to appreciate and try to understand the complexity of that relationship within a **family systems** model. According to this perspective, all family members and their behaviors are interconnected. Everything that happens to one family member potentially has an impact on everyone else in the family (Olson & DeFrain, 1994). Family relationships are described in terms of subsystems (husband-wife, parent-child, siblings), family cohesion (togetherness), and flexibility (ability to change). While much of the earlier research focused on how parents influence infants, we now recognize that parents are influenced by infants, and that parent-child relationships are influenced by mother-father and other relationships within the family. Parents and infants are also influenced by their relations with people in the larger sociocultural network. Thus, the outcomes of parenting must be viewed as the result of complex interactions between numerous sources of influence.

CURRENT TRENDS IN THE AMERICAN FAMILY

The form and structure of the American family have changed dramatically in recent decades. A diversity of family forms is emerging to replace the traditional family form made up of the breadwinner father and the homemaker mother. Current variations include dual-worker families, single-parent families, and blended or step families. Increasing divorce rates, the movement of women into the labor force, increased rates of teenage pregnancy, decreasing family size, and numerous other social changes through the years have contributed to the transformation. Changes that have significant implications for infant development are the increases in the number of single-parent families and the number of working mothers.

Single-Parent Families. The increase in the number of **single-parent families** during the past two decades has been dramatic. The proportion of single-parent families in the United States increased from 13 percent of all family groups with children younger than 18 in 1970 to 31 percent in 2000 (U.S. Census Bureau, 2001). This represents more than a 50 percent increase in the single-parent population between 1970 and 2000. Of the 31 percent of single-parent families, 26 percent are headed by women and the remaining 5 percent are headed by men. Those households headed by single women were more likely to include more than one child than those maintained by men. An important trend for female-headed households is the increase in women who have never been married. Divorced women are more likely to have higher levels of education and income than women who have never been married. White women are more likely to be divorced (50 percent) than have a child out of wedlock (30 percent), whereas black women are more likely to have a child out of wedlock (65 percent) than be divorced (17 percent).

The rise in the number of single-parent households can be attributed mainly to increases in rates of divorce and separation (U.S. Bureau of the Census, 1995). Also, the likelihood of a remarriage after divorce has declined while there has been an increase in the average number of years between divorce and remarriage (Taeuber, 1996).

Impact of Single-Parent Families. Does it make any difference whether an infant grows up in a single-parent family or a two-parent family? It is not easy to answer that question because single-parent families vary widely. For example, a family headed by a 16-year-old mother of an unplanned infant represents a different family unit than that of a 30-year-old single mother of an adopted infant. To some extent, a single-parent family may represent a transition from one family form to another. While a large number of families may be classified as single-parent households at some point, this designation may be of short duration because of marriage or remarriage (T. Roberts, 1994). However, many single-parent families share similar problems, including financial instability, inadequate alternative child care, and a high level of stress. The extent to which these and other adverse conditions exist is likely to determine the degree to which infant development is negatively affected by being reared by a single parent. In many instances, single parents have a support network of family members, neighbors, and friends who supplement the caregiving process.

Eiduson and colleagues (1982) compared infants who were reared from birth in single-mother families with infants reared in traditional two-parent families and alternative families (communal and unmarried social-contract families). A variety of psychological variables, including attachment, cognitive functioning, and social adjustment, were assessed repeatedly during the infant's first three years. No significant differences between the single-mother infants and infants reared in the other families were discovered. There is little additional research that directly addresses the impact of the single-parent family on infants. Consequently, studies dealing with the effects of divorce, stress, and father absence on children must be examined for additional information on this issue.

Effects of Divorce. Because of their cognitive immaturity, very young infants are expected to be less affected by some of the trauma caused by

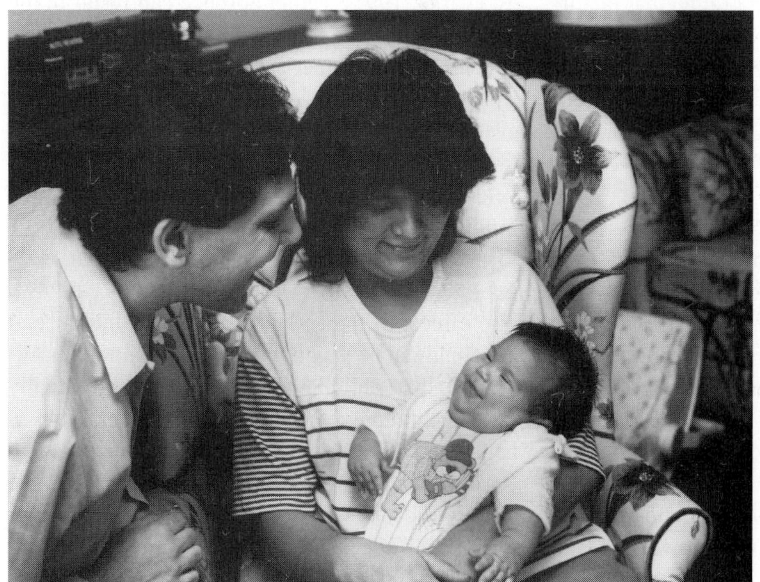

The number of infants who are reared in two-parent families has declined.

divorce. However, their immaturity and greater dependency needs may actually make them developmentally more vulnerable to the effects of divorce in some ways. Few studies have isolated the effects of divorce that takes place when the children are infants. Santrock (1970, 1972) assessed the effects of divorce on children who were under age 2 when the divorce occurred. These children displayed less basic trust, more guilt and shame, less industry, and more feelings of inferiority as they grew older. Other researchers found that children of parents who divorced early displayed behavior problems at preschool-age (Shaw, Winslow, & Flanagan, 1999).

When divorce occurs during infancy, there may also be negative effects upon intellectual development and achievements later in life. Studies on preschool-age children show that boys may be slightly more vulnerable to the effects of divorce on social adjustment than girls (Amato & Keith, 1991). Some studies indicate that younger children are considerably less burdened by divorce than older children (Guttmann, 1993).The extent to which divorce has negative consequences for the development of infants and young children is likely to be determined by the level of parental conflict and stress, the support system, and adequacy of parenting prior to and following the divorce. One group of researchers found that factors such as the mother's income, education, ethnicity, child-rearing beliefs, and depressive symptoms tended to be better predictors of adjustment problems than the divorce alone (Clarke-Stewart, Vandell, & McCartney et al., 2000).

Effects of Stress. Single parents experience far greater levels of tension, stress, and conflict in coping with the practical problems of living than parents in intact families. This is particularly true when infants are involved. Some of the most prevalent stresses include economic problems, finding adequate child care, and simply having time and energy to devote to children (Hetherington, 1979).

Wallerstein and Kelly (1980) found that the stress and conflict that accompany divorce result in a **diminished parenting effect** whereby the parents' ability to maintain interaction and communication with their children is lessened. These findings are consistent with the results of other studies. In a laboratory setting, parents were more critical and irritable with their toddlers when they were mildly stressed while performing a task than when the parents were not preoccupied (Zussman, 1980). Hetherington, Cox, and Cox (1982) found that during the first year after divorce, mothers tend to decrease their responsiveness and affection to their children.

The most important factor in the ability of single-parent families to cope with stress appears to be the support system available in the extended family network and in society. For example, Belsky (1999a) found that parent-child attachment relationships were affected by social support satisfaction, the number of people to provide support, and work-family support-interference. When adequate economic resources, assistance with child care, housing, and the emotional support of a kinship and social network are available, the potential stresses and problems faced by single-parent families are dramatically reduced (Hetherington, 1979).

Effects of Father Absence. A father may be absent from the home because of death, divorce, desertion, working arrangements, or lack of interest (Parke, 1995). Father absence can result in the loss of economic, parental, and community resources (McClanahan & Teitler, 1999). The quality and the degree of the father's involvement, even in the first year of life, are important factors in the child's sex role, personality, and mental development (Biller, 1981). Studies show that male infants whose fathers are absent tend to score lower on tests of cognitive performance than male infants whose fathers are consistently available. The effects of fathers' absence on the intellectual development of daughters apparently do not occur until later in childhood (Parke, 1995). Eventually the educational achievement of boys and girls is negatively affected (McClanahan & Teitler, 1999)

Apparently father absence does more damage when it occurs during infancy than at later ages (Lamb, 1976). Wachs and Gruen (1982) concluded that boys raised without fathers may have problems establishing appropriate sex-role behavior, such as a tendency to be less masculine or to display an exaggerated masculinity. The effects are particularly noticeable if the separation occurred before 5 years of age. Sex-role development of girls is also negatively affected by father absence, but the effects are not usually observed until adolescence.

Santrock (1970) found that fifth-grade boys who experienced father absence before the age of 2 had more personality problems than boys who lost their fathers at a later age. The boys who experienced father absence during infancy were less trusting, less industrious, and exhibited more feelings of inferiority than boys who were without fathers between 3 and 5 years of age. A study conducted on the Caribbean island of Barbados revealed that school-age males had same-sex identification problems if their father had been absent during the first two years of life (R. Burton, 1972). Other studies have found early father absence to be associated with increased susceptibility to a variety of behavioral and psychological problems (Biller, 1981).

Maternal Employment. The percentage of working mothers in the United States with children under 3 years of age has risen steadily during the past three decades from 33 percent in 1975 to 60.7 percent in 1999 (U.S. Census Bureau, 2000; U.S. Department of Labor, 2000). The labor force participation rate of mothers with an infant under 1 year of age is a little lower (55 percent in the year 2000) (U.S. Census Bureau, 2001). The increase in the number of working mothers has been fueled by a variety of social and economic forces, including changes in gender roles, family values, and increases in the cost of living.

Effects of Maternal Employment. The dramatic increase in maternal employment has generated questions and concerns about how it will affect the development of infants and young children. Many research studies have been conducted on this issue with conflicting results. Some studies report negative effects of maternal employment on infants' cognitive development, on language development of boys (Chase-Lansdale, Michael, & Desai, 1991), and on child-maternal attachment (Barglow, Vaughn, & Molitor, 1987; Benn, 1986; Lamb, 1982b). Other studies report no effects on cognitive development, social competence, behavioral adjustment (Gottfried, 1991; Hock, 1980; Zimmerman & Bernstein, 1983), or child-maternal attachment (Easterbrooks & Goldberg, 1985; Stifter, Coulehan, & Fish, 1993; Weinraub, Jaeger, & Hoffman, 1990).

Researchers have also reported that maternal employment does not adversely affect the mental and motor development of relatively healthy preterm infants at 18 months of age (Youngblut, Loveland-Cherry, & Horan, 1994). Positive effects of maternal employment during the child's first three years have been associated with second-grade reading achievement of children from low-income families (Vandell & Ramanan, 1992). A recent long-term study (Gottfried et al., 1999) has found no relationship between maternal employment and child development.

The contradictory results of research studies on the effects of maternal employment on infant development are not surprising in view of the complexities involved in studying this issue. When comparisons are made between the developmental characteristics of infants being reared by employed mothers versus infants of unemployed mothers, there are numerous environmental and attitudinal factors that can make a difference in the outcomes. Maternal employment status affects infant development only to the extent that it alters family interrelationships and the home environment (Gottfried, 1991; L. Hoffman, 1989). For example, job-related unhappiness and stress may have a "spillover" effect whereby the mother is less nurturing with an infant.

Maternal employment status is less likely to have a negative impact on infant development if the mother has a choice about working (Youngblut et al., 1994), is satisfied with her job and work role, has a satisfactory child-care arrangement, and does not experience separation anxiety when leaving her infant in alternative child care (Lamb, 1982b; Weinraub et al., 1990; Zaslow, Rabinovich, & Sualsky, 1991). Of these variables, researchers have devoted most of their attention to how nonparental child care affects infant development.

Child-Care Arrangements. Working parents choose from a variety of options when making a child-care arrangement. Their choices are influenced by a variety of factors, including cost/affordability, convenience, age of the child, and availability. Approximately 27 percent of children of families in the United States younger than 3 years are cared for by a parent (while at work or by the other parent). Another 27 percent are cared for by a relative. Smaller proportions of young children are found in day care centers (22 percent) and the homes of non-relative family child-care providers (17 percent) (Capizzano, Adams, & Sorenstein, 2001). Although fewer infants are enrolled in day-care centers, this is the fastest-growing type of day care offered to the general public.

Effects of Infant Day Care. Questions and concerns about possible negative effects of nonmaternal care on infants have generated numerous research studies during the past three decades. The earliest studies, conducted in the late 1960s and early 1970s, were limited mostly to high-quality day-care centers designed specifically for research purposes. Since that time additional studies have emerged that are more representative of the type and quality of care available to and utilized by the general public. In addition, more recent studies have taken into consideration a more complex set of variables, including child-care quality, family characteristics, and child-rearing attitudes. In spite of the problems and limitations of the studies, there are a number of consistent findings on how day care affects various aspects of infant development.

Physical Development. In general, day care has not been perceived as a threat to normal physical growth, so very little research has been done in this area. The limited research available indicates that infants from poor families who participate in good-quality day care experience positive gains in height, weight, and motor performance. The physical growth of infants from middle-class families apparently is not affected by day care (Clarke-Stewart & Fein, 1983).

Health. Infants who attend any type of day care with more than three other infants can be expected to be sick more frequently than infants who do not participate in day care. They have more incidents of colds, flu, and other respiratory illnesses than infants who stay at home (Kendall, 1983; Strangert, 1976). In addition, type B influenzae, hepatitis A, and diarrhea are some of the most common and persistent health problems that are associated with day care. Young infants are more susceptible to more frequent and severe

Group day care is a common experience for infants from many contemporary families.

infections due to immune system immaturity, incomplete immunization, and increased exposure (Link, Kernested, & Ford-Jones, 1993). The transmission of diarrhea and hepatitis is usually the result of the breakdown of proper sanitation practices, such as hand washing after diaper changes (Snow, 1983; Trump & Karasic, 1983).

Safety. Studies on the magnitude of accidental injuries to infants and children who participate in out-of-home care are limited mainly to day-care centers. Child-care injury rates for infants are usually not distinguished from rates for older children. Although rates of injuries requiring medical treatment vary widely from study to study, injury rates of children in day care compare favorably with rates of children injured at home or elsewhere. On the basis of existing studies it has been estimated that 33 to 48 percent fewer serious injuries take place in day-care centers than at home or in other places (Snow et al., 1992).

Social Development. The results of studies that have assessed the effects of day care on social development have produced a mixed picture. While some studies have found no differences between home-reared and day-care subjects, others suggest that day care can have both positive and negative effects on social behavior. Some researchers report that children who were enrolled in day care as infants have a tendency to display more aggression and other negative interactions with peers, and are less obedient than children who did not participate in day care (Belsky, 1988, 1999b). Other researchers have found that children who participated in day care as infants were no more aggressive than peers who received care at home (Lamb, 1998).

On the positive side, day-care children have been found to exhibit more social competence in interacting with peers and adults (Snow, 1983). More positive behaviors are noted when the day-care quality is high and caregivers are responsive to the children's needs (Elicker, Fortner-Wood, & Noppe, 1999; Hestenes, Kontos, & Bryan, 1993; Lamb, 1998). Quality care has also been shown to support the development of children's play behaviors (Howes, 1997b; Howes & Smith, 1995), as well as improving other social skills (McCartney et al., 1997; Peisner-Feinberg & Burchinal, 1997).

Emotional Development. Research on the effects of day care on emotional development has been limited mostly to studies on the infant's attachment to the mother. The possibility that nonmaternal child care adversely affects the infant's attachment to the mother has been the subject of intense concern by scientists as well as parents. Numerous research studies on this issue have produced contradictory conclusions. There are studies indicating that infant day care does not negatively affect attachment behavior (e.g. Field et al., 1988; Kagan et al., 1978; Rauh et al., 2000). However, other researchers have concluded that infants under 1 year of age who are enrolled in day care for more than 20 hours per week are at-risk for forming emotionally insecure attachments with their mothers (Belsky & Rovine, 1988; Lamb, Sternberg, & Prodromidis, 1992; Scher & Mayseless, 2000).

In 1988, the National Institute of Child Health and Human Development (NICHD) initiated a large-scale long-term study to resolve the controversy over whether there is an association between nonmaternal infant care and infant-mother attachments. The ongoing NICHD Early Child Care Research Network (1996) study includes leading child-care researchers from 14 universities throughout the United States. In 1991, infants from approximately 1,300 families were enrolled when they were 1 month old. The infants and families represent diverse backgrounds in terms of race, maternal education, maternal employment status, family income, and family structure.

The results of the study clearly indicate that nonparental child care does not, in and of itself, threaten the security of infant-mother attachment. When assessed at 15 months of age, infants who were enrolled in various forms of out-of-home care did not differ in security of attachment from infants who were cared for at home by a parent. However, certain child-care conditions, in combination with certain home environments, apparently increase the likelihood that day care will adversely affect the attachment relationship. There was consistent evidence that infants who were enrolled in poor quality care and unstable child care for more than 10 hours per week were more likely to be insecurely attached *if* their mothers were low in sensitivity and unresponsive to their needs. Overall, the results of the NICHD study as well as other research findings provide reassurance to working parents that day care does not ordinarily interfere with parent-infant attachment. After reviewing all the noteworthy studies on the consequences of day care, Lamb (1998) concluded that "children are not inevitably harmed just because they experience nonparental care" (p. 73).

Cognitive and Language Development. Through the years research findings have consistently demonstrated that stimulation provided in a high-quality day-care program has positive effects on the cognitive development of infants from economically disadvantaged families. Early studies that focused on infants and children from middle-class families tended to conclude that good quality day-care has no obvious harmful or beneficial effects on the intellectual development of those subjects. However, recent studies (Burchinal et al., 1996; Clarke-Stewart, Vandell, Burchinal, 2000; Dunn, Beach, & Kontos, 1994; Kontos & Wilcox-Herzog, 1997; NICHD Early Child Care Research Network, 1999) have found that various types of good-quality day care contributed to significant gains in cognitive and language development for children from all economic backgrounds during the first three years of life. Higher child-care quality was consistently related to better developmental outcomes. Poorer-quality child care is likely to have effects on cognitive development. However, the effect may vary depending on how the day-care quality compares with the quality of care that infants would receive at home (Lamb, 1998).

Day-Care Quality. The most critical factor in considering the effects of day care on infants is the quality of the care that is provided. Under certain conditions, infants and toddlers who attend higher-quality day-care centers have been identified as more likely to be securely attached to their caregivers and more socially oriented than infants in poor or minimally adequate care (Howes, Philips, & Whitebook, 1992; NICHD Early Child Care Research Network, 1996). In addition, the quality of center day care has been associated with cognitive and language development during infancy (Burchinal et al., 1996; NICHD Early Child Care Research Network, 1997).

The quality of child care varies widely among facilities. The quality of care was rated on a scale from poor to superior in a study of 50 nonprofit and 50 for-profit randomly chosen centers in California, Colorado, Connecticut, and North Carolina (Cost, Quality, & Outcomes Team, 1995). The investigators concluded that quality of infant/toddler care at most U.S. child-care centers does not meet the needs for health, safety, warm relationships, and learning. Generally, nonprofit facilities (e.g., municipal agencies, universities, public schools, and employer-sponsored centers) were rated as superior in quality to other facilities. Unfortunately, the availability of these facilities is very limited.

Much less is known about the quality of family day care in which care is provided in a home other than the child's residence. These facilities are more difficult to identify and study because they are less visible and accessible to researchers. A government-sponsored national day-care home study (Fosberg, 1981) found that the quality of family day care varies considerably among facilities. Generally, homes that were sponsored by a government or nonprofit agency provided better care than homes that were simply registered or licensed or not regulated at all.

Components of Day-Care Quality. Researchers and caregivers have identified many of the factors that are associated with day-care quality. There is general agreement on the major components of day-care quality that can be regulated through government agencies. These features include staff-child ratio, group size, caregiver training, basic health and safety requirements, and adequate indoor and outdoor space. Staff wages, staff turnover, and parent involvement are also important indicators of day-care quality, but are not typically included in day-care regulations. Additional components of day-care quality include caregiver sensitivity and responsiveness to infant needs and a developmentally appropriate curriculum.

Ratios and Group Size. The maximum number of infants that can be adequately cared for by one caregiver is generally considered to be three or four for infants and five for toddlers (National Association for the Education of Young Children (NAEYC), 1991; Ruopp et al., 1979). The maximum recommended group sizes are: six for precrawling infants; nine for infants who are mobile (up to 18 months); and twelve for 18 months to 3 years of age (Lally et al., 1995). Smaller group size, however, has been associated with more positive outcomes for children (Elicker et al., 1999; Howes et al., 1992). Although child-care center licensing regulations for staff-child ratios and group size have improved in recent years, licensing laws in most states still do not require day-care facilities to meet recommended standards of quality (Children's Defense Fund, 2000). In some states, one adult may be allowed to care for as many as eight babies. The caregiver-infant ratio is the major factor affecting the cost of care. Staff salaries are the most expensive part of day care, so when more personnel are employed, the cost of care increases. Thus, most day-care facilities do not maintain higher standards than those required by law.

Caregiver Qualifications. Another important factor in assessing the quality of infant day care is the qualifications of the provider. Researchers have found that day-care staff with education and training that relates to understanding and meeting the needs of infants provide better care with superior results than caregivers without appropriate training (Fosberg, 1981; Honig, 1995; Howes, 1997a; Ruopp et al., 1979). Effective interpersonal skills along with commitment and concern for infants and their families are also important caregiver qualifications (Clarke-Stewart, 1982). There is no financial incentive, however, for caregivers to seek more education. Apparently the more education that caregivers attain, the lower their salaries are in relation to others with similar levels of education (Whitebook, Sakai, & Howes, 1997). Only a few states require day-care providers to have any specialized training or preparation in the care of infants, although most states include in-service training requirements in their child-care licensing regulations (McGaha, Snow, & Teleki, 2001; Snow, Teleki, & Reguero de-Atiles, 1996).

Parent Involvement. High-quality day-care programs also include parent involvement and participation as a major component. The more parents are involved in the day-care program, the more children benefit (Zigler & Turner, 1982). Parents can become involved in an infant-toddler day-care program in numerous ways, including serving on an advisory board, as a program observer, or helping with special projects. Regular communication between parent and caregiver is viewed as an essential feature of good day care. Unfortunately, parents average only about seven minutes per day in their child's day-care center (Zigler & Turner, 1982). Most of the parent-caregiver contacts occur at "transition points" when children arrive and depart (Powell, 1978).

Staff Turnover. Continuity and stability of caregivers and caregiving arrangements appear to be very important considerations for infants, especially when they are in the peak period for stranger anxiety. Although not all of the research studies have found negative consequences associated with frequent changes in caregivers (e.g., Schiller, 1980), conventional wisdom and much of the research support this conclusion (e.g., Cummings, 1980; Lally et al., 1995; NICHD, 1996). The child's family situation is an important variable that affects the outcome of care in any event. Continuity of care is apparently more important for infants who receive inadequate attention at home (NICHD, 1999).

Infants experience discontinuity of care when they are moved from one child-care arrangement to another, when a caregiver leaves a program, or when an infant is changed from one caregiver to another within a facility. Shifting infants from one caregiver to another as often as every six to nine months is a common practice in child-care centers (Lally et al., 1995). Day-care facilities typically have staff-turnover problems because of low wages and lack of fringe benefits. Staff-turnover rates are highest in facilities that pay the lowest wages (Whitebook et al., 1997). Teaching staff earning the lowest wages are twice as likely to leave their jobs as those earning the highest wage (Whitebook, Howes, & Philips, 1989). Among the unregulatable components of day-care quality, staff wages is the most important predictor of the quality of care infants and children receive (Scarr, Eisenberg, & Deater-Deckard, 1994).

Assessment of Day-Care Quality. Day-care quality is usually assessed by comparing the regulatable components to the ideal standards discussed previously. Researchers have found that a variety of factors should be used in assessing day-care quality (Scarr et al., 1994). The **Infant-Toddler Environment Rating Scale (ITERS)** (Harms, Cryer, & Clifford, 1990) is an instrument that can be used to provide an environmental assessment of center-based day care for children under 30 months of age. The ITERS includes 35 items on such "process" factors as personal-care routines, furnishings, learning activities, and caregiver-infant interactions. An overall score and scores on seven subscales can be obtained.

EARLY-INTERVENTION PROGRAMS

As a part of the war on poverty initiated by the federal government in the 1960s, a variety of early-intervention programs were developed for infants and their parents. These programs were designed primarily to prevent the decline in intelligence scores that often results from environmental deprivation. Many of these efforts were designed as experimental programs to test the effectiveness of intervention in general as well as specific educational models (Beller, 1979). Some of the programs were designed to teach parents how to teach their infants. Other programs focused directly on providing stimulation for the infants. The programs also varied on whether the activities were conducted on an individual basis in the home or in groups at a center. A few model programs were developed in the form of centers designed to work both with parents and their infants.

The first intervention programs were directed primarily at infants considered to be developmentally at-risk because of the effects of poverty. More recent programs have been developed to include infants affected by prematurity, genetic disorders, hearing loss, visual impairment, or other conditions that threaten growth and development (Trohanis, Cox, & Meyer, 1982).

Lasting Effects of Early Intervention. The results of early-intervention programs are consistent in demonstrating positive short-range effects on the development of economically disadvantaged infants (Beller, 1979). In fact, research suggests that intervention is most effective for infants with low-quality home environments (Bradley, Burchinal, & Casey, 2001). To determine whether or not these benefits last, investigators from 12 early-intervention programs pooled their information and conducted a joint follow-up study. Their participants were aged 9 to 19 at the time. The findings clearly show that the early-intervention programs had long-lasting beneficial effects (Lazar & Darlington, 1979, 1982). The children who participated in the early-intervention programs were more likely than the control children to perform better in their schools in the following ways:

1. The number of children assigned to special-education classes was reduced by approximately 50 percent.
2. The number of children failing a grade in school was reduced.
3. The program participants achieved superior scores on fourth-grade math tests. There was also a trend toward increased scores on fourth-grade reading tests.
4. The children who received the intervention surpassed their controls on IQ tests for up to three years after the programs ended. The participants of the three programs, which involved infants and toddlers, maintained superior IQ scores approximately 10 to 15 years after the programs ended.

In addition, mothers' attitudes toward school performance and their vocational hopes for their children were affected in positive ways.

More recently, follow-up results of the Carolina Abecederian Project have provided additional support for the long-term effectiveness of early intervention. This project was a well-designed experiment to determine the extent to which the detrimental effects of poverty could be prevented through an intensive educational program beginning in infancy (F. Campbell & Ramey, 1994). The researchers found that, at age 21, the children who had been enrolled in the intervention project maintained a cognitive and academic advantage over the control subjects who had not received the early educational program (F. Campbell et al., 2001). The study supports the theory that, for children from impoverished environments, the earlier in the life span intervention is begun, the greater its benefits are likely to be. A long-term follow-up study of another early-intervention program found that its benefits were still evident when the graduates were 27 years old. In comparison to subjects in a control group, the program participants had significantly higher levels of schooling, higher wages, higher percentages of home ownership, with lower percentages receiving social services or being arrested (Schweinhart, Barnes, & Weikart, 1993).

Current Programs. Early-intervention programs for infants and toddlers who are at-risk for developmental problems have become widespread throughout the United States, encompassing rural, urban, and suburban areas (Hanson, 1996b). The program delivery models vary from home-based to center-based to a combination of home- and center-based services. Services are provided by a variety of professionals and agencies with heavy emphasis placed upon family involvement, transdisciplinary programming, and interagency coordination.

THE HOME ENVIRONMENT

The quality of the environment within the home is a critical factor affecting the infant's development. The home environment is directly related to the developmental status of the infant (Gottfried, 1985). What are the characteristics of a favorable home environment for infant development? Betty Caldwell, a nationally recognized expert in infant development and child care, has developed a list of the six environmental characteristics of homes that are most likely to foster early development (Caldwell & Bradley, 1979):

1. Emotional and verbal responsivity of the mother.
2. Avoidance of restriction and punishment.
3. Organization of the physical and temporal (day-to-day) environment.
4. Provisions of appropriate play materials, for example, books, toys, music, and games.
5. Maternal (parental) involvement with the child.
6. Opportunities for variety in daily stimulation.

These characteristics have been incorporated into the **HOME Inventory** (Caldwell & Bradley, 1979) that has been used widely in infant research and developmental-screening programs to measure the quality of home environments. The two most important home-environment characteristics that are related to intellectual and language development during infancy are the quantity and quality of parent-infant relations and the availability of play materials (See applications section at end of this chapter) (Bradley, 1994; Bradley et al., 1989; Gottfried, 1985). Homes that rate highly on those qualities tend to produce infants who score highest on measures of cognitive performance, language development, and social competency.

Characteristics of Parent-Infant Relations. In spite of the changes that have occurred in the American family structure, the mother continues to serve as the primary caregiver. Even when the mother is employed, the father spends less time caring for the baby than the mother (Belsky & Volling, 1987; Darling-Fisher & Tiedje, 1990). Mothers average spending 65 to 80 percent more time than fathers in one-to-one interactions with their babies (Parke, 1995). Fathers and mothers differ not only in the amount of time they spend with their infants, but in their styles of interaction. A greater proportion of father-infant interactions are spent in play and social interactions,

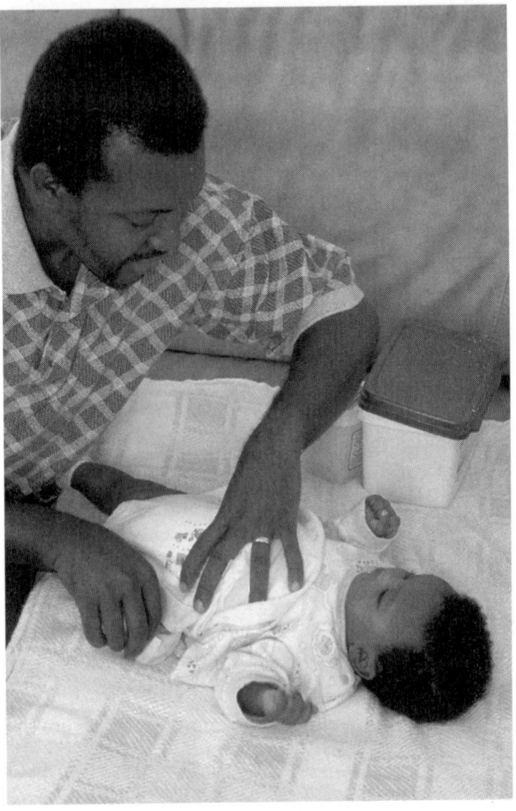

Fathers can be as competent as mothers in meeting the needs of an infant, although they engage in caregiving activities less often.

whereas mothers are more involved in routine caregiving activities (Bailey, 1994; Hossain & Roopnarine, 1994). However, this does not mean that fathers are less competent caregivers than mothers. Studies have shown that fathers are as successful as mothers in interpreting a baby's signals and in responding to its needs (Parke & Tinsley, 1987).

In some ways fathers and mothers treat daughters differently from sons. Some studies report that boys are handled more roughly and receive more physical punishment from both parents than girls (Huston, 1983). Other studies report that both parents more often reject, criticize, challenge, control, and reprimand their daughters than their sons (Cowan, Cowan, & Kerig, 1993). Grant (1994) reviewed nine studies that found differences in the mother-infant interaction on the basis of the gender. The overall conclusions were that mothers tended to stimulate or arouse (e.g., burping, handling) their male infants, while mothers of female infants tended to gently caress and stroke their infants.

Fathers tend to play with infants in different ways than mothers. They are more likely to engage in physical play by bouncing their infants, moving the infant's limbs, and engaging in rough-and-tumble games. In contrast, mothers are more likely to engage in quieter, more conventional playful interactions with toys and games, such as peekaboo (Parke & Tinsley, 1987). Some studies report that fathers are more directly involved in the rearing of sons than they are daughters (Lamb, 1981b). Other researchers report that fathers provide less physical contact, overall, for their male infants than for their female infants (Shields & Sparling, 1993).

The reason why fathers sometimes differ from mothers in the treatment of sons and daughters may be related to divergent parenting styles and marital conflict. Cowan and his co-researchers (1993) found that the more husbands and wives differ in parenting styles, the more likely their parenting is affected by whether the baby is a boy or a girl. Fathers were found to be more authoritarian with their daughters than their sons if the mother displayed a different style of parenting. In families where there was marital conflict, the difference between the way fathers treated their sons and daughters was intensified.

How Infants Influence Parental Responses. Infants initiate many of the parent-child interactions and are highly effective in gaining parental attention (Maccoby & Martin, 1983). The young infant's sighs, cries, smiles, gaze, state of alertness, helplessness, and "baby face" are some of the characteristics to which parents respond. Yet not all of their responses are positive. Parents typically do not respond as positively to infants with physical impairments, to preterm infants, to noncuddlers, or to difficult infants as they do to infants perceived as displaying more positive characteristics (Maccoby & Martin, 1983; Osofsky &

Fathers tend to engage in "rough and tumble" play with their infants.

Connors, 1979). Infants are very adaptive, however, and tend to alter many of their responses to match parental behaviors.

How Infants Influence Marital Relations. With the birth of children, the husband-wife relationship changes. The family system changes with the birth of each child (Stafford & Dainton, 1995). For many couples, the birth of the first child constitutes a crisis that disrupts the marital relationship. For others, the "blessed event" requires only minor adjustments (Dyer, 1963; Hobbs, 1968). In most marriages, though, the quality of the husband-wife relationship is apparently affected for better or worse. Approximately 12 percent of a group of 250 married couples experienced a severe decline in marital satisfaction following the birth of the first baby (Belsky & Kelly, 1994). Thirty-eight percent of the couples reported a moderate decline of marital quality. There was no change in marital satisfaction for 30 percent of the couples, while 19 percent felt that their marriage improved.

A number of factors determine the extent to which infants affect the marriage relationship. Couples who are older and who have been married for longer periods of time tend to have fewer problems adjusting to parenthood (Belsky, 1981). The quality of the marriage before the baby is born is another major factor. The parent relationship with the infant is also an important factor. Gloger, Gabriele, and Huerkamp (1998) found higher levels of marital satisfaction when there was a secure mother-infant attachment. Couples who report the highest levels of marital satisfaction before pregnancy tend to remain the happiest after the baby is born (Schneck, 1986). The number of children and the years between their birthdays also make a difference. Finally, the individual characteristics of an infant are probably the most important factor in determining how the marriage is affected. Parents of babies who cry more frequently and who are more active tend to be more stressed than parents of less demanding, quieter babies (Russell, 1974).

Marital Relationships and Parenting. The quality of the marriage has important implications for the quality of parenting the infant receives. Belsky found that "in marriages where marital quality declines the most, the bond between mother and child is weakest" (cited in Schneck, 1986, p. 12). Harmonious marriage relationships have been found to be associated with secure toddler-parent attachments, and marital discord with insecure attachments (Easterbrooks & Goldberg, 1990). Studies have also shown that marital tension and conflict have a negative impact on the mother's ability to enjoy her baby, to regard it with affection, to be competent as a parent, and to achieve a high quality of infant-mother attachment (Belsky, 1981; Parke & Tinsley, 1987). For example, higher rates of negative behaviors between the father and mother have been found to be associated with a larger number of negative behaviors directed by the mother to the baby (Pederson, Anderson, & Cain, 1980). Some researchers have reported stronger associations between marital quality and father-infant relationships than mother-infant relationships, but others found a strong link for mothers as well (Crockenberg & Leerkes, 2000).

The father's involvement in caregiving, playfulness, satisfaction with fatherhood, and competence in caregiving are also linked to the quality of the marriage (Belsky, 1979; Dickie & Matheson, 1984; Feldman, Nash, & Aschenbrenner, 1983). A happy and supportive marital relationship is apparently even more important for the father-infant relationship than it is for the mother-infant relationship. The father may depend more on the mother's support because of uncertainties about how to care for an infant and reluctance to intrude into what is traditionally perceived as the mother's territory (Parke & Tinsley, 1987). Initial differences in parenting styles may be intensified by marital conflict (Cowan et al., 1993), or marital conflict may be intensified by differences in parenting styles. Fathers and mothers may influence infant behavior through the **co-parenting relationship.** That is, the degree to which both parents agree or disagree with each other parent can undermine or support a decision. Hostile-competitive co-parenting may result in more aggressive and other negative child behaviors (Crockenberg & Leerkes, 2000).

When fathers spend more time in parenting, both parents benefit. Willoughby and Glidden (1995) found higher participation of fathers in the care of children with disabilities to be associated with greater marital satisfaction for mothers as well as fathers. Those findings are consistent with other studies showing that higher levels of father involvement with typically developing children are linked to enhanced marital satisfaction. However, researchers have trouble deciding whether greater marital satisfaction results from more father participation, or whether higher levels of marital satisfaction contribute to increased father participation. The cause-effect relationship may be circular. Fathers who have a higher level of marital satisfaction may tend to become more involved in meeting the needs of their children and enhance marriage satisfaction in the process.

Cultural and Ethnic Diversity in Parenting. On a worldwide scale, parents in all cultures share a common set of goals in their concern for the physical health and survival of their infants and efforts to maximize their future social adjustment and future economic welfare (Levine, 1980). However, the specific child-rearing attitudes and strategies parents use in implementing these goals vary widely around the world. In many parts of the world, such as Kenya and South America, infants are held and carried most of the time. Parenting styles are relaxed and casual. Attention is devoted to meeting the baby's physical needs, but efforts are not made to stimulate precocious social or intellectual development (Levine, 1980). In contrast, many American parents are less involved physically with their infants but are more concerned about social and intellectual stimulation. Child-rearing practices vary widely within, as well as between, ethnic and cultural groups. Parents from around the world vary in their perceptions of mechanisms responsible for infant behavior, beliefs about how infants should be treated, educational practices, and patterns of interaction.

In the United States, most of the research on father-infant and mother-infant interactions has been conducted among middle-class Caucasian families. However, experts predict that by the middle of the 21st century the United States will no longer have any one dominant ethnic group (Chang & Pulido, 1994). Fortunately, information is slowly beginning to accumulate on intracultural and intercultural variations in parenting values and practices among various racial and ethnic groups (see Garcia Coll, Meyer, & Brillon, 1995). Professionals who work with infants and parents in various settings need to understand and be sensitive to different cultural child-rearing practices and values in order to improve communication and establish appropriate child-care, early-intervention, or other programs.

African-American Parents. Studies of infant caregiving and interaction among African American families are finding patterns that differ, but not dramatically, from those observed in other racial groups. African American mothers, like mothers from other racial classifications in the United States, are typically the primary caregiver. However, the rate of involvement in child care by African American fathers varies from rates identified for Caucasian American fathers. In one study of intact, middle-class African American families, fathers reported spending 42 percent as much time as mothers in primary caregiving routines. Whether the mother was employed part time or full time did not make any difference (Hossain & Roopnarine, 1994). By comparison, other studies report middle-class Caucasian fathers spend about 33 percent as much time as mothers in caregiving activities when both parents are employed (Lamb, 1987). African American fathers, compared with African American mothers, rate themselves as less involved in certain caregiving interactions such as bedtime routines, feeding, comforting a crying infant, or singing to an infant (Hossain & Roopnarine, 1994).

African American parents tend to emphasize the importance of family ties. Studies reviewed by Garcia Coll and others (1995) indicate that African American families place a high value on socializing children to respect, obey, and learn from elders in the family and community. Grandparents, other family members, and members from the community tend to support parents in the provision of child care, protection, guidance, and discipline.

Other Minority Parents. Native American and Hispanic American (or Latino) families tend to adopt a nurturant, relaxed, and permissive style in rearing infants (Garcia Coll et al., 1995). Responsibilities for child care are typically shared among parents, extended-family members, siblings, and members of the community in both groups. Native American infants are encouraged to master self-care skills early. Mutual dependence, responsibility, respect for others, courage, optimism, respect for nature, and a spiritual orientation are values that are commonly emphasized in the socialization of infants and children (Olson & DeFrain, 1994). Hispanic Americans also socialize their infants to be interdependent with family members rather than independent and individualistic. Asian American parents tend to be lenient, nurturant, and permissive with infants and young children. However, as children get older, their parents impose stricter standards of discipline and encourage self-control, obedience, and emotional maturity (Garcia Coll et al., 1995). Research studies on parenting in lesbian and gay families are very limited, especially in relation to parenting infants (West & Turner, 1995). The results of existing studies have found no evidence to indicate that the gay and lesbian parenting practices and child-rearing results differ in noticeable ways from those of heterosexual parents (Patterson, 1995).

Importance of Grandparents. In most families throughout the world grandparents play an important role in infant development. Grandparents, especially grandmothers, influence the development of infants indirectly through the emotional, economic, and other forms of support they provide parents. Grandparents also directly influence the development of infants through contact and interaction (Crockenberg, Lyons-Ruth, & Dickstein, 1993). The attachment between grandparents and grandchildren is second only to the emotional connection between parent and child (Woodard, 1997). In some cases, grandparents may be more influential than the infant's parents. Although parents across cultures often complain about grandparents being overindulgent and interfering in discipline (Broude, 1995), parents typically value and appreciate the role of grandparents. For many single, adolescent mothers, grandparents are the most important source of support, and often function as the infant's primary caregiver.

The same is true of grandparents of children with disabilities (Heller, Hsieh, & Rowitz, 2000). Grandparents also serve an important function of providing care for working parents at nontraditional times of the day (Hunts & Avery, 1998). Research indicates that support from grandparents is associated with more nurturant, sensitive, and responsive caregiving by the infant's mother (Crockenberg et al., 1993). In many families, infants appear to be attached to parents and grandparents alike. Studies also show that the involvement of grandmothers in the care of infants is typically associated with positive developmental outcomes, but is most apparent in cases where parent resources and other sources of support are limited (Crockenberg et al., 1993).

Parenting Infants With Special Needs. Infants who are born with a developmentally challenging condition (e.g., prematurity, Down syndrome, cerebral palsy) display behavioral and physical characteristics that affect interactional patterns with their caregivers. Infants with disabilities tend to be less responsive, less active, and provide less distinct behavioral cues than typically developing infants. For example, infants with Down syndrome engage in less eye contact and less vocal turn taking with their caregivers than other infants (Widerstrom et al., 1991). Parents may misinterpret their signals and provide excessive stimulation during feeding and other caregiving activities in an effort to elicit responses. On the other hand, because these infants physically appear to be more fragile and less cuddly, parents may provide less stroking, holding, or other nurturing interactions.

Hanson (1996a) reviewed research studies on parent interactions with infants affected by cognitive impairments, physical disabilities, or other developmental challenges. Mothers of cognitively impaired infants tended to use more structure or directive language than mothers of typically developing infants in their parent-to-infant interactions. Mothers of infants with hearing deficits exhibited less flexible, less approving, more intrusive, and overprotective interaction patterns as compared with mothers of infants without hearing loss. Mothers of infants with vision problems or physical disabilities also tended to exhibit problems in their caregiving behaviors (Meadow-Orlans, 1995). Fathers of boys with autism or other communication disorders have been observed participating less in child-care activities than fathers of boys without disabilities (Bristol, Gallagher, & Schopler, 1988). Shields and Sparling (1993) found that, when compared with fathers of healthy infants, fathers of sick and low birth weight infants provided less physical contact and affectional touch. Other studies (see Darke & Goldberg, 1994), however, suggest that fathers of preterm infants and other infants with special needs are more involved in the care of their infants than are fathers whose babies are healthy. In all cases, though, mothers of infants with special needs tend to bear a larger share of the work and psychological stress involved in parenting than do fathers (Darke & Goldberg, 1994).

In spite of the increased demands involved in parenting infants with disabilities, both mothers and fathers adjust remarkably well. In fact, parents report that having a child with a disability produces positive changes, such as personal growth, improved relations with others, and changes in philosophical or religious values (Scorgie & Sobsey, 2000). Caregiver-infant interactions are best when caregivers understand and adjust to the characteristics and special needs of infants with developmental problems. Hanson (1996b) recommends that intervention programs assist parents in interpreting the infant's unique signaling system, reading and understanding their infant's cues, and providing appropriate interactional responses.

MANAGING INFANT BEHAVIOR: DISCIPLINE

Discipline is an essential part of child rearing. In its broadest meaning, **discipline** refers to the process of teaching and learning that fosters human growth and development (Dodson, 1970; DuBois, 1952). Discipline gives young children a sense of security by letting them know what they can and cannot do. Children gain approval from others by learning to behave according to socially accepted standards. Discipline thus facilitates the development of self-esteem. Appropriate discipline also fosters achievement motivation and the development of a conscience. The ultimate goal of discipline, though, is the development of self-discipline. Infants begin life with little ability to control their own behavior. They depend upon their caregivers to guide them through the process of establishing impulse control and self-regulation.

Discipline and behavior control are usually not a major concern of parents during the early months of life. Excessive crying and fussing are the behaviors that present the most problems for caregivers before infants begin to move around. As they learn to creep and walk, infants begin to explore the environment and begin to "get out of bounds." As discussed previously, biting, hitting, temper tantrums, failure to comply with requests, clinging, and other types of negative behavior are problem behaviors that develop during the toddler stage. Parents and other caregivers are then faced with decisions about how much freedom to allow, what limits to set, and what methods of discipline and guidance to use.

Setting Limits. Parental expectations of infant behavior and limits must be reasonable to be most effective. Arbitrary and unnecessary limits contribute to negativism, noncompliance, and parent-child conflict. Generally, limits should be designed to (1) ensure the child's health and safety; (2) protect the health, safety, and rights of others; (3) prevent the destruction of property; and (4) teach the moral and social values of the family and society.

Realistic behavioral expectations can be established only if adults keep in mind the age-level characteristics, needs, and limited abilities of infants and toddlers. Cognitive immaturity and limited language ability prevent infants from understanding and complying with adults' wishes, as well as from communicating their own desires. Their struggle to establish autonomy frequently results in negative responses to adult requests. Toddlers need physical activity and freedom of movement. Thus, they have difficulty sitting still and keeping quiet. Infants and toddlers are very egocentric, which means that they view things only from their own point of view. For example, to the parent bath water is used for bathing, but to an infant bath water is something used for playing.

Children need to be informed of the limits that are set and the expectations their caregivers hold. They react to ambiguity with confusion and should not be expected to conform to unclear limits. Toward the end of the first year, infants can begin to understand simple restrictions, such as the meaning of "No." As language development proceeds, verbal explanations can become a little more complex. For young children, it is more important to explain *what* they should do rather than *why* (Greenfield & Tronick, 1980). When possible, directions should be stated in a positive form that tells an infant what to do instead of what not to do ("Keep the sand in the sandbox!").

Strategies for Guiding Behavior. Once limits have been clearly established, they need to be consistently enforced. However, this should be done in positive ways that "preserve the self-respect of the parent as well as the child" (Ginott, 1965, p. 96). Infants need to be protected from inappropriate teasing, neglect, disapproval, or punishment (Ramey & Ramey, 1999). The restrictions are applied firmly and kindly without excessive anger or force and without attacking the personality of the child. Children need to be given the right to have feelings, just as adults. Their feelings can be accepted even though the behavior is objectionable. Name-calling and personality attacks, such as "you stupid brat," should never be used. Chamberlain and Patterson (1995) have identified four types of discipline that have been consistently linked with negative child-rearing outcomes: (1) inconsistent discipline; (2) irritable, explosive discipline; (3) low supervision and involvement; and (4) inflexible, rigid discipline.

Adults have numerous options for enforcing limits and guiding the behavior of their children. Those discussed here are among the strategies usually recommended for positive guidance of infants and toddlers. Keep in mind, however, that no single technique is equally effective with all children. A child's compliance will vary with the person making the request, the situation, and other factors such as how tired the child is at the time. The temperament of the infant is also an important factor in how resourceful an adult has to be.

Distraction and Redirection. Infants who are crying or engaged in unacceptable activities can be distracted or diverted to another activity. For example, young infants can sometimes be distracted by being held in front of a mirror or a window. They can be moved to a new, more appropriate location. Alternative activities and toys can be provided as substitutes for those that are prohibited. When Tanya was 18 months old, she was found playing in the toilet bowl. Her mother's response was "You need to play somewhere else." She then took Tanya to her room and found some toys for her to play with. Whenever possible, children should be given choices. "Do you want to play here or go outside?" However, a choice should not be given if it is not really available or acceptable.

Environmental Control. Many problem behaviors can be avoided if the environment is properly structured. An infant needs a place to play that is childproof. Breakable objects and other valuables should be placed where infants cannot reach them. Safety hazards should be eliminated. An adequate supply of age-appropriate toys and interesting activities should be provided to keep the child busy. Nine-month-old Jamal opened a kitchen cabinet and pulled out the pots and pans from the bottom shelves. Jamal's mother put fasteners on the cabinet doors to keep him away from her cooking utensils. She also put some old pots and pans in a cabinet that she left open so Jamal could play with them.

Modeling. It is important for adults to model the behaviors they want to teach. For example, the best way to teach children to use good manners is for the adult to practice them in caregiving interactions. When adults say "Please" and "Thank you" when making requests, the child will eventually reciprocate. Young children are more likely to imitate a model that is warm and nurturing than one that is cold and aloof.

Positive Reinforcement. Children tend to repeat behaviors that are reinforced with a social reinforcer such as praise, a hug, or a smile. Parents and caregivers are generally encouraged to praise desirable behavior and ignore, as much as possible, behaviors they don't want to encourage. However, praise or other social reinforcers should be sincere and nonmanipulative. Reinforcement should be perceived as a means of fostering the infant's self-esteem rather than simply as a means to achieve behavior control (Seefeldt, 1987).

To be most effective, praise must be given immediately after the behavior. Praise is also most effective when it is a recognition of the child's specific behavior (Ginott, 1965) ("Thank you for sharing your toy! That was a nice thing to do!"). General praise that addresses the child's personality is less helpful ("You're the best child!").

Time-out. The use of **time-out** to discipline toddlers is another option available to parents and caregivers. In this procedure, a child who is being disruptive is removed from the situation and given a chance to calm down. In some cases, the child is taken to another room and isolated for a while. After a brief interval, the child may return to the situation or resume another activity. This gives the child who is out of control a chance to regain equilibrium and self-control. It is unrealistic, however, to expect an infant or a toddler to sit in a specified place for more than a few seconds. Time-out should be viewed as a teaching act and an opportunity for the infant to establish self-control rather than as a punishment.

Punishment. The use of punishment in controlling the behavior of infants and toddlers is controversial. Scolding, spanking, withdrawal of love, isolation, and other negative responses to a child's behavior are types of **punishment** commonly used. Punishment is the least desirable means of behavior control. Holden (1983) observed the strategies mothers used in controlling the behavior of 2-year-old infants. Some of the mothers used scolding or reprimands when the infant misbehaved. Other mothers used preventive measures such as engaging the child in conversation to control behavior. The mothers who used preventive measures had fewer problems and less conflict with their infants.

Most parents feel that there are times when punishment is necessary, but it should be brief and clearly linked to what the child has done (Laishley, 1983). Punishment is effective in suppressing some behavior, but that does not mean that the behavior is eliminated. Punishment may produce undesirable side effects, such as associating the punishment with the parent. Punishment does not foster the development of internal control and can lead to excessive reliance on external authority for behavioral inhibition (Maccoby, 1980). Punishment is most effective when it immediately follows the problem behavior and when it is consistent. It is also more effective when administered by someone who has a warm and caring relationship with the child (Hetherington & Parke, 1979).

Spanking is the most controversial type of punishment. Most child-rearing experts (e.g., Brazelton, 1992; Ginott, 1965) recommend that parents avoid the use of spanking. For example, Ginott (1965) argues that spanking is ineffective and should be avoided: "If spanking is so effective, why do we have such uneasy feelings about it. . . . What is wrong with spanking is the lessons it demonstrates. It teaches children undesirable methods of dealing with frustration. It dramatically tells them: when you are angry—hit!" (p. 107). Ginott's argument is illustrated by the cartoon that shows a father vigorously spanking his son. The caption reads: "That will teach you to hit your younger sister!" The father is right. It will. In actual practice, the majority of parents use spanking as a method of discipline out of a sense of frustration if for no other reason. However, if parents are resourceful, they can find more positive means of behavior control.

Love Withdrawal. One of the most common methods used by parents to control a child's behavior is **love withdrawal.** The parent expresses anger and disappointment when the child misbehaves: "I don't like you when you cry like that!" The parent follows up by isolating the child emotionally. The child's efforts to communicate are ignored as the parent turns away from the child, refusing to speak or listen. The parent may even threaten to leave (Maccoby, 1980). Withdrawal of love is punitive and implicitly says to the child, "If you don't please me, I won't love you!" The results of love withdrawal are mostly negative. It produces a high level of arousal and anxiety in children and does not lead to the establishment of internal control (M. Hoffman, 1970). Discipline begins with the loving care that a baby receives (Keister, 1973), so the very foundation of discipline is threatened by the use of love withdrawal.

Parental Attitudes. The effectiveness of any disciplinary technique depends largely upon the nature of the parent-child relationship. Discipline is administered in the context of parental attitudes. The message and meaning of the disciplinary action, especially punishment, are determined to a large extent by the attitude of the disciplinarian. Parental attitudes can be placed on a continuum ranging from love and acceptance to hostility and rejection. The most competent children are reared by parents who use positive methods to control behavior within the context of a warm and loving attitude (M. Hoffman, 1981). This combination of authority and positive attitudes tends to result in children who are self-reliant, self-confident, curious, and happy (Becker, 1964).

SUMMARY

Family Systems Perspectives

- Many scholars believe it is important to view the complexity of parent-infant relationships from a family systems model. According to this perspective, emphasis is placed upon the reciprocal and complex nature of relationships in which infants, parents, and other family members influence each other's behavior and are subject to many other sources of influence.

Current Trends in the American Family

- Dramatic increases in the number of single-parent families and the number of employed mothers represent changes in the structure of the American family that have affected the ways infants are reared.
- High rates of divorce and unwed motherhood are the main causes of the increased number of single-parent families. Most single-parent families with infants are headed by divorced mothers.
- Single-parent families share similar problems, including financial instability, inadequate alternative child care, and a high level of stress. The effects of single parenting are likely to depend upon the extent to which these or other adverse conditions exist.
- Infants are especially vulnerable to the effects of divorce.

APPLICATIONS: SELECTING TOYS AND MATERIALS

Choosing a baby's toys and play materials is as important as choosing the baby's clothing. However, the task is not easy because of the almost endless variety of toys available. Some general criteria should be considered by parents and caregivers in selecting toys and materials for infants and toddlers:

- Toys and materials should be appropriate for the child's age and developmental level. Fortunately, infants are adaptable and play with toys in their own way. Information about toys for infants, recommended according to age, is readily available in numerous publications (e.g., Aston, 1984; Greenfield & Tronick, 1980; B. White, 1985). Many toy manufacturers label their toys according to a general age range.
- Toys and materials should provide a challenge to the child without being impossible to master. Adults cannot always predict which toys will present an optimum challenge. However, given a reasonable variety of toys, an infant will select the ones that are most appealing.
- All toys and play materials should be free from safety hazards (see Chapter 5).
- The infant's toy collection should be balanced and comprehensive. There should be a variety of toys to cover each area of development, including small and large muscle, sensorimotor, eye-hand coordination, social, emotional, language, and cognitive as well as imagination and creativity.
- The infant's toy collection should be built around the basics. It should include playthings that can be used in a variety of ways and that are universal and timeless favorites, such as balls, blocks, puzzles, books, records, dolls, and stuffed animals.
- Toys should be cost effective. A toy should be durable, sturdy, and worth the investment. In some cases this may mean paying more for a better quality toy and perhaps buying fewer toys. For example, although a wooden puzzle costs more than a cardboard puzzle, the wooden puzzle is a better buy because it lasts longer and "works" better. Parents do not need to purchase a lot of expensive educational toys and materials. Old pots and pans, spools, cans, and other common household items make excellent play materials.
- Toys should match the available storage and be easily accessible to the infant. Shelves are better than a toy box for organizing and storing toys. Toys should be rotated from time to time. When an infant has grown tired of a toy, it should be stored away and reintroduced at a later time.

- The extra stress and conflict experienced by single-parent families are frequently accompanied by a diminished-parenting effect.
- Father absence during infancy has been associated with difficulty in sex-role, intellectual, and personality development. Males appear to be more adversely affected by father absence than females.
- Apparently maternal employment does not ordinarily have negative effects on infant development, provided the mother has a choice about working, likes her work, has a satisfactory child-care arrangement, and does not experience separation anxiety when leaving her infant in alternative child care.
- Good-quality day care for infants has no harmful effect on most aspects of infant development. It has been found to be beneficial to the physical and cognitive development of infants from economically deprived families. However, infants who participate in day care are sick more frequently than infants who stay at home. Infants are no more likely to be injured at a day-care setting than they are at home. Day care may increase aggressiveness as an infant gets older.
- Nonparental child care does not threaten the security of infant-mother attachment, unless infants are exposed to poor quality, unstable child care and their mothers are typically unresponsive to their needs.
- The components of good quality day care include (1) an adequate caregiver-infant ratio and limited

group size, (2) well-qualified caregivers, (3) parental involvement, and (4) continuity of caregivers.

- The **Infant-Toddler Environment Rating Scale** is an instrument that can be used, in combination with other standards, to assess the quality of center-based day care for infants.

Early-Intervention Programs

- Various types of early-intervention programs were established in the 1960s to facilitate the development of infants from low-income families. The long-term results of those programs show that early-intervention can be effective in alleviating the effects of an impoverished environment. Early-intervention programs for infants and toddlers have become widespread throughout the United States.

The Home Environment

- Two important characteristics of the home environment that are related to infant cognitive and language development are parent-infant interactions and the provision of adequate play materials.
- In most American families, the mother continues to be the primary caregiver. However, fathers can be just as capable as mothers in taking care of an infant. Fathers and mothers use different styles in playing and interacting with their infants.
- The quality of a marital relationship tends to decline slightly and level off after the birth of a baby. Couples who have been married longer, couples who were older when they married, and couples who have a relatively high level of marital satisfaction before pregnancy have the least trouble adjusting to parenthood.
- The decline in the quality of marital relationships is accompanied by a decline in the quality of parenting.
- Adults who work with infants and parents in various settings need to understand how child-rearing values and practices vary within, as well as between, racial, ethnic, and cultural groups.
- Grandparents play an important role in infant development through the emotional, economic, and other forms of support they provide parents as well as their direct contact and interactions with infants.
- Infants who have special needs display behavioral and physical characteristics that affect interactional patterns with their caregivers. Mothers and fathers tend to adjust remarkably well to the increased demands.

Managing Infant Behavior: Discipline

- Positive discipline is an essential part of effective parent-infant relationships. Useful strategies for guiding the behavior of infants include distraction and redirection, controlling the environment, modeling, positive reinforcement, and the use of time-out. The use of spanking and love withdrawal as means of behavior control should be avoided.

KEY TERMS

family systems
single-parent families
diminished parenting effect
Infant-Toddler Environment Rating Scale (ITERS)
HOME Inventory
co-parenting relationship
discipline
time-out
punishment
spanking
love withdrawal

INFORMATION ON THE WEB*

www.nccic.org The National Child Care Information Center disseminates information on this site about child-care research, funding, promising practices, and a variety of frequently asked questions. Links are available to organizations serving child-care and related professions and state child-care agencies.

www.tnpc.com The National Parenting Center's site provides parents with information on a variety of topics related to child rearing. Links to a number of other sites that provide information on parenting issues are highlighted.

*Web sites are subject to change.

GLOSSARY

Accident. An occurrence in a sequence of events that produces unintended injury, death, or property damage.
Accommodation. The process of changing existing patterns of thought or behavior to conform to new information or experiences.
Acquired Immune Deficiency Syndrome (AIDS). A disease that attacks the immune system, caused by infection with the human immunodeficiency virus (HIV).
Adaptation. The processes by which an individual adjusts and changes to get along in the environment; includes assimilation and accommodation.
Adaptive Behaviors. Self-care activities such as feeding, dressing, and toileting.
Affect. The subjective feeling and expressive components of emotions.
Affordances. What the environment provides to individuals for action.
Alberta Infant Motor Scale (AIMS). A tool designed to evaluate motor performance of infants from birth to 18 months of age.
Ambivalent Attachment. A pattern of attachment in which the infant is upset when the caregiver leaves, and upon reunion with the caregiver, alternately clings to and resists the caregiver.
Amniocentesis. The procedure in which a sample of amniotic fluid is withdrawn from the amniotic sac through a hollow needle for laboratory analysis.
Amnion; Amniotic Sac. The inner fluid-filled membrane, resembling a plastic bag, that encloses the developing embryo or fetus; the "bag of waters."
Anoxia. A condition in which the tissues of the body are not receiving an adequate supply of oxygen.
Apgar Scale. A test administered 1 minute and again 5 minutes after birth to check the physiological condition of the infant.
Apnea. A pause in breathing for 20 seconds or longer.
Appropriate for Gestational Age. Infants whose weight is at an expected level for their gestational age.
Assessment of Preterm Infant Behavior (APIB) Scale. One of the most widely used instruments for evaluating the developmental status of preterm infants.
Assimilation. The process of incorporating new information into existing patterns of thought or action.
Asynchronous Growth. Development of different parts of the body at different rates.
Asynchronous Interactions. Social interactions that are not reciprocal or mutual.
At-Risk. A condition whereby infants have been exposed, or may have been exposed, to hazards that are likely to result in developmental delay or atypical development.
Attachment. A relatively enduring emotional tie to another person.
Avoidant Attachment. A pattern of attachment in which the infant does not protest when the caregiver leaves and ignores the caregiver when he/she returns.
Axon. Transmitter of nerve impulses that extends from the cell body of the neuron.
Babbling. Sound play consisting of the repetition of consonants and vowels in alternating sequences; thought to be the forerunner of the first meaningful utterances.
Babinski Reflex. An involuntary movement in which the toes fan inward toward the bottom of the foot when the inner side of the infant's foot is rubbed from heel to toe.
Baby diary. A daily record of an infant's behavior recorded by an adult observer, usually a parent scientist.
Babyproof the Environment. An attempt to prevent injuries to infants by checking the environment for infant safety.
Back to Sleep Campaign. A public awareness campaign to increase knowledge about sudden infant death syndrome and to promote the practice of placing infants in the supine (back) position to sleep.
Battelle Developmental Inventory. An instrument for assessing development, including social skills.
Bayley Scales of Infant Development–II. A widely used norm-referenced instrument for the assessment of cognitive and motor performance of infants from 1 month to 42 months of age.
Behavioral Observation Audiometry (BOA). A technique that involves testing infant hearing through observation of the child's reactions to sounds.
Behavioral Theories. Theories that stress the importance of the environment and experience in shaping the human infant.
Bilirubin. A pigment formed when red blood cells are destroyed. High levels lead to jaundice.
Binocular Cues. Cues that are available when both eyes focus on an object.
Birthing Rooms. Birthing facilities that more closely resemble the home environment than a hospital room.
Blastocyst. A fertilized ovum about the time it enters the uterus and a central cavity is formed inside.
Body Mass Index. A guideline for determining whether a child is underweight or overweight in relation to height.
Bonding. The process by which a parent forms an emotional attachment to an infant.
Bottle–Mouth Syndrome. A pattern of severe tooth decay teeth that is caused by the pooling of milk or other sugary liquids around the teeth; commonly found among children who are habitually given a bottle to nurse while going to sleep.
Boundary of Viability. The earliest age at which infants can be born and survive.

Braxton Hicks Contractions. Mild contractions of the uterus that occur before true labor begins; sometimes referred to as false labor.
Brazelton Neonatal Behavior Assessment Scale. An instrument used to assess the basic functioning of the newborn infant's nervous system and behavioral response capacities.
Breech Position. The birth of an infant with the buttocks, feet, or knees as the part that emerges first.
Bronchopulmonary Dysplasia (BPD). A chronic lung disease that affects preterm infants.
Caesarean Section (C-section). Childbirth by means of a surgical incision through the abdomen and uterus.
Canonical babbling. An advanced form of babbling that consists of well-formed vowel and consonant sound combinations.
Capacitation. A 7–hour period of conditioning in which sperm become capable of fertilizing an ovum.
Caregiver. A person, such as a parent, nurse, or day-care worker, who provides care for an infant.
Catch-up Growth. The ability of the individual to achieve normal growth potential after a period of malnutrition, intrauterine crowding, illness, or other adversity.
Cattell Infant Intelligence Scale. An instrument used to assess intelligence in infants ages 2 months to 30 months.
Cephalocaudal Principle. The principle that growth and development proceed from the upper part of the body to the lower extremities.
Cerebral Palsy. A developmental disorder caused by brain damage; the effects vary from mild motor problems involving one side of the body to severe impairment involving the trunk and all four extremities.
Cervical Pregnancy. A pregnancy in which the fertilized ovum is implanted in or close to the cervix.
Cervix. The mouth, or opening, of the uterus (womb).
Child Neglect. The willful failure of parents or other designated caregivers to meet the child's basic needs for food, clothing, shelter, medical treatment, and affection.
Chorion. The outer prenatal membrane that encloses the developing baby. One side of the chorion becomes attached to the uterus as the placenta.
Chorionic Villus Sampling (CVS). The procedure whereby a sample of tissue from the chorion is removed and tested for genetic defects.
Circular Reaction. The term Piaget used to describe a continuous response that stimulates its own repetition.
Classical Conditioning. A procedure in which a neutral stimulus and a stimulus that automatically evokes a response are presented at approximately the same time. Eventually, the presentation of the neutral stimulus alone evokes the response.
Cognition. All the mental processes such as thinking, remembering, perceiving, learning, and concept formation.
Cognitive Developmental Theories. Theories that emphasize the interaction between genetic inheritance and environmental factors in understanding the development of cognitive processes.
Colic. A condition that causes an infant to cry, with distinctive sounds, inconsolably for long periods of time, day in and day out, as if in pain.
Competence Motivation. The tendency to seek out and master the most challenging aspects of the environment; a human characteristic considered by some theorists to be innate.
Conductive Hearing Loss. A hearing deficit that results from abnormalities in the ear structure or fluid in the middle ear.
Congenital Malformation. A defect present at birth.
Contingency. A situation in which the behavior of an individual is dependent upon the behavior of another person or some other environmental stimuli.
Conversational Turn Taking. Waiting for a turn and responding in the course of conversation.
Cooing. Vowel like, rhythmic sounds made by infants during the early part of the prespeech stage.
Co-parenting Relationship. The degree to which both parents agree or disagree with each other.
Cordocentesis; also **Percutaneous Umbilical Cord Sampling (PUBS).** A procedure by which a long needle is inserted through the mother's abdomen into a vein in the umbilical cord to obtain a sample of fetal blood to test for disorders of development.
Cortisol. A hormone contained in human saliva that varies in relation to stress levels.
Cosleeping or **Bed Sharing.** The practice of allowing an infant to sleep in the same bed with the mother, or father, or both.
Couvade. A term used to refer to the behavior that is typical of expectant or new fathers, usually related to magical or religious beliefs that are meant to protect the mother and baby.
Crawling. Locomotion with the head and chest raised while the stomach maintains contact with the surface of the floor.
Creeping. Locomotion on hands and knees or hands and feet.
Crib Talk. Monologues toddlers use to talk to themselves, usually just before going to sleep.
Cri du Chat Syndrome. A disorder caused by a missing section of chromosome No. 5, characterized by a cry that resembles the meowing of a cat.
Criterion-Referenced Instruments. Tests used to assess an infant's ability to achieve specific, previously determined skills without comparing one infant with a group of other same-age infants.
Critical Period. The span of time when a developing organism is most likely to be permanently influenced by environmental factors.
Cross–modal Transfer. The transfer of information from one sensory system to other sensory systems.
Crowning. The point during childbirth when the top of the baby's head becomes visible at the vaginal opening.
Cruising. A characteristic of infant movement in which the infant moves around, usually sideways, holding on to furniture or other objects.
Crying. A state of arousal produced by the nervous system triggered by some form of biological threat.
Cystic Fibrosis. A recessively inherited genetic disorder that affects the mucous, sweat, tear, and salivary glands, causing congestion in the breathing passages.

Deciduous Teeth. The first set of 20 teeth developed by an infant, which are replaced by 32 permanent teeth; also called primary, temporary, baby, or milk teeth.
Deferred Imitation. Imitation of a model that is no longer present.
Dendrites. Treelike branches that extend from the cell body of the neuron. They serve as receptors of nerve impulses.
Developmental Systems Theories. See **Dynamic Systems Approach.**
Denver II. One of the most widely used norm-referenced screening tests for infants and children up to 6 years of age.
Depth Perception. The ability to see objects in three dimensions, judging the size and distance of objects and perceiving heights of drop-offs.
Diarrhea. An increase in the frequency, fluidity, and volume of bowel movements.
Difficult Child. A pattern of temperament characterized by irregularity, difficulty in adjusting to new situations, frequent crying, and difficulty in being soothed.
Dilation. The process by which the cervix opens to its widest capacity to allow a baby to be born.
Diminished Parenting Effect. A situation following divorce in which the parents' ability to maintain interaction and communication with their children is lessened.
Direct Perception. The view that infants are preattuned to perceive the world without cognitive inference.
Discipline. Procedures used by parents and other adults to guide, correct, punish, and control the behavior of children.
Dishabituation. The renewal of interest in a stimulus arising from a noticeable change in the stimulus characteristics.
Disorders of Attachment. A controversial term used to by some therapists to classify problems resulting from the failure to form adequate attachments during infancy. Attachment disorders include aggressive, disruptive behaviors, or the inability to form and maintain close relationships later in life.
Disorganized/Disoriented Attachment. A pattern of attachment in which the infant exhibits extreme internal conflict.
Dominant Gene. A gene carrying a trait that is always expressed.
Down Syndrome. A developmental disorder caused by the presence of an extra chromosome No. 21, or an extra amount of No. 21 chromosomal material.
Dynamic Systems Approach. A theoretical perspective based on the view that complex and changing biological and social systems interact in dynamic (energetic, forceful) ways to bring about the development of new abilities and behaviors (especially motor skills).
Easy Child. A pattern of temperament characterized by regularity, a positive response to new situations, quick adaptation to change, and a generally positive mood.
Echolalia. The tendency of an infant to repeat the same sounds over and over.
Ecological Self. Knowledge about self that is obtained through perception of body experiences.
Ectoderm. The external embryonic layer of cells that forms the nervous system, backbone, the skin, hair, nails, and parts of the eyes and ears.
Ectopic Pregnancy. A pregnancy in which the fertilized ovum becomes implanted outside the uterus.
Effacement. The process during labor through which the cervix becomes thinner and shorter.
Ego. The term used by Freud to label the rational, or thinking, component of personality.
Egocentrism. The inability to see things from another person's point of view.
Elicited Imitation. A technique to study memory in which an action is modeled and the infant is encouraged to imitate the action.
Embryo. The developing infant from about 2 weeks after conception until the end of the eighth week of pregnancy.
Emotion. Feelings; complex internal states consisting of perceptions, thoughts, body responses, and impulses.
Emotion Regulation. The capacity of individuals to monitor and control their emotional states and emotional reactions in order to accomplish their goals.
Empathic Concern. Feelings and behaviors that are a combination of sympathy and empathy.
Empathy. Feeling as, or sharing the same emotion that another person is experiencing at a given time.
Empiricists. Theorists who believe that infants come into the world with no knowledge and are shaped primarily by experience.
Endoderm. The external embryonic layer of cells that will develop into the digestive tract, respiratory system, liver, and various glands.
Endogenous Smile. Spontaneous smile, usually observed when an infant is sleeping, that is triggered by internal body processes.
Entrainment. The momentum of interactional sequences.
Epidural Block. A method of pain relief in which a local anesthetic is delivered through a thin tube inserted in the epidural space between two lower spinal vertebrae, which reduces all sensation from the waist to the feet.
Epiphyses. Ossification centers that form near the end of the long bones.
Episiotomy. A surgical incision made in the tissue between the vagina and the rectum to facilitate childbirth and prevent tearing of the tissue.
Equilibrium. The term Piaget used to describe a state of balance between assimilation and accommodation.
Established Risk. A category used to classify infants who have been diagnosed with a condition known to result in developmental delay or atypical development.
Exogenous Smile. Smiling behavior elicited by stimuli outside the infant's body.
Experience-Dependent. Term used to express the idea that new synaptic connections in the brain are dependent on exposure to certain experiences.
Experience-Expectant. Term referring to the notion that brain pathways are ready and waiting for certain experiences within a given time period.
Expressive Speech. The meaningful vocal utterances and sounds composed and expressed by an individual in communication with others.
Expressive Style. A communication style in which a toddler uses speech that is socially oriented, consisting mainly of pronouns and actions words.

Family Systems. A theoretical perspective based on the belief that all family members and their behaviors are interconnected.

Fertilization Age. A reference point for calculating the length of pregnancy based on the date the sperm fertilized the ovum.

Fetal Alcohol Effects (FAE). The term used in cases where prenatal alcohol exposure has been more limited and the observable effects are not as severe as full-blown fetal alcohol syndrome.

Fetal Alcohol Syndrome (FAS). Congenital disabilities, such as overall growth retardation, facial malformations, inadequate brain growth, heart defects, motor problems, skeletal defects, hyperactivity, and other difficulties, resulting from excessive maternal alcohol consumption during pregnancy.

Fetus. An unborn infant from the beginning of the ninth prenatal week until birth.

Fine-Tuning. Facilitating language acquisition using techniques such as prompting, echoing, and expansion.

FISH Test. A technique for detecting chromosomal abnormalities in which a laser light is used to separate fetal cells in the mother's blood from the mother's cells.

Fontanels. The soft spots in the young infant's skull that harden and disappear as the separate pieces of the skull grow together.

Food Guide Pyramid for Young Children. The Department of Agriculture's recommendations concerning the basic food groups.

Forceps. An instrument, shaped like tongs, sometimes used in difficult deliveries to help the baby emerge from the birth canal.

Full-Term. Born between 37 and 42 weeks of gestational age.

Functional-Relational Play. The second stage of sensorimotor play; characterized by the infant's ability to play with two or more objects at the same time in ways that are increasingly appropriate to the relationships of the objects.

Gastrulation. The process through which the three germ layers of the developing embryo are formed.

Gentlest Intervention. An approach that focuses on using minimal stimulation to infants in the NICU.

General to Specific. According to this developmental trend, control over general movements of the body develop before specific movements are mastered.

Gesell Developmental Schedules. A tool for determining the integrity and functional maturity of the nervous system between 1 month and 6 years of age.

Gestational Age. The age of the infant calculated from the estimated date of fertilization of the ovum until birth.

Glial Cells. See neuroglial.

Golden Age of Pregnancy. The years between ages 20 and 35 years when women are less likely to experience complications during pregnancy.

Goodness-of-Fit. The extent to which the caregiving style of the parents appropriately matches the temperament of the infant.

Guided Participation. The process by which children develop through involvement in the cultural practices of their community.

Habituation. The weakening or decline of responsiveness to a stimulus over a period of time.

Haemophilus Influenzae Type B (Hib). A virus that can result in meningitis, pneumonia, and severe infections of the skin, throat, ears, joints, and bloodstream.

Haptic Perception. The perceptual process by which infants acquire information about the properties of objects through touch and handling sensations.

Hepatitis. An inflammation of the liver caused by viruses, toxic substances, or drugs.

Hierarchical Integration. The process whereby the simplest abilities and skills develop first and become more complex as they are combined to form more elaborate movements.

Hitching. Locomotion in a sitting position.

Holophrase. A single word considered to be equivalent to a whole phrase or a complete sentence.

Home Birth. Birth that occurs at home rather than in a hospital setting.

HOME Inventory. An instrument that is designed to measure the quality of home environments, including six characteristics.

Human Growth Hormone (HGH). A substance produced by the thyroid gland that is necessary for normal body growth.

Huntington's Chorea. A dominantly inherited genetic disorder characterized by a progressive degeneration of the nervous system.

Hydrocephaly. A condition in which the infant has an excessive amount of cerebrospinal fluid.

Hypertonia. Muscle tone that is too stiff and rigid.

Hypotonia. Muscle tone that is too limp and floppy.

Id. The term Freud used to represent the personality component consisting of the basic instincts and physiological urges, such as hunger, thirst, and sex.

Idioglossia. A private communication system that emerges between twins.

Imitation. Repeating the actions of others.

Infancy. The period between birth and 3 years.

Infant. A child who is between the ages of birth and 3 years.

Infant Temperament Questionnaire. A tool used to assess infant temperament.

Infant-Toddler Environment Rating Scale (ITERS). An instrument used to provide an environmental assessment of center-based day-care classrooms for children under 30 months of age.

Infantile Autism or **Autistic Disorder.** An extreme psychological disorder characterized by a lack of responsiveness to other people, failure to communicate, and other social or emotional disabilities.

Information Processing Approach. An approach to cognitive development in which the functions of the brain are viewed as being somewhat analogous to the internal operations of a computer.

Injury Control. An attempt to prevent injury.

Intelligence. The ability to think, learn, remember, and solve problems.

Intelligence Quotient (IQ). The score derived from an intelligence test that is typically calculated as: Mental age (Test Score) divided by Chronological Age × 100.

Interactional Synchrony. Behavioral exchanges between a caregiver and an infant that are reciprocal, harmonious, and mutually rewarding.
Interactionist. A theorist who believes that growth and development are the result of the interaction between hereditary and environmental forces.
Internal Working Model. The mental and emotional understandings and expectations about oneself and other people in the world that serve as a "script" or a guide for interpersonal relationships.
Interpersonal Play. The type of play that involves face-to-face interactions, social games, or routines during which infants have opportunities to enjoy and practice socially appropriate ways of interaction and communication.
Interpersonal Self. Knowledge about self that is obtained through social experiences.
Intersensory Perception or **Intermodal Perception.** The ability to combine information from different senses.
Intrauterine. Inside the uterus.
Iron Deficiency Anemia. A low supply of red blood cell mass caused by an inadequate amount of iron in the diet.
Jargon. Long strings of sophisticated babbling sounds frequently made with gestures and eye contact, also called **conversational babble.**
Jaundice. A yellowish appearance of the skin caused by excessive bilirubin, a pigment formed when the red blood cells are destroyed by disease or by the aging of the blood cells.
Joint Attention. Communication episodes during which infant and caregiver focus on the same object, sounds, or events.
Kangaroo Care. An approach in which the mother holds the infant between her breasts so that the baby has self-regulatory access to breast-feeding.
Klinefelter Syndrome. A developmental disorder that occurs when a male child is born with two X chromosomes and one Y chromosome.
Kwashiorkor. A severe form of malnutrition caused by insufficient protein in the diet.
Labor. The process of childbirth.
Labor Contraction. The tightening and shortening of the muscles in the uterus during the process of childbirth.
Lamaze Method. The most widely used approach to childbirth education in the United States. The approach focuses on empowering expectant parents to become active participants in the birth process and to minimize the medical management of childbirth.
Language. Vocal utterances, nonverbal behavior, written expressions, and other behaviors used in the process of communication.
Lanugo. The fine hair that covers the fetus from approximately the 20th week until the 7th month of pregnancy.
Large for Gestational Age. Infants whose weight is more than expected for gestational age.
Lateralization. The process by which the different hemispheres of the brain take on special functions.
Learning. The process of acquiring knowledge or skills through experience.
Leboyer Method. A set of procedures used in the delivery room to minimize the trauma of birth on an infant.
Lightening. The point prior to the onset of labor when the baby's head "drops," or moves into the mother's pelvic opening, thereby reducing pressure on the mother's diaphragm.
Locomotion. The ability to move from place to place.
Long-Term Memory. Information that is stored in the mind indefinitely.
Love Withdrawal. A discipline technique in which the parent expresses anger and disappointment and isolates the child emotionally when the child misbehaves.
Low Birth-Weight. Term used for a baby who weighs less than 5½ pounds at birth.
Malnutrition. A condition in which there is either a deficit or an excess of one or more essential nutrients needed by the body's tissues.
Marasmus. A severe form of malnutrition caused by insufficient food intake in general, but a deficiency of calories in particular.
Maternity Centers. See birthing rooms.
Maturationist (also Maturational Theory). The position of theorists who believe that growth and development result from the aging process that is largely controlled by a genetic timetable.
Meconium. The greenish black substance eliminated in the baby's first bowel movement.
Meiosis. The process through which the body forms reproductive cells (sperm and ovum) by reducing the number of chromosomes from 46 to 23.
Mesoderm. The middle layer of embryonic cells that form the circulatory, excretory, and reproductive systems, skeleton, muscles, and connecting tissues.
Microcephaly. A condition in which the head and brain are underdeveloped.
Miscarriage. Spontaneous abortion; termination of pregnancy.
Mitosis. The formation of body cells containing 46 chromosomes for tissue growth and replacement.
Monocular Cues. Cues that can be perceived through one eye working alone.
Moral Development. Learning and internalizing rules and principles that govern human behavior.
Moro Reflex. An involuntary response in which the infant quickly stretches out the arms and brings them inward in a hugging motion when a loud noise or sudden loss of support occurs.
Morphemes. The smallest units of meaning in a language.
Morphology. The way sounds are combined to form words and other units of meaning.
Morula. The fertilized ovum, or zygote, after a mulberry-shaped cluster of 12 to 16 cells has formed at approximately the third day after fertilization.
Motherese. The vocal expressions characteristically used by mothers in talking to their infants, also referred to as **baby talk** (See also **parentese.**)
Motor Biases. The tendency of infants to practice the newest body movements they have learned.
Movement Assessment of Infants (MAI). A tool designed to identify infants with cerebral palsy and other motor problems.

Muscle Strength. The amount of force that the muscles in a particular body part can exert while pushing or pulling against resistance.
Muscle Tone. The amount of tension in the muscles when the body is in a state of rest.
Mutual Regulation. The process whereby infant and caregiver responses control and influence each other's feelings and behavior.
Myelin. A fatty substance produced by the glial cells that forms a sheath around the nerve fibers.
Myelination. The formation of a fatty tissue covering, called myelin, over the nerve cells.
Nativists (also Nativistic theory). Theorists who believe infants are genetically endowed with some basic ideas, feelings, personality, and other characteristics that provide the foundation for future growth and development.
Necrotizing Enterocolitis. A disease that threatens the life of preterm infants, caused by an inadequate blood flow to the intestines or infectious bacteria.
Neonatal Period. See newborn period.
Neonate. The newborn baby from birth through the first two weeks of life.
Neuroglia (Glial). Central nervous systems cells that serve as connecting links between the neurons and the blood supply.
Neurons. Basic nerve cells that transmit impulses and control central nervous system functions.
Neurotransmitters. Brain chemicals that facilitate the transmission of signals within the central nervous system.
Neurulation. The process through which the central nervous system begins to develop during the prenatal period.
Newborn Period. The first two weeks of life after birth.
Niche-Picking. A term used to describe the tendency of children to seek out experiences that fit their genetic predispositions.
Nonorganic Failure to Thrive (NOFTT). Growth failure due to physical and emotional neglect.
Norm-Referenced Tests. Assessment instruments that provide specific scores or ratings that can be used to compare an infant with the performance of other infants of the same age.
Norms. Typical patterns of growth and development.
Novelty. A new or unfamiliar stimulus.
Non-rapid-eye-movement (NREM) sleep. A sleep state in which the baby's eyes do not display patterns of movement beneath the eyelids.
Nutrition. The process by which the body takes in and uses food and other digestible substances.
Objective Self-Awareness. The capacity of infants to "know that they know" and to "remember that they remember."
Object Permanence. The concept of an object as being present somewhere, even if it cannot always be seen, touched, or heard.
Object Play. The type of play that involves toys and play materials; characterized by little, if any, interaction with others.
Olfactory System. The system of the sense of smell.
Operant Conditioning. The process by which behavior is repeated or changed as the result of a reward or punishment that is given as a consequence for a particular response.
Ossification. The process by which cartilage hardens into bone.
Otitis Media. Inflammation of the middle ear.
Otitis Media With Effusion. Inflammation of the middle ear that persists after earaches and other signs or symptoms have disappeared.
Otoacoustic Emissions Test. A test in which a probe is placed into each ear canal, allowing for the detection of hearing loss.
Overextended Words. Words that are overgeneralized to apply to situations, objects, or persons not included in the conventional adult meaning.
Overinvolved Parenting. A parent-child relationship characterized by physical and/or psychological intrusiveness, interference with infant goals, overcontrol, and developmentally inappropriate demands by the caregiver.
Ovum. The reproductive cell produced by the female.
Palmar Grasp Reflex. An involuntary grasp that is elicted by placing a small object in the palm of the baby's hand.
Parentese. The characteristic vocal expressions used by parents, including fathers, in talking to their infants. (See also **motherese.**)
Parent-Infant Relationship Global Assessment Scale (PIR-GAS). A tool used for assessing the strengths of relationships, as well as the severity of a relationship disorder.
Peers. Individuals of about the same age or developmental level who interact with each other in some way; equals.
Perceived Personal Effectance. The extent to which infants perceive that they control what happens in their environment.
Perception. The process through which information gathered by the senses is interpreted by the brain.
Personality. The relatively enduring patterns of behavior and personal qualities that establish one's individuality.
Pertussis (Whooping Cough). An acute infectious disease characterized by mucous discharge from the nose and later repeated attacks of coughing.
Phenylketonuria (PKU). A major recessive genetic disorder which prevents an infant from producing an enzyme necessary for the digestion of an amino acid (phenylalanine) found in milk and many other foods.
Phonemes. The basic units of sounds in a language that are combined to form words.
Phonology. The distinctive sound features of speech and the rules for their combinations.
Physical Abuse. Nonaccidental physical injury as a result of acts or omissions on the part of parents or guardians.
Placenta. The organ or membrane attached to the unborn baby's umbilical cord on one side and the mother's uterine lining on the other. The baby receives nutrients and oxygen and gets rid of waste products through the placenta.
Placental Previa. A condition in which the placenta is attached too close to the cervix, resulting in a risk of early placental separation and maternal bleeding.
Polio. An acute infectious disease caused by a virus inflammation of the gray matter of the spinal cord, sometimes resulting in paralysis.
Polygenic Inheritance. Inherited characteristics that result from the combined effects of multiple genes.

Postterm; Postmature. Term used to classify an infant born after 42 weeks of gestational age.
Posture. The adjustment and maintenance of the body position in relation to the forces of gravity.
Potential Risk. A category used to classify infants who have been exposed to adverse biological and/or environmental conditions that have the potential for causing developmental problems.
Pragmatics. The practical aspects of language including the affective and social components; how language is used to relate to others and to get one's needs met.
Prehension. The ability to grasp with the fingers and thumb.
Prereaching. The first stage of reaching during which infants reflexively reach for or swat at objects with little or no motor coordination or control.
Prespeech Sounds. Sounds, such as crying, cooing, and babbling, that emerge before speech.
Pretend (Symbolic) Play. Play that involves imagination of real-world objects and experiences.
Preterm; Premature. Terms used to classify an infant born before 37 weeks of gestational age.
Primary Yolk Sac. A large cavity that is formed alongside the embryo. As the amniotic sac increases in size, the primary yolk sac decreases in size and forms the secondary yolk sac.
Private Speech. In Vygotsky's theory, the inner speech or "self-talk" that emerges around 30 months of age and is used for self-communication in solving problems and regulating one's own behavior.
Prosocial Behaviors. A variety of positive, socially desirable activities that benefit others.
Protein Energy Malnutrition (PEM). Malnutrition due to an inadequate supply of protein that can result in growth retardation or failure and possibly mental disabilities.
Proxemics. The use of space in communication.
Proximodistal Principle. The principle that growth and development proceed from the central parts of the body to the outer extremities.
Pseudoimitation. An early form of imitation that is based on a response the child has already demonstrated or finds easy to mimic.
Psychoanalytic and **Psychosocial Theories.** Theories that stress the importance of early experiences and the role of emotions in shaping human personality and behavior.
Punishment. A discipline technique that involves a negative response to the child's behavior.
Quickening. The first movements of the fetus that are felt by the mother.
Recall Memory. The ability to retrieve information from the memory in the absence of direct sensory perceptions of the stimulus in question.
Receptive-Emergent Language Test-2 (REEL-2). A checklist that is used to screen infants from 1 to 36 months of age for potential delays in receptive and expressive language skills.
Receptive Speech. The meanings and understandings that are attached to the vocal expressions of others.
Recessive Gene. A gene carrying traits that are expressed only if the gene is paired with the identical recessive gene.
Recognition Memory. The ability to determine whether a stimulus has been previously encountered; the ability to recognize the correct stimulus (answer) when given a choice.
Referential Style. A communication style in which a toddler mainly uses words to share information about objects, one word at a time.
Reflex. An automatic, involuntary response to a stimulus.
Relative Maturity Percentages. Rough estimates of adult height based on current height.
Rapid-eye-movement (REM) sleep. Sleep characterized by rapid movements of the eyes from side to side beneath the eyelids due to increased brain wave activity.
Resilient Infants. Infants who have good developmental outcomes while living under stressful conditions.
Respiratory Distress Syndrome (RDS). A disease of preterm infants caused by a deficiency of surfactant, a substance necessary for efficient breathing.
Retinopathy of Prematurity (ROP). A disease of preterm and low birth weight infants caused by exposure to excess oxygen or other adverse conditions, causing scarring of the eye tissue and possibly blindness.
Rh factor. A type of protein found in human blood that can result in blood incompatibility if it is present in the blood of a fetus (Rh positive) but not in blood of the mother (Rh negative).
Rhythmical Stereotypy. A type of repetitive, rhythmical movement sometimes used by infants to prepare for more advanced and better-coordinated motor activities.
Rooming-in. The practice of allowing the newborn baby to stay in the mother's room rather than in the hospital nursery.
Rooting Reflex. An involuntary response in which a newborn infant moves the head in search of something on which to suck; can be elicited by a touch on the cheek.
Scaffolding. The term used to describe how adults use special structures of language, social encouragement, and tutoring to promote children's learning.
Scheme. The term Piaget used to label a pattern or unit of thought or action.
Secondary Yolk Sac. Formed from the primary yolk sac, the secondary yolk sac is instrumental in the transfer of nutrients to the human embryo prior to the placental connection with the mother.
Secure Base. A caregiver whose presence serves as a support for exploration.
Securely Attached; Secure Attachment. A pattern of attachment in which an infant is easily comforted after having been upset; a securely attached infant uses the caregiver as a secure base for exploration.
Self-Awareness. The perception or awareness of oneself as a distinct individual with an existence and identity separate from other people and objects.
Self-Concept. The sum total, or composite picture, of how one perceives oneself as an individual.
Self-Definition. The ability to define oneself in terms of age, size, gender, personal pronouns, and other verbal labels.
Self-Esteem. The evaluation an individual makes of the self-concept, including positive and negative thoughts and feelings.

Self-Recognition. The ability of infants to recognize their own images in mirrors, pictures, videotapes, and other forms.
Semantics. The definitions of words and the meanings of words as they are used in relation to other words.
Semisolid Food. The thin, strained food that is typically introduced as the baby's first nonmilk food.
Sensations. Sources of information about the environment taken in through the senses.
Sensorial Hearing Loss. A type of hearing deficit that results from abnormality of the inner ear, or failure of the nerves to carry sound signals from the inner ear to the brain.
Sensorimotor Period. The first two years of life when the infant relates to the world by coordinating information from the senses with motor activities of the body.
Sensorimotor Play. Play that is focused on body movements that provide sensory pleasure.
Sensory Integration Dysfunction. An inability to integrate information from different sensory systems.
Sensory Memory. Information from immediate sensory impressions that is stored in the mind for an instant.
Sensory Register. The immediate sensory impressions that persist for a brief interval after a stimulus is gone.
Separation Anxiety. Emotional distress resulting from an infant's separation from a parent or other attachment figure.
Separation-Individuation. The process by which an infant achieves a sense of separateness from the mother.
Sex-Linked Disorders. A variety of hereditary disorders that are caused by defective genes carried on the sex chromosomes.
Shaken Impact Syndrome. Violent shaking of an infant leading to an impact or movement of the brain inside the skull that causes damage to the brain, eyes, or other parts of the head and neck.
Shaken Infant Syndrome. See **shaken impact syndrome.**
Short-Term Memory. The ability to recall information that is stored for a brief period of time, usually about a minute.
Sickle Cell Anemia. A recessively inherited blood disease that produces malformed red blood cells and weakens resistance to infection and other symptoms.
Slow-to-Warm-Up Child. A pattern of temperament characterized by mild intensity of reactions and a negative response to new situations but adaptation over time.
Small for Gestational Age. Infants who weigh less than 90 percent of infants with the same gestational age.
Social Competence. The ability to use environmental and personal resources to get one's needs met and to achieve a satisfactory developmental outcome.
Social Contextual Theories. Theories that posit human beings are, to a large extent, the products of their social and cultural worlds.
Socialization. The process through which a person acquires the attitudes, behaviors, and skills needed to get along in a given society.
Socialization of Emotions. The process by which the infants' emotions are influenced, over time, by the responses of parents and other caregivers.
Social Referencing. The use of behavioral cues or indicators displayed by others in deciding how to respond in a situation in which the decision is not clear.
Somites. The budlike segments in the developing embryo from which the skeleton is formed.
Sound Localization. Identifying the direction from which a sound originates.
Spanking. A discipline technique in which the adult physically punishes the child.
Speech. The vocal or spoken component of language.
Spermatozoa. The reproductive cell produced by the male.
State of Arousal. The degree to which an infant is awake, alert, active, or sleeping.
Stepping Reflex. An involuntary response in which an infant takes rhythmic steps forward, when held upright, with bare feet touching a surface.
Stranger Anxiety. A negative emotional response to a stranger characterized by withdrawal, avoidance, crying, or other signs of distress.
Streptococcus Pneumoniae (Pneumococcus). A strain of bacteria that is the leading cause of pneumonia, bacterial meningitis, sinusitis, and bloodstream and middle ear infections.
Subitization. A perceptual process that people apply in looking at three or four objects and knowing how many there are without going through the process of enumeration.
Subjective Self-Awareness. The awareness of oneself as distinguished from other people and objects in the world.
Sucking Reflex. An involuntary movement in which the infant sucks when the mouth is touched.
Sudden Infant Death Syndrome (SIDS). The sudden, unexpected death of an infant for which no adequate medical explanation can be found.
Superego. The term Freud used to label the personality component that consists of the moral principles and social standards; includes the conscience and the ideal self.
Symbolic Play. The use of pretend games and/or objects to represent something else.
Sympathy. Feelings of sorrow and compassion for another person who is in pain and distress.
Synapses. Connections between the neurons in the brain.
Synaptogenesis. The formation of synapses, or connections, between the neurons via their dendrites and axons.
Syntax. Rules that govern the ways words can be combined to form sentences or meaningful phrases.
Tabula Rasa. The notion proposed by John Locke that newborn infants are a blank slate, that is, passive creatures molded by experiences.
Tay-Sachs Disease. A recessively inherited fatal disease that causes the nervous system to degenerate.
Telegraphic Speech. Linguistic utterances or sentences of limited length that use word order to convey meaning; conjunctions and other nonessential parts of speech are omitted, as in a telegram.
Temperament. The stable behavioral and emotional reactions that appear early and are influenced in part by heredity.
Teratogen. Any substance that can produce a developmental abnormality in an embryo or a fetus.
Test of Sensory Function in Infants. An instrument for assessing sensory processing and reactive abilities of infants.
Theory of Mind. The ability to consider the psychological states of other people.

Thermography. A technique using infrared photographic equipment to detect changes in facial skin surface temperature associated with a change in an infant's emotional state.
Thinking. A process that occurs between input and output of information in humans that includes elementary knowledge and memory.
Thyroxine. A hormone produced by the thyroid gland that is necessary for normal physical growth.
Time-out. A discipline technique in which the child is removed from the situation and given a chance to calm down.
Toddler. An infant who is in the early stage of walking; covers the period of time from approximately 18 months to 3 years of age.
Tonic Neck Reflex. A reflex, present at birth, that causes one side of the body to be dominant. The infant assumes a "fencing" position when lying on stomach or back.
Transactional Perspective. The theory in which developmental outcomes are viewed as the result of reciprocal influences between the child and the environment.
Transdisciplinary Play-Based Assessment (TPBA). A method of assessing the development of infants and young children by a team of professionals and a parent who observe the child in a play session structured in various ways.
Transition Phase. The most difficult time in labor in which the contractions are stronger, last longer, and increase in intensity.
True Social Smile. A voluntary smile that emerges as a result of social stimulation.
Turner Syndrome. A developmental disorder that occurs when a female infant is born with only one sex (X) chromosome.
Ultrasound. A commonly used technique for prenatal assessment whereby high-frequency sound waves are bounced off the fetus to form a live video image called a sonogram.
Umbilical Cord. The ropelike cord containing two arteries and one vein, connecting the unborn infant to the placenta.
Underextended Words. Words that are used too narrowly and specifically.
Underinvolved Parenting. A parent-child relationship characterized by unresponsiveness and insensitivity to infant cues, and low-quality care on the part of parents.
Unintentional Injury. An injury that is not caused on purpose.
Uzgiris-Hunt Ordinal Scales of Psychological Development. An assessment instrument consisting of six subscales based on Piaget's description of cognitive development during infancy; the test items are arranged, or ordered, according to their level of difficulty.
Vacuum Extractor. A device consisting of a metal or plastic cup that is attached to the top of the baby's head to assist in the birth process.
Vagal Tone. A particular measure of heart rate variability controlled by the vagus nerve of the brain that is considered to be an indicator of changes in emotional states and other psychological functions.
Varicella (Chicken pox). An acute, contagious viral disease, usually of young children, characterized by fever and blisters.
Verbal Self. Self-concept that emerges through the use of verbal labels.
Vernix Caseosa. The whitish, oily substance that covers the fetus to protect the skin from the amniotic fluid.
Vestibular Stimulation. Sensory information related to the body's movement and degree of balance.
Vineland Adaptive Behavior Scales. An instrument to assess the ability of individuals to take care of themselves and get along with others from birth to adulthood.
Violation of Expectation Method. A research technique in which infants are presented with an impossible event to determine if they are surprised when the event appears to take place.
Visual Accommodation. The ability to bring objects into focus at various distances.
Visual Acuity. The ability to see objects clearly.
Visual Cliff. A device used to test depth perception in infants.
Visual Evoked Responses. A technique that measures brain waves in response to visual stimulation.
Visually Directed Reaching. The regulation of grasping/manipulative responses through intensified visual activity.
Visual Preference Technique. An innovative method developed by Robert Fantz to study visual perception by means of a special apparatus equipped with a peephole and a "looking chamber."
Visual Reinforcement Audiometry (VRA). A technique used to test hearing that involves pairing auditory and visual stimuli in a variety of ways.
Vocabulary Spurt. A rapid increase in the number of words added to infant vocabulary between 18 and 24 months.
Weaning. The process by which milk-fed infants gradually become accustomed to the range of food characteristic of the society into which they are born.
Working Memory. Information that the brain is actively working on at the moment.
Zone of Proximal Development (ZPD). In Vygotsky's theory, the range of tasks and concepts that a child cannot accomplish alone but is capable of mastering with the help of an adult or a more advanced peer.
Zygote. A fertilized ovum.

REFERENCES

Abbott, S. (1992). Holding on and pushing away: Comparative perspectives on an eastern Kentucky child-rearing practice. *Ethos, 20,* 33–65.

Abel, E. (1983). *Marihuana, tobacco, alcohol, and reproduction.* Boca Raton, FL: CRC.

Abravanel, E., & DeYong, N. (1991). Does object modeling elicit imitative-like gestures from young infants? *Journal of Experimental Child Psychology, 52,* 22–40.

Abravanel, E., & Sigafoos, A.D. (1984). Exploring the presence of imitation during early infancy. *Child Development, 55,* 381–392.

Acredolo, L., & Goodwyn, S. (1996). *Baby signs: How to talk to your baby before your baby can talk.* Chicago: Contemporary.

Acredolo, L., & Goodwyn, S. (1997). Furthering our understanding of what humans understand. *Human Development, 40*(1), 25–31.

Acredolo, L., & Goodwyn, S. (2000). Verbal labels and gestural routines in parental communication with young children. *Journal of Nonverbal Behavior, 24,* 63–79.

Adams, R., Courage, M., & Mercer, M. (1994). Systematic measurement of human neonatal color vision. *Vision Research, 34,* 1691–1701.

Adams, R., & Maurer, D. (1983, April). *A demonstration of color perception in the newborn.* Paper presented at the Society for Research in Child Development, Detroit, MI.

Adams, R., & Maurer, D. (1984, April). *The use of habituation to study newborns' color vision.* Paper presented at the 4th International Conference on Infant Studies, New York.

Adams, R., Maurer, D., & Davis, M. (1986). Newborns' discrimination of chromatic from achromatic stimuli. *Journal of Experimental Child Psychology, 41,* 167–281.

Adamson, L. (1995). *Communication development in infancy.* Madison, WI: Brown & Benchmark.

Adelson, E., & Fraiberg, S. (1974). Gross motor development in infants blind from birth. *Child Development, 45,* 114–126.

Ainsworth, M. (1967). *Infancy in Uganda: Infant care and the growth of attachment.* Baltimore: Johns Hopkins Press.

Ainsworth, M., Blehar, M., Waters, E., & Wall, S. (1978). *Patterns of attachment.* Hillsdale, NJ: Erlbaum.

Akerman, B., & Thomassen, P. (1991). Four-year follow-up of locomotor and language development in 34 twin pairs. *Acta Geneticae Medicae et Gemellologiaem, 40,* 21–27.

Alan Guttmacher Institute. (1981). *Teenage pregnancy: The problem that hasn't gone away.* New York: Author.

Albus, K.E., & Dozier, M. (1999). Indiscriminate friendliness and terror of strangers in infancy: Contributions from the study of infants in foster care. *Infant Mental Health Journal, 20*(1), 30–41.

Alexy, B., & Martin, A. (1994). Breastfeeding: Perceived barriers and benefits/enhancers in a rural and urban setting. *Public Health Nursing, 11,* 214–218.

Allen, M. (1993). An overview of long-term outcome. In F. Witter & L. Keith (Eds.), *Textbook of prematurity* (pp. 371–383). Boston: Little, Brown.

Allen, M., Donohue, P., & Dusman, A. (1993). The limit of viability—neonatal outcome at 22 to 25 weeks gestation. *New England Journal of Medicine, 329,* 1597–1601.

Allen, W. P. (1996). Folic acid in the prevention of birth defects. *Current Opinion in Pediatrics, 8,* 630–634.

Alm, B., Wennergren, G., Norvenius, G., Skjaerven, R., Oyen, N., Helwig-Larsen, K., Lagerkrantz, H., & Irgens, L. (1999). Caffeine and alcohol risk factors for sudden infant death syndrome. Nordic epidemiological SIDS study. *Archives of Disease in Childhood, 81,* 107–111.

Almli, C.R., Ball, R.H., & Wheeler, M.E. (2001). Human fetal and neonatal movement patterns: Gender differences and fetal-to-neonatal continuity. *Developmental Psychobiology, 38*(4), 252–273.

Als, H. (1982). Manual for the assessment of preterm infants' behavior (APIB). In H. Fitzgerald, B. Lester, & M. Yogman (Eds.), *Theory and research in behavioral pediatrics* (Vol. 1, pp. 65–132). New York: Plenum.

Amato, P., & Keith, B. (1991). Parental divorce and well-being of children: A meta-analysis. *Psychological Bulletin, 110,* 26–46.

American Academy of Pediatrics. (1985). Prolonged infantile apnea. *Pediatrics, 76,* 129–130.

American Academy of Pediatrics (1986). Committee on Practice and Ambulatory Medicine. Vision screening and eye examination in children. *Pediatrics, 77,* 918.

American Academy of Pediatrics. (1993). *Toilet training: Guidelines for parents.* [Brochure]. Elk Grove, IL: Author.

American Academy of Pediatrics. (1996). Task force report on infant positioning and SIDS. Positioning and sudden infant death syndrome (SIDS): Update. *Pediatrics, 98,* 1216–1218.

American Academy of Pediatrics (2000). Task force report on infant sleep position and sudden infant death syndrome. Changing concepts of sudden infant death syndrome: Implications for infant sleeping environment and sleep position. *Pediatrics, 105,* 650–656.

Andersen, R., Bale, J., Blackman, J., & Murph, J. (1994). *Infections in children: A sourcebook for child-care providers* (2nd ed.). Gaithersburg, MD: Aspen.

Anderson, D. (1993). Nutrition for premature infants. In P. McQueen & C. Lang (Eds.), *Handbook of pediatric nutrition* (pp. 83–106). Gaithersburg, MD: Aspen.

Angleitner, A., & Ostendorf, F. (1994). Temperament and the big five factors of personality. In C. Halverson, G. Kohnstamm, & R. Martin (Eds.), *The developing structure of temperament and personality from infancy to adulthood* (pp. 69–90). Hillsdale, NJ: Erlbaum.

Anisfeld, M. (1996). Only tongue protrusion modeling is matched by neonates. *Developmental Review, 16,* 149–161.

Annis, L. (1978). *The child before birth.* Ithaca, NY: Cornell University Press.

Anson, B. (Ed). (1966). Morris' human anatomy (12th ed.). New York: McGraw-Hill.

Appleton, T., Clifton, R., & Goldberg, S. (1975). The development of behavioral competence in infancy. In F. Horowitz (Ed.), *Review of child development research* (Vol. 4, pp. 101–186). Chicago: University of Chicago Press.

Arnold, J. (1996). Otitis media and its complications. In W. Nelson, R. Behrman, R. Kliegman, & A. Arving (Eds.), *Nelson's textbook of pediatrics* (15th ed., pp. 1814–1819). Philadelphia: Saunders.

Arterberry, M.E. (1995). Perception of object number through an aperture by human infants. *Infant Behavior and Development, 20,* 359–362.

Arterberry, M.E. (1997). Perception of object properties over time. In C. Rovee-Collier & L.P. Lipsitt, (Eds.), *Advances in Infancy Research, 11,* 219–268.

Arterberry, M., Craton, L., & Yonas, A. (1993). Infants' sensitivity to motion-carried information for depth and object properties. In C. Granrud (Ed.), *Visual perception and cognition in infancy* (pp. 225–234). Hillsdale, NJ: Erlbaum.

Arvin, A. (2001). Varicella vaccine: The first six years. *New England Journal of Medicine, 344,* 1007–1009.

Asher, S., Erdley, C., & Gabriel, S. (1994). Peer relations. In M. Rutter & D. Hay (Eds.), *Development through the lifespan: A handbook for clinicians* (pp. 456–488). Oxford, England: Blackwell.

Ashmead, D., & Perlmutter, M. (1980). Infant memory in everyday life. In M. Perlmutter (Ed.), *New directions for child development: Children's memory* (Vol. 10, pp. 1–16). San Francisco: Jossey-Bass.

Aslin, R. (1981). Development of smooth pursuit in human infants. In D.F. Fischer, R.A. Monty, & W.J. Senders, (Eds.), *Eye movements: Cognition and visual perception* (pp. 31–51). Hillsdale, NJ: Erlbaum

Aslin, R. (1993). Perception of visual direction in human infants. In C. Granrud (Ed.), *Visual perception and cognition in infancy* (pp. 91–119). Hillsdale, NJ: Erlbaum.

Aslin, R., Pisoni, D., & Jusczyk, P. (1983). Auditory development and speech perception in infancy. In P. H. Mussen (Ed.), *Handbook of child psychology: Vol. 2. Infancy and developmental psychobiology* (4th ed., pp. 573–688). New York: Wiley.

Associated Press. (1997, June 8). Better floss: Bad gums tied to heart attacks and premature births. *The Daily Reflector* (Greenville, NC), p. A4.

Aston, A. (1984). *Toys that teach your child.* Charlotte, NC: East Woods Press.

Atkinson, J. (1995). Through the eyes of an infant. In R. Gregory, J. Harris, P. Heard, & D. Rose (Eds.), *The artful eye* (pp. 141–156). New York: Oxford University Press.

Avery, M. (1995). Out of the vortex: Neonatologists' treatment decisions for newborns at risk for HIV [Editorial]. *American Journal of Public Health, 85,* 1484–1485.

Avery, M., & First, L. (1994). *Pediatric medicine* (2nd ed.). Baltimore: Williams & Wilkins.

Baca, M. (2001, March 20). Beyond da-da. *The Raleigh News and Observer,* 1E, 3E.

Bachman, J. (1983). Prenatal care and the normal pregnant woman. *Primary care, 10* (2), 145–160.

Bahrick, L.E., (1995). Intermodal origins of self-perception. In P. Rochat (Ed.), *The self in infancy: Theory and research* (pp. 349–373). Amsterdam: North Holland-Elsevier.

Bahrick, L.E. (2000). Increasing specificity in the development of intermodal perception. In D.W. Muir & A. Slater, (Eds.), *Infant development: The essential readings* (pp. 119–136). Oxford, England: Blackwell.

Bahrick, L.E., & Lickliter, R. (2000). Intersensory redundancy guides attentional selectivity and perceptual learning in infancy. *Developmental Psychology, 36,* 190–201.

Bahrick, L.E., Moss, L., & Fadil, C. (1996). Development of visual self-recognition in infancy. *Ecological Psychology, 8*(3), 189–208.

Bahrick, L. E., & Pickens, J. (1994). Amodal relations: The basis for intermodal perception and learning in infancy. In D. Lewkowicz & R. Lickliter (Eds.), *The development of intersensory perception: Comparative perspectives* (pp. 205–233). Hillsdale, NJ: Erlbaum.

Baildum, E., Hillier, V., Menon, S., Bamford, F., Moore, W., & Ward, B. (2000). Attention to infants in the first year. *Child Care, Health and Development, 26*(3), 199–216.

Bailey, W. (1994). A longitudinal study of fathers: Involvement with young children: Infancy to age 5 years. *Journal of Genetic Psychology, 155,* 331–339.

Baillargeon, R. (1993). The object concept revisited: New directions in the investigation of infants' physical knowledge. In C. Granrud (Ed.), *Visual perception and cognition in infancy* (pp. 265–315). Hillsdale, NJ: Erlbaum.

Baillargeon, R. (1994). How do infants learn about the physical world. *Current Directions in Psychological Science, 3,* 133–140.

Bakker, P. (1987). Autonomous language of twins. *Acta Geneticae Medicae et Gemellologiaem, 36,* 233–238.

Baldwin, A. (1967). *Theories of child development.* New York: Wiley.

Bale, J. (1990). The neurologic complications of AIDS in infants and young children. *Infants and Young Children, 3,* 15–23.

Ballachanda, B. (1995). *The human ear canal.* San Diego: Singular.

Ballard, J., Khoury, J., Wedig, K., Wang, L., Eilers-Walshman, B., & Lipp, R. (1991). New Ballard Score expanded to include extremely premature infants. *Journal of Pediatrics,* 119, 417–423.

Bandura, A. (1977). *Social learning theory.* Englewood Cliffs, NJ: Prentice Hall.

Bangs, T. (1982). *Language and learning disorders of the preacademic child* (2nd ed.). Englewood Cliffs, NJ: Prentice Hall.

Banks, M. (1980). The development of visual accommodation during early infancy. *Child Development, 51,* 646–666.

Banks, M., Aslin, R., & Letson, R. (1975). Sensitive period for the development of binocular vision. *Science, 190,* 675–677.

Banks, M., & Bennett, P. (1991). Anatomical and physiological constraints on neonatal visual sensitivity and determinants of fixation behavior. In M. Weiss & P. Zalazo (Eds.), *Newborn attention: Biological constraints on the influence of experience* (pp. 177–217). Norwood, NJ: Ablex.

Banks, M., & Salapatek, P. (1983). Infant visual perception. In P. Mussen (Ed.), *Handbook of child psychology: Vol. 2. Infancy and developmental psychobiology* (4th ed., pp. 435–571). New York: Wiley.

Banks, M., & Shannon, E. (1993). Spatial and chromatic visual efficiency in human neonates. In C. Granrud (Ed.), *Visual perception and cognition in infancy* (pp. 1–46). Hillsdale, NJ: Erlbaum.

Barglow, P., Vaughn, B., & Moliter, N. (1987). Effects of maternal absence due to employment on the quality of infant-mother attachment in a low-risk sample. *Child Development, 58,* 945–954.

Barness, L., & Curran, J. (1996). Nutrition. In W. Nelson, R. Behrman, R. Kleigman, & A. Arving (Eds.), *Nelson textbook of pediatrics* (15th ed., pp. 141–172). Philadelphia: Saunders.

Barnet, A., & Barnet R. (1998). *The youngest minds.* New York: Touchstone.

Baron-Cohen, S. (1994). Development of a theory of mind: Where would we be without the intentional stance? In M. Rutter & D. Hay (Eds.), *Development through life* (pp. 303–318). Oxford, England: Blackwell.

Barr, H., Streissguth, A., Martin, D., & Herman, C. (1984). Infant size at 8 months of age: Relationship to maternal use of alcohol, nicotine, and caffeine during pregnancy. *Pediatrics, 74,* 336–341.

Baruffi, G., Dellinger, W., Stobino, D., Rudolph, A., Timmons, R., & Ross, A. (1984). A study of pregnancy outcomes in a maternity center and a tertiary care hospital. *American Journal of Public Health, 74,* 973–978.

Bates, E., Benigni, L., Bretherton, I., Camaioni, L., & Volterra, V. (1977). From gesture to the first word: On cognitive and social prerequisites. In M. Lewis & L. Rosenblum (Eds.), *Interaction, conversation and the development of language* (pp. 247–317). New York: Wiley.

Bates, E., O'Connell, B., & Shore, C. (1987). Language and communication in infancy. In J. Osofsky (Ed.), *Handbook of infant development* (2nd ed., pp. 149–203). New York: Wiley.

Bates, J. (1980). The concept of difficult temperament. *Merrill-Palmer Quarterly, 25,* 299–319.

Bates, J. (1987). Temperament in infancy. In J. Osofsky (Ed.), *Handbook of infant development* (2nd ed., pp. 1101–1149). New York: Wiley.

Bates, J. (1994). Introduction. In J. Bates & T. Wachs (Eds.), *Temperament: Individual differences at the interface of biology and behavior* (pp. 1–14). Washington, DC: American Psychological Association.

Bates, J., & Bayles, K. (1984). Objective and subjective components in mothers' perceptions of their children from age 6 months to 3 years. *Merrill-Palmer Quarterly, 30,* 111–129.

Bates, J., Wachs, T., & Emde, R. (1994). Toward practical uses for biological concepts of temperament. In J. Bates & T. Wachs (Eds.), *Temperament: Individual differences at the interface of biology and behavior* (pp. 275–306). Washington, DC: American Psychological Association.

Batshaw, M. (1997). Understanding your chromosomes. In M. Batshaw (Ed.), *Children with disabilities* (4th ed., pp 3–33). Baltimore: Brookes.

Bauer, P. (1996). What do infants recall of their lives? Memory for specific events by one- to two-year-olds. *American Psychologist, 51,* 29–41.

Bauer, P., & Hertsgaard, L. (1993). Increasing steps in recall of events: Factors facilitating immediate and long-term memory in 13.5 and 16.5-month-old children. *Child Development, 64,* 1204–1223.

Bauer, P., & Wewerka, S. (1995). One- to two-year-olds recall of events: The more expressed, the more impressed. *Journal of Developmental Psychology, 59,* 475–496.

Bax, M., Hart, H., & Jenkins, S. (1990). *Child development and health.* Oxford, England: Blackwell.

Bayley, N. (1935). The development of motor abilities during the first three years. *Monographs of the Society of Research in Child Development, 1* (Serial No. 1).

Bayley, N. (1965). Comparisons of mental and motor tests scores for ages 1–15 months by sex, birth order, race, geographical location, and education of parents. *Child Development, 36,* 379–411.

Bayley, N. (1969). *Bayley Scales of Infant Development.* New York: Psychological Corp.

Bayley, N. (1993). *Bayley Scales of Infant Development–II* (2nd ed.). San Antonio: Psychological Corp.

Bayley, N., & Schaefer, E. (1964). Correlations of maternal and child behaviors with the development of mental abilities: Data from the Berkeley Growth Study. *Monographs of the Society for Research in Child Development, 29* (6, Serial No. 97).

Bear, M.F., Connors, B.W., & Paradiso, M.A. (2001). *Neurosciences: Exploring the brain* (2nd ed.). Baltimore: Lippincott Williams & Wilkins.

Beauchamp, G., & Cowart, B. (1986, March). When tots taste salt. *Science, 86,* 10.

Beauchamp, G.K., Cowart, B.I., Mennella, J.A., & Marsh, R.R. (1994). Infant salt taste: Developmental, methodological and contextual factors. *Developmental Psychobiology, 27,* 353–365.

Beauchamp, G., & Moran, M. (1984). Acceptance of sweet and salty tastes in 2-year-old children. *Appetite, 5,* 291–305.

Beck, S. (1979). *Baby talk: How your child learns to speak.* New York: New American Library.

Becker, W. (1964). Consequences of different kinds of parental discipline. In M. Hoffman & L. Hoffman (Eds.), *Review of child development research* (Vol. 1, pp. 169–208). New York: Russell Sage Foundation.

Bee H. (2000). *The developing child* (9th ed.). Boston: Allyn & Bacon.

Bee, W., Barnard, K., Eyeres, S., Gray, C., Hammond, M., Spietz, A., Snyder, C., & Clark, B. (1982). Prediction of IQ and language skill from perinatal status, child performance, family circumstances and mother-infant interaction. *Child Development, 53,* 1134–1156.

Beedle, G. (1984). Teeth. In C. Kempe, H. Silver, & D. O'Brien (Eds.), *Current pediatric diagnosis and treatment* (8th ed., pp. 290–293). Los Altos, CA: Lange.

Begley, S. (1996, February 19). Your child's brain. *Newsweek, 127,* 55–61.

Begley, S. (1997, Spring/Summer). How to build a baby's brain. *Newsweek: Special Edition,* 28–32.

Behrman, R., & Vaughan, V. (1983). *Nelson textbook of pediatrics* (12th ed.). Philadelphia: Saunders.

Bell, S., & Ainsworth, D. (1972). Infant crying and maternal responsiveness. *Child Development, 43,* 1171–1190.

Beller, E. (1979). Early intervention programs. In J. Osofsky (Ed.), *Handbook of infant development* (pp. 852–894). New York: Wiley.

Belsky, J. (1979). The interrelation of parental and spousal behavior during infancy in transitional nuclear families: An exploratory analysis. *Journal of Marriage and the Family, 41,* 62–68.

Belsky, J. (1981). Early human experience: A family perspective. *Developmental Psychology, 17,* 3–23.

Belsky, J. (1988). The "effects" of infant day care reconsidered. *Early Childhood Research Quarterly, 3,* 235–272.

Belsky, J. (1999a). Infant-parent attachment. In L. Balter & C. Tamis-Lemonda (Eds.), *Child psychology: A handbook of contemporary issues* (pp. 45–63). Philadelphia: Psychology Press.

Belsky, J. (1999b). Quantity of nonmaternal care and boys' problem behavior/adjustment at ages 3 and 5: Exploring the mediating role of parenting. *Psychiatry: Interpersonal and Biological Processes, 62*(1), 1–20.

Belsky, J., & Kelly, J. (1994). *The transition to parenthood.* New York: Delacorte.

Belsky, J., & Most, R. (1981). From exploration to play: A cross-sectional study of infant free play behavior. *Developmental Psychology, 17,* 630–639.

Belsky, J., & Rovine, M. (1988). Nonmaternal care in the first year of life and the security of infant-parent attachment security. *Child Development, 59,* 157–167.

Belsky, J., & Volling, B. (1987). Mothering, fathering, and marital interaction in the family triad: Exploring family systems processes. In P. Berman & F. Pedersen (Eds.), *Men's transition to parenthood: Longitudinal studies of early family experience* (pp. 37–63). Hillsdale, NJ: Erlbaum.

Bench, J., Collyer, Y., Langford, C., & Toms, R. (1972). A comparison between the neonatal sound-evoked startle response and the head-drop (Moro) reflex. *Developmental Medicine and Child Neurology, 14,* 308–314.

Benenson, J. (1996). Gender differences in the development of relationships. In G. Noam & K. Fischer (Eds.), *Development and vulnerability in close relationships* (pp. 263–286). Mahwah, NJ: Erlbaum.

Benirschke, K. (1995). The biology of the twinning process: How placentation influences outcome. *Seminars in Perinatology, 19,* 342–350.

Benn, R. (1986). Factors promoting secure attachment relationships between employed mothers and their sons. *Child Development, 57,* 1224–1231.

Bennett, F. (1987). The effectiveness of early intervention for infants at increased biologic risk. In M. Guralnick & F. Bennett (Eds.), *The effectiveness of early intervention for at-risk and handicapped children* (pp. 79–112). New York: Academic.

Benson, R., & Pernoll, M. (1994). *Handbook of obstetrics and gynecology* (9th ed.). New York: McGraw-Hill.

Berg, W., Adkinson, C., & Strock, B. (1973). Duration and frequency of periods of alertness in neonates. *Developmental Psychology, 15,* 760–769.

Berk, L. (1996). *Infants, children, and adolescents* (2nd ed.). Boston: Allyn & Bacon.

Berk, L., & Winsler, A. (1995). *Scaffolding children's learning. Vygotsky and early childhood education.* Washington, DC: National Association for the Education of Young Children.

Bernbaum, J., & Batshaw, M. (1997). Born too soon, born too small. In M. Batshaw & Y. Perret (Eds.), *Children with handicaps: A medical primer* (4th ed., pp. 115–139). Baltimore: Brookes.

Bernhardt, J. (1987). Sensory capabilities of the fetus. *Maternal Child Nursing Journal, 12,* 44–46.

Berry, K. (1975). Developmental study of recognition of antecedents of infant vocalizations. *Perceptual and Motor Skills, 41,* 400–402.

Bertenthal, B., & Campos, J. (1987). New directions in the study of experience. *Child Development, 58,* 560–567.

Bertenthal, B., & Campos, J. (1990). A systems approach to the organizing effects of self-produced locomotion during infancy. In C. Rovee-Collier & L. Lipsitt (Eds.), *Advances in infancy research* (Vol. 6, pp. 1–60). Norwood, NJ: Ablex.

Bertenthal, B., Campos, J., & Bennett, K. (1984). Self-produced locomotion: An organizer of emotional, cognitive, and social development in infancy. In R. Emde & R. Harmon (Eds.), *Continuities and discontinuities of development* (pp. 195–207). New York: Plenum.

Bertenthal, B., & Fischer, K. (1978). Development of self-recognition in the infant. *Developmental Psychology, 14,* 14–50.

Bhatt, R. (1997). The interface between perception and cognition: Feature detection, visual pop-out effects, feature integration, and long-term memory in infancy. In C. Rovee-Collier & L.P. Lipsitt, (Eds.), *Advances in infancy research,* (Vol. 11, 143–191).

Bhatt, R., & Waters, S. (1998). Perception of three-dimensional cues in early infancy. *Journal of Experimental Child Psychology, 70,* 207–224.

Billeaud, F. (1993). *Communication disorders in infants and toddlers.* Boston: Andover.

Biller, H. (1981). Father absence, divorce and personality development. In M. Lamb (Ed.), *The role of the father in child development* (2nd ed., pp. 489–552). New York: Wiley.

Birch, L., & Marlin, D. (1982). I don't like it; I never tried it: Effects of exposure on two-year-old children's food preferences. *Appetite, 3,* 353–360.

Birnholz, J., & Benacerraf, B. (1983). The development of fetal hearing. *Science, 222,* 516–518.

Bischof-Kohler, D. (1991). The development of empathy in infants. In M. Lamb & H. Keller (Eds.), *Infant development: Perspectives from German-speaking countries* (pp. 245–274). Hillsdale, NJ: Erlbaum.

Blair, P., Fleming, P., Bensley, D., Smith, I., Bacon, C., Taylor, E., Berry, J., Golding, J., & Tripp, J. (1996). Smoking and the sudden infant death syndrome: Results from 1993–5 case-control study for confidential inquiry into stillbirths and deaths in infancy. *British Medical Journal. 313,* 195–198.

Blanche, S., Mayaux, M., Rouzioux, C., Teglas, J., Firtion, G., Monpoux, F., Ciraru-Virgneron, N., Meier, F., Triciore, J., & Courpotin, C. (1994). Relation of the course of HIV infection in children to the severity of the disease in their mothers at the time of delivery. *New England Journal of Medicine, 330,* 308–312.

Blass, E., & Ciaramitaro, V. (1994). A new look at some old mechanisms in human newborns. *Monographs of the Society for Research in Child Development, 59* (1, Serial No. 239).

Blass, E., Ganchrow, J., & Steiner, J. (1984). Classical conditioning in newborn humans 2–48 hours of age. *Infant Behavior and Development, 7,* 223–235. Norwood, NJ: Ablex.

Bloch, H., & Carchon, I. (1992). On the onset of eye-head coordination in infants. *Behavioural Brain Research, 49,* 85–90.

Bloom, L. (1973). *One word at a time: The use of single word utterances before syntax.* The Hague, The Netherlands: Mouton.

Bloom, L. (1993). *The transition from infancy to language.* New York: Cambridge.

Bloom, L. (1998). Language acquisition in its developmental context. In W. Damon, D. Kuhn, & R. Siegler (Eds.), *Child psychology* (5th ed., pp. 309–370). New York: Wiley.

Bohannon, J. (1993). Theoretical approaches to language acquisition. In J. Berko Gleason (Ed.), *The development of language* (3rd. ed, pp. 239–297). New York: Macmillan.

Boklage, C. (1980). The sinisitral blastocyst: An embryonic perspective on the development of brain-function asymetries. In J. Herron (Ed.), *Neuropsychology of left-handedness* (pp. 115–137). New York: Academic Press.

Boland, M., & Oleske, J. (1995). The health care needs of infants and children: An epidemiological perspective. In N. Boyd-Franklin, G. Steiner, & M. Boland (Eds.), *Children and families with HIV/AIDS: Psychosocial and therapeutic issues* (pp. 19–51). New York: Guilford.

Boring, E. (1923, June). Intelligence as the tests test it. *New Republic, 35,* 35–37.

Bornstein, M. (1981). Psychological studies of color perception in human infants: Habituation, discrimination and categorization, recognition, and conceptualization. In L. Lipsitt (Ed.), *Advances in infancy research* (Vol. 1, pp. 2–40). Norwood, NJ: Ablex.

Bornstein, M. (1988). Perception across the life cycle. In M.H. Bornstein & M.E. Lamb (Eds.), *Developmental psychology: An advanced text* (pp. 151–204). Hillsdale, NJ: Erlbaum.

Bornstein, M., & Arterberry, M. (1999). Perceptual development. In M. Bornstein & M. Lamb (Eds.), *Developmental psychology: An advanced text* (4th ed., pp. 231–274). Mahwah, NJ: Erlbaum

Bornstein, M., & Lamb, M. (1992). *Development in infancy* (3rd ed.). New York: McGraw-Hill.

Borovsky, D., & Rovee-Collier, C. (1990). Contextual constraints on memory retrieval at six-months. *Child Development,* 61, 1569–1583.

Bossey, J. (1980). Development of olfactory and related structures in staged human embroyos. *Anatomy of Embryology, 161,* 225–236.

Bowen, C. (2001). Speech and language development in infants and young children. Retrieved August 9, 2001 from http: www.//members.tripod.com/Caroline_Bowen/devel1.htm.

Bowen, S., & Miller, B. (1980). Paternal attachment behavior as related to presence or absence at delivery and parenthood classes: A pilot study. *Nursing Research, 29,* 307–311.

Bower, H. (1999). New research demolishes link between MMR vaccine and autism. *British Medical Journal, 318,* 1643–1649.

Bower, T. (1977b). *A primer of infant development.* San Francisco: Freeman.

Bower, T.(1977a). Blind babies see with their ears. *New Scientist, 73,* 255–257.

Bower, T. (1982). *Development in infancy* (2nd ed.). San Francisco: Freeman.

Bower, T., Broughton, J., & Moore, M. (1970). Demonstration of intention in the reaching behavior of neonate humans. *Nature, 228,* 679–681.

Bowerman, M. (1978). The acquisition of word meaning: An investigation into some current conflicts. In N. Waterson & C.E. Snow, (Eds.), *The development of communication* (pp. 263–287). New York: Wiley.

Bowlby, J. (1969). *Attachment and loss. Vol. 1: Attachment.* New York: Basic.

Boyson-Bardies, B. (1994). Speech development: Contributions from cross-linguistic studies. In A. Vyt, H. Bloch, & M. Bornstein (Eds.), *Early child development in the French tradition: Contributions from current research* (pp. 191–206). Hillsdale, NJ: Erlbaum.

Brackbill, Y., McManus, K., & Woodard, L. (1985). *Medication in maternity: Infant exposure and maternal information.* Ann Arbor: University of Michigan.

Bradley, L. (1995). Changing American birth through childbirth education. *Parent Education and Counseling, 25,* 75–82.

Bradley, R. (1972). Development of the taste bud and gustatory papilae in human fetuses. In J. Bosma (Ed.), *The third symposium of oral sensation and perception: The mouth of the infant* (pp. 137–162). Springfield, IL: Thomas.

Bradley, R. (1974). *Husband coached childbirth.* New York: Harper & Row.

Bradley, R. (1994). The HOME Inventory: Review and reflections. In H. Reese (Ed.), *Advances in child development and behavior* (Vol. 25, pp. 241–288). San Diego: Academic.

Bradley, R., Burchinal, M., & Casey, P. (2001). Early intervention: The moderating role of the home environment. *Applied Developmental Science, 5*(1), 2–8.

Bradley, R., Rock, S., Barnard, K., Gray, C., Hammon, M., Mitchel, S., Siegel, L., Ramey, C., Gottfried, A., & Johnson, D. (1989). Home environment and cognitive development in the first 3 years of life: A collaborative study involving six sites and three ethnic groups in North America. *Developmental Psychology, 25,* 217–235.

Brambati, B., & Oldrini, A. (1986). Methods of chorionic villus sampling. In B. Brambati, G. Simoni, & S. Fabro (Eds.), *Chorionic villus sampling* (pp. 73–97). New York: Dekker.

Braungart, J., Plomin, R., Defries, J., & Fulker, D. (1992). Genetic influence on tester-rated infant temperament as assessed by Bayley's Infant Behavior Record: Nonadoptive and adoptive siblings and twins. *Developmental Psychology, 28,* 40–47.

Brazelton, T. (1973). Neonatal behavioral assessment scale. *Clinics in Developmental Medicine,* No. 50. Philadelphia: Lippincott.

Brazelton, T. (1992). *Touchpoints.* Reading, MA: Addison-Wesley.

Brazelton, T., & Cramer, B. (1990). *The earliest relationship.* Reading, MA: Addison-Wesley.

Bredberg, G. (1985). The anatomy of the developing ear. In S. Trehub & B. Schmeiter (Eds.), *Auditory development in infancy* (pp. 3–20). New York: Plenum Press.

Bremner, J. (1988). *Infancy.* New York: Basil Blackwell.

Bremner, J. (1998). From perception to action: The early development of knowledge. In F. Simion and G. Butterworth (Eds.), *The development of sensory, motor and cognitive capacities in early infancy: From perception to cognition* (pp. 239–255).

Brennan, W., Ames, E., & Moore, R. (1966). Age differences in infants' attention patterns to different complexities. *Science, 151,* 354–356.

Bretherton, I. (1996). Internal working models of attachment relationships as related to resilient coping. In G. Noam & K. Fischer (Eds.), *Development and vulnerability in close relationships* (pp. 3–27). Mahwah, NJ: Erlbaum.

Bretherton, I., Beeghly-Smith, M., Williamson, C., & McNew, S. (1980, April). *"I hurt your feelings cause I was mean to you." Toddlers' person knowledge as expressed in their language.* Paper presented at the meeting of the International Conference on Infant Studies. New Haven, CT.

Bretherton, I., & Waters, E. (Eds.). (1985). Growing points of attachment theory and research. *Monographs of the Society of Research in Child Development, 50* (1–2, Serial No. 209).

Briggs, J. (1970). *Never in anger: Portrait of an Eskimo family.* Cambridge, MA: Harvard University.

Bristol, M., Gallagher, J., & Schopler, E. (1988). Mothers and fathers of young developmentally disabled and nondisabled boys: Adaptation and spousal support. *Developmental Psychology, 24,* 441–451.

Bromwich, R. (1980). *Working with parents and infants: An interactional approach.* Baltimore: University Park Press.

Bronfenbrenner, U. (1979). *The ecology of human development.*Cambridge, MA: Harvard University.

Bronson, G. (1972). Infants' reactions to unfamiliar persons and novel objects. *Monographs of the Society for Research in Child Development, 37* (3, Serial No. 148).

Brookhart, J., & Hock, E. (1976). The effects of experimental context and experimental background on infants' behavior toward their mothers and strangers. *Child Development, 47,* 333–340.

Brooks, J., & Lewis, M. (1976a). Infants' response to strangers: Midget, adult and child. *Child Development, 47,* 323–332.

Brooks, J., & Lewis, M. (1976b, July). *Visual self-recognition in infancy: Contingency and the self-other distinction.* Paper presented at the Southeastern Conference 21st International Congress, Paris.

Brooks-Gunn, J., & Lewis, M. (1979). The effects of age and sex on infants' playroom behavior. *Journal of Genetic Psychology, 134,* 99–105.

Brooks-Gunn, J., & Lewis, M. (1982). The development of self-knowledge. In C. Kropp & J. Krakow (Eds.), *The child: Development in a social context* (pp. 333–387). Reading, MA: Addison-Wesley.

Brooten, D., & Jordan, C. (1983). Caffeine and pregnancy: A research review and recommendations for clinical practice. *JOGN Nursing, 12*(2), 190–195.

Broude, G. (1995). *Growing up: A cross-cultural encyclopedia.* Santa Barbara, CA: ABC-CLIO.

Brown, R. (1973). *A first language: The early stages.* Cambridge, MA: Harvard University Press.

Brown, R. (1977). Introduction. In C. E. Snow & C. Ferguson (Eds.), *Talking to children* (pp. 1–27). London: Cambridge University Press.

Brown, R., & Fraser, C. (1963). The acquisition of syntax. In C. Cofer & B. Musgrave (Eds.), *Verbal behavior and learning: Problems and processes* (pp. 158–197). New York: McGraw-Hill.

Browne, S., & Miller, B. (1980). Paternal attachment behavior as related to presence during delivery and preparenthood classes. *Nursing Research, 29,* 307–311.

Brownell, C., & Brown, E. (1992). Peers and play in infants and toddlers. In V. Van Hasselt & M. Hersen (Eds.), *Handbook of social development: A lifespan perspective* (pp. 183–200). New York: Plenum.

Brownell, C., & Kopp, C. (1991). Common threads, diverse solutions: Concluding commentary. *Developmental Review, 11,* 288–303.

Bruck, K. (1961). Temperature regulation in the newborn infant. *Biologic Neonatorum, 3,* 65–119.

Bruer, J. (1999). *The myth of the first three years.* New York: Free Press.

Brunelle, J., & Carlos, J. (1990). Recent trends in dental caries in U.S. children and the effects of water fluoridation. *Journal of Dental Research, 69,* 723–727.

Bruner, J. (1978). Learning the mother tongue. *Human Nature, 1,* 42–49.

Bruner, J. (1982). The formats of language acquisition. *American Journal of Semiotics, 1,* 1–16.

Bruner, J. (1983). *Child's talk.* New York: Norton.

Bryden, M., & Steenhuis, R. (1991). The assessment of handedness in children. In J. Obrzut & G. Hynd (Eds.), *A handbook of issues, methods, and practice* (pp. 411–436). San Diego: Academic.

Bryen, D. (1982). *Inquiries into child language.* Boston: Allyn & Bacon.

Buchsbaum, H., & Emde, R. (1990). Play narratives in thirty-six-month-old children: Early moral development and family relationships. *Psychoanalytic Study of the Child, 40,* 129–155.

Burchinal, M., Roberts, J., Nabors, L., & Bryant, D. (1996). Quality of center child care and infant cognitive and language development. *Child Development, 67,* 606–620.

Burlingham, D. (1964). Hearing and its role in the development of the blind. *Psychoanalytic Study of the Child, 19,* 95–112.

Burlington wife has miracle baby. (1979, July 17). *The Raleigh News and Observer,* p. 6.

Burnett, C., & Johnson, E. (1971). Development of gait in childhood: Part 2. *Developmental Medicine and Child Neurology, 13,* 207.

Burton, B., Schulz, C., Angle, B., & Burd, L. (1995). An increased incidence of haemangiomas in infants born following chorionic villus sampling (CVS). *Prenatal Diagnosis, 15,* 209–214.

Burton, R. (1972). Cross-sex identity in Barbados. *Developmental Psychology, 6,* 365–374.

Bushnell, E. (1985). The decline of visually guided reaching during infancy. *Infant Behavior and Development, 8,* 139–155.

Bushnell, E. (1998). The origins of face perception. In F. Simion & G. Butterworth, (Eds.), *The development of sensory, motor and cognitive capacities in early infancy: From perception to cognition* (pp. 69–86). East Sussex, UK: Psychology Press.

Bushnell, E., & Boudreau, J. (1991). The development of haptic perception during infancy. In M. Heller & W. Schiff (Eds.), *The psychology of touch* (pp. 139–161). Hillsdale, NJ: Erlbaum.

Bushnell, E., & Boudreau, J. (1993). Motor development and the mind: The potential role of motor abilities as a determinant of aspects of perceptual development. *Child Development, 64,* 1005–1021.

Bushnell, I., & Sai, F. (1987). *Neonatal recognition of mother's face.* University of Glasgow Report 87/1.

Buss, A. (1989). Temperaments as personality traits. In G. Kohnstamn, J. Bates, & M. Rothbart (Eds.), *Temperament in childhood* (pp. 49–58). New York: Wiley.

Buss, A., & Plomin, R. (1975). *A temperament theory of personality.* New York: Wiley.

Butterfield, E., & Sipperstein, G. (1974). Influence of contingent auditory stimulation upon nonnutritional suckle. In J.

Bosma (Ed.), *Third symposium on oral sensation and perception: The mouth of the infant* (pp. 313–334). Springfield, IL: Thomas.

Butterfield, J., & Covey, M. (1962). Letter to the Editor: Practical epigram of the Apgar Score. *Journal of the American Medical Association, 181,* 353.

Butterfield, P. (1996). The partners in parenting education program: A new option in parent education. *Zero to Three, 17*(1), 3–10.

Butterworth, G. (1998). What is special about pointing in babies. In F. Simion & G. Butterworth (Eds.), *The development of sensory, motor and cognitive capacities in early infancy* (pp. 171–190). East Sussex, England: Psychology Press.

Butterworth, G., & Hopkins, B. (1993). Origins of handedness. *Developmental Medicine and Child Neurology, 35,* 177–184.

Byard, R. (1994). Is co-sleeping in infancy a desirable or dangerous practice? *Journal of Paediatrics and Child Health, 30,* 198–199.

Byers, T., Graham, S., Rzepka, T., & Marshall, J. (1985). Lactation and breast cancer. *American Journal of Epidemiology, 121,* 644–674.

Bzoch, K., & League, R. (1991) *The Receptive-Emergent Language Test–2.* Los Angeles: Western Psychological Services.

Caldwell, B., & Bradley, R. (1979). *Home observation for measurement of the environment.* Little Rock: University of Arkansas.

Callen, P., & Filley, R. (1990). Amniotic fluid evaluation. In M. Harrison, M. Golbus, & R. Filly (Eds.), *The unborn patient: Prenatal diagnosis and treatment* (2nd ed., pp. 139–149). Philadelphia: Saunders.

Campbell, A., Shirley, L., Heywood, C., & Crook, C. (2000). Infants' visual preference for sex-congruent babies, children, toys and activities: A longitudinal study. *British Journal of Developmental Psychology, 18*(4), 479–498.

Campbell, D., & Eaton, W. (1999). Sex differences in the activity level of infants. *Infant and Child Development, 8,* 1–17.

Campbell, F., Pungello, E., Miller-Johnson, S., Burchinal, M., & Ramey, C. (2001). The development of cognitive and academic abilities: Growth curves from an early childhood educational experiment. *Developmental Psychology, 37,* 231–242.

Campbell, F., & Ramey, C. (1994). Effects of early intervention on intellectual and academic achievement: A follow-up study of children from low-income families. *Child Development, 65,* 684–698.

Campos, J., Barrett, K., Lamb, M., Goldsmith, H., & Stenberg, C. (1983). Socioemotional development. In P. Mussen (Ed.), *Handbook of child psychology: Vol. 2. Infancy and developmental psychobiology* (4th ed., pp. 784–915). New York: Wiley.

Campos, J., Bertenthal, B., & Kermoian, R. (1992). Early experience and emotional development: The emergence of wariness of heights. *Psychological Science, 3,* 61–64.

Campos, J., Campos, R., & Barrett, K. (1989). Emergent themes in the study of emotional development and emotion regulation. *Developmental Psychology, 25,* 394–402.

Campos, J., Kermoian, R., & Zumbahlen, M. (1992). Socioemotional transformations in the family system following infant crawling onset. *New Directions for Child Development, 55* (Spring), 25–56.

Campos, J., & Stenberg, C. (1981). Perception, appraisal, and emotion: The onset of social referencing. In M. Lamb & L. Sherrod (Eds.), *Infant social cognition: Empirical and theoretical considerations* (pp. 273–314). Hillsdale, NJ: Erlbaum.

Canadian Paediatric Society Nutrition Committee. (1979). Infant feeding. *Canadian Journal of Public Health, 70,* 376–385.

Capizzano, J., Adams, G., & Sorenstein, G. (2000). Child care arrangements for children under five: Variations across the states. Number B–7 in Series: *New federalism: National Survey of America's Families.* Urban Institute. Retrieved October 20, 2001from http://newfederalism.urban.org/html/series b/b7.html

Capute, A., Shapiro, B., Palmer, F., Ross, A., & Wachtel, R. (1985). Normal gross motor development: The influence of race, sex, and socioeconomic status. *Developmental Medicine and Child Neurology, 27,* 635–643.

Carey, S. (1996). Perceptual classification and expertise. In R. Gelman & T. Au (Eds.), *Perceptual and cognitive development* (pp. 49–69). San Diego: Academic.

Carey, W., & McDevitt, S. (1978). Revision of the Infant Temperament Questionnaire. *Pediatrics, 61,* 735–739.

Carlson, B. (1999). Human embryology and developmental biology (2nd ed.). St. Louis: Mosby.

Carlson, V., Cicchetti, D., Barnett, D., & Braunwald, K. (1989). Disorganized/disoriented attachment relationships in maltreated children. *Developmental Psychology, 25,* 525–531.

Carr, D. (1971). Chromosome studies on selected spontaneous abortions: Polyploidy in man. *Journal of Medical Genetics, 8,* 164.

Casaer, P. (1992). Development of motor functions: A developmental-neurological approach. In A. Kalverboer, B. Hopkins, & R. Geuze (Eds.), *Motor development in early and later childhood: Longitudinal approaches* (pp. 125–136). Cambridge, England: Cambridge University.

Cataldo, C. (1983). *Infants and toddler programs: A guide to very early education programs.* Reading, MA: Addison-Wesley.

Cattell, P. (1940). *The measurement of intelligence of infants and young children.* New York: Psychological Corp.

Caudill, W., & Schooler, C. (1973). Child behavior and child rearing in Japan and the United States: An interim report. *Journal of Nervous and Mental Disease, 157,* 323–338.

Centers for Disease Control and Prevention (CDC). (1996). Sudden infant death syndrome—United States, 1983–1994. *Morbidity and Mortality Report, 45,* 859–861.

Centers for Disease Control and Prevention (CDC). (2000). Preventing pneumococcal disease among infants and young children: Recommendations of the Advisory Committee on Immunization Practices. *Morbidity and Mortality Weekly Report, 49*(RR-9), 1–37.

Centers for Disease Control and Prevention (CDC). (2001, January 12). Recommended childhood immunization schedule; United States, 2001. *Morbidity and Mortality Weekly Report, 50*(01), 7–10, 19.

Centers for Disease Control and Prevention (CDC). (2002). Body mass index-for age. Retrieved February 10, 2002 from http://www.cdc.gov/nccdphp/dnpa/bmi/bmi-for-age.htm.

Chamberlain, P., & Patterson, G. (1995). Discipline and child compliance in parenting. In M. Bornstein (Ed.), *Handbook of parenting* (Vol. 4, pp. 205–225). Mahwah, NJ: Erlbaum.

Chandler, L., Andrews, M., & Swanson, M. (1980). *Movement assessment of infants: A manual.* Rolling Bay, WA: Infant Movement Research.

Chang, H., & Pulido, D. (1994). The critical importance of cultural and linguistic continuity for infants and toddlers. *Zero to Three, 15*(2), 9–11.

Charman, T., Baron-Cohen, S., Swettenham, J., Baird, G., Cox, A., & Drew, A. (2001). Testing joint attention, imitation, and play as infancy precursors to language and theory of mind. *Cognitive Development, 15*(4), 481–498.

Charman, T., Swettenham, J., Baron-Cohen, S., Cox, A., Baird, G., & Drew, A. (2000). An experimental investigation of social-cognitive abilities in infants with autism: Clinical implications. In D. Muir & A. Slater (Eds.), *Infant development: The essential readings in development psychology* (pp. 343–363). Malden, MA: Blackwell.

Charney, R. (1980). Speech roles and the development of personal pronouns. *Journal of Child Language, 7,* 509–528.

Charpak, N., Ruiz-Pelaez, J., Figueroa de C, Z., & Charpak, Y. (1997). Kangaroo mother versus traditional care for newborn infants ≤2000 grams: A randomized, controlled trial. *Pediatrics, 100,* 682–688.

Chase-Lansdale, P., Michael, R., & Desai, S. (1991). Maternal employment during infancy. In J. Lerner & N. Galambos (Eds.), *Employed mothers and their children: An analysis of "Children of the national longitudinal survey of youth"* (pp. 37–62). New York: Garland.

Chase-Lansdale, P., & Owen, M. (1987). Maternal employment in a family context: Effects of infant-mother and infant-father attachment. *Child Development, 58,* 1505–1512.

Chess, S., Thomas, A., & Birch, H. (1965). *Your child is a person.* New York: Viking.

Child, I. (1968). Personality in culture. In E. Borgatta & W. Lambert (Eds.), *Handbook of personality theory and research* (pp. 82–145). Chicago: Rand McNally.

Children's Defense Fund. (2001). *The state of America's children: 2001 yearbook.* Washington, DC: Author.

Chinitz, S. (1995). Intervention with children with developmental disabilities and attachment disorders. *Developmental and Behavioral Pediatrics, 16*(3), S17–S20.

Chisholm, J. (1981). Prenatal influences on aboriginal-white Australian differences in neonatal irritability. *Ethology and Sociobiology, 2,* 67–73.

Chomsky, N. (1968). *Language and mind.* New York: Harcourt, Brace, Jovanovich.

Chomsky, N. (1975). *Reflections on language.* New York: Pantheon.

Chugani, H. (1993). Positron emission tomography scanning: Applications in newborns. *Clinics in Perinatology, 20,* 395–409.

Cicchetti, D. (1991). Fractures in the crystal: Developmental psychopathology and the emergence of self. *Developmental Review, 11,* 271–287.

Cicchetti, D., Ganiban, J., & Barnett, D. (1991). Contributions from the study of high-risk populations to understanding the development of emotion regulation. In J. Garber & K. Dodge (Eds.), *The development of emotion regulation and dysregulation* (pp. 15–48). New York: Cambridge University.

Ciaranello, R.D. (2002). The neurobiology of infantile autism. *National Alliance for Research on Schizophrenia and Depression (NARSAD) Research Newsletter.* Abstract retrieved February 12, 2002 from NASRD Web site: http://www.mhsource.com/narsad/pub/archautism.html.

Clark, D., Kreutzberg, J., & Chee, F. (1977). Vestibular stimulation influence on motor development in infants. *Science, 196,* 1228–1229.

Clark, E. (1973). What's in a word: On the child's acquisition of semantics in his first language. In T. Moore (Ed.), *Cognitive development and the acquisition of language* (pp. 65–110). New York: Academic Press.

Clark, E. (1995). Language acquisition: The lexicon and syntax. In J. Miller & P. Eimas (Eds.), *Speech, language, and communication* (pp. 303–337). San Diego: Academic.

Clark, H., & Clark, E. (1977). *Psychology and language.* New York: Harcourt, Brace, Jovanovich.

Clarke, S., & Taffel, S. (1995). Changes in cesarean delivery in the United States, 1988 and 1993. *Birth, 22,* 63–67.

Clarke-Stewart, A. (1982). *Daycare.* Cambridge, MA: Harvard University Press.

Clarke-Stewart, A., & Fein, G. (1983). Early childhood programs. In P. Mussen (Ed.), *Handbook of child psychology: Vol. 2. Infancy and developmental psychobiology* (4th ed., pp. 917–999). New York: Wiley.

Clarke-Stewart, K., Vandell, D., Burchinal, M., O'Brien, M., & McCartney, K. (2000). Do features of child care homes affect children's development? Unpublished paper, University of California, Irvine.

Clarke-Stewart, K., Vandell, D., McCartney, K., Owen, M., & Booth, C. (2000). Effects of parental separation and divorce on very young children. *Journal of Family Psychology, 14*(2), 304–326.

Clements, D. (1998). Haemophilus influenzae type b. In S. Katz, A. Gershon, & C. Wilfert (Eds.), *Krugman's infectious diseases of children* (10th ed., pp. 140–156), St. Louis, MO: Mosby.

Clifton, R., Perris, E., & Bullinger, A. (1991). Infants' perception of auditory space. *Developmental Psychology, 27,* 187–197.

Cobo-Lewis, A., Oller, D., Lynch, M., & Levine, S. (1995). Milestones in typically developing infants and infants with Down syndrome. *American Journal of Mental Retardation, 100,* 456–467.

Cockburn, F. (1984). The newborn. In J. Forfar & G. Arneil (Eds.), *Textbook of pediatrics* (3rd ed.), (Vol. 1, pp. 117–258). New York: Churchill Livingstone.

Cogan, R. (1980). Effects of childbirth preparation. *Clinical Obstetrics and Gynecology, 23,* 1–14.

Cole, P., Michel, M., & Teti, L. (1994). The development of emotion regulation and dysregulation: A clinical perspective. In N. Fox (Ed.), *Monographs of the Society for Research in Child Development, 59,* 73–100 (Serial No. 240).

Collin, M., Halsey, C., & Anderson, C. (1991). Emerging developmental sequelae in the 'normal' extremely low birth weight infant. *Pediatrics, 88,* 115–120.

Collins, E., & Turner, G. (1975). Maternal effects of regular salicylate in gestation in pregnancy. *Lancet, 2,* 335–337.

Columbo, J.(1993). *Infant cognition: Predicting later intellectual functioning.* Newbury Park, CA: Sage.

Comer, J., & Poussaint, A. (1976). *Black child care.* New York: Pocket Books.

Committee on Injury and Poison Prevention. American Academy of Pediatrics. (1995). Injuries associated with infant walkers. *Pediatrics, 95,* 778–779.

Committee on Nutrition. American Academy of Pediatrics. (1976). Commentary on breast-feeding and infant formulas, including proposed standards for formulas. *Pediatrics, 57,* 287–285.

Committee on Nutrition. American Academy of Pediatrics. (1998). *Pediatric nutrition handbook* (4th ed.). Elk Grove Village, IL: American Academy of Pediatrics.

Committee to Study the Prevention of Low Birth Weight. (1985). *Preventing Low Birth Weight.* Washington, DC: National Academy Press.

Condon, W., & Sander, L. (1974). Synchrony demonstrated between movements of the neonate and adult speech. *Child Development, 45,* 456–462.

Condry, J., & Condry, S. (1976). Sex differences: A study of the eye of the beholder. *Child Development, 47,* 812–819.

Connolly, K., & Stratton, P. (1969). An exploration of some parameters affecting classical conditioning in the neonate. *Child Development, 40,* 431–441.

Connor, F., Williamson, G., & Siepp, J. (Eds.). (1978). *Program guide for infants and toddlers with neuromotor and other developmental disabilities.* New York: Teachers College Press.

Cooksey, N. (1995). Pica and olfactory cravings of pregnancy: How deep are the secrets. *Birth, 22,* 129–136.

Coopersmith, S. (1967). *The antecedents of self-esteem.* San Francisco: Freeman.

Coplan, J. (1995). Normal speech and language development. *Pediatrics in Review, 16,* 91–100.

Corkum, V., & Moore, C. (1995). Development of joint visual attention in infants. In C. Moore & J. Dunham (Eds.), *Joint attention: Its origins and role in development* (pp. 61–83). Hillsdale, NJ: Erlbaum.

Cornelius, M., Taylor, P., Geva, D., & Day, N. (1995). Prenatal tobacco exposure and marijuana use among adolescents: Effects on offspring gestational age, growth, and morphology. *Pediatrics, 95,* 738–743.

Corsaro, W., & Eder, D. (1990). Children's peer cultures. *Annual Review of Sociology, 16,* 197–220.

Cost, Quality, & Outcomes Team. (1995). *Cost, quality, and child outcomes in child care centers: Executive summary* (2nd ed.). Denver, CO: University of Denver.

Courage, M., & Adams, R. (1990). Visual acuity assessment from birth to three years old using the acuity card procedures: Cross-sectional and longitudinal samples. *Optometry and Vision Science, 67,* 713–718.

Courage, M., & Adams, R. (1997). Visual acuity in extremely low birth weight infants. *Developmental and Behavioral Pediatrics (18),* 4–12.

Coustan, D. (1995a). Obstetric analgesia and anesthesia. In D. Coustan, R. Haning, & D. Singer (Eds.), *Human reproduction: Growth and development* (pp. 327–340). Boston: Little, Brown.

Coustan, D. (1995b). Obstetric complications. In D. Coustan, R. Haning, & D. Singer (Eds.), *Human reproduction: Growth and development,* (pp. 431–455). Boston: Little, Brown.

Cowan, P., Cowan, C., & Kerig, P. (1993). Mothers, fathers, sons, and daughters: Gender differences in family formation and parenting style. In P. Cowan, D. Field, D. Hansen, A. Skolnick, & G. Swanson (Eds.), *Family, self, and society* (pp. 165–195). Hillsdale, NJ: Erlbaum.

Craig, K., Hadjistavropoulos, H., Grunau, R., & Whitfield, M. (1994). A comparison of two measures of facial activity during pain in the newborn child. *Journal of Pediatric Psychology, 19,* 305–318.

Craig, K., Whitfield, M., & Grunau, R., Linton, J., & Hadjistavropoulos, H. (1993). Pain in the preterm neonate: Behavioral and physiological indices. *Pain, 52,* 287–299.

Crais, E., & Roberts, J. (1996). Assessing communication skills. In M. McLean, D. Bailey, & M. Wolery (Eds.), *Assessing infants and toddlers with special needs* (pp. 334–397). Columbus, OH: Merrill.

Cratty, B. (1979). *Perceptual and motor development in infants and young children* (2nd ed.). Englewood Cliffs, NJ: Prentice Hall.

Crockenberg, S. (1987). Predictors and correlates of anger toward and punitive control of toddlers by adolescent mothers. *Child Development, 58,* 964–975.

Crockenberg, S., & Leerkes, E. (2000). Infant social and emotional development in family context. In C. Zenah, Jr. (Ed.), *Handbook of infant mental health* (2nd ed.; pp. 60–90). New York: Guilford.

Crockenberg, S., Lyons-Ruth, K., & Dickstein, S. (1993). The family context of infant mental health: II. Infant development in multiple family relationships. In C. Zeanah, Jr (Ed.), *Handbook of infant mental health* (pp. 38–55). NewYork: Guilford.

Crook, C. (1977). Taste and the temporal organization of neonatal sucking. In J. Weiffenbach (Ed.), *Taste and development: The genesis of sweet preference* (pp. 146–158). Bethesda, MD: National Institutes of Health. (DHEW Pub. No. NIH 771068).

Cruttenden, A. (1970). A phonetic study of babbling. *British Journal of Disorders in Communication, 5,* 110–118.

Cryer, D., Harms, T., & Bourland, B. (1987). *Addison-Wesley active learning series: Active learning for infants.* Menlo Park, CA: Addison-Wesley

Cummings, E. (1980). Caregiver stability and day care. *Developmental Psychology, 16,* 31–37.

Cummings, M., & Cicchetti, D. (1990). Toward a transactional model of relations between attachment and depression. In M. Greenberg, D. Cicchetti, & E. Cummings, *Attachment in the preschool years: Theory, research and intervention* (pp. 339–372). Chicago: University of Chicago.

Curtiss, S. (1977). *Genie.* New York: Academic Press.

Daehler, M., & Greco, C. (1985). Memory in very young children. In M. Pressley & C. Brainerd (Eds.), *Cognitive learning and memory in children* (pp. 49–79). New York: Springer-Verlag.

Dahl, R., Scher, M., Williamson, T., Robles, N., & Day, N. (1995). A longitudinal study of prenatal marijuana use. Effects on sleep and arousal at age 3 years. *Archives of Pediatric and Adolescent Medicine, 149,* 145–150.

Dale, P. (1976). *Language and development* (2nd ed.). New York: Holt, Rinehart & Winston.

D'Alton, M. (1994). Prenatal diagnostic procedures. *Seminars in Perinatology, 18,* 140–162.

Damon, W., & Hart, D. (1982). The development of self-understanding from infancy through adolescence. *Child Development, 53,* 841–864.

Daniels, D., & Plomin, R. (1985). Differential experience of siblings in the same family. *Developmental Psychology, 21,* 747–760.

Darke, P., & Goldberg, S. (1994). Father-infant interaction and parent stress with healthy and medically compromised infants. *Infant Behavior and Development, 17,* 3–14.

Darley, F., & Winitz, H. (1961). Age of the first word: Review of research. *Journal of Speech and Hearing Disorders, 26,* 272–290.

Darling-Fisher, C., & Tiedje, L. (1990). The impact of maternal employment characteristics on fathers' participation in child care. *Family Relations, 39,* 20–26.

Darwin, C. (1877). A biographical sketch of an infant. *Mind, 2,* 285–294.

Davis, B., Moon, R., Sachs, H., & Ottolini, M. (1998). Effects of sleep position on infant motor development. *Pediatrics, 102,* 1135–1140.

Davis, J., & Rovee-Collier, C. (1983). Alleviated forgetting of a learned contingency in 8-week-old infants. *Developmental Psychology, 19,* 353–365.

Day, N., & Richardson, G. (1991). Prenatal alcohol exposure: A continuum of effects. *Seminars in Perinatology, 15,* 271–279.

Day, R. (1967). Factors influencing offspring. *American Journal of Diseases of Children, 142,* 6.

Dayton, G.O., & Jones, M.H. (1964). Analysis of characteristics of fixation reflex in infants by use of direct current electrooculography. *Neurology, 14,* 1152–1156.

Decarie, G., & Ricard, G. (1996). Revisiting Piaget revisited. In G. Noam & K. Fischer (Eds.), *Development and vulnerability in close relationships* (pp. 113–132). Mahwah, NJ: Erlbaum.

Decarie, T. (1969). A study of the mental and emotional development of the thalidomide child. In B. Foss (Ed.), *Determinants of infant behavior* (Vol. 4, pp. 110–114) London: Methuen.

DeCasper, A., & Fifer, W. (1980). Of human bonding: Newborns prefer their mothers' voices. *Science, 208,* 1174–1176.

DeCasper, A., & Prescott, P. (1984). Human newborns' perception of male voices: Preference, discrimination and reinforcing value. *Developmental Psychobiology, 17,* 481–491.

DeCasper, A., & Spence, M. (1986). Prenatal maternal speech influences newborns' perception of speech sounds. *Infant Behavior and Development, 9,* 133–150.

DeGangi, G., & Greenspan, S. (1989). *Test of Sensory Functions in Infants.* Los Angeles, CA: Western Psychological Services.

DeHart, G., Sroufe, L., & Cooper, R. (2000). *Child development: Its nature and course* (4th ed.). Boston: McGraw-Hill.

DeKaban, A. (1970). *Neurology of early childhood.* Baltimore: Williams & Wilkins.

de Mause, L. (1974). The evolution of childhood. In L. de Mause (Ed.), *The history of childhood* (pp. 1–73). New York: Psychohistory Press.

Denham, S.A. (1998). *Emotional development in young children.* New York: Guilford Press.

Dennis, W. (1941). Infant development under conditions of restricted practice and of minimal social stimulation. *Genetic Psychology Monographs, 23,* 143–191.

D'Entremont, B., & Muir, D. (1999). Infant responses to adult happy and sad vocal and facial expressions during face-to-face interactions. *Infant Behavior and Development, 22*(4), 527–539.

Derryberry, D., & Rothbart, M. (1984). Emotions, attention and temperament. In C. Izard, J. Kagan, & R. Zajonc (Eds.), *Emotions, cognition, and behavior* (pp. 132–166). London: Cambridge University Press.

Desmond, M., Wilson, G., Alt, E., & Fisher, E. (1980). The very low birth weight infant after discharge from intensive care: Anticipatory health care and developmental course. *Current Problems in Pediatrics, 10,* 1–59.

Desor, J., Maller, O., & Andrews, K. (1975). Ingestive responses of human newborns to salty, sour and bitter stimuli. *Journal of Comparative and Physiological Psychology, 89,* 966–970.

Desor, J., Maller, O., & Greene, L. (1977). Preference for sweet in humans: Infant children and adults. In J. Wiffenbach (Ed.), *Taste and development: The genesis of sweet preference* (pp. 161–172). Bethesda, MD: National Institutes of Health. (DHEW Pub. No. NIH 77–1068).

Desrochers, S., Morissette, P., & Ricard, M. (1995). Two perspectives on pointing in infancy. In C. Moore & J. Dunham (Eds.), *Joint attention: Its origins and role in development* (pp. 85–101). Hillsdale, NJ: Erlbaum.

de Villiers, J., & de Villiers, P. (1978). *Language acquisition.* Cambridge, MA: Harvard University Press.

de Villiers, J., & de Villiers, P. (1979). *Early language.* Cambridge, MA: Harvard University Press.

DeVries, M.W. (1984). Temperament and infant mortality among the Masai of East Africa. *American Journal of Psychiatry, 141,* 1189–1194.

de Waal, F. (1999). The end of nature versus nurture. *Scientific American, 281*(6), 94–99.

Dewey, C., Fleming, P., Golding, J., & ALSPAC Study Team. (1998). Does the supine sleeping position have any adverse effects on the child? II. Development in the first 18 months. *Pediatrics, 101*(1), e5. Retrieved February 17, 2002, from http://www.pediatrics.org/cgi/content/full/101/1/e5

Dewey, K., Heinig, J., & Nommsen-Rivers, L. (1995). Differences in morbidity between breast-fed and formula-fed infants. *Journal of Pediatrics, 126,* 696–702.

Dickie, J., & Matheson, P. (1984, August). *Mother-father-infant: Who needs support.* Paper presented at the meeting of the American Psychological Association, Toronto, Ontario.

Dick-Read, G. (1972). *The practice of natural childbirth.* New York: Harper & Row.

Dobbing, J. (1976). Vulnerable periods in brain growth and somatic growth. In D. Roberts & A. Thomson (Eds.), *The biology of human fetal growth* (pp. 137–147). New York: Halsted Press.

Dobbing, J. (1993). Nutrition, the developing brain and intelligence. *Professional Care of Mother and Child, 3,* 64–69.

Dobbing, J., & Smart, J. (1974). Vulnerability of developing brain and behavior. *British Medical Bulletin, 30,* 164.

Dodson, F. (1970). *How to parent.* New York: Signet.

Draper, P., & Cashdan, E. (1988). Technological change and child behavior among the young. *Ethnology, 27,* 339–365.

Drillien, C. (1964). *The growth and development of the prematurely born infant.* Edinburgh, Scotland: Livingstone.

Dryden, R. (1978). *Before birth.* London: Heinemann.

DuBois, F. (1952). The security of discipline. *Mental Hygiene, 36,* 353–372.

Dubowitz, L., Dubowitz, V., & Goldberg, C. (1970). Clinical assessment of gestational age in the newborn infant. *Journal of Pediatrics, 77,* 1–10.

Dunham, P., Dunham, F., & Curwin, A. (1993). Joint-attentional states and lexical acquisition at 18 months. *Developmental Psychology, 29,* 827–831.

Dunham, P., & Dunham, R. (1992). Lexical development during middle infancy: A mutually driven infant-caregiver process. *Developmental Psychology, 28,* 414–420.

Dunn, J. (1986). Pretend play in a family. In A. Gottfried & C. Brown (Eds.), *Play interactions* (pp. 149–162). Lexington, MA: Heath.

Dunn, J. (1987). The beginnings of moral understanding: Development in the second year. In J. Kagan & S. Lamb (Eds.), *The emergence of morality in young children* (pp. 91–112). Chicago: University of Chicago.

Dunn, J. (1988). *The beginnings of social understanding.* Oxford, England: Basil Blackwell.

Dunn, L., Beach, S.A., & Kontos, S. (1994). Quality of the literacy environment in day care and children's development. *Journal of Research in Childhood Education, 9,* 24–34.

Dunnihoo, D. (1992). *Fundamentals of gynecology and obstetrics* (2nd ed.). Philadelphia: Lippincott.

Dunst, C. (1980). *A clinical and educational manual for use with the Uzgiris and Hunt Scales of infant psychological development.* Austin, TX: Pro-Ed.

Durand, A. (1992). The safety of home birth: The farm study. *American Journal of Public Health, 82,* 450–452.

Dwyer, T., & Ponsonby, A. (1995). SIDS epidemiology and incidence. *Pediatric Annals, 24,* 350–356.

Dyer, E. (1963). Parenthood as crisis: A restudy. *Marriage and Family Living, 25,* 488–496.

Eagan, B., Whelan-Williams, S., & Brooks, W. (1985). The abuse of infants by manual shaking: Medical, social and legal issues. *Florida Medical Association Journal, 72,* 503–507.

Easterbrooks, M., & Goldberg, W. (1985). Effects of early maternal employment on toddlers, mothers, and fathers. *Developmental Psychology, 21,* 774–783.

Easterbrooks, M., & Goldberg, W. (1990). Security of toddler-parent attachment: Relation to sociopersonality functioning during kindergarten. In M. Greenberg, D. Cicchetti, & E. Cummings, *Attachment in the preschool years: Theory, research and intervention* (pp. 221–244). Chicago: University of Chicago.

Echols, C. H., Crowhurst, M. J., & Childers, J. B. (1997). Perception of rhythmic units in speech by infants and adults. *Journal of Memory and Language, 52,* 1135–1145.

Eckerman, K., & Whatley, J. (1977). Toys and social interaction between infant peers. *Child Development, 48,* 1146–1156.

Edwards, C. (1995). Parenting toddlers. In M. Bornstein (Ed.), *Handbook of parenting* (Vol. 1, pp. 41–64). Mahwah, NJ: Erlbaum.

Eichorn, D. (1979). Physical development: Current foci of research. In J. Osofsky (Ed.), *Handbook of infant development* (pp. 253–282). New York: Wiley.

Eiduson, B., Kornfein, M., Zimmerman, I., & Weisner, T. (1982). Comparative socialization practices in traditional and alternative families. In M. Lamb (Ed.), *Nontraditional families: Parenting and child development* (pp. 315–346). Hillsdale, NJ: Erlbaum.

Eilers, R., & Minifie, F. (1975). Fricative discrimination in early infancy. *Journal of Speech and Hearing Research, 18,* 158–167.

Eimas, P., Siqueland, E., Juzcyk, P., & Vigorito, J. (1971). Speech perception in early infancy. *Science, 171,* 303–306.

Eisenberg, R. (1976). *Auditory competence in early life.* Baltimore: University Park Press.

Eliason, M., & Williams, J. (1990). Fetal alcohol syndrome and the neonate. *Journal of Perinatal and Neonatal Nursing, 3,* 64–72.

Elicker, J., Fortner-Wood, C., & Noppe, I.C. (1999). The context of infant attachment in family child care. *Journal of Applied Developmental Psychology, 20,* 319–336.

Eliot, L. (1999). *What's going on in there? How the brain and mind develop in the first five years of life.* New York: Bantam.

Elkind, D. (1981). *The hurried child: Growing up too fast too soon.* Reading, MA: Addison-Wesley.

Emde, R. (1996). Thinking about intervention and improving early socioemotional development: Recent trends in policy and knowledge. *Zero to Three, 17*(1), 11–16.

Emde, R., Biringen, Z., Clyman, R., & Oppenheim, D. (1991). The moral self of infancy: Affective core and procedural knowledge. *Developmental Review, 11,* 251–270.

Emde, R., Gaensbauer, T., & Harmon, R. (1976). Emotional expression in infancy: A bio-behavioral study. *Psychological Isssues* (Vol.10. No.1, Monograph 37). New York: International Universities Press.

Emde, R., Johnson, W., & Easterbrooks, M. (1987). The do's and don'ts of early moral development: Psychoanalytic tradition and current research. In J. Kagan & S. Lamb (Eds.), *The emergence of morality in young children* (pp. 245–277). Chicago: University of Chicago.

Ensher, G., & Clark, D. (1994). *Newborns at risk: Medical care and psychoeducational intervention* (2nd ed.). Gaithersberg, MD: Aspen.

Entwisle, D., & Doering, S. (1981). *The first birth.* Baltimore: Johns Hopkins University.

Eppler, M., Adolph, K., & Weiner, T. (1996). The developmental relationship between infants' exploration and action on slanted surfaces. *Infant Behavior and Development, 19,* 259–264.

Epstein, H. (1978). Growth spurts during brain development: Implications for educational policy and posture. In J. Chall & A. Mirsky (Eds.), *Education and the brain: The seventy-seventh yearbook of the National Society for the Study of Education* (pp. 343–370). Chicago: University of Chicago Press.

Erikson, E. (1963). *Childhood and society* (2nd ed.). New York: Wiley.

Eskola, J., Kilpi, T., Palmu, A., Jokinen, J., Haapakoski, J., Herva, E., et al., (2001). Efficacy of a pneumococcal conjugate vaccine against acute otitis media. *New England Journal of Medicine, 344*(6), 403–409.

Ervin-Tripp, S. (1966). Language development. In L. Hoffman & M. Hoffman (Eds.), *Review of child development research* (Vol. 2, pp. 55–105). New York: Russell Sage Foundation.

Espenschade, A., & Eckert, H. (1967). *Motor development.* Columbus, OH: Merrill.

Etaugh, C., Grinnel, K., & Etaugh, A. (1989). Development of gender labeling: Effect of age pictured children. *Sex Roles, 21,* 769–773.

Evans, G., & Hall, J. (1976). The older sperm. *Ms., 4* (7), 48–50.

Evans, G. W., Maxwell, I., & Hart, B. (1999). Parental language and verbal responsiveness to children in crowded homes. *Developmental Psychology, 35,* 1020–1023.

Eyler, F., & Behnke, M. (1999). Early development of infants exposed to drugs prenatally. *Clinic in Perinatology, 26,* 107–151.

Fabes, R., & Martin, C. (2000). *Exploring child development: Transactions and transformations.* Boston: Allyn & Bacon.

Fagan, J. (1971). Infants' recognition memory for a series of visual stimuli. *Journal of Experimental Child Psychology, 11,* 244–250.

Fagard, J. (1990). The development of bimanual coordination. In C. Bard, M. Fleury, & L. Hay (Eds.), *Development of eye-hand coordination across the life span* (pp. 262–282). Columbia: University of South Carolina.

Fagot, B. (1995). Parenting boys and girls. In M. Bornstein (Ed.), *Handbook of parenting* (Vol. 1, pp. 163–183). Mahwah, NJ: Erlbaum.

Fagot, B., & Hagan, R. (1991). Observations of parent reactions to sex-stereotyped behaviors: Age and sex effects. *Child Development, 62,* 617–628.

Fagot, B., & Leinbach, M. (1989). The young child's gender schema: Environmental input, internal organization. *Child Development, 60,* 663–672.

Fagot, B., & Leinbach, M. (1993). Gender-role development in young children: From discrimination to labeling. *Developmental Review, 13,* 205–224.

Fantz, R. (1958). Pattern vision in young infants. *Psychological Review, 8,* 43–49.

Fawcett, A. (2001, July 19). Infant signs. *The* (Greenville NC) *Daily Reflector,* pp. D1–2.

Feldman, S., Nash, S., & Aschenbrenner, B. (1983). Antecedents of fathering. *Child Development, 54,* 1628–1636.

Fenichel, E. (1996). Editor's note. *Zero to Three, 17*(1), 2.

Fenson, L., Dale, P., Reznick, S., Bates, E., Thal, D., & Pethick, S. (1994). Variability in early communicative development. *Monographs of the Society for Research in Child Development, 59* (5, Serial No. 242).

Fenson, L., Dale, P., Reznick, S., Thal, D., Bates, E., Hartung, J., Pethick, S., & Reilly, J. (1993). *MacArthur Communication Development Inventories.* San Diego, CA: Singular Publishing Group.

Fenson, L., Kagan, J., Kearsley, R., & Zelazo, P. (1976). The developmental progression of manipulative play in the first two years. *Child Development, 47,* 232–236.

Fernald, A. (1984). The perceptual and affective salience of mothers' speech to infants. In L. Feagans, C. Garvey, & R. Golinkoff (Eds.), *The origins and growth of communication* (pp. 5–29). Norwood, NJ: Ablex.

Fernald, A. (1989). Intonation and communicative intent in mother's speech to infants: Is the melody the message? *Child Development, 60,* 1497–1510.

Fernald, A., Taeschner, T., Dunn, J., Papousek, M., Boyson-Bardies, B., & Fukui, I. (1989). A cross-language study of prosodic modifications in mothers' and fathers' speech to preverbal infants. *Journal of Child Language, 16,* 477–501.

Fetters, L. (1996). Motor development. In M. Hanson (Ed.), *Atypical infant development* (2nd. ed., pp. 403–450). Austin, TX: Pro-Ed.

Field, T. (1990). *Infancy.* Cambridge, MA: Harvard University.

Field, T. (1995). Massage therapy for infants and children. *Developmental and Behavioral Pediatrics, 16,* 105–111.

Field, T. (2000). Preterm infants benefit from early intervention. In J. Osofsky & H. Fitzgerald (Eds.), *WAIMH handbook on infant mental health* (Vol. 4, pp. 296–325). New York: Wiley.

Field, T., Cohen, D., Garcia, R., & Greenberg, R. (1984). Mother-stranger face discrimination by the newborn. *Infant Behavior and Development, 7,* 19–25.

Field, T., Masi, W., Goldstein, S., Perry, S., & Parl, S. (1988). Infant day care facilitates preschool social behavior. *Early Childhood Research Quarterly, 3,* 341–359.

Fifer, W.P., & Moon, C. (1989). Psychobiology of newborn auditory preferences. *Seminars in Perinatology, 13,* 430–433.

Filer, L. (1990). Iron needs during rapid growth and mental development. *Journal of Pediatrics. 117,* S143–146.

Filer, L. (1995). Iron deficiency. In F. Lifshitz (Ed.), *Childhood nutrition* (pp. 53–59). Boca Raton, FL: CRC.

Finberg, L., Kiley, J., & Luttrell, C. (1963). Mass accidental salt poisoning in infancy. *Journal of the American Medical Association, 184,* 121–124.

Finkelstein, N., Dent, C., Gallagher, J., & Ramey, C. (1978). Social behavior of infants and toddlers in a daycare environment. *Developmental Psychology, 14,* 257–262.

Fiscus, S., Adimora, A., Schoenbach, V., Lim. W., McKinney, R., Rupar, D., Kenny, J., Woods, C., & Wilfert, C. (1996). Perinatal HIV infection and the effect of Zidovudine therapy on transmission in rural and urban counties. *Journal of the American Medical Association, 275,* 1483–1488.

Fish, M. (1998). Negative emotionality and positive/social behavior in rural Appalachian infants: Predictions from caregiver and infant characteristics. *Infant Behavior and Development, 21*(4), 685–698.

Fleischer, K. (1955). Unterschugen zur entuicklung der inneohrfunktion (intrauterine kindsbewegungen nach schallreizen). *Laryngologie, Rhinologie, Otologie, 34,* 733–740.

Fogel, A. (2001). *Infancy: Infant, family, and society* (4th ed.). Belmont, CA: Wadsworth

Foman, S. (1993). *Nutrition of normal infants.* St. Louis, MO: Mosby.

Fontaine, R. (1984). Imitative skills between birth and six months. *Infant Behavior and Development, 7,* 232–333.

Ford, R., Schluter, P., Mitchell, E., Taylor, B., Scragg, R., & Stewart, A. (1998). Heavy caffeine intake in pregnancy and sudden infant death syndrome. *Archives of Disease in Childhood, 78,* 9–13.

Fosberg, S. (1981). *Family day care in the United States: Summary of findings* (Vol. 1). Final report of the national day care home study. Cambridge, MA: ABT Associates.

Fowler, W. (1980). *Infant and child care: A guide to education in group settings.* Boston: Allyn & Bacon.

Fox, M., & Porges, S. (1985). The relation between neonatal heart period patterns and developmental outcome. *Child Development, 56,* 28–37.

Fox, N. (1985). The organization of cerebral lateralization during infancy. *Infant Mental Health Journal, 6,* 175–184.

Fox, N. (1998). Temperament and regulation of emotion in the first year of life. In J.Warhol (Ed.), *New perspectives in emotional regulation* (pp. 17–28). Skillman, NJ: Johnson & Johnson.

Fox, N.A., Henderson, H.A., Rubin, K.H., Calkins, S.D., & Schmidt, L.A. (2001). Continuity and discontinuity of behavioral inhibition and exuberance: Psychophysiological and behavioral influences across the first four years of life. *Child Development, 72*(1), 1–21.

Fraiberg, S. (1971). Interaction in infancy: A program for blind infants. *Journal of the American Academy of Child Psychiatry, 10,* 381–405.

Fraiberg, S. (1974). Blind infants and their mothers: An examination of the sign system. In M. Lewis & L. Rosenblum

(Eds.), *The effect of the infant on its caregivers* (pp. 215–232). New York: Wiley.

Fraiberg, S. (1977). *Insights from the blind.* New York: Basic Books.

Fraiberg, S., & Freedman, D.A. (1964). Studies in the ego development of the congenitally blind child. *Psychoanalytic Study of the Child, 21,* 327–357.

Fraiberg, S., Smith, M., & Adelson, E. (1969). An educational program for blind infants. *Journal of Special Education, 3,* 121–139.

Frank, D., Bauchner, H., Parker, S., Huber, A., Kyei-Aboagyke, K., Cabral, H., & Zuckerman, B. (1990). Neonatal body proportionality and body composition after in utero exposure to cocaine and marijuana. *Journal of Pediatrics. 117,* 622–626.

Frankel, K.A., & Bates, J.E. (1990). Mother-toddler problem-solving: Antecedents in attachment, home behavior, and temperament. *Child Development, 61,* 810–819.

Frankenburg, W., Dodds, J., Archer, P., Bresnick, B., Mashka, P., Edelman, N., & Shapiro, H. (1992). *Denver II* (2nd ed.). Denver, CO: Denver Developmental Materials, Inc.

Frankenburg, W., Dodds, J., & Fandal, A. (1973). *Denver Developmental Screening Test.* Denver, CO: Denver Developmental Materials, Inc.

Freed, E., Steinschneider, A., Glassman, M., & Winn, K. (1994). Sudden infant death syndrome prevention and an understanding of selected clinical issues. *Pediatric Clinics of North America, 41,* 967–989.

Freud, S. (1917). *Psychopathology of everyday life.* New York: Macmillan.

Freud, S. (1940). *An outline of psychoanalysis.* New York: Norton.

Fried, P., & Makin., J. (1987). Neonatal behavioral correlates of prenatal exposure to marijuana, cigarettes, and alcohol in a low risk population. *Neurobehavioral Toxicology ad Teratology.* 79–85.

Freedman, D. (1981). Ethnic differences in babies. In E. Hetherington & R. Parke (Eds.), *Contemporary readings in child psychology* (pp. 6–12). New York: McGraw-Hill.

Friedman, J., & Polifka, J. (1994). *Teratogenic effects of drugs: A resource for clinicians.* Baltimore: Johns Hopkins.

Furuno, S., O'Reilly, K., Hosaka, C., Inatsuka, T., Zeisloft-Falbey, B., & Allman, T. (1988). *Hawaii Early Learning Profile (HELP).* Palo Alto, CA: Vort.

Gallahue, D. (1982). *Understanding motor development in children.* New York: Wiley.

Garcia, J. (1999). *Sign with your baby; How to communicate with your infants before they can speak.* Northlight Communications.

Garcia Coll, C., & Meyer, E. (1993). The sociocultural context of infant development. In C. Zeanah (Ed.), *Handbook of infant mental health* (pp. 56–69). New York: Guilford.

Garcia Coll, C., Meyer, E., & Brillon, L. (1995). Ethnic and minority parenting. In M. Bornstein (Ed.), *Handbook of parenting* (Vol. 2, pp. 189–210). Mahwah, NJ: Erlbaum.

Garmel, S., & D'Alton, M. (1994). Diagnostic ultrasound in pregnancy: An overview. *Seminars in Perinatology, 18,* 117–132.

Garn, S. (1966). Body size and its implication. In L. Hoffman & M. Hoffman (Eds.), *Review of child development research* (Vol. 2, pp. 529–566). New York: Russell Sage Foundation.

Gasser, R. (1975). *Atlas of human embryos.* New York: Harper & Row.

Gellis, S., & Kagan, B. (1986). *Current pediatric therapy.* Philadelphia: Saunders.

Gerber, M. (1981). What is appropriate curriculum for infants and toddlers? In B. Weissbound & J. Musick (Eds.), *Infants: Their social environments* (pp. 77–85). Washington, DC: National Association for the Education of Young Children.

Gershon, A., & LaRussa, P. (1992). Varicella-zoster virus infections. In S. Krugman, S. Katz, A. Gershon, & C. Wilfert (Eds.), *Infectious diseases of children* (9th ed., pp. 587–614). St. Louis: Mosby.

Gesell, A. (1925). *The mental growth of the preschool child.* New York: MacMillan.

Gesell, A. (1940). *The first five years of life: A guide to the study of preschool child.* New York: Harper & Brothers.

Gesell, A. (1945). *The embryology of behavior.* New York: Harper.

Gesell, A. (1954). The ontogenesis of infant behavior. In L. Carmichael (Ed.), *Manual of child psychology* (2nd ed., pp. 335–373). New York: Wiley.

Gesell, A., & Ilg, F. (1937). *Feeding behavior of infants.* Philadelphia: Lippincott.

Gesell, A., & Thompson, H. (1934). *Infant behavior: Its genesis and growth.* New York: McGraw-Hill.

Gestwicki, C. (1999). *Developmentally appropriate practice: Curriculum and development in early education.* Albany, NY: Delmar Publishers.

Giattino, J., & Hogan, J. (1975). Analysis of father's speech to his language learning child. *Journal of Speech and Hearing Disorders, 40,* 524–537.

Gibb, W. (1998). The role of prostaglandins in human parturition. *Ann Med, 30,* 235–241.

Gibson, D., Sheps, S., Schechter, M., & McCormick, A. (1990). Retinopathy of prematurity-induced blindness: Birthweight-specific survival and the new epidemic. *Pediatrics, 86,* 405–412. American Psychological Association.

Gibson, E. (1969). *Principles of perceptual learning and development.* New York: Appleton.

Gibson, E. (1992). How to think about perceptual learning: Twenty-five years later. In H. Pick, P. Van Den Broek, & D. Knill (Eds.), *Cognition: Conceptual and methodological issues* (pp. 215–237). Washington, DC: Appleton.

Gibson, E. (1995). Exploratory behavior in the development of perceiving, acting, and the acquiring of knowledge. In C. Rovee-Collier and L.P. Lipsitt (Eds.), *Advances in infancy research* Vol. 9, (pp. xxi–lxi). Norwood, NJ: Ablex.

Gibson, E., & Pick, A. (2000). *An ecological approach to perceptual learning and development.* New York, NY: Oxford University Press.

Gibson, E., & Walk, R. (1960). The "visual cliff." *Scientific American, 202,* 64–71.

Gibson, J. (1979). *The ecological approaches to visual perception.* Hillsdale, NJ: Erlbaum

Ginott, H. (1965). *Between parent and child.* New York: Macmillan.

Glassman, M. (1994). All things being equal: The two roads of Piaget and Vygotsky. *Developmental Review, 14,* 186–214.

Gleason, C., & Durand, D. (1993). Respiratory complications. In F. Witter & L. Keith (Eds.), *Textbook of prematurity* (pp. 279–303). Boston: Little, Brown.

Gleason, J. (1993). Studying language development. In J. Gleason (Ed.), *The development of language* (3rd ed., pp. 1–37). New York: Macmillan.

Gloger, T., Gabriele, S., & Huerkamp, M. (1998). Relationship change at the transition to parenthood and security of infant-mother attachment. *International Journal of Behavioral Development, 22*(3), 633–655.

Gold, E. (1996). Almost extinct diseases: Measles, mumps, rubella, and pertussis. *Pediatrics in Review, 17,* 120–127.

Golden, M., & Birns, B. (1976). Social class and infant intelligence. In M. Lewis (Ed.), *Origins of intelligence: Infancy and early childhood* (pp. 299–352). New York: Plenum.

Goldfield, B. (1987). The contributions of child and caregiver to referential and expressive language. *Applied Psycholinguistics, 8,* 267–280.

Goldman, A. (1984). Drugs and the mechanism of the drug induced teratogenesis. In L. Stern (Ed.), *Drug use in pregnancy* (pp. 68–98). Balgowlah, Australia: ADIS Health Science.

Goldman, A. (1998). Variation in timing and eruption of tooth formation and eruption. In S. Ultijaszek, F. Johnston, & M. Preece (Eds.), *The Cambridge encyclopedia of human growth and development* (pp. 209–210). Cambridge, England: Cambridge University.

Goldsmith, H. (1983). *Emotionality in infant twins: Longitudinal results.* Abstracts of the Fourth International Congress on Twin Studies. London.

Goldsmith, H., & Alansky, J. (1987). Maternal and infant temperamental predictors of attachment: A metaanalytic review. *Journal of Consulting and Clinical Psychology, 55,* 805–816.

Goldsmith, H., & Rothbart, M. (1991). Contemporary instruments for assessing temperament by questionnaire and in the laboratory. In J. Streulau & A. Anglettner (Eds.), *Explorations in temperament* (pp. 249–272). New York: Plenum.

Golub, M. (1996). Labor analgesia and infant brain development. *Pharmacology of Biochemical Behavior, 55,* 619–628.

Gonzalez-Mena, J., & Eyer, D. (1980). *Infancy and caregiving.* Palo Alto, CA: Mayfield.

Gonzalez-Mena, J., & Eyer, D. (1997). *Infants, toddlers, and caregivers* (4th ed.). Mountain View, CA: Mayfield.

Goodwyn, S., & Acredolo, L. (1993). Symbolic gesture versus word: Is there a modality advantage for onset of symbol use. *Child Development, 64,* 688–701.

Goodwyn, S., & Acredolo, L. (1998). Encouraging symbolic gestures: A new perspective on the relationship between gesture and speech. In J. Iverson & S. Goldin-Meadows (Eds.), *The nature and functions of gesture in children's communications* (pp. 61–73). San Francisco: Jossey-Bass.

Gopnik, A., Meltzoff, A., & Kuhl, P. (1999). *The scientist in the crib: What early learning tells us about the mind.* New York: Perennial.

Gormican, A., Valentine, J., & Satter, E. (1980). Relationships of maternal weight gain and infant birthweight. *Journal of the American Dietetic Association, 77,* 662–668.

Gotlin, R., Kappy, M., Eisenbarth, G., & Chase, P. (1995). Endocrine disorders. In W. Hay, J. Groothuis, A. Hayward, & M. Levin (Eds.), *Current pediatric diagnosis and treatment* (12th ed., pp. 881–883). Norwalk, CT: Appleton.

Gottfried, A. (1984). Touch as an organizer of human development. In C. Brown (Ed.), *The many facets of touch* (pp. 114–120). Skillman, NJ: Johnson & Johnson.

Gottfried, A. (1985). The relationship of play materials and parental involvement to young children's development. In C. Brown & A. Gottfried (Eds.), *Play interactions: The role of toys and parental involvement in children's development* (pp. 181–185). Somerville, NJ: Johnson & Johnson.

Gottfried, A. (1991). Maternal employment in the family setting: Developmental and environmental issues. In J. Lerner & N. Galambos (Eds.), *Employed mothers and their children: An analysis of "Children of the national longitudinal survey of youth"* (pp. 63–84). New York: Garland.

Gottfried, A., Bathurst, K., & Killian, C. (1999). Maternal and dual-earner employment: Family environment, adaptations, and the developmental impingement perspective. In M. Lamb (Ed.), *Parenting and child development in "nontraditional" families* (pp. 15–37). Mahwah, NJ: Erlbaum.

Graeber, J., & Schwartz, T. (1993). In F. Witter & L. Keith (Eds.), *Textbook of prematurity* (pp. 321–332). Boston: Little, Brown.

Granrud, C., & Yonas, A. (1984). Infants perception of pictorial specified interposition. *Journal of Experimental Child Psychology, 37,* 500–511.

Granrud, C., Yonas, A., & Opland, E. (1985). Infants' sensitivity to depth cue of shading. *Perception and Psychophysics, 37,* 415–419.

Granrud, C., Yonas, A., Smith, I., Arterberry, M., Gliksman, M., & Sorknes, A. (1984). Infants' sensitivity to accretion and deletion of texture and information for depth at an edge. *Child Development, 55,* 1630–1636.

Grant, V. (1994). Sex of infant differences in mother-infant interaction: A reinterpretation of past findings. *Developmental Review, 14,* 1–26.

Grasselli, R., & Hegner, P. (1980). *Playful parenting.* New York: Putman.

Greco, C., Rovee-Collier, C., Hayne, H., Greisler, P., & Earley, L. (1986). Ontogeny of early event memory: I. Forgetting and retrieval by 2- and 3-month-olds. *Infant Behavior and Development, 9,* 441–461.

Greenberg, M.T. (1999). Attachment and psychopathology in childhood. In J. Cassidy & P.R. Shaver (Eds.), *Handbook of attachment: Theory, research, and clinical implications* (pp. 469–496). New York: Guilford.

Greenfield, P., & Tronick, E. (1980). *Infant curriculum: The Bromley-Heath Guide to the care of infants in groups* (rev. ed.). Santa Monica, CA: Goodyear.

Greenough, W., Black, J., & Wallace, C. (1987). Experience and brain development. *Child Development, 58,* 539–559.

Greenspan, S., & Greenspan, N. (1985). *First feelings: Milestones in the emotional development of your baby and child.* New York: Viking.

Greenspan, S., & Meisels, S. (1996). Toward a new vision for the developmental assessment of infants and young children. In S. Meisels and E. Fenichel (Eds.), *New visions for the developmental assessment of infants and young children* (pp. 11–26). Washington, DC: Zero to Three.

Grolnick, W.S., Kurowski, C.O., McMenamy, J.M., Rivkin, I., & Bridges, L.J. (1998). Mothers' strategies for regulating their toddlers' distress. *Infant Behavior and Development, 21*(3), 437–450.

Groome, L. Swiber, M., Bentz, L., Holland, S., & Atterbury, J. (1995). Maternal anxiety during pregnancy: Effect on fetal behavior at 38 to 40 weeks of gestation. *Developmental and Behavioral Pediatrics, 16,* 391–396.

Guerrero, V., & Rojas, O. (1975). Spontaneous abortion and aging of human ova and spermatozoa. *New England Journal of Medicine, 293,* 573–575.

Guillory, A., Self, P., & Paden, L. (1980, April). *Odor sensitivity in one month infants.* Paper presented at the International Conference on Infant Studies, New Haven, CT.

Gunnar, M. (1978). Changing a frightening toy into a pleasant toy by allowing the infant to control its actions. *Developmental Psychology, 14,* 157–162.

Gunnar, M. (1980). Control, warning signals and distress in infancy. *Developmental Psychology, 16,* 281–289.

Gunnar, M. (1994). Psychoendocrine studies of temperament and stress in early childhood: Expanding current models. In J. Bates & T. Wachs (Eds.), *Temperament: Individual differences at the interface of biology and behavior* (pp. 175–198). Washington, DC: American Psychological Association.

Gunnar, M., Brodersen, L., Krueger, K., & Rigatuso, R. (1996). Dampening of behavioral and adrenocortical reactivity during early infancy: Normative changes and individual differences. *Child Development, 67,* 877–889.

Guntheroth, W. (1995). *Crib death: The sudden infant death syndrome* (3rd ed.). Armonk, NY: Futura.

Gurney, J. (1979). The young child: Protein-energy malnutrition. In D. Jelliffe & E. Jelliffe (Eds.), *Nutrition and growth* (pp. 185–216). New York: Plenum.

Guttmann, J. (1993). *Divorce in psychosocial perspective: Theory and research.* Hillsdale, NJ: Erlbaum.

Hagekull, B. (1994). Infant temperament and early childhood functioning: Possible relations to the five-factor model. In C. Halverson, G. Kohnstamm, & R. Martin (Eds.), *The developing structure of temperament and personality from infancy to adulthood* (pp. 227–240). Hillsdale, NJ: Erlbaum.

Hainline, L. (1998). The development of basic visual abilities. In A. Slater (Ed.), *Perceptual development: Visual, auditory and speech perception in infancy.* Hove, England: Psychology Press.

Hainline, L., & Lemerise, E. (1982). Infants' scanning of geometric forms varying in size. *Journal of Experimental Child Psychology, 33,* 235–256.

Hains, S.M.J., & Muir, D.W. (1996). Infant sensitivity to adult eye direction. *Child Development, 67,* 1940–1951.

Haith, M. (1979). Visual competence in early infancy. In R. Held, H. Leibowitz, & H. Teuber (Eds.), *Handbook of sensory physiology: Vol. 8. Perception* (pp. 311–356). Berlin: Springer-Verlag.

Haith, M., & Benson, J. (1998). Infant cognition. In W. Damon (Ed.-in-Chief), D. Kuhn & R. Siegler (Vol. Eds.), *Handbook of child psychology, Vol 2: Cognition, perception, and language* (pp. 199–254). New York: Wiley.

Haith, M., Bergman, T., & Moore, M. (1977). Eye contact and face scanning in early infancy. *Science, 198,* 853–855.

Hall, C., & Lindzey, G. (1978). *Theories of personality* (3rd ed.). New York: Wiley.

Hall, D. (1985). The outlook for low birth weight babies. *The Practitioner, 229,* 779–783.

Hall, E. (1969). *The hidden dimension.* New York: Doubleday.

Hall, G. (1891). Notes on the study of infants. *The Pedagogical Seminary,* 1, 127–138.

Halliday, M. (1975). *Learning how to speak: Explorations in the development of language.* New York: Elsevier.

Halpern, L.F., Garcia-Coll, C.T., Meyer, E.C., & Bendersky, K. (2000). The contributions of temperament and maternal responsiveness to the mental development of small-for-gestational-age and appropriate-for-gestational-age infants. *Journal of Applied Developmental Psychology, 21*(2), 199–224.

Halpern, R. (1993). Poverty and infant development. In C. Zeanah, Jr. (Ed.). *Handbook of infant mental health* (pp. 73–86), New York: Guilford.

Halverson, H. (1931). An experimental study of the prehension in infants by means of systematic cinema records. *Genetic Psychology Monographs, 10,* 107–286.

Hamilton, M. (1984). *Basic maternity nursing* (5th ed.). St. Louis, MO: Mosby.

Hanawalt, B. (1977). Childrearing among the lower classes of late medieval England. *Journal of Interdisciplinary History, 8,* 1–22.

Hanlon, H.W., Thatcher, R.W., & Cline, M.J. (1999). Gender differences in the development of EEG coherence in normal children. *Developmental Neuropsychology, 16*(3), 479–506.

Hanna, E., & Meltzoff, A. (1993). Peer imitation by toddlers in laboratory, home, and day-care contexts: Implications for social learning and memory. *Developmental Psychology, 29,* 701–710.

Hanson, M. (1996a). Early interactions: The family context. In M. Hanson (Ed.), *Atypical infant development* (2nd ed., pp. 235–272). Austin, TX: Pro-Ed.

Hanson, M. (1996b). Early intervention: Models and practices. In M. Hanson (Ed.), *Atypical infant development* (2nd ed., pp. 451–476). Austin, TX: Pro-Ed.

Harkins, D., & Uzgiris, I. (1991). Hand use matching between mothers and infants during the first year. *Infant Behavior and Development, 14,* 289–298.

Harlow, H., & Zimmerman, R. (1959). Affectional responses in the infant monkey. *Science, 130,* 431–432.

Harms, T., Cryer, D., & Clifford, R. (1990). *The Infant and Toddler Environmental Rating Scale.* New York: Teachers College.

Harrigan-Hamamoto, K. (1983). *Pain in infants.* Unpublished master's thesis, California State University, Long Beach.

Harris, E. (1998). Dental maturation. In S. Ultijaszek, F. Johnston, & M. Preece (Eds.), *The Cambridge encyclopedia of human growth and development* (pp. 45–48). Cambridge, United Kingdom: Cambridge University.

Harris, G., & Booth, D.A. (1987). Infants' preference for salt in food: Its dependence upon recent dietary experience. *Journal of Reproductive and Infant Psychology, 5,* 97–104.

Harris, J. (1998). *The nurture assumption.* New York: Free Press.

Hart, B., & Risley, T. (1995). *Meaningful differences in the everyday experience of young American children.* Baltimore: Brookes.

Hartshorn, K., & Rovee-Collier, C. (1997). Infant learning and long-term memory at 6 months: A confirming analysis. *Developmental Psychobiology, 30,* 71–85.

Hartup, W. (1983). Peer relations. In P. Mussen (Ed.), *Handbook of child psychology: Vol. 4. Socialization, personality and development* (4th ed., pp. 103–196). New York: Wiley.

Harvey, E., Boife, J., Honeyman, M., & Flannery, J. (1985). Prenatal x-ray exposure and childhood cancer in twins. *New England Journal of Medicine, 312,* 541–545.

Harwood, R.L., Miller, J.G., & Irizarry, N.L. (1995). *Culture and attachment: Perceptions of the child in context.* New York, NY: The Guilford Press.

Haslett, B., & Sampter, W. (1997). *Children communicating: The first 5 years.* Mahwah, NJ: Erlbaum.

Hassid, P. (1984). *Textbook for childbirth educators* (2nd ed.). Philadelphia: Lippincott.

Hauth, J., Goldeberg, R., Andrews, W., DuBard, M., & Cooper, R. (1995). Reduced incidence of preterm delivery with metronidazole and erythromycin in women with bacterial vaginosis. *New England Journal of Medicine. 333,* 1732–1735.

Hawkins, J., & Higgins, L. (1981). *Maternal and gynecological nursing.* Philadelphia: Lippincott.

Hay, D. (1994). Prosocial development. *Journal of Child Psychology and Psychiatry, 35,* 29–71.

Hay, D., Caplan, M., Castle, J., & Stimson, C. (1991). Does sharing become increasingly rational in the second year of life? *Developmental Psychology, 27,* 987–993.

Hay, D., Castle, J., & Davies, L. (2000). Toddlers' use of force against familiar peers: A precursor of serious aggression? *Child Development, 71*(2), 457–467.

Hay, D., Castle, J., Davies, L., Demetriou, H., & Stimson, C. (1999). Prosocial action in very early childhood. *Journal of Child Psychology and Psychiatry and Allied Disciplines, 40*(6), 905–916.

Hay, D., Castle., & Jewett, J. (1994). Character development. In M. Rutter & D. Hay (1994), *Development through the lifespan: A handbook for clinicians* (pp. 319–349). Oxford, England: Blackwell.

Hay, D., Castle, J., Stimson, C., & Davies, L. (1995). The social contruction of character in toddlerhood. In M. Killen & D. Hart (Eds.), *Morality in everyday life* (pp. 23–51). New York: Cambridge University.

Haywood, K. (1993). *Life span motor development* (2nd ed.). Champaign, IL: Human Kinetics.

Health Watch. (1997, January 7). *NBC Nightly News.* New York: NBC.

Hecaen, H., & Ajuriagurra, J. (1964). *Left-handedness: Manual superiority and cerebral dominance.* New York: Grune & Stratton.

Heidelise, A., Tronick, E., Lester, B., & Brazelton, T. (1979). Specific neonatal measures: The Brazelton Neonatal Behavioral Assessment Scale. In J. Osofsky (Ed.), *Handbook of infant development* (pp. 185–215). New York: Wiley.

Hein, A., & Held, R. (1967). Dissociation of the visual placing response into elicited and guided components. *Science, 158,* 390–392.

Held, R. (1993). What can rates of development tell us about underlying mechanisms. In C. Granrud (Ed.), *Visual perception and cognition in infancy* (pp. 75–89). Hillsdale, NJ: Erlbaum.

Held, R., & Bauer, J.A. (1974). Development of sensorially-guided reaching in infant monkeys. *Brain Research, 71,* 265–271.

Held, R., & Hein, A. (1963). A movement-produced stimulation in the development of visually guided behavior. *Journal of Comparative Physiological Psychology, 56,* 872–876.

Heller, T., Hsieh, K., & Rowitz, L. (2000). Grandparents as supports to mothers of persons with intellectual disability. *Journal of Gerontological Social Work, 33*(4), 23–34.

Helms, D., & Turner, J. (1976). *Exploring child behavior: Basic principles.* Philadelphia: Saunders.

Henig, R., & Fletcher, A. (1983). *Your premature baby.* New York: Rawson Associates.

Hermes, P. (1981, February 10). WD medical update: Crib death. *Woman's Day, 43,* 14, 16–17.

Hershenson, M. (1964). Visual discrimination in the human newborn. *Journal of Comparative and Physiological Psychology, 58,* 270–276.

Hestenes, L.L., Kontos, S., & Bryan, Y. (1993). Children's emotional expression in child care centers varying in quality. *Early Childhood Research Quarterly, 8,* 295–307.

Hetherington, E. (1979). Divorce: A child's perspective. *American Psychologist, 34,* 851–858.

Hetherington, E., Cox, M., & Cox, R. (1982). Effects of divorce on parents and children. In M. Lamb (Ed.), *Nontraditional families* (pp. 233–288). Hillsdale, NJ: Erlbaum.

Hetherington, E., & Parke, R. (1979). *Child psychology: A contemporary viewpoint* (2nd ed.). New York: McGraw-Hill.

Hill, L., & Breckle, R. (1983). Current uses of ultrasound in obstetrics. *Primary Care, 10*(2), 205–223.

Hill, L., & Kleinberg, F. (1984a). Effects of drugs and chemicals on the fetus and newborn (First of two parts). *Mayo Clinic Proceedings, 59,* 707–716.

Hill, L., & Kleinberg, F. (1984b). Effects of drugs and chemicals on the fetus and newborn (Second of two parts). *Mayo Clinic Proceedings, 59,* 755–765.

Hillier, S., Nugent, R., Eschenbach, D., Krohn, M., Gibbs, R., Martin, D., Cotch, M., Edelman, R., Pastorek, J., Rao, V., McNellis, D., Regan, J., Carey, J., & Klebanoff, M. (1995). Association between bacterial vaginosis and preterm delivery of a low-birthweight infant. *New England Journal of Medicine, 333,* 1737–1742.

Himmelberger, D., Brown, B., & Cohen, E. (1978). Cigarette smoking during pregnancy and the occurrence of spontaneous abortion and congenital abnormality. *Journal of Epidemiology, 108,* 470.

Hinde, R. (1982). Attachment: Some conceptual and ethnic influences upon socialization. In P.H. Mussen (Ed.), *The place of attachment in human behavior* (pp. 60–76). London: Tavistock.

Hinton, S., & Kerwin, D. (1981). *Maternal, infant and child nutrition.* Chapel Hill, NC: Health Services Consortium.

Hjelle, L., & Ziegler, D. (1976). *Personality theories: Basic assumptions and research applications.* New York: McGraw-Hill.

Hobbs, D. (1968). Transition to parenthood: A replication and extension. *Journal of Marriage and the Family, 30,* 413–417.

Hock, E. (1980). Working and nonworking mothers and their infants: A comparative study of maternal caregiving characteristics and infant social behavior. *Merrill-Palmer Quarterly, 26,* 79–101.

Hodapp, R., & Mueller, E. (1982). Early social development. In B. Wolman (Ed.), *Handbook of developmental psychology* (pp. 284–300). Englewood Cliffs, NJ: Prentice Hall.

Hoffman, L. (1989). Effects of maternal employment in the two-parent family. *American Psychologist, 44,* 283–292.

Hoffman, M. (1970). Moral development. In P. Mussen (Ed.), *Carmichael's handbook of child psychology* (Vol. 2, pp. 261–359). New York: Wiley.

Hoffman, M. (1981). Development of moral thought, feeling and behavior. In E. Hetherington & R. Parke (Eds.), *Contemporary readings in child psychology* (2nd ed., pp. 366–373). New York: McGraw-Hill.

Hogge, W. (1990). Teratology. In I. Merkatz & J. Thompson (Eds.), *New perspectives on prenatal care* (pp. 117–121). New York: Elsevier.

Hogue, C., & Hargraves, M. (1995). Preterm birth in the African-American community. *Seminars in Perinatology, 19*(4), 255–262.

Holden, G. (1983). Avoiding conflict: Mothers as tacticians in the supermarket. *Child Development, 50,* 1020–1035.

Holmes, S., Reef, S., Hadler, S., Williams, W., & Wharton, M. (1996). Recommendations of the Advisory Committee on Immunization Practices. *Morbidity and Mortality Weekly Report, 45*(RR–11), 1–23.

Holst, M. (1998). Developmental and behavioral effects of iron-deficiency anemia. *Nutrition Today, 33*(1), 27–37.

Honig. A. (1993). Mental health for babies: What do theory and research teach us? *Young Children, 48*(3), 69–76.

Honig, A. (1995). Choosing child care for young children. In M. Bornstein (Ed.), *Handbook of parenting* (Vol. 4, pp. 411–435). Mahwah, NJ: Erlbaum.

Hook, E., & Lindsjo, A. (1978). Down's syndrome in live births by single year maternal age interval in a Swedish study: Comparison with results from a New York study. *American Journal of Human Genetics, 30,* 19–27.

Hooker, D. (1952). *The prenatal origin of behavior.* Lawrence: University of Kansas.

Hopkins, B., & Westra, T. (1988). Maternal handling and motor development: An intracultural study. *Genetic, Social, and General Psychology Monographs, 114,* 377–420.

Hopper, H., & Naremore, R. (1978). *Children's speech: A practical introduction to communication development* (2nd ed.). New York: Harper & Row.

Horowitz, F. (1982). Methods of assessment for high-risk and handicapped infants. In C. Ramey & P. Trohanis (Eds.), *Finding and educating high-risk and handicapped infants* (pp. 101–118). Baltimore: University Park Press.

Hossain, Z., & Roopnarine, J. (1994). African-American fathers' involvement with infants: Relationship to their functional style, support, education, and income. *Infant Behavior and Development, 17,* 175–184.

Hottinger, W. (1977). Motor development: Conception to age five. In C. Corbin (Ed.), *A textbook of motor development* (pp. 1–28). Dubuque, IA: Brown.

Howes, C. (1987). Peer interaction of young children. *Monographs of the Society for Research in Child Development, 53*(1, Serial No. 217).

Howes, C. (1997a). Children's experiences in center-based child care as a function of teacher background and adult-child ratio. *Merrill Palmer Quarterly, 43,* 404–425.

Howes, C. (1997b). Teacher sensitivity, children's attachment and play with peers. *Early Education and Development, 8*(1), 41–49.

Howes, C., & Olenick, M. (1986). Family and child care influences on toddler's compliance. *Child Development, 57,* 202–216.

Howes, C., Philips, D., & Whitebook, M. (1992). Thresholds of quality: Implications for the social development of children in center-based child care. *Child Development, 63,* 449–460.

Howes, C., & Smith, E. (1995). Relations among child care quality, teacher behavior, children's play activities, emotional security, and cognitive activity in child care. *Early Childhood Research Quarterly, 10,* 381–404.

Hronsky, S., & Emory, E. (1987). Neurobehavioral effects of caffeine on the neonate. *Infant Behavior and Development, 10,* 61–80.

Hubel, D., & Wiesel, T. (1959). Receptive fields of single neurons in the cat's striate cortex. *Journal of Physiology, 148,* 574–591.

Hubel, D., & Wiesel, T. (1963). Single-cell responses in striate cortex of kittens deprived of vision in one eye. *Journal of Neurophysiology, 26,* 1003–1017.

Hubel, D., & Wiesel, T. (1965). Receptive fields and functional architecture in two nonstriate visual areas (18 and 19) of the cat. *Journal of Neurophysiology, 28,* 229–289.

Hubel, D., & Wiesel, T. (1970). The period of susceptibility to the physiological effects of unilateral eye closure in kittens. *Journal of Physiology, 206,* 419–436.

Hunts, H.J.H., & Avery, R.J. (1998). Relatives as child care givers: After hours support for nontraditional workers. *Journal of Family and Economic Issues, 19*(4), 315–341.

Hunziker, U., & Barr, R. (1986). Increased carrying reduces infant crying: A randomized control trial. *Pediatrics, 43,* 641–648.

Huston, A. (1983). Sex-typing. In P. Mussen (Ed.), *Handbook of child psychology: Vol. 4. Socialization, personality and development* (4th ed., pp. 387–367). New York: Wiley.

Huttenlocher, J. (1994). Synaptogenesis in human cerebral cortex. In G. Dawson & K. Fischer (Eds.), *Human behavior and the developing brain* (pp. 137–152). New York: Guilford.

Huttenlocher, J. (1999). Language input and language growth. In N. Fox, L. Leavitt, & J. Warhol (Eds.), *The role of early experience in development* (pp. 69–82). Skillman, NJ: Johnson & Johnson.

Hyvarinen, L. (1988). *Vision in children: Normal and abnormal.* Meaford, Ontario, Canada: Canadian Deaf-Blind & Rubella Association.

Illingworth, R. (1991). *Normal child: Some problems of the early years and their treatment* (10th ed.). London: Churchill Livingstone.

Irwin, O. C. (1948). Infant speech: Development of vowel sounds. *Journal of Speech and Hearing Disorders, 13,* 31–34.

Isabella, R., & Belsky, J. (1991). Interactional synchrony and the origins of infant-mother attachment: A replication study. *Child Development, 62,* 373–384.

Iverson, J., Tencer, H., & Goldin-Meadow, S. (2000). The relation between gesture and speech in congenitally blind and sighted language-learners. *Journal of Nonverbal Behavior,* 24, 105–230.

Izard, C. (1977). *Human emotions.* New York: Plenum.

Izard, C. (1979). *The maximally discriminative facial movement coding system (Max).* Newark: University of Delaware, Instructional Resources Center.

Izard, C. (1993), Organizational and motivational functions of discrete emotions. In M. Lewis & J. Haviland (Eds.), *Handbook of emotions* (pp. 631–641). New York: Guilford.

Izard, C., & Malatesta, C. (1987). Perspectives on emotional development: Differential emotions theory of early emotional development. In J. Osofsky (Ed.), *Handbook of infant development* (2nd ed., pp. 494–554). New York: Wiley.

Jacklin, C., & Maccoby, E. (1983). Issues of gender differentiation in normal development. In M. Levine, W. Carey, A. Crocker, & R. Gross (Eds.), *Developmental-behavioral pediatrics* (pp. 175–184). Philadelphia: Saunders.

Jacobson, J., Tianen, R., Wille, D., & Aytck, D. (1986). Infant-mother attachments and early peer relations: The assessment of behavior in an interactive context. In E. Mueller & C. Cooper (Eds.), *Process and outcome in peer relations* (pp. 57–78). New York: Academic Press.

James, T. (1985). Editorial comment: Crib death. *Journal of the American College of Cardiology, 5,* 1185–1187.

Jensen, A. (1969). How much can we boost IQ and scholastic achievement? *Harvard Educational Review, 39,* 1–123.

Jirasek, J. (1983). *Atlas of human prenatal morphogenesis.* Boston: Martinus Nijhoff.

Johnson, C. (1996). Nonorganic failure to thrive. In W. Nelson, R. Behrman, R. Kliegman, & A. Arving (Eds.), *Nelson's textbook of pediatrics* (15th ed., pp. 119–120). Philadelphia: Saunders.

Johnson, J., & Ershler, J. (1982). Curricular effects on the play of preschoolers. In D. Pepler & K. Rubin (Eds.), *Contributions to human development: Vol. 5. The play of children: Current theory and research* (pp. 130–143). Basel, Switzerland: S. Karger.

Johnson, M., Dziurawiee, S., Ellis, H., & Morton, J. (1991). Newborns' preferential tracking of face-like stimuli and its subsequent decline. *Cognition, 40,* 1–19.

Johnson, S.P. (1997). Young infants' perception of object unity: Implications for development of attentional and cognitive skills. *Current Directions in Psychological Science, 6,* 5–11.

Johnson-Martin, N., Jens, K., Attermeier, S., & Hacker, B. (1991). *The Carolina Curriculum for Infants and Toddlers with Special Needs (*2nd ed.). Baltimore, MD: Paul H. Brookes.

Johnston, P. (1998). *The newborn child* (8th ed.). New York: Churchill Livingstone.

Jones, S.S., & Hong, H.W. (2001). Onset of voluntary communication: Smiling looks to mother. *Infancy, 2*(3), 353–370.

Juscyck, P. (1995). Language acquisition: Speech sounds and the beginning of phonology. In J. Miller & P. Eimas (Eds.). *Speech, language, and communication* (pp. 263–301). San Diego: Academic.

Jusczyk, P.W., Houston, D., & Goodman, M. (1998). Speech perception during the first year. In A. Slater, (Ed.), *Perceptual development: Visual, auditory, and speech perception in infancy* (pp. 357–388). East Sussex, England: Psychology Press.

Jusczyk, P.W., Luce, P.A., & Charles Luce, J. (1994). Infants' sensitivity to phonotactic patterns in the native language. *Journal of Memory and Language, 33,* 630–645.

Kagan, J. (1979). Overview: Perspectives on human infancy. In J. Osofsky (Ed.), *Handbook of infant development* (pp. 1–25). New York: Wiley.

Kagan, J. (1981a). *The second year: The emergence of self awareness.* Cambridge, MA: Harvard University Press.

Kagan, J. (1981b). Universals in human development. In R. H. Munroe, R. L. Munroe, & B. Whiting (Eds.), *Handbook of cross-cultural human development* (pp. 53–62). New York: Garland.

Kagan, J. (1994). *Galen's prophecy: Temperament and human nature.* New York: Basic Books.

Kagan, J., Kearsley, R., & Zelazo, P. (1978). *Infancy: Its place in human development.* Cambridge, MA: Harvard University Press.

Kagan, J., & Klein, R. (1973). Cross-cultural perspectives on early development. *American Psychologist, 28,* 947–961.

Kajuira, H., Cowart, J., & Beauchamp, G.K. (1992). Early developmental changes in bitter taste responses in human infants. *Developmental Psychobiology, 25,* 375–386.

Kalkwarf, H., & Specker, B. (1995). Bone mineral loss during lactation and recovery after weaning. *Obestretics and Gynegology, 86,* 26.

Kaminer, R., & Jedrysek, E. (1983). Age of walking and mental retardation. *American Journal of Public Health, 73,* 1094–1096.

Kaplan-Sanoff, M., Parker, S., & Zuckerman, B. (1991). Poverty and early childhood development: What do we know and what should we do? *Infants and Young Children, 4,* 68–76.

Karnes, M. (1982). *You and your small wonder: Book II.* Circle Pines, MN: American Guidance Service.

Kaufman, J., & Zigler, E. (1987). Do abused children become abusive parents? *American Journal of Orthopsychiatry, 57,* 186–192.

Kaufmann-Hayoz, R. (1991). Perceptual development. In M. Lamb & H. Keller, (Eds.), *Infant development: Perspectives from German-speaking countries* (pp. 219–243).

Kaye, K. (1980). Why we don't talk "baby talk" to babies. *Journal of Child Language, 7,* 489–507.

Kazura, K. (2000). Fathers' qualitative and quantitative involvement: An investigation of attachment, play, and social interactions. *Journal of Mens' Studies, 9*(1), 41–57.

Keister, M. (1973). *Discipline: The secret heart of child care.* Greensboro: The University of North Carolina at Greensboro.

Kellman, P., & Spelke, E. (1983). Perception of partly occluded objects in infancy. *Cognitive Psychology, 15,* 483–454.

Kelly, D., & Shannon, D. (1982). Sudden infant death syndrome and near sudden infant death syndrome: A review of the literature, 1964–1982. *Pediatric Clinics of North America, 29,* 1241–1261.

Kempe, C., & Helfer, R. (1972). *Helping the battered child and his family.* Philadelphia: Lippincott.

Kendall, E. (1983). Child care and disease: What's the risk. *Young Children, 38*(5), 68–77.

Kent, R. (1980). Articulatory and acoustic perspectives on speech development. In A. Reilly (Ed.), *The communication game: Perspectives on the development of speech, language and nonverbal communication skills* (pp. 38–48). Skillman, NJ: Johnson & Johnson.

Kilkenny M., & Lumley, J. (1994). Ethnic differences in the incidence of the sudden infant death syndrome in Victoria, Australia 1985–1989. *Paediatric and Perinatal Epidemiology, 8,* 27–40.

King, W., & Seegmiller, B. (1973). Performance of 14- to 22-month-old black firstborn male infants on two tests of cognitive development. *Developmental Psychology, 8,* 317–326.

Kinsbourne, M. (1978). *Asymmetrical function of the brain.* London: Cambridge University.

Kisilevsky, B.S., Muir, D.W., & Low, J.A. (2000). Maturation of human fetal responses to vibroacoustic stimulation. In D.W. Muir & A. Slater, (Eds.), *Infant development: The essential readings* (pp. 72–92). Oxford, England: Blackwell Publishers.

Klaus, M., & Kennell, J. (1976). *Maternal-infant bonding.* St. Louis, MO: Mosby.

Klaus, M., & Kennell, J. (1982). *Parent-infant bonding* (2nd ed.). St. Louis, MO: Mosby.

Klein, J. (1992). Otitis media. In S. Krugman, S. Katz, A. Gershon, & C. Wilfert, (Eds.), *Infectious diseases of children* (9th ed.; pp. 285–293). St. Louis: Mosby.

Knight-Ridder News Service. (1991, May 24). 13-ounce baby holding his own in Florida hospital. *The Raleigh News and Observer,* p. 4.

Knobloch, H., Stevens, F., & Malone, A. (1980). *Manual of developmental diagnosis.* New York: Harper & Row.

Kochanska, G. (2001). Emotional development in children with different attachment histories: The first three years. *Child Development, 72*(2), 474–490.

Kochanska, G., Coy, K.C., & Murray, K.T. (2001). The development of self-regulation in the first four years of life. *Child Development, 72*(4), 1091–1111.

Kolb, B. (1989). Brain development, plasticity, and behavior. *American Psychologist, 44,* 1203–1212.

Kolb, B. (1999). Neuroanatomy and development overview. In N. Fox, L. Leavitt, & J. Warhol (Eds.), *The role of early experience in development* (pp. 5–14). Skillman, NJ: Johnson & Johnson.

Kolb, B., & Whishaw, I. (1990). *Fundamentals of human neuropsychology* (3rd ed.). New York: Freeman.

Komaroff, A. (1999). *The Harvard medical school family health guide.* New York: Simon & Schuster.

Kontos, S., & Wilcox-Herzog, A. (1997). Influences on children's competence in early childhood classrooms. *Early Childhood Research Quarterly, 12,* 247–262.

Kopp, C. (1992). Emotional distress and control in young children. *New Directions for Child Development, 55*(Spring), 41–56.

Kopp, C., & Brownell, C. (1991). The development of self: The first 3 years. *Developmental Review, 11,* 195–196.

Kopp, C., & Krakow, J. (1982). *The child: Development in a social context.* Reading, MA: Addison-Wesley.

Kostelnik, M., Whiren, A., Soderman, A., Stein, L., & Gregory, K. (2002). *Guiding children's social development* (4th ed.). Albany, NY: Delmar.

Krashen, S. (1973). Lateralization, language learning, and the critical period: Some new evidence. *Language Learning, 23*(1), 63–74.

Kroenfeld, J., & Glick, D. (1995). Unintentional injury: A major health problem for young children and youth. *Journal of Family and Economic Issues, 16,* 353–393.

Kuhl, P. (1981). Auditory category formation and developmental speech perception. In R. Stark (Ed.), *Language behavior in infancy and early childhood* (pp. 165–183). New York: Elsevier.

Kuhl, P. (1999). The role of experience in early language development: Linguistic experience alters the perception and production of speech. In N. Fox, L. Leavitt, & J. Warhol (Eds.), *The role of early experience in development* (pp. 101–121). Skillman, NJ: Johnson & Johnson.

Kuhl, P., & Meltzoff, A. (1982). The bimodal perception of speech in infancy. *Science, 218,* 1138–1141.

Kullander, S., & Kaellen, B. (1971). A prospective study of smoking and pregnancy. *Acta Obstetrics and Gynecology of Scandinavia, 50,* 83.

Ladd, G., & Le Sieur, K. (1995). Parents and peer relationships. In M. Bornstein (Ed.), *Handbook of parenting* (Vol. 4, pp. 377–409). Mahwah, NJ: Erlbaum.

Lagercrantz, H., & Slotkin, T. (1986). The stress of being born. *Scientific American, 254,* 100–108.

Lagerspetz, K., Nygard, M., & Strandwick, C. (1971). The effects of training in crawling on the motor and mental development of infants. *Scandinavian Journal of Psychology, 12,* 192–197.

Laible, D.J., & Thompson, R.A. (2000). Attachment and self-organization. In M.D. Lewis & I. Granic (Eds.), *Emotion, development, and self-organization* (pp. 298–323). Cambridge, UK: Cambridge University Press.

Laishley, J. (1983). *Working with young children.* London: Edward Arnold.

Lally, J., Griffin, A., Fenichel, E., Segal, M., Szanton, E., & Weissbourd, B. (1995). *Caring for infants and toddlers in groups.* Arlington, VA: Zero to Three/ NationalCenter.

Lamaze, F. (1970). *Painless childbirth: The Lamaze method.* Chicago: Henry Regency.

Lamb, M. (1976). *The role of the father in child development.* New York: Wiley.

Lamb, M. (1981a). Developing trust and perceived effectance in infancy. In L. Lipsitt (Ed.), *Advances in infancy research* (Vol. 1, pp. 101–127). Norwood, NJ: Ablex.

Lamb, M. (1981b). Fathers and child development: An integrative review. In M. Lamb (Ed.), *The role of the father in child development* (2nd ed., pp. 1–73). New York: Wiley.

Lamb, M. (1982a). Early context and maternal-infant bonding: One decade later. *Pediatrics, 70,* 763–768.

Lamb, M. (1982b). Maternal employment and child development: A review. In M. Lamb (Ed.), *Nontraditional families: Parenting and child development* (pp. 45–69). Hillsdale, NJ: Erlbaum.

Lamb, M. (1982c). Parent-infant interaction, attachment and socioemotional development in infancy. In R. Emde & R. Harmon (Eds.), *The development of attachment and affiliative systems* (pp. 195–214). New York: Plenum.

Lamb, M. (Ed.). (1987). *The father's role: Cross-cultural perspectives.* Hillsdale, NJ: Erlbaum.

Lamb, M. (1998). Nonparental child care: Context, quality, correlates, and consequences. In W. Damon (Ed.-in-Chief), I. Siegel & K. A. Renninger (Vol. Eds.), *Handbook of child psychology, Vol 4: Child psychology and practice* (pp. 73–133). New York: Wiley.

Lamb, M., & Bornstein, M. (1987). *Development in infancy: An introduction* (2nd ed.). New York: Random House.

Lamb, M., & Campos, J. (1982). *Development in infancy.* New York: Random House.

Lamb, M., Sternberg, K., & Prodromidis, M. (1992). Nonmaternal care and the security of infant-mother attachment: A reanalysis of the data. *Infant Behavior and Development, 15,* 71–83.

Langer, W. (1975). Infanticide: A historical survey. In L. deMause (Ed.), *The new psychohistory* (pp. 55–67). New York: Psychohistory Press.

Langlois, J., Roggman, L., Casey, R., Ritter, J., Reiser-Dammer, L., & Jenkins, V. (1987). Infant preferences for attractive faces: Rudiments of a stereotype? *Developmental Psychology, 23,* 363–369.

Lasky, R. E., Syrdal–Lasky, A., & Klein, R. E. (1975). VOT discrimination by four—to six—and a half–month old infants from Spanish environments. *Journal of Experimental Child Psychology, 20,* 215–225.

Lazar, I., & Darlington, R. (1979). *Lasting effects after preschool: Summary report.* (DHEW Publication No. OHDS 79–30179). Washington, DC: U.S. Department of Health, Education and Welfare.

Lazar, I., & Darlington, R. (1982). Lasting effects of an early education. *Monographs of the Society for Research in Child Development, 47* (2–3, Serial No. 195).

Leach, P. (1976). *Babyhood.* New York: Knopf.

Leavitt, L. (1980). The development of speech comprehension and speech production. In A. Reilly (Ed.), *The communication game: Perspectives on the development of speech, language and non-verbal communication skills* (pp. 21–30). Skillman, NJ: Johnson & Johnson.

Leavitt, R., & Eheart, B. (1985). *Toddler day care: A guide to responsive caregiving.* Lexington, MA: Heath.

Leboyer, F. (1975). *Birth without violence.* New York: Knopf.

Lecaunet, J. (1998). Foetal responses to auditory and speech stimuli. In. A. Slater, (Ed.), *Perceptual development: Visual, auditory, and speech perception in infancy* (pp. 317–355). East Sussex, England: Psychology Press.

Lecanuet, J. P., Graniere-Deferre, C., Jacquet, A.Y., & DeCasper, A.J. (2000). Fetal discrimination of low-pitched musical notes. *Developmental Psychobiology, 36,* 29–39.

Lechat, M., Borlee, I., Bouckaert, A., & Mission, C. (1980). Caffeine study (letter to the editor). *Science, 207,* 1296–1297.

LeDoux, J. (1993). Emotional networks in the brain. In M. Lewis & J. Haviland (Eds.), *Handbook of emotions* (pp. 109–118). New York: Guilford.

Lee, Y., & Jessee, P (1997). Taiwanese infants' and toddlers' interactions with a baby in a group setting. *Early Child Development and Care, 134,* 75–87.

Lee-Parritz, A., & Heffner, L. (1995). Gestational diabetes. In F. Brown & J. Hare (Eds.), *Diabetes complicating pregnancy* (pp. 15–40). New York: Wiley.

Legerstee, M.(1991). The role of person and object in eliciting early imitation. *Journal of Experimental Child Psychology, 51,* 423–433.

Lehane, S. (1976). *Help your baby learn.* Englewood Cliffs, NJ: Prentice Hall.

Leibel, R. (1991). Obesity. In O. Brunser, F. Carrazza, M. Gracey, B. Nichols, & J. Senterre (Eds.), *Clinical nutrition of the young child* (pp. 155–166). New York: Raven.

Lickona, T. (1983). Raising good children. New York: Bantam.

Lieberman, A.F., & Zeanah, C.H. (1995). Disorders of attachment in infancy. *Child and Adolescent Psychiatric Clinics of North America, 4,* 571–687.

Leifer, G. (1999). *Thompson's introduction to maternity and pediatric nursing* (3rd ed.). Philadelphia: Saunders.

Lempers, J., Flavell, E., & Flavell, J. (1977). The development in very young children of tacit knowledge concerning visual perception. *Genetic Psychology Monographs, 95,* 3–53.

Lenneberg, E. (1967). *Biological foundations of language.* New York: Wiley.

Lenneberg, E., Rebelsky, G., & Nichols, I. (1965). The vocalizations of infants born to deaf and hearing parents. *Human Development, 8,* 23–27.

Lester, B. (1985). There's more to crying than meets the ear. In B. Lester & C. Boukydis (Eds.), *Infant crying: Theoretical and research perspectives* (pp. 1–27). New York: Plenum.

Lester, B., & Boukydis, C. (1992). No language but a cry. In H. Papousek, U. Jurgens, & M. Papousek, (Eds.), *Nonverbal vocal communication* (pp. 45 –173). New York: Cambridge University.

Lester, B., Boukydis, C., Garcia Coll, C., Hole, W., & Peucker, M. (1992). Infantile colic: Acoustic cry characteristics, maternal perception of cry, and temperament. *Infant Behavior and Development, 15,* 15–26.

Lester, B., & Dreher, M. (1989). Effects of marijuana use during pregnancy on newborn cry. *Child Development, 60,* 765–771.

Leventhal, A., & Lipsitt, L. (1964). Adaptation, pitch discrimination, and sound localization in the neonate. *Child Development, 35,* 759–767.

Leventhal, J. (1996). Child maltreatment: Neglect to abuse. In A. Rudolph, J. Hoffman, & C. Rudolph (Eds.), *Rudolph's pediatrics* (20th ed., pp. 145–152). Stamford, CT: Appleton & Lange.

Levin, G. (1983). *Child psychology.* Monterey, CA: Brooks/Cole.

Levine, R. (1980). A cross-cultural perspective on parenting. In M. Fantini & R. Cardenas (Eds.), *Parenting in a multicultural society* (pp. 17–40). New York: Longman.

Levitt, M. (1991). Attachment and close relationships: A lifespan perspective. In J. Gewirtz & W. Kurtines (Eds), *Intersections with attachment* (pp. 183–205). Hillsdale, NJ: Erlbaum.

Levy, J. (1973). *The baby exercise book.* New York: Random House.

Levy, M., & Koren, G. (1992). Clinical toxicology of the neonate. *Seminars in Perinatology, 16*(1), 63–75.

Lewis, M. (1991). Ways of knowing: Objective self-awareness or consciousness. *Developmental Review, 11,* 231–244.

Lewis, M. (1993). The emergence of human emotions. In M. Lewis & J. Haviland (Eds.), *Handbook of Emotions* (pp. 223–246). New York: Guilford.

Lewis, M., & Brooks, J. (1974). Self, others and fear: Infant's reactions to people. In M. Lewis & L. Rosenblum (Eds.), *The origins of fear* (pp. 195–227). New York: Wiley.

Lewis, M., & Brooks, J. (1978). Self-knowledge in emotional development. In M. Lewis & L. Rosenblum (Eds.), *The development of affect* (pp. 205–226). New York: Plenum.

Lewis, M., & Brooks-Gunn, J. (1979). *Social cognition and the acquisition of self.* New York: Plenum.

Lewis, M., & Freedle, R. (1973). Mother-infant dyad: The cradle of meaning. In P. Pliner, L. Krames, & T. Alloway (Eds.), *Communication and affect: Language and thought* (pp. 127–155). New York: Academic Press.

Lewis, M., & Michalson, L. (1983). *Children's emotions and moods: Developmental theory and measurement.* New York: Plenum.

Lewis, M., & Saarni, C. (1985). Culture and emotions. In M. Lewis & C. Saarni (Eds.), *The socialization of emotions* (pp. 1–17). New York: Plenum.

Lewis, M., Stanger, C., & Sullivan, M. (1989). Deception in 3-year-olds. *Developmental Psychology, 25,* 439–443.

Lewkowicz, D. (1996). Infants' response to the audible and visible properties of the human face: 1. Role of the lexical-syntactic content, temporal synchrony, gender, and manner of speech. *Developmental Psychology, 32,* 347–366.

Lilly, C.M., Craig, K.D., & Grunau, R.E. (1997). The expression of pain in infants and toddlers: Developmental changes in facial expression. *Pain, 72,* 161–170.

Linder, T. (1993). *Transdisciplinary play-based assessment* (rev. ed.). Baltimore: Brookes.

Lindfors, J. (1980). *Children's language and learning.* Englewood Cliffs, NJ: Prentice Hall.

Link, A., Kernested, D., & Ford-Jones, E. (1993). Young infants. In L. Donowitz (Ed.), *Infection control in the childcare center and preschool* (pp. 23–29). Baltimore: Williams & Wilkins.

Linn, P., Horowitz, F., & Fox, H. (1985). Stimulation in the NICU: Is more necessarily better? *Clinics in Perinatology, 12,* 407–422.

Linn, S., Schoenbaum, S., Monson, R., Rosner, B., Subblefield, P., & Ryan, K. (1982). No association between coffee consumption and adverse outcomes of pregnancy. *New England Journal of Medicine, 306,* 141–145.

Linn, S., Schoenbaum, S., Monson, R., Rosner, B., Stubblefield, P., & Ryan, K. (1983). The association of marijuana use with outcome of pregnancy. *American Journal of Public Health, 73,* 1161–1164.

Lipsitt, L. (1977). Taste in human neonates: Its effect on sucking and heart rate. In J. Weiffenbach (Ed.), *Taste and development: The genesis of sweet preference* (pp. 125–141). Bethesda: MD: National Institutes of Health. (DHEW Pub. No. NIH 77–1068).

Lipsitt, L., Engen, T., & Kaye, H. (1963). Developmental changes in the olfactory threshold of the neonate. *Child Development, 34,* 371–376.

Lipsitt, L., & Levy, N. (1959). Electrotactual threshold in the neonate. *Child Development, 30,* 547–554.

Lisker, L., & Abramson, A.S. (1970). The voicing dimension: Some experiments in comparative phonetics. In *Proceedings of the 6th International Congress of Phonetic Sciences* (pp. 563–567). Prague: Academia.

Litovsky, R., & Clifton, R. (1992). Use of sound-pressure level in auditory distance discrimination by 6-month-old infants. *Journal of the Acoustical Society of America, 92,* 794–802.

Little, A., Lipsitt, L., & Rovee-Collier, C. (1984). Classical conditioning and retention of the infant's eyelid response: Effects of age and interstimulus interval. *Journal of Experimental Child Psychology, 37,* 512–524.

Littman, H., Medendorp, S., & Goldfarb, J. (1994). The decision to breast-feed. *Clinical Pediatrics, 33,* 214–219.

Locke, J. (1961). *An essay concerning human understanding.* London: Dent. (Original work published 1690).

Lorenz, K. (1965). *Evolution and modification of behavior.* Chicago: University of Chicago Press.

Lourenco, O., & Machado, A. (1996). In defense of Piaget's theory: A reply to 10 common criticisms. *Psychological Review, 103,* 143–164.

Lowrey, C. (1978). *Growth and development of children* (7th ed.). Chicago: Medical Yearbook.

Lowrey, C. (1986). *Growth and development of children* (8th ed.). Chicago: Medical Yearbook.

Lozoff, B., Wolff, A., & Davis, N. (1984). Cosleeping in urban families with young children in the United States. *Pediatrics, 74,* 171–182.

Lu, G., & Goldenberg, R. (2000). Current concepts on the pathogenesis and markers of preterm births. *Clinics in Perinatology, 27,* 263–283.

Lubchenco, L., Hansman, C., Dressler, M., & Boyd, E. (1963). Intrauterine growth as estimated from liveborn birthweight data at 24 to 42 weeks of gestation. *Pediatrics, 32,* 793–796.

Lucas, A., Morley, L., & Cole, T. (1992). Breast milk and subsequent intelligence quotient in children born preterm. *Lancet, 339,* 261–264.

Lunt, R., & Law, D. (1974). A review of the chronology of eruption of deciduous teeth. *Journal of the American Dental Association, 89,* 872–879.

Lutz, D., & Sternberg, R. (1999). Cognitive development. In M. Bornstein & M. Lamb (Eds.), *Developmental psychology: An advanced text* (4th ed., pp. 275–311). Mahwah, NJ: Erlbaum.

Maccoby, E. (1980). *Social development: Psychological growth and the parent-child relationship.* New York: Harcourt, Brace, Jovanovich.

Maccoby, E. (1990). Gender and relationships: A developmental acount. *American Psychologist, 45,* 513–520.

Maccoby, E., & Feldman, S. (1972). Mother-attachment and stranger-reaction patterns in the third year of life. *Monographs of the Society for Research in Child Development, 37*(1, Serial No. 146).

Maccoby, E., & Martin, J. (1983). Socialization in the context of the family. In P. Mussen (Ed.), *Handbook of child psychology: Vol. 4. Socialization, personality and social development* (4th ed., pp. 1–101). New York: Wiley.

Mace, J.W., Goodman, S.I., Centerwall, W.R., & Chinnock, R.F. (1976). The child with an unusual odor: A clinical resume. *Clinical Pediatrics, 15,* 57–62.

MacFarlane, J. (1975). Olfaction in the development of social preferences in the human neonate. In *Parent-infant interaction: Ciba Foundation Symposium 33* (new series; pp. 103–117). Amsterdam: Elsevier.

Machado, J., & Meyer-Botnarescue, H. (1997). *Student teaching guide: Early childhood practicum guide* (3rd ed.). Albany, NY: Delmar.

Mackey, M. (1995). Women's evaluation of their childbirth performance. *Maternal-Child Nursing Journal, 23,* 57–72.

MacMillan, H., MacMillan, J., & Oxford, D. (1993). Periodic health examinations, 1993 update: 1. Primary prevention of child maltreatment. *Canadian Medical Association Journal, 148,* 151–163.

Main, M., & Hesse, E. (1990). Parents' unresolved traumatic experiences are related to infant disorganized attachment status. In M. Greenberg, D. Cicchetti, & E. Cummings (Eds.), *Attachment in the preschool years: Theory, research and intervention* (pp. 161–220). Chicago: University of Chicago.

Main, M., Kaplan, N., & Cassidy, J. (1985). Security in infancy, childhood, and adulthood: A move to the level of representation. In I. Bretherton & E. Waters (Eds.), Growing points of attachment theory and research (pp. 66–104). *Monographs of the Society for Research in Child Development, 50*(1–2, Serial No. 209).

Malatesta, C., & Haviland, J. (1982). Learning display rules: The socialization of emotion expression in infancy. *Child Development, 53,* 991–1003.

Malatesta, C., & Haviland, J. (1985). Signals, symbols and socialization: The modification of emotional expression in human development. In M. Lewis & C. Saarni (Eds.), *The socialization of emotions* (pp. 89–116). New York: Plenum.

Malina, R. (1973). Physical development factors in motor performance. In C. Corbin (Ed.), *A textbook of motor development* (pp. 36–46). Dubuque, IA: Brown.

Malina, R., & Bouchard, C. (1991). *Growth, maturation, and physical activity.* Champaign, IL: Human Kinetics.

Mandel, D.R., Jusczyk, P.W., & Pisoni, D.B. (1995). Infants' recognition of the sound patterns of their own names. *Psychological Science, 6,* 314–317.

Mandler, J. (1984). Representation and recall in infancy. In M. Moscovitch (Ed.), *Advances in the study of communication and affect: Vol. 9. Infant memory* (pp. 75–101). New York: Plenum.

Mandler, J. (1990). A new perspective on cognitive development in infancy. *American Scientist, 78,* 236–243.

Manion, J. (1977). A study of fathers and infant caretaking. *Birth and the Family Journal, 4,* 174–178.

Manke, B., Saudino, K., & Grant, J. (2001). Extreme analyses of observed temperament dimensions. In R. Emde & J. Hewitt (Eds), *Infancy to early childhood: Genetic and environmental influences on developmental change.* New York: Oxford University.

Mans, L., Cicchetti, D., & Sroufe, L. (1978). Mirror reactions of Down's syndrome infants and toddlers: Cognitive underpinnings of self-recognition. *Child Development, 49,* 1247–1250.

Maone, T.R., Mattes, R.D., Bernbaum, J.C., & Beauchamp, G.K. (1990). A new method for delivering a taste without fluids to preterm and term infants. *Developmental Psychobiology, 23,* 179–191.

Maratos, O. (1998). Neonatal, early and later imitation: Same order phenomena? In F. Simion & G. Butterworth, (Eds.), *The development of sensory, motor and cognitive capacities in early infancy: From perception to cognition* (pp. 145–160). East Sussex, UK: Psychology Press.

Marks, M. (1985). *Pediatric infectious diseases for the practitioner.* New York: Springer-Verlag.

Marotz, L., Cross, M., & Rush, J. (2001). *Health, safety, and nutrition* (5th ed.). Albany, NY: Delmar.

Martin, A. (1996, February 9). Now that's a lot of babies: Multiple births take off. *The Raleigh News and Observer,* p. 6D.

Martin, E., & Beal, V. (1978). *Robert's nutrition work with children* (4th ed.). Chicago: University of Chicago Press.

Martinez, G., & Dodd, D. (1983). 1981 milk feeding patterns in the United States during the first 12 months of life. *Pediatrics, 71,* 166–170.

Marzollo, J. (1977). *Super tot: Creative activities for children from one to three.* New York: Harper & Row.

Matsungaga, E., Tonomura, A., Oishi, H., & Kikuchi, Y. (1978). Re-examination of paternal age effect in Down syndrome. *Human Genetics, 40,* 259–268.

Matthews, T., MacDorman, M., & Menacker, F. (2002). Infant mortality statistics from the 1999 period linked birth/infant death data set. *National Vital Statistics Reports, 50*(4), 1–27.

Maurer, D., & Barrera, M. (1981). Infants' perception of natural and distorted arrangements of a schematic face. *Child Development, 52,* 196–202.

Mawhinney, S., & Pagano, M. (1994). Distribution of the latency period for perinatally acquired AIDS. *Statistics in Medicine, 13,* 2031–2042.

Mayhall, P., & Norgard, K. (1983). *Child abuse and neglect.* New York: Wiley.

Maziade, M., Boudreault, M., Cote, R., & Thivierge, J. (1986). Influence of gentle birth delivery procedures and other perinatal circumstances on infant temperament: Developmental and social implications. *The Journal of Pediatrics, 108,* 134–136.

McCall, R. (1974). Exploratory manipulation and play in the human infant. *Monographs of the Society of Research in Child Development, 39* (2, Serial No. 155).

McCall, R., & Melson, W. (1970). Complexity, contour, and area as determinants of attention in infants. *Developmental Psychology, 3,* 343–349.

McCarthy, D. (1954). Language development in children. In L. Carmichael (Ed.), *Manual of child psychology* (pp. 492–630). New York: Wiley.

McCartney, K., Scarr, S., Rocheleau, A., Phillips, D., Abbot-Shim, M., Eisenberg, M., Keefe, N., Rosenthal, S., & Ruh, J. (1997). Teacher-child interaction and child-care auspices as predictors of social outcomes in infants, toddlers, and preschoolers. *Merrill Palmer Quarterly, 43,* 426–450.

McClanahan, S., & Teitler, J. (1999). The consequences of father absence. In M.E. Lamb (Ed.), *Parenting and child development in "nontraditional" families* (pp. 83–102). Mahwah, NJ: Erlbaum.

McClenaghan, B., & Gallahue, D. (1978). *Fundamental movement: A developmental and remedial approach.* Philadelphia: Saunders.

McCormick, C., & Maurer, D. (1988). Unimanual hand preferences in 6-month-olds: Consistency and relation to familial-handedness. *Infant Behavior and Development, 11,* 21–29.

McCormick, K. (1996). Assessing cognitive development. In M. McLean, D. Bailey, & M. Wolery (Eds.), *Assessing infants and children with special needs* (2nd ed., pp. 268–304). Columbus, OH: Merrill.

McDonald, K. (1980). Enhancing a child's positive self-concept. In T. Yawkey (Ed.), *The self-concept of the young child* (pp. 51–61). Provo, UT: Brigham Young University Press.

McDonald, R., & Avery, D. (1983). *Dentistry for the child and adolescent* (4th ed.). St. Louis, MO: Mosby.

McGaha, C.G., Snow, C.W., & Teleki, J.K. (2001). Family child care in the United States: A comparative analysis of 1981 and 1998 state regulations. *Early Childhood Education Journal, 28*(4), 251–255.

McGraw, M. (1935). *Growth: A study of Johnny and Jimmy.* New York: Appleton-Century-Crofts.

McGraw, M. (1966). *The neuromuscular maturation of the human infant.* New York: Hafner.

McIntire, D., Bloom, S., Casey, B., & Leveno, K. (1999). Birth weight in relation to morbidity and mortality among newborn infants. *New England Journal of Medicine, 340,* 1234–1238.

McKenna, J., & Mosko, S. (1993). Evolution and infant sleep: An experimental study of infant-parent cosleeping and its implication for SIDS. *Acta Paediatrics, Supplement 389,* 31–36.

McKenna, J., Mosko, S., Richard, C., Drummond, S., Hunt, L., Cetel, M., & Arpaia, J. (1994). Experimental studies of infant-parent cosleeping: Mutual physiological and behavioral influences and their relevance to SIDS. *Early Human Development, 38,* 187–201.

McLaren, D., & Burman, D. (1982). *Textbook of paediatric nutrition* (2nd ed.). London: Churchill Livingstone.

McLean, M., Bailey, D., & Wolery, M. (1996). *Assessing infants and preschoolers with special needs* (2nd ed). Englewood Cliffs, NJ: Merrill.

McNeil, D. (1970). The development of language. In P. Mussen (Ed.), *Carmichael's manual of child psychology* (Vol. 1, pp. 1061–1161). New York: Wiley.

Meadow-Orlans, K. (1995). Parenting with a sensory or physical disability. In M. Bornstein (Ed.), *Handbook of parenting* (Vol. 4, pp. 57–84). Mahwah, NJ: Erlbaum.

Mehl, M., & Peterson, G. (1981). Home birth versus hospital birth: Comparisons of outcomes of matched populations. In P. Ahmed (Ed.), *Pregnancy, childbirth, and parenthood* (pp. 315–334). New York: Elsevier.

Meier, J., & Malone, P. (1979). *Facilitating children's development* (Vol. 1). Baltimore: University Park Press.

Meisels, S. (1996). Charting the continuum of assessment and intervention. In S. Meisels & E. Fenichel (Eds.), *New visions for the developmental assessment of infants and young children* (pp. 27–52). Washington, DC: Zero to Three.

Meltzoff, A. (1988a). Infant imitation and memory: Nine-months-olds in immediate and deferred tests. *Child Development, 59,* 217–225.

Meltzoff, A. (1988b). Infant imitation after a 1-week delay: Long-term memory for novel acts and multiple stimuli. *Developmental Psychology, 24,* 470–476.

Meltzoff, A., & Borton, R. (1979). Intermodal matching by human neonates. *Nature, 282,* 403–404.

Meltzoff, A., & Gopnik, A. (1994). The role of imitation in understanding persons and developing a theory of mind. In S. Baron-Cohen, H. Tager-Flusberg et al. (Eds.), *Understanding other minds: Perspectives from autism* (pp. 335–366). New York: Oxford University Press.

Meltzoff, A., Kuhl, P., & Moore, M. (1991). Perception, respresentation, and the control of action in newborns and young infants: Toward a new synthesis. In M. Weiss & P. Zelazo (Eds.), *Newborn attention: Biological constraints and the influence of experience* (pp. 377–412). Norwood, NJ: Ablex.

Meltzoff, A., & Moore, M. (1977). Imitation of facial and normal gestures of human neonates. *Science, 198,* 75–78.

Meltzoff, A., & Moore, M. (1983). Newborns imitate adult facial gestures. *Child Development, 54,* 702–709.

Meltzoff, A., & Moore, M. (1989). Imitation in newborns: Exploring the range of gestures imitated and the underlying mechanisms. *Developmental Psychology, 25,* 954–962.

Meltzoff, A., & Moore, M. (1992). Early imitation within a functional framework: The importance of person identity, movement, and development. *Infant Behavior and Development, 15,* 479–505.

Meltzoff, A., & Moore, M. (1994). Imitation, memory, and representation of persons. *Infant Behavior and Development, 17,* 83–99.

Melzack, R. (1984). The myth of painless childbirth. *Pain, 19,* 321–337.

Mendelson, M., & Haith, M. (1976). The relation between audition and vision in the human newborn. *Monographs of the Society for Research in Child Development, 41* (Whole No. 167).

Menn, L., & Stoel-Gammon, C. (1993). Phonological development: Learning sound patterns. In J. Gleason (Ed.), *The development of language* (3rd ed., pp. 65–113). New York: Macmillan.

Mennella, J. (2001). Regulation of milk intake after exposure to alcohol in mother's milk. *Alcoholism: Clinical and Experimental Research, 25*(4), 590–593.

Mennella, J., & Beauchamp, G. (1991a). Maternal diet alters the sensory qualities of human milk and the nursling's behavior. *Pediatrics, 88,* 737–744.

Mennella, J., & Beauchamp, G. (1991b). The transfer of alcohol to human milk: Effects on flavor and the infants' behavior. *New England Journal of Medicine, 325,* 981–985.

Mennella, J., & Beauchamp, G. (1993a). Beer, breastfeeding, and folklore. *Developmental Psychobiology, 26,* 459–466.

Mennella, J., & Beauchamp, G. (1993b). Early flavor experiences: When do they start? *Zero to Three, 14*(2), 1–7.

Mennella, J., & Beauchamp, G. (1998). Infants' exploration of scented toys: Effects of prior experience. *Chemical Senses, 23,* 11–17.

Mennella, J., Johnson, A., & Beauchamp, G. (1995). Garlic ingestion by pregnant women alters the odor of amniotic fluid. *Chemical Senses, 20,* 207–209.

Menyuk, P. (1982). Language development. In C. Kopp & J. Krakow (Eds.), *The child: Development in a social context* (pp. 282–331). Reading, MA: Addison-Wesley.

Meryash, D. (1995). Genetics. In D. Coustan, R. Haning, & D. Singer (Eds.), *Human reproduction: Growth and development* (pp. 99–120). Boston: Little, Brown.

Michalson, L., & Lewis, M. (1985). What do children know about emotions and when do they know it? In M. Lewis & C. Saarni (Eds.), *The socialization of emotions* (pp. 117–139). New York: Plenum.

Milgrom, J., Westley, D., & McCloud, P. (1995). Do infants of depressed mothers cry more that other infants? *Journal of Paediatrics and Child Health, 31,* 218–221.

Miller, J., & Eimas, P. (1983). Studies on the categorization of speech by infants. *Cognition, 13,* 135–165.

Miller, P. (1993). *Theories of developmental psychology* (3rd ed.). New York: Freeman.

Miller, S. (1987). *Developmental research methods.* Englewood Cliffs, NJ: Prentice Hall.

Mistretta, C.M., & Bradley, R.M. (1975). Taste and swallowing in utero: A discussion of fetal sensory function. *British Medical Bulletin, 31,* 80–84.

Miyake, K., Campos, J., Kagan, J., & Bradshaw, D. (1986). Issues in socioemotional development in Japan. In H. Azuma, I. Hakuta, & H. Stevenson (Eds.), *Kodomo: Child development and education in Japan* (pp. 239–261). San Francisco: Freeman.

Miyake, K., Chen, S., & Campos, J. (1985). Infant temperament, mothers mode of interaction, and attachment in Japan: An interim report. In I. Bretherton & E. Waters (Eds.), *Growing points of attachment theory and research* (pp. 276–297). Monographs of the Society for Research in Child Development, 50, (1–2, Serial No. 209).

Mizukami, K., Kobayashi, N., Ishii, T., Iwati, H. (1990). First selective attachment begins in early infancy: A study using telethermography. *Behavior and Development, 13,* 257–271.

Modi, N. (1999). The role of early experience in infant development: Enhancing outcome after birth. In N. Fox, L. Leavitt, & J. Warhol (Eds.), *The role of early experience in development* (pp. 267–282). Skillman, NJ: Johnson & Johnson.

Moffitt, A. (1971). Consonant cue perception by 20–24 week-old infants. *Child Development, 42,* 717–731.

Monckeberg, F. (1991). Protein energy malnutrition: Marasmus. In O. Brunser, F. Carrazza, M. Gracey, B. Nichols, & J. Senterre. (Eds.), *Clinical nutrition of the young child* (pp. 121–132). New York: Raven.

Mondschein, E.R., Adolph, K.E., & Tamis-LeMonda, C.S. (2000). Gender bias in mothers' expectations about infant crawling. *Journal of Experimental Child Psychology, 77*(4), 304–316.

Montagu, A. (1964). *Life before birth.* New York: American Library.

Montagu, A. (1971). *Touching: The human significance of skin.* New York: Columbia University Press.

Monto, M. (1996). Lamaze and Bradley childbirth classes: Contrasting perspectives toward the medical model of birth. *Birth, 23,* 193–201.

Moon, C., & Fifer, W.P. (1990). Newborns prefer a prenatal version of mother's voice. *Infant Behavior and Development, 13,* 530.

Moon, C., Panneton-Cooper, R., & Fifer, W. (1993). Two-day-olds prefer their native language. *Infant Behavior and Development, 16,* 495–500.

Moore, K. (1983). *Before we are born* (2nd ed.). Philadelphia: Saunders.

Moore, K., & Persaud, T. (1998). *The developing human: Clinically oriented embryology* (6th ed.). Philadelphia, Saunders.

Moore, M. (1978). *Realities in childbearing.* Philadelphia: Saunders.

Morelli, G., Oppenheim, D., Rogoff, B., & Goldsmith, D. (1992). Cultural variations in infants' sleeping arrangements: Questions of independence. *Developmental Psychology, 28,* 604–613.

Morelli, G., Rogoff, B., Oppenheim, D., & Goldsmith, D. (1992). Cultural variations in infants' sleeping arrangements: Questions of independence. *Developmental Psychology, 28,* 604–613.

Morelli, G., & Tronick, E. (1991). Efe multiple caretaking and attachment. In J. Gewirtz & W. Kurtines (Eds.), *Intersections with attachment* (pp. 41–51). Hillsdale, NJ: Erlbaum.

Morisset, C., Barnard, K., & Booth, C. (1995). Toddlers' language development: Sex differences within social risk. *Developmental Psychology, 31,* 851–865.

Morse, P. (1972). The discrimination of speech and nonspeech stimuli in early infancy. *Journal of Child Language, 6,* 199–204.

Morton, J., & Johnson, M. (1991). CONSPEC and CONLERN: A two-process theory of infant face recognition. *Psychological Review, 98,* 164–181.

Moss-Salentijn, L., & Hendricks-Klyvert, M. (1990*). Dental and oral tissues: An introduction* (3rd ed.). Philadelphia: Lea & Febiger.

Mrazek, P. (1993). Maltreatment and infant development. In C. Zeanah (Ed.), *Handbook of infant mental health* (pp. 159–172). New York: Guilford.

Mruk, C. (1999). *Self esteem: Research theory and practice* (2nd ed.). New York: Springer.

Mueller, C. (1996). Multidisciplinary research of multimodal stimulation of premature infants: An integrative review of the literature. *Maternal-Child Nursing Journal, 24,* 18–31.

Mueller, E., & Vandell, D. (1979). Infant-infant interaction. In J. Osofsky (Ed.). *Handbook of infant development* (pp. 591–622). New York: Wiley.

Mueller, W. (2001). Oral medicine and dentisty. In W. Hay, A. Hayward, M. Levin, & J. Sondheimer (Eds.), *Current pediatric diagnosis and treatment* (15th ed, pp. 390–399). New York: Lange.

Muir, D. (1985). The development of infants' auditory spatial sensitivity. In S. Trehub & B. Schneider (Eds.), *Auditory development in infancy* (pp. 51–84). New York: Plenum.

Muir, D., & Field, J. (1979). Newborn infants orient to sound. *Child Development, 50,* 431–436.

Murphy, K., & Smyth, C. (1962). Response of fetus to auditory stimulation. *Lancet, 1,* 972–973.

Murphy, L. (1983). Issues in the development of emotion in infancy. In R. Plutchik & H. Kellerman (Eds.), *Emotion: theory, research and experience: (Vol. 2). Emotions in early development* (pp. 1–34). New York: Academic Press.

Mussen, P., Conger, J., & Kagan, J. (1974). *Child development and personality* (4th ed.). New York: Harper & Row.

Myers, M., Fifer, W., Grose-Fifer, J., Sahni, R., Stark, R., & Schulze, K. (1997). "A novel quantitative measure of Trace-alternat EEG activity and its association with sleep states of preterm infants." *Developmental Psychobiology, 31,* 167–174.

Nadel, J., Carchon, I., Kervella, C., Marcelli, D., & Reserbat-Plantey, D. (1999). Expectancies for social contingency in 2-month-olds. *Developmental Science, 2*(2), 164–173.

Naeye, R. (1979). Weight gain and the outcome of pregnancy. *American Journal of Obstetrics and Gynecology, 135,* 3–9.

Naeye, R. (1983). Maternal age, obstetric complications and the outcome of pregnancy. *Obstetrics and Gynecology, 61,* 210–216.

Nanez, J. (1988). Perception of impending collision in 3- to 6-week-old human infants. *Infant Behavior and Development, 11,* 447–463.

Nash, M. (1997, February 3). Fertile minds. *Time, 149,* 48–56.

Nathanson, L. (1994). *The portable pediatrican for parents.* New York: Harper/Collins.

National Association for the Education of Young Children (NAEYC). (1991). *Accreditation criteria and procedures of the National Academy of Early Childhood Programs* (rev. ed.). Washington, DC: Author.

National Center for Health Statistics. (1976, June). NCHS Growth Charts, 1976. *Monthly Vital Statistics Report,* (Vol. 25, No. 3, Supplement, HRA 76–1120). Rockville, MD: U.S. Department of Health, Education and Welfare.

National Center for Health Statistics. (2000). *CDC Growth Charts: United States.* Retrieved from http://www.cdc.gov/growthcharts

National Institute of Neurological Disorders and Strokes. (1999). *Autism* (Fact Sheet). NIH Publication No. 96–1877. Bethesda, MD: National Institues of Health. Retrieved from http://www.ninds.nih.gov/health_and_medical/pubs/autism.htm

National Safety Council. (2000). *Injury facts.* Chicago: Author.

Needham, R. (1996). Assessment of growth. In W. R. Behrman, R. Kleigman, & A. Arving (Eds.), *Nelson's textbook of pediatrics* (15th ed., pp. 63–67). Philadelphia: Saunders.

Needleman, R. (1996). Fetal growth and development. In W. Nelson, R. Behrman, R. Kliegman, & A. Arving (Eds.), *Nelson's textbook of pediatrics* (15th ed., pp. 33–36). Philadelphia: Saunders.

Neisser, U. (1967). *Cognitive psychology.* New York, NY: Appleton-Century-Crofts.

Neisser, U. (1991). Two perceptually given aspects of the self and their development. *Developmental Review, 11,* 197–209.

Nelms, B., & Mullins, R. (1982). *Growth and development: A primary care approach.* Englewood Cliffs, NJ: Prentice Hall.

Nelson, K. (1973). Structure and strategy in learning to talk. *Monographs of the Society for Research in Child Development, 38* (Whole No. 149).

Nelson, K. (Ed.). (1989). *Narratives from the crib.* Cambridge, MA: Harvard.

Nelson, L. (1996). Disorders of the eye. In W. Nelson, R. Behrman, R. Kleigman, & A. Arvin (Eds.), *Nelson's textbook of pediatrics* (15th ed., pp. 1746–1747). Philadelphia: Saunders.

Nelson, N., Enkin, M., Saigel, S., Bennet, K., Milner, R., & Sackett, D. (1980). A randomized clinical trial of the Leboyer approach to childbirth. *New England Journal of Medicine, 202,* 655–660.

Newberger, J. (1997). New brain development research: A wonderful opportunity to build public support for early childhood education. *Young Children, 52,*(4), 4–9.

Newborg, J., Stock, J., Wnek, L., Guiduabaldi, J., & Sviniski, J. (1988). *Battelle Developmental Inventory Screening test.* Chicago: Riverside.

Newell, K. (1984). Physical constraints to motor development. In J. Thomas (Ed.), *Motor development during childhood and adolescence* (pp. 105–122). Minneapolis: Burgess.

Newport, E. (1990). Maturational constraints on language learning. *Cognitive Science, 14,* 11–28.

Newport, E., Gleitman, H., & Gleitman, L. (1977). Mother I'd rather do it myself: Some effects and non-effects of maternal speech style. In C.E. Snow & C. Ferguson (Eds.), *Talking to children* (pp. 109–149). London: Cambridge University Press.

NICHD Early Child Care Research Network. (1996, April). *Infant child care and attachment security: Results of the NICHD study of early child care.* Symposium, International Conference on Infant Studies, Providence, RI.

NICHD Early Child Care Research Network (1997, April). *Mother-child interaction and cognitive outcomes associated with early child care: Results of the NICHD study.* Poster symposium, Society for Research in Child Development, Washington, DC.

NICHD Early Child Care Research Network. (1999). Child care and mother-child interaction in the first three years of life. *Developmental Psychology, 35*(6), 1399–1413.

Nicoll, A., Newell, M., Van Praag, V., Van de Perre, P., & Peckham, C. (1994). Infant feeding policy and practice in the presence of HIV-1 infection. *Current Science, 9,* 107–119.

Niebyl, J. (1982). *Drug use in pregnancy.* Philadelphia: Lea & Febiger.

Nilsson, L., & Hamberger, L. (1990). *A child is born.* New York: Delacorte.

Novak, J., & Broom, B. (1999). *Ingall's and Salerno's maternal and child health nursing* (9th ed.). St. Louis, MO: Mosby.

Nowakowski, R. (1987) Basic concepts of CNS development. *Child Development, 58,* 568–595.

Oates, R. (1996). *The spectrum of child abuse: Assessment, treatment, and prevention.* New York: Bruner/ Mazel.

Obler, K. (1985). Language through the life-span. In J. Gleason (Ed.), *The development of language* (pp. 277–305). Columbus, OH: Merrill.

O'Brien, M. (1992). Gender identity and sex roles. In V. Van Hassselt & M. Hersen (Eds.), *Handbook of social development* (pp. 325–345). New York: Plenum.

O'Brien, M. (1997). *Inclusive child care for infants and toddlers: Meeting individual and special needs.* Baltimore: Brookes.

O'Connor, T.G., Bredenkamp, D., & Rutter, M. (1999). Attachment disturbances and disorders in children exposed to early severe deprivation. *Infant Mental Health Journal, 20*(1), 10–29.

Odom, S., & Munson, L. (1996). Assessing social performance. In M. McLean, D. Bailey, & M. Wolery (Eds.), *Assessing infants and preschoolers with special needs* (2nd ed., pp. 398–434). Columbus, OH: Merrill.

Oleske, J. (1994). The many needs of the HIV-infected child. *Hospital Practice, 29,* 81–87.

Oller, D., & Eilers, R. (1982). Similarity in Spanish and English learning babies. *Journal of Child Language, 9,* 565–577.

Oller, D., Eilers, R., Neal, R., & Schwartz, H. (1999). Precursors to speech in infancy: The prediction of speech and language disorders. *Journal of Communication Disorders, 32,* 223–245.

Oller, D., Willmar, L., Doyle, W., & Ross, C. (1976). Infant babbling and speech. *Journal of Child Language, 3,* 1–12.

Olney, R., & Scholnick, E. (1976). Adult judgements of age and linguistic differences in infant vocalizations. *Journal of Child Language, 3,* 145–156.

Olsen, J., Pereira, A., & Olsen, S. (1991). Does maternal smoking modify the effect of alcohol on fetal growth? *American Journal of Public Health, 81,* 69–73.

Olson, D., & DeFrain, J. (1994). *Marriage and the family: Diversity and strengths.* Mountain View, CA: Mayfield.

Olson, G., & Strauss, M. (1984). The development of infant memory. In M. Moscovitch (Ed.), *Advances in the study of communication and affect: Vol. 9. Infant memory* (pp. 29–48). New York: Plenum.

Olson, H. (1994). The effects of prenatal alcohol exposure on child development. *Infants and Young Children, 6,* 10–25.

Osofsky, J., & Connors, K. (1979). Mother-infant interaction: An integrative review. In J. Osofsky (Ed.), *Handbook of infant development* (pp. 519–548). New York: Wiley.

Osofsky, J., & Jackson, B. (1994). Parenting in violent environments. *Zero to Three, 14* (3), 8–12.

Otake, M., & Schull, W. (1984). In utero exposure to A-bomb radiation and mental retardation: A reassessment. *British Journal of Radiology, 57,* 409–414.

Overby, K. (1996). Pediatric health supervision. In A. Rudolph, J. Hoffman, & C. Rudolph (Eds.), *Rudolph's pediatrics* (20th ed., pp. 26–30). Stamford, CT: Appleton & Lange.

Oxorn, H. (1980). *Oxorn-Foote human labor and birth* (4th ed.). New York: Appleton-Century-Crofts.

Padilla, A., & Lindholm, K. (1976). Acquisition of bilingualism: A descriptive analysis of the linguistic structures of Spanish/English speaking children. In H. Keller (Ed.), *Bilingualism in the bicentennial and beyond* (pp. 97–142). New York: Bilingual Review Press.

Painter, G. (1971). *Teach your baby.* New York: Simon & Schuster.

Palmer, F., Capute, A., & Shapiro, B. (1988). Mandated interventions and clinical trials: A time of proof. *Developmental and Behavioral Pediatrics, 9,* 79–81.

Panneton, R., & DeCasper, A. (1982, March). *Newborns are sensitive to temporal and behavioral contingencies.* Paper presented at the meeting of the International Conference on Infant Studies, Austin, TX.

Panskepp, J. (1993). Neurochemical control of moods and emotions: Amino acids and neuropeptides. In M. Lewis & J. Haviland (Eds.), *Handbook of emotions* (pp. 87–107). New York: Guilford.

Panskepp, J. (2000). The neurodynamics of emotions: An evolutionary-neurodevelopmental view. In M.D. Lewis & I. Granic (Eds.), *Emotion, development, and self organization* (pp. 236–264). Cambridge, England: Cambridge University Press.

Pansky, B. (1982). *Review of medical embryology.* New York: Macmillan.

Papalia, D., Olds, S., & Feldman, R. (2002). *A child's world* (9th ed). Boston: McGraw-Hill.

Papousek, M., & Papousek, H. (1991). Early verbalizations as precursors of language development. In M. Lamb & H. Keller (Eds.), *Infant development: Perspectives from German speaking countries* (pp. 299–328). Hillsdale, NJ: Erlbaum.

Papousek, M., Papousek, H., & Harris, B. (1987). The emergence of play in parent-infant interactions. In D. Gorlitz & J. Wohlwill (Eds.), *Curiosity, imagination, and play* (pp. 215–246). Hillsdale, NJ: Erlbaum.

Parke, R. (1989). Social development in infancy: A 25-year perspective. In H. Reese (Ed.), *Advances in child development and behavior* (Vol. 21, pp. 1–35). New York: Academic.

Parke, R. (1995). Fathers and families. In M. Bornstein (Ed.), *Handbook of parenting* (Vol. 3, pp. 27–63). Mahwah, NJ: Erlbaum.

Parke, R. (1996). *Fatherhood.* Cambridge, MA: Harvard University.

Parke, R., & O'Leary, S. (1976). Family interaction in the newborn period. In K. Riegal & J. Meacham (Eds.), *The developing individual in a changing world. Vol. 2: Social and environmental issues* (pp. 49–62). The Hague, The Netherlands: Mouton.

Parke, R., & Sawin, D. (1977, March). *The family in early infancy: Social interactional and attitudinal analysis.* Paper presented at the Society for Research in Child Development, New Orleans.

Parke, R., & Tinsley, B. (1987). Family interaction in infancy. In J. Osofsky (Ed.), *Handbook of infant development* (2nd ed., pp. 579–641). New York: Wiley.

Parks, W. (1996). Human immunodeficiency virus. In W. Nelson, R. Behrman, R. Kliegman, & A. Arving (Eds.), *Nelson's textbook of pediatrics* (15th ed., pp. 916–919). Philadelphia: Saunders.

Parmelee, A., & Sigman, M. (1983). Perinatal brain development and behavior. In P. H. Mussen (Ed.), *Handbook of child development* (3rd ed., Vol. 2, pp. 95–157). New York: Wiley.

Patterson, C. (1995). Lesbian and gay parenthood. In M. Bornstein (Ed.), *Handbook of parenting* (Vol. 3, pp. 255–274). Mahwah, NJ: Erlbaum.

Pederson, F., Anderson, B., & Cain, R. (1980). Parent-infant and husband-wife interactions observed at age five months. In F. Pederson (Ed.), *The father-infant relationship* (pp. 71–86). New York: Praeger.

Peeples, D., & Teller, D. (1975). Color vision in two month old human infants. *Science, 189,* 1102–1103.

Peisner-Feinberg, E.S., & Burchinal, M.R. (1997). Relations between preschool children's child-care experiences and concurrent development: The cost, quality, and outcomes study. *Merrill Palmer Quarterly, 43,* 451–477.

Pelaez-Nogueras, M., Field, T., Gewirtz, J.L., Cigales, M., Gonzalez, A., Sanchez, A., & Richardson, S.C. (1997). The effects of systematic stroking versus tickling and poking on infant attention and affective behavior. *Journal of Applied Developmental Psychology, 18,* 169–178.

Pellegrino, L. (1997). Cerebral palsy. In M. Batshaw (Ed.), *Children with disabilities* (4th ed., pp. 499–528). Baltimore: Brookes.

Peperkamp, S., & Mehler, J. (1999). Signed and spoken language. *Language and Speech. 42,* 333–346.

Perris, E., & Clifton, R. (1988). Reaching in the dark toward sound as a measure of auditory localization in infants. *Infant Behavior and Development, 11,* 473–491.

Peterson, C. (1974). *A child grows up.* New York: Alfred.

Petitto, L., & Marentette, P. (1991). Babbling in the manual mode: Evidence from the ontogeny of language. *Science, 251,* 1493–1496.

Phillips, W., Baron-Cohen, S., & Rutter, M. (1992). The role of eye contact in goal detection: Evidence from normal infants and children with autism or mental handicap. *Development and Psychopathology, 4*(3), 375–383.

Piaget, J. (1929). *The child's conception of the world.* New York: Harcourt & Brace.

Piaget, J. (1952). *The origins of intelligence in children* (M. Cook, Trans.). New York: International Universities Press.

Piaget, J. (1954). *The construction of reality in the child.* New York: Basic Books.

Piaget, J. (1962). *Play, dreams and imitation in childhood.* New York: Norton.

Pickens, J. (1994). Perception of auditory-visual distance relations by 5-month-old infants. *Developmental Psychology, 30,* 537–544.

Pikler, E. (1968). Some contributions to the study of gross motor development of children. *Journal of Genetic Psychology, 113,* 27–39.

Piper, M., & Darrah, J. (1993). *Motor assessment in the developing infant.* Philadelphia: W. B. Saunders.

Pipes, P. (1982). Nutrition in infancy and childhood. *Primary Care, 9,* 497–516.

Pipes, P. (1997). Infant feeding and nutrition. In C. Trahms & P. Pipes (Eds.), *Nutrition in infancy and childhood* (6th ed., pp. 98–129). New York: WCB/McGraw-Hill

Pipp-Siegel, S., & Pressman, L. (1996). Developing a sense of self and others. *Zero to Three, 17*(1), 17–24.

Plomin, R., Chipuer, H., & Loehlin, J. (1990). Behavior genetics and personality. In L. Pervin (Ed.), *Handbook of personality theory and research* (pp. 222–243). New York: Guilford.

Plomin, R., & DeFries, J. (1980). Genetics and intelligence: Recent data. *Intelligence, 4,* 15–24.

Plomin, R., & DeFries, J. (1985). *Origins of individual differences in infancy: The Colorado Adoption Project.* New York: Academic Press.

Plomin, R., DeFries, J., & McClearn, G. (1990). *Behavioral genetics: A primer.* New York: Freeman.

Plomin, R., & Saudino, K. (1994). Quantitative genetics and molecular genetics. In J. Bates & T. Wachs (Eds.), *Temperament: Individual differences at the interface of biology and behavior* (pp. 143–171). Washington, DC: American Psychological Association.

Pollock, L. (1983). *Forgotten children: Parent-child relations from 1500 to 1900.* Cambridge, London: Cambridge University Press.

Powell, D. (1978). Correlates of parent-teacher communication frequency and diversity. *Journal of Educational Research, 71,* 331–341.

Press, B., & Greenspan, S. (1985a). Ned and Dan: The development of a toddler friendship. *Children Today, 14,* 24–29.

Press, B., & Greenspan, S. (1985b). The toddler group: A setting for adaptive social-emotional development of disadvantaged one- and two-year-olds in a peer group. *Zero to Three, 5*(4), 6–11.

Pressman, E., DiePietro, J., Costigan, K., Shupe, A., & Johnson, T. (1998). Fetal neurobehavioral development: Association with socioeconomic class and fetal sex. *Developmental Psychobiology, 33,* 79–91.

Preyer, W. (1888). *The mind of the child: Part 1. The senses and the will.* New York: Appleton-Century-Crofts.

Pritchard, J., MacDonald, P., & Gant, N. (1985). *Williams obstetrics* (17th ed.). Norwalk, CT: Appleton-Century-Crofts.

Provence, S. (1967). *Guide for the care of infants in groups.* New York: Child Welfare League of America.

Prudden, B. (1964). *How to keep your child fit from birth to six.* New York: Harper & Row.

Prudden, S., & Sussman, J. (1972). *Suzy Prudden's creative fitness for baby and child.* New York: Morrow.

Pruett, K. (1998). Attachment: Role of the father. In J. Warhol (Ed.), *New perspectives in emotional regulation* (pp. 71–91). Skillman, NJ: Johnson & Johnson.

Pulaski, M. (1978). *Your baby's mind and how it grows.* New York: Harper & Row.

Ramey, C., & Ramey, S. (1999). *Right from birth: Building your child's foundation for life.* New York: Goodard.

Ranly, D. (1980). *A synopsis of craniofacial growth.* New York: Appleton-Century-Crofts.

Rappoport, D. (1976). Pour une naissance sans violence: Resultats d'une premiere enquete. (For a birth without violence: Results of a first inquiry.) *Bulletin Psychologie, 29,* 552–560.

Rauh, H., Ziegenhain, U., Mueller, B., & Wijnroks, L. (2000). Stability and change in infant-mother attachment in the second year of life: Relations to parenting quality and varying degrees of day-care experience. In P.M. Crittenden & A.H. Claussen (Eds), *The organization of attachment relationships: Maturation, culture, and context* (pp. 251–276). New York: Cambridge University Press.

Rauscher, F., & Shaw, G. (1998). Key components of the Mozart Effect. *Perceptual and Motor Skills, 86,* 835–841.

Redshaw, M., Rivers, R., & Rosenblatt, B. (1985). *Born too early: Special care for your preterm infant.* Oxford, England: Oxford University Press.

Reimish, J. (1981). Prenatal exposure to synthetic progestins increases potential for aggression in humans. *Science, 211,* 1171–1173.

Reinisch, E., & Minear, R. (1978). *Health of the preschool child.* New York: Wiley.

Reissland, N. (1988). Neonatal imitation in the first hour of life: Observations in rural Napal. *Developmental Psychology, 24,* 464–469.

Rhodes, G., Sumich, A., & Byatt, G. (1999). Are average facial configurations attractive only because of their symmetry? *Psychological Science, 10,* 52–58.

Ridenour, M. (1978). Programs to optimize infant motor development. In M. Ridenour (Ed.), *Motor development: Issues and implications* (pp. 39–61). Princeton, NJ: Princeton Book Co.

Rimell, F., Thome, A., Stool, S., Reilly, J., Rider, G., & Wilson, C. (1995). Characteristics of objects that cause choking in children. *JAMA, 274,* 1763–1766.

Rivara, F., & Brownstein, D. (1996). In W. Nelson, R. Behrman, R. Kliegman, & A. Arving (Eds.), *Nelson's textbook of pediatrics* (15th ed., pp. 226–232). Philadelphia: Saunders.

Roberts, L. (1991). FISHing cuts the angst in amniocentesis. *Science, 254,* 378–379.

Roberts, T. (1994). *A systems perspective on parenting.* Pacific Grove, CA: Brooks/Cole.

Robinson, J., & Glaves, L. (1996). Supporting emotion regulation and emotional availability through home visitation. *Zero to Three, 17*(1), 31–35.

Rochat, P. (2001). *The infant's world.* Cambridge, MA: Harvard University Press.

Rochat, P., & Hespos, S. (1997). Differential rooting response by neonates: Evidence for an early sense of self. *Early Development and Parenting, 6*(3–4), 105–112.

Rochat, P., Querido, J.G., & Striano, T. (1999). Emerging sensitivity to the timing and structure of protoconversation in early infancy. *Developmental Psychology, 35*(4), 950–957.

Rock, A., Trainor, L., & Addison, T. (1999). Distinctive messages in infant-directed lullabies and play songs. *Developmental Psychology, 35*(2), 527–534.

Rogan, W., & Gladen, B. (1993). Breast-feeding and cognitive development. *Early Human Development, 31,* 181–193.

Rogoff, B. (1990). *Apprenticeship in thinking: Cognitive development in social context.* New York: Oxford University Press.

Rogoff, B., Mistry, J., Goncu, A., & Mosier, C. (1993). Guided participation in cultural activity by toddlers and caregivers. *Monographs of the Society for Research in Child Development, 58*(8, Serial No. 236).

Rogoff, B., & Morelli, G. (1989). Perspectives on children's development from cultural psychology. *American Psychologist, 44,* 343–348.

Roopnarine, J., & Field, T. (1983). Peer-directed behaviors of infants and toddlers during nursery school play. *Infant Behavior and Development, 6,* 133–138.

Roquer, J., Figueras, J., & Jimenez, R. (1995). Influence on fetal growth of exposure to tobacco smoke during pregnancy. *Acta Paediatrics, 84,* 118–121.

Rose, N., & Mennuti, M. (1995). Periconceptual folic acid supplementation as a social intervention. *Seminars in Perinatology, 19,* 243–254.

Rose, S. (1984). Preterm responses to passive, active, and social touch. In C. Brown (Ed.), *The many facets of touch* (pp. 91–106). Skillman, NJ: Johnson & Johnson.

Rose, S. (1994). From hand to eye: Findings and issues in infant cross-modal transfer. In D. Lewkowicz & R. Lickliter (Eds.), *The development of intersensory perception: Comparative perspectives* (pp. 265–284). Hillsdale, NJ: Erlbaum.

Rose, S., & Ruff, H. (1987). Cross modal abilities in human infants. In J. Osofsky (Ed.), *Handbook of infant development* (2nd ed., pp. 318–362). New York: Wiley.

Rosen, K., & Rothbaum, F. (1993). Quality of parental caregiving and security of attachment. *Developmental Psychology, 29,* 358–357.

Rosenblatt, K., & Thomas, D. (1993). Lactation and the risk of epithelial ovarian cancer. *International Journal of Epidemiology, 22,* 192–197.

Rosenblith, J., & Sims-Knight, J. (1985). *In the beginning: Development in the first two years of life.* Monterey, CA: Brooks/Cole.

Rosenstein, D., & Oster, H. (1990). Differential facial responses to four basic tastes in newborns. *Child Development, 59,* 1555–1568.

Rosenzweig, M., Bennett, E., & Diamond, M. (1972). Brain changes in response to experience. *Scientific American, 226,* 22–29.

Ross, H. (1974). Forms of exploratory behavior in young children. In B. Foss (Ed.), *New perspectives in child development* (pp. 138–163). Harmondsworth, England: Penguin.

Ross, H., & Lollis, S. (1987). Communication with infant social games. *Developmental Psychology, 23,* 241–248.

Rothbart, M. (1981). Measurement of temperament in infancy. *Child Development, 52,* 569–578.

Rothbart, M. (1982). The concept of difficult temperament. *Merrill-Palmer Quarterly, 28,* 35–39.

Rothbart, M., & Derryberry, D. (1981). Development of individual differences in temperament. In M. Lamb & A. Brown (Eds.), *Advances in developmental psychology* (Vol. 1, pp. 37–86). Hillsdale, N J: Erlbaum.

Rothbart, M.K., Derryberry, D., & Hershey, K. (2000). Stability of temperament in childhood: Laboratory infant assessment to parent report at seven years. In V.J. Molfese & D.L. Molfese (Eds.), *Temperament and personality development across the lifespan* (pp. 85–119). Mahwah, NJ: Erlbaum.

Rothman, K., Moore, P., Singer, M., Nguyen, U., Mannino, S., & Milunsky, A. (1995). Teratogenicity of high vitamin A intake. *New England Journal of Medicine, 333,* 1372–1373.

Roucoux, A., Culee, C., & Roucoux, M. (1983). Development of fixation and pursuit eye movements in human infants. *Behavioural Brain Research, 10,* 133–139.

Rovee-Collier, C. (1999). The development of infant memory. *Current Directions in Psychological Science, 8,* 80–85.

Rovee-Collier, C., & Shyi, C. (1992). A functional and cognitive analysis of infant long-term retention. In C. Howe, C. Brainerd, & V. Reyna (Eds.), *Development of long-term retention* (pp. 3–55). New York: Springer-Verlag.

Rugh, R., & Shettles, L. (1971). *From conception to birth.* New York: Harper & Row.

Ruopp, R., Travers, J., Glantz, F., & Coelen, C. (1979). *Children at the center: Final report of the national day care study* (Vol. 1). Cambridge, MA: ABT Associates.

Russell, C. (1974). Transition to parenthood: Problems and gratifications. *Journal of Marriage and the Family, 36,* 294–301.

Russell, M. (1976). Human olfactory communication. *Nature, 260,* 520–522.

Rust, O., & Morrison, J. (1993). Surveillance for onset of preterm labor and prophylactic therapy. In F. Witter & L. Keith (Eds.), *Textbook of prematurity* (pp. 47–64), Boston: Little, Brown.

Rutkowska, J. (1993). *The computational infant.* New York: Harvester/Wheatsheaf.

Rutstein, R., Conlon, C., & Batshaw, M. (1997). HIV and AIDS: From mother to child. In M. Batshaw., & Y. Perret (Eds.), *Children with handicaps: A medical primer* (4th. ed., pp. 163–181). Baltimore: Brookes.

Rutter, M. (1985). Family and school influences on cognitive development. *Journal of Child Psychology and Psychiatry, 26,* 683–704.

Rutter, M. (1987). Continuities and discontinuities from infancy. In J. Osofsky (Ed.), *Handbook of infant development* (2nd ed., pp. 1256–1296). New York: Wiley.

Ryan, A. (2000). *Ross Mothers Survey.* Dayton, OH: Ross Products Division, Abbott Laboratories.

Ryan, R.M., Kuhl, J., & Deci, E.L. (1997). Nature and autonomy: An organizational view of social and neurobiological aspects of self-regulation in behavior and development. *Development and Psychopathology, 9,* 701–728.

Sachs, J. (1993). The emergence of intentional communication. In J. Gleason (Ed.), *The development of language* (3rd ed., pp. 39–64). New York: Macmillan.

Sachs, J., & Devlin, J. (1976). Young children's use of age appropriate speech styles in social interaction and role playing. *Journal of Child Language, 3,* 81–98.

Sadler, T. (1990). *Langman's medical embryology* (6th ed.). Baltimore: Williams & Wilkins.

Sagi, A. (1981). Mothers' and non-mothers' identification of infant cries. *Infant Behavior and Development, 4,* 37–40.

Salisbury, G., & Hart, R. (1970). Gamete aging and its consequences. *Biology of Reproduction, 2* (Supplement), 1.

Sameroff, A. (1968). The components of sucking in the human newborn. *Journal of Experimental Psychology, 6,* 607–623.

Sameroff, A. (1993). Models of development and developmental risk. In C. Zeanah (Ed.), *Handbook of infant mental health* (pp. 3–13). New York: Guilford.

Sameroff, A., & Cavanagh, P. (1979). Learning in infancy: A developmental perspective. In J. Osofsky (Ed.), *Handbook of infant development* (pp. 344–392). New York: Wiley.

Sammons, W., & Lewis, J. (1985). *Premature babies: A different beginning.* St. Louis: Mosby.

Sanson, A., Oberklaid, F., Pedlow., R., & Prior, M. (1991). Risk indicators: Assessment of infancy predictors of preschool behavioral maladjustment. *Journal of Child Psychology and Psychiatry, 32,* 609–626.

Santos, J., Arrendo, J., & Vitale, J. (1983). Nutrition, infection and immunity. *Pediatric Annals, 12,* 182–194.

Santrock, J. (1970). Influence of onset and type of parental absence on the first Ericksonian crisis. *Developmental Psychology, 3,* 272–274.

Santrock, J. (1972). Relation of type and onset of father absence to cognitive development. *Child Development, 42,* 1721–1734.

Satter, E. (2000). *Child of mine: Feeding with love and good sense* (rev. ed.). Palo Alto, CA: Bull.

Satter, E. (1990). The feeding relationship: Problems and interventions. *Journal of Pediatrics, 117,* S181–189.

Saudino, K., & Eaton, W. (1991). Infant temperament and genetics: An objective twin study of motor activity level. *Child Development, 62,* 1167–1174.

Savitz, D., Schwingl, P., & Skeels, R. (1991). Influence of paternal age, smoking and alcohol consumption on congenital anomalies. *Teratology, 44,* 429–440.

Scarr, S., Eisenberg, M., & Deater-Deckerd, K. (1994). Measurement of quality in child care centers. *Early Childhood Research Quarterly, 9,* 131–151.

Scarr, S., & McCartney, K. (1983). How people make their own environments: A theory of genotype *A*E environment effects. *Child Development, 54,* 424–435.

Scarr, S., & Salapatek, P. (1970). Patterns of fear development during infancy. *Merrill-Palmer Quarterly, 16,* 53–90.

Scarr, S., & Weinberg, R. (1978, April). Attitudes, interests and IQ. *Human Nature, 1,* 29–36.

Scarr-Salapatek, S. (1983). An evolutionary perspective on infant intelligence: Species patterns and individual variation. In M. Lewis (Ed.), *Origins of intelligence* (2nd ed., pp. 191–223). New York: Plenum.

Schaffer, H. (1979). Acquiring the concept of dialogue. In M. Bornstein & W. Kessen (Eds.), *Psychological development from infancy* (pp. 279–306). Hillsdale, NJ: Erlbaum.

Schanler, R., & Hurst, N. (1994). Human milk for the hospitalized preterm infant. *Seminars in Perinatology, 18,* 476–484.

Scher, A., & Mayseless, O. (2000). Mothers of anxious/ambivalent infants: Maternal characteristics and child-care context. *Child Development, 71*(6), 1629–1639.

Scherz, R. (1981). Fatal motor vehicle accidents of child passengers from birth to four years of age in Washington state. *Pediatrics, 68,* 572–575.

Schiff, W., Benasich, A., & Bornstein, M. (1989). Infant sensitivity to audiovisually coherent events. *Psychological Research, 51,* 102–106.

Schiller, J. (1980). *Child care alternatives and emotional well being.* New York: Pregena.

Schmitt, B., & Berman, S. (1984). Ear, nose and throat. In H. Kempe, H. Silver, and D. O'Brien (Eds.), *Current pediatric diagnosis and treatment* (8th ed., pp. 297–328). Los Altos, CA: Lange.

Schmitt, B., & Roxann, H. (1994). Ambulatory pediatrics. In W. Hay, J. Groothuis, A. Hayward, & M. Levin. *Current pediatric diagnosis & treatment* (12th ed., pp. 283–315). Norwalk, CT: Appleton & Lange.

Schneck, M. (1986, April). And baby makes three. *Human Development Research at Penn State, 3,* 10–12.

Schneider, B., Atkinson, L., & Tardif, C. (2001). Child-parent attachment and children's peer relations: A quantitative review. *Developmental Psychology, 37,* 86–100.

Schneider, W., & Bjorklund, D. (1998). Memory. In W. Damon (Ed.-in-Chief), D. Kuhn & R. Siegler (Vol. Eds.), *Handbook of child psychology, Vol 2: Cognition, perception, and language* (pp. 467–522). New York: Wiley.

Schneider-Rosen, K., & Wenz-Goss, M. (1990). Patterns of compliance from eighteen to thirty months of age. *Child Development, 61,* 104–112.

Schore, A.N. (2000). The self-organization of the right brain and the neurobiology of emotional development. In M.D. Lewis & I. Granic (Eds.), *Emotion, development, and self-organization* (pp. 155–185). Cambridge, England: Cambridge University Press.

Schweinhart, L., Barnes, H., & Weikart, D. (1993). *Significant benefits: The High/Scope Perry preschool study through age 27. Monographs of the High/Scope Educational Research Foundation Number 10.* Ypsilanti, MI: High/Scope.

Scorgie, K., & Sobsey, D. (2000). Transformational outcomes associated with parenting children who have disabilities. *Mental Retardation, 38*(3), 195–206.

Scott, E., Jan, J., & Freeman, R. (1977). *Can't your child see?* Baltimore: University Park Press.

Scrutton, D. (1969). Footprint sequences of normal children under five years old. *Developmental Medicine and Child Neurology, 115,* 44–51.

Sears, C. J. (1994). Recognizing and coping with tactile defensiveness in young children. *Infants and Young Children: An Interdisciplinary Journal of Special Care Practices, 6,* 47–53.

Seefeldt, C. (1987). Praise—good or bad? *Dimensions, 15* (4), 18–20.

Senter, S. (1983). *Infant communication: Learning to understand your baby.* Irvine, CA: National Pediatric Support Services.

Shafer, V.J., Shucard, D.W., & Jaeger, J.J. (1999). Electrophysiological indices of cerebral specialization and the role of prosody in language acquisition. *Developmental Neuropsychology, 15,* 73–109.

Shaw, D.S., Winslow, E.B., & Flanagan, C. (1999). A prospective study of the effects of marital status and family relations on young children's adjustment among African American and European American families. *Child Development, 70*(3), 742–755.

Shelov, S. (1998). *The American Academy of Pediatrics: Caring for your baby and young child* (rev. ed.). New York: Bantam.

Shepherd, T. (1991). *Catalog of teratogenic agents* (7th ed.). Baltimore: Johns Hopkins.

Shepherd-Look, D. (1982). Sex differentiation and the development of sex roles. In B. Wolman (Ed.), *Handbook of developmental psychology* (pp. 403–433). Englewood Cliffs, NJ: Prentice Hall.

Sherrod, K., Vietze, P., & Friedman, C. (1978). *Infancy.* Monterey, CA: Brooks/Cole.

Shields, M., & Sparling, J. (1993). Fathers' play and touch behaviors with their three-month-old infants. *Physical & Occupational Therapy in Pediatrics, 13,* 39–59.

Shirley, M. (1931). *The first two years: A study of twenty-five babies: Vol. 1. Postural and locomotor development.* Minneapolis: University of Minnesota Press.

Shoemaker, W., & Tower, W. (1970). Out of the oven and into the winner's circle. *Sports Illustrated, 32,* 20–25.

Siegler, R. (1993). *Children's thinking* (2nd ed.). Englewood Cliffs, NJ: Prentice-Hall.

Siegler, R. (1998). *Children's thinking* (3rd ed.). Upper Saddler River, NJ: Prentice-Hall.

Silberg, J. (1993). *Games to play with babies* (rev ed.). Beltsville, MD: Gryphon.

Silver, H. (1984). Growth and development. In C. Kempe, H. Silver, & D. O'Brien (Eds.), *Current pediatric diagnosis and treatment.* (8th ed., pp. 9–25). Los Altos, CA: Lange.

Sinclair, D. (1978). *Human growth after birth* (3rd ed.). New York: Oxford University Press.

Sinclair, H. (1994). Early cognitive development and the contribution of peer integration: A Piagetian view. In S. Friedman & H. Haywood (Eds.), *Developmental follow-up* (pp. 129–138). San Diego: Academic.

Singer, D. (1995). Human embryogenesis. In D. Coustan, R. Haning, & D. Singer (Eds.), *Human reproduction: Growth and development* (pp. 27–98). Boston: Little, Brown.

Siqueland, E. (1968). Reinforcement and extinction in human newborns. *Journal of Experimental Child Psychology, 6,* 431–442.

Skinner, B. (1957). *Verbal behavior.* New York: Appleton-Century-Crofts.

Skinner, B. (1961). *Cumulative record.* New York: Appleton-Century.

Skinner, B. (1972). *The shaping of a behaviorist.* New York: Knopf.

Slater, A. (2000). Visual perception in the young infant: Early organization and rapid learning. In D. Muir & A. Slater (Eds.), *Infant development: The essential readings* (pp. 95–116). Oxford, England: Blackwell.

Slater, A., Mattock, A., & Brown, E. (1990). Size constancy at birth: Newborn infants' responses to retinal and real size. *Journal of Experimental Child Psychology, 49,* 314–322.

Slater, A., & Morison, V. (1985). Shape constancy and slant perception at birth. *Perception, 14,* 337–344.

Slater, A., von der Schulenberg, C., Brown, E., Badenoch, M., Butterworth, G., Parsons, S., & Samuels, C. (1998). Newborn infants prefer attractive faces. *Infant Behavior and Development, 21,* 345–354.

Slocum, D., & James, S. (1968). Biomechanics of running. *Journal of the American Medical Association, 97,* 205.

Smedler, A., Faxelius, G., Bremme, K., & Lagerstrom, M. (1992). Psychological development in children born with very low birth weight after severe intrauterine growth retardation: A 10-year follow-up study. *Acta Paediatrics, 81,* 197–203.

Smelser, N., & Smelser, W. (1963). *Personality and social systems.* New York: Wiley.

Smetana, J.G., Kochanska, G., & Chuang, S. (2000). Mothers' conceptions of everyday rules for young toddlers: A longitudinal investigation. *Merrill Palmer Quarterly, 46*(3), 391–416.

Smith, L. (1996, July 26). 'Attachment disorder' hot diagnosis of troubled kids. *The Raleigh News and Observer,* p. D4.

Smith, M. (1926). An investigation of the development of the sentence and the extent of the vocabulary in young children. *University of Iowa Studies in Child Welfare, 3,* No. 5.

Smith, N. (1973). *The acquisition of phonology: A case study.* Cambridge, England: Cambridge University Press.

Smith, P. (1989). Assessing motor skills. In D. Bailey & M. Wolery (Eds.), *Assessing infants and preschoolers with handicaps* (pp. 301–338). Columbus, OH: Merrill.

Smith, R. (1999). The timing of birth. *Scientific Americam, 280,* 68–75.

Smoll, F. (1982). Developmental kinesiology. In J. Kelso & J. Clark (Eds.), *The development of movement control and co-ordination.* New York: Wiley.

Smotherman, W.P. (1982). In utero chemosensory experience alters taste preferences and corticosterone responsiveness. *Behavioral and Neural Biology, 36,* 61–68.

Snow, C. E. (1977). The development of conversation between mothers and babies. *Journal of Child Language, 4,* 1–22.

Snow, C.W. (1983, November). *As the twig is bent: A review of research on the consequences of day care with implications for caregiving.* Paper presented at the annual meeting of the National Association for the Education of Young Children, Atlanta, GA. (Eric Document Reproduction Service No. Ed 238–590).

Snow, C.W., Teleki, J., Cline, D., & Dunn, K. (1992). Is day care safe? A review of research on accidental injuries. *Day Care and Early Education, 19*(3), 28–31.

Snow, C.W., Teleki, J., & Reguero de-Atiles, J. (1996). Child care licensing standards in the United States: 1981 to 1995. *Young Children, 51(6),* 36–41.

Snyder, L., Bates, E., & Bretherton, I. (1981). Content and context in early lexical development. *Journal of Child Language, 8,* 565–582.

Soken, N., & Pick, A. (1992). Intermodal perception of happy and angry expressive behaviors by seven-month-old infants. *Child Development, 63,* 787–795.

Soutullo, D., Hernandez, M., & Bahrick, L. (1992, May). *Infants bimodal perception of adult and child faces and voices.* Presented at the International Conference on Infant Studies, Miami Beach, FL.

Sparling, J., & Lewis, I. (1979). *Learning games for the first three years.* New York: Berkley Books.

Sparrow, S., Balla, D., & Cicchetti, D. (1984). *Interview edition, expanded form manual, Vineland adaptive behavior scales.* Circle Pines, MN: American Guidance Service.

Spelke, E. (1979). Perceiving bimodally specified events in infancy. *Developmental Psychology, 15,* 626–636.

Spelke, E., & Hermer, L. (1996). Early cognitive development: Objects and space. In R. Gelman & T. Au (Eds.), *Perceptual and cognitive development* (pp. 71–114). San Diego, CA: Academic.

Spelt, D. (1948). The conditioning of the human fetus in utero. *Journal of Experimental Psychology, 38,* 375–376.

Sperry, L., & Sperry, D. (1995). Young children's presentations of self in conversational narration. *New Directions for Child Development, 69*(Fall), 47–60.

Spitz, R. (1945). Hospitalism. *Psychoanalytic Study of the Child, 1,* 45–74.

Spitz, R., Emde, R., & Metcalf, D. (1970). Further prototypes of ego formation: A working paper from a research project on early development. *The Psychoanalytic Study of the Child, 25,* 417–441.

Spock, B., & Rothenberg, M. (1992). *Dr. Spock's baby and child care* (6th ed.). New York: Pocket.

Spreen, O., Risser, A., & Edgell, D. (1995). *Developmental neurology.* New York: Oxford University Press.

Sroufe, L. (1977). *Knowing and enjoying your baby.* Englewood Cliffs, NJ: Prentice Hall.

Sroufe, L. (1979). Socioemotional development. In J. Osofsky (Ed.), *Handbook of infant development* (pp. 462–516). New York: Wiley.

Sroufe, L. (1996). *Emotional development.* New York: Cambridge University Press.

Sroufe, L., & Waters, E. (1976). The ontogenesis of smiling and laughing: A perspective on the organization of development in infancy. *Psychological Review, 83,* 173–189.

Sroufe, L., & Wunsch, J. (1972). The development of laughter in the first year of life. *Child Development, 43,* 1326–1344.

Stafford, L., & Dainton, M. (1995). Parent-child communication within the family system. In T. Socha & G. Stamp (Eds.), *Parents, children, and communication* (pp. 3–21). Mahwah, NJ: Erlbaum.

Stangler, S., Huber, C., & Routh, D. (1980). *Screening growth and development of preschool children.* New York: McGraw-Hill.

Stansbury, K., & Gunnar, M. (1994). Adrenocortical activity and emotion regulation. In N. Fox (Ed.), The development of emotion regulation: Biological and behavioral considerations. *Monographs of the Society for Research in Child Development* (pp. 108–134), *59* (Serial No. 240).

Stark, R. (1978). Features of infant sounds: The emergence of cooing. *Journal of Child Language, 5,* 379–390.

Stark, R. (1979). Prespeech segmental feature development. In P. Fletcher & M. Garman (Eds.), *Language acquisition* (pp. 15–32). Cambridge, England: Cambridge University Press.

Starr, R. (1979). Child abuse. *American Psychologist, 34,* 872–878.

Stechler, G., & Halton, A. (1982). Prenatal influences on human development. In B. Wolman (Ed.), *Handbook of developmental psychology* (pp. 175–189). Englewood Cliffs, NJ: Prentice Hall.

Steele, K., Bass, K., & Crook, M. (1999). The mystery of the Mozart Effect: Failure to replicate. *Psychological Science, 10,* 366–369.

Stein, Z., Susser, M., Saenger, G., & Morolla, F. (1974). *Famine and human development: The Dutch hunger winter of 1944–1945.* New York: Oxford University Press.

Steiner, J. (1977). Facial expressions of the neonate indicating the hedonics of food related chemical stimuli. In J. Weiffenbach, (Ed.), *Taste and development: The genesis of sweet preference* (pp. 173–204). Bethesda, MD: National Institute of Health. (DHEW Pub. No. NIH 77–1068).

Steinmetz, J. (1994). Brain substrates of motion and temperament. In J. Bates & T. Wachs (Eds.), *Temperament: Individual differences at the interface of biology and behavior* (pp. 17–45). Washington, DC: American Psychological Association.

Stenberg, C., & Campos, J. (1990). The development of anger expressions in infancy. In N. Stein, B. Leventhal, & T. Trabasco (Eds.), *Psychological and biological approaches to emotion* (pp. 247–282). Hillsdale, NJ: Erlbaum.

Stene, J., Fischer, G., Stene, E., Mikkelesen, M., & Petersen, E. (1977). Paternal age effect in Down's syndrome. *American Human Genetics, 40,* 299–306.

Stern, D. (1985). *The interpersonal world of the infant.* New York: Basic Books.

Steuer, F. (1994). *The psychological development of children.* Pacific Grove, CA: Brooks/Cole.

Stewart, J., Manchester, D., & Sujansky, E. (1995). Genetics and dysmorphology. In W. Hay, J. Groothuis, A. Hayward, & M. Levin (Eds.), *Current pediatric diagnosis and treatment* (12th ed., pp. 947–987). Norwalk, CT: Lange.

Stifter, C., Coulehan, C., & Fish, M. (1993). Linking employment to attachment: The mediating effects of maternal separation anxiety and interactive behavior. *Child Development, 64,* 1451–1460.

Stifter, C., Spinrad, T., & Braungart-Ricker, J. (1999). Toward a developmental model of child compliance: The role of emotion regulation in infancy. *Child Development, 70,* 21–32.

Stipek, D., Gralinski, J., & Kopp, C. (1990). Self-concept development in the toddler years. *Developmental Psychology, 26,* 972–977.

Strangert, K. (1976). Respiratory illness in preschool children with different forms of day care. *Pediatrics, 57,* 219–229.

Streeter, L.A. (1976). Language perception of two-month old infants shows effects of both innate mechanisms and experience. *Nature, 259,* 39–41.

Strelau, J. (1994). The concepts of arousal and arousability as used in temperament studies. In J. Bates & T. Wachs (Eds.), *Temperament: Individual differences at the interface of biology and behavior* (pp. 117–141). Washington, DC: American Psychological Association.

Streri, A., & Spelke, E. (1988). Haptic perception of objects in infancy. *Cognitive Psychology, 20,* 1–23.

Streri, A., & Spelke, E. (1989). Effects of motion and figural goodness on haptic object perception in infancy. *Child Development, 60,* 1111–1125.

Suomi, S. (1982). Biological foundations and developmental psychobiology. In C. Kopp & J. Krakow (Eds.), *The child: Development in a social context* (pp. 42–91). Reading, MA: Addison.

Super, C. (1981). Behavioral development in infancy. In R. H. Munroe, R. L. Munroe, & B. Whiting (Eds.), *Handbook of cross-cultural human development* (pp. 181–270). New York: Garland.

Super, C., & Harkness, S. (1982). The development of affect in infancy and early childhood. In D. Wagner & H. Stevenson (Eds.), *Cultural perspectives in child development* (pp. 1–19). San Francisco: Freeman.

Svejda, M., Campos, J., & Emde, R. (1980). Mother-infant "bonding": Failure to generalize. *Child Development, 51,* 775–779.

Svedjda, M., Pannabecker, B, & Emde, R. (1982). Parent-to-infant attachment: A critique of the "early bonding model." In R. Emde & R. Harmon (Eds.), *The development of attachment and cognitive systems* (pp. 83–93). New York: Plenum.

Swain, I., Zelazo, P., & Clifton, R. (1993). Newborn infants' memory for speech sounds retained over 24 hours. *Developmental Psychology, 29,* 312–323.

Taber-Flusberg, H. (1994). Language development. In M. Rutter and D. Hay (Eds.), *Development through life: A handbook for clinicians* (pp. 212–238). London: Blackwell.

Taddio, A., Katz, J., Ilersich, A.L., & Koren, G. (1997). Effect of neonatal circumcision on pain response during subsequent routine vaccination. *Lancet, 349,* 599–603.

Taeuber, C. (1996). *Statistical handbook on women in America* (2nd ed.). Phoenix, AZ: Oryx.

Tanner, J. (1990). *Fetus into man.* Cambridge, MA: Harvard University.

Tantam, D. (1992). Characterizing the fundamental social handicap in autism. *Acta Paedopsychiatrica: International Journal of Child and Adolescent Psychiatry, 55*(2), 83–91.

Tatzer, E., Schubert, M., Timisch, W., & Simbruner, G. (1985). Discrimination of taste preference for sweet in premature babies. *Early Human Development, 12,* 23–30.

Taubman, B. (1984). Clinical trial of the treatment of colic by modification of parent-infant interaction. *Pediatrics, 74,* 998–1003.

Teller, D., & Lindsey, D. (1993). Motion nulling techniques and infant color vision. In C. Granrud (Ed.), *Visual perception and cognition in infancy* (pp. 47–73). Hillsdale, NJ: Erlbaum.

Teplin, S. (1995). Visual impairment in infants and young children. *Infants and Young Children, 8,* 18–51.

Tesh, J., & Glover, T. (1969). Aging of rabbit spermatozoa in the male and its effect on fertility. *Journal of Reproductive Fertility, 20,* 573.

Thelen, E. (1981). Rythmical behavior in infancy: An ethological perspective. *Developmental Psychology, 17,* 237–257.

Thelen, E. (1995). Motor development: A new synthesis. *American Psychologist, 50,* 79–95.

Thelen, E. (2000). Motor development as a foundation and future source of developmental psychology. *International Journal of Behavioral Development, 24,* 385–397.

Thelen, E., Fisher, D., & Ridley-Johnson, R. (1984). The relationship between physical growth and a newborn reflex. *Infant Behavior and Development, 7,* 479–493.

Thelen, E., & Fogel, A. (1989). Toward an action-based theory of infant development. In J. Lockman & N. Hazen (Eds.), *Action in social context: Perspectives on early development* (pp. 23–64). New York: Plenum.

Thelen, E., & Smith, L. (1998). Dynamic system theories. In R. M. Lerner (Ed.) & W. Damon (Ed.-in-Chief), *Handbook of child psychology: Vol. 1. Theoretical models of human development* (5th ed., pp. 563–634). New York: Wiley.

Thelen, E., & Spencer, J. (1998). Postural control during reaching in young infants: A dynamic systems approach. *Neuroscience and Biobehavioral Reviews, 22,* 507–514.

Thelen, E., Ulrich, B., & Jensen, J. (1989). The developmental origins of locomotion. In M. Woollacott & A. Shumway-Cook (Eds.), *The development of posture and gait across the lifespan* (pp. 25–47). Columbia: University of South Carolina Press.

Thoman, E. (1993). Obligation and option in the premature nursery. *Developmental Review, 13,* 1–30.

Thomas, A., & Chess, S. (1977). *Temperament and development.* New York: Brunner/Mazel.

Thomas, A., & Chess, S. (1985). The behavioral study of temperament. In J. Strelau, F. Farley, & A. Gale (Eds.), *The biological bases of personality and behavior: Vol. 1. Theories, measurement, techniques and development* (pp. 213–225). Washington, DC: Hemisphere.

Thomas, R. (1996). *Comparing theories of child development* (4th ed.). Pacific Grove, CA: Brooks/Cole.

Thompson, M., McInnes, R., & Willard, H. (1991). *Thompson & Thompson: Genetics in Medicine* (5th ed.). Philadelphia: Saunders.

Thompson, R. (1994). Emotion regulation: A theme in search of definition. In N. Fox (Ed.), The development of emotion regulation: Biological and behavioral considerations. *Monographs of the Society for Research in Child Development* (pp. 25–52), *59* (Serial No. 240).

Thompson, R. (1999b). Personality and social development. In L. Balter & C. Tamis-LeMonda (Eds.), *Child psychology: A handbook of contemporary issues* (pp. 375–409). Philadelphia: Psychology Press.

Thompson, R. (1999a). Early attachment and later behavior. In J. Cassidy & P. Shaver (Eds.), *Handbook of attachment* (pp. 265–286). New York: Guilford.

Thompson, R., & Lamb, M. (1984). Infants, mothers, families and strangers. In M. Lewis (Ed.), *Beyond the dyad* (pp. 195–221). New York: Plenum.

Tiedemann, D. (1787/1972). Observations on the mental development of a child. In W. Dennis (Ed.), *Historical readings in developmental psychology* (pp. 11–31). New York: Appleton-Century-Crofts.

Tizard, I. (1995). *Immunology: An introduction* (4th ed.). Philadelphia: Saunders.

Toda, S., & Fogel, A. (1993). Infant response to the still-face situation at 3 and 6 months. *Developmental Psychology, 29,* 532–538.

Tomasello, M. (1995). Joint attention as social cognition. In C. Moore & P. Dunham (Eds.), *Joint attention: Its origins and role in development* (pp. 103–130). Hillsdale, NJ: Erlbaum.

Townsend, T. (1993). Hepatitis A; Hepatitis B. In L. Donowitz (Ed.), *Infection control in the child care center and preschool* (2nd ed., pp. 151–156). Baltimore: Williams & Wilkins.

Trahams, C., & Pipes, P. (1997). Nutrient needs of infants and children. In C. Trahms & P. Pipes (Eds.), *Nutrition in infancy and childhood* (6th ed., pp. 35–67). New York: WCB/McGraw-Hill.

Treem, W. (1994). Infant colic: A pediatric gastroenterologist's perspective. *Pediatric Clinics of North America, 41,* 1121–1138.

Trehub, S., Trainor, L., & Unyk, A. (1993). Music and speech processing in the first year of life. In H. Reese (Ed.), *Advances in child development and behavior* (Vol. 24, pp. 1–35). San Diego, CA: Academic.

Tremblay, R. (2001). The development of physical aggression during childhood and the prediction of later dangerousness. In G. Pinard & L. Pagani (Eds.), *Clinical assessment of dangerousness: Empirical contributions* (pp. 47–65). New York: Cambridge University Press.

Trevarthen, C. (1978). The psychobiology of speech development. *Neurosciences Research Program Bulletin, 12* (4), 570–585.

Trevarthen, C. (1988). Universal co-operative motives: How infants begin to know the language and culture of their parents. In G. Jahoda & I.M. Lewis (Eds.), *Acquiring culture: Cross cultural studies in child development.* London: Helm.

Trohanis, P., Cox, J., & Meyer, R. (1982). A report on selected demonstration programs for infant intervention. In C. Ramey & P. Trohanis (Eds.), *Finding and educating high-risk and handicapped infants* (pp. 137–191). Baltimore: University Park Press.

Tronick, E. (1989). Emotions and emotional communication. *American Psychologist, 44,* 112–118.

Trotter, R. (1987). You've come a long way, baby. *Psychology Today, 21*(5), 34–45.

Troyer, L., & Parisi, V. (1993). Management of Labor in T. Moore, R. Reiter, R. Rebar, & V. Baker (Eds.), *Gynecology and obstetrics: A longitudinal approach* (pp. 575–590). New York: Churchill Livingstone.

Trump, C., & Karasic, R. (1983). Management of communicable diseases in day care centers. *Pediatric Annals, 12,* 219–229.

Turner, G., & Collins, E. (1975). Fetal effects of regular salicylate ingestion in pregnancy. *Lancet, 2,* 338–339.

Tweedie, J. (1987). *Children's hearing problems: Their significance, detection, and management.* Bristol, England: Wright.

Ungerer, J., Brody, L., & Zelazo, P. (1978). Long-term memory for speech in 2-4-week-old infants. *Infant Behavior and Development, 1,* 177–186.

United Nations Children's Fund (1996). *The progress of nations 1996.* New York: UNICEF.

U.S. Census Bureau. (2000). *Statistical Abstract of the United States* (120th ed.). Washington, DC: U.S. Government Printing Office.

U.S. Census Bureau. (2001, October 18). Press release: Labor force participation for mothers with infants declines for first time. Retrieved from http://www.census.gov/Press-Release/www/2001/cb01–170.html

U.S. Department of Health and Human Services. (2001). *Child maltreatment 1999: Reports from the states to the national child abuse and neglect data system.* Washington, DC: U.S. Government Printing Office.

U.S. Department of Health, Education, and Welfare (1972). *Tips for tots.* DHEW Publication No. (FDA) 73–7012. Washington, DC: U.S. Government Printing Office.

U.S. Department of Labor. Work and Family Team. (2000, April). Work-related child care statistics. Retrieved from http://www.dol.gov/dol/wb/childcare/ccstats.htm

Uzgiris, I. (1967). Ordinality in the development of schemes for relating to objects. In J. Hellmuth (Ed.), *Exceptional infant: Vol. 1. The normal infant* (pp. 315–334). New York: Bruner/Mazel.

Uzgiris, I., & Hunt, I. (1975). *Assessment in infancy.* Urbana, IL: University of Illinois Press.

Uzgiris, I., & Raeff, C. (1995). Play in parent-child interactions. In M. Bornstein (Ed.), *Handbook of parenting* (Vol. 4, pp. 353–376). Mahwah, NJ: Erlbaum.

Valadian, I., & Porter, D. (1977). *Physical growth and development.* Boston: Little, Brown.

Vance, M. L., & Mauras, N. (1999). Growth hormone therapy in adults and children. *New England Journal of Medicine, 341,* 1206–1216.

Vandell, D., & Mueller, E. (1980). Peer play and friendships during the first two years. In H. Foot, A. Chapman, & J. Smith (Eds.), *Friendship and social relations in children* (pp. 181–208). New York: Wiley.

Vandell, D., & Ramanan, J. (1992). Effects of early and recent maternal employment on children from low-income families. *Child Development, 63,* 938–949.

Vandell, D., & Wilson, K. (1987). Infants' interactions with mother, sibling, and peer contacts: Contrasts and relations between interaction systems. *Child Development, 58,* 176–186.

Vandell, D., Wilson, K., & Buchanan, N. (1980). Peer interaction in the first year of life: An examination of its structure, content and sensitivity to toys. *Child Development, 51,* 481–488.

Vander Vliet, W., & Hafez, E. (1974). Surviving and aging of spermatozoa: A review. *American Journal of Obstetrics and Gynecology, 118,* 1006.

Van-Egeren, L., Barratt, M., & Roach, M. (2001). Mother-infant responsiveness: Timing, mutual regulation, and interactional context. *Developmental Psychology, 37*(5), 684–697.

Van Ijzendoorn, M., & Kroonenberg, P. (1988). Cross-cultural patterns of attachment: A meta-analysis of the Strange Situation. *Child Development, 59,* 147–156.

Varendi, H., Porter, R.H., & Winberg, J. (1997). Natural odour preferences of newborn infants change over time. *Acta Paediatrica, 86,* 985–990.

Vedam, S., & Kolodji, Y. (1995). Guidelines for client selection in the home birth midwifery practice. *Journal of Nurse-Midwifery, 40,* 508–521.

Ventura, S., Martin, J., Curtin, S., Menacker, F., & Hamilton, B. (2001). Births: Final data for 1999. *National Vital Statistics for 1999. 49*(1), 1–15.

Verba, M. (1994). The beginnings of collaboration in peer interaction. *Human Development, 37,* 125–139.

Vintner, A. (1985). *L'imitation chez le nouveau-ne.* Neuchatel and Paris Delachaux et Niestle.

Von Hofsten, C. (1982). Eye-hand coordination in the newborn. *Developmental Psychology, 18,* 450–461.

Von Hofsten, C. (1984). Developmental changes in the organization of prereaching movements. *Developmental Psychology, 20,* 378–388.

Von Hofsten, C. (1992). Studying the development of goal-directed behavior. In A. Kalverboer, B. Hopkins, & R. Geuze (Eds.), *Motor development in early and later childhood: Longitudinal approaches* (pp. 89–108). Cambridge, England: Cambridge University.

Von Hofsten, C., & Rosander, K. (1996). The development of gaze control and predictive tracking in young infants. *Vision Research, 36,* 81–96.

Von Hofsten, C., & Rosander, K. (1997). Development of smooth pursuit tracking in young infants. *Vision Research, 37,* 1799–1810.

Von Hofsten, C., & Rosander, K. (1998). The establishment of gaze control in early infancy. In F. Simion & G. Butterworth (Eds.), *The development of sensory, motor and cognitive capacities in early infancy: From perception to cognition* (pp. 49–66). East Sussex, England: Psychology Press.

Vorhees, C., & Mollnow, E. (1987). Behavioral teratogenesis: Long term influences on behavior from early exposure to environmental agents. In J. Osofosky (Ed.), *Handbook of infant development* (pp. 913–971). New York: Wiley.

Vulliamy, D. (1982). *The newborn child* (5th ed.). London: Churchill Livingstone.

Vygotsky, L. (1962). *Thought and language.* Cambridge, MA: MIT Press.

Vygotsky, L. (1978). *Mind in society: The development of higher mental processes.* Cambridge, MA: Harvard University Press.

Wachs, T. (1999). The what, why, and how of temperament. In L. Balter & C. Tamis-LeMonda (Eds.), *Child psychology: A handbook of contemporary issues* (pp. 23–44). Philadelphia: Psychology Press.

Wachs, T., & Gruen, G. (1982). *Early experiences and human development.* New York: Plenum.

Wakefield, A. (1998). Ileal-lymphoid-nodular hyperplasia, non-specific colitis, and pervasive developmental disorder in children. *Lancet, 351,* 637–649.

Walco, G., Cassidy, R., Schechter, N. (1994). Pain, hurt, and harm: The ethics of pain control in infants and children. *New England Journal of Medicine, 331,* 541–544.

Walco, G., & Harkins, S. (1999). Lifespan developmental approaches to pain. In R.G. Gatchel & D.C. Turk, (Eds.), *Psychosocial factors in pain* (pp. 107–117), New York:Guilford.

Walden, T., & Garber, J. (1994). Emotional development. In M. Rutter & D. Hay (Eds.), *Development through the lifespan: A handbook for clinicians* (pp. 403–455). Oxford, England: Blackwell.

Walk, R., & Gibson, E. (1961). A comparative and analytical study of visual depth perception. *Psychological Monographs,* 75 (Whole No. 519).

Walker-Andrews, A. (1994). Taxonomy for intermodal relations. In D. Lewkowicz & R. Lickliter (Eds.), *The development of intersensory perception: Comparative perspectives* (pp. 39–56). Hillsdale, NJ: Erlbaum.

Wallerstein, J., & Kelly, J. (1980). *Surviving the break-up: How children and parents cope with divorce.* New York: Basic Books.

Ward, C.D., & Cooper, R.P. (1999). A lack of evidence in 4-month-old human infants for paternal voice preference. *Developmental Psychobiology, 35,* 49–59.

Ward, M., Lee, S., & Lipper, E. (2000). Failure-to-thrive is associated with disorganized infant-mother attachment and unresolved maternal attachment. *Infant Mental Health Journal, 21*(6), 428–442.

Wasserman, G., & Stern, D. (1978). An early manifestation of differential behavior toward children of the same and opposite sex. *Journal of Genetic Psychology, 133,* 129–137.

Wasz-Hocket, O., Lind, J., Vucrenkoski, V., Partenen, T., & Valanne, E. (1968). The infant cry: A spectrographic and auditory analysis. *Clinics in Developmental Medicine, 29.* London: Heinemann.

Waters, E., Hamilton, C., & Weinfield, N. (2000). The stability of attachment security from infancy to adolescence and early adulthood: General introduction. *Child Development, 71,* 678–683.

Waters, E., & Sroufe, L. (1983). Social competence as a developmental construct. *Developmental Review, 3,* 79–97.

Watson, J. (1924). *Behaviorism.* New York: Norton

Watson, R., & Stone, B. (1997, Spring/Summer). You've come a long way baby. *Newsweek: Special Edition,* 41–44.

Wechsler, D. (1944). *The measurement of adult intelligence* (3rd ed). Baltimore: Williams & Wilkins.

Weinberg, M., Tronick, E., Colin, J., & Olson, K. (1999). Gender differences in emotional expressivity and self-regulation during early infancy. *Developmental Psychology, 35,* 175–188.

Weiner, I., & Elkind, D. (1972). *Child development: A core approach.* New York: Wiley.

Weinraub, M., Clements, L., Sockloff, A., Ethridge, T., Gracely, E., & Meyers, B. (1984). The development of sex role stereotypes in the third year: Relationships to gender identity, sex typed toy preferences. *Child Development, 55,* 1493–1503.

Weinraub, M., Jaeger, E., & Hoffman, L. (1990). Predicting infant outcome in families of employed and nonemployed mothers. In N. Fox & G. Fein (Eds.), *Infant day care: The current debate* (pp. 127–144). Norwood, NJ: Ablex.

Weir, R. (1966). Some questions on the child's learning of phonology. In F. Smith & G. Miller (Eds.), *The genesis of language* (pp. 153–169). Cambridge, MA: MIT.

Weiser, M. (1982). *Group care and education of infants and toddlers.* St. Louis, MO: Mosby.

Weiss, S., Wilson, P., Hertenstein, M., & Campos, R. (2000). The tactile context of a mother's caregiving: Implications for attachment of low birth weight infants. *Infant Behavior and Development, 23*(1), 91–111.

Weissbluth, M., & Green, O. (1984). Plasma progesterone concentrations and infant temperament. *Developmental and Behavioral Pediatrics, 5,* 251–253.

Wekselman, K., Spiering, K., Hetteberg, C., Kenner, C., & Flandermeyer, A. (1995). Fetal alcohol syndrome from infancy through childhood: A review of the literature. *Journal of Pediatric Nursing, 10,* 296–303.

Wellman, B. (1937). Motor achievements of preschool children. *Childhood Education, 13,* 311–316.

Wellman, H. (1994). Early understanding of mind: The normal case. In S. Baron-Cohen, H. Tager-Flusberg, & D. Cohen (Eds.), *Understanding other minds* (pp. 10–39). New York: Oxford University Press.

Werker, J. (2000). Becoming a native listener. In D. Muir & A. Slater, (Eds.), *Infant development: The essential readings* (pp. 149–162). Oxford, England: Blackwell.

Werker, J.F., & Lalonde, C.E. (1988). The development of speech perception: Initial capabilities and the emergence of phonemic categories. *Developmental Psychology, 24,* 672–683.

Werker, J., & Tees, R. (1984). Cross-language speech perception: Evidence for perceptual reorganization during the first year of life. *Infant Behavior and Development,* 49–63.

Werner, E. (1979). *Cross-cultural child development.* (Vol. 7). Monterey, CA: Brooks/Cole.

Werner, E. (2000). Protective factors and individual resilience. In J. Shonkoff & S. Meidels (Eds.), *Handbook of early childhood intervention* (2nd ed., pp. 115–132). New York: Cambridge University Press.

Werner, E., & Smith, R. (1992). *Overcoming the odds: High risk children from birth to adulthood.* Ithaca, NY: Cornell University.

Werner, L., & VandenBos, G. (1993). Developmental psychoacoustics: What infants and children hear. *Hospital and Community Psychiatry, 44,* 624–626.

West, R., & Turner, L. (1995). Communication in lesbian and gay families: Building a descriptive base. In T. Socha & G. Stamp (Eds.), *Parents, children, and communication* (pp. 147–169). Mahwah, NJ: Erlbaum.

Whaley, K. (1990). The emergence of social play in infancy: A proposed developmental sequence of infant-adult play. *Early Childhood Research Quarterly, 5,* 347–358.

Whaley, K., & Rubenstein, T. (1994). How toddlers "do" friendship: A descriptive analysis of naturally occuring friendships in a group child care setting. *Journal of Social and Personal Relationships, 11,* 383–400.

Wheeler, C. (1995). Labour: Normal and dysfunctional. In D. Coustan, R. Haning, & D. Singer (Eds.), *Human reproduction: Growth and development* (pp. 291–305). Boston: Little, Brown.

Whetnal, E. & Fry, D. (1964). *The deaf child.* London: Heinemann.

White, B. (1975). *The first three years of life.* Englewood Cliffs, NJ: Prentice Hall.

White, B. (1985). *The first three years of life* (rev. ed.). Englewood Cliffs, NJ: Prentice Hall.

White, B., & Watts, J. (1973). *Experience and environment* (Vol. 1). Englewood Cliffs, NJ: Prentice Hall.

White, R. (1959). Motivation reconsidered: The concept of competence. *Psychological Review, 66,* 297–333.

Whitebook, M., Howes, C., & Philips, D. (1989). *Who cares? Child care teachers and the quality of care in America. Executive summary of the national child care staffing study.* Oakland, CA: Child Care Employee Project.

Whitebook, M., Sakai, L., & Howes, C. (1997). NAEYC accreditation as a strategy for improving child care quality: An assessment. Washington, DC: Final Report, National Center for the Early Childhood Work Force.

Whitehurst, G. (1982). Language development. In B. Wolman (Ed.), *Handbook of developmental psychology* (pp. 367–386). Englewood Cliffs, NJ: Prentice Hall.

Whorf, B. (1956). *Language, thought and reality.* Cambridge, MA: MIT Press.

Wickstrom, R. (1983). *Fundamental motor patterns* (3rd ed.). Philadelphia: Lee & Febiger.

Widerstrom, A., Mowder, B., & Sandall, S. (1991). *At-risk and handicapped newborns and infants: Development, assessment, and intervention.* Englewood Cliffs, NJ: Prentice-Hall.

Wiesenfeld, A., Malatesta, C., & Deloache, L. (1981). Differential parental response to familiar and unfamiliar infant distress signals. *Infant Behavior and Development, 4,* 281–295.

Williams, H. (1983). *Perceptual and motor development.* Englewood Cliffs, NJ: Prentice Hall.

Willinger, M. (1995). SIDS prevention. *Pediatric Annals, 24,* 358–364.

Willinger, M., James, L., & Catz, C. (1991). Defining sudden infant death syndrome (SIDS). *Developmental Pediatric Pathology, 11,* 677–684.

Willoughby, J., & Glidden, L. (1995). Fathers helping out: Shared child care and marital satisfaction of parents of children with disabilities. *American Journal on Mental Retardation, 95,* 399–406.

Wingert, P., & Underwood, A. (1997, Spring/Summer). "Hey—look out world, here I come." *Newsweek: Special Edition,* 12–15.

Winick, M. (1979). Nutrition and brain development. In F. Balli (Ed.), *Nutritional problems in childhood.* Padova, Italy: Piccin Medical Books.

Woelfel, J. (1984). *Dental anatomy* (3rd ed.). Philadelphia: Lea & Febiger.

Wolff, P. (1963). Observations on the early development of smiling. In B. Foss (Ed.), *Determinants of infant behavior* (Vol. 2, pp. 113–138). London: Methuen.

Wolff, P. (1966). The causes, controls, and organization of behavior in the neonate. *Psychological Issues, 5* (1, Whole No. 17), 7–11.

Wolff, P. (1969). The natural history of crying and other vocalizations in early infancy. In B. Foss (Ed.), *Determinants of infant behavior* (Vol. 4, pp. 81–109). London: Methuen.

Wolk, S., Zeanah, C., Garcia Coll, C., & Carr, S. (1992). Factors affecting parents' perception of temperament in early infancy. *American Journal of Orthopsychiatry, 62,* 71–82.

Wood, B. (1976). *Children and communication: Verbal and nonverbal language development.* Englewood Cliffs, NJ: Prentice Hall.

Wood, B., & Walker-Smith, J. (1981). *Mackeith's infant feeding and feeding difficulties* (6th ed.). London: Churchill Livingstone.

Wood, N., Marlow, N., Costeloe, K., Wilkinson, A., & Andrew, R. (2000). Neurologic and developmental disability after extremely preterm birth. *New England Journal of Medicine¸343,* 378–384.

Woodard, K. (1997, Spring/Summer). A grandparent's role. *Newsweek: Special Edition,* pp. 81–82.

Woollacott, M. (1992). Early postnatal development of posture control: Normal and abnormal aspects. In A. Kalverboer, B. Hopkins, & R. Geuze (Eds.), *Motor development in early and later childhood: Longitudinal approaches* (pp. 89–108). Cambridge, England: Cambridge University Press.

World Health Organization/UNICEF. (1981). *Infant and young child feeding: Current issues.* Geneva, Switzerland: Author.

World Health Organization. (1985). *Treatment and prevention of acute diarrhoea.* Geneva: Author.

Worthington-Roberts, B., & Williams, S. (1996). *Nutrition throughout the life cycle* (3rd ed.). St. Louis, MO.: Mosby.

Wortley, P., Lindegren, M., & Fleming, P. (2001, May 11). Successful implementatiom of perinatal HIV prevention guidelines. *MMWR, 50*(RR06), 15–28.

Wortman, C., Loftus, E., & Marshall, M. (1992). *Psychology (4th ed.).* New York: Mc-Graw Hill.

Wyly, M. (1995). *Premature infants and their families: Developmental interventions.* San Diego, CA: Singular.

Wynbrandt, J., & Ludman, M. (1991). *The encyclopedia of genetic disorders and birth defects.* New York: Facts on File.

Wynn, K. (1992). Addition and subtraction by human infants. *Nature, 357,* 52–53.

Yarrow, L. (1979). Emotional development. *American Psychologist, 34,* 951–957.

Young, S.K., Fox, N.A., & Zahn-Waxler, C. (1999). The relations between temperament and empathy in 2-year-olds. *Developmental Psychology, 35*(5), 1189–1197.

Young, S., Schmitz, S., Corley, R., & Fuller, D. (2001). Language and cognition. In R. Emde & J. Hewitt (Eds.), *Infancy to early childhood* (pp. 221–240). New York: Oxford University Press.

Youngblut, J., Loveland-Cherry, C., & Horan, M. (1994). Maternal employment effects on families and preterm infants at 18 months. *Nursing Research, 43,* 331–337.

Zach, U., & Keller, H. (1999). Patterns of attachment-exploration balance of 1-year-old infants from the United States and Northern Germany. *Journal of Cross-Cultural Psychology, 30*(3), 381–388.

Zahn-Waxler, C., Cummings, E., & Cooperman, G. (1984). Emotional development in childhood. In G. Whitehurst (Ed.), *Annuals of child development* (Vol. 1, pp. 45–106). Greenwich, CT: JAI Press.

Zahn-Waxler, C., & Radke-Yarrow, M. (1990). The origins of empathic concern. *Motivation and Emotion, 14,* 107–130.

Zahn-Waxler, C., Schiro, K., Robinson, J.L., Emde, R.N., & Schmitz, S. (2001). Empathy and prosocial patterns in young MZ and DZ twins: Development and genetic and environmental influences. In R.N. Emde & J.K. Hewitt (Eds.), *Infancy to early childhood: Genetic and environmental influences on developmental change* (pp. 141–162). New York: Oxford University Press.

Zarbatany, L., & Lamb, M. (1985). Social referencing as a function of information source: Mothers versus strangers. *Infant Behavior and Development, 8,* 25–33.

Zaslow, M., Rabinovich, B., & Sualsky, J. (1991). From maternal employment to child outcomes: Preexisting group difference and moderating variables. In J. Lerner & N. Galambos (Eds.), *Employed mothers and their children: An analysis of "Children of the national longitudinal survey of youth"* (pp. 237–290). New York: Garland.

Zelazo, P., Zelazo, N., & Kolb, S. (1972). Walking in the newborn. *Science, 176,* 314–315.

Zero to Three/National Center for Clinical Infant Programs. (1994). *Diagnostic classification: 0–3: Diagnostic classification of mental health and developmental disorders of infancy and early childhood.* Arlington, VA: Author.

Zeskind, P. (1983). Cross-cultural differences in maternal perceptions of cries of low- and high-risk infants. *Child Development, 54,* 1119–1128.

Zeskind, P., & Marshall, T. (1991). Temporal organization in neonatal arousal: Systems, oscillations, and development. In M. Weiss & P. Zelazo (Eds.), *Newborn attention: Biological constraints and the influence of experiences* (pp. 22–62). Norwood, NJ: Ablex.

Zeskind, P., Sale, J., Maio, M., Huntington, M., & Wiseman, J. (1984, April). *Adult perceptions of pain and hunger cries:*

A synchrony arousal. Paper presented at the International Conference on Infant Studies, New York.

Zhang, Y., Kreger, B., Dorgan, J., Cupples, L., Myers, R., Splansky, G., Schatzkin, A., & Ellison, R. (1999). Parental age at child's birth and son's risk of prostate cancer: The Framington Study. *American Journal of Epidemiology, 150(11),* 1208–1212.

Zigler, E., & Turner, P. (1982). Parents and day care workers: A failed partnership? In E. Zigler & A. Gordon (Eds.), *Day care: Scientific and social policy issues* (pp. 174–182). Boston: Auburn House.

Zimmerman, I., & Bernstein, M. (1983). Parental work patterns in alternative families: Influence on child development. *American Journal of Orthopsychiatry, 53,* 418–425.

Ziv, Y., Aviezer, O., Gini, M., Sagi, A., & Koren-Karie, N. (2000). Emotional availability in the mother-infant dyad as related to the quality of infant-mother attachment relationship. *Attachment and Human Development, 2*(2), 149–169.

Zlatnik, F. (1995). Normal labor and delivery. In J. Scott, P. DiSaia, C. Hammond, & W. Spellacy (Eds.), *Danforth's obstetrics and gynecology* (7th ed., pp. 105–128). Philadelphia: Lippincott.

Zuckerman, B., Bauchner, H., & Parker, S. (1990). Maternal depressive symptoms during pregnancy and newborn irritability. *Journal of Developmental and Behavioral Pediatrics, 11,* 190–194.

Zuckerman, B., Frank, D., Hingson, R., Amaro, H., Levenson, S., Kayne, H., Parker, S., Vinci, R., Aboagye, K., Fried, L., Cabral, H., Tiemperi, R., & Bauchner, H. (1989). Effects of maternal marijuana and cocaine use on fetal growth. *New England Journal of Medicine, 320,* 762–768.

Zussman, J. (1980). Situational determinants of parental behavior: Effects of competing cognitive activity. *Child Development, 51,* 792–800.

Zwelling, E. (1996). Childbirth education in the 1990's and beyond. *JOGN, 25,* 425–432.

Appendix 1

Birth to 36 months: Boys
Length-for-age and Weight-for-age percentiles

NAME ______________________

RECORD # ____________

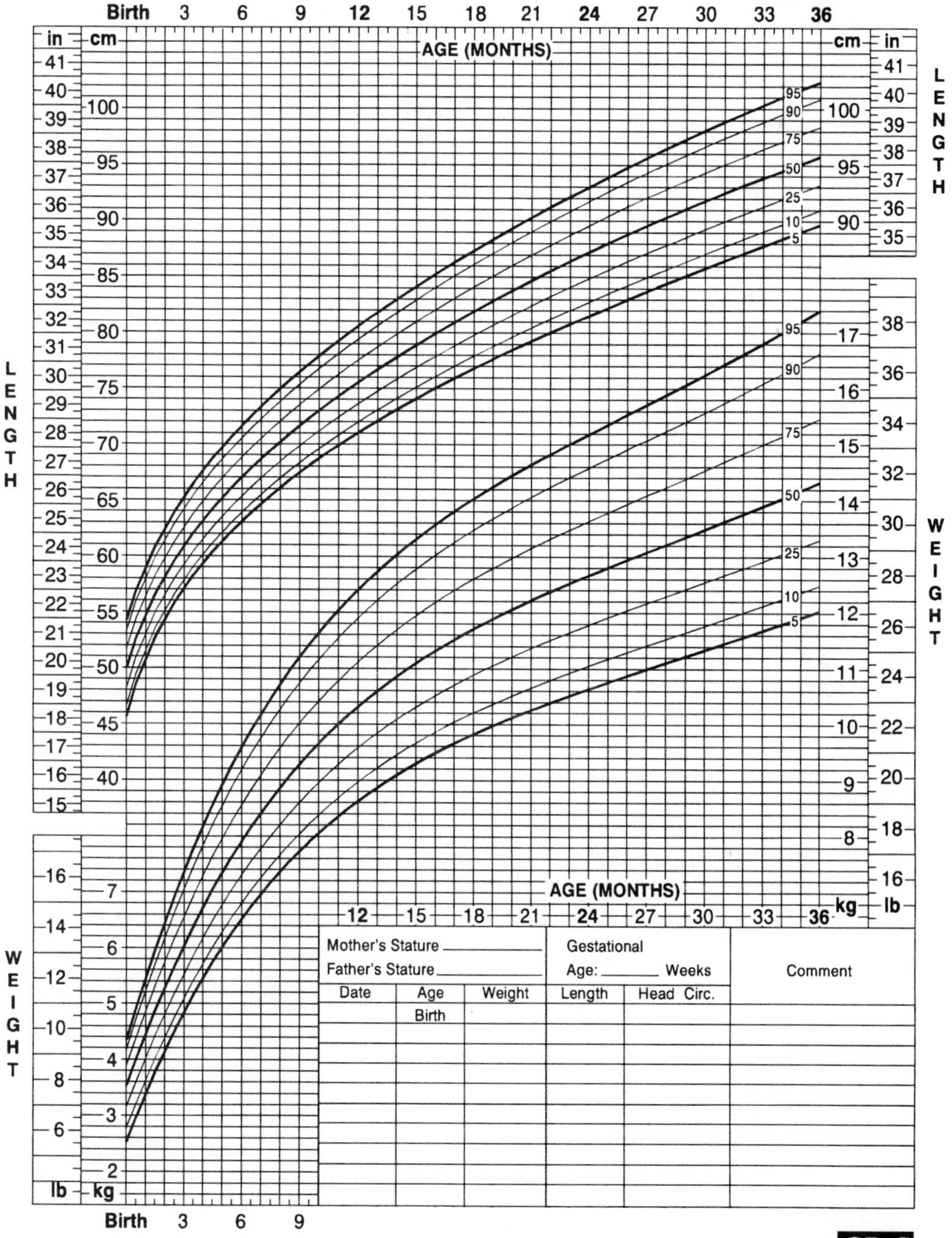

Birth 3 6 9 12 15 18 21 24 27 30 33 36

AGE (MONTHS)

LENGTH

in: 15 16 17 18 19 20 21 22 23 24 25 26 27 28 29 30 31 32 33 34 35 36 37 38 39 40 41

cm: 40 45 50 55 60 65 70 75 80 85 90 95 100

Percentiles: 95 90 75 50 25 10 5

WEIGHT

kg: 2 3 4 5 6 7 8 9 10 11 12 13 14 15 16 17

lb: 6 8 10 12 14 16 18 20 22 24 26 28 30 32 34 36 38

Percentiles: 95 90 75 50 25 10 5

AGE (MONTHS)

12 15 18 21 24 27 30 33 36

Birth 3 6 9

Mother's Stature ______ Father's Stature ______			Gestational Age: ______ Weeks		Comment
Date	Age	Weight	Length	Head Circ.	
	Birth				

Revised November 21, 2000.

SOURCE: Developed by the National Center for Health Statistics in collaboration with the National Center for Chronic Disease Prevention and Health Promotion (2000).

http://www.cdc.gov/growthcharts

Appendix 2

Birth to 36 months: Girls
Length-for-age and Weight-for-age percentiles

NAME ______________________

RECORD # ____________

Birth 3 6 9 12 15 18 21 24 27 30 33 36

AGE (MONTHS)

LENGTH (in / cm) — percentile curves 5, 10, 25, 50, 75, 90, 95

WEIGHT (lb / kg) — percentile curves 5, 10, 25, 50, 75, 90, 95

Mother's Stature ________			Gestational		Comment
Father's Stature ________			Age: ______ Weeks		
Date	Age	Weight	Length	Head Circ.	
	Birth				

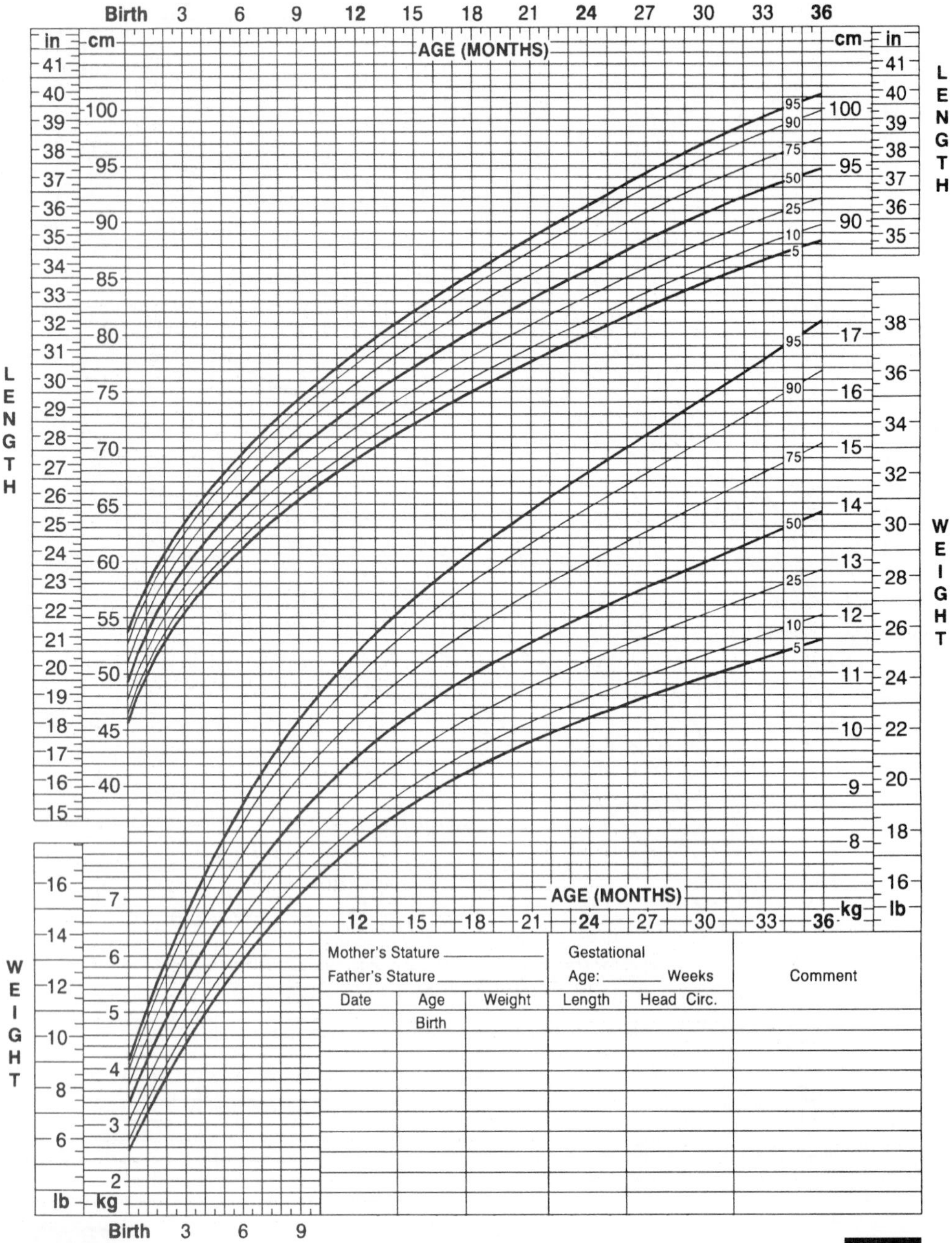

Revised April 20, 2001.

SOURCE: Developed by the National Center for Health Statistics in collaboration with the National Center for Chronic Disease Prevention and Health Promotion (2000).
http://www.cdc.gov/growthcharts

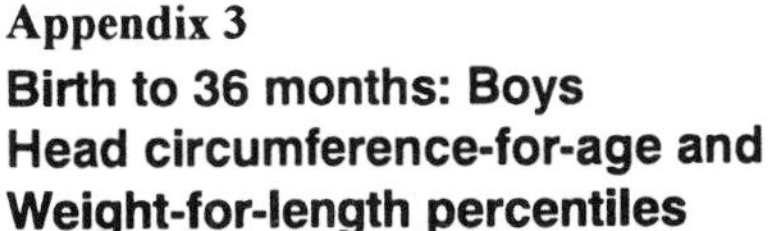

Appendix 3

Birth to 36 months: Boys
Head circumference-for-age and
Weight-for-length percentiles

NAME ______________________

RECORD # ____________

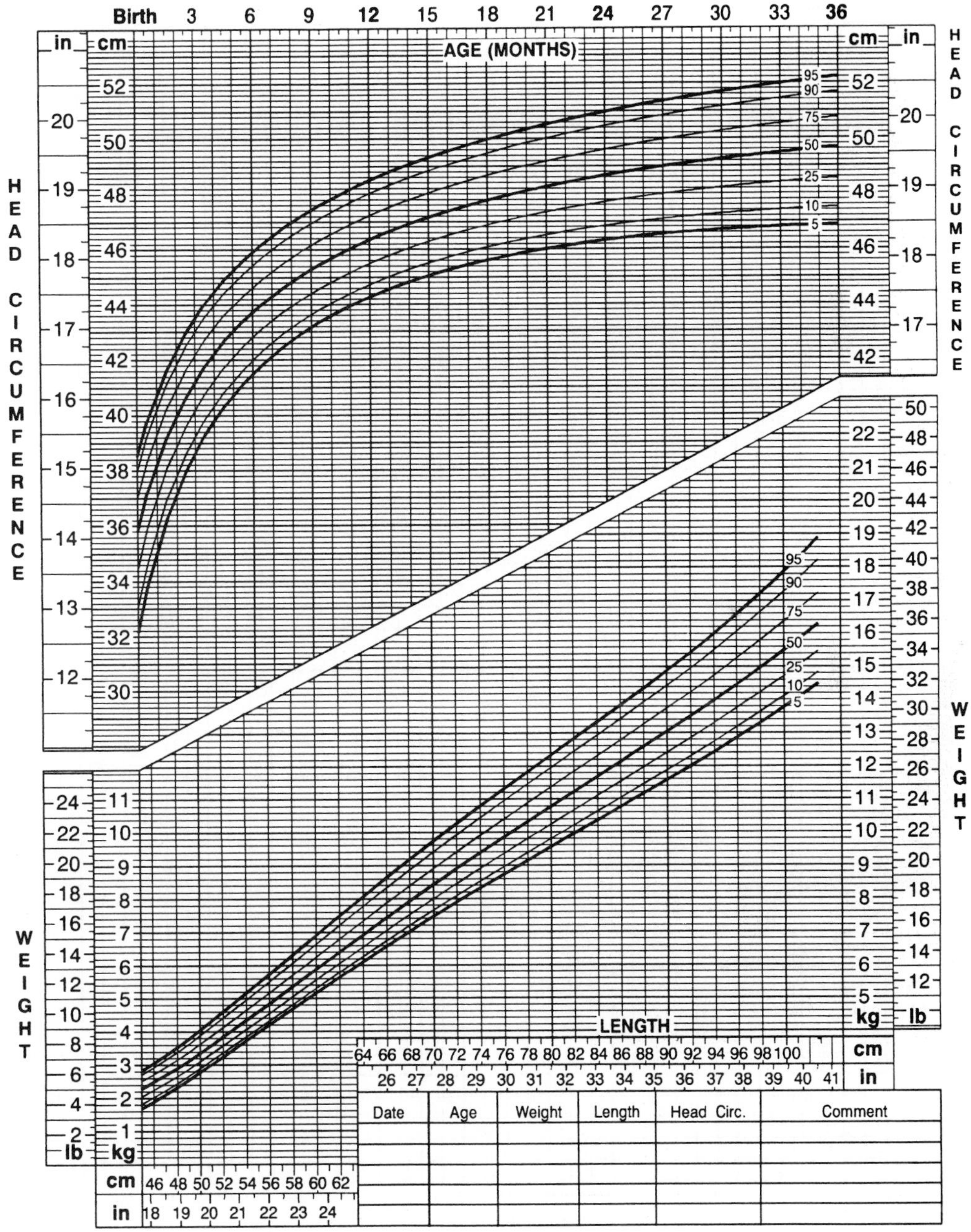

Birth 3 6 9 12 15 18 21 24 27 30 33 36

AGE (MONTHS)

HEAD CIRCUMFERENCE

in: 12 13 14 15 16 17 18 19 20

cm: 30 32 34 36 38 40 42 44 46 48 50 52

95 90 75 50 25 10 5

WEIGHT

kg: 1 2 3 4 5 6 7 8 9 10 11 12 13 14 15 16 17 18 19 20 21 22

lb: 2 4 6 8 10 12 14 16 18 20 22 24 26 28 30 32 34 36 38 40 42 44 46 48 50

LENGTH

cm: 46 48 50 52 54 56 58 60 62 64 66 68 70 72 74 76 78 80 82 84 86 88 90 92 94 96 98 100

in: 18 19 20 21 22 23 24 25 26 27 28 29 30 31 32 33 34 35 36 37 38 39 40 41

Date	Age	Weight	Length	Head Circ.	Comment

SOURCE: Developed by the National Center for Health Statistics in collaboration with the National Center for Chronic Disease Prevention and Health Promotion (2000). http://www.cdc.gov/growthcharts

Appendix 4

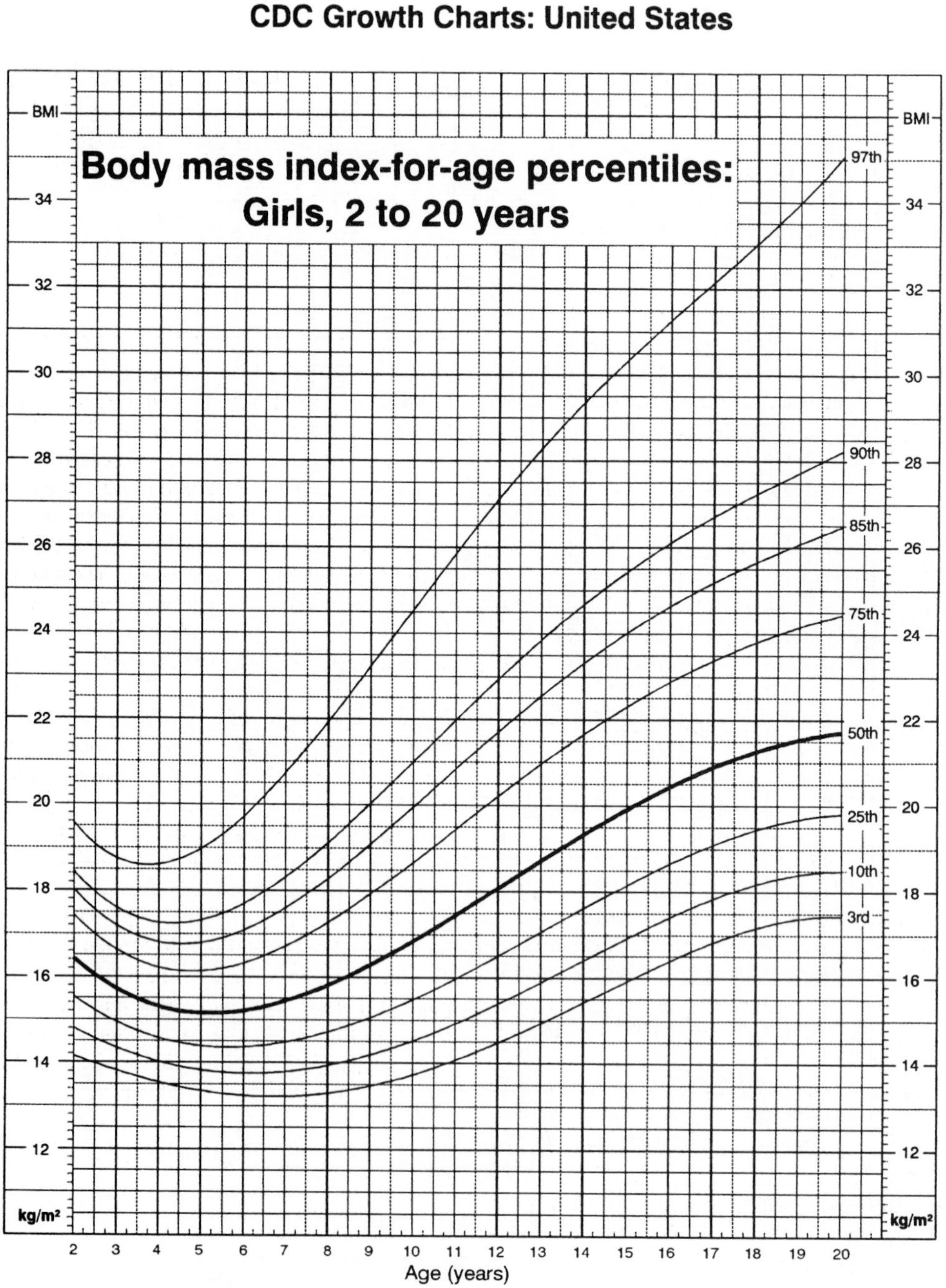

CDC Growth Charts: United States

Body mass index-for-age percentiles: Girls, 2 to 20 years

BMI

34
32
30
28
26
24
22
20
18
16
14
12

kg/m²

97th
90th
85th
75th
50th
25th
10th
3rd

2 3 4 5 6 7 8 9 10 11 12 13 14 15 16 17 18 19 20

Age (years)

SOURCE: Developed by the National Center for Health Statistics in collaboration with the National Center for Chronic Disease Prevention and Health Promotion (2000).

CREDITS

CHAPTER OPENING QUOTATIONS

Chapter 1. Shakespeare, W. S. (1623/1952). "As you like it." In G. Harrison (Ed.), *Shakespeare: The Complete Works.* New York: Harcourt, Brace, p. 789.

Chapter 2. MacDonald, G. (1924). *At the Back of the North Wind.* New York: Macmillan, p. 321. Reprinted by permission.

Chapter 3. First Quotation: Blake, W. (1757/1827). "Infant Sorrow" in *Songs of Experience.* In David V. Erdman, commentary by Harold Bloom (1965). *The Poetry and Prose of William Blake.* New York: Doubleday & Company, Inc.

Second Quotation: From an American Greeting card. Used by permission of American Greetings Corp., Cleveland, OH.

Chapter 4. An English proverb. In W. Mieler (1986). *The Prentice Hall Encyclopedia of World Proverbs.* Englewood Cliffs, NJ: Prentice Hall, p. 71.

Chapter 5. First Quotation: Anthony, E. (1947). "Advice to small children" in *Every Dog Has His Say.* New York: Watson-Guptill. Reprinted by permission.

Second Quotation: Lamb, M. (1903). "The first tooth." In E. Lucas (Ed.), *The Works of Charles and Mary Lamb* (Vol. 3; p. 362). London: Methuen. (Reprinted by AMS Press, New York, 1968). Reprinted by permission of Methuen & Co.

Chapter 6. Kierkegaard, S. (1948). *Purity of Heart is to Will One Thing.* Trans. D. Steere. New York: Harper & Row, p. 85. Reprinted by permission.

Chapter 7. An original poem by Charles W. Snow.

Chapter 8. Holland, J. (1879). "Bitter-sweet" from *The Complete Poetical Writings of J. G. Holland* (New York: Charles Scribner's Sons, 1879). Reprinted by permission.

Chapter 9. Psalm 8:2; Matthew 21:16. *The Holy Bible.* King James Version.

Chapter 10. Prelutsky, J. (1983). *The Random House Book of Poetry for Children.* New York: Random House, p. 117. Reprinted by permission of the author.

Chapter 11. Barrie, J. (1949). *Peter Pan.* New York: Charles Scribner's Sons, p. 36.

Chapter 12. "Animula" from *Collected Poems 1909–1962* by T. S. Eliot, copyright © 1936 by Harcourt Brace Jovanovich, Inc., copyright © 1963, 1964 by T. S. Eliot. Reprinted by permission of the publisher and Faber and Faber, Ltd.

Chapter 13. Gibran, K. (1972). *The Prophet.* New York: Alfred A. Knopf, p. 17. Reprinted by permission.

PHOTOGRAPHS

Page 23: National Library of Medicine; Dr. Landrum B. Shettles; **page 25:** Dr. Landrum B. Shettles; **page 29:** From the Journal of the American Medical Association, 1976, Vol. 235, 1458-1460. Courtesy, James W. Hanson, M.D.; **page 35:** GE Medical Systems; **page 45:** E. Mandelmann/World Health Organization; **page 49:** Shirley Zeiberg/Pearson Education/PH College; **page 51:** Teri Stratford; **page 54:** Laima Druskis/Pearson Education/PH College; **page 68:** Charles W. Snow; **page 71:** Teri Stratford; **page 85:** World Health Organization; **page 94:** Shirley Zeiberg/Pearson Education/PH College; **page 97:** J. Abcede/World Health Organization; **page 100:** H.Oomen/World Health Organization; **page 106:** United Nations; **page 111:** Ken Karp/Pearson Education/PH College; **page 113:** Teri Stratford; **page 118:** Teri Stratford; **page 136:** Mrs. Robin Palmer; **page 138:** Cindy McGaha; **page 148:** Photoquest, Inc.; **page 161:** Charles W. Snow; **page 172:** Photo Researchers, Inc; **page 175:** Erika Stone/Photo Researchers, Inc.; **page 193:** Teri Stratford; **page 199:** Gerber Products Company; **page 201:** Teri Stratford; **page 209:** L. Morris/Photoquest, Inc.; **page 212:** Shirley Zeiberg/Pearson Education/PH College; **page 228:** Ken Karp/Pearson Education/PH College; **page 233:** Shirley Zeiberg/Pearson Education/PH College; **page 243:** Shirley Zeiberg/Pearson Education/PH College; **page 246:** Lawrence Migdale/Photo Researchers, Inc.; **page 252:** Laura Dwight/PhotoEdit.

Subject Index

NAME INDEX